Fodor's

ARIZONA

Welcome to Arizona

From the vastness of the Grand Canyon to Sedona's red rocks and the living Sonoran Desert, Arizona's landscapes are breathtaking. The state's spectacular canyons, blooming deserts, raging rivers, petrified forests, and scenic mountains enthrall lovers of the outdoors in pursuit of hiking, rafting, golf, or picturesque spots to watch the sunset. But there's more to Arizona than beautiful vistas, including its world-renowned spas and rich native cultures. As you plan your upcoming travels to Arizona, please confirm that places are still open and let us know when we need to make updates by writing to us at this address: editors@fodors.com.

TOP REASONS TO GO

★ **Grand Canyon:** Whether you hike, raft, or drive it, you shouldn't miss it.

★ **Native American Heritage:** There's no better place to appreciate these thriving cultures.

★ **Big Flavors:** Blending Native American and Southwestern spices, Arizona's cuisine pops.

★ **Road Trips:** The wide-open spaces of Arizona dazzle anew with every turn.

★ **Stunning Landscapes:** From Sedona's red rocks to Monument Valley, beauty reigns.

★ **Outdoor Experiences:** Canyons, deserts, and mountains offer adventures aplenty.

Contents

Fodor's Features

Chapter 1

EXPERIENCE ARIZONA

25 ULTIMATE EXPERIENCES

Arizona offers terrific experiences that should be on every traveler's list. Here are Fodor's top picks for a memorable trip.

1 Hike the Grand Canyon

Seeing the canyon for the first time is an astounding experience. Witness the sandstone canyon walls, pine and fir forests, mesas, plateaus, volcanic features, and the Colorado River far below. *(Ch. 4)*

2 Go Rafting on the Colorado River

Rafting down the Colorado River, through the Grand Canyon, is an iconic Arizona experience. Jostle your joints on a day trip, or splurge on a multiday adventure. *(Ch. 4)*

3 Discover the Beauty of Cacti at the Desert Botanical Garden

Offering an up-close view of more than 4,000 species of desert flora, the garden is a glorious rebuttal to any claims that deserts are void of life. *(Ch. 3)*

4 View Native American Art

The Heard Museum has the most comprehensive collection of Native American art in the world, including paintings, textiles, pottery, and jewelry. *(Ch. 3)*

5 Explore One of Nature's Masterpieces

Canyon de Chelly National Monument is the home of pueblo ruins that date back to AD 350 and a Navajo community that lives along the canyon's floor. *(Ch. 6)*

6 Play Rounds of Golf in Scottsdale

No other city can offer the caliber of golf courses quite like Scottsdale. Most on-site pro shops can outfit you with all the gear you need for your day on the greens. *(Ch. 3)*

7 Visit the Wild West in Tombstone

The Wild West spirit is very much alive in towns such as Tombstone and Bisbee, where the mining boom gave way to outlaws and shoot-outs. *(Ch. 9)*

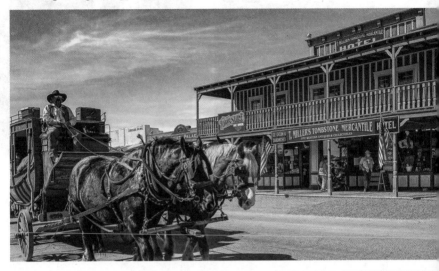

8 Stop at the Painted Desert

Forget your impression of brown desert land; this one is awash in color, from deep red hues to lovely lavender. It's like the sunset imprinted itself on the land. *(Ch. 7)*

9 Shop for Local Crafts

Trading posts are traditional hubs of commerce with everything from tchotchkes to fine works of art. Hubbell Trading Post near Canyon de Chelly is outstanding. *(Ch. 6)*

10 Experience the Magic of Antelope Canyon

A narrow, red, sandstone slot canyon of petrified dunes make you question texture and matter. How can rock look liquid? How can something so smooth also be fierce? *(Ch. 6)*

11 Get your Kicks on Route 66

Classic American Route 66 runs from Seligman to Kingman. Enjoy the beautiful scenery and stop for lunch at a drive-in. Remember, it's all about the journey. *(Ch. 5, 10)*

12 Discover the Beauty of Sedona

With stunning red rock formations—Cathedral Rock, Bear Mountain, Courthouse Rock, Bell Rock—reaching up into an almost-always blue sky, Sedona is a mystical place. *(Ch. 5)*

13 Relax in Style at a World-Class Spa

Put away your phone and grab a warm robe. Arizona's spas are world-renowned, and offer treatments ranging from massages to facials, scrubs to wraps. Doing nothing is perfect. *(Ch. 5)*

14 See Montezuma Castle National Monument

This 600-year-old structure was named by explorers who thought it had been erected by the Aztecs. Sinagua Native Americans built the five-story, 20-room cliff dwelling. *(Ch. 5)*

15 Gaze at the Cacti of Saguaro National Park

Emblems of the Southwest, these amazing cacti have a life span of up to 200 years and can extend to 60 feet tall. They don't produce their first arm until around age 50. *(Ch. 8)*

16 Play in the Desert

Wonderfully kid-friendly, the Arizona-Sonora Desert Museum is equal parts museum, zoo, aquarium, and botanical garden, with every type of desert creature imaginable. *(Ch. 8)*

17 Tour Kartchner Caverns

Walk through the underground passages of this living, wet cave system to see multicolor limestone formations and one of the world's longest soda straw stalactites. *(Ch. 9)*

18 Explore the Petrified Forest

Witness colors and textures from millennia past and glimpse at 500-year-old petroglyphs. The Blue Mesa trail is an easy walk past blue and purple hills and rock. *(Ch. 7)*

19 Check out the Art Scene in Tucson

Thanks to its Western roots, university-town vibe, and pop-culture connection to film, Tucson is an artist's haven. Top billing goes to Tucson Museum of Art and MOCA. *(Ch. 8)*

20 Eat Excellent Mexican Food

Chimichangas, enchiladas, chilaquiles, tacos, mole, spicy and mild salsas, and, of course, lots of margaritas—a trip to Arizona without indulging in Mexican food is just wrong. *(Ch. 3)*

21 Go Camping

Pitch a tent or rent a rustic cabin to unplug from city life and connect to Arizona's land. Notable locations include Sedona and the Apache-Sitgreaves National Forest. *(Ch. 5, 7)*

22 Make a Splash on Lake Havasu

Miles of shoreline draw Arizonans to this playground for water recreation, where you can zip around with Jet Skis or relax in a houseboat rental. *(Ch. 10)*

23 Stargaze

The Milky Way stretches over the desert sky like a chiffon scarf across the celestial sphere. Get a closer look through telescopes at Lowell Observatory or Kitt Peak. *(Ch. 5, 9)*

24 Experience Picture-Perfect Monument Valley

This remarkably remote region of Arizona and Utah is impossible to view in a single frame. A scenic 17-mile strip of Valley Drive will have you channeling Ansel Adams. *(Ch. 6)*

25 Try Arizona Wine

Grapes grow well in Sonoita, a burgeoning wine region where you can hop from vineyard to vineyard and decide on the area's merits for yourself. *(Ch. 9)*

WHAT'S WHERE

1 Phoenix, Scottsdale, and Tempe. Rising where the Sonoran Desert meets the Superstition Mountains, the Valley of the Sun is filled with resorts and spas, shops and restaurants, and more than 200 golf courses.

2 Grand Canyon National Park. Whether you select the popular South Rim or the remote North Rim, don't just peer over the edge—take the plunge into the canyon on foot or on a raft trip.

3 North-Central Arizona. Cool, laid-back towns here are as bewitching as the high-country landscape they inhabit. There are quaint escapes such as Prescott and Jerome, Sedona with its red-rock buttes, and the vibrant university town of Flagstaff.

4 Northeast Arizona. This remote area includes the stunning surroundings of Monument Valley. Alongside today's Navajo and Hopi communities, Canyon de Chelly and Navajo National Monument are reminders of how ancient peoples lived with the land.

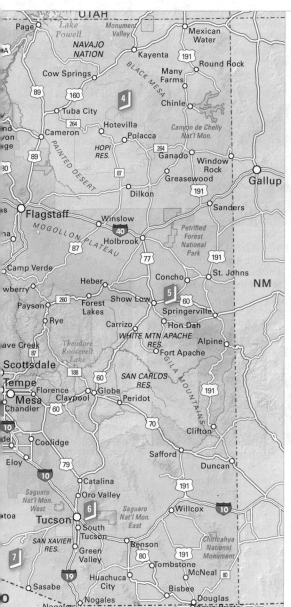

5 Eastern Arizona. Summer visitors flock to the lush, green White Mountains and the warm colors of the Painted Desert. Petrified Forest National Park features trees that stood when dinosaurs walked the Earth.

6 Tucson. The modern history of Arizona begins here, where Hispanic, Anglo, and Native American cultures became intertwined in the 17th century. Farther out, city slickers enjoy horseback rides at some of the region's many guest ranches, or luxury pampering at world-class spas.

7 Southern Arizona. Splendid mountain and desert scenery evokes the romanticized spirit of the Wild West. Enduring pockets of westward expansion are the largest draw today: notorious Tombstone and the mining boomtown Bisbee.

8 Northwest Arizona and Southeast Nevada. This corner of Arizona includes Lake Havasu City and London Bridge; old-fashioned Americana around Kingman on legendary Route 66; and Hoover Dam and Laughlin's casinos, a short jaunt away in Nevada.

Best Hikes in Arizona

PINNACLE PEAK
One of the most popular trails in the greater Phoenix area, this moderate city of Scottsdale climb is accessible year-round. It's 3.5 miles out and back, and offers some fantastic views of the Valley. As part of the Sonoran Desert, it also offers the chance to spot desert flora and fauna such as desert tortoises and towering cacti. *(Ch. 3)*

BRIGHT ANGEL TRAIL
The grandaddy of all Grand Canyon trails, Bright Angel is among the most popular of the South Rim. The full 9.5 miles to the bottom of the canyon is moderately difficult and features many switchbacks, beautiful vistas, and diverse plant and animal life. *(Ch. 4)*

HAVASU FALLS
Descend 3,000 feet to splashing pools of turquoise water on this multiday, 19-mile hike, one of the most beautiful in the Grand Canyon area (if not the U.S.). It's entirely within the Havasupai tribal lands, so visitors must obtain permits far in advance before embarking on their journey with a tour guide. *(Ch. 4)*

WALNUT CANYON NATIONAL MONUMENT
Two trails strewn with ancient cliff dwellings offer a chance to step back in time just outside of Flagstaff. The 1-mile Island Trail's 7,000-foot elevation makes it extremely difficult, but the easier Rim Trail is relatively level and has lovely views. *(Ch. 5)*

HUMPHREYS PEAK
Located north of Flagstaff, Mount Humphreys is home to the highest perch in the state and one of its most strenuous hikes. Ascending 3,000 feet on the 10-mile round trip through the alpine tundra is no cake walk, but the view is certainly worth the climb. *(Ch. 5)*

CATHEDRAL ROCK

Sedona's most popular trail is a non-technical but vigorous 1.2-mile round trip known for its 360-degree views of red rock. Just a five-minute drive away is iconic Bell Rock, with its own 3.6-mile trail. *(Ch. 5)*

HORSESHOE BEND TRAIL

For a bird's-eye view of the bending Colorado River, come to this striking trail near Page. While it is generally easy, hikers should be aware that the 1.4-mile trail is mostly sandy gravel, and there are no rails along the cliffs. *(Ch. 6)*

CAMELBACK MOUNTAIN

One of Phoenix's iconic landmarks is also one of its most notable places to hike. The 1.23 miles to the summit is a difficult climb, and it's imperative to bring plenty of water as well as sun protection—first responders have had to rescue hikers who suffer from heat exhaustion in summer. *(Ch. 3)*

BEAR CANYON TRAIL

This 7.8-mile round-trip hike that leads to the Seven Falls in the Sabino Canyon Recreation Area of Tucson is a feast for the eyes, and only moderately difficult. Pass saguaro cacti, ocotillo, cholla, palo verde, and rock formations before coming to the waterfalls. You might need to traverse some water, so wear shoes you can stand to get muddy. *(Ch. 8)*

NAVAJO NATIONAL MONUMENT

Located in northeastern Arizona within the Navajo Nation, the Navajo National Monument offers three memorable self-guided trails. One, the paved Sandal Trail, allows you to view breathtaking Betatakin cliff dwellings that were carved into the natural sandstone alcoves around AD 1250–1300. (Ch. 6)

What to Eat and Drink in Arizona

MACHACA BEEF

When you're at a Mexican restaurant in Arizona, order the machaca. This slow-cooked, shredded beef seasoned with peppers and onions is tender and delicious, whether it's rolled into an enchilada, folded into a chimichanga, or spooned into a taco.

ARIZONA WINE

While Arizona is perhaps better known for its citrus and cotton, it is also home to a growing wine industry. The areas of Sonoita, about an hour south of Tucson, and the Verde Valley, about an hour north of Phoenix, boast vineyards and a product that's gaining popularity.

HATCH CHILES

You needn't fear the hatch chile, but you should respect it. These heat-seeking flavor bombs hail from the Hatch Valley of New Mexico, and are the chiles of choice at restaurants across Arizona. Spicy, smoky, and a little sweet, they give a kick to dishes like pozole, salsa, and chili.

FRY BREAD

This flat, deep-fried dough is usually served sprinkled with powdered sugar or honey (a similar, smaller version called a sopapilla is on most Mexican restaurants' dessert menus). It's served hot, and can be pulled apart by hand. Fry bread also is offered as an entrée, topped with meat, cheese, and garnish.

CHEESE CRISP

You'll know someone is an Arizona local if they call an open-faced quesadilla a cheese crisp. This simple, delicious, crunchy and cheesy dish is a favorite of Arizona kids.

CHIMICHANGA

Legend says that the founders of Phoenix's famous Macayo's Mexican restaurants created the chimichanga by accident when a *burro* (the local term for burrito) was dropped into a deep fryer. Today it's a classic, usually containing meat and cheese and topped with sauce and sour cream.

SUN TEA

What sweet tea is to the South, sun tea is to Arizona. Rather than boil water over a stove or in a kettle, locals simply place a gallon-sized jar of water with tea bags outside to bake in the hot Arizona sun. Simple and refreshing.

NOPALES

One of a few cactus delicacies is *nopales* (prickly pear cactus pads), which taste like a tart and sticky green bean and can be served sautéed, fried, or raw.

TAMALES

Families order platters of this traditional dish by the dozen during the holidays, but you can enjoy them year-round. Much like burros or enchiladas, tamales feature a filling (usually meat, but not always) surrounded by a shell. While tortillas are used for burros and enchiladas, tamales have a corn-based wrapper, and they're steamed in an actual corn husk, which you should unfold and discard (or use as a plate) before digging into the filling.

GREEN CHILE SAUCE

The mother sauce of the Southwest, green chile sauce makes everything more delicious. Over an enchilada? Sure. Atop a chimichanga? Brings out the flavor. Much like salsa, its depth of flavor and heat can vary by chef, but green chile sauce is generally mild and thick, containing chiles, sauteed onions, and spices.

SONORAN HOT DOG

The Sonoran Dog is like no other hot dog; this amalgam of Mexican and American flavors is wrapped in bacon, tucked in a *bolillo* (fluffy bun), and topped with condiments like pinto beans, jalapeño salsa, onions, mayo, and mustard. You'll find one easily in Phoenix and Tucson.

POZOLE

Hominy (dried corn) is the star of this traditional Mexican stew of hearty broth and meat. A similar recipe that originated in the Hopi community is made with lamb, hominy, and carrots and served with thinly layered *piki* bread, made with blue corn.

PRICKLY PEAR MARGARITA

When you take your first sip of a bright, magenta-hued prickly pear margarita, you'll wonder how the original ever existed without it. The prickly pear cactus produces the wonderful, sweet fruit that's used to accent beverages, desserts, and even entrées.

What to Buy in Arizona

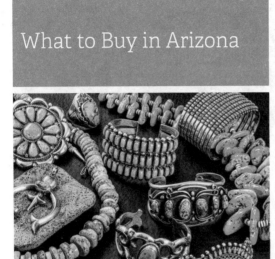

TURQUOISE JEWELRY

Arizona is a leading producer of turquoise, and the gem has been used in the creation of necklaces, rings, bracelets, and earrings by native cultures for ages. To be sure your item is authentically handcrafted by a local artisan, consider buying direct at trading posts in northern Arizona.

BELLS FROM ARCOSANTI

Handcrafted ceramic and bronze wind-bells have made the town of Arcosanti famous the world over. Stop by the studio in Phoenix's Paradise Valley and watch artisans make the bells, or visit the community north of the city.

PRINTS

A vintage print from the Grand Canyon Conservancy, the official nonprofit partner of the beloved national park, isn't just a reminder of your trip to the canyon—it also helps fund park upkeep. If you're more of a photography fan, pick up an iconic calendar from the *Arizona Highways* magazine, a big hit for those who love Arizona's vistas and a nice reminder of warmer or sunnier times.

PRICKLY PEAR CANDY

Satisfy your sweet tooth with a bite—or two, or three—of candy made from the sweet fruit of the cactus. Usually packaged as bright red gummies or as jawbreaker-style pieces, it makes for an affordable and transportable treat. The Cactus Candy Company is one well known brand—look for their bright yellow packaging.

CACTUS
Small, desktop-sized cacti can be a perfect memento from a trip to Arizona. Available at most gift shops, these little living pieces of the desert require almost no water or maintenance. Perhaps most important for your fingers, they come boxed, too.

NAVAJO RUGS
Colorful rugs and blankets, locally woven with intricate designs, are available at the Hubbell Trading Post. A purchase supports local artisans and serves as the perfect foundation for your road trip picnic.

GREEN CHILES
Whether you find them in a freeze-dried bag, sautéed, in a jar, or fresh from the grocer, green chiles are perhaps the best way to transport the flavor of Arizona back to your home. Pick up a cookbook during your journey so you can recreate your favorite dishes.

Western Boots

WESTERN BOOTS
Dressy or casual, simple or snazzy, cowboy boots aren't just for ranch life. A good pair can be an investment, but can last a lifetime. Check out some of the boutiques in Old Town Scottsdale, or Western wear shops across the state. Complete the look with a cowboy or sun hat to protect from strong Arizona rays.

SALSA
In a state that hosts salsa festivals (in Phoenix, Tucson, and Maricopa) and has a dedicated Salsa Trail from Globe to Tucson, you could say Arizona knows a thing or two about salsa. Buy from local brands like Arizona Salsa & Spice Company or Southwest Specialty Food Inc. to complete your crunchy, salty, spicy road-trip snack.

CITRUS
Grade schoolers in Arizona learn about the five "C"s of the state: copper, cotton, cattle, citrus, and climate. Orange groves are so plentiful in parts of Phoenix, the evening air smells of orange blossoms for weeks in March. Ship yourself a box of Arizona-grown citrus—it's one of the most delicious wintertime souvenirs.

Day Trips From Phoenix

SEDONA

Loved for its majestic red rocks, its spiritual energy, and its fantastic resorts and spas, Sedona is unlike any other town in America. Take the active route and explore Oak Creek Canyon and the surrounding area on foot or by bike or jeep, or indulge in the luxe life at a world-class spa, restaurant, or art gallery. *1½ hours from Phoenix. (Ch. 5)*

THE APACHE TRAIL

A drive along this 42-mile route will lead you to beauty, solitude, and unforgettable views, from the Superstition Mountains to Tortilla Flat. Start your day drive at Apache Junction. *1 hour to Apache Junction from Phoenix. (Ch. 3)*

CASA GRANDE RUINS NATIONAL MONUMENT

One of the best-preserved sites of the ancestral Sonoran Desert people, the Great House at Casa Grande Ruins dates to around 1300. Guided tours teach visitors about the Hohokam people and their once-thriving community in the desert. *1 hour from Phoenix. (Ch. 3)*

VERDE VALLEY

A short drive from the bustle of Phoenix, the Verde Valley is a great area for unwinding and relaxing. Tour a local winery, visit Jerome's historic downtown, or take a trip on the Verde Canyon Scenic Railroad. Stop by Montezuma Castle on your drive back to the city. *1½ hours from Phoenix. (Ch. 5)*

MONTEZUMA CASTLE NATIONAL MONUMENT

This national monument north of Phoenix features preserved dwellings of the Sinagua people dating to approximately 1100. The National Park Service calls the site a "20-room high-rise apartment," proving that prime real estate is always worth a look. *1½ hours from Phoenix. (Ch. 5)*

SAGUARO NATIONAL PARK

Arizonans revere the saguaro cactus. Its iconic branches take an estimated 50 to 70 years to grow, and their lifespan is typically 150 years. The Saguaro National Park in Tucson lets visitors see the saguaro, and the wildlife that thrives with it, in its natural state. Take a drive, enjoy a hike, and gaze at one of nature's masterpieces. *2 hours from Phoenix. (Ch. 8)*

KARTCHNER CAVERNS STATE PARK

This subterranean wonder south of Tucson wasn't discovered until 1974, but Mother Nature spent 200,000 years making it. Featuring more than 2½ miles of caves, the site is one of Arizona's most amazing. *2½ hours from Phoenix. (Ch. 9)*

KITT PEAK NATIONAL OBSERVATORY

Stargazers flock to Tucson to visit Kitt Peak's astronomical observatory and ponder the heavens with the help of high-powered telescopes. The sight of the Milky Way lighting up the sky will be one you won't soon forget. *2½ hours from Phoenix. (Ch. 9)*

METEOR CRATER

About 50,000 years ago, an iron-nickel asteroid measuring 150 feet across crashed into Earth about a half-hour east of what is now Flagstaff. Today, you can tour the site, which is about a mile across. NASA says it's "unusually well preserved." *3 hours from Phoenix. (Ch. 5)*

ROUTE 66

This famous roadway's stretch in Arizona traverses some of the state's most scenic areas. Visit Holbrook, take in prehistoric sites such as the Petrified Forest and Painted Desert, and stand on a corner in Winslow. Head to Seligman, and experience all the perfectly wonderful kitsch that Route 66 embodies. *3 hours to Winslow from Phoenix. (Ch. 5, 10)*

Arizona with Kids

CHOOSING A DESTINATION

You can make your trip one for adventure, education, or good ol' play time. Stay close to the urban areas surrounding Phoenix or Tucson if you want to revel in water parks, swimming pools, and resort children's programs. Travel north to Sedona, where you can see **Snoopy Rock,** before exploring the wonder that is the **Grand Canyon.** If you're looking for an educational journey, don't forget to stop by Phoenix's **Heard Museum** for an introduction to Native American cultures, or spend some quality time in Northeast Arizona at **Monument Valley** or **Canyon de Chelly,** two geological marvels.

CHOOSING A PLACE TO STAY

This is the Old West, after all, and there's a great deal of "roughing it" that you could experience by staying at campsites, dude ranches, or motels near the Grand Canyon or Northeast Arizona. Don't expect to always have great mobile phone reception or cable TV.

The cities of Arizona, however, have some of the most heralded resorts in the world. In Phoenix check out the **Arizona Grand Resort,** which has an extensive water park. Posh resorts like the **JW Marriott Desert Ridge** and the **Westin Kierland Resort & Spa** have special kids-only programs that include evening "dive-in" movies and daytime sports and recreation instruction.

OUTDOOR ACTIVITIES

With its majestic landscapes and sites that are right out of a Hollywood script, you're going to be spending a lot of your time in Arizona outside. Be sure to take advantage of the national parks' **Junior Ranger Programs.** Of course, there's nothing quite as up close and personal

as a hike down the **Grand Canyon,** an adventurous rafting trip down the **Colorado River,** or a walk back in time through **Kartchner Caverns State Park.** Let your kids make the most of their digital cameras while they document the journey. If you prefer something slightly less adventurous, be sure to check out **Oak Creek Canyon** in Sedona, and cool off at **Slide Rock State Park.** On one of your nights away from the city, take advantage of your location and search for constellations as you stargaze.

INDOOR ACTIVITIES

On hot summer days, choose indoor activities for the afternoon, when the sun is at its most intense, and your kids are likely to be their most impatient. This might be a good time to head to Downtown Phoenix and check out the **Children's Museum of Phoenix,** the **Heard Museum,** the **Phoenix Art Museum,** and the **Arizona Science Center,** all of which are steps away from the city's light-rail system. If you're in the cooler country, take advantage of nighttime programs and events at **Lowell Observatory** in Flagstaff, where you can watch the stars in relative comfort.

ROAD TRIP TIPS

Chances are, you'll explore most of Arizona by car. There are kid-friendly stops along the way from Phoenix to Sedona or the Grand Canyon, including **Meteor Crater** and **Montezuma Castle,** that can help break up your hours in the car. Children and adults alike can be quite stunned by how quickly Arizona's landscape changes. Your child could start the day in the desert, and wake up from a nap driving through a ponderosa-pine winter wonderland in Eastern Arizona.

Arizona Today

COVID-19 RECOVERY

In the spring of 2020, the United States (including Arizona) was gravely impacted by the COVID-19 virus. Businesses were forced to shut down and travel stopped in an attempt to curb its spread. Even though the state was relatively quick to reopen, many restaurants, hotels, shops, bars, and even cultural institutions have since closed for good. The Navajo Nation was hit especially hard. While the longterm effects on Arizona's tourism is still largely unknown, we expect more than the usual number of businesses to close. If you're planning a visit, remember to call ahead to verify open hours, and to make sure the property is still in operation.

ENVIRONMENT

Over a decade of droughts in the area has made that water a precious resource to residents, especially as the state's population continues to grow. While Lake Powell is recovering, Lake Mead remains at record-low levels, and meager snowfall in the high country is making ski season more of a celebration than an expectation. Nevertheless, the Valley of the Sun is becoming more conscious of its water usage, including an uptick in artificial lawns and natural landscapes in residential yards throughout Phoenix, while golf courses optimize every drop of water, and many are installing low-flow showerheads that use a quarter of the water normally used in a shower. State agencies have been preparing for the future by leveraging canal systems and groundwater. The Central Arizona Project has banked years' worth of water, and residential and commercial construction projects have built-in environmental conservation mandates. All hotels now display "save the water" placards asking you to keep towels an extra day or two. Every drop saved helps.

FOOD

A decade or two ago, you didn't necessarily come to Arizona to eat well. Today, however, renowned chefs are making their mark across the state in every imaginable style, from pizzerias and wine bars to Mexican food and molecular gastronomy. Nobuo at Teeter House in Downtown Phoenix features fine Japanese cuisine crafted by the delicate hands of Nobuo Fukuda. Chris Bianco's pizzas at Pizzeria Bianco in Phoenix are among the best in the state, while Silvana Salcido Esparza has elevated Mexican food to a whole new level at her revered Barrio Café, also in Phoenix. Wineries across the state are also gaining a strong reputation for offering unique blends and tasting rooms. A trip along the Verde Valley Wine Trail makes for an excellent afternoon, as does a visit farther south to Sonoita or Willcox.

TRANSPORTATION

As Arizona's population continues to grow, public transportation cannot be ignored. The Phoenix area took a big step forward with a light-rail system that has cemented Downtown Phoenix as a go-to entertainment district and transformed the way thousands commute to and visit the city. Thanks to the Sky Train at Sky Harbor International Airport, it's now possible to visit and enjoy Phoenix without a car. More transit lines are planned through 2032. Further, the city's bike-share program has 700 bikes available at 70 stops throughout Phoenix, Tempe, and Mesa. Improved freeways are also planned from a wider and more efficient drive south to Tucson to improved roads north to Sedona, Flagstaff, and beyond to the Grand Canyon.

What to Watch and Read

ARIZONA DOCUMENTARIES

Whether you want to learn about the Grand Canyon, Arizona's efforts to manage its water, or famous national figures such as Barry Goldwater or Sandra Day O'Connor, Arizona PBS has a collection well worth navigating ⊕ *azpbs.org/tv/arizonacollection*.

TOMBSTONE (1993)

Much of the filming for this movie about lawman Wyatt Earp and his notorious gunfight at the O.K. Corral occurred at Old Tucson Studios, a favorite shooting location for decades of Western TV and movies. The film is good inspiration for a trip to Tombstone or Bisbee.

RAISING ARIZONA (1987)

This classic oddball comedy by the Coen brothers was filmed all over the Valley of the Sun. One particularly memorable site in the film, the adobe home, is the Jokake Inn on the grounds of The Phoenician resort.

JERRY MAGUIRE (1996)

For a time, this film about a sports agent played by Tom Cruise gave perhaps the most positive depiction of professional football in Phoenix. Locals filled the stands at Sun Devil Stadium for the filming of Rod Tidwell's famous catch.

PSYCHO (1960)

The early scenes of this iconic Hitchcock thriller feature downtown Phoenix in 1960. Some overhead shots offer an excellent view of what downtown looked like back then, and an appreciation for the buildings that remain.

THE BEAN TREES (1988)

A fictional Arizona mining town is the setting for Barbara Kingsolver's novel, which weaves together themes of politics, race, culture, and ultimately, humanity. If you like Kingsolver's work, read its sequel, *Pigs in Heaven*, or *Animal Dreams*, also set in Arizona.

LAUGHING BOY: A NAVAJO LOVE STORY (1929)

Winner of the Pulitzer prize, this novel by Oliver La Farge is a tale of love, identity, family, and the inherent clashes that occur with them.

THE DEVIL'S HIGHWAY: A TRUE STORY (2004)

This Pulitzer finalist by Luis Alberto Urrea chronicles the true story of Mexican immigrants and their travels through the desert in Arizona.

LAZY B: GROWING UP ON A CATTLE RANCH IN THE AMERICAN SOUTHWEST (2003)

The first woman to serve on the Supreme Court was an Arizona girl through and through. In this memoir, co-written with her brother Alan, Sandra Day O'Connor discusses growing up on the Lazy B ranch. The story is one of self-sustenance, fortitude, and independence—traits that helped O'Connor as she blazed her own trail in law.

RIDERS OF THE PURPLE SAGE (1912)

This classic tale of cowboys and their Old West adventures is one of the primary reasons author Zane Grey is so beloved in Arizona. His tales of the frontier and adventure helped to shape the narrative of the American cowboy.

MONKEY WRENCH GANG (1975)

A man returns from Vietnam to discover the desert he loved has been paved, cleared, mined, and dammed. His response makes this novel by Edward Abbey a favorite of counterculturists.

VALLEY 101 PODCAST

If you're more of a listener than a reader or a watcher, check out this local podcast, presented by *The Arizona Republic*, which answers listener questions about the oddities (and wonders) that abound in the Valley of the Sun.

ARIZONA LANDSCAPE ADVENTURES

Arizona's spectacular landscape dominates the eye and floods the senses. No place else in the world has so many unique and bizarre geological features—and the canyons, deserts, and mountains are more than just a backdrop for your journey. To understand and experience the land, you must get outdoors and be willing to accept nature on its own terms.

ARIZONA'S NATURAL FEATURES

Oak Creek Canyon, near Sedona

The diversity that these regions contain, not just in terrain but in flora and fauna, is unparalleled in the Lower 48. Resourceful plants and animals teach us so much about adapting to our surroundings and learning from nature. Some humans have also learned to survive in these harsh environments, but for most of us even a brief foray into Arizona's landscapes can be an adventure.

Canyons, mountains, and deserts are all closely related in the state's basic regions:

■ The northern section is part of the **Colorado Plateau**, a high-elevation region characterized by glowing red rocks and impossibly graceful slot canyons. It is also home to the Grand Canyon.

■ Along the state's southwestern corridor is the **Basin and Range Province**, where cactus-littered deserts and scrubby valleys rise abruptly to the San Francisco Peaks and Chiricahua Mountains.

■ In between, the **Central Highlands** contain mountain ranges where peaks drop away to canyons and desert grasslands, such as the easily accessible Saguaro National Park and the Arizona-Sonora Desert Museum.

NEVADA

SHIVWITS PLATEAU

KANAB PLATEAU

Lake Mead

LAKE MEAD NAT'L RECREATION AREA

GRAND WASH CLIFFS

Lake Mohave

BLACK MTS

Kingman

HUALAPAI MOUNTAIN PARK

Bullhead City

HUALAPAI MTS

Lake Havasu

Lake Havasu City

CALIFORNIA

Alamo Lake

Colorado River

Elevation in feet

10,000

6,000

4,000

2,000

500

MAP AND ACTIVITY KEY

Canyons
Deserts
Mountains
--- Arizona Trail
Birding
Desert Plants
Horse/Mule
Mountain Biking
Photography
Rafting
Rock Climbing
Walking/Hiking

*For details on outfitters and activities, see corresponding chapters.

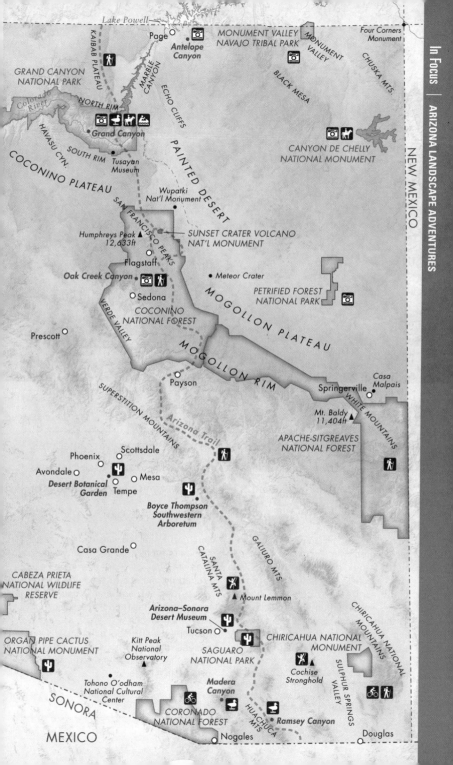

Lake Powell
Page
KAIBAB PLATEAU
GRAND CANYON NATIONAL PARK
Colorado River
NORTH RIM
HAVASU CYN.
COCONINO PLATEAU
SOUTH RIM
Grand Canyon
Tusayan Museum
MARBLE CANYON
ECHO CLIFFS
San Francisco Peaks
PAINTED DESERT

MONUMENT VALLEY NAVAJO TRIBAL PARK
Four Corners Monument
Antelope Canyon
MONUMENT VALLEY
BLACK MESA
CHUSKA MTS.
CANYON DE CHELLY NATIONAL MONUMENT
NEW MEXICO

Wupatki Nat'l Monument
Humphreys Peak 12,633ft
SUNSET CRATER VOLCANO NAT'L MONUMENT
Flagstaff
Oak Creek Canyon
Sedona
Meteor Crater
PETRIFIED FOREST NATIONAL PARK
COCONINO NATIONAL FOREST
VERDE VALLEY
MOGOLLON PLATEAU
Prescott
MOGOLLON RIM
Payson
SUPERSTITION MOUNTAINS
Springerville
Casa Malpais
WHITE MOUNTAINS
Mt. Baldy 11,404ft
APACHE-SITGREAVES NATIONAL FOREST

Arizona Trail
Scottsdale
Phoenix
Avondale
Desert Botanical Garden
Mesa
Tempe
Boyce Thompson Southwestern Arboretum
GALIURO MTS

Casa Grande
CABEZA PRIETA NATIONAL WILDLIFE RESERVE
SANTA CATALINA MTS
Mount Lemmon
Arizona–Sonora Desert Museum
Tucson
Kitt Peak National Observatory
SAGUARO NATIONAL PARK
CHIRICAHUA NATIONAL MONUMENT
CHIRICAHUA NATIONAL MOUNTAINS
ORGAN PIPE CACTUS NATIONAL MONUMENT
Tohono O'odham National Cultural Center
Cochise Stronghold
SULPHUR SPRINGS VALLEY
SONORA
CORONADO NATIONAL FOREST
Madera Canyon
HUACHUCA MTS
Ramsey Canyon
Douglas
MEXICO
Nogales

CANYONS

While the Grand Canyon lives up to its impressive reputation, it is one of many such precious places in Arizona. Each canyon is a unique classroom of geology, where you can see the results of millions of years of shifts in the land.

More than 500 million years ago, a vast sea covered what is now Arizona. Sediments formed in thick layers as the sea rose and fell. Subsequent movement in the earth's crust created mountain ranges and lifted up entire sections of northern Arizona. Erosion and downcutting by rivers created deep canyons, uncovering layers of sandstone, shale, and limestone.

Forces of water and wind work to create some of Arizona's signature landscapes. High-elevation plateaus are continually eroded by rain, ice, rivers and groundwater, chipping and cracking the soft rock to form mesas and buttes, isolated hills or formations with steep sides and flat tops. What's the difference? One general rule of thumb is that a mesa is wider than it is high, while a butte is taller than it is high.

Some Grand Canyon excursions, such as mule tours (top) and rafting (opposite), are so popular they are booked up to a year in advance.

You can get your ecology credits here, too. As elevation changes from canyon floor to rim, so do the plants and animals. You can easily pass through four different biomes in a day's hike. Riparian communities on the canyon floor give way to a desert scrub, then to pinyon and Ponderosa pine forests. Where elevation exceeds 8,000 feet, spruce-fir forests make you feel as if you've somehow been transported to Canada.

ANCIENT PEOPLE AND THE LAND
Archaeologists have uncovered artifacts that show that people have lived in the Grand Canyon for at least 4,000 years. Tools, fire pits, cave paintings, and other remains indicate the presence of hunter-gatherers called the Archaic people, descendants of prehistoric indigenous tribes. You can see some "Archaic origami" stick figures on display at the Tusayan Museum at the South Rim.

TOP CANYON EXPERIENCES

WHITEWATER RAFTING
It's the rivers that helped create the canyons, after all, so spending time on the water is to spend time imagining the steady flow that carved out these works of natural art. About two dozen outfitters offer trips on the Colorado River through or near the Grand Canyon. Some sections are quiet and gentle, others rage and roil.

HORSE AND MULE TOURS
The best way to get a sense of the sheer scale of canyons is to be humbled by them—which means that you have to get to the bottom and look up. Hiking can be arduous, so many tour operators and parks offer horse or mule expeditions.

BIRDING
The entire state offers magnificent birding, but two extremes stand out. In the Grand Canyon, you can spot the enormous California condor's nine-foot wingspan since it was re-introduced in the 1990s. In the canyons of southeast Arizona, birders congregate in summer time to search for tiny hummingbirds.

BEYOND THE GRAND CANYON

In the northeast corner of Arizona, **Canyon de Chelly National Monument**, a National Park on Navajo Tribal Trust Land, rivals the Grand Canyon in natural splendor and can't be beat for cultural significance. People have been in residence here continuously since prehistoric times.

Antelope Canyon, called the world's most photographed slot canyon, is near Page in northern Arizona. You'll need an authorized guide to hike into this narrow sandstone canyon, which is inside the Navajo Nation.

Just north of Sedona in north-central Arizona, you can drive through **Oak Creek Canyon**. Stop along the way to take a closer look at the red sandstone cliffs and buttes.

WORTH NOTING
- Canyon X, northeast Arizona
- Havasu Canyon, Grand Canyon
- Ramsey Canyon, southern Arizona
- Madera Canyon, southern Arizona
- Walnut Canyon National Monument, North-Central Arizona

DESERTS

Deserts are full of mystery, surprises, and stories of plants, animals, and people overcoming odds to survive and flourish. Track down a rare desert bloom, listen to the screech of an owl, or hear the hiss of a rattlesnake and you'll get a sense of the unique beauty and power of the landscape.

Just one of Arizona's claims to nature's hall of fame is as the only state to have all four of the major deserts in the United States within its borders. The Great Basin, the nation's largest cold desert, spills down to touch the northernmost areas of Arizona. In northwest Arizona, low shrubs such as yucca and the Joshua Tree dominate the small Mojave Desert, a hot desert, which has the nation's lowest elevation and highest temperatures. Only a few skinny fingers of the Chihuahan Desert grasslands stretch into the state's southeast corner. Arizona's largest desert, the Sonoran, is unusual with its biseasonal rainfall, mild winters, and subtropical climate that give rise to a diversity rarely seen in a desert environment.

Although deserts may look barren from a distance, a closer look reveals classic saguaros (top) and blooming prickly pear cacti (opposite).

And then there's the Painted Desert, not actually a true desert. In this high, dry region of the Colorado Plateau, colorful layers of sedimentary rocks are buckled and pitched up in grand steps, and carved into canyons and other-worldly rock formations.

ANCIENT PEOPLE AND THE LAND

Thousands of years ago, native people learned to live and thrive in the Sonoran Desert, creating canals to irrigate crops, migrating with the seasons from low valleys to cooler mountains, and harvesting desert plants. Today, the 20,000-plus members of the Tohono O'odham Nation live on more than 2.8 million acres in southwestern Arizona. To see handicrafts by tribal members and sample local food, stop by San Xavier Plaza in Tucson.

TOP DESERT EXPERIENCES

WALKING AND HIKING
Whether you're on a gentle nature stroll or a challenging scramble up a mountain, take the time for a scavenger hunt. Seek out a blooming teddy bear cholla, find a whiptail lizard sunning on a rock, or listen for the howl of a coyote at dusk.

PHOTOGRAPHY
The desert has a singular beauty that changes as the light shifts from scorching midday to shadowy dusk to evocative moonshine. With practice you can learn how to capture the best images of sweeping horizons, wildflowers, horses, cowboys, and even the wings of a hummingbird.

VIEWING DESERT PLANTS
Throughout the dry desert landscape, hardy succulents—water-retaining plants including cactus—are well-adapted to the extreme conditions. In wild parks and botanical gardens, you can observe bizzare-looking forms like the Joshua Tree as well as the more familiar saguaro, prickly pear, and barrel cactus.

TOP DESTINATIONS

Part zoo, part botanical garden, part natural history museum, the popular **Arizona-Sonora Desert Museum** allows you to sample the wildlife of the Sonoran Desert in downtown Tucson.

If you've got a little more time and energy, head for **Saguaro National Park** near Tucson. Its two districts have wonderful outdoor opportunities. For vistas of abundant cacti, try the Valley View Overlook.

For a true desert wilderness experience, head southwest to **Organ Pipe Cactus National Monument**, where organ pipe, saguaro, chollo, ocotillo, creosote, and other succulent plants flourish. Hike a trail, bike the 21-mile Ajo Mountain Drive, or camp here for pure serenity.

WORTH NOTING
- Desert Botanical Garden, Phoenix
- Boyce Thompson Arboretum, east of Phoenix
- Cabeza Prieta National Wildlife Refuge, southern Arizona
- Petrified Forest National Park, eastern Arizona

MOUNTAINS

What goes down, must come up. As Arizona's deserts and canyons were formed, so were mountain ranges. Mountain peaks reaching above 4,000 feet in elevation can be found in all parts of the state except the southwest corner.

Ancient rocky ranges with high meadows and cool alpine lakes, cratered volcanic peaks, and desert mountains that fall away to river gorges in deep canyons—Arizona has it all. The diversity of wildlife is immense and you really can travel from a cactus-covered desert to a snow-covered mountain peak in a day. The same geologic forces that created canyons—tectonic to volcanic to glacial activity—have left the state with mountains both old and young.

The rising and falling of the land created not just ranges but also isolated high-elevation areas in southern Arizona. Dubbed "sky islands," a collection of 40 forested mountain groups with lush vegetation at the top and their accompanying canyons below is surrounded by deserts or grasslands. The confluence of desert and forest communities has created habitats for rare and endemic species, and wildlife-watching opportunities are truly

In warm weather, mountains can be cool escapes. Multi-use trails for bikers and hikers criss-cross the area near Sedona (top) and Flagstaff (opposite).

unparalleled. And in eastern Arizona, the pine-covered White Mountains are a cool respite for many outdoor adventures.

ANCIENT PEOPLE AND THE LAND

As Arizona's prehistoric inhabitants evolved from hunting and gathering to agriculture, one group made its home in the forested mountain ranges and nearby valleys: the Mogollon. About 2,000 years ago, early Mogollon people hunted mountain game and gathered fruits, berries, and seeds from alpine meadows and forests to supplement what crops they could grow in the lower valleys. At Casa Malpais, in Springerville, remains of a 16-acre pueblo complex include what is thought to be a Mogollon solstice observatory, built around AD 1200.

TOP MOUNTAIN EXPERIENCES

MOUNTAIN BIKING

You can join a group ride with one of many biking clubs, take a guided tour, or venture out on your own. Recommended spots include: the Elephant Head Trail in Coronado National Forest, and trails in the Coconino National Forest, between Sedona and Flagstaff.

HIKING THE ARIZONA TRAIL

One of the eleven National Scenic Trails, this long-distance route covers about 800 miles from Mexico to Utah. People commonly take one section at a time. The trail takes you through major mountain ranges, from the Huachucas and Santa Rita in the south, through the Superstition Wilderness and over the San Francisco Peaks.

ROCK CLIMBING

Southern Arizona rock formations and towering cliffs are a great place to learn the basics of climbing. Take a course and start with basic bouldering, then learn how to rope up for multi-pitch climbs. Mount Lemmon and Cochise Stronghold, both near Tucson, are popular climbing spots.

TOP DESTINATIONS

Just north of Flagstaff, the volcanic **San Francisco Peaks** can be experienced by foot, mountain bike, horse, or even ski lift. Humphrey's Peak, the state's highest spot at 12,633 feet, is a rewarding trek for experienced hikers.

Erosion has carved out a "Wonderland of Rocks" at **Chiricahua National Monument** in the southeastern section of the state. A perfect example of a sky island, this is considered one of the most ecologically diverse regions in the entire country.

About 1,000 years ago, a series of violent erruptions formed **Sunset Crater Volcano National Monument** and destroyed plants for five miles. Now, you can hike on a lava flow, climb a cinder cone, and see signs of life regenerating.

WORTH NOTING

- Apache-Sitgreaves National Forest, eastern Arizona
- White Mountains, eastern Arizona
- Superstition Wilderness, Phoenix
- Hualapai Mountain Park, northwest Arizona
- Santa Catalina Mountains, Tucson

DISTINCTIVE ANIMALS OF ARIZONA

❶ Coatimundi

These high-energy mammals combine a long ringed tail like a monkey's, a snout like an anteater's, the lumbering walk of a bear, and the mask of a raccoon. Members of the raccoon family, they live in large social groups. Normally tree dwellers, in mountainous southeastern Arizona these nonstop foragers can make dens in caves and crevices.

❷ Desert bighorn sheep

Found primarily in the mountains of the Sonoran and Mojave Deserts, the sheep favor steep slopes and canyon walls. Unique padded hooves allow them to grab the surface of the rock. Males use their large curved horns for fighting and to break open cactus, a common food for the large grazers.

❸ Elegant trogon

This rare, distinctive bird migrates from Mexico to southeast Arizona's mountains and canyons in the summer. The foot-long birds make their nests in dead or dying sycamore trees in cavities created by woodpeckers. The colorful male has an emerald green back and throat, with a bright red breast and a white breast band.

❹ Gila woodpecker

One of the Sonoran Desert's signature species, this woodpecker works away at the saguaro cactus, creating cavities that serve as homes for itself and other animals, including owls, rats, lizards purple martins, and other birds. The very common birds don't hammer just to make holes; they also use sound to mark their territory.

❺ Western diamondback rattlesnake

Reptiles are plentiful in all of Arizona's deserts, and while most are fascinating and beautiful, the rattlesnakes can also be very dangerous. The Western Diamondback, with its triangular-shaped head and black and white ringed tail, is active late afternoon and at night, and will strike if it's disturbed. Tread carefully!

DISTINCTIVE PLANTS OF ARIZONA

⑥ Ocotillo

Common in both the Sonoran and Chihuahuan Deserts, this tall woody shrub has long, thin, spiny stems that rise up out of a short trunk. Reddish orange flowers bloom at the tips of these stems in spring, providing nectar—and energy—to migrating hummingbirds.

⑦ Ponderosa pine

Forests of these tall stately pines cover high-elevation areas on the Colorado Plateau, and in some cases pure stands stretch for thousands of acres—such as the one from Flagstaff along the Mogollon Rim to the White Mountains. Growing more than 100 feet tall, this tree provides food and shelter to many animals and birds.

⑧ Rocky Mountain iris

There's nothing quite like a mountain meadow in May, when blooming alpine wildflowers herald the season. Among the lupines, paintbrushes, lilies, and poppies, look for the Rocky Mountain iris between 6,000 and 9,000 feet elevation.

Growing one or two feet high, the stems produce one to four delicate purple flowers with accents of yellow and white.

⑨ Saguaro cactus

This iconic plant plays such a vital role in the Sonoran Desert, providing food and shelter to bats, bees, and birds. A giant, columnar cactus, with short stout arms that point to the sky, it can grow to be 40 feet tall or higher, with an average life span of 150 years. Its large, creamy white flowers bloom by night in late April and May, harbingers of the red juicy fruit.

⑩ Yellow palo verde (foothill palo verde)

Look for this twiggy, thorny shrub on rocky hillsides. Its green bark contains chlorophyll, so it can still carry on with photosynthesis even when the shrub's leaves drop off during the dry season. The palo verde is the primary nurse plant for the saguaro cactus, providing shade for its seedlings.

A GEOLOGY PRIMER

Left: dramatic spires at the Chiricahuas. Top right: Rainbow Bridge, the world's longest natural bridge. Lower right: Monument Valley's Mittens and Merrick Butte.

ARCH This type of opening in a rock wall forms either through erosion, when wind and sand wear away the rock face, or through the freezing action of water. When water enters spaces or joints in a rock and freezes, the expansion of the ice can crack off chunks of rock.

BRIDGE If an opening through a rock is created by water flowing beneath it, it is called a bridge. You can see many natural bridges in Arizona, such as Rainbow Bridge near Lake Powell and Devil's Bridge near Sedona.

BUTTE A butte is what remains when a mesa erodes. You can see good examples of this formation in Monument Valley in northeast Arizona.

CAVES Natural underground chambers that open to the surface give you an opportunity to descend below the Earth's surface and learn about the forces of heat and water upon rocks and minerals. Kartchner Caverns, south of Tucson, is a living cave where water still flows, dissolving minerals and creating beautiful formations.

MESA A mesa, or hill with a smooth, flat, tablelike top (mesa means "table" in Spanish), is a clear example of how hard rock stands higher and protects the soft rock beneath. A single mesa may cover hundreds of square miles of land. There are many mesas in the Hopi Reservation, including the villages of First, Second, and Third Mesa.

MONUMENT This general term applies to geologic formations that are much taller than they are wide, or to formations that resemble man-made structures. These are what give Monument Valley its name.

PETRIFIED WOOD If you want to know what the desert of the Southwest used to look like, picture the Florida Everglades populated with giant dragonflies and smaller species of dinosaurs. Arizona's Petrified Forest offers a glimpse of the once lush, tropical world. Stumps and logs from the ancient woodland are now turned to rock because they were immersed in water and sealed away from the air, so normal decay did not occur. Instead, the preserved wood gradually hardened as silica, or sand, filtered into its porous spaces, almost like cement. Erosion was among the geological processes that exposed the wood.

SPIRE As a butte erodes, it may become one or more spires. You can see wonderful examples of these rock formations in southern Arizona's Chiricahua National Monument.

Chapter 2

TRAVEL SMART

Updated by
Mara Levin

★ **CAPITAL:**
Phoenix

👫 **POPULATION:**
7.3 million

💬 **LANGUAGE:**
English

$ **CURRENCY:**
U.S. Dollar

⚠ **EMERGENCIES:**
911

📧 **AREA CODES:**
480, 602, 623 (Phoenix
area); 520 (Tucson and
points south); 928 (Northern
Arizona)

🚗 **DRIVING:**
On the right

🕙 **TIME:**
3 hours behind New York
during daylight saving time

⚡ **ELECTRICITY:**
120–220 v/60 cycles; plugs
have two or three rectangu-
lar prongs

🌐 **WEB RESOURCES:**
www.visitarizona.com
nps.gov/grca

✈ **AIRPORTS:**
PHX, TUS

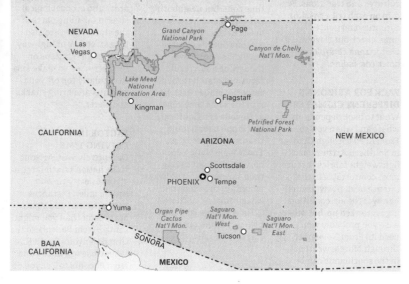

Know Before You Go

From iconic desert scenes, where coyotes howl under saguaro-studded moonscapes, to sacred Native American sites, red rocks, pine forests, and the wondrous Grand Canyon, Arizona's diversity in weather, nature, and cultural history is vast. How do you choose what to see, when to go, and how to pack? Here's how to make the most of your trip.

PLAN AHEAD FOR VISITS TO TRIBAL LANDS

Arizona has 22 Native American tribes, each with its own government and culture. Most tribes have websites or phone information lines, and it's best to contact them before a trip. Many areas, like Antelope Canyon and Canyon de Chelly, require a guide from the tribe to take you on a tour; others require a permit for hiking, biking, taking photos, or filming in scenic areas. Always be respectful of individual cultures and traditions. For info on each tribe's visitor activities and guidelines, check out ⊕ www. visitarizona.com/places/american-indian.

PACK FOR ARIZONA'S DIFFERENT CLIMATES

What to pack depends on where and when you go. From April through October in Southern Arizona, pack lightweight fabrics that are most comfortable in the intense heat. (A sweater is handy if the air-conditioning is cranked up, but otherwise you probably won't need it.) From November through March, weather in the southlands can be more capricious, with rainy or cold snaps followed by a string of balmy 75°F days. As you go north, Sedona and Prescott boast a mild four-seasons climate. Flagstaff and the Grand Canyon rims get plenty of snow, with winter temps averaging 20–40°F, so bring clothing you can layer. If you hike down into the canyon, the temperature rises as you descend.

BE AWARE OF THE TIME ZONE

Arizona is in the mountain time zone, but neighboring California and Nevada are in the Pacific time zone. Arizona doesn't observe daylight saving time, though, and as a result, from mid-March through early November Arizona is in the same time zone as Nevada and California and is one hour behind Utah and New Mexico. The Navajo Nation does observe daylight saving time, however, so it's always mountain time zone on Navajo lands. Confused? ⊕ Timeanddate.com can help you figure out the correct time anywhere.

STAY HYDRATED

Sure, it's a dry heat, and you probably won't *feel* too uncomfortable, but dehydration and heatstroke are real and serious threats in the Sonoran Desert, with high temps and super-low humidity (the average is only 6 %). Heed the advice of locals: drink plenty of water or sports drinks (remembering that coffee and alcohol will dehydrate you) and stay inside, or in shade, between the peak sun hours of noon and 4 pm. Heed the advice of your mom, too: wear a hat and use sunscreen.

RENT A CAR

Wide open spaces mean there's a lot of territory to cover in these parts, and public transportation is sparse. Unless you are hunkering down at a resort or taking a guided tour up to Sedona or the Grand Canyon, renting a car is the best way to explore Arizona. Many of the top sights are nature areas and archaeological sites in far-flung parts of the state. There are also long stretches of highway without gas stations or food services, so make sure to regularly top off your gas tank and bring snacks and water.

FACTOR IN DRIVING TIME

Deceptively vast, Arizona is the nation's sixth-largest state at nearly 114,000 square miles. Distances between cities and sights are greater than you might think—from Phoenix to the Grand Canyon's South Rim takes close to 4 hours, and from Phoenix to Canyon de

Chelly or Monument Valley is a 5-hour drive. (If you start in Tucson, add 2 hours to these estimates.) Sedona is 2 hours from Phoenix and 4 hours from Phoenix; make sure to leave time for hiking or a jeep tour when you get there. Day trips are more of an option in Southern Arizona, where historical towns and winery tours are 1–2 hours from Tucson.

SAVE TWO DAYS FOR THE GRAND CANYON

The average visitor to the Grand Canyon spends only half a day in the park. We do not recommend this! In order to savor the awesome views and take part in all the activities on offer—rafting, hiking, mule rides, biking, and more—plan to spend at least two days in the park. You can stay in one of the canyon's campgrounds or lodges, or base yourself in a nearby town such as Tusayan. At the very least, stay for sunset.

LEAVE NO TRACE

With more than 11,000 archaeological sites and 50 national and state parks, there's a lot of Arizona to love—and to preserve for future generations. Do your part to respect the land by leaving it as you found it. Don't take anything from or mark on the sites, always ask permission before taking photos on tribal lands, and consider eco-friendly hotels.

BE PREPARED FOR EXTREMES

You can start your day in 90°F heat in Phoenix and end it in near-freezing temperatures at the rim of the Grand Canyon. Be sure to plan accordingly for the weather: if driving in the desert in summer, keep bottled water in the car; in winter in the high country, be prepared for icy roads. And remember that violent flash floods and dust storms can pepper the desert during the summer monsoons. Storms usually pass quickly.

DON'T EXPECT TO STAY OUT LATE

If you are visiting from a big city like New York, Chicago, or Los Angeles, you may be surprised that even in larger cities like Phoenix and Tucson, many restaurants close at 9 pm and eateries in the smaller towns are shuttered even earlier. Some bars and craft breweries also keep shorter hours, closing by midnight. Best not to put off dinner to linger by the pool.

LEARN THE LINGO

There are a few regional terms that might crop up on your trip. If you see *burro* on a menu, know it's the proper name for a burrito here. *Flag* is a shortened version of Flagstaff. And if a dust storm rolls through (pay close attention to the National Weather Service), you might hear it referred to as a *haboob*, the same type of storm that rolls over Sudan.

FIND BARGAINS IN THE OFF SEASON

When is the best time to visit Arizona? It's complicated. January through April is high season in Phoenix and Tucson. Prices for lodging and golf are significantly higher (and in Tucson, it's hard to find any accommodations during the first two weeks in February, when the Gem & Mineral Show comes to town). Bargains can be found, even at the fancy resorts, during summer months, because it's very hot and outdoor activities are limited. The north-central parts of the state, including the Grand Canyon, have their high season during the summer, and it's crucial to make summer reservations well in advance for activities and lodging in the Grand Canyon (and gateway cities). Sedona is popular almost year-round, with only a brief lull in January, but rates are highest in spring and fall.

BE CAUTIOUS AT THE MEXICAN BORDER

Many Arizonans fondly recall the days when they could drive down to the border town of Nogales, Mexico, with only a passport and shop for bargains or enjoy lunch. The current situation is not so tourist-friendly; high crime and drug-related violence in the Mexican state of Sonora have caused many shops and restaurants to close, and the U. S. State Department advises travelers to reconsider crossing the border. If you do enter, you will need a passport and FMM (Multiple Immigration Form) visa, which is free for stays up to 7 days and $500 for up to 180 days. Roadside checkpoints are set up along Arizona highways north of the border, where your car will be briefly inspected.

Getting Here

Most visitors to Arizona arrive either by car via one of the main east–west interstates, I–40, I–10, or I–8, or by air into the state's major airport in Phoenix. (Smaller but still significant numbers fly into Tucson.) Most visitors who arrive by air rent cars; public transportation is limited and limiting, and this vast state is ideally suited for car touring. The state's highways are well maintained, have minimal congestion outside of Phoenix, and have high speed limits (up to 75 mph on interstates); so traveling even significant distances by car isn't a great challenge, and the scenery throughout most of the state is stunning.

✈ Air

Despite its high passenger volume, lines at the check-in counters and security checkpoints at Phoenix Sky Harbor Airport are usually brisk and efficient, although during busy periods (spring break, holiday weekends, etc.) you should anticipate longer waits and arrive at the airport 30 to 60 minutes earlier than you would otherwise. Because Phoenix is a hub for Southwest and American Airlines, it has direct flights to most major U.S. cities and a number of international destinations elsewhere in North America (Calgary, Cancún, Edmonton, Guadalajara, Mexico City, Puerto Vallarta, Toronto, Vancouver, and San José, Costa Rica, among them), as well as nonstop service to London on British Airways.

Sample flying times from major cities are: one hour from Los Angeles, three hours from Chicago, and five hours from New York City. Keep in mind that several destinations have only seasonal nonstop service from Phoenix (usually from midautumn through midspring).

AIRPORTS

Major gateways to Arizona include Phoenix Sky Harbor International (PHX), about 3 miles southeast of Phoenix city center, and Tucson International Airport (TUS), about 8½ miles south of Tucson's central business area.

Phoenix Sky Harbor International Airport is one of the busiest airports in the world for takeoffs and landings but rarely suffers from congestion or lengthy lines. Its spacious, modern terminals are easily navigated, with plenty of dining options as well as free Wi-Fi. Sky Harbor's three passenger terminals are connected by the free Sky Train, which runs regularly throughout the day and also links to the 44th St./Washington METRO Light Rail station. Shuttle vans to the rental-car center stop outside each terminal.

Tucson International Airport has one terminal that has a smattering of restaurants and free Wi-Fi. Although it services far fewer passengers per day than Sky Harbor, it does offer nonstop flights to Chicago, Atlanta, Denver, and a number of cities around the western half of the country.

FLIGHTS

Phoenix is a hub for Southwest Airlines and American Airlines; these carriers, as well as the other major U.S. airlines, offer direct flights into and out of Phoenix to most of the country's larger metro areas. Nonstop international destinations from Phoenix include London and many cities in Mexico and Canada. From Tucson, Southwest has direct flights to Chicago, Denver, Las Vegas, Los Angeles, and San Diego, and American Airlines has numerous daily connections to Dallas and Chicago and between Tucson and Phoenix. United and Delta have a few daily flights in and out of Tucson as well.

Among the smaller carriers, Alaska Airlines has direct service from Phoenix and Tucson to Portland and Seattle. Frontier connects Phoenix with Denver. Hawaiian Airlines flies from Phoenix to Hawaii. JetBlue has service from Phoenix to Boston and New York. Sun Country Airlines has seasonal service from Phoenix to Minneapolis. Canada's WestJet connects Phoenix directly with most major cities in western Canada. Low-cost carrier Spirit Airlines has direct service to Denver, Chicago, and Minneapolis. A discount Mexican airline, Volaris, flies from Phoenix nonstop to Guadalajara, with connecting flights to Mexico City and Cancun.

Within Arizona, American Airlines flies from Phoenix to Flagstaff and Yuma. For air travel to smaller Arizona cities, Contour Airlines flies from Phoenix to Page and Boutique Air has service to Show Low. Scenic Airlines flies from Las Vegas to the Grand Canyon.

🚗 Car

A car is a necessity in Arizona, as even bigger cities are challenging to get around in using public transportation. Distances are considerable, but you can make excellent time on long stretches of interstate and other four-lane highways with speed limits of up to 75 mph (even rural two-lane highways often have speed limits of 65 mph). In cities, freeway limits are between 55 mph and 65 mph. If you venture off major thoroughfares, slow down. Many rural roadways have no shoulders; on many twisting and turning mountain roads speed limits dip to 25 mph, and police officers often patrol heavily near entrances to small town centers, where speed limits drop precipitously. For the most part, the scenery you'll take in while driving makes road-tripping worth the time and effort.

At some point you'll probably pass through one or more of the state's 22 Native American reservations. Roads and other areas within reservation boundaries are under the jurisdiction of reservation police and governed by separate rules and regulations. Observe all signs, and respect Native Americans' privacy. Be careful not to hit any animals, which often wander onto the roads; the fines can be very high.

Note that in Phoenix certain lanes on interstates are restricted to carpools and multi-occupant vehicles. Seat belts are required at all times. Tickets can be given for failing to comply. Driving with a blood-alcohol level higher than 0.08 will result in arrest and seizure of your driver's license. Fines are severe. Radar detectors are legal in Arizona, but note that talking on handheld phones and texting while driving is illegal in Phoenix and Tucson, and state police do pull drivers over for both.

Always strap children under age five into approved child-safety seats. In Arizona children must wear seat belts regardless of where they're seated. In Arizona you may turn right at a red light after stopping if there's no oncoming traffic.

CAR RENTAL
Car-rental rates in Phoenix typically begin around $45 a day or $250 a week for an economy car with air-conditioning, automatic transmission, and unlimited mileage—rates vary according to supply and demand, tending to be lower in summer and often dramatically higher in winter. This doesn't include taxes and fees on car rentals, which can range from about 15% to 50%, depending on pickup location. The base tax rate at Sky Harbor Airport is about 30%. When you add the daily fees (which are about $6 or more a day), taxes and fees can add up to almost half the cost of the car rental. Taxes at nonairport locations are typically around 25% or less.

Getting Here

Typical Travel Times

	Hours by Car	Distance
Phoenix–Flagstaff	2	145 miles
Phoenix–Grand Canyon South Rim	4	229 miles
Phoenix–Lake Mead/Hoover Dam	4½	260 miles
Phoenix–Monument Valley	5½	322 miles
Phoenix–Yuma	3	185 miles
Tucson–Phoenix	2	120 miles

Check the Internet or local papers for discounts and deals. Local rental agencies also frequently offer lower rates.

Most agencies in Arizona won't rent to you if you're under the age of 21, and several major agencies won't rent to anyone under 25.

In Arizona the car-rental agency's insurance is primary; therefore, the company must pay for damage to third parties up to a preset legal limit, beyond which your own liability insurance kicks in.

GASOLINE

Gas stations, many of them open 24 hours, are widely available in larger towns and cities and along interstates. Nevertheless, you'll encounter some mighty lonely and long stretches of highway in certain remote sections of Arizona; in these areas it's not uncommon to travel 50 or 60 miles between service stations. It's prudent to play it safe when exploring the far-flung corners of the state and keep your tank at least half full. Gas prices in Arizona are slightly higher than the national average but generally lower than in neighboring Nevada and California.

PARKING

Parking is plentiful and either free or very inexpensive in most Arizona towns, even Phoenix and Tucson. During very busy times, however, such as holidays, parking in smaller popular places like Sedona, Flagstaff, Scottsdale, and Bisbee can prove a little challenging.

ROAD CONDITIONS

The highways in Arizona are well maintained, but there are some natural conditions to keep in mind.

Desert heat. Vehicles and passengers should be well equipped for searing summer heat in the low desert. If you're planning to drive through the desert, make sure you carry plenty of water, a good spare tire, a jack, radiator coolant, a cell phone, and emergency supplies. If you get stranded, stay with your vehicle and wait for help to arrive.

Dust storms. Dust storms are common on the highways and interstates that traverse the open desert (Interstate 10 statewide, and Interstate 8 between Casa Grande and Yuma). These usually occur from May to mid-September, causing extremely low visibility. They also occur occasionally in northeast Arizona around the Navajo and Hopi regions. If you're on the highway, pull as far off the road as possible, turn on your headlights to stay visible, and wait for the storm to subside.

Flash floods. Warnings about flash floods shouldn't be taken lightly. Sudden downpours send torrents of water racing into low-lying areas so dry that they're unable to absorb such a huge quantity of water quickly. The result can be powerful walls of water suddenly descending upon these low-lying areas, devastating anything in their paths. If you see rain clouds or thunderstorms coming, stay away from dry riverbeds (also called arroyos or washes). If you find yourself in one, get out quickly. If you're with a car in a long gully, leave your car and climb out of the gully. You simply won't be able to outdrive a speeding wave—the idea is to get to higher ground immediately when it rains. Major highways are mostly flood-proof, but some smaller roads dip through washes; most roads that traverse these low-lying areas will have flood warning signs, which should be seriously heeded during rainstorms. Washes filled with water shouldn't be crossed unless you can see the bottom. By all means, don't camp in these areas at any time, interesting as they may seem.

Fragile desert life. The dry and easily desecrated desert floor takes centuries to overcome human damage. Consequently, it's illegal for four-wheel-drive and all-terrain vehicles and motorcycles to travel off established roadways.

Winter snow and ice. First-timers to Arizona sometimes doubt the intensity and prevalence of icy and snowy winter weather in the state's higher elevations: the Interstate 40 corridor, Grand Canyon region, north-central and northeast Arizona, as well as some high-elevation communities in eastern Arizona. It's not uncommon for Phoenix to enjoy dry weather and temperatures in the 50s and 60s, while Flagstaff—just 140 miles north—is getting heavy snow and high winds. Facilities at the North Rim of the Grand Canyon are closed from mid-October through mid-May, and the road to the North Rim usually closes by or before December 1. Always check on weather conditions before planning trips to northern and eastern Arizona from late fall through mid-spring.

RIDE-SHARING

Uber and Lyft operate in Arizona's most populous cities (Phoenix, Tucson, Prescott, Flagstaff, and Yuma) as well as at the Phoenix and Tucson airports. Taxis are your best bet in Sedona and Arizona's small towns.

ROADSIDE EMERGENCIES

In the event of a roadside emergency, call 911. Depending on the location, either the state police or the county sheriff's department will respond. Call the city or village police department if you encounter trouble within the limits of a municipality. Native American reservations have tribal police headquarters, and rangers assist travelers within U.S. Forest Service boundaries.

🚆 Train

Amtrak's *Southwest Chief* operates daily between Los Angeles and Chicago, stopping in Needles, California (near the Arizona border), Kingman, Williams Junction (from which bus transfers are available to the scenic Grand Canyon Railway), Flagstaff, Winslow, and Gallup, New Mexico (near the Arizona border). The *Sunset Limited* travels three times each week between Los Angeles and New Orleans, with stops at Yuma, Maricopa (about 25 miles south of Phoenix), Tucson, and Benson. There's a connecting bus (a three-hour trip) between Flagstaff and Phoenix.

Essentials

Dining

Two distinct cultures—Native American and Sonoran—have had the greatest influence on native Arizona cuisine. Chiles, beans, corn, tortillas, and squash are common ingredients for those restaurants that specialize in regional cuisine (cactus is just as tasty but less common). Mom-and-pop taquerías are abundant, especially in the southern part of the state. In Phoenix, Tucson, Sedona, Flagstaff, and increasingly Bisbee, Prescott, Lake Havasu City, and a growing number of smaller communities, you'll find hip, intriguing restaurants specializing in contemporary American and Southwestern cuisine—often with an emphasis on local produce and meats—as well as some excellent purveyors of Asian cuisine, with Thai, Chinese, Vietnamese, and Japanese leading the way.

RESERVATIONS

Regardless of where you are, it's a good idea to make a reservation if you can. In some places—top resort restaurants in Scottsdale and Tucson, for example—it's expected. (Large parties should always call ahead to check the reservations policy.)

Online reservation services, such as OpenTable, make it easy to book a table before you even leave home.

WINES, BEER, AND SPIRITS

Although Arizona isn't typically associated with viticulture, the region southeast of Tucson, stretching to the Mexico border, has several microclimates ideal for wine growing. The iron- and calcium-rich soil is similar to that of the Burgundy region in France and, combined with the temperate weather and lower-key atmosphere, has enticed more than two dozen independent and family-run wineries to open in the past two decades in the Elgin, Sonoita, and Willcox areas. A somewhat more nascent but increasingly respected crop of vineyards have developed north of Phoenix, in the Verde Valley around Sedona. Microbreweries are another fast-growing presence in Arizona, with a number of good ones in Phoenix, Tucson, Sedona, and Flagstaff, and other notables in Lake Havasu City, Prescott, Bisbee, and a few other towns.

In Arizona you must be 21 to buy alcohol. Bars and liquor stores are open daily, including Sunday, but must stop selling alcohol at 2 am. Smoking is prohibited in bars and restaurants that serve food. You'll find beer, wine, and alcohol at most supermarkets. Possession and consumption of alcoholic beverages is illegal on Native American reservations.

⊕ Health

ANIMAL BITES

Wherever you're walking in desert areas, particularly between April and October, keep a lookout for rattlesnakes. You're likely not to have any problems if you maintain distance from snakes that you see—they can strike only half of their length, so a 6-foot clearance should allow you to remain unharmed, especially if you don't provoke them. If a rattler bites you, don't panic. Get to a hospital within two to three hours of the bite. Try to keep the area that has been bitten below heart level, and stay calm, as increased heart rate can spread venom more quickly. Keep in mind that 30% to 40% of bites are dry bites, where the snake uses no venom (still, get thee to a hospital). Avoid night hikes without rangers, when snakes are on the prowl and less visible.

Scorpions and Gila monsters are no less of a concern, though they strike only when provoked. To avoid scorpion encounters, look before touching: never place your hands where you can't see, such as under rocks and in holes. Likewise, if you move a rock to sit down, make sure that scorpions haven't been exposed. Campers should shake out shoes in the morning, since scorpions like warm, moist places. If you're bitten, see a ranger about symptoms that may develop. Chances are good that you won't need to go to a hospital. Children are a different case, however: scorpion stings can be fatal for them. Always try to keep an eye on what they may be getting their hands into to avoid the scorpion's sting.

Gila monsters are relatively rare and bites are even rarer, but bear in mind that the reptiles are most active between April and June. Should a member of your party be bitten, it's most important to release the Gila monster's jaws as soon as possible to minimize the amount of venom released. This can usually be achieved with a stick, an open flame, or immersion of the animal in water.

COVID-19

A novel coronavirus brought all travel to a virtual standstill in the first half of 2020. Although the illness is mild in most people, some experience severe and even life-threatening complications. Once travel started up again, albeit slowly and cautiously, travelers were asked to be particularly careful about hygiene and to avoid any unnecessary travel, especially if they are sick.

Older adults, especially those over 65, have a greater chance of having severe complications from COVID-19. The same is true for people with weaker immune systems or those living with some types of medical conditions, including diabetes, asthma, heart disease, cancer, HIV/AIDS, kidney disease, and liver disease.

Starting two weeks before a trip, anyone planning to travel should be on the lookout for some of the following symptoms: cough, fever, chills, trouble breathing, muscle pain, sore throat, and new loss of smell or taste. If you experience any of these symptoms, you should not travel at all.

And to protect yourself during travel, do your best to avoid contact with people showing symptoms. Wash your hands often with soap and water. Limit your time in public places, and, when you are out and about, wear a cloth face mask that covers your nose and mouth. Indeed, a mask may be required in some places, such as on an airplane or in a confined space like a theater, where you share the space with a lot of people.

You may wish to bring extra supplies, such as disinfecting wipes, hand sanitizer (12-ounce bottles were allowed in carry-on luggage at this writing), and a first-aid kit with a thermometer.

Given how abruptly travel was curtailed in March 2020, it is wise to consider protecting yourself by purchasing a travel insurance policy that will reimburse you for any costs related to COVID-19-related cancellations. Not all travel insurance policies protect against pandemic-related cancellations, so always read the fine print.

DEHYDRATION

This underestimated danger can be serious, especially considering that one of the first major symptoms is the inability to swallow. It may be the easiest hazard to avoid, however; simply drink every 10–15 minutes, up to a gallon of water per day when outside in summer, and keep well hydrated other times of year, too, as even cool winter days can be very dry.

Essentials

HYPOTHERMIA

Temperatures in Arizona can vary widely from day to night—as much as 40°F. Be sure to bring enough warm clothing for hiking and camping, along with wet-weather gear. It's always a good idea to pack an extra set of clothes in a large, waterproof plastic bag that would stay dry in any situation. Exposure to the degree that body temperature dips below 95°F produces the following symptoms: chills, tiredness, then uncontrollable shivering and irrational behavior, with the victim not always recognizing that he or she is cold. If someone in your party is suffering from any of these symptoms, wrap him or her in blankets and/or a warm sleeping bag immediately and try to keep him or her awake. The fastest way to raise body temperature is through skin-to-skin contact in a sleeping bag. Drinking warm liquids also helps.

SUN EXPOSURE

Wear a hat and sunglasses and put on sunblock to protect against the burning Arizona sun. Try to minimize your sun exposure during the peak hours of noon to 4 pm, and watch out for heatstroke. Symptoms include headache, dizziness, and fatigue, which can turn into convulsions and unconsciousness and can lead to death. If someone in your party develops any of these conditions, have one person seek emergency help while others move the victim into the shade and wrap him or her in wet clothing (is a stream nearby?) to cool down.

Immunizations

There are no immunization requirements for visitors traveling to the United States for tourism.

Lodging

Arizona's hotels and motels run the gamut from world-class resorts to budget chains and from historic inns, bed-and-breakfasts, and mountain lodges to dude ranches, campgrounds, houseboat rentals, and RV parks. Make reservations well in advance for the high season—winter in the desert and summer in the high country. A few areas, such as Sedona and the Grand Canyon's South Rim, stay relatively busy year-round, so book as soon as you can. Tremendous bargains can be found off-season, especially in the Phoenix and Tucson areas in summer, when even the most exclusive establishments may cut their rates by half or more.

Phoenix and Tucson have the most variety of accommodations in the state, with Flagstaff offering the largest number in the northern part of the state. Lodgings in Sedona and in some of the smaller, more exclusive desert communities can be pricey, but there are inexpensive chains in or near just about every resort-oriented destination. That said, even the budget chains in these areas can have rates in at least the upper double-digits.

The Grand Canyon area is relatively pricey, but camping, cabins, and dorm-style resorts on or near the national park grounds offer lower rates. ■TIP➔ **If you plan to stay at the Grand Canyon, make lodging reservations as far as a year in advance—especially if you're looking to visit in summer.** You might have a more relaxing visit, and find better prices, in one of the gateway cities: Tusayan, Williams, and Flagstaff to the south, and Jacob Lake, Fredonia, and Kanab, Utah, to the north. Of all of these, Flagstaff has the best variety of lodging options in all price ranges.

Our local writers vet every hotel to recommend the best overnights in each price category, from budget to expensive. Unless otherwise specified, you can expect a private bath and TV in your room.

BED-AND-BREAKFASTS

Arizona is one of the better destinations in the country when it comes to B&Bs. You'll find luxurious Spanish colonial–style compounds and restored Victorian inns in the more upscale destinations, such as Tucson, Sedona, Flagstaff, and Prescott, as well as less fancy lodges virtually everywhere. BnBfinder.com is an online resource that lists many B&Bs throughout the state. Most of the regional visitor center websites, such as ⊕ visitsedona.com and ⊕ discoverbisbee. com, also list B&Bs and cottage rentals.

DUDE–GUEST RANCHES

Guest ranches afford visitors a close encounter with cowboy culture, activities, and cooking. Most of the properties are situated either near Tucson or in Wickenburg, northwest of Phoenix. Some are resort-style compounds where guests are pampered, whereas smaller, family-run ranches expect *everyone* to join in the chores. Horseback riding and other outdoor recreational activities are emphasized. Many dude ranches are closed in summer. The Arizona Dude Ranch Association provides names and addresses of member ranches and their facilities and policies.

💲 Money

Prices throughout this guide are given for adults. Substantially reduced fees are almost always available for children, students, and senior citizens.

Item	Average Cost
Cup of Coffee	$3
Glass of Wine	$9
Pint of Beer	$6
Sandwich	$9
One-mile Taxi Ride in Phoenix	$7
Museum Admission	$12

🖾 Packing

Pack casual clothing and resort wear for a trip to Arizona; how many layers you bring depends on what time of year you visit and where you plan to go. Stay cool in the intense desert heat of Southern Arizona with cotton fabrics and light colors. T-shirts, polo shirts, sundresses, and lightweight shorts, trousers, skirts, and blouses are useful year-round in all but the higher-elevation parts of the state, where cooler temperatures mandate warmer garb. Pack a sweater for chilly desert nights during the winter. Bring sun hats, swimsuits, sandals, and sunscreen—essential warm-weather items. Bring warm layers, including sweaters and a warm jacket, November through April in the high country—anywhere around Flagstaff, at the Grand Canyon, and in the White Mountains. And don't forget jeans and sneakers or sturdy walking shoes year-round.

SHIPPING SPORTING EQUIPMENT

If you're driving here, lugging your gear isn't much of a hassle. But travelers arriving by plane may find hauling bags of golf clubs or mountain bikes a bit daunting. Luggage Forward specializes in shipping gear door-to-door. The service isn't cheap, but it's highly reliable and convenient.

Essentials

🌐 Passport

All visitors to the United States are required to have a passport that is valid for six months beyond your expected period of stay. Passports are also necessary for travel into Mexico.

➕ Safety

Arizona's track record in terms of crime is not unlike that of other U.S. states, and property crime is a little higher than average in Phoenix and Tucson. In these big cities you should take the same precautions you would anywhere—be aware of what's going on around you, stick to well-lighted and populous areas, and quickly move away from any situation or people that might be threatening. Wherever you go, don't leave anything valuable in your car.

■TIP➜ Check the U.S. government travel advisory before you plan a trip to the Mexico border towns. Visitors should take extra precautions.

💲 Taxes

Arizona state sales tax (called a transaction privilege tax), which applies to all purchases except food in grocery stores, is 5.6%. Individual counties and municipalities, however, then add their own sales taxes, which add another few percentage points, making some Arizona cities' sales taxes among the highest in the country, including Tucson (8.7%) and Phoenix (8.3%). Sales taxes don't apply on Native American reservations.

💲 Tipping

The customary tip for taxi drivers is 15%–20%, with a minimum of $2. Bellhops are usually given $1–$2 per bag. Hotel maids should be tipped $2 per day of your stay. A doorman who hails a cab can be tipped $1–$2. You should also tip your hotel concierge for services rendered; the size of the tip depends on the difficulty of your request, as well as the quality of the concierge's work. For an ordinary dinner reservation or tour arrangements, $3–$5 should do; if the concierge scores seats at a popular restaurant or show, or performs unusual services (getting your laptop repaired, finding a good pet-sitter, etc.), $10 or more is appropriate.

Waiters should be tipped 15%–20%. Many restaurants add a gratuity to the bill for parties of six or more; if so, tipping beyond this amount is optional. Ask what the percentage is if the menu or bill doesn't state it. Tip $1 per drink you order at the bar, though if at an upscale establishment, those $15 martinis warrant at least a $2 tip.

🔤 Visa

Except for citizens of Canada and Bermuda, most visitors to the United States must have a visa. If you are from one of the 39 designated members of the Visa Waiver Program, then you only require an ESTA (Electronic System for Travel Authorization) as long as you are staying for 90 days or less. However, nationals of Visa Waiver nations who have traveled to Iran, Iraq, Libya, Somalia, Sudan, Syria, or Yemen no longer qualify for ESTA. Also, if you have been denied a visa to visit the United States, your application for the ESTA program most likely will be denied.

🔍 Visitor Information

⇨ *For local tourism information, see specific chapters and towns.* Many of Arizona's Native American reservations have websites and helpful information. Some require permits for visiting certain areas.

ONLINE RESOURCES

Information of particular interest to outdoorsy types can be found on the website for Arizona State Parks. The National Park Service website has links to 26 NPS sites in the state. There's also a handful of excellent general-interest sites related to travel in Arizona.

📅 When to Go

Low Season: If you're on a budget, the posh desert resorts drop their prices—sometimes by more than half—June through September. The South Rim of the Grand Canyon and Sedona are busy year-round but least busy during the winter months. Remember that the North Rim of the Grand Canyon is closed in winter, from mid-October to mid-May.

Shoulder Season: Spring is a near-perfect time to visit; wildflowers are best from March until May in Southern Arizona and May-June in the higher elevations. Prices for lodging in Phoenix and Tucson can still be high through April, as the weather is glorious for golfing, hiking and biking; May is less expensive, though a bit warmer in the desert. Fall is a great shoulder season in terms of both budget and weather in all parts of the state: lodging costs less, and it's balmy in the desert regions and pleasantly crisp in the mountains up north.

High Season: High season at the resorts of Phoenix and Tucson is winter, when the snowbirds fly south. Expect the best temperatures—and the highest prices—January through March, when nearly every weekend is filled with outdoor festivals. Also take note that areas such as eastern Arizona are most popular with summer travelers, so many shops and restaurants are closed in the winter months.

WEATHER

For a statewide excursion, keep in mind that Arizona's climate is extreme. Although a winter visit might be most comfortable in Phoenix, remember that the Grand Canyon, Flagstaff, and Sedona—Arizona's high country—will be quite cold then.

Phoenix averages 325 sunny days and 7 inches of precipitation annually. The high mountains see about 25 inches of rain. The Grand Canyon is usually cool at the rim and about 20°F warmer on the floor. The North Rim is generally about 10°F cooler than the South Rim, which is open year-round. Temperatures in valley areas like Phoenix and Tucson average about 60°F to 70°F in the daytime in winter and between 100°F and 115°F in summer. Flagstaff and Sedona stay much cooler, dropping into the 30s and 40s in winter and leveling off at 80°F to 90°F in summer.

Best Tours

ARCHAEOLOGY

Archaeological Conservancy. This esteemed organization offers a number of multiday tours covering significant sites around the country, including one or two Southwest trips each year that may involve sites in Arizona. Additionally, the conservancy oversees and offers visits to a pair of archaeological preserves in Arizona: Sherwood Ranch Pueblo in Apache County and Mission Guevavi in Santa Cruz County. ☎ 505/266–1540 ⊕ www.archaeo-logicalconservancy.org ⌨ From $2295.

BICYCLING

A number of companies offer extensive bike tours that cover parts of the Southwest. ■ TIP→ **Most airlines accommodate bikes as luggage, provided they're dismantled and boxed.**

Bicycle Adventures. This Washington-based company offers a very popular six-day bike excursion, the Arizona Sonora Bike Tour, through Tucson's Saguaro National Park and down through Tombstone and Bisbee. Lodgings each night are at high-end resorts and hotels throughout the region. ☎ 800/443–6060 ⊕ www.bicycleadven-tures.com ⌨ From $2998.

Magpie Cycling. Although specializing in tours around southeastern Utah, this Moab-based outfitter does have an exciting five-day mountain-biking trip around the North Rim of the Grand Canyon. ☎ 435/259–4464 ⊕ magpiecycling.com ⌨ From $1175.

REI Co-op Adventure Center Arizona. The Scottsdale-based branch of this dependable national outfitter offers a variety of bike trips and outdoor adventures throughout the state, including half-day and full-day mountain-biking rides through the Sonoran Desert, road-biking tours, kayaking, and hiking tours. ☎ 480/945–2881, 866/455–1601 ⊕ www.destinations.rei.com ⌨ From $60.

GOLF

Golfpac. This company specializing in custom golf-vacation planning arranges trips all over the world, with Phoenix and Scottsdale among its most popular destinations. Rates include golf and lodging. ☎ 888/848–8941, 407/260–2288 ⊕ www.golfpactravel.com ⌨ From $250.

HIKING

REI Co-op Adventure Center Arizona. This reliable company's Arizona branch, based in Scottsdale, offers multiday and half-day hiking (as well as kayaking and rafting) excursions through some of the state's most dramatic scenery, from the Grand Canyon to Havasupai. ☎ 480/945–2881, 866/455–1601 ⊕ destinations.rei.com ⌨ From $60.

Timberline Adventures. This Colorado-based company has multiday hiking tours in the Grand Canyon as well as in Chiricahua National Monument and the Sonoran Desert near Tucson. ☎ 303/664–8388, 800/417–2453 ⊕ www.timber-line-adventures.com ⌨ From $2050.

NATIVE AMERICAN HISTORY

Native American Journeys. You can explore a number of parts of the state important to indigenous peoples—the Grand Canyon, Hopi Country, Antelope Canyon, Canyon de Chelly, Monument Valley—on one-day hiking or float trips offered by this first-rate company based in Sedona. ☎ 928/204–5506, 877/367–2383 ⊕ na-tiveamericanjourneys.com ⌨ From $199.

NATURAL HISTORY

Naturalist Journeys. Seven-day tours by this Arizona-based outfitter emphasize birding and wildlife, and venture into southeastern Arizona on small group trips. ☎ 520/558–1146, 866/900–1146 ⊕ www.naturalistjourneys.com ✉ From $2390.

Off the Beaten Path. Founded in 1986, this company offers small and customized group tours in northern Arizona and elsewhere in the Southwest, including a six-night tour covering the Grand Canyon, Lake Powell, Antelope Canyon, and Zion National Park (in southern Utah) and a six-night Puebloan Mystery tour exploring Canyon de.Chelly and New Mexico's Chaco Canyon. ☎ 406/586–1311, 888/436–4285 ⊕ www.offthebeatenpath.com ✉ From $2950.

Smithsonian Journeys. Trip options through the distinguished Smithsonian include a five-day tour of world-renowned astronomy research centers in Southern Arizona and a 10-day hiking trip in the Grand Canyon, Bryce Canyon, and Zion national parks. ☎ 855/330–1542 ⊕ www.smithsonianjourneys.org ✉ From $3590.

Victor Emanuel Nature Tours. Also known as VENT Birding Tours, this excellent, world-renowned tour operator that emphasizes bird-watching has been going strong since 1976, offering four or five different multiday tours during winter in Southeastern Arizona. ☎ 512/328–5221, 800/328–8368 ⊕ www.ventbird.com ✉ From $2795.

RIVER-RAFTING

Rafting on the Colorado River through the Grand Canyon is a once-in-a-lifetime experience for many who try it. Numerous reliable companies offer rafting tours through the canyon; see the Grand Canyon National Park chapter for details on the variety of rafting trips offered.

Action Whitewater Adventures. This company, founded in 1955, leads multiday rafting itineraries through the upper Grand Canyon, starting at Marble Canyon. The cost includes the flight from Las Vegas. ☎ 801/375–4111, 800/453–1482 ⊕ riverguide.com ✉ From $1419.

Aramark Wilderness River Adventures. Based in Page, and part of the respected Aramark Parks and Destinations brand, this rafting company has trips through the Grand Canyon as well as from Moab, Utah, to Lake Powell on the Arizona border. Both motorized and paddle options are available. ☎ 800/992–8022 ⊕ www.riveradventures.com ✉ From $1235.

OARS. This California-based company is highly respected for its rafting adventures through the Grand Canyon, which last from 5 to 18 days. ☎ 209/736–4677, 800/346–6277 ⊕ www.oars.com ✉ From $2649.

Western River Expeditions. This Utah-based company's three-, four-, six-, and seven-day rafting trips through the Grand Canyon are geared to all ability levels, with the shorter adventures best for beginners. ☎ 801/942–6669, 866/904–1160 ⊕ www.westernriver.com ✉ From $1470.

Great Itineraries

Arizona Road Trip: Phoenix and the Grand Canyon, 7 Days

A week in Arizona can take you from the beauty of the Sonoran Desert and its towering saguaros to the famous red rocks of Sedona and the majesty of the Grand Canyon. You'll get a sense of the state's history, culture, and awe-inspiring landmarks, with time to spare for some serious pampering and playtime.

DAYS 1 AND 2: PHOENIX AND THE VALLEY OF THE SUN

The metropolitan Phoenix area is the best place to begin your trip to Arizona, with a wealth of hotels and resorts. Reserve a day in the Valley and visit the Heard Museum and Desert Botanical Garden; don't forget to stop by one of the area's popular Mexican restaurants for dinner. If time permits, stroll through Old Town Scottsdale's tempting art galleries. If you have kids, can't-miss stops include the Children's Museum of Phoenix and the Phoenix Zoo; either will take up a half day and wear your little ones out. Depending on your remaining time in the Valley, you can escape to a spa for a day of pampering, go for a hike and explore, get out your golf clubs and hit the links, or—if the season is right—catch a Major League Baseball spring-training game.

Logistics: Sky Harbor International Airport is located at the center of the city and is 20 minutes away from most of the Valley's major resorts. Plan on driving everywhere in the greater Phoenix area, as public transportation is nearly nonexistent. The Valley of the Sun is a large area, but Phoenix itself is remarkably simple to navigate. Designed on a grid, numbered streets run north–south and named streets (Camelback Road, Glendale Avenue) run east–west. Grand Avenue, running about 20 miles from Downtown Phoenix to Sun City, is the only diagonal. If you need to know which direction you're facing, you can see South Mountain, conveniently looming in the south, from nearly any point in the city.

DAYS 3 AND 4: SEDONA AND THE RED ROCKS

The unusual red rock formations in Sedona are a key destination for most visitors to Arizona, and it's no wonder. The shades of red and pink in the towering rocks are like none other. In one day, you can get a good grasp of the beauty of the city, although it's easy to spend several days just soaking it in. Visit Chapel of the Holy Cross and sites such as Bell Rock, Cathedral Rock, Oak Creek Canyon, and Slide Rock State Park (especially if it's warm out). If you feel like a thrill, take a jeep tour and explore the landscape in a bumpy and unforgettable adventure. Sedona is famous for its spas and retreats, so book an hour for a creek-side massage or a guided meditation.

Logistics: The drive to Sedona from Phoenix takes about two hours; longer during the weekend when many commute away from the heat. Take Interstate 17 north to State Route 179, which takes you straight into Sedona and its beautiful red rocks. Some find the alternate route more scenic; exit Interstate 17 earlier, taking AZ 260 to AZ 89A.

DAYS 5 AND 6: THE GRAND CANYON SOUTH RIM

The sight of the Grand Canyon's immense beauty has taken many a visitor's breath away. It's also larger than you might imagine: just driving from the popular South Rim to the North Rim takes about five hours. The South Rim is typically the best location for first-time visitors; it's open 365 days a year and has more tourist-friendly facilities, while the North Rim is extremely secluded and only open half the year. Make sure you catch a sunset or sunrise view during your visit. A night, or even just dinner, at grand El Tovar Hotel won't disappoint, but book your reservation early (up to six months ahead). Outdoors enthusiasts will want to reserve several days to hike and explore the canyon; less ambitious travelers can comfortably see the area in one or two days. If you have specific goals, whether it's a rafting trip or dining and lodging, be sure to book very early—reservations are essential.

Logistics: Reaching the South Rim from Sedona takes at least two hours. In Sedona, take AZ 89A through Oak Creek Canyon to Flagstaff. There, take Interstate 40 west to Williams, and then take AZ 64 to the South Rim.

DAY 7: FLAGSTAFF, PRESCOTT, AND JEROME

The drive south back to Phoenix can feel like a long haul (it will take half the day), but there are plenty of spots to stretch your legs and take in more of the state. Be sure to check your departure time at Sky Harbor Airport, and reserve at least two hours to return your rental car and get through security. If there's time along the drive back, check out Flagstaff, a college town with a love for the outdoors and the stars; Prescott, with its Whiskey Row and Victorian homes; and Jerome, a charming artists' community built on a steep hillside. Closer to Phoenix, stop at Montezuma Castle National Monument for one last glimpse of history, and maybe a souvenir.

Great Itineraries

The Best of Southern Arizona, 7 Days

While it's easy to think of the Grand Canyon and Sedona as the go-to sites in Arizona, they're really only the beginning. To truly appreciate the full beauty of the state, bypass the high country and instead head south to Tucson and its neighboring towns. There, you'll see undisturbed saguaro cacti by the hundreds, explore historic caverns, and enjoy quaint artists' communities.

While Tucson does have an international airport, it often isn't as convenient as Phoenix. Typically fares are lower in Phoenix as more flights fly into the city. Plus starting your journey in the Valley gives the perfect opportunity to view the yin and yang of Arizona: urban, sprawling Phoenix and its quiet but charming smaller neighbor to the south, Tucson.

DAYS 1 AND 2: PHOENIX AND THE VALLEY OF THE SUN

Start your trip by immersing yourself in the basics of the desert. First, visit the Heard Museum, regarded as the finest collection of Native American art in the nation. Then head east about 20 minutes and explore the Desert Botanical Garden, where you'll see desert plants in all shapes and colors, and discover that the native landscape is more diverse and beautiful than a thorny cactus. For dinner enjoy a spicy and hearty Mexican meal; be sure to order something filled with machaca beef and covered in green sauce. You won't regret it. In the morning head outdoors for a hike or a balloon ride, or even have a little grown-up playtime at one of Phoenix's many luxurious spas or manicured golf courses. In the evening explore Old Town Scottsdale. Stroll the streets, window-shop for art (you'll be tempted), and then dine at a fine restaurant.

DAY 3: TUCSON

Just two hours from Phoenix by car, Tucson offers a change of pace. Cooler (literally about 10 degrees cooler), smaller, and more natural, Tucson just has a different vibe. Get a feel for the area by visiting the indoor-outdoor Arizona-Sonora Desert Museum, where you'll see plants, animals, art, and more. Kids might enjoy a couple of hours at the nearby Old Tucson Studios. After lunch, head south to Mission San Xavier del Bac, the oldest Catholic Church in the United States.

Logistics: Tucson is about two hours by car from Phoenix. Take Interstate 10 south.

DAY 4: THE WILD WEST

The Old West is alive and well in Southern Arizona. Historic Tombstone, of Wyatt Earp and the O.K. Corral fame, is just an hour outside of Tucson. Visit the Tombstone Historama to get a feel for the town and its history, and then watch a reenactment of the O.K. Corral gunfight. Spend the night in nearby Bisbee, an artists' haven and a great site for shopping, or return to Tucson if metropolitan comforts are more to your liking.

Logistics: Tombstone is about an hour southeast of Tucson. Take Interstate 10 east to AZ 80 to reach Tombstone. Bisbee is farther along AZ 80, just about a half hour outside of Tombstone, and an hour and a half from Tucson.

DAY 5: KARTCHNER CAVERNS STATE PARK

The most impressive cave system in Arizona, and quite possibly the country, was a secret until 1999. Only discovered in 1974 and then kept hidden from the public for some 25 years, Kartchner Caverns State Park is a wet cave system comprising 13,000 feet of passages and two chambers. Reservations are essential, and you'll have to choose between a tour of the Big Room or

Phoenix and the Valley of the Sun · Scottsdale · Sabino Canyon · Saguaro National Park West · Saguaro National Park East · Tucson · Benson · Kartchner Caverns State Park · Tombstone · Sonoita · The Wild West · Bisbee

MEXICO

the Rotunda/Throne Room. There's an on-site café, so don't worry about packing provisions. But plan on making a relatively long drive home—whether that's Tucson or Bisbee—for dinner.

Logistics: To reach Kartchner Caverns State Park, take Interstate 10 to Benson, which is a half hour east of Tucson. Take AZ 90 south for 9 miles to reach the park.

DAY 6: WINE IN SONOITA
The earth of Southern Arizona's Santa Cruz Valley happens to be ideal for winemaking, and Sonoita has become the center of this growing area of wineries. Callaghan Vineyards is a popular stop, thanks to its award-winning Fumé Blanc. Get a good meal before heading back to Tucson.

Logistics: The Sonoita area is about an hour from Tucson. Take Interstate 10 to AZ 83 and drive south to AZ 82. Vineyards are located along AZ 83 and AZ 82.

DAY 7: SAGUARO NATIONAL PARK OR SABINO CANYON
Before heading back to Phoenix for your departure, visit either Saguaro National Park or Sabino Canyon. If you don't feel like walking, both East and West districts of Saguaro have a scenic drive, and Sabino Canyon has an open-air tram. There you can view one of the densest populations of the iconic saguaro cactus, the most protected and beloved inhabitants of the state; they can reach 50 feet in height and live up to 200 years. Bring food and water for your visit, even if your only plan is to explore by car. Hikes vary from easy to strenuous and will bring you closer to the saguaro-filled hillsides. Allow two hours to return to Phoenix, and two hours to return your rental car and get through the terminal at the airport.

Logistics: Saguaro National Park is split into two halves on either side of Tucson, each about a half hour from the heart of the city. To reach the west section of the park, take Speedway Boulevard west of Interstate 10. Its name will change to Gates Pass Road. Follow it to Kinney Road and turn right to the park's entrance. To reach the east side of the park, take Speedway Boulevard east to Houghton Road. Go south on Houghton to Old Spanish Trail. Turn left and drive to the park entrance. Sabino Canyon is in the northeast corner of Tucson. From Interstate 10, take Ina Road, which becomes Sunrise Drive. Take Sunrise Drive to its end point at Sabino Canyon Rd. Turn left, then right into the park entrance.

Contacts

Air

Phoenix Sky Harbor International. ☎ 602/273–3300 ⊕ www.skyharbor.com. **Tucson International Airport.** ☎ 520/573–8100 ⊕ www.flytucson.com.

🚗 Car

TRAFFIC Arizona Department of Public Safety. ☎ 602/223–2000 ⊕ www.azdps.gov. **Arizona Department of Transportation.** ☎ 511 for Arizona road info from within the state, 888/411–7623 for Arizona road info from outside state ⊕ www.az511.gov.

ROADSIDE EMERGENCIES Arizona Automobile Association. (*AAA*). ☎ 800/222–4357 ⊕ www.az.aaa.com.

🚆 Train

Amtrak. ☎ 800/872–7245 ⊕ www.amtrak.com.

➕ Health

NextCare Urgent Care ✉ 1701 E Thomas Rd., Phoenix ☎ 602/845-4445.

Southern Arizona Urgent Care. ✉ 446 N Campbell Ave., #130, Tucson ☎ 520/305-3900.

Lodging

BED-AND-BREAKFAST RESERVATIONS BnB Finder.com. ☎ 888/469–6663 ⊕ www.bnbfinder.com.

CAMPING RESERVATIONS Recreation.gov. ☎ 877/444–6777 ⊕ www.recreation.gov.

DUDE RANCHES Arizona Dude Ranch Association. ⊕ www.azdra.com.

📦 Packing

LUGGAGE TRANSPORT Luggage Forward. ☎ 617/482–1100 ⊕ www.luggageforward.com.

➕ Safety

U.S. TRAVEL ADVISORIES Transportation Security Administration. (*TSA*). ☎ 866/289–9673 ⊕ www.tsa.gov. **U.S. Department of State.** ⊕ travel.state.gov.

📍 Visitor Information

Arizona Office of Tourism. ☎ 866/275–5816, 602/364–3700 ⊕ www.visitarizona.com.

NATIVE AMERICAN CONTACTS Discover Navajo. ⊕ www.discovernavajo.com. **Gila River Indian Community.** ⊕ www.gilariver.

org. **Hopi Tribe Arts Trail.** ☎ 928/283–4500 ⊕ www.hopiartstrail.com. **Salt River Pima-Maricopa Indian Community.** ☎ 480/362–2700 ⊕ www.discoversaltriver.com. **Tohono O'odham Nation.** ☎ 520/383–0211 ⊕ www.tonation-nsn.gov. **White Mountain Apache Nation.** ☎ 928/338–4346 ⊕ www.whitemountainapache.org.

PARK ESSENTIALS Arizona State Parks. ☎ 602/542–4174, 800/285–3703 ⊕ www.azstateparks.com. **Grand Canyon National Park.** ✉ Grand Canyon Visitor Center, 450 Hwy. 64, Grand Canyon Village ☎ 928/638-7888 General Visitor Information, 928/638-7875 Backcountry Information Center, 928/638-7843 River Permits Office ⊕ www.nps.gov/grca. **National Park Service.** ☎ 202/208–3818 ⊕ www.nps.gov.

ONLINE RESOURCES Arizona Craft Brewers Guild. ⊕ chooseazbrews.com. **Arizona Wine Growers Association.** ☎ 623/236–2338 ⊕ arizonawine.org. **AzCentral.com.** ⊕ www.azcentral.com. **Flagstaff Live.** ⊕ azdailysun.com/flaglive. **GayArizona.com.** ⊕ gayarizona.com. **Phoenix.** *New Times.* ⊕ www.phoenixnewtimes.com. **Tucson Weekly.** ⊕ www.tucsonweekly.com.

Chapter 3

PHOENIX, SCOTTSDALE, AND TEMPE

Updated by
Elise Riley

3

⦿ Sights	🍴 Restaurants	🛏 Hotels	🛍 Shopping	🍸 Nightlife
★★★★☆	★★★★★	★★★★★	★★★★★	★★★★☆

WELCOME TO PHOENIX, SCOTTSDALE, AND TEMPE

TOP REASONS TO GO

★ **Resort spas:** With dozens of outstanding desert spas, Phoenix has massaged and wrapped its way to the top of the relaxation destinations list.

★ **Shops and restaurants:** Boutiques, art galleries, and gift shops throughout Scottsdale and along the Camelback Corridor offer yet another way to retreat and relax in the Valley of the Sun. A thriving restaurant scene provides a perfect end to a day of retail therapy.

★ **The Heard Museum:** This small but world-renowned museum elegantly celebrates Native American people, culture, art, and history.

★ **The great outdoors:** Sure there's urban sprawl, but Phoenix also has cool and accessible places to get away from it all, like the Desert Botanical Garden, Papago Park, Tempe Town Lake, and mountain and desert preserves.

★ **Golf:** All year long, links lovers can take their pick of top-rated public and private courses—many with incredibly spectacular views.

It can be useful to think of Phoenix as a flower with petals (other communities) growing in every direction from the bud of Sky Harbor Airport. The East Valley includes Scottsdale, Paradise Valley, Ahwatukee, Tempe, Mesa, Fountain Hills, and Apache Junction. To the southeast are Chandler and Gilbert. The West Valley includes Glendale, Sun City, Peoria, and Litchfield Park.

Central Avenue, which runs north and south through the heart of Downtown Phoenix, is the city's east–west dividing line. Everything east of Central is considered the East Valley and everything west of Central is the West Valley.

1 Phoenix. As the site of Arizona's government operations and the state's largest concentration of skyscrapers, Downtown Phoenix used to be strictly business. Nowadays it's home to some of the Valley's major museums, galleries, performance venues and sports arenas, plenty of high-rise homeowners, and a light-rail system

that's changing the face of the city. Greater Phoenix offers an unusual mix of attractions that includes historic neighborhoods, acres of mountain preserves, and cultural centers. Hike a couple of peaks, visit the animals at the Phoenix Zoo, zoom over to the Heard Museum, and then relax at a luxury mountainside resort—all in one day.

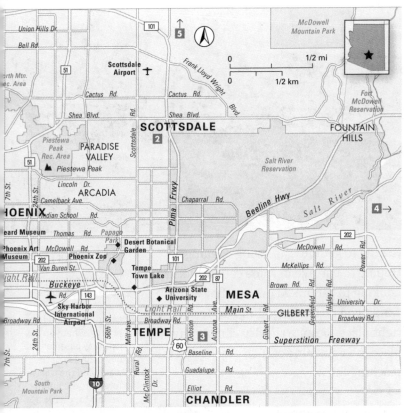

2 Scottsdale. Once an upscale Phoenix sibling, it now flies solo as a top American destination. Scottsdale is a bastion of high-end and specialty shopping, historic sites, elite resorts, restaurants, spas, and golf greens next to desert views.

3 Tempe, Mesa, and Chandler. Known collectively as part of the East Valley, these three small cities make up much of the eastern half of metro Phoenix. Tempe is equal parts party and performance as the home of Arizona State University and a creative melting pot of residents.

4 Side Trips Near Phoenix. Venture an hour and a half outside the city to get an authentic taste of the West with dude ranches, villages trapped in time, artists' havens, and luxury retreats.

5 The Apache Trail. A road trip for anyone who likes off-the-beaten-path adventures, this 150-mile drive is both scenic and, at times, a bit scary.

VALLEY OF THE SUN GOLF: DRIVING AMBITION

It's easy to find greens in the Valley of the Sun.

Itching to get into the swing of things? Hoping to partake in some course work? Looking to get linked in? In other words, would you rather be golfing? You're in the right place. Despite the dry climate this place is a gold mine of lush greens and far-reaching fairways.

Golf is one of Arizona's leading draws for locals and visitors from around the world. Golf is a big business in the Valley of the Sun, evidenced by the more than 200 courses that consume much of the area and surround some of its finest resorts. Locally based golf companies include PING, which makes golf equipment and apparel, and Dixon Golf, which specializes in balls (and also makes apparel). The Phoenix Open is an annual tournament and weeklong party that takes place in North Scottsdale at the renowned Tournament Players Club (TPC). All of this means there are courses that cater to nearly every skill set and budget. The biggest difficulty is often finding a place and time to play, especially during the busy winter season, when temperatures are mild.

TEE-TIME TIPS

Because most courses now offer advance booking as well as online demand pricing, what you pay can vary based on the hour, the day of the week, and the weather forecast. You might be able to reserve a tee time 60–90 days in advance by calling a resort concierge or the course's pro shop. For municipal courses, visit ⊕ *www.phoenix. gov/parks*. To see a list of every course in the Valley, check out ⊕ *www.azgolf.org*.

PLAN AHEAD

Call well ahead for tee times during the cooler months from January to April, especially for popular courses. In summer, it's not uncommon to schedule a round before dawn. If you're booking a room at a resort with a course, book your tee time then, too. Last-minute tee times are sometimes available through online reservation services, depending on the season.

PERFECT YOUR GOLF SWING

Feel like you need to swing like a pro before you take on the Valley of the Sun's premier golf courses? Troon North has a solution: the **Callaway Golf Performance Center** (☎ *480/585–5300* ⊕ *www.troonnorthgolf.com*) is a state-of-the-art facility that analyzes your swing and fits your clubs with 3D imagery and software designed by the experts at Callaway. Golf greats like Phil Mickelson use similar technologies to perfect their games. With only a handful of facilities like this in the country, it's definitely worth checking out.

SAVINGS TIPS

Encanto Park and Papago Golf Course are just two of the city and public courses that are a great value. Check course websites for discounts. Some golf courses offer a discounted twilight rate—and the weather is often much

The Tournament Players Club (TPC) at the Fairmont Scottsdale Princess Resort

more amenable at this time of day. Fees drop dramatically in summer, but remember that afternoon heat can be sweltering.

"GREENER" GREENS

Short of creating sand and cactus courses, desert golf facilities are hard-pressed to answer the eco-friendly call, but some are making strides in chipping away their carbon cleat-print. Most courses now use reclaimed water and are experimenting with low-water grasses.

GROUPS TO GUIDE YOU

Package deals abound at resorts as well as through booking agencies like **Arizona Golf Adventures** (☎ *800/398–8100* ⊕ *www.arizonagolfadventures. com*), who will plan and schedule a nonstop golf holiday for you. For a copy of the *Arizona Golf Guide*, contact the **Arizona Golf Association** (☎ *602/944–3035 or 800/458–8484* ⊕ *www.azgolf. org*).

The setting at The Boulders

3

Phoenix, Scottsdale, and Tempe VALLEY OF THE SUN GOLF: DRIVING AMBITION

The Valley of the Sun, otherwise known as metro Phoenix (i.e., Phoenix and all its suburbs, including Tempe and Scottsdale), is named for its 325-plus days of sunshine each year. Although many come to Phoenix for the golf and the weather, the Valley has much to offer by way of shopping, outdoor activities, and nightlife. The best of the latter is in Scottsdale and the East Valley with their trendy clubs, old-time saloons, and upscale wine bars.

The Valley marks the northern tip of the Sonoran Desert, a prehistoric seabed that extends into northwestern Mexico with a landscape offering much more than just cacti. Palo verde and mesquite trees, creosote bushes, brittle bush, and agave dot the land, which is accustomed to being scorched by temperatures in excess of 100°F for weeks at a time. Late summer brings precious rain as monsoon storms illuminate the sky with lightning shows and the desert exudes the scent of creosote. Spring sets the Valley blooming, and the giant saguaros are crowned with white flowers for a short time in May—in the evening and cool early mornings—and masses of vibrant wildflowers fill desert crevices and span mountain landscapes.

Phoenix, Scottsdale, and Tempe Planner

When to Go

It's a common misconception that Phoenix forever hovers around 100°F. That might hold true from May to October, but the winter months have been known to push the mercury down to 35°F. The city also has experienced consecutive days of nonstop rain. Such instances are rare, but it's good to be prepared and check weather reports before you pack.

Phoenix can get pretty darn hot in summer, so plan your outdoor activities for the cooler parts of the day and save the air-conditioned stuff for when it's needed: the Heard Museum is not only a must-see, it's also inside, as are the nearby Phoenix Art Museum and many other popular attractions.

FESTIVALS AND EVENTS

Arizona State Fair

FESTIVALS | FAMILY | Come for classic fair fun, including a petting zoo, farm animals, and a rockin' concert stage every October. ☎ 602/252–6771 ⊕ azstatefair.com.

Barrett-Jackson

FESTIVALS | This fabulous car auction attracts thousands every January. ☎ 480/421–6694 ⊕ www.barrett-jackson.com.

The Heard Museum World Championship Hoop Dance Contest

DANCE | FAMILY | Every February, the Heard Museum hosts the spectacular Annual World Hoop Dance Championship, with traditional music and costumes. ☎ 602/252–8840 ⊕ www.heard.org.

Indian Fair & Market

CULTURAL FESTIVALS | FAMILY | More than 700 Native American artists and artisans are showcased at the Heard Museum for this annual March event. ☎ 602/252–8840 ⊕ www.heard.org.

★ Las Noches de las Luminarias

FESTIVALS | FAMILY | Adjacent to the twinkling zoo, the Desert Botanical Garden lights up every night during Las Noches de las Luminarias, when thousands of luminarias (paper bags with lights inside) line the garden's pathways. Stroll, listen to live music, and enjoy the beauty of the desert. Tickets sell out quickly, so be sure to make a reservation for this annual event in December. ☎ 480/941–1225 ⊕ www.dbg.org.

The Parada del Sol Parade and Rodeo

FESTIVALS | FAMILY | This February horse-drawn parade and festival is an Arizona tradition featuring cowboys, cowgirls, horses, and floats. ☎ 480/990–3179 ⊕ paradadelsol.net.

Rock 'n' Roll Marathon

MUSIC | Live bands line the marathon course and a concert follows the 26.2-mile race that attracts runners each January. ⊕ www.runrocknroll.com/en/events/arizona.

Russo and Steele

FESTIVALS | Every January, the Russo and Steele auction features some of the most sought-after vehicles in the world. ☎ 602/252–2697 ⊕ russoandsteele.com.

Scottsdale Arts Festival

ARTS FESTIVALS | FAMILY | This weekend event is jam-packed with arts and crafts—and music every March. ☎ 480/499–8587 ⊕ scottsdaleartsfestival.org.

Scottsdale Culinary Festival

FESTIVALS | FAMILY | Foodies from across the Valley mark their calendars for this outdoor weekend festival in April, which offers creations from some of the best chefs in town. ☎ 480/656–9940 ⊕ scottsdaleculinaryfest.org.

Waste Management Phoenix Open

FESTIVALS | Formerly the Phoenix Open, this January golf tournament is the "Greatest Show on Grass." ☎ 602/870–0163 ⊕ wmphoenixopen.com.

ZooLights

FESTIVALS | FAMILY | The Phoenix Zoo celebrates the holidays each year from Thanksgiving through New Year's with ZooLights. ☎ 602/286–3800 ⊕ www.phoenixzoo.org.

Planning Your Time

Three to five days is an optimal amount of time to spend in Phoenix if you want to relax, get outside to hike or golf, and see the main sites like the Heard Museum and Scottsdale. Extra time will allow you to make some interesting side trips to nearby places like Arcosanti, Wickenburg, Cave Creek, and Carefree.

Remember that the Valley of the Sun is sprawling, so planning ahead will help you save time and gas. If you're heading to the Heard Museum in Downtown Phoenix, for instance, you might want to visit the nearby Arizona Science Center and/or the Phoenix Art Museum, too, both of which are close to the light-rail line. If you're going to Taliesin West, do so before or after spending time in Scottsdale.

■ TIP➜ If you're driving to the Grand Canyon from Phoenix, allow at least two full days, with a minimum drive time of four hours each way. You can always anticipate slow-moving traffic on Interstate 17, but in the afternoon and evening on Friday and Sunday, lengthy standstills are almost guaranteed, so plan ahead if you have a flight to catch.

Getting Here and Around

AIR

Phoenix Sky Harbor International Airport (PHX) is served by most major airlines and is the largest airport in the area. The Phoenix airport is a 15-minute drive from Downtown Phoenix or Tempe, and 30 minutes from North Scottsdale. Phoenix-Mesa Gateway Airport (AZA) is smaller and serves regional carriers. It's about a 45-minute drive to either Downtown Phoenix or North Scottsdale. Super-Shuttle vans service both airports and take up to seven passengers to different destinations. One-way fares from either airport range from about $15 to $50.

AIR CONTACTS Phoenix-Mesa Gateway Airport. (*AZA*) ☎ *480/988–7600* ⊕ *www.gatewayairport.com.* **Phoenix Sky Harbor International Airport.** (*PHX*) ☎ *602/273–3300* ⊕ *www.skyharbor.com.* **SuperShuttle.** ☎ *800/258–3826* ⊕ *www. supershuttle.com.*

CAR

To get around Phoenix, *you will need a car.* Only the major downtown areas of Phoenix, Scottsdale, and Tempe are pedestrian-friendly. Don't expect to nab a rental car without a reservation, especially from January to April.

Roads in Phoenix and its suburbs are laid out on an 800-square-mile grid. Grand Avenue, running 20 miles from Downtown Phoenix to Sun City, is the only diagonal. Central Avenue is the main north–south axis: all roads parallel to and west of Central are numbered avenues; all roads parallel to and east of Central are numbered streets. The numbering begins at Central and increases in each direction.

PUBLIC TRANSPORTATION

The Valley's light-rail system is convenient for exploring Downtown Phoenix museums or the area near Arizona State University. The fare is $4 per day, and multiday passes are available. Phoenix runs a free Downtown Area Shuttle (DASH).

CONTACTS Valley Metro. ☎ *602/253–5000* ⊕ *www.valleymetro.org.*

TAXI

Taxi fares are unregulated in Phoenix, except at the airport. The 800-square-mile metro area is so large that one-way fares in excess of $50 are not uncommon. Except within a compact area, travel by taxi isn't recommended. Taxis charge about $5 for the first mile and $3 per mile thereafter, not including tips.

CONTACTS Checker/Yellow Cab. ☎ *480/888–8888* ⊕ *www.yellowcabaz. com.*

RIDE-SHARE

Ride-share services such as Uber and Lyft are widely available in Phoenix, Scottsdale, and Tempe. At the Phoenix Sky Harbor and Phoenix-Mesa Gateway airports, signs direct visitors toward approved ride-share pickup areas. Prices

Where Should I Stay?

	Neighborhood Vibe	Pros	Cons
Downtown Phoenix	Big-name hotel chains in an urban setting; good nightlife.	Close to major venues for sports and entertainment.	Expensive parking; heavy convention crowds.
Camelback Corridor	Luxurious resorts perfect for a getaway.	Fantastic service and amenities; great dining nearby.	Costly resorts; you need a car.
North Central Phoenix	Intimate, nontouristy feel.	Good access to museums, attractions, and freeways.	Some properties lack amenities.
Paradise Valley	The ultimate in luxury getaways.	Five-star service, spas, and dining.	You'll pay for all that luxury.
Greater Scottsdale	Where West meets chic; a haven for pleasure seekers.	Beautiful desert views; hip.	Minimum 30-minute drive from the airport.
Tempe	Great for younger travelers or families visiting college students nearby.	Less expensive; only a few minutes from the airport.	Few resorts offer luxury amenities.

are generally cheaper than for regular taxis, but both companies require you to install an app on your mobile phone and register a credit card for payments.

Hotels

The Valley of the Sun now offers locals and visitors some of the country's best choices when it comes to funky, high-fashion accommodations. Developers and hoteliers have taken advantage of the Valley's wide-open spaces to introduce supersize, luxury resorts like the Westin Kierland and the JW Marriott Desert Ridge, offering everything from their own golf courses and water parks to four-star restaurants and shopping villages. Places like the retro-hip Hotel Valley Ho and the sleek, mountainside Sanctuary on Camelback Mountain have brought Arizona to the forefront of luxury-hotel style. Regal resorts like The Phoenician, the Four Seasons, the romantic Royal Palms Resort, and the Moroccan-inspired Omni Scottsdale keep lodging grounded in traditional, unsurpassed elegance, while plenty of boutique and business hotels keep it grounded in price.

Downtown Phoenix properties tend to be business hotels, close to the heart of the city and the convention centers—and often closer to the average vacationer's budget. Many properties here cater to corporate travelers during the week, but the lively weekend events in Downtown Phoenix are more than enough to entice leisure travelers. With more than 60,000 hotel rooms in the metro area, you can take your pick of anything from a luxurious resort to a guest ranch to an extended-stay hotel. For a true Western experience, guest-ranch territory is 70 miles northwest in the town of Wickenburg.

Don't be surprised if you see a "Resort Fee" on your checkout statement. Most Valley hotels charge these fees, which range from $20 to $30 per day and cover such amenities as parking, in-room Wi-Fi, daily newspapers, in-room coffee/tea, fitness centers, pools, and more. Ask your hotel for a complete description of what the resort fee covers.

Restaurants

Phoenix and its surroundings have met-amorphosed into a melting pot for every type of cuisine imaginable: Northern to Tuscan Italian; mom-and-pop to Mexico City Mexican; low-key Cuban to high-end French- and Greek-inspired Southwest-ern; Japanese- to Spanish-style tapas; and kosher to American classics with subtle ethnic twists.

Eateries like La Grande Orange grocery are revolutionizing Phoenix's "fast-food" concept with gourmet takeout. Four-star cuisine, some concocted by celebrity chefs, also awaits all over the Valley, from Kai in Chandler to Scottsdale's Bourbon Steak. Dotted with massive strip malls, Phoenix's outskirts are becoming a haven of corporate eateries, but don't worry, there's plenty of divine, independent dining for all tastes and all trends in between.

Many of the best restaurants in the Valley are in resorts, camouflaged behind court-yard walls, or tucked away in shopping malls. Newer, upscale eateries are clus-tered along the Camelback Corridor—a veritable restaurant row, running west to east from Phoenix to Scottsdale—and in Scottsdale itself. Great Mexican food can be found throughout the Valley, but the most authentic spots are in North Central and South Phoenix.

Restaurants change hours, locations, chefs, prices, and menus frequently, so it's best to call ahead to confirm. Show up without a reservation during tourist season (November through mid-March), and you may have to head for a fast-food drive-through window to avoid an hour-long wait for a table.

Hotel and restaurant reviews have been shortened. For full information, visit Fodors.com.

Dining and Lodging Prices in U.S. Dollars

	$	$$	$$$	$$$$
RESTAURANTS				
	Under $13	$13–$20	$21–$30	Over $30
HOTELS				
	Under $151	$151–$225	$226–$350	Over $350

Nightlife

From brewpubs, sports bars, and cof-feehouses to dance clubs and country venues, Phoenix offers nightlife of all types. Nightclubs, comedy clubs, upscale lounges, and wine bars abound in Down-town Phoenix and along Camelback Road in North Central Phoenix.

Among music and dancing styles, coun-try-and-western has the longest tradition here. Jazz venues, rock clubs, and hotel lounges are also numerous and varied. Phoenix continues to get trendier and more cosmopolitan, so behind the bar you're just as likely to find a mixologist as a bartender. There are also dozens of LGBTQ+ bars, primarily on 7th Avenue, 7th Street, and the stretch of Camelback Road between the two.

You can find listings and reviews in the *New Times* free weekly newspaper, distrib-uted Wednesday, or in the *Arizona Repub-lic,* also online at ⊕ *www.azcentral.com,* the paper's website. The local gay scene is covered in *Echo Magazine,* ⊕ *echomag. com,* which you can pick up all over town.

Performing Arts

For weekly listings of theater, arts, and music, check out Thursday's *Arizona Republic,* pick up a free issue of the inde-pendent weekly *New Times,* or check out *Where Phoenix/Scottsdale Magazine,* available free in most hotels.

Shopping

In Phoenix, old meets new: upscale stores, one-of-a-kind shops, and outlet malls sell the latest fashions, but you can also find cowboy collectibles, handwoven rugs, traditional folk art, and contemporary turquoise jewelry.

It's Scottsdale that steals the shopping spotlight. Inspired by the region's rich cultural traditions, contemporary artists have flourished here, making Scottsdale—a city with more art galleries than gas stations—one of the Southwest's largest art centers alongside Santa Fe, New Mexico. If you're looking for luxury, whether that's in the form of a priceless work of art or a perfectly fitting pair of jeans, head to Scottsdale. Filled with luxury boutiques and more than enough sites to purchase a pair of cowboy boots, Scottsdale takes Western chic to a whole new level.

The East Valley cities of Tempe and Chandler are Phoenix's version of suburbia, offering large shopping malls that cater to families and teens. But don't knock 'em until you've tried 'em.

Tours

If you'd like a break from driving, consider a tour to see the Valley's top attractions. Reservations are a must year-round.

Open Road Tours
GUIDED TOURS | This operator offers excursions to Sedona and the Grand Canyon, Phoenix city tours, and Native American–culture trips to the Salt River Pima–Maricopa Indian Reservation. ☎ 602/997–6474, 855/563–8830 ⊕ open-roadtoursusa.com ✆ From $79.

Vaughan's Southwest Tours
GUIDED TOURS | This 4½-hour city tour stops at the Pueblo Grande Museum, Mummy Mountain, and Old Town Scottsdale. Vaughan's tours use custom vans and accommodate groups of up to 11 passengers. The company will also take you east to the Apache Trail, or on day trips north to Sedona or the Grand Canyon. ☎ 602/971–1381, 800/513–1381 ⊕ www.southwesttours.com ✆ From $70.

Visitor Information

Most Valley cities have tourism centers where you can get maps or excursion suggestions.

CONTACTS Experience Scottsdale. ⊠ Scottsdale Fashion Square, 7014 E. Camelback Rd., Camelback Corridor ⊹ Near food court ☎ 800/782–1117, 480/421–1004 ⊕ www.experiencescottsdale.com. Greater Phoenix Convention & Visitors Bureau. ⊠ Phoenix Convention Center West Building, 125 N. 2nd St., Suite 120, Downtown Phoenix ☎ 877/225–5749, 602/254–6500 ⊕ www.visitphoenix.com. Tempe Tourism. ⊠ 222 S. Mill Ave., Suite 120, Tempe ☎ 800/283–6734, 480/894–8158 ⊕ www.tempetourism.com.

Phoenix

The nation's fifth-largest city is a bustling metropolis, still growing past its boundaries. Warm weather, stunning sunsets, year-round golf and sports, and delicious cuisine have beckoned visitors to Phoenix for generations. Despite the modern urban sprawl, the city, particularly its historic central corridor, still retains its charm. Visit a museum or hit the links, enjoy a meal or a drink on a patio, and take in the sunshine. There's a reason it's called the Valley of the Sun.

GETTING HERE AND AROUND
There are lots of parking options in Downtown Phoenix, and they're listed on the free map provided by Downtown Phoenix Partnership, available in many local restaurants (⊕ www.downtownphoenix.com). Many Downtown Phoenix sites are served by the light-rail

system or the free DASH (Downtown Area Shuttle) bus service.

Beyond Downtown Phoenix, although the city has some public transportation, it's best to explore the Valley by car.

TIMING
Artlink Phoenix First Fridays
On the first Friday of every month galleries stay open late and crowds converge to view the work of emerging and established artists, listen to live music, and see impromptu street performances. It's an excellent way to check out the Phoenix arts scene. ⊕ *artlinkphx.org/ first-fridays.*

Downtown Phoenix

◉ Sights

While Downtown Phoenix used to be a sleepy area that shut down after 5 pm, today it is humming long past midnight year-round. There are restaurants and bars; apartments and loft spaces; cultural and sports facilities, including Jefferson Street's Chase Field and Talking Stick Resort Arena; and large areas for conventions and trade shows. It's retained a mix of past and present, too, as restored homes in Heritage Square, from the original townsite, give an idea of how far the city has come since its inception around the turn of the 20th century.

Arizona Science Center
MUSEUM | FAMILY | With more than 300 hands-on exhibits, this is the venue for science-related exploration. You can pilot a simulated airplane flight, travel through the human body, navigate your way through the solar system in the Dorrance Planetarium, and watch a movie in a giant, five-story IMAX theater. ⊠ *600 E. Washington St., Downtown Phoenix* ☏ *602/716–2000* ⊕ *www.azscience.org* ⊠ *Museum $20; museum, IMAX, planetarium, and exhibition $44.*

Children's Museum of Phoenix
MUSEUM | FAMILY | A playground for kids of all ages, this museum features hands-on exhibits where children learn by playing. Venture through the "noodle forest," relax in the book loft, or get a crash course in economics by role-playing at the on-site market. ⊠ *215 N. 7th St., Downtown Phoenix* ☏ *602/253–0501* ⊕ *childrensmuseumofphoenix.org* ⊠ *$15* ⊗ *Closed Mon.*

Heritage Square
PLAZA | In a parklike setting from 5th to 7th streets between Monroe and Adams streets, this city-owned block contains the only remaining houses from the original Phoenix townsite. On the south side of the square, along Adams Street, stand several houses built between 1899 and 1901. The Bouvier Teeter House has a Victorian-style tea room, and the Thomas House and Baird Machine Shop are now Pizzeria Bianco, one of the area's most popular eateries. ⊠ *Downtown Phoenix* ☏ *602/261–8063* ⊕ *heritagesquarephx. org.*

Rosson House Museum
HOUSE | This 1895 Queen Anne Victorian is the queen of Heritage Square. Built by a physician who served a brief term as mayor, it's the sole survivor among fewer than two dozen Victorians erected in Phoenix. It was bought and restored by the city in 1974. ⊠ *113 N. 6th St., Downtown Phoenix* ☏ *602/262–5070* ⊕ *www. heritagesquarephx.org* ⊠ *$12* ⊗ *Closed Mon.–Thurs.*

ⓧ Restaurants

The Arrogant Butcher
$$$ | MODERN AMERICAN | The attention-grabbing name is intentional, as is the in-your-face decor and cuisine of this Downtown Phoenix not-quite-bar, not-quite-restaurant. It's noisy, but that's part of the charm: you'll sit next to couples on their first date, bachelorette parties, families having a reunion,

Sights

1 Arizona Science Center....... D4
2 Children's Museum of Phoenix..... D3
3 Heritage Square...... D4
4 Rosson House Museum.... D4

Restaurants

1 The Arrogant Butcher..... B4
2 Blue Hound Kitchen & Cocktails.... B4
3 Matt's Big Breakfast... C2
4 Mrs. White's Golden Rule Café......... D4
5 Nobuo at Teeter House........ D4
6 Pizzeria Bianco...... D4

Hotels

1 Hyatt Regency Phoenix..... C4
2 Kimpton Hotel Palomar Phoenix..... B4
3 Renaissance Phoenix Downtown.. B4
4 Sheraton Phoenix Downtown.. C3

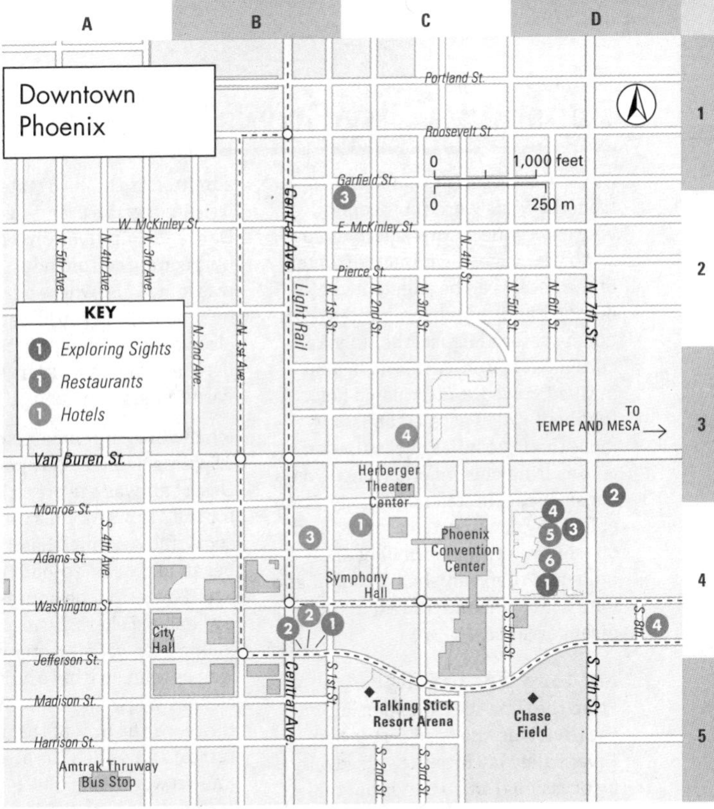

and concertgoers who are prepping their vocal cords for an upcoming show. **Known for:** shareable appetizers; party atmosphere; attentive service. $ *Average main: $23* ✉ *2 E. Jefferson St., Downtown Phoenix* ☎ *602/324–8502* 🌐 *www.foxrc.com/restaurants/the-arrogant-butcher.*

Blue Hound Kitchen & Cocktails

$$$ | **MODERN AMERICAN** | Located inside the Hotel Palomar Phoenix, this restaurant is a great place for cocktails or appetizers before a show and, if you have the time, a fantastic meal. The menu of elevated American cuisine changes frequently. **Known for:** intentionally peculiar cocktails; deviled eggs; great brunch. $ *Average main: $24* ✉ *Hotel Palomar Phoenix, 2 E. Jefferson St., Downtown Phoenix* ☎ *602/258–0231* 🌐 *www.bluehoundkitchen.com.*

★ Matt's Big Breakfast

$ | **AMERICAN** | Fresh, filling, and simply fantastic, the food at this itty-bitty, retro cool diner is a great way to start any day, especially when you have time to walk or sleep it off afterward. Ingredients like hearty bacon strips, jams, and whole-grain breads come from local sources, and each one is of the highest quality. **Known for:** extra-thick pancakes; a worthwhile wait for a table; making otherwise simple breakfast food extraordinary. $ *Average main: $11* ✉ *825 N. 1st St., Downtown Phoenix* ☎ *602/254–1074* 🌐 *mattsbigbreakfast.com* 🕒 *No dinner.*

Mrs. White's Golden Rule Café

$$ | **SOUTHERN** | This plain yellow building has been the best place in town for true Southern cooking for more than 50 years. The humble lunch counter and few surrounding tables are the setting in which

Phoenix: A City Grows in the Desert

As the Hohokam (the name comes from the Pima word for "people who have gone before") discovered 2,300 years ago, the miracle of water in the desert can be augmented by human hands. Having migrated from northwestern Mexico, the Hohokam cultivated cotton, corn, and beans in tilled, rowed, and irrigated fields for about 1,700 years, establishing more than 300 miles of canals—an engineering phenomenon when you consider the limited technology available. They constructed a great town on whose ruins modern Phoenix is built, and then vanished. Drought and long winters are attributed to their disappearance.

Modern Beginnings

From the time the Hohokam left until the Civil War, the once-fertile Salt River valley lay forgotten, used only by occasional small bands of Pima and Maricopa. Then in 1865 the U.S. Army established Fort McDowell in the mountains to the east, where the Verde River flows into the Salt River. To feed the men and the horses stationed there, a former Confederate Army officer reopened the Hohokam canals in 1867. Within a year, fields bright with barley and pumpkins earned the area the name Pumpkin-ville. By 1870 the 300 residents had decided that their new city would arise from the ancient Hohokam site, just as the mythical phoenix rose from its own ashes.

A City on the Rise

Phoenix would grow indeed. Within 20 years it had become large enough—its population was about 3,000—to wrest the title of territorial capital from Prescott. By 1912, when Arizona was admitted as the 48th state, the area, irrigated by the brand-new Roosevelt Dam and Salt River Project, had a burgeoning cotton industry. Copper was mined elsewhere but traded in Phoenix, and cattle were raised elsewhere but slaughtered and packed here in the country's largest stock-yards outside Chicago.

Meanwhile, the climate, so long a crippling liability, became an asset. Desert air was the prescribed therapy for the respiratory ills rampant in the sooty, factory-filled East; Scottsdale began in 1901 as "30-odd tents and a half-dozen adobe houses" put up by health seekers. By 1930 travelers looking for warm winter recreation as well as rejuvenating aridity filled the elegant Wigwam Resort and Arizona Biltmore, the first of the many luxury retreats for which the area is now known worldwide. The 1950s brought residential air-conditioning, an invention that made the summers bearable for the growing workforce of the burgeoning technology industry.

Phoenix Today

The Valley is very much a work still in progress, and historians are quick to point out that never in the world's history has a metropolis grown from "nothing" to attain the status of Phoenix in such a short period of time. At the heart of all the bustle, though, is a way of life that keeps its own pace: Phoenix is one of the world's largest small towns—where people dress informally and where the rugged, Old West spirit lives on in many of the Valley's nooks and crannies despite the sprawling growth. And if summer heat can be overwhelming, at least it has the restorative effect of slowing things down to an enjoyable pace.

to enjoy rich entrées, including fried chicken, catfish, and oxtail. **Known for:** best soul food in Phoenix; a "don't judge a book by its cover" location; hearty portions. $ *Average main: $15* ✉ *808 E. Jefferson St., Downtown Phoenix* ☎ *602/262–9256.*

★ Nobuo at Teeter House

$$ | **JAPANESE** | The creations chef Nobuo Fukuda arranges on your plate might look too beautiful to eat, but it's okay—feel free to devour them. These Japanese fusion dishes (this is no sushi joint) are alive with color and texture, all served in a quaint house built in 1899. **Known for:** elaborate plating; attentive service; shareable plates, like the standout pork belly. $ *Average main: $20* ✉ *622 E. Adams St., Downtown Phoenix* ☎ *602/254–0600* 🌐 *www.nobuofukuda.com* 🕒 *Closed Mon.*

Pizzeria Bianco

$$ | **PIZZA** | Brooklyn native Chris Bianco became famous for his pizza made with passion in this small establishment on Heritage Square. His wood-fired thin-crust creations incorporate the finest and freshest ingredients, including house-made mozzarella cheese. **Known for:** simply perfect pizza; permanent line out the door; "must-visit" status. $ *Average main: $16* ✉ *623 E. Adams St., Downtown Phoenix* ☎ *602/258–8300* 🌐 *www.pizzeriabianco.com.*

🛏 Hotels

Hyatt Regency Phoenix

$$$ | **HOTEL** | The convenience of Downtown Phoenix's light rail makes this convention-center hotel an attractive destination for vacationers, too. **Pros:** business amenities; light-rail access; views from revolving restaurant. **Cons:** atrium blocks view on floors 8–10; parking gets pricey; can feel dated, even with updated furnishings. $ *Rooms from: $299* ✉ *122 N. 2nd St., Downtown Phoenix* ☎ *602/252–1234* 🌐 *phoenix.hyatt.com* 🛏 *693 rooms* 🍴 *No meals.*

★ Kimpton Hotel Palomar Phoenix

$$$$ | **HOTEL** | Hip and unabashedly quirky, this urban hotel has kicked up Phoenix's cool factor a few notches and offers a compelling reason to stay in Downtown. **Pros:** modern and luxurious furnishings; great Downtown views; attentive staff; evening wine reception; pets welcome. **Cons:** costly parking; rowdy atmosphere could be tiresome; missing the luxe amenities of nearby, grand resorts. $ *Rooms from: $369* ✉ *2 E. Jefferson St., Downtown Phoenix* ☎ *602/253–6633, 877/488–1908* 🌐 *www.hotelpalomar-phoenix.com* 🛏 *242 rooms* 🍴 *No meals.*

Renaissance Phoenix Downtown

$$$ | **HOTEL** | One of the city's architectural marvels, this Downtown Marriott has an appealing mix of classic comfort and modern accommodations. **Pros:** prime location for light-rail travel; great lobby bar; modern, but still has history. **Cons:** primarily oriented to business travelers; ongoing renovations are sometimes noticeable; expansive lobby can feel a bit impersonal. $ *Rooms from: $249* ✉ *50 E. Adams St., Downtown Phoenix* ☎ *602/333–0000, 800/309–8138* 🌐 *www.marriott.com* 🛏 *527 rooms* 🍴 *No meals.*

Sheraton Phoenix Downtown

$$$ | **HOTEL** | The grande dame of Downtown Phoenix hotels has positioned itself as the go-to residence of convention goers, but its service and proximity to sports and arts venues make it desirable for leisure travelers as well. **Pros:** can't-beat location within walking distance of almost everything desirable in Downtown; great lobby for lounging or meeting people; high level of personal attention for such a large property. **Cons:** long and impersonal hallways; expensive parking; limited outdoor space. $ *Rooms from: $299* ✉ *340 N. 3rd St., Downtown Phoenix* ☎ *602/262–2500, 866/837–4213* 🌐 *www.sheratonphoenixdowntown.com* 🛏 *1,003 rooms* 🍴 *No meals.*

♈ Nightlife

CityScape

GATHERING PLACES | The best place to take part in Downtown Phoenix's thriving nightlife offers a mix of clubs, entertainment, restaurants, and shopping, all within steps of hotels and sports arenas. ⊠ *1 E. Washington St., Downtown Phoenix* ⊕ *cityscapephoenix.com.*

Fez

BARS/PUBS | This place is a stylish restaurant by day and a LGBTQ+ hot spot by night. The sleek interior and fancy drinks make you feel uptown, while the happy-hour prices and location keep this place grounded. ⊠ *105 W. Portland St., Downtown Phoenix* ☎ *602/287–8700* ⊕ *www.fezoncentral.com.*

Lux Central

CAFES—NIGHTLIFE | Decorated with local art and retro furniture, Lux is an eclectic gathering place where artists, architects, and Downtown businesspeople enjoy excellent classic European espresso drinks. ⊠ *4400 N. Central Ave., Downtown Phoenix* ☎ *602/327–1396* ⊕ *www. luxcoffee.com.*

Majerle's Sports Grill

BARS/PUBS | Operated by former Phoenix Suns basketball player Dan Majerle, this sports bar offers a comprehensive menu for pre- and postgame celebrations as well as some of the best people-watching potential in town. ⊠ *24 N. 2nd St., Downtown Phoenix* ☎ *602/253–0118* ⊕ *majerles.com.*

Seamus McCaffrey's Irish Pub

BARS/PUBS | Enjoy one of the dozen European brews on draft at this fun and friendly place. It also has one of the largest scotch collections in Arizona. A small kitchen turns out traditional Irish fare. ⊠ *18 W. Monroe St., Downtown Phoenix* ☎ *602/253–6081* ⊕ *www.seamusmccaffreys.com.*

Stand Up Live

COMEDY CLUBS | This Downtown Phoenix comedy club features national acts. ⊠ *CityScape, 50 W. Jefferson St., Downtown Phoenix* ☎ *480/719–6100* ⊕ *standuplive.com.*

♦ Performing Arts

Ak-Chin Pavilion

CONCERTS | This outdoor amphitheater books major live concerts. ⊠ *2121 N. 83rd Ave., West Phoenix* ☎ *602/254–7200* ⊕ *ak-chinpavilion.com.*

Arizona Federal Theatre

ARTS CENTERS | Phoenix's high-tech, state-of-the-art entertainment venue morphs from an intimate Broadway stage setup to a concert hall seating 5,000. There are great views from almost every seat. ⊠ *400 W. Washington St., Downtown Phoenix* ☎ *602/379–2800* ⊕ *www.arizonafederaltheatre.com.*

Arizona Opera

MUSIC | This company stages an opera season in both Tucson and Phoenix. The Phoenix season runs from October to March at Symphony Hall and the Orpheum Theatre. ☎ *602/266–7464* ⊕ *www.azopera.org.*

Arizona Theatre Company

THEATER | Based in Tucson, the Arizona Theatre Company also performs at the Herberger Theater Center. Productions, held from September through June, range from classic dramas to musicals and new works by emerging playwrights. ⊠ *222 E. Monroe, Downtown Phoenix* ☎ *602/256–6995* ⊕ *www.arizonatheatre.org.*

Ballet Arizona

DANCE | The state's professional ballet company presents a full season of classical and contemporary works (including pieces commissioned for the company) in Tucson and Phoenix. The season runs from October through May. ☎ *602/381–1096* ⊕ *balletaz.org.*

The Black Theatre Troupe

THEATER | This troupe presents original and contemporary dramas and musical revues, as well as adventurous adaptations, between September and May. ⊠ *Helen K. Mason Performing Arts Center, 1333 E. Washington St., Downtown Phoenix* ☎ *602/258–8129* ⊕ *www.blacktheatretroupe.org.*

Crescent Ballroom

CONCERTS | This small music venue only accommodates 350 people, but has a loyal following for its eclectic calendar of indie acts. The lounge is open nightly. ⊠ *308 N. 2nd Ave., Downtown Phoenix* ☎ *602/716–2222* ⊕ *www.crescentphx.com.*

Great Arizona Puppet Theater

PUPPET SHOWS | **FAMILY** | A yearlong cycle of inventive puppet productions is held in a historic building featuring lots of theater and exhibit space. ⊠ *302 W. Latham St., Downtown Phoenix* ☎ *602/262–2050* ⊕ *www.azpuppets.org.*

Herberger Theater Center

ARTS CENTERS | The home of the Arizona Theatre Company and other local theater companies also hosts performances of visiting dance troupes, orchestras, and Broadway shows. ⊠ *222 E. Monroe St., Downtown Phoenix* ☎ *602/252–8497* ⊕ *www.herbergertheater.org.*

Orpheum Theatre

ARTS CENTERS | The Spanish-colonial Orpheum Theatre, built in 1927 and renovated throughout the '90s, is a glamorous venue showcasing ballet, theater, and film festivals. The Phoenix Convention Center coordinates ticketing for the facility. ⊠ *203 W. Adams St., Downtown Phoenix* ☎ *602/262–7272* ⊕ *www.phoenixconventioncenter.com.*

Phoenix Symphony

MUSIC | The resident company at Symphony Hall, the Phoenix Symphony features orchestral works from classical and contemporary composers, a chamber series, composer festivals, and outdoor pops concerts. The season runs September through May. ⊠ *75 N. 2nd St., Downtown Phoenix* ☎ *602/495–1999, 800/776–9080* ⊕ *www.phoenixsymphony.org.*

Symphony Hall

ARTS CENTERS | The Phoenix Symphony and Arizona Opera perform here. ⊠ *75 N. 2nd St., Downtown Phoenix* ☎ *602/495–1999* ⊕ *www.phoenixsymphony.org.*

Camelback Corridor

A hub of boutique retail stores, fine dining establishments, and upscale resorts, the Camelback Corridor stretches from North Central Phoenix into Arcadia, Paradise Valley, and Scottsdale. This is a more mature area of the Valley, where neighborhoods were born from citrus groves.

◉ Sights

★ Camelback Mountain

MOUNTAIN—SIGHT | Named for its resemblance to a camel's hump, Phoenix's most iconic landmark is also one of its most popular hiking destinations. Its two trails, Echo Canyon Trail and Cholla Trail, are both difficult to climb but lead to stunning panoramic views of the Valley. Even if you don't hike, you can still spot the towering peak from many restaurants and hotels in the Camelback Corridor and Paradise Valley neighborhoods. The mountain is a 20-minute drive from Downtown Phoenix. ■ **TIP→ Dogs are not allowed on the trails.** **For more information on hiking, see Activities.** ⊠ *Echo Canyon Trailhead, 4925 E. McDonald Dr., Camelback Corridor* ☎ *602/534–5867* ⊕ *www.phoenix.gov/parks.*

3

Phoenix, Scottsdale, and Tempe PHOENIX

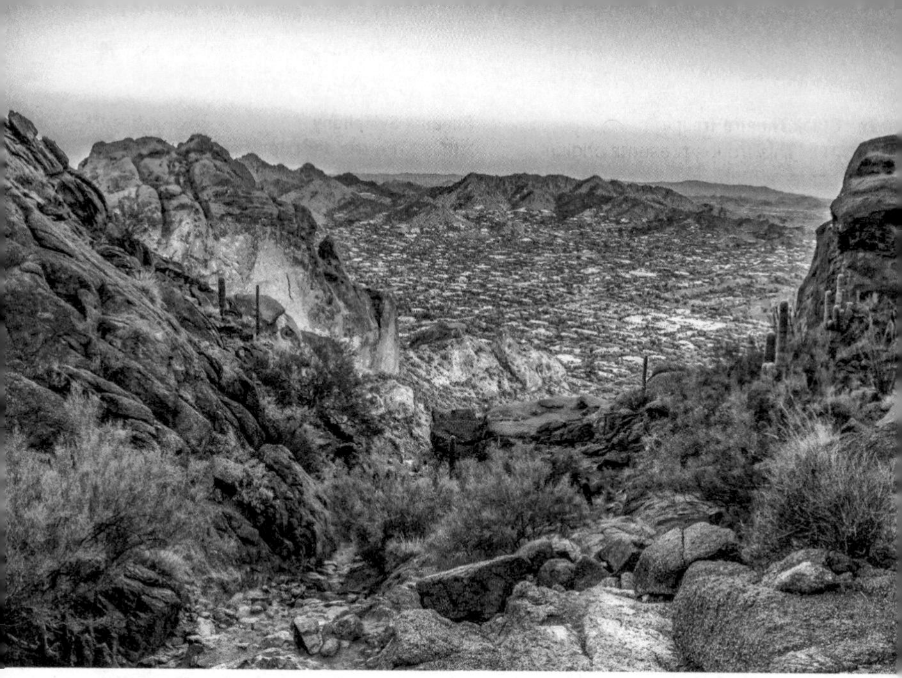

The sun rises over Camelback Mountain, one of the most popular hiking spots in Greater Phoenix.

Shemer Art Center

MUSEUM | Revolving exhibits of current Arizona artists, who have agreed to donate one of their pieces to the center's permanent collection, are displayed in this former residence near the Phoenician resort. The collection is largely contemporary, and exhibits change every month or so. ✉ *5005 E. Camelback Rd., Camelback Corridor* ☎ *602/262–4727* 🌐 *shemerart-center.org* 🎫 *$7* 🕓 *Closed Sun.*

🍴 Restaurants

Set at the southern base of Camelback Mountain, the Camelback Corridor, as it's come to be known, is home to some of the best independent dining establishments in Phoenix. From gastropubs to see-and-be-seen delights, some of the best noshing can be found within these few square miles.

Beckett's Table

$$$ | **MODERN AMERICAN** | With a menu full of comfort food far better than any Mom could make, Beckett's Table combines elegance with tradition. The menu changes frequently, but long-standing favorites include cast iron chicken and tender short ribs with a red wine reduction. **Known for:** difficulty choosing between an entrée or multiple appetizers; a diverse, all-ages crowd; lots of bacon on the dessert menu (really). [$] *Average main: $23* ✉ *3737 E. Indian School Rd., Camelback Corridor* ☎ *602/954–1700* 🌐 *beckettstable.com* 🕓 *Closed Mon. and Tues. No lunch.*

★ Chelsea's Kitchen

$$$ | **AMERICAN** | With its hip, Pacific Northwest–chic interior and a patio that feels more like a secret garden, Chelsea's Kitchen can easily make you forget you're dining in the desert. Expect a wait on the weekends but don't fret: it's an opportunity to grab a drink on the patio bar. **Known for:** delightfully rowdy patio dining; weekend brunch; changing specials. [$] *Average main: $30* ✉ *5040 N. 40th St., Camelback Corridor* ☎ *602/957–2555* 🌐 *www.chelseaskitchenaz.com.*

★ J&G Steakhouse

$$$$ | STEAKHOUSE | This is more than a steak house; it's an experience. The menu changes seasonally, but if you're lucky enough to be here when the sweet-corn ravioli is available, stop, order, and savor. **Known for:** its balcony, one of the most romantic spots in town; fast, quiet service; extensive wine list. $ *Average main: $47* ✉ *The Phoenician, 6000 E. Camelback Rd., Camelback Corridor* ☎ *480/214–8000* ⊕ *www.jgsteakhouse-escottsdale.com* ⊗ *No lunch.*

★ La Grande Orange

$$ | AMERICAN | This San Francisco–inspired grocery and eatery sells artisanal nosh and novelty items, along with a formidable selection of wines. Valley residents flock to LGO, as they call it, to see and be seen, and to feast on mouthwatering sandwiches, pizzas, salads, and decadent breads and desserts. **Known for:** guests arriving via bicycle; pet-friendly patio; plentiful gluten-free options. $ *Average main: $15* ✉ *4410 N. 40th St., Camelback Corridor* ☎ *602/840–7777* ⊕ *www.lagrandeorangegrocery.com.*

★ T. Cook's at the Royal Palms

$$$$ | MEDITERRANEAN | One of the finest restaurants in the Valley, T. Cook's exudes romance, from the floor-to-ceiling windows with dramatic views of Camelback Mountain to its 1930s-style Spanish-colonial architecture and decor. **Known for:** palm trees in dining room that extend through the ceiling; one of the nicest brunches in town; diverse Mediterranean-inspired menu. $ *Average main: $47* ✉ *Royal Palms Resort & Spa, 5200 E. Camelback Rd., Camelback Corridor* ☎ *602/808–0766* ⊕ *royalpalmshotel.com/tcooks.*

Tomaso's

$$$$ | ITALIAN | In a town where restaurants come and go almost overnight, Tomaso's has been a favorite since 1977, and for good reason. Chef Tomaso Maggiore learned to cook at the family's restaurant in Palermo, Sicily, and honed his skills at the Culinary Institute of Rome.

Known for: decades-long reputation for good food; well-heeled crowd; authenticity. $ *Average main: $32* ✉ *3225 E. Camelback Rd., Camelback Corridor* ☎ *602/956–0836* ⊕ *www.tomasos.com* ⊗ *No lunch weekends.*

Vincent on Camelback

$$$$ | ECLECTIC | Chef Vincent Guerithault is best known for creating French food with a Southwestern touch. The menu changes daily, and it's all delicious. **Known for:** romantic ambience; parking lot so small, valet is all but required; meals that can last two hours or longer (if you want). $ *Average main: $40* ✉ *3930 E. Camelback Rd., Camelback Corridor* ☎ *602/224–0225* ⊕ *www.vincentsoncamelback.com* ⊗ *No dinner Sun. and Mon.*

🛏 Hotels

Arizona Biltmore Resort & Spa

$$$$ | RESORT | Designed by Frank Lloyd Wright's colleague Albert Chase McArthur, the Biltmore has been Phoenix's premier resort since it opened in 1929. **Pros:** centrally located; stately; historic charm. **Cons:** finding a parking spot near your room can be a headache; hard to find lounge chairs at some pools; low ceilings in the resort's more-historic areas. $ *Rooms from: $519* ✉ *2400 E. Missouri Ave., Camelback Corridor* ☎ *602/955–6600, 800/950–0086* ⊕ *www.arizonabiltmore.com* ⇋ *738 rooms* ⦿ *No meals.*

Courtyard Phoenix Camelback

$$$ | HOTEL | Public areas in this four-story hotel are mostly glass and tile, while rooms are tastefully done with light-color walls and accents like plush duvets, ample storage, and desk space to work. **Pros:** great value; within walking distance of great shopping and dining; lap pool and Jacuzzi. **Cons:** few frills; business-oriented; limited restaurant service. $ *Rooms from: $265* ✉ *2101 E. Camelback Rd., Camelback Corridor* ☎ *602/955–5200, 800/321–2211* ⊕ *courtyard.marriott.com* ⇋ *167 rooms* ⦿ *No meals.*

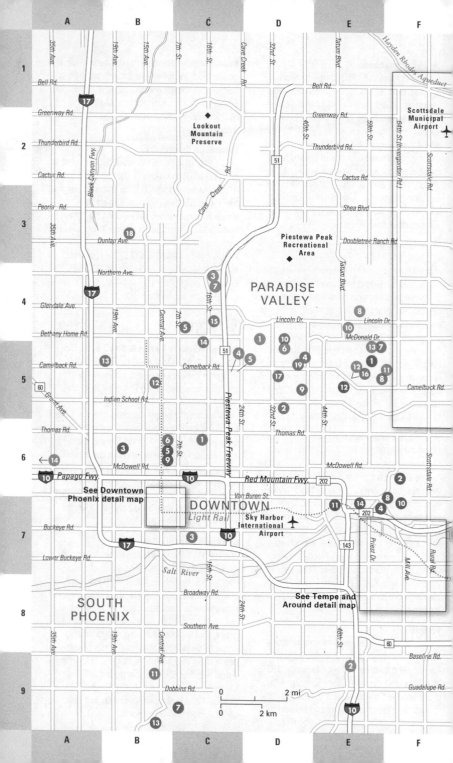

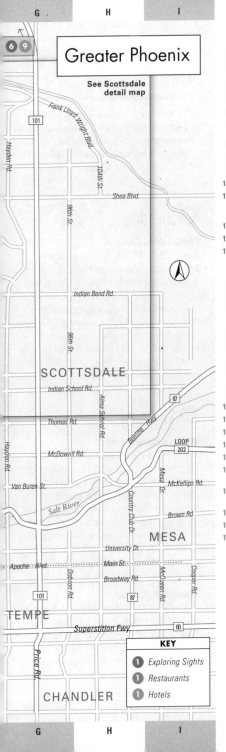

Greater Phoenix

See Scottsdale
detail map

SCOTTSDALE

MESA

TEMPE

CHANDLER

Sights ▼

1 Camelback Mountain ... **E5**
2 Desert
  Botanical Garden........ **F6**
3 Encanto Park........... **B6**
4 Hall of Flame **E7**
5 Heard Museum **B6**
6 Musical Instrument
  Museum (MIM) **G1**
7 Mystery Castle........... **C9**
8 Papago Park............. **F6**
9 Phoenix Art Museum... **B6**
10 Phoenix Zoo **F7**
11 Pueblo Grande
  Museum and
  Archaeological Park **E7**
12 Shemer Art Center....... **E5**
13 South Mountain Park... **B9**
14 Tovrea Castle............. **E7**

Restaurants ▼

1 Barrio Café **C6**
2 Beckett's Table.......... **D5**
3 Carolina's
  Mexican Food............ **C7**
4 Chelsea's Kitchen....... **D5**
5 Christo's Ristorante...... **C4**
6 Durant's **B6**
7 elements.................. **E5**
8 J&G Steakhouse.......... **E5**
9 La Grande Orange **D5**
10 Lon's at the Hermosa... **D4**
11 Los Dos Molinos **B9**
12 Pane Bianco............. **B5**
13 Pepe's Taco Villa........ **B5**
14 Phoenix City Grille **C4**
15 Richardson's Cuisine of
  New Mexico **C4**
16 T. Cook's at the
  Royal Palms **E5**
17 Tomaso's................. **D5**
18 Via Delosantos.......... **B3**
19 Vincent on
  Camelback.............. **D5**

Hotels ▼

1 Arizona Biltmore
  Resort & Spa **D4**
2 Arizona Grand
  Resort **E9**
3 Best Western Plus
  Inn Suites.................. **C4**
4 Courtyard Phoenix
  Camelback................ **C5**
5 Hampton Inn
  Phoenix-Biltmore **C5**
6 Hermosa Inn.............. **D5**
7 Hilton Phoenix Resort
  at the Peak **C4**
8 JW Marriott
  Camelback Inn
  Resort & Spa **E4**
9 JW Marriott
  Desert Ridge
  Resort & Spa **G1**
10 Omni Scottsdale
  Resort & Spa at
  Montelucia **E4**
11 The Phoenician **F5**
12 Royal Palms
  Resort and Spa........... **E5**
13 Sanctuary on
  Camelback Mountain
  Resort & Spa **E5**
14 Wigwam Resort.......... **A6**

KEY

1 *Exploring Sights*
1 *Restaurants*
1 *Hotels*

Hampton Inn Phoenix-Biltmore

$$$ | **HOTEL** | Conveniently located one block off Camelback Road, this four-story hotel is great for business travelers, with spacious and accommodating rooms appointed with comfortable yet modern furnishings. **Pros:** great value; central location; modern conveniences. **Cons:** pool area is clearly visible from the parking lot and street; breakfast just ok; no restaurant on-site. $ *Rooms from: $310* ✉ *2310 E. Highland Ave., Camelback Corridor* ☎ *602/956–5221* ⊕ *hamptoninn3.hilton. com* ⇆ *120 rooms* ❍| *Free breakfast.*

★ The Phoenician

$$$$ | **RESORT** | **FAMILY** | In a town where luxurious, expensive resorts are the rule, the Phoenician still stands apart, primarily in the realm of service. **Pros:** has everything you'd expect from a luxury resort, and then some; highest industry standards; fantastic pools. **Cons:** high prices, even in the off-season; casual, comfortable decor can feel a little skimpy for the price; elevators can be confusing. $ *Rooms from: $819* ✉ *6000 E. Camelback Rd., Camelback Corridor* ☎ *480/941–8200, 800/888–8234* ⊕ *www.thephoenician.com* ⇆ *645 rooms* ❍| *No meals.*

★ Royal Palms Resort and Spa

$$$$ | **RESORT** | Once the home of Cunard Steamship executive Delos T. Cooke, this Mediterranean-style resort has a stately row of the namesake palms at its entrance, courtyards with fountains, and individually designed rooms that feel more like mini casitas than basic hotel rooms. **Pros:** great for romantic getaways; houses a cozy cigar lounge, renowned restaurant, and open-air spa; impeccable service. **Cons:** expensive; only one pool, and it's small; it's really easy to miss the entrance off of busy Camelback Road. $ *Rooms from: $499* ✉ *5200 E. Camelback Rd., Camelback Corridor* ☎ *602/840–3610, 800/672–6011* ⊕ *www.royalpalmshotel. com* ⇆ *119 rooms* ❍| *No meals.*

Farmers' Markets 🛍

To find the fresh wares of a Valley farmers' market, visit ⊕ *www.arizonacommunityfarmersmarkets.com*, a comprehensive calendar listing of markets located across the area.

🍸 Nightlife

Postino Wine Cafe

BARS/PUBS | Postino has grown from a small neighborhood haunt into several separate destinations throughout the Valley. More than 40 wines are poured by the glass. Order a few grazing items off the menu (the bruschetta is unmatched by any in the Valley) and settle in, or carry out a bottle of wine, hunk of cheese, and loaf of bread for a twilight picnic. ✉ *3939 E. Campbell Ave., Camelback Corridor* ☎ *602/852–3939* ⊕ *www.postinowinecafe.com.*

🛍 Shopping

Biltmore Fashion Park

SHOPPING CENTERS/MALLS | Macy's, Saks Fifth Avenue, and Ralph Lauren anchor more than 70 stores and upscale boutiques in this posh, parklike setting. It's accessible from the Camelback Esplanade and The Camby hotel by a pedestrian tunnel that runs beneath Camelback Road. ✉ *2502 E. Camelback Rd., Camelback Corridor* ☎ *602/955–8400* ⊕ *www. shopbiltmore.com.*

Camelback Market

OUTDOOR/FLEA/GREEN MARKETS | On Saturday from 9 am to 1 pm, October through May, some of the Valley's tastiest creations, from crepes to paella, can be found in the parking lot of Vincent on Camelback. The market also sells imported olive oil and honey. ✉ *3930 E. Camelback Rd., Camelback Corridor* ⊕ *www.vincentsoncamelback.com.*

Cornelia Park

GIFTS/SOUVENIRS | If Alice in Wonderland decided to open a store, this would be it. An eclectic mix of home furnishings, gifts, and touches of whimsy, this boutique is one of the best places in the Valley to find a treasure or a gift. ✉ *Biltmore Fashion Park, 2502 E. Camelback Rd., Camelback Corridor* ☎ *602/955–3195* ⊕ *www.corneliapark.com.*

The French Bee

GIFTS/SOUVENIRS | Michael Hansen made a name for himself as a designer of jaw-dropping silk floral arrangements. Those talents eventually turned into the French Bee, a wonderland of flowers, vases, and home furnishings. It's a visual delight. ✉ *3833 E. Indian School Rd., Camelback Corridor* ☎ *602/954–2024* ⊕ *www.thefrenchbee.com.*

My Sister's Closet

CLOTHING | What began as an idea in this Camelback Corridor space turned into a revolution of resale clothing and furnishings. My Sister's Closet offers upscale resale clothing, shoes, and accessories. Its sister store, My Sister's Attic, has resale furniture. There are locations across the Valley, but this is the primary store. You could find a luxury handbag for a third of the price, or a designer suit for pennies on the dollar. All items are guaranteed authentic. ✉ *Town & Country Shopping Center, 4869 N. 20th St., Camelback Corridor* ☎ *602/954–6080* ⊕ *www.mysisterscloset.com.*

North Central Phoenix

One of the oldest and most traditional areas of Phoenix, the North Central corridor is located just north of Downtown Phoenix. Decades ago, this was the area Downtown's workers called home. Now that millions call Phoenix home,

North Central has a bit of a "frozen in time" quality. Seventh Avenue is a hub for shopping—particularly resale home furnishings and decor. Seventh Street, meanwhile, has emerged as the go-to area for dining. This might be "old Phoenix," but it's thriving.

◉ Sights

Encanto Park

AMUSEMENT PARK/WATER PARK | FAMILY | Urban Encanto (Spanish for "enchanted") Park covers 222 acres at the heart of one of Phoenix's oldest residential neighborhoods. There are many attractions, including picnic areas, a lagoon where you can paddleboat and canoe, a municipal swimming pool, a nature trail, Enchanted Island amusement park (⊕ *www.enchantedisland.com*), fishing in the park's lake, and two public golf courses. ✉ *1202 W. Encanto Blvd., North Central Phoenix* ☎ *602/261–8991* ⊕ *www.phoenix.gov/parks* ✉ *Park free, Enchanted Island rides $5 each or $22 for a daily pass.*

★ Heard Museum

MUSEUM | FAMILY | Pioneer settlers Dwight and Maie Heard built a Spanish colonial–style building on their property to house their collection of Southwestern art. Today the staggering collection includes such exhibits as a Navajo hogan dwelling and rooms filled with art, pottery, jewelry, kachinas, and textiles. The Heard also actively supports contemporary Native American artists and displays their work. Annual events include the World Championship Hoop Dance Contest in February and the Indian Fair & Market in March. Children enjoy the interactive art-making exhibits. ■ TIP→ **The museum also has an incredible gift shop with authentic, high-quality goods purchased directly from Native American artists.** ✉ *2301 N. Central Ave., North Central Phoenix* ☎ *602/252–8840* ⊕ *www.heard.org* ✉ *$18* ⊗ *Closed Mon.*

Off the Beaten Path

Deer Valley Petroglyph Preserve. Any visit to Arizona requires a viewing of petroglyphs, and the Deer Valley Rock Art Center is one of the best in the state. Its proximity to the Valley makes it a no-brainer stop, and it's the largest concentration of ancient petroglyphs in the metropolitan Phoenix area. Some 1,500 of the cryptic symbols are here, left behind by Native American cultures that lived in the Valley (or passed through) during the last 1,000 years. After watching a video about the petroglyphs, pick up a pair of binoculars ($1) and an informative trail map and set out on the ¼-mile path. Telescopes point to some of the most skillful petroglyphs; they range from human and animal forms to more abstract figures. ⊠ *3711 W. Deer Valley Rd., Phoenix* ☎ *623/582–8007* ⊕ *shesc.asu.edu/dvpp* 🎟 *$9* ⊗ *Closed May–Sept. Closed Sun. and Mon.*

Phoenix Art Museum ·

MUSEUM | FAMILY | This museum is one of the most visually appealing pieces of architecture in the Southwest. Basking in natural light, the museum makes great use of its modern, open space by tastefully fitting more than 17,000 works of art from around the world—including sculptures by Frederic Remington and paintings by Georgia O'Keeffe, Thomas Moran, and Maxfield Parrish—within its soaring concrete walls. The museum hosts more than 20 significant exhibitions annually and has one of the most acclaimed fashion collections in the country. ⊠ *1625 N. Central Ave., North Central Phoenix* ☎ *602/257–1222* ⊕ *www.phxart. org* 🎟 *$13; free Wed. 3–9, 1st Fri. of month 6 pm–10 pm, and 2nd weekend of month* ⊗ *Closed Mon.*

🍴 Restaurants

★ Barrio Café

$$ | MEXICAN | Chef Silvana Salcido Esparza has taken Mexican cuisine to a new level, routinely winning accolades for modern specialties such as *cochinita pibil,* 12-hour slow-roasted pork with red achiote and sour orange, and *chiles en nogada,* a delicious traditional dish from central Mexico featuring a spicy poblano pepper stuffed with fruit, chicken, and raisins. In short, this is no taco joint. **Known for:** extensive agua fresca (fruit water) menu; fine Mexican cuisine—not a burrito stand; exterior covered with murals. 💲 *Average main: $20* ⊠ *2814 N. 16th St., North Central Phoenix* ☎ *602/636–0240* ⊕ *www.barriocafe.com* ⊗ *Closed Mon.*

Carolina's Mexican Food

$ | MEXICAN | This small, nondescript restaurant in North Phoenix makes the most delicious, thin-as-air flour tortillas imaginable. In-the-know locals have been lining up at Carolina's for years to partake of the homey, inexpensive Mexican food, so it makes sense that she expanded from the original Downtown Phoenix location to let a little more of the Valley in on the action. **Known for:** lines out the door; paper-plate, no-silverware service; one of the most efficient kitchens in town. 💲 *Average main: $6* ⊠ *2126 E. Cactus Rd., North Central Phoenix* ☎ *602/275–8231* ⊕ *www.carolinasmexicanfood.com* ⊗ *Closed Sun.*

Christo's Ristorante

$$$ | ITALIAN | Don't judge this book by its cover: cozy and unassuming in a Phoenix strip mall, Christo's keeps its tables filled with loyal customers who enjoy fine Italian cuisine. Attentive servers ensure that your water glass never empties, and folks rave about the fresh seafood dishes, the roasted rack of lamb, the veal, and the delicious pasta dishes. **Known for:** waitstaff that remembers your name; friendly, neighborhood ambience; high-caliber food. $ *Average main: $25* ⊠ *6327 N. 7th St., North Central Phoenix* ☎ *602/264–1784* ⊕ *www.christosristorante.com* ⊗ *Closed Sun. No lunch Sat.*

★ Durant's

$$$$ | STEAKHOUSE | Durant's has endured in the same location since 1950 with the same menu and waiters who've been on staff for decades, making it one of Phoenix's legendary eating establishments. Supreme steaks, chops, and fresh seafood, including lobster tail and oysters Rockefeller, dominate here; when the restaurant once tried to update its menu, regulars protested so furiously the idea was shelved. **Known for:** looking like it's frozen in the 1950s (in a good way); steak, lobster, and jumbo martinis; guilt-free daytime drinking. $ *Average main: $41* ⊠ *2611 N. Central Ave., at Virginia, North Central Phoenix* ☎ *602/264–5967* ⊕ *www.durantsaz.com* ⊗ *No lunch weekends.*

★ Pane Bianco

$$ | ITALIAN | Chef-owner Chris Bianco is known for his pizza-making skills, but it turns out he creates to-die-for sandwiches, too. This no-frills eatery offers three sandwiches and just as many salads, but don't let the small menu fool you: they're all delicious. **Known for:** walk-in and walk-out brown-bagging; some of the best bread in the city; mozzarella sandwich. $ *Average main: $14* ⊠ *4404 N. Central Ave., North Central Phoenix* ☎ *602/234–2100* ⊕ *www.pizzeriabianco.com* ⊗ *No dinner. Closed Sun.*

Pepe's Taco Villa

$ | MEXICAN | FAMILY | The neighborhood's not fancy, and neither is this restaurant, but in a town with a lot of gringo-ized south-of-the-border fare, this is the real friendly, real deal. Tacos *rancheros*—spicy, shredded pork lathered with aromatic adobo paste—are a dream, as are the green-corn tamales and Monterrey tacos filled with imported *machacado* (air-dried beef). **Known for:** waitstaff that happily gives recommendations; squeeze-bottles of salsa at your table; possibly the best chiles rellenos in Arizona. $ *Average main: $12* ⊠ *2108 W. Camelback Rd., North Central Phoenix* ☎ *602/242–0379* ⊗ *No dinner Sun. Closed Mon.*

Phoenix City Grille

$$$ | AMERICAN | FAMILY | This North Central Phoenix neighborhood eatery has amassed a loyal following over more than 25 years. From burgers to pasta, all of the quintessentially American fare served here is infused with a hint of the Southwest. **Known for:** rotating dining room art depicting Arizona's landscape; table dedicated to former Arizona Governor Rose Mofford, who dined here frequently; griddled corn cakes with green chiles. $ *Average main: $22* ⊠ *5816 N. 16th St., North Central Phoenix* ☎ *602/266–3001* ⊕ *www.phoenixcitygrille.com.*

★ Richardson's Cuisine of New Mexico

$$$$ | SOUTHWESTERN | Richardson's lures back locals with heat-filled dishes that test the limits of your palate—but not in a threatening way. This is fine New Mexican cuisine, which means everything (including heat and quality) is ratcheted up about three notches. **Known for:** small, cozy booths; prickly pear margaritas; beef-tenderloin chile relleno. $ *Average main: $36* ⊠ *6335 N. 16th St., North Central Phoenix* ☎ *602/287–8900* ⊕ *richardsonsnm.com.*

Via Delosantos

$$ | MEXICAN | The family-owned restaurant looks a little rough around the edges outside, but it's what's inside that counts—an accommodating staff, an enormous and authentic Mexican menu, and one of the best-tasting and best-priced house margaritas in town. Entrées are ample and include more than just tired combinations of beef, beans, and cheese. **Known for:** kitchy cerveza advertisements in every corner; ample tequila

menu; chicken delosantos. $ *Average main: $13* ✉ *9120 N. Central Ave., North Central Phoenix* ☎ *602/997–6239.*

🛏 Hotels

Best Western Plus Inn Suites

$$ | HOTEL | A comfortable base for travel, this affordable hotel is within a short drive of great recreation areas (Piestewa Peak) and great dining options, and is less than 1 mile from AZ 51, meaning quick and easy access to major freeways, Valley shopping, and Sky Harbor Airport. **Pros:** the price is right, especially for the area; pet-friendly; clean rooms and friendly staff. **Cons:** amenities aren't on par with nearby resorts; on a busy corner that can be a challenge during rush hour; rowdy pool-goers can make for noisy evenings. $ *Rooms from: $159* ✉ *1615 E. Northern Ave., North Central Phoenix* ☎ *602/997–6285* ⊕ *www.bestwestern. com* ↪ *109 rooms* ⦿ *Free breakfast.*

★ Hilton Phoenix Resort at the Peak

$$$ | RESORT | FAMILY | The highlight of this family-oriented, all-suite hotel is the 9-acre River Ranch Water Park; it has swimming pools with waterfalls, a 130-foot waterslide, and a 1,000-foot "river" that winds past a miniature golf course, tennis courts, and artificial buttes. **Pros:** adjacent to the Phoenix Mountain Preserve, making it an ideal base for hiking and biking trips; affordable alternative to luxury resorts nearby; family-friendly. **Cons:** finding a parking spot can be a challenge; rooms near lobby are noisy; buildings are so spread out, it can be a hike to get a meal. $ *Rooms from: $229* ✉ *7677 N. 16th St., North Central Phoenix* ☎ *602/997–2626, 800/947–9784* ⊕ *www.hiltonphoenixresortatthepeak. com* ↪ *563 units* ⦿ *No meals.*

🍸 Nightlife

The Cash Nightclub and Lounge

BARS/PUBS | This LGBTQ-friendly bar draws an eclectic clientele and features music just as diverse, from country to Latin. ✉ *2140 E. McDowell Rd., North Central Phoenix* ☎ *602/244–9943* ⊕ *www.cashnightclub.com.*

Charlie's

BARS/PUBS | A longtime favorite of local gay men, Charlie's has a country-western look (cowboy hats are the accessory of choice) and friendly staff. ✉ *727 W. Camelback Rd., North Central Phoenix* ☎ *602/265–0224* ⊕ *www.charliesphoenix.com.*

Rhythm Room

MUSIC CLUBS | Excellent local and national rock and blues artists perform here seven nights a week. ✉ *1019 E. Indian School Rd., North Central Phoenix* ☎ *602/265–4842* ⊕ *www.rhythmroom.com.*

🎭 Performing Arts

Phoenix Theatre

THEATER | Across the courtyard from the Phoenix Art Museum, Phoenix Theatre stages musical and dramatic performances. ✉ *100 E. McDowell Rd., North Central Phoenix* ☎ *602/254–2151* ⊕ *www. phoenixtheatre.com.*

🛍 Shopping

AJ's Fine Foods

FOOD/CANDY | The Valley's grandest upscale grocery store, AJ's is a great place to fill your basket with exclusive local creations ranging from salsas and sauces to spice mixes. It's possible to spend hours at any of the 10 identical Valley locations. It's also possible to spend far more money than you would at an average grocery store, but the vast inventory of unusual products and one-stop shopping experience make it all worthwhile. The wine selection is among the best in town, and the sommelier-quality staff will gladly offer suggestions. Be sure to partake of the bistro's fresh, chef-prepared food offerings, including homemade soups, salad, pizza, specialty sandwiches, and gourmet take-out entrées. ⊠ *5017 N. Central Ave., North Central Phoenix* ☎ *602/230–7015* ⊕ *www.ajsfinefoods.com.*

★ The Heard Museum Shop

CRAFTS | The shop at the Heard Museum is hands-down the best place in town for Southwestern Native American and other crafts, both traditional and modern. Prices tend to be high, but quality is assured, with many one-of-a-kind items among the collection of rugs, kachina dolls, pottery, and other crafts; there's also a wide selection of lower-priced gifts. ⊠ *2301 N. Central Ave., North Central Phoenix* ☎ *602/252–8840* ⊕ *www.heard.org.*

Modern Manor

ANTIQUES/COLLECTIBLES | If you're searching for modern, minimalist, or retro furnishings and accessories, Modern Manor might have the item to indulge your inner Don Draper. And, their in-house bar and restaurant can satisfy your "it's 5:00 somewhere" mid-shopping hankering. ⊠ *4130 N. 7th Ave., North Central Phoenix* ☎ *602/266– 3376* ⊕ *modernmanorphx.com.*

Sweet Salvage

ANTIQUES/COLLECTIBLES | Shopping resale stores for home furnishings can be a frustrating experience: you go through lots of what you don't want in the hope that you'll find that oh-so-perfect something. Sweet Salvage works to improve those odds, opening for just four days a month (the third Thursday through Sunday of each month) so its showroom is loaded with quality items that meet their standards. Each month features a different theme, and their loyal followers eagerly anticipate what's next. ⊠ *4678 N. 7th Ave., North Central Phoenix* ☎ *602/279–2996* ⊕ *sweetsalvage.net.*

Vintage Finds 🛍

In certain parts of the Valley "old" is the new "new." The Melrose District, on 7th Avenue between Indian School and Camelback Roads in Central Phoenix, is banking on its Old Phoenix charm in a slow but steady race to become the next hip historic neighborhood. New faces on old buildings are the perfect welcome mat for progress with forthcoming lofts, condos, eateries, and big plans for public art, but the overall charm is anchored by its variety of vintage stores. Hours are generally 10–5, and many stores are closed Monday and Tuesday.

North Phoenix

Desert Ridge is a bustling area on the far northern edge of Phoenix and Scottsdale. The area developed around 2000, and it's now home to thousands of Valley residents. It's where you'll find the Mayo Clinic, the Musical Instrument Museum, and Paradise Valley's JW Marriott Desert Ridge Resort & Spa.

◉ Sights

★ Musical Instrument Museum (MIM)

MUSEUM | FAMILY | A fun destination for even casual music fans, the museum offers a rare display of music and instruments going back hundreds of years— including more than 15,000 instruments and artifacts from across the globe. Special galleries highlight video demonstrations as well as audio tracks that showcase the sounds that instruments, both primitive and contemporary, create. There's even an Experience Gallery where kids can make their own music. ⊠ *4725 E. Mayo Blvd., North Phoenix* ☎ *480/478– 6000* ⊕ *www.mim.org* 🎟 *$20.*

Hotels

JW Marriott Desert Ridge Resort & Spa
$$$$ | **RESORT** | **FAMILY** | Arizona's largest resort has an immense entryway with floor-to-ceiling windows that allow the sandstone lobby, the Sonoran Desert, and the resort's amazing water features to meld together perfectly. **Pros:** perfect for luxuriating with family or groups; close to north Valley restaurants, entertainment, and attractions; so many amenities, there's no need to leave the property. **Cons:** large size makes it a bit impersonal; lots of walking and stairs required to get anywhere; on-site dining has a steep price tag. [$] *Rooms from: $399* ✉ *5350 E. Marriott Dr., North Phoenix* ☎ *480/293–5000, 800/835–6206* 🌐 *www.jwdesertridgeresort.com* 🛏 *950 rooms* 🍴 *No meals.*

Paradise Valley

One of the smallest communities in the Valley of the Sun, Paradise Valley is known to locals as one of the premier places to live. For visitors, it's equally luxurious. Many of the area's finest resorts and restaurants are located here.

Restaurants

elements
$$$$ | **ECLECTIC** | Perched on the side of Camelback Mountain at the Sanctuary resort, this stylish modern restaurant offers breathtaking desert-sunset and city-light views. They're the perfect complement to the culinary delights that fuse hearty American traditions and Asian flavors. **Known for:** romantic views at sunset; creations of chef Beau MacMillan. [$] *Average main: $43* ✉ *Sanctuary on Camelback Mountain, 5700 E. McDonald Dr., Paradise Valley* ☎ *480/948–2100* 🌐 *sanctuaryoncamelback.com/dining/elements.*

Go Antiquing

The central-Phoenix corridor, between 7th Street and 7th Avenue, has many antiques stores. Most shops sit north of Thomas and south of Camelback. Prices, though reasonable, are firm at most shops.

Lon's at the Hermosa
$$$$ | **AMERICAN** | In an adobe hacienda hand-built by cowboy artist Lon Megargee, this romantic spot has sweeping vistas of Camelback Mountain and the perfect patio for after-dinner drinks under the stars. Megargee's art and cowboy memorabilia decorate the dining room. **Known for:** quiet, intimate setting; cowboy candy bar dessert; weekend brunch. [$] *Average main: $41* ✉ *Hermosa Inn, 5532 N. Palo Cristi Dr., Paradise Valley* ☎ *602/955–7878* 🌐 *www.hermosainn.com/lons.*

Hotels

Hermosa Inn
$$$$ | **HOTEL** | On 6 acres of lushly landscaped desert, the Hermosa is a blessedly peaceful alternative to some of the larger resorts nearby. **Pros:** luxurious but cozy; pet-friendly; fantastic restaurant. **Cons:** neighborhood location means you'll have to drive to get anywhere; lacks some luxury amenities of larger resorts nearby; although delicious, only one restaurant. [$] *Rooms from: $399* ✉ *5532 N. Palo Cristi Rd., Paradise Valley* ☎ *602/955–8614, 800/241–1210* 🌐 *www.hermosainn.com* 🛏 *43 casitas* 🍴 *No meals.*

JW Marriott Camelback Inn Resort & Spa
$$$$ | **RESORT** | Built on 125 acres in the mid-1930s and gorgeously renovated to keep its cowboy character, this hacienda-style resort remains top-notch and was the first JW Marriott ever established.

Pros: stunning place to catch a sunset; world-class spa and golf course; imbued with a sense of history. **Cons:** noisy neighbors are easily heard at night; pool is small for a resort of this stature; some buildings and fixtures can feel a bit old. [$] *Rooms from: $574* ✉ *5402 E. Lincoln Dr., Paradise Valley* ☎ *480/948–1700, 800/242–2635* 🌐 *www.camelbackinn.com* 🛏 *453 rooms* 🍴 *No meals.*

Omni Scottsdale Resort & Spa at Montelucia

$$$$ | **RESORT** | This luxury resort brings a touch of the Mediterranean to Paradise Valley with its exquisite dark furnishings and light stone work, impeccable Joya Spa, pool pavilion, and Spanish-inspired wedding chapel. **Pros:** semi-urban getaway with stellar sunset views; good restaurant; beautiful pool area. **Cons:** while the grounds are beautiful, the layout is boxy, awkward, and confusing; parking not included in the resort fee; hosts many large conferences. [$] *Rooms from: $439* ✉ *4949 E. Lincoln Dr., Paradise Valley* ☎ *480/627–3200, 888/444–6664* 🌐 *www.omnihotels.com* 🛏 *293 rooms* 🍴 *No meals.*

★ Sanctuary on Camelback Mountain Resort & Spa

$$$$ | **HOTEL** | This luxurious boutique hotel is the only resort on the north slope of Camelback Mountain; secluded mountain casitas have chic modern furnishings, which contrast with the breathtaking views of Camelback Mountain, the Praying Monk (from some vantages), and the setting western sun. **Pros:** secluded location in one of the most bustling areas of Phoenix; unparalleled views of Camelback's Praying Monk rock; great restaurant, pool, and spa. **Cons:** walking between buildings can mean conquering slopes or flights of stairs; not kid-friendly; grounds very dark at night. [$] *Rooms from: $659* ✉ *5700 E. McDonald Dr., Paradise Valley* ☎ *480/948–2100, 800/245–2051* 🌐 *www.sanctuaryaz.com* 🛏 *116 rooms* 🍴 *No meals.*

Nightlife

★ Jade Bar

BARS/PUBS | This spot has spectacular views of Paradise Valley and Camelback Mountain; an upscale, modern bar lined with windows; and a relaxing fireplace-lighted patio. ✉ *Sanctuary on Camelback Mountain, 5700 E. McDonald Dr., Paradise Valley* ☎ *480/948–2100* 🌐 *www.sanctuaryoncamelback.com.*

Shopping

★ Cosanti Originals

CRAFTS | This is the studio where architect Paolo Soleri's famous bronze and ceramic wind chimes are made and sold. You can watch the craftspeople at work, then pick out your own—prices are surprisingly reasonable. ✉ *6433 Doubletree Ranch Rd., Paradise Valley* ☎ *800/752–3187, 480/948–6145* 🌐 *www.cosanti.com.*

Papago Park

A historic and cultural hub for the Valley, Papago Park showcases the history—and the exceptional urban planning—of the Valley of the Sun. It's home to the tomb of George W. P. Hunt, Arizona's first governor, as well as one of the city's largest parks, the Phoenix Zoo, the Desert Botanical Garden, and hundreds of acres for recreation.

Sights

★ Desert Botanical Garden

GARDEN | **FAMILY** | Opened in 1939 to conserve and showcase the ecology of the desert, these 150 acres contain more than 4,000 different species of cacti, succulents, trees, and flowers. A stroll along the ½-mile "Plants and People of the Sonoran Desert" trail is a fascinating lesson in environmental adaptations. Kid-centric activity areas encourage tactile play and exploration. Specialized tours are available at an extra cost; check online for times and

The Mystery Castle in South Phoenix is full of quirky, unusual artifacts.

prices. ■ TIP→ **The Desert Botanical Garden stays open late, to 8 pm year-round, and it's particularly lovely when lighted by the setting sun or by moonlight. You can plan for a cool, late visit after a full day of activities.** ✉ *1201 N. Galvin Pkwy., Phoenix* ☎ *480/941–1225* ⊕ *www.dbg.org* ⛶ *$15.*

Hall of Flame

MUSEUM | FAMILY | Retired firefighters lead tours through nearly 100 restored fire engines and tell harrowing tales of the "world's most dangerous profession." The museum has the world's largest collection of firefighting equipment, and children can climb on a 1916 engine, operate alarm systems, and learn fire safety from the pros. Helmets, badges, and other firefighting-related articles from as far back as 1725 are on display. ✉ *6101 E. Van Buren St., Phoenix* ☎ *602/275–3473* ⊕ *www.hallofflame.org* ⛶ *$10* ⊗ *Closed Sun. and Mon.*

Papago Park

CITY PARK | FAMILY | An amalgam of hilly desert terrain, streams, and lagoons, this park has picnic ramadas (shaded, open-air shelters), a golf course, a playground, hiking and biking trails, and even largemouth bass and trout fishing. (An urban fishing license is required for anglers ages 15 and over. Visit ⊕ *www.azgfd. gov* for more information.) The hike up to landmark **Hole-in-the-Rock**—a natural observatory used by the native Hohokam to devise a calendar system—is steep and rocky, and a much easier climb up than down. **Governor Hunt's Tomb,** the white pyramid at the top of Ramada 16, commemorates the former Arizona leader and provides a lovely view. ✉ *625 N. Galvin Pkwy., Phoenix* ☎ *602/495–5458* ⊕ *www.phoenix.gov/parks* ⛶ *Free.*

Phoenix Zoo

ZOO | FAMILY | Four designated trails wind through this 125-acre zoo, replicating such habitats as an African savanna and a tropical rain forest. Meerkats, warthogs, desert bighorn sheep, and the endangered Arabian oryx are among the species here. The zoo is full of interactive stops for kids of all sizes. Harmony Farm introduces youngsters to small mammals, and a stop at the Big Red Barn petting zoo provides a chance to interact with goats, cows, and more. ■ **TIP→ In December the zoo stays open late (until 10) for the popular "ZooLights" exhibit, which transforms the area into an enchanted forest of more than 225 million twinkling lights, many in the shape of the zoo's residents.** Starry Safari Friday Nights in summer are fun, too. ⊠ *455 N. Galvin Pkwy., Phoenix* ☎ *602/273–1341* ⊕ *www. phoenixzoo.org* ⊠ *$25.*

South Phoenix

Although Phoenix has grown well outside its municipal borders, there still are plenty of historical sites to visit close to Downtown Phoenix and near Phoenix Sky Harbor airport.

 ## Sights

Mystery Castle

HOUSE | FAMILY | At the foot of South Mountain lies a curious dwelling built from desert rocks by Boyce Gulley, who came to Arizona to cure his tuberculosis. Full of fascinating oddities, the castle has 18 rooms with 13 fireplaces, a downstairs grotto tavern, and a quirky collection of Southwestern antiques. The pump organ belonged to Elsie, the "Widow of Tombstone," who buried six husbands under suspicious circumstances. ⊠ *800 E. Mineral Rd., South Phoenix* ☎ *602/268–1581* ⊕ *www.mymystery- castle.com* ⊠ *$10* ☉ *Closed June–Sept. Closed Mon.–Wed.*

Pueblo Grande Museum and Archaeological Park

ARCHAEOLOGICAL SITE | FAMILY | Phoenix's only national landmark, this park was once the site of a 500-acre Hohokam village supporting about 1,000 people and containing homes, storage rooms, cemeteries, and ball courts. Three exhibition galleries hold displays on the Hohokam culture and archaeological methods. View the 10-minute orientation video before heading out on the ½-mile Ruin Trail past excavated sites that give a hint of Hohokam savvy: there's a building whose corner doorway was perfectly placed for watching the summer-solstice sunrise. Children especially like the hands-on interactive learning center. Guided tours by appointment only. ⊠ *4619 E. Washington St., South Phoenix* ☎ *602/495–0900* ⊕ *phoenix.gov/parks/arts-culture-history/ pueblo-grande* ⊠ *$6* ☉ *May–Sept. closed Sun. and Mon.*

South Mountain Park

NATIONAL/STATE PARK | The world's largest city park (almost 17,000 acres) offers a wilderness of mountain-desert trails for hikers, bikers, and horseback riders— and a great place to view sunsets. The Environmental Center has a model of the park as well as displays detailing its history, from the time of the ancient Hohokam people to gold seekers. Roads climb past picnic ramadas constructed by the Civilian Conservation Corps, winding through desert flora to the trailheads. Look for ancient petroglyphs, try to spot a desert cottontail rabbit or chuckwalla lizard, or simply stroll among the desert vegetation. Maps of all scenic drives as well as hiking, mountain biking, and horseback trails are available at the Gatehouse Entrance just inside the park boundary. ⊠ *10919 S. Central Ave., South Phoenix* ☎ *602/495–5458* ⊕ *www.phoenix.gov/ parks* ⊠ *Free.*

Did You Know?

Saguaro cacti are found all over the Valley of the Sun, including the Desert Botanical Garden in Phoenix.

Tovrea Castle
CASTLE/PALACE | Get a glimpse of what Phoenix was like a century ago by touring the extensive grounds and the two floors of the castle, constructed in the 1920s and early 1930s. Unfortunately, the cupola—the castle's "crown"—doesn't meet fire codes, so visitors can't get the 360-degree views that cattle baron E. A. Tovrea enjoyed. A Phoenix landmark, this 44-acre site in central Phoenix is managed jointly by the city of Phoenix and a group of loyal preservationists. ■ **TIP→ Reservations are required, and tickets go on sale months in advance; plan ahead to avoid disappointment.** ✉ *5025 E. Van Buren St., South Phoenix* ☎ *602/256–3221* 🌐 *tovreacastletours.com* 🎟 *$20* 🕒 *Closed July and Aug. Closed Mon.–Thurs.*

🍴 Restaurants

Just a few minutes from Downtown Phoenix, South Phoenix includes one of the most heralded Mexican restaurants in Los Dos Molinos.

Los Dos Molinos
$$ | **MEXICAN** | This fun restaurant is a must-do dining experience if you want true New Mexican–style food. New Mexico chiles form the backbone and fiery breath of the dishes here. **Known for:** "You order it, you own it" menu warning; La Rosa margaritas to cool your mouth; hacienda setting with outdoor seating. [$] *Average main: $14* ✉ *8646 S. Central Ave., South Phoenix* ☎ *602/243–9113* 🌐 *losdosmolinosphoenix.com* 🕒 *Closed Sun. and Mon.*

Papago Salado 👁

The word *papago*, meaning "bean eater," was a name given by 16th-century Spanish explorers to the Hohokam, a vanished native people of the Phoenix area. Farmers of the desert, the Hohokam lived in central Arizona from about 300 BC to AD 1450, when their civilization abandoned the Salt River (Rio Salado) valley, leaving behind the remnants of their villages and also a complex system of irrigation canals.

🛏 Hotels

Arizona Grand Resort
$$$$ | **RESORT** | **FAMILY** | This beautiful all-suites resort next to South Mountain Park is home to Oasis, one of the largest water parks in the country, and one of the Valley's more challenging golf courses. **Pros:** great family or large-group location; all rooms are suites; plenty of activities to entertain you. **Cons:** huge property can be overwhelming; freeway noise could be a problem in some rooms; lacking in luxury. [$] *Rooms from: $369* ✉ *8000 S. Arizona Grand Pkwy., South Phoenix* ☎ *602/438–9000, 866/267–1321* 🌐 *www.arizonagrandresort.com* 🚪 *744 suites* 🍽 *No meals.*

🎭 Performing Arts

Celebrity Theatre
ARTS CENTERS | This 2,600-seat theater-in-the-round hosts concerts and other live performances. ✉ *440 N. 32nd St., South Phoenix* ☎ *602/267–1600* 🌐 *www.celebritytheatre.com.*

Litchfield Park

Although it's known today as a suburb of Phoenix, Litchfield Park has welcomed visitors for almost a century. Back then, it was a winter retreat for executives in the tire industry.

🛏 Hotels

Wigwam Resort

$$$ | **RESORT** | Built in 1918 as a retreat for executives of the Goodyear Company, the grand Wigwam Resort maintains its historical character while delivering a modern-day luxury experience. **Pros:** although only a few minutes from Downtown Phoenix, this resort feels away from it all; great service; a true retreat with a calm atmosphere. **Cons:** odd resort layout makes it a challenge to find anything; rooms can teeter the fence between old historic charm and just plain "old"; 30-minute drive to central Phoenix and popular attractions. $ *Rooms from: $350* ⊠ *300 E. Wigwam Blvd., Litchfield Park* ☎ *623/935–3811* ⊕ *wigwamarizona. com* ➭ *331 rooms* ❝◯❞ *No meals.*

Glendale

Sports fans might recognize Glendale as the home of State Farm Stadium, the site for Arizona Cardinals games as well as the Fiesta Bowl.

👜 Shopping

Glendale Old Towne & Catlin Court

ANTIQUES/COLLECTIBLES | This antiques district has a plethora of shops and restaurants in colorful, century-old bungalows. Stroll the pedestrian-friendly streets and window-shop, or have lunch at one of the neighborhood eateries to fuel up for some retail therapy. ⊠ *59th and Glendale Aves., Glendale.*

Activities

The mountains surrounding the Valley of the Sun are among its greatest assets, and outdoors enthusiasts have plenty of options within the city limits to pursue hiking, bird-watching, or mountain-biking passions. Piestewa Peak, north of Downtown Phoenix, is popular with hikers, and Camelback Mountain and the Papago Peaks are landmarks between Phoenix and the East Valley. South of Downtown are the much less lofty peaks of South Mountain Park, which separates the Valley from the rest of the Sonoran Desert.

Central Arizona's dry desert heat imposes particular restraints on outdoor endeavors—even in winter, hikers and cyclists should wear lightweight opaque clothing, a hat or visor, and high UV–rated sunglasses, and should carry a quart of water for each hour of activity. The intensity of the sun makes strong sunscreen (SPF 30 or higher) a must, and don't forget to apply it to your hands and feet. ■**TIP**➔ **From May 1 to October 1 you shouldn't jog or hike from one hour after sunrise until a half hour before sunset.** During these times the air is so hot and dry that your body will lose moisture at a dangerous, potentially lethal rate. And keep your eyes peeled in natural desert areas; rattlesnakes and scorpions could be on the prowl.

BALLOONING

A sunrise or sunset hot-air-balloon ascent is a remarkable desert sightseeing experience. The average fee is $200 per person, and hotel pickup is usually included. Because flight paths and landing sites vary with wind speed and direction, a roving land crew follows each balloon in flight. Time in the air is generally between 1 and 1½ hours, but allow 3 hours for the total excursion.

A hot air balloon ride over Phoenix affords striking desert views.

★ Hot Air Expeditions

BALLOONING | This is the best ballooning in Phoenix. Flights are long, the staff are charming, and the gourmet snacks, catered by the acclaimed Vincent restaurant, are out of this world. ✉ *Phoenix* ☎ *480/502–6999, 800/831–7610* ⊕ *www. hotairexpeditions.com* ⛴ *From $179.*

BICYCLING

There are plenty of gorgeous areas for biking in the Phoenix area, but riding in the streets isn't recommended, as there are few adequate bike lanes in the city. Popular parks such as South Mountain Park and the Tempe Town Lake have miles of trails. ■ **TIP**→ **Note that the desert climate can be tough on cyclists, so make sure you're prepared with lots of water.**

Phoenix Parks and Recreation

BICYCLING | The Parks and Recreation department has detailed maps of Valley bike paths. ☎ *602/262–6862* ⊕ *www. phoenix.gov/parks.*

Trail 100

BICYCLING | This trail runs throughout the Phoenix Mountain preserve; it's just the thing for mountain bikers. ✉ *North Central Phoenix* ⊕ *Enter at Dreamy Draw park, just east of intersection of Northern Ave. and 16th St.* ☎ *602/262–6862* ⊕ *www.phoenix.gov/parks.*

FOUR-WHEELING

Taking a jeep through the backcountry has become a popular way to experience the desert's saguaro-covered mountains and curious rock formations. Prices start at around $100 per person.

Desert Dog Offroad Adventures

FOUR-WHEELING | This operator heads out on half- and full-day Humvee, dune buggy, and ATV tours to the Four Peaks Wilderness Area in Tonto National Forest and the Sonoran Desert. ☎ *480/837–3966* ⊕ *www.azadventures.com* ⛴ *From $145.*

Baseball's Spring Training

For dyed-in-the-wool baseball fans there's no better place than the Valley of the Sun. Baseball has become nearly a year-round activity in the Phoenix area, beginning with spring training in late February and continuing through the Arizona Fall League championships in mid-November.

Spring

Today the Cactus League consists of 15 Major League teams that play at stadiums across the Valley. Ticket prices are reasonable, around $15 for bleacher seats and $20 to $30 for reserved seats. Many stadiums have lawn-seating areas in the outfield where you can spread a blanket and bring a picnic. Cactus League stadiums are more intimate than big-league parks, and players often come right up to the stands to say hello and to sign autographs.

Tickets for some teams go on sale as early as December. Brochures listing game schedules and ticket information are available from the **Cactus League**'s website (⊕ *www.cactus-league.com*).

Summer

During the regular Major League season, the hometown Arizona Diamondbacks (⊕ *www.azdiamond-backs.com*) play on natural grass at Chase Field in the heart of Downtown Phoenix. The stadium is a technological wonder; if the weather's a little too warm outside, they close the roof and turn on gigantic air-conditioners. You can tour the stadium except on afternoon-game days and holidays.

Fall

At the conclusion of the regular season, the Arizona Fall League runs until the week before Thanksgiving. Each major-league team sends six of its most talented young prospects to compete with other young promising players—180 players in all. There are six teams in the league, broken down into two divisions. It's a great way to see future Hall of Famers in their early years. Tickets for Fall League games are $8.

Call **Scottsdale Stadium** (☎ *480/312–2586*), one of the league's host sites, for ticket information.

Wayward Wind Desert Tours

FOUR-WHEELING | This operator ventures down to the Verde River on its own trail and offers wilderness cookouts for large groups. ☎ *602/867–7825, 800/804–0480* ⊕ *www.waywardwind-tours.com* ⊠ *From $110.*

Wild West Jeep Tours

FOUR-WHEELING | Special permits allow Wild West Jeep Tours to conduct four-wheel excursions in Tonto National Forest, which, in addition to a wild ride, lets you also visit 1,000-year-old Native American sites. ☎ *480/922–0144* ⊕ *www.wildwestjeeptours.com* ⊠ *From $99.*

GOLF

Arizona has more golf courses per capita than any other state west of the Mississippi River, making it one of the most popular golf destinations in the United States. The sport is also one of Arizona's major industries, and greens fees can run from $35 at a public course to more than $500 at some of the premier golfing spots. Pricing can vary greatly—online reservation systems automatically adjust pricing by demand, day of the week, hour, and even the weather. New courses seem to pop up routinely: there are more than 200 in the Valley (some lighted at night), and the PGA's Southwest section has its headquarters here.

MUNICIPAL COURSES
Encanto Park
GOLF | The 9-hole course and 18-hole course at Encanto Park are among the most affordable in the Valley. ☒ 2775 N. 15th Ave., North Central Phoenix ☎ 602/262–6862 ⊕ www.phoenix.gov/parks/golf ⊠ $20 for 9 holes, $50 for 18 holes ⌘ 9 holes, 1710 yards, par 30; 18 holes, 6404 yards, par 70.

Papago Golf Course
GOLF | Phoenix's best municipal course—considered the best public course in the state—is low-priced (compared to its private, ritzy neighbors) and has 18 holes. ☒ 5595 E. Moreland St., Phoenix ☎ 602/275–8428 ⊕ phoenix.gov/parks/golf ⊠ $95 ⌘ 18 holes, 7333 yards, par 72.

PUBLIC COURSES
Hillcrest Golf Club
GOLF | With 18 holes on 179 acres of well-designed turf, Hillcrest Golf Club is the best course in the Sun Cities. ☒ 20002 Star Ridge Dr., Sun City West ☎ 623/584–1500 ⊕ www.hillcrestgolfclub.com ⊠ $70 ⌘ 18 holes, 7002 yards, par 72.

Raven Golf Club—Phoenix
GOLF | Thousands of Aleppo pines and Lombardy poplars at this course make it a cool, shady 18-hole haven for summertime golfers. ☒ 3636 E. Baseline Rd., South Phoenix ☎ 602/243–3636 ⊕ www.ravenphx.com ⊠ $200 ⌘ 18 holes, 7078 yards, par 72.

RESORT COURSES
Arizona Biltmore Country Club
GOLF | The granddaddy of Valley golf courses, Arizona Biltmore Country Club has two 18-hole PGA championship courses, lessons, and clinics. ☒ Arizona Biltmore Resort & Spa, 24th St. and Missouri Ave., Camelback Corridor ☎ 602/955–9655 ⊕ www.arizonabiltmore.com ⊠ $159 ⌘ Adobe: 18 holes, 6430 yards, par 71; Links: 18 holes, 6300 yards, par 71.

Camelback Golf Club
GOLF | Challenging water holes and layouts make the two 18-hole courses at the JW Marriott's Camelback Golf Club among the best in the area. ☒ JW Marriott Camelback Inn, 7847 N. Mockingbird La., Paradise Valley ☎ 480/948–1700 ⊕ www.camelbackinn.com ⊠ Padre $259, Ambiente $299 ⌘ Padre: 18 holes, 6903 yards, par 72; Ambiente: 18 holes, 7221 yards, par 72.

Lookout Mountain Golf Club
GOLF | This property at the Pointe Hilton Tapatio Cliffs has pristine greens and beautiful mountain views. ☒ Pointe Hilton Tapatio Cliffs, 11111 N. 7th St., North Central Phoenix ☎ 602/866–6356 ⊕ www.tapatiocliffshilton.com ⊠ $329 ⌘ 18 holes, 6515 yards, par 72.

★ The Phoenician Golf Club
GOLF | Set at the base of Camelback Mountain, the Phoenician's Phil Smith-designed course debuted in 2018 and is one of the most aesthetically beautiful courses in the Valley. ☒ The Phoenician, 6000 E. Camelback Rd., Camelback Corridor ☎ 480/941–8200 ⊕ www.thephoenician.com ⊠ $250 ⌘ 18 holes, 6518 yards, par 71.

The Wigwam
GOLF | This country club is the home of the famous Gold Course, as well as two other 18-hole courses. ☒ 300 E. Wigwam Blvd., Litchfield Park ☎ 623/935–3811 ⊕ wigwamarizona.com ⊠ $139 ⌘ Gold Course: 18 holes, 7345 yards, par 72; Blue Course: 18 holes, 6373 yards, par 70; Red Course: 18 holes, 6852 yards, par 72.

HIKING
One of the best ways to see the beauty of the Valley of the Sun is from above, so hikers of all calibers seek a vantage point in the mountains surrounding the flat Valley. A short drive from Downtown Phoenix, South Mountain Park is the jewel of the city's mountain park preserves, with more than 60 miles

of marked trails for hikers, horseback riders, and mountain bikers. ■TIP→ **No matter the season, be sure to bring sunscreen, a hat, plenty of water, and a camera to capture a dazzling sunset. It's always a good idea to tell someone where you'll be and when you plan to return.**

Camelback Mountain and Echo Canyon Recreation Area

HIKING/WALKING | This recreation area has intermediate to difficult hikes up the Valley's most outstanding central landmark. *Difficult.* ⊠ *Tatum Blvd. and McDonald Dr., Paradise Valley* ☎ *602/262–6862 for Phoenix Parks and Recreation* ⊕ *www. phoenix.gov/parks.*

Papago Park

HIKING/WALKING | FAMILY | The peaks of Papago Park were sacred sites for the Hohokam. The soft-sandstone formations contain accessible caves, some petroglyphs, and splendid views of much of the Valley. The park's most popular sunset viewpoint is Hole-in-the-Rock, a chamber formation on the east side of the park. This is a good spot for family hikes. *Easy.* ⊠ *625 N. Galvin Pkwy., Phoenix* ☎ *602/262–6862* ⊕ *www.phoenix.gov/parks.*

Phoenix Mountain Preserve System

HIKING/WALKING | Much of Phoenix's famous mountains and hiking trails are part of the Phoenix Mountain Preserve, a series of mountains that encircles the Valley. The city's park rangers can help plan your hikes. ☎ *602/262–6862* ⊕ *www.phoenix.gov/parks.*

Piestewa Peak

HIKING/WALKING | Just north of Lincoln Drive, Piestewa Peak has a series of trails for all levels of hikers. It's a great place to get views of Downtown Phoenix. Allow about 1½ hours for each direction. *Moderate.* ⊠ *2701 E. Piestewa Peak Dr., North Central Phoenix* ☎ *602/262–6862* ⊕ *www.phoenix.gov/parks.*

★ Waterfall Trail

HIKING/WALKING | FAMILY | Part of the 25 miles of trails available at the White Tank Mountain Regional Park, this short and easy trail is kid-friendly. Strollers and wheelchairs roll along easily to Petroglyph Plaza, which boasts 1,500-year-old boulder carvings—dozens are in clear view from the trail. From there the trail takes a rockier but manageable course to a waterfall, which, depending on area rainfall, can be cascading, creeping, or completely dry. Stop at the visitor center to view desert reptiles (safely held in aquariums) such as king and gopher snakes. *Easy.* ⊠ *20304 W. White Tank Mountain Rd., Waddell* ☎ *623/935–2505* ⊕ *www.maricopacountyparks.net.*

HORSEBACK RIDING

More than two dozen stables and equestrian-tour outfitters in the Valley attest to the saddle's enduring importance in Arizona—even in this auto-dominated metropolis. Stables offer rides for an hour, a whole day, and even overnight adventures. Some local resorts can arrange for lessons on-site or at nearby stables.

Ponderosa Stables

HORSEBACK RIDING | Enjoy your South Mountain experience from a higher perch by renting horses at this nearby stable. The private company rents its land from the City of Phoenix, and will take you on an excursion or send you on one of your own. ⊠ *10215 S. Central Ave., South Phoenix* ☎ *602/268–1261* ⊕ *www.arizona-horses.com* ⚐ *From $40.*

SAILPLANING–SOARING

Northwest Sky Sports

FLYING/SKYDIVING/SOARING | Scenic sailplane rides from this company last from 15 to 60 minutes. ⊠ *8700 W. Carefree Hwy., Peoria* ☎ *602/284–9777* ⊕ *www. nwskysports.com* ⚐ *From $165.*

SPAS

There's no better place for relaxation than at one of Phoenix's rejuvenating resort spas. Many feature Native American–inspired treatments and use indigenous ingredients such as agave and desert clay. In resort spas, you can indulge in such treats as private, rooftop pools, Swiss showers, eucalyptus-scented steam rooms, plunge pools, and more. Most also offer fitness classes and state-of-the-art workout facilities. Why book just a treatment when you could instead enjoy a whole day of pampering?

■TIP➔ Be sure to ask about gratuity when you book your spa treatment. Many resorts automatically add 20% gratuity to the bill. To save a little money, consider booking a multitreatment package. Often these packages include built-in discounts and gratuity—you could save up to 20% on your total bill.

CAMELBACK CORRIDOR
Alvadora at the Royal Palms Resort & Spa
FITNESS/HEALTH CLUBS | The full-service Alvadora Spa is intimate; its couples' treatment rooms feature private patios, as well as showers and tubs. Public areas include tranquil courtyards and retreat areas that offer repose under the warm desert sun or in air-conditioned comfort. Treatments incorporate herbs, flowers, oils, and minerals from the Mediterranean—a nod to the resort's architecture—as well as orange-infused massages and facials, which are fitting, as the property was an orange grove before the resort's construction. ⊠ 5200 E. Camelback Rd., Camelback Corridor ☎ 602/977–6400 ⊕ www.royalpalmshotel.com.

PARADISE VALLEY
Joya Spa at Omni Scottsdale Resort
FITNESS/HEALTH CLUBS | This two-story spa offers a stairway to the heavens. Everything here is meticulously hand-crafted, handpicked, or hand-placed to summon the healing spirits. Inspired by the resort's Spanish and Moroccan designs, the spa features plush seating areas, quiet lounges with privacy draping,

and a public sundeck. Offering Arizona's only hammam, the spa encourages visitors to linger and absorb the tranquil surroundings—the location at the base of Camelback Mountain doesn't hurt. ⊠ 4949 E. Lincoln Dr., Paradise Valley ☎ 480/627–3200, 888/691–5692 ⊕ www.joyaspa.com.

Sanctuary Spa at Sanctuary on Camelback Mountain Resort
FITNESS/HEALTH CLUBS | Savvy spa-goers continue to select Sanctuary as their destination of choice, and with good reason. This sleek spa has 12 Asian-inspired indoor-outdoor treatment rooms nestled at the base of Camelback Mountain. A meditation garden is the perfect place to reflect and relax before or after your treatment. ⊠ 5700 E. McDonald Dr., Paradise Valley ☎ 480/607–2326, 800/245–2051 ⊕ www.sanctuaryoncamelback.com.

Scottsdale

Scottsdale is 12 miles (19.31 km) northeast of Phoenix.

Reveling in its reputation as the "West's Most Western Town," Scottsdale prides itself in its roots—dude ranches, cowboy-boot outfitters, and horseback riding. But don't fool yourself: this is a luxury traveler's paradise. Fine resorts, world-class dining, manicured golf courses, a thriving arts community, and some of the best (and most expensive) shopping in the state make Scottsdale an adult's playground.

Nationally known art galleries, souvenir shops, and a funky Old Town fill downtown Scottsdale. Visit Native American jewelry and crafts stores, or hobnob with the international art set at galleries and interior-design shops.

GETTING HERE AND AROUND
Although your tour of the downtown area can easily be completed on foot, there's a regular, free trolley service (☎ 480/312–3111 ⊕ www.scottsdaleaz.gov/trolley).

TIMING

If you have limited time in the area, spend a half day in Old Town Scottsdale and the rest of the day at Taliesin West.

Scottsdale ArtWalk

Every Thursday evening (except Thanksgiving) from 7 to 9, the galleries along Main Street and Marshall Way stay open for this indoor-outdoor celebration of the arts. Tour the galleries, watch street performers, and grab a bite to eat. 🌐 *www.scottsdalegalleries.com.*

Central Scottsdale

The West's Most Western Town earned its nickname largely because of central Scottsdale, a collection of art galleries, cowboy hat and boot outfitters, and some of the finest dining in the Valley of the Sun.

🍴 Restaurants

Chez Vous

$ | **BISTRO** | An authentic French creperie tucked into a Scottsdale shopping center, Chez Vous transports just enough Paris to make diners say "Merci" instead of "Thank you" throughout the meal. Owners Richard and Isabelle Horvath make and serve the food, and their accents are undeniably legit. **Known for:** locals trying to speak French with the owners; rubbernecking to see what other diners ordered; crepes, quiche, and tartes. [$] *Average main: $11* ✉ *8787 N. Scottsdale Rd., Central Scottsdale* ☎ *480/433–2575* 🌐 *www.chezvous.restaurant* 🕓 *Closed Mon. No dinner.*

Rancho Pinot

$$$$ | **ECLECTIC** | The attention to quality here makes this one of the town's most lauded dining spots. The minimalist cowboy decor and almost secret-handshake location are forgotten upon the first bite of food and replaced with taste-bud heaven. **Known for:** seeing your meal prepared in the open kitchen; neighborhood vibe, despite its Valley-wide draw; locally grown ingredients. [$] *Average main: $31* ✉ *6208 N. Scottsdale Rd., Central Scottsdale* ✥ *Northwest of Trader Joe's in Lincoln Village Shops* ☎ *480/367–8030* 🌐 *www.ranchopinot.com* 🕓 *Closed Sun. and Mon. May–Sept., and 1st 2 wks of July. No lunch.*

🛏 Hotels

Holiday Inn Express Scottsdale North

$$ | **HOTEL** | **FAMILY** | This hotel has a great location along the Scottsdale Road corridor, with trendy restaurants and shopping opportunities within easy walking distance, making it a comfortable, affordable, and family-friendly option. **Pros:** free shuttle; excellent for the price in this area; free breakfast, parking, and Wi-Fi. **Cons:** these affordable rooms can't meet the high-scale standards of nearby hotels and resorts; while the hotel is quiet, the surrounding area is not; caters more to business travelers. [$] *Rooms from: $225* ✉ *7350 E. Gold Dust Rd., at Scottsdale Rd., Central Scottsdale* ☎ *480/596–6559, 888/465–4329* 🌐 *www.hiexpress.com* 🛏 *122 rooms* 🍴 *Free breakfast.*

★ Hyatt Regency Scottsdale Resort and Spa at Gainey Ranch

$$$$ | **RESORT** | **FAMILY** | While staying here, it's easy to imagine that you're relaxing at an oceanside resort instead of in the desert; shaded by towering palms and with manicured gardens and paths, the property has water everywhere—a large pool area has a beach, three-story waterslide, waterfalls, and a lagoon. **Pros:** gondola rides at night; oasis atmosphere; live entertainment in the lobby bar. **Cons:** if you're early to bed, avoid a room near the lobby; it's enormous; frustrating parking lot logistics. [$] *Rooms from: $379* ✉ *7500 E. Doubletree Ranch Rd., Central Scottsdale* ☎ *480/444–1234* 🌐 *scottsdale.regency.hyatt.com* 🛏 *493 rooms* 🍴 *No meals.*

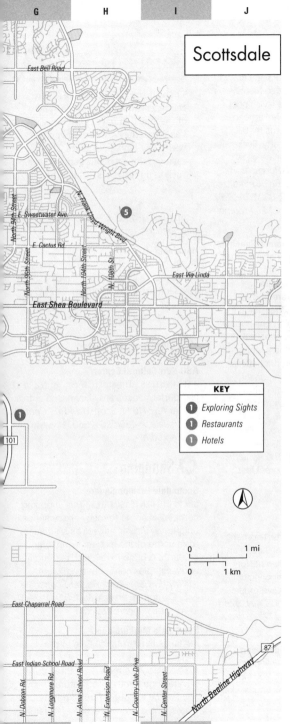

Scottsdale

KEY

1 Exploring Sights
1 Restaurants
1 Hotels

The Scott Resort & Spa

$$$$ | **HOTEL** | Popular with the Spring Training and bachelor/bachelorette party crowd, the Scott—both trendy and eco-friendly—is a place built for fun. **Pros:** the lavish pool and lounge area are considered among the area's nicest; special rooms for tall people; it can be a 24-hour party. **Cons:** no elevator; interior hallways can be noisy; it can be a 24-hour party. [$] *Rooms from: $369* ✉ *4925 N. Scottsdale Rd., Central Scottsdale* ☎ *480/945–7666, 800/528–7867* 🌐 *www.thescottresort.com* 🛏 *204 rooms* 🍴 *No meals.*

Sonesta Suites Scottsdale Gainey Ranch

$$$ | **HOTEL** | **FAMILY** | Directly adjacent to the Gainey Village development, with boutique shopping, upscale dining, and a spa, this hotel is a rare find for both amenities and price. **Pros:** ideal for large family or group travel; convenient location next to much higher-priced resorts; breakfast buffet and evening hors d'oeuvres included in price. **Cons:** comfortable but fairly generic decor; must leave property to enjoy recreation amenities (except pool); has more of extended-stay apartment vibe than a vacation resort. [$] *Rooms from: $319* ✉ *7300 E. Gainey Suites Dr., Central Scottsdale* ☎ *480/922–6969* 🌐 *sonesta.com* 🛏 *162 suites* 🍴 *Free breakfast.*

Nightlife

Casino Arizona

CASINOS | You'll get a full entertainment experience here with a steak house and buffet, concerts and other live performances, and plenty of gaming including blackjack and keno. There's live music and dancing most nights. ✉ *524 N. 92nd St., Scottsdale* ☎ *480/850–7777* 🌐 *www.casinoarizona.com.*

Casino Arizona at Talking Stick Resort

CASINOS | Locals come here for blackjack, poker, keno, more than 200 slot machines, and a dash of Las Vegas–like nightlife. ✉ *9800 E. Indian Bend Rd., Scottsdale* ☎ *480/850–7777* 🌐 *www.talkingstickresort.com.*

Gambling

There are casinos on Native American reservations around the Valley of the Sun. Compared with those in Las Vegas, they are smaller venues with a low-key atmosphere. The casinos follow Arizona gaming laws, such as no cash bets—chips only.

Handlebar-J

DANCE CLUBS | This lively restaurant and bar attracts a Western line-dancing, 10-gallon-hat-wearing crowd. ✉ *7116 E. Becker La., Scottsdale* ☎ *480/948–0110* 🌐 *www.handlebarj.com.*

Performing Arts

ASU Kerr Cultural Center

ARTS CENTERS | Theater, dance, music, and jazz performances are showcased at this center. ✉ *6110 N. Scottsdale Rd., Central Scottsdale* ☎ *480/596–2660* 🌐 *www.asukerr.com.*

Shopping

Scottsdale Fashion Square

SHOPPING CENTERS/MALLS | This shopping complex is home to many luxury shops unique to Arizona, as well as boutiques from some of the biggest luxury brands on earth. A huge food court, restaurants, and a cineplex complete the picture. ✉ *7014 E. Camelback Rd., at Scottsdale Rd., Central Scottsdale* ☎ *480/941–2140* 🌐 *www.fashionsquare.com.*

Scottsdale Marketplace

ANTIQUES/COLLECTIBLES | One of the largest antiques stores in the Valley, this marketplace has more than three dozen privately run booths that feature Asian and French antiques, furnishings, housewares, and a large selection of Western goods. ✉ *6310 N. Scottsdale Rd., Central Scottsdale* ☎ *480/368–5720* 🌐 *scottsdale-marketplace.com.*

North Scottsdale

Away from the bustle of Old Town and the city center, North Scottsdale is a haven for hikers and adventure seekers as well as those who value luxury. It's home to some of the area's finest restaurants and, unsurprisingly, the priciest real estate around.

👁 Sights

Butterfly Wonderland

NATURE PRESERVE | FAMILY | The largest butterfly pavilion in the United States gives kids (and their parents) a close-up view of thousands of butterflies in a temperature-controlled rain forest environment. You should also make time to check out the honeybee exhibit and the 3D theater. ✉ *9500 E. Via De Ventura, North Scottsdale* ☎ *480/800–3000* 🌐 *butterflywonderland.com* 🎟 *$25.*

★ Pinnacle Peak Park

TRAIL | This popular trailhead with jaw-dropping views of the Valley is a good spot to picnic, rock climb, bike, or hike in a beautiful desert environment. The moderately difficult trail is 3.5 miles out and back, winding up a mountain strewn with boulders and towering saguaro cacti. **■ TIP→ Dogs are not allowed on the trail. For more information on hiking, see Activities.** ✉ *26802 N. 102nd Way, North Scottsdale* ☎ *480/312-0990* 🌐 *www.scottsdaleaz.gov/parks.*

★ Taliesin West

HOUSE | Ten years after visiting Arizona in 1927 to consult on designs for the Biltmore hotel, architect Frank Lloyd Wright chose 600 acres of rugged Sonoran Desert at the foothills of the McDowell Mountains as the site for his permanent winter residence. Today it's a National Historic Landmark. Wright and apprentices constructed a desert camp here using organic architecture to integrate the buildings with their natural surroundings. In addition to the living quarters, drafting studio, and small apartments of the Apprentice Court, Taliesin West has two theaters, a music pavilion, and the Sun Trap—sleeping spaces surrounding an open patio and fireplace. Five guided tours are offered, ranging from a 90-minute "insights" tour to a three-hour behind-the-scenes tour, with other tours offered seasonally; all visitors must be accompanied by a guide. **■ TIP→ Wear comfortable shoes for walking.**

To reach Taliesin West, drive north on the 101 Freeway to Frank Lloyd Wright Boulevard. Follow Frank Lloyd Wright Boulevard for a few miles to the entrance at the corner of Cactus Road. ✉ *12621 Frank Lloyd Wright Blvd., North Scottsdale* ☎ *888/516–0811, 480/860–2700* 🌐 *franklloydwright.org/taliesin-west* 🎟 *$38–$75.*

🍴 Restaurants

★ Bourbon Steak

$$$$ | STEAKHOUSE | This upscale steak restaurant run by top-rated chef Michael Mina lives up to the royal reputation of the Fairmont Scottsdale Princess. Its severe but stunning stone-and-glass entrance lets people know they are in for something serious—seriously good. **Known for:** "go-to" status for birthdays, anniversaries, proposals; extra-attentive service; expensive cuts of Kobe beef. [$] *Average main: $68* ✉ *Fairmont Scottsdale Princess, 7575 E. Princess Dr., North Scottsdale* ☎ *480/585–4848* 🌐 *www.scottsdaleprincess.com/dining/bourbon-steak* 🕑 *No lunch.*

Deseo

$$$$ | LATIN AMERICAN | Tucked away in the Westin Kierland Resort, this gem, designed and inspired by Douglas Rodriguez, the founder of Nuevo Latino

Frank Lloyd Wright's Taliesin West

More than just an artist's retreat and workshop, Taliesin West and the surrounding desert still inspire both visitors and architects who study here. Frank Lloyd Wright once said, "The desert abhors the straight, hard line." Though much of Wright's most famed work is based on such lines, this sprawling compound takes its environment into consideration as few desert structures do. Taliesin West mirrors the jagged shapes and earthen colors of its mountain backdrop and desert surroundings. Even Wright's interior pieces of "origami" furniture assume the mountain's unpredictable shapes.

Arizona Inspiration
Wright first came to Phoenix from Wisconsin in 1927 to act as a consultant to architect Albert Chase McArthur on the now famed Arizona Biltmore. Later Wright was also hired to design a new hotel in what is currently Phoenix South Mountain Park. Wright and his working entourage returned to the Valley and, instead of residing in apartments, they built a camp of asymmetrical cabins with canvas roofs that maximized but pleasantly diffused light, and blended into the rugged mountain backdrop.

When the hotel project failed due to the stock market crash of 1929, Wright and his crew returned to Taliesin, his Wisconsin home and site of his architectural fellowship, and the camp was disassembled and carted away. But the concept of his humble worker village would remain in Wright's creative consciousness, and a decade later the renowned architect found an appropriate plot of land north of Scottsdale.

Natural Construction
Built upon foundations of caliche, known as nature's own concrete, and painted in crimson and amber hues that highlight the "desert masonry," the buildings seem to adhere naturally to the landscape. The asymmetrical roofs resemble those of Wright's South Mountain camp and were covered with canvas for many years before Wright added glass. Supported by painted-steel-and-redwood beams, they face the sun-filled sky like the hard shell of a desert animal that seems to be comfortable here despite all the odds against its survival.

Architectural Legacy
The more-than-80-year-old property and its structures, which Wright envisioned as a "little fleet of ships," are perhaps some of the best nonnative examples of organic architecture. They also serve as desert building blocks for future generations of Wright protégés—some perhaps schooled on these very grounds—to balance man and Mother Nature.

---

cuisine, serves the best ceviche in town. Start with the muddle bar, where you can sip an assortment of creative mojitos that go beyond a hint of mint. **Known for:** the "chocolate cigar" dessert, almost too pretty to eat; one of the most extensive seafood menus in the city; top-notch ceviche. $ *Average main: $34* ⊠ *Westin Kierland Resort & Spa, 6902 E. Greenway Pkwy., North Scottsdale* ☎ *480/624–1202* ⊕ *kierlandresort.com* ⊙ *No lunch.*

Taliesin West was Frank Lloyd Wright's winter residence. The original Taliesin in Wisconsin was his summer home.

Hotels

Fairmont Scottsdale Princess

$$$$ | **RESORT** | **FAMILY** | Home of the Tournament Players Club Stadium golf course and the Phoenix Open, this resort covers 450 breathtakingly landscaped acres of desert. **Pros:** upscale favorite, especially for families; excellent spa and rooftop pool; some of the city's best restaurants are here. **Cons:** sprawling campus can be difficult to navigate; a bit far from popular Scottsdale attractions; shade is a limited commodity around pools and paths. [$] *Rooms from: $699* ✉ *7575 E. Princess Dr., North Scottsdale* ☎ *480/585–4848* 🌐 *www.scottsdaleprincess.com* 🛏 *750 rooms* 🍴 *No meals.*

★ **Four Seasons Resort Scottsdale at Troon North**

$$$$ | **RESORT** | A resort in every sense of the word, Four Seasons Scottsdale is tucked in the shadows of Pinnacle Peak, near the popular hiking trail, and features large, casita-style rooms with separate sitting and sleeping areas as well as fireplaces and balconies or patios. **Pros:** amazing service; breathtaking views; peaceful, calm atmosphere. **Cons:** far from everything; awkward parking situation necessitates valet service; very dark at night. [$] *Rooms from: $680* ✉ *10600 E. Crescent Moon Dr., North Scottsdale* ☎ *480/515–5700, 866/207–9696* 🌐 *www.fourseasons.com/scottsdale* 🛏 *210 rooms* 🍴 *No meals.*

Holiday Inn Hotel & Suites Scottsdale North-Airpark

$$$ | **HOTEL** | Located right off the 101 freeway, this affordable hotel is a convenient base of operations; cool and modern throughout, it has clean, large, simply decorated rooms. **Pros:** clean and spacious rooms; comfortable beds; good price for Scottsdale. **Cons:** more practical than perfect; primarily for business clientele; long drive to most popular attractions. [$] *Rooms from: $227* ✉ *14255 N. 87th St., North Scottsdale* ☎ *480/922–6500, 888/465–4329* 🌐 *holidayinn.com* 🛏 *117 rooms* 🍴 *No meals.*

Old Town Scottsdale's waterfront is lined with shops and restaurants.

★ Westin Kierland Resort & Spa

$$$$ | RESORT | FAMILY | Original artwork by Arizona artists is displayed throughout the public spaces of the Westin Kierland, and the spacious rooms have balconies or patios with views of the mountains or the resort's water park and tubing river. **Pros:** on-site Scotch library; walking distance to Kierland Commons boutiques and restaurants; fantastic children's programs. **Cons:** rooms lack personality; adults' pool very close to kids' area; steep parking prices. ⓢ *Rooms from: $409* ✉ *6902 E. Greenway Pkwy., North Scottsdale* ☎ *480/624–1000, 800/354–5892* ⊕ *www.kierlandresort.com* ⇗ *732 rooms* ❖ *No meals.*

🛍 Shopping

Kierland Commons

SHOPPING CENTERS/MALLS | Next to the Westin Kierland Resort is one of the city's most popular shopping areas. "Urban village" is the catchphrase for this outdoor pedestrian mall with restaurants and upscale chain retailers. ✉ *15205 N. Kierland Blvd., North Scottsdale* ☎ *480/348–1577* ⊕ *www.kierlandcommons.com.*

Scottsdale Quarter

SHOPPING CENTERS/MALLS | This outdoor mall creates a one-two punch for shoppers in search of fantastic food and dining. Catch a movie, or grab an ice cream cone and window shop. ✉ *15279 N. Scottsdale Rd., North Scottsdale* ☎ *480/270–8123* ⊕ *scottsdalequarter.com.*

Old Town

One of the most pedestrian-friendly areas of the Valley, Old Town Scottsdale is great for travelers. Stroll by (or through) art galleries and souvenir shops, saddle up to a bar, or feast on some of the area's most beloved cuisine.

Sights

Old Town Scottsdale

HISTORIC SITE | Known as "the West's Most Western Town," this area has rustic storefronts and wooden sidewalks alongside some of the best dining and window-shopping in town. It can be exceptionally touristy in some areas, but it's also the closest you'll come to the "Old West" as it was 80 years ago. High-quality jewelry and Mexican imports are sold alongside kitschy souvenirs. ✉ *Main St. from Scottsdale Rd. to Brown Ave., Old Town.*

Scottsdale Museum of Contemporary Art

MUSEUM | SMoCA, the Scottsdale Museum of Contemporary Art is often referred to as a "museum without walls." There's a good museum store here for unusual jewelry and stationery, posters, and art books. New installations are planned every few months, with an emphasis on contemporary art, architecture, and design. ✉ *7374 E. 2nd St., Old Town* ☎ *480/874–4666* 🌐 *smoca.org* 🎟 *$10, free Thurs. and second Sat. each month* ⏲ *Closed Mon.*

Restaurants

Citizen Public House

$$$$ | MODERN AMERICAN | With its hip Scottsdale address, central see-and-be-seen bar, and—most important—its menu of modern twists on traditional favorites, this place is the epitome of "cool." While the entrées are finger-licking good, you can enjoy one of the best meals of your life by simply ordering a series of appetizers to share. Don't-miss items include the pork belly spätzle and the mac 'n' cheese with gorgonzola and Emmental. **Known for:** bacon-fat popcorn; a libations menu that goes well beyond cosmos and Manhattans; chopped salad with a side of Phoenix culinary history. [$] *Average main: $35* ✉ *711 E. 5th Ave., Old Town* ☎ *480/398–4208* 🌐 *www.citizenpublichouse.com* ⏲ *No lunch.*

Malee's Thai Bistro

$$ | THAI | This cozy but fashionable eatery in the heart of Scottsdale's Main Street Arts District serves sophisticated, Thai-inspired fare. Try the crispy *pla*: flash-fried whitefish fillets with fresh cilantro and sweet jalapeño garlic sauce. **Known for:** a Valley institution for nearly 30 years; often the first stop in a night of reveling in Old Town; Arizona heat-wave red curry. [$] *Average main: $19* ✉ *7131 E. Main St., Old Town* ☎ *480/947–6042* 🌐 *www.maleesonmain.com* ⏲ *Closed Sun.*

The Mission

$$$$ | SOUTHWESTERN | The food will take your taste buds to new levels at this dark and sophisticated space adjacent to a historic Catholic mission. Sit at the elegant bar or fireside on the patio, and enjoy an avocado margarita with supreme starters or sides. **Known for:** elevating everyday food like guacamole into something divine; beautifully plated dishes; weekend brunch. [$] *Average main: $32* ✉ *3815 N. Brown Ave., Old Town* ☎ *480/636–5005* 🌐 *www.themissionaz.com.*

Olive & Ivy

$$$ | MEDITERRANEAN | Tucked into the south side of the high-traffic, high-priced Scottsdale waterfront complex, Olive & Ivy is a pleasant surprise. By day the light comes from the wall of windows that look out onto the ample patio with cozy couches and fire pits; by night the giant space becomes intimate with dim, designer lighting. **Known for:** being a great date-night destination; pedestrian-friendly location; Mediterranean flavors. [$] *Average main: $27* ✉ *7135 E. Camelback Rd., Suite 195, Old Town* ☎ *480/751–2200* 🌐 *oliveandivyrestaurant.com.*

★ Sugar Bowl Ice Cream Parlor

$ | DINER | FAMILY | This iconic Scottsdale destination transports you back in time to a 1950s malt shop, complete with great burgers and lots of yummy ice-cream confections. **Known for:** iconic Family Circus cartoons on the walls; the "Spectacular Banana Bowl," which children try in vain to conquer; being one of the few spots that hasn't changed in decades. $ *Average main: $9* ✉ *4005 N. Scottsdale Rd., Old Town* 📞 *480/946–0051* ⊕ *www.sugar-bowlscottsdale.com.*

Sushi Roku

$$$$ | SUSHI | It's hard to decide which is more entertaining at this hub of Scottsdale nightlife: sitting at the sushi bar and watching the chefs prepare works of edible art, or relaxing in a booth and people-watching. This is see-and-be-seen dining, but it's also one of the best places to enjoy sushi. **Known for:** dishes that are as colorful as they are delicious; sake flights; the katana roll (spicy tuna with shrimp tempura topped by tuna and yellowtail). $ *Average main: $31* ✉ *W Scottsdale, 7277 E. Camelback Rd., Old Town* 📞 *480/970–2121* ⊕ *sushiroku.com.*

 Hotels

Hotel Valley Ho

$$$ | HOTEL | When it originally opened in 1956, this hotel was a hangout for celebrities, including Natalie Wood, Robert Wagner, and Tony Curtis, but it remains a hot spot today, especially the main pool. **Pros:** retro decor; great history; trendy, youthful style. **Cons:** busy location; occasionally rowdy weekend crowd; the retro vibe can feel a bit dated, too. $ *Rooms from: $299* ✉ *6850 E. Main St., Old Town* 📞 *480/248–2000, 866/882–4484* ⊕ *www.hotelvalleyho.com* 🛏 *241 rooms* ⦿ *No meals.*

W Scottsdale

$$$$ | HOTEL | A taste of youthful but sophisticated elegance, this hot-spot hotel in the heart of Scottsdale's shopping and social scene caters to the wants and needs of the fashionable but fickle traveler with "Whatever/Whenever" service that provides guests with anything

they want ("as long as it's legal!"). **Pros:** unpretentious elegance right across from Scottsdale Fashion Square; exudes a hip, urban vibe that, quite frankly, isn't common in Phoenix; posh pool and spa. **Cons:** can get a little noisy at night; little to no sound or privacy barrier between bathroom and sleeping area; if you're not a fan of sushi, you need to go off-site to eat. $ *Rooms from: $490* ✉ *7277 E. Camelback Rd., Old Town* 📞 *480/970–2100* ⊕ *www.wscottsdalehotel.com* 🛏 *263 rooms* ⦿ *No meals.*

🌙 Nightlife

AZ88

BARS/PUBS | This spot is great for feasting on huge portions of food and lavish quantities of liquor, but also for feasting your eyes on the fabulous people who flock here on weekend nights. It's a great stop before and after an Old Town event or a night of partying. ✉ *Scottsdale Civic Center, 7353 Scottsdale Mall, Old Town* 📞 *480/994–5576* ⊕ *www.az88.com.*

BsWest

BARS/PUBS | Tucked behind a shopping center on Scottsdale's main shopping drag, BsWest draws a stylish, well-heeled LGBTQ+ crowd. ✉ *7125 E. 5th Ave., Old Town* 📞 *480/945–9028* ⊕ *www.facebook.com/bswest.scottsdale.*

Kazimierz Wine & Whiskey Bar

WINE BARS—NIGHTLIFE | Snuggle up with a friend—or make some new friends—while sampling from a selection of wines from around the world and more than 200 whiskeys. Enjoy live music nightly. ✉ *7137 E. Stetson Dr., Old Town* 📞 *480/946–3004* ⊕ *kazbarscottsdale.com.*

Salty Senorita

BARS/PUBS | This spot is known more for its extensive margarita selection and lively patio crowd than for its food. The restaurant-bar touts 51 different margaritas—with some recipes so secret they won't tell you what goes in them. Try the

El Presidente or the Chupacabra. ✉ *3748 N. Scottsdale Rd., Old Town* ☎ *480/947–2116* ⊕ *www.saltysenorita.com.*

🎭 Performing Arts

Scottsdale Center for the Performing Arts
ARTS CENTERS | Performances at this cultural and entertainment complex typically emphasize contemporary art and artists. You might be able to catch a comical, interactive performance of the long-running *Late Night Catechism*, or an installation of modern dance or music. The acclaimed Scottsdale Arts Festival is held annually here in March. ✉ *7380 E. 2nd St., Old Town* ☎ *480/499–8587* ⊕ *scottsdaleperformingarts.org.*

🛍 Shopping

5th Avenue
SHOPPING NEIGHBORHOODS | Whether you seek handmade Native American arts and crafts, casual clothing, or cacti, you'll find it here. ✉ *5th Ave. between Civic Center Rd. and Stetson Dr., Old Town.*

Gilbert Ortega Gallery
CRAFTS | This retailer has many Native American shops throughout Scottsdale. Prices are steep, but the products are authentic and the selection is among the best in town. ✉ *3925 N. Scottsdale Rd., Old Town* ☎ *480/990–1808.*

Kactus Jock
GIFTS/SOUVENIRS | This somewhat kitschy Arizona souvenir store sells food, T-shirts, and some art. ✉ *7229 E. Main St., Old Town* ☎ *480/945–6691* ⊕ *www.kactusjock.com.*

Main Street Arts District
SHOPPING NEIGHBORHOODS | Gallery after gallery displays artwork in myriad styles—contemporary, Western realism, Native American, and traditional. Several antiques shops are also here; specialties include porcelain and china, jewelry, and Oriental rugs. ✉ *Old Town* ✛ *Bounded by Main St. and 1st Ave., Scottsdale Rd. and 69th St.*

Marshall Way Arts District
SHOPPING NEIGHBORHOODS | Galleries that exhibit predominantly contemporary art line the blocks of Marshall Way north of Indian School Road, and upscale gift and jewelry stores can be found here, too. Farther north on Marshall Way across 3rd Avenue are more art galleries and creative stores with a Southwestern flair. ✉ *Marshall Way, from Indian School Rd. to 5th Ave., Old Town.*

★ Wilde Meyer Gallery
ART GALLERIES | With locations in Scottsdale and Tucson, this is the place to go for the true colors of the Southwest. In addition to one-of-a-kind paintings, the galleries also feature rustic, fine-art imports from around the state and the world, including furniture, sculptures, and jewelry. ✉ *4142 N. Marshall Way, Old Town* ☎ *480/945–2323* ⊕ *wildemeyer.com.*

🏃 Activities

MULTISPORT OUTFITTERS
REI Co-Op Adventures
TOUR—SPORTS | The personable staff leads half-day, full-day, and multiday adventures for hikers, bikers, rafters, and kayakers. Guides are extremely knowledgeable about local flora and fauna. Or, you can rent a road bike or a mountain bike to explore the area's mountain regions, parks, and canal paths. ✉ *Scottsdale* ☎ *480/945–2881, 866/455–1601* ⊕ *destinations.rei.com/arizona* 🏷 *Full day with guide from $240.*

BICYCLING
Indian Bend Wash Greenbelt
BICYCLING | This multiuse park system has paths suitable for bikes winding among its golf courses and ponds. ✉ *Along Hayden Rd., from Shea Blvd. south to Indian School Rd., Scottsdale* ☎ *480/312–7275* ⊕ *www.scottsdaleaz.gov/parks/greenbelt.*

Pinnacle Peak

BICYCLING | This is a popular place to take bikes for the ride north to Carefree and Cave Creek, or east and south over the mountain pass and down to the Verde River, toward Fountain Hills. ⊠ *26802 N. 102nd Way, North Scottsdale* ⊹ *25 miles northeast of Downtown Phoenix* ☎ *480/312–0990* ⊕ *www.scottsdaleaz. gov/parks/pinnacle-peak-park.*

GOLF

Grayhawk

GOLF | This 36-hole course has beautiful mountain views. In summer the greens fee is much lower. ⊠ *8620 E. Thompson Peak Pkwy., North Scottsdale* ☎ *480/502–1800* ⊕ *grayhawkgolf.com* ⊠ *$260* ⸙ *Talon: 18 holes, 6973 yards, par 72; Raptor: 18 holes, 7151 yards, par 72.*

SunRidge Canyon

GOLF | East of Scottsdale, SunRidge Canyon is a great 18-hole course for both the low handicapper and those who score above 100. The incredible mountain views are almost distracting. ⊠ *13100 N. Sunridge Dr., Fountain Hills* ☎ *480/837–5100* ⊕ *www.sunridgegolf.com* ⊠ *$165* ⸙ *18 holes, 6823 yards, par 71.*

Tournament Players Club of Scottsdale

GOLF | This 36-hole course is the site of the PGA Waste Management Phoenix Open, which takes place in January/ February. ⊠ *Fairmont Scottsdale Princess Resort, 17020 N. Hayden Rd., North Scottsdale* ☎ *480/585–4334, 888/400–4001* ⊕ *www.tpc.com* ⊠ *Stadium $300, Champions $175* ⸙ *Stadium: 18 holes, 7261 yards, par 71; Champions: 18 holes, 7115 yards, par 71.*

★ Troon North

GOLF | Long considered one of the finest golf courses in the country, a visit to Troon North is a must for any golfer that wants to experience a desert course. The multimillion-dollar views add to the experience at this perfectly maintained 36-hole course. ⊠ *10320 E. Dynamite Blvd., North Scottsdale* ☎ *480/585–7700*

⊕ *www.troonnorthgolf.com* ⊠ *$275* ⸙ *Monument: 18 holes, 7039 yards, par 72; Pinnacle: 18 holes, 7009 yards, par 71.*

HIKING

Lost Dog Wash Trail

HIKING/WALKING | Part of the continually expanding McDowell Sonoran Preserve (⊕ *www.mcdowellsonoran.org*), Lost Dog Wash Trail is a mostly gentle 4½-mile round trip that will get you away from the bustle of the city in a hurry. The trailhead has restrooms and a map that shows a series of trails for varying skill levels. *Easy.* ⊠ *12601 N. 124th St., north of Shea Blvd., North Scottsdale* ☎ *480/312–7013* ⊕ *www.scottsdaleaz.gov/preserve.*

★ Pinnacle Peak Trail

HIKING/WALKING | This is a well-maintained trail offering a moderately challenging 3½-mile round-trip hike—or a horseback experience for those who care to round one up at the local stables. Interpretive programs and trail signs along the way describe the geology, flora, fauna, and cultural history of the area. *Moderate.* ⊠ *26802 N. 102nd Way, North Scottsdale* ⊹ *1 mile south of Dynamite and Alma School Rds.* ☎ *480/312–0990* ⊕ *www.scottsdaleaz.gov/parks/ pinnacle-peak-park.*

HORSEBACK RIDING

Arizona Cowboy College

HORSEBACK RIDING | The wranglers here will teach you everything you need to know about ridin', ropin', and ranchin' in one- and three-day courses. ⊠ *30208 N. 152nd St., North Scottsdale* ☎ *480/471–3151* ⊕ *www.cowboycollege.com* ⊠ *From $450.*

MacDonald's Ranch

HORSEBACK RIDING | **FAMILY** | This ranch offers one- and two-hour trail rides and guided breakfast, lunch, and dinner rides through desert foothills above Scottsdale. ⊠ *26540 N. Scottsdale Rd., North Scottsdale* ☎ *480/585–0239* ⊕ *www.macdonaldsranch.com* ⊠ *From $55.*

SPAS

Four Seasons Troon North Spa

FITNESS/HEALTH CLUBS | Although most think of the Four Seasons Troon North as an escape for golfers, its spa proves that there's relaxation to be had away from the links. There are, however, treatments especially for golfers, including a massage that incorporates warm golf balls and stretching to relieve a subpar day. ✉ *10600 E. Crescent Moon Dr., North Scottsdale* ☎ *480/515–5700* ⊕ *www.fourseasons.com/scottsdale.*

La Vidorra Spa at The Scott Resort

FITNESS/HEALTH CLUBS | With its relaxing interior, La Vidorra focuses on repairing and restoring from within by relying on plant science and a combination of Eastern and Western spa philosophies. Keeping with the resort's green efforts, spa treatments incorporate natural products that are hypoallergenic and are not animal-tested. Your wallet will get some relaxation, too; although La Vidorra is one of the smallest resort spas in town, it's also one of the more affordable. ✉ *The Scott Resort, 4925 N. Scottsdale Rd., Central Scottsdale* ☎ *480/424–6072* ⊕ *www.thescottresort.com.*

The Spa at JW Marriott Camelback Inn

FITNESS/HEALTH CLUBS | One of the Valley's most popular spas blends Mediterranean and desert themes. Trained therapists will scrub, wrap, and polish your body to perfection and use the finest products to massage your muscles and cleanse your pores. You'll want all the pampering after a private session with one of the resort's trainers who specialize in Pilates and gyrokinesis. Refuel at the on-site café, and finish your day at the outdoor heated lap pool. ✉ *5402 E. Lincoln Dr., Central Scottsdale* ☎ *480/596–7040, 800/922–2635* ⊕ *www.camelbackspa.com.*

★ Spa Avania at the Hyatt Regency Scottsdale at Gainey Ranch

FITNESS/HEALTH CLUBS | The gorgeous stone-tiled facility seeks to cleanse the body of unnatural stimuli and give equilibrium through the senses, the way nature intended. Conclude your day with a dip in the mineral pool, and inhale your worries away in the eucalyptus steam room. By day's end, you will indeed feel rejuvenated and back in rhythm. ✉ *7500 E. Doubletree Ranch Rd., Central Scottsdale* ☎ *480/444–1234* ⊕ *scottsdale.regency.hyatt.com.*

VH Spa at the Hotel Valley Ho

FITNESS/HEALTH CLUBS | At the always-hip Hotel Valley Ho, guests should feel comfortable entrusting renovation of the body and soul to the mod, colorful glass VH (Vitality Health) Spa. You can boost your treatments with a "flight" of anti-oxidants—what other people might call a glass of wine—because, hey, this is a vacation after all. If you don't feel like venturing south to the spa, get the five-star treatment in a private poolside cabana. Guests can choose in-room treatments. ✉ *6850 E. Main St., Old Town* ☎ *480/248–2000* ⊕ *www.hotelvalleyho.com.*

★ Well & Being Spa, Fairmont Scottsdale Princess

FITNESS/HEALTH CLUBS | Perhaps one of the most romantic spa settings in the Valley, Well & Being Spa is an ideal retreat for couples. A three-story experience, the spa offers more water than seems possible in a desert. Enjoy an afternoon at the rooftop pool—which also includes private cabanas—or cuddle with your loved one under the powerful waterfall that connects the men's and women's locker facilities. Inside, the locker rooms feature plunge pools and hot tubs, aromatherapy rooms, saunas, and steam rooms. ✉ *Fairmont Scottsdale Princess Resort, 7575 E. Princess Dr., North Scottsdale* ☎ *480/585–4848* ⊕ *www.fairmont.com/scottsdale/spa.*

TENNIS

Scottsdale Ranch Park & Tennis Center

TENNIS | Lessons are available at this city facility, which has 18 lighted courts. ✉ *10400 E. Via Linda, North Scottsdale* ☎ *480/312–7774* ⊕ *www.scottsdaleaz.gov/parks/scottsdale-ranch-park.*

Tempe, Mesa, and Chandler

Tempe is 11 miles (18 km) southeast of Phoenix.

Tempe, Mesa, and Chandler are part of the East Valley, a term for the collection of suburbs located east of Phoenix. Because of their close proximity and similarities, it helps to think of them as one area. The East Valley is a great destination for families traveling with children. It has excellent museums and cultural centers—and also happens to be home to the finest restaurant in the state.

Most notably, Tempe is the home of Arizona State University's main campus and a thriving student population. A 20-minute drive from Phoenix, tree- and brick-lined Mill Avenue is the main drag, filled with student hangouts, bookstores, boutiques, eateries, and a repertory movie house. There are always things to do or see, and plenty of music venues and fun, casual dining spots.

The banks of the Rio Salado in Tempe are the site of a commercial and entertainment district, and Tempe Town Lake—a 2-mile-long waterway created by inflatable dams in a flood-control channel—which is open for boating. There are biking and jogging paths on the perimeter.

Mesa, Arizona's third-largest city, has long been considered Phoenix's under-achieving sibling. Today, it's making a name for itself. An arts center—reachable by the Valley's light-rail system—showcases theatre, dance, singers and comedians nightly. And its museums offer a closer look into Arizona and its ancient history.

Chandler, another suburb of the East Valley, is home to the annual Ostrich Festival, casinos, and fine restaurants.

GETTING HERE AND AROUND

Street parking is hard to find, especially amid all the construction, but there are plenty of public parking garages. Some merchants validate parking for reduced parking charges. The Orbit free shuttle does a loop around Arizona State University, with stops at Mill Avenue and Sun Devil Stadium. The light rail also stops at 3rd Street and Mill Avenue.

TIMING

Tempe Festival of the Arts

This free festival on Mill Avenue is held twice a year in early December and March/April; it has all sorts of interesting arts and crafts from local artisans. ⊕ *www.tempefestivalofthearts.com.*

◉ Sights

Arizona State University and nearby Mill Avenue are the heart of Tempe. Stroll along Mill, and you'll see Tempe in a nutshell: students, galleries, clubs and bars, and independent shops. It's also the location of some of the Valley's most inspired architecture. The inverted pyramid that is Tempe City Hall, on 5th Street, one block east of Mill Avenue, was constructed by local architects Rolf Osland and Michael Goodwin not just to win design awards (which they have), but also to shield city workers from the desert sun. The pyramid is built mainly of bronzed glass and stainless steel, and the point disappears in a sunken courtyard lushly landscaped with jacaranda, ivy, and flowers, out of which the pyramid widens to the sky; stand underneath and gaze up for a weird fish-eye perspective.

Arizona Museum of Natural History

MUSEUM | FAMILY | Kids young and old get a thrill out of the largest collection of dinosaur fossils in the state. You can also pan for gold and see changing exhibits from around the world. ✉ *53 N. Macdonald St., Mesa* 🕾 *480/644–2230* ⊕ *arizonamuseumofnaturalhistory.org* 🎟 *$12* 🕙 *Closed Mon.*

Tempe is home to Arizona State University, the largest university in the Southwest.

Arizona State University

COLLEGE | What began in 1886 as the Tempe Normal School for Teachers, a four-room redbrick building and 20-acre cow pasture, is now the 750-acre Tempe campus of ASU, the largest university in the Southwest. The university has five campuses across the Valley, with the Tempe campus serving as headquarters. As you walk around campus, you'll wind past public art and innovative architecture—including a music building that bears a strong resemblance to a wedding cake, designed by Taliesin students to echo Frank Lloyd Wright's Gammage Auditorium, and a law library shaped like an open book—and end up at Sun Devil Stadium, which is carved out of a mountain and cradled between the Tempe buttes. ⊠ *Tempe* ☎ *480/965–9011* ⊕ *www.asu.edu.*

Arizona State University Art Museum

MUSEUM | This museum is in the gray-purple stucco Nelson Fine Arts Center, just north of Gammage Auditorium on the Arizona State campus. For a relatively small museum, it has an extensive collection, including 19th- and 20th-century paintings and sculptures by masters such as Winslow Homer, Edward Hopper, Georgia O'Keeffe, and Rockwell Kent. Works by faculty and student artists are also on display, and there's a gift shop. ⊠ *Nelson Fine Arts Center, Mill Ave. and 10th St., Tempe* ☎ *480/965–2787* ⊕ *asuartmuseum.asu. edu* ⊠ *Free* ☉ *Closed Sun. and Mon.*

LEGOLAND Discovery Center

AMUSEMENT PARK/WATER PARK | **FAMILY** | Imagine thousands of square feet full of LEGO bricks, and not having to clean up any of them. No, it's not a dream—it's LEGOLAND. Kids can see giant LEGO creations as well as play, build, and watch. ■**TIP→ Buy a dual ticket with the adjoining Sea Life Arizona Aquarium and save on admission.** ⊠ *Arizona Mills, 5000 Arizona Mills Cir., Tempe* ☎ *855/450– 0558* ⊕ *arizona.legolanddiscoverycenter. com* ⊠ *$20* ☉ *Closed Tues.*

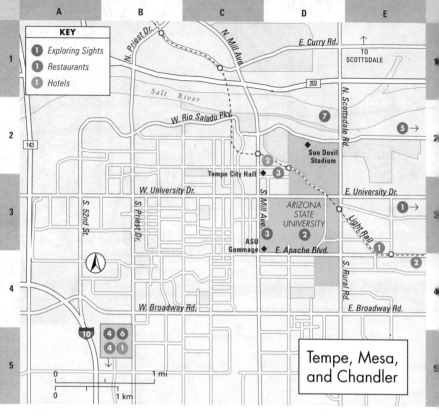

Sights ▼

1 Arizona Museum of
  Natural History........... **E3**
2 Arizona State
  University................ **D3**
3 Arizona State University
  Art Museum............. **D3**
4 LEGOLAND
  Discovery Center **B5**
5 Mesa Grande
  Cultural Park **E2**
6 Sea Life Arizona **B5**
7 Tempe Town Lake....... **D2**

Restaurants ▼

1 Curry Corner.............. **E3**
2 Haji Baba **E4**
3 House of Tricks.......... **D2**
4 Kai **B5**

Hotels ▼

1 Sheraton Grand at
  Wild Horse Pass........ **B5**
2 Tempe Mission
  Palms..................... **D2**

Mesa Grande Cultural Park

ARCHAEOLOGICAL SITE | FAMILY | Unpreserved in the middle of the city for years, this amazing, six-acre historic site features a group of Hohokam structures dating to 1400–1100 BC. Once protected only by locals and the occasional landowner, it's now operated by the Arizona Museum of Natural History. ✉ *1000 N. Date St., Mesa* ☎ *480/644–3075* 🌐 *arizonamuseumofnaturalhistory.org* 🎟 *$5* 🕒 *Closed mid-May–mid-Oct. Closed Mon. and Tues.*

Sea Life Arizona

ZOO | FAMILY | Some 5,000 creatures including sharks, stingrays, eels, and a giant octopus call this underwater menagerie home. A 165,000-gallon tank with a 360-degree viewing tunnel is the first of its kind. Who says there's no water in the desert? **■TIP→ Buy a dual ticket with the adjoining LEGOLAND Discovery Center and save on admission.** ✉ *Arizona Mills, 5000 Arizona Mills Cir., Tempe* ☎ *480/478–7600, 855/450–0559* 🌐 *www.visitsealife.com/arizona* 🎟 *$20.*

Tempe Town Lake

BODY OF WATER | FAMILY | The human-made Town Lake has turned downtown Tempe into a commercial and urban-living hot spot, and attracts college students and Valley residents of all ages. Little ones enjoy the Beach Park, and fishermen appreciate the rainbow trout–stocked lake. You also can rent a boat and tour the lake on your own. ✉ *550 E. Tempe Town Lake, Tempe* ☎ *480/350–5200* 🌐 *www.tempe.gov/lake* 🎟 *Free.*

🍴 Restaurants

Home to Arizona State University, Tempe is synonymous with college energy. Mill Avenue is a hub of clubs, movie theaters, and restaurants. Nearby Chandler is home to one of the best restaurants in the Greater Phoenix area.

Curry Corner

$ | INDIAN | In the shadow of Arizona State University, Curry Corner serves some of the best Indian food in town. The naan is plentiful at this mom-and-pop eatery, and the chicken tikka masala is the house specialty. **Known for:** clientele that skews "college"; late-night snacks (open until 10:30); fast and affordable food. [$] *Average main: $10* ✉ *1212 E. Apache Blvd., Tempe* ☎ *480/894–1276* 🌐 *currycornertempe.com.*

Haji Baba

$ | MIDDLE EASTERN | This casual treasure is a hole-in-the-wall Middle Eastern favorite that gets consistent rave reviews. The reasonably priced menu includes hummus, *lebni* (fresh cheese made from yogurt), fabulous falafel, gyros, shawarma, and kebab plates, all served by a friendly and efficient staff. **Known for:** feeding a decent percentage of ASU faculty; the grocery store, almost as busy as the restaurant; hearty servings of chicken shawarma. [$] *Average main: $10* ✉ *1513 E. Apache Blvd., Tempe* ☎ *480/894–1905* 🕒 *No dinner Sun.*

★ **House of Tricks**

$$$ | CONTEMPORARY | There's nothing up the sleeves of Robert and Robin Trick, who work magic on their ever-changing eclectic menu. One of the Valley's most unusual dining venues, the restaurant encompasses an utterly charming 1920s home and a separate brick-and-adobe-style house originally built in 1903, adjoined by an intimate wooden deck and outdoor patio shaded by a canopy of grapevines and trees. **Known for:** idyllic location in the middle of a college campus; outdoor patio dining under twinkling lights; menu that adapts to the season and the whims of the chef. [$] *Average main: $27* ✉ *114 E. 7th St., Tempe* ☎ *480/968–1114* 🌐 *www.houseoftricks.com* 🕒 *Closed Sun.*

★ Kai

$$$$ | **SOUTHWESTERN** | One of the finest restaurants in all of the Valley, the prestigious Kai ("seed" in the Pima language) uses indigenous ingredients from local tribal farms to create innovative Southwestern cuisine. The seasonal menu reflects the restaurant's natural setting on the Gila River Indian Community. **Known for:** unparalleled, orchestrated service that's worth a drive to Chandler; a "dinner and a show" experience with every meal; huge windows that show off mountain and desert views at sunset. $ *Average main: $53* ✉ *Sheraton Grand at Wild Horse Pass, 5594 W. Wild Horse Pass Blvd., Chandler* ☎ *602/225–0100* ⊕ *www.wildhorsepass.com* ⊗ *Closed Sun. and Mon. No lunch.*

Hotels

Sheraton Grand at Wild Horse Pass

$$$$ | **RESORT** | **FAMILY** | The culture and heritage of the Pima and Maricopa tribes are reflected in every aspect of this tranquil property on the grounds of the Gila River Indian community, 11 miles south of Sky Harbor Airport. **Pros:** great views and service; peaceful; good for families and older travelers looking to escape urban chaos. **Cons:** conferences can sometimes overrun the place; beautiful hand-hewn guest-room doors are loud when they slam shut; long walk to reach most guest rooms from the lobby. $ *Rooms from: $379* ✉ *5594 W. Wild Horse Pass Blvd., Chandler* ☎ *602/225–0100* ⊕ *www.wildhorsepass. com* ⇥ *500 rooms* ⧑ *No meals.*

Tempe Mission Palms

$$$$ | **HOTEL** | A handsome, casual lobby and an energetic young staff set the tone at this three-story courtyard hotel with comfortable, Southwestern-style rooms. **Pros:** nice hotel with friendly service and a rooftop pool; right at the center of ASU and Mill Avenue activity; mere minutes from the airport. **Cons:** all that activity can be bad for light sleepers; a bit dated overall; few amenities. $ *Rooms from: $359*

✉ *60 E. 5th St., Tempe* ☎ *480/894–1400, 800/547–8705* ⊕ *www.destinationhotels. com/tempe-mission-palms* ⇥ *303 rooms* ⧑ *No meals.*

Nightlife

Aura

DANCE CLUBS | Boasting the largest dance floor on Mill Ave., Aura offers 5,000 square feet of space to let loose. Given its location near campus, it's no surprise that Aura is a favorite of ASU students. If you need a vibe that's a little more post-college, opt for a VIP table and bottle service. ✉ *411 S. Mill Ave., Tempe* ☎ *602/210–2872* ⊕ *auratempe.com.*

Casey Moore's Oyster House

BARS/PUBS | A laid-back institution where students, hippies, and families come together, Casey Moore's occupies a 1910 house rumored to be haunted by ghosts. Enjoy more than two dozen beers on tap and fresh oysters at this Irish pub-style favorite. ✉ *850 S. Ash Ave., Tempe* ☎ *480/968–9935* ⊕ *caseymooresoysterhouse.godaddysites.com.*

Four Peaks Brewing Company

BREWPUBS/BEER GARDENS | This beer spot is the former redbrick home of Bordens Creamery. Wash down pub grub—pizza, wings, and burgers—with an ample supply of house-made brews on tap (including some seasonal specialties). ✉ *1340 E. 8th St., Tempe* ☎ *480/303–9967* ⊕ *www. fourpeaks.com.*

The Monastery

BARS/PUBS | Grill your own burgers and nosh on picnic food at this casual beer and wine pub. You can also play horseshoes, chess, or volleyball. ✉ *4810 E. McKellips, Mesa* ☎ *480/474–4477* ⊕ *www.themonasterybar.com.*

SanTan Brewing Company

BREWPUBS/BEER GARDENS | If you're in Chandler, come here for good food with great beer and an energetic pub atmosphere without the tired, hole-in-the-wall, or overly commercial feel. Wash down some SanTan wings and a stuffed burger with a SanTan IPA. ✉ *8 San Marcos Pl., Chandler* ☎ *480/917–8700* ⊕ *santanbrewing.com.*

The Tempe Improv
COMEDY CLUBS | Part of a national chain, The Tempe Improv showcases better-known headliners from Thursday to Sunday. Get here early for good seats. ✉ *930 E. University Dr., Tempe* ☎ *480/921–9877* ⊕ *tempeimprov.com.*

Wild Horse Pass Hotel & Casino
CASINOS | Part of the Wild Horse Pass resort, this place includes 500 slots, live poker, blackjack, and keno. ✉ *5040 Wild Horse Pass Blvd., Chandler* ☎ *800/946–4452* ⊕ *playatgila.com.*

🎭 Performing Arts

ASU Gammage
ARTS CENTERS | Frank Lloyd Wright designed the ASU Gammage Auditorium, which presents more Broadway shows outside the Big Apple than any other venue in the nation. ✉ *Arizona State University, Mill Ave. at Apache Blvd., Tempe* ☎ *480/965–3434* ⊕ *www.asugammage.com.*

Chandler Center for the Arts
ARTS CENTERS | FAMILY | The schedule here includes some of the nation's most popular touring performances for families and children. ✉ *250 N. Arizona Ave., Chandler* ☎ *480/782–2680* ⊕ *www.chandlercenter.org.*

Childsplay
THEATER | FAMILY | The state's theater company for young audiences and families holds performances during the school year at Tempe Center for the Arts. ✉ *Tempe Center for the Arts, 700 W. Rio Salado Pkwy., Tempe* ☎ *480/921–5700* ⊕ *www.childsplayaz.org.*

Marquee Theatre
THEATER | This venue hosts mainly headlining rock 'n' roll entertainers. ✉ *730 N. Mill Ave., Tempe* ☎ *480/829–0607* ⊕ *luckymanonline.com.*

Mesa Arts Center
ARTS CENTERS | This arts organization is one of the Valley's top destinations for exhibits, visual-art performances, and A-list concerts. ✉ *1 E. Main St., Mesa* ☎ *480/644–6500* ⊕ *www.mesaartscenter.com.*

Tempe Center for the Arts
ARTS CENTERS | This small, architecturally interesting arts center at the edge of Tempe Town Lake has become a great source of local pride. Visual art, music, theater, and dance featuring local, regional, and international talent are showcased in a state-of-the-art, 600-seat proscenium theater, a 200-seat studio theater, and a 3,500-square-foot gallery. ✉ *700 W. Rio Salado Pkwy., Tempe* ☎ *480/350–2822* ⊕ *www.tempecenterforthearts.com.*

🛍 Shopping

Changing Hands Bookstore
BOOKS/STATIONERY | This bookstore has a large selection of new and used books and often features special book signings and other events with authors. ✉ *6428 S. McClintock Dr., Tempe* ☎ *480/730–0205* ⊕ *www.changinghands.com.*

Mill Avenue Shops
SHOPPING NEIGHBORHOODS | Named for the landmark Hayden Flour Mill, this is one of the Valley's favorite walk-and-shop experiences. Directly west of the Arizona State University campus and just steps from a light-rail stop, Mill Avenue is an active melting pot of students, artists, residents, and tourists. Shops include some locally owned stores and midrange chains, as well as many bars and restaurants. The Valley Art Theater is a Mill Avenue institution and Tempe's home of indie cinema. ✉ *Mill Ave., Tempe* ✛ *Between Rio Salado Pkwy. and University Dr.* ☎ *480/355–6060* ⊕ *www.downtowntempe.com.*

River tubers that float down Salt River sometimes spot wild horses.

Saba's Western Wear

CLOTHING | For nearly 100 years, the Saba family has outfitted Arizonans and visitors alike with authentic Western wear. Just a single store remains, in downtown Chandler, but it's worth a drive if you're searching for boots and authentic cowboy garb including jeans, shirts, and belts. If you can't find a boot here, you're just not made for them. ⊠ *67 W. Boston St., Chandler* ☎ *480/963–4496* ⊕ *www. sabasofchandler.com.*

🏃 Activities

GOLF

★ Gold Canyon Golf Club

GOLF | Near Apache Junction in the East Valley, Gold Canyon Golf Club offers fantastic views of the Superstition Mountains and challenging golf. ⊠ *6100 S. King's Ranch Rd., Gold Canyon* ☎ *480/982–9090, 800/827–5281* ⊕ *gcgr. com* 🏌 *Dinosaur Mountain: $225; Sidewinder: $130* 🏌 *Dinosaur Mountain: 18 holes, 6653 yards, par 70; Sidewinder: 18 holes, 6533 yards, par 71.*

Ocotillo Golf Club

GOLF | There's water in play on nearly all 27 holes at Ocotillo Golf Club, which was designed around 95 acres of man-made lakes. ⊠ *3751 S. Clubhouse Dr., Chandler* ☎ *480/917–6660* ⊕ *www.ocotillogolf. com* 🏌 *$119* 🏌 *Blue/Gold: 18 holes, 7016 yards, par 72; White/Gold: 18 holes, 6804 yards, par 71; Blue/White: 18 holes, 6782 yards, par 71.*

HORSEBACK RIDING
★ OK Corral Stables

HORSEBACK RIDING | Half-, one-, two-, and four-hour horseback trail rides and steak cookouts are available from this company, which also runs one- to three-day horse-packing trips. They have the oldest pack station in the history of the Superstition Mountains, and all their guides are U.S. Forest Service–licensed. ⊠ *5470 E Apache Trail, Apache Junction* ☎ *480/982–4040* ⊕ *www.okcorrals.com* 🏌 *From $40.*

SPAS
Aji Spa at the Sheraton Grand at Wild Horse Pass

FITNESS/HEALTH CLUBS | A gem on the grounds of the Gila River Indian community, Aji incorporates its Native American surroundings into every aspect of the spa, from the name (*aji* is Pima for sanctuary) to its Sonoran design and treatments. A complete spa experience awaits, from the plunge pool to the steam room and exercise facilities. Enjoy lunch at the always-healthy spa café, and relax poolside at the coed patio that overlooks the resort and surrounding desert. ⊠ *Sheraton Grand at Wild Horse Pass, 5594 W. Wild Horse Pass Blvd., Chandler* ☎ *602/225–0100* ⊕ *www.wildhorsepass.com.*

TUBING

The Valley may not be known for its wealth of water, but locals manage to make the most of what there is. A popular summer stop is the northeast side of the Salt River, where sun worshippers can rent an inner tube and float down the river for an afternoon. Tubing season runs from May to September. Several Valley outfitters rent tubes. Make sure you bring lots of sunscreen, a hat, water—and a rope for attaching your cooler to a tube.

Salt River Recreation

WATER SPORTS | This outfitter offers shuttle-bus service to and from your starting point and rents tubes for $19 for the day. It's open during summer months only. ⊠ *Usery Pass and Power Rd., Mesa* ☎ *480/984–3305* ⊕ *www.saltrivertubing.com.*

Side Trips Near Phoenix

There are a number of interesting sights within a 1- to 1½-hour drive of Phoenix. To the north, the thriving artist communities of Carefree and Cave Creek are popular Western attractions. Arcosanti and Wickenburg are half- or full-day trips from Phoenix. Stop along the way to visit the petroglyphs of Deer Valley Rock Art Center and the reenactments of Arizona territorial life at the Pioneer Living History Village. You also might consider Arcosanti and Wickenburg as stopovers on the way to or from Flagstaff, Prescott, or Sedona.

South of Phoenix, an hour's drive takes you back to prehistoric times and the site of Arizona's first known civilization at Casa Grande Ruins National Monument, a vivid reminder of the Hohokam who began farming this area more than 1,500 years ago.

Pioneer Living History Village

25 miles north of Downtown Phoenix.

It's easy to wonder what places in Arizona were like 100 years ago or more. A trip to the Pioneer Living History Village provides an answer. Here you can get a glimpse at 19th-century desert living.

GETTING HERE AND AROUND

Take Interstate 17 north from Downtown Phoenix for 25 miles. Just north of Carefree Highway (AZ 74), take Exit 225, and turn left on Pioneer Road to get to the entrance.

◉ Sights

Pioneer Living History Museum

MUSEUM VILLAGE | FAMILY | This museum contains 28 original and reconstructed buildings from throughout territorial Arizona. Costumed guides filter through the bank, schoolhouse, jail, and print shop, as well as the Pioneer Opera House, where classic melodramas are performed daily. It's popular with the grade-school field-trip set, and it's your lucky day if you can tag along for their tour of the site. ⊠ *3901 W. Pioneer Rd., Pioneer* ☎ *623/465–1052* ⊕ *www.pioneeraz.org* ⊠ *$10* ⊙ *Closed Mon. and Tues.*

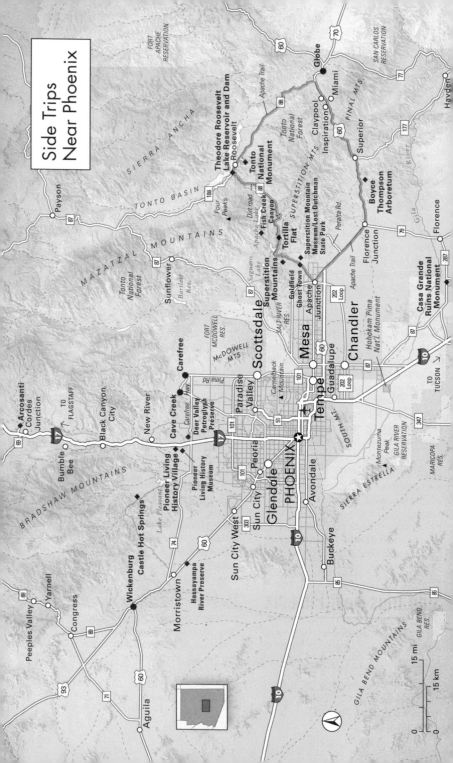

Side Trips Near Phoenix

Cave Creek and Carefree

30 miles north of Downtown Phoenix.

Some 30 miles north of Phoenix, resting high in the Sonoran Desert at an elevation of 2,500 feet, the towns of Cave Creek and Carefree hearken back to a lifestyle far different from that of their more populous neighbors to the south.

Cave Creek got its start with the discovery of gold in the region. When the mines and claims "played out," the cattlemen arrived, and the sounds of horse hooves and lowing cattle replaced those of miners' picks. The area grew slowly and independently from Phoenix to the south, until a paved road connected the two in 1952. Today the mile-long main stretch of town on Cave Creek Road is a great spot to have some hot chili and cold beer, try on Western duds, or learn the two-step in a "cowboy" bar. You're likely to run into folks dressed in cowboy hats, boots, and bold belt buckles. Horseback riders and horse-drawn wagons have the right of way here, and the 25 mph speed limit is strictly enforced by county deputies. You can amble up the hill and rent a horse for a trip into the Tonto National Forest in search of some long-forgotten native petroglyphs, or take a jeep tour out to the forest.

Just about the time the dirt-road era ended in Cave Creek, planners were sketching out a new community, which became neighboring Carefree. The world's largest sundial, at the town's center, is surrounded by galleries, artists' workshops, and cafés. Today Cave Creek and Carefree sit cheek by jowl—but the former has beans, beef, biscuits, and beer, while the latter doesn't hestitate to flaunt its luxury.

GETTING HERE AND AROUND

Follow Interstate 17 north of Downtown Phoenix for 15 miles. Exit at Carefree Highway (AZ 74) and turn right, then go 12 miles. Turn left onto Cave Creek Road and go 3 miles to downtown Cave Creek, then another 4 miles on Cave Creek Road to Carefree. Pick up maps and information about the area at the Chamber of Commerce.

ESSENTIALS

VISITOR INFORMATION Carefree–Cave Creek Chamber of Commerce. ✉ *748 Easy St., Carefree* ☎ *480/488–3381* 🌐 *www.carefreecavecreek.org.*

Sights

Cave Creek Museum

MUSEUM | Exhibits at the Cave Creek Museum depict pioneer living, mining, and ranching. See an original 1920s tuberculosis cabin and a collection of artifacts from the Hohokam and Yavapai tribes. ✉ *6140 E. Skyline Dr., Cave Creek* ☎ *480/488–2764* 🌐 *www.cavecreekmuseum.org* 🎟 *$7* 🕓 *Closed June–Sept. Closed Mon. and Tues.*

Frontier Town

NEIGHBORHOOD | **FAMILY** | The pseudo-Western Frontier Town has wooden sidewalks, ramshackle buildings, and souvenir shops. ✉ *6245 E. Cave Creek Rd., Cave Creek* 🎟 *Free.*

Restaurants

Horny Toad Restaurant

$$$ | **AMERICAN** | Cave Creek's oldest restaurant is a rustic spot for barbecued pork ribs and steak, but the real star is the fried chicken. The quirky menu features a range of fare from soup "de joor" to Icelandic cod and carne asada. **Known for:** kid-friendly environment; a bit of a Cave Creek–meets–Woodstock feel; homemade barbecue sauce. [$] *Average main: $22* ✉ *6738 E. Cave Creek Rd., Cave Creek* ☎ *480/488–9542* 🌐 *www.thehornytoad.com.*

Tonto Bar & Grill at Rancho Mañana

$$$$ | **AMERICAN** | Old West ambience emanates from every corner of the Tonto Bar & Grill, from the hand-carved ceiling beams to the *latilla*-covered (stick-covered) patios with views of the pristine Sonoran Desert. Try the cowboy Cobb salad or the Tonto burger piled with fried onions and cheddar for lunch; root beer–braised short ribs or onion-crusted walleye are good choices at dinner. **Known for:** eclectic fare far beyond Cave Creek cowboy grub; almost year-round comfortable dining on the patio; menu featuring Native American and Southwest ingredients. [$] *Average main: $38* ✉ *5736 E. Rancho Manana Blvd., Cave Creek* ☎ *480/488–0698* 🌐 *tontobarandgrill.com.*

Hotels

★ Boulders Resort & Spa
$$$$ | RESORT | One of the country's top resorts hides amid hill-size, 12-million-year-old granite boulders and the picturesque Sonoran Desert. **Pros:** remote desert getaway; even standard accommodations are luxurious; exceptional service, spa, and golfing. **Cons:** on-site dining is priced above average; minimum 45-minute drive to Phoenix attractions; few non-pool-related dining options for a resort of its caliber. [$] *Rooms from: $429* ✉ *34631 N. Tom Darlington Dr., Carefree* ☎ *480/488–9009, 888/579–2631* 🌐 *www.theboulders.com* 🛏 *218 units* 🍴 *No meals.*

Nightlife

Buffalo Chip Saloon
BARS/PUBS | Watch real cowboys and cowgirls two-step to live music at this saloon, where you can also gorge on mesquite-grilled chicken and buffalo chips (hot, homemade potato chips). Reservations are suggested for the all-you-can-eat Friday-night fish fry, which draws crowds. There's live music and dancing just about every night. ✉ *6811 E. Cave Creek Rd., Cave Creek* ☎ *480/488–9118* 🌐 *buffalochipsaloon.com.*

Harold's Cave Creek Corral
BARS/PUBS | Harold's has two full bars, a huge dance floor with live bands on weekends, a game room, TVs, and a restaurant serving some of the best ribs in the Valley. It's also the go-to place to watch Pittsburgh Steelers games during the NFL season. ✉ *6895 E. Cave Creek Rd., Cave Creek* ☎ *480/488–1906* 🌐 *www.haroldscorral.com.*

Activities

The Boulders Golf Club
GOLF | There are two championship 18-hole courses at this club, which has one of the most unique settings in the Valley. The Jay Morrish–designed courses wind around the granite boulders for which the resort is named. ✉ *Boulders Resort & Spa, 34631 N. Tom Darlington Dr., Carefree* ☎ *480/488–9009, 888/579–2631* 🌐 *www.theboulders.com* 🎫 *$259* ⛳ *North Course: 18 holes, 6959 yards, par 72; South Course: 18 holes, 6917 yards, par 71.*

★ The Spa at the Boulders Resort
FITNESS/HEALTH CLUBS | If you're seeking the serenity of the desert, this is the place. Influenced by Asian and Native American cultures, the soothing Southwestern spa is divided into two wings—east for relaxation and west for activity, which includes a movement studio for Pilates, tai chi, and yoga. Walk through the outdoor, Hopi-inspired tranquility labyrinth, or schedule a visit with the spa's resident astrologer. The services menu includes traditional treatments such as massages and facials, as well as signature experiences such as chakra balancing, emotional balancing, and detoxification. ✉ *Boulders Resort & Spa, 34631 N. Tom Darlington Dr., Carefree* ☎ *480/595–3500* 🌐 *www.theboulders.com/spa-at-the-boulders.*

Spur Cross Stables
HORSEBACK RIDING | FAMILY | Well-cared-for horses will take you on one- to six-hour rides to the high Sonoran Desert of the Spur Cross Preserve and the Tonto National Forest. Some rides include visits to petroglyph sites and a saddlebag lunch. ✉ *44029 Spur Cross Rd., Cave*

Creek ☎ 480/488–9117, 800/758–9530 🌐 *arizonahorsebackadventures.com* 🎟 *From $50.*

Castle Hot Springs

50 miles northwest of Downtown Phoenix.

A stay at the luxurious, secluded Castle Hot Springs resort is well worth the hour-long drive from Downtown Phoenix. Reopened in 2020 after a long renovation, the iconic desert retreat has been around since 1896, drawing visitors with its wellness activities and natural hot springs.

GETTING HERE AND AROUND

Follow Interstate 17 north from Phoenix and AZ-74 W to N. Castle Hot Springs Rd. in Peoria. Then drive to N. Castle Hot Springs Rd. in Yavapai County.

Hotels

★ Castle Hot Springs

$$$$ | RESORT | A true desert oasis an hour north of Phoenix, this luxurious and historic 1,100-acre ranch set in the heart of the Sonoran Desert offers private cabins and exclusive access to mineral hot springs. **Pros:** luxurious amenities; plenty of activities including free yoga and tours; exclusive access to hot springs. **Cons:** far from the action; spa services and alcohol are an additional charge; pricey, but you get a lot for your money. [$] *Rooms from: $650* ✉ *5050 East Castle Hot Springs Rd.* ☎ *877/600-1137* 🌐 *www.castlehotsprings.com* 🛏 *34 rooms* 🍴 *All-inclusive.*

Activities

Lake Pleasant Regional Park

PARK—SPORTS-OUTDOORS | Lake Pleasant Regional Park is one of the most scenic water recreational areas in the Valley of the Sun. Recreational opportunities include camping, boating, fishing, hiking, swimming, picnicking, and wildlife-viewing. At the visitor center you can learn the history of the area. With the city lights of Phoenix in the distance, this is a great place for stargazing. ✉ *41835 N. Castle Hot Springs Rd., Morristown* ✣ *Northwest of Carefree Hwy. and Castle Hot Springs Rd.* ☎ *928/501–1710* 🌐 *www.maricopacountyparks.net* 🎟 *$7 per car.*

Wickenburg

70 miles northwest of Downtown Phoenix.

This town, land of guest ranches and tall tales, is named for Henry Wickenburg, whose nearby Vulture Mine was the richest gold strike in the Arizona Territory. In the late 1800s Wickenburg was a booming mining town on the banks of the Hassayampa River, with a seemingly endless supply of gold, copper, and silver. Nowadays Wickenburg's Old West history attracts visitors hoping to awaken their inner cowboy to its guest ranches.

GETTING HERE AND AROUND

Follow Interstate 17 north from Phoenix for about 15 miles to the Carefree Highway (AZ 74) junction. About 30 miles west on AZ 74, take U.S. 89/93 north and go another 10 miles to Wickenburg.

Maps for self-guided walking tours of the town's historic buildings are available at the Wickenburg Chamber of Commerce, in the town's old Santa Fe Depot.

VISITOR INFORMATION

CONTACTS Wickenburg Chamber of Commerce. ✉ *216 N. Frontier St.* ☎ *928/684–5479* 🌐 *www.wickenburgchamber.com.*

Sights

Desert Caballeros Western Museum

MUSEUM | FAMILY | One of the best collections of Western art in the nation includes paintings and sculpture by Frederic Remington, Albert Bierstadt, Joe Beeler (founder of the Cowboy Artists of America), and others. Kids enjoy the re-creation of a turn-of-the-20th-century Main Street that includes a general store, period clothing, and a large collection of cowboy gear. ✉ *21 N. Frontier St.* ☎ *928/684–2272* 🌐 *www.westernmuseum.org* 🎟 *$12* 🕒 *Closed Mon. June–Aug.*

Hassayampa River Preserve

NATURE PRESERVE | Self-guided trails wind through lush cottonwood-willow forests, mesquite trees, and around a 4-acre, spring-fed pond and marsh habitat. Waterfowl, herons, and Arizona's rarest raptors shelter here. ✉ *49614 U.S. 60* ✥ *3 miles southeast of Wickenburg* ☎ *928/684–2772* 🌐 *maricopacountyparks.net* 🎟 *$5* 🕒 *Closed Mon.–Wed.*

Jail Tree

JAIL | Prisoners were chained to this now 200-year-old mesquite tree on the northeast corner of Wickenburg Way and Tegner Street. The desert heat sometimes finished them off before their sentences were served. ✉ *Wickenburg.*

Restaurants

Anita's Cocina

$$ | **MEXICAN** | A favorite for locals or those just passing through, Anita's Cocina serves reliable Mexican fare including fresh tamales for lunch or dinner and warm, sugary *sopapillas* (piping-hot, fried pastry pillows) for dessert. **Known for:** the spot for dinner in Wickenburg; charming Western decor; tamales. [$] *Average main: $13* ✉ *57 N. Valentine St.* ☎ *928/684–5777* 🌐 *www.anitascocina.com.*

Hotels

★ Rancho de los Caballeros

$$$$ | **RESORT** | **FAMILY** | This 20,000-acre property combines the guest-ranch experience with first-class amenities. **Pros:** large rooms, casitas, and suites; abundant activity roster; a great place for family gatherings. **Cons:** remote location; long hikes to rooms; might not interest those who don't like golf or horseback riding. [$] *Rooms from: $495* ✉ *1551 S. Vulture Mine Rd.* ☎ *928/684–5484, 800/684–5030* 🌐 *www.ranchodeloscaballeros.com* 🕒 *Closed mid-May–early Oct.* 🛏 *79 rooms* 🍴 *All meals.*

Arcosanti

65 miles north of Downtown Phoenix.

Off the beaten path near Cordes Junction is the unusual community started by Italian architect Paolo Soleri, Arcosanti. Tourists visit partially to stretch their legs and see the grounds, but mostly to buy a sought-after wind chime.

GETTING HERE AND AROUND

From Phoenix, take Interstate 17 north 65 miles to Exit 262 (Cordes Junction). Follow the partly paved road 2½ miles northeast to the community.

Sights

Arcosanti

TOWN | The evolving complex and community of Arcosanti was masterminded by Italian architect Paolo Soleri to be a self-sustaining habitat in which architecture and ecology function in symbiosis. Building began in 1970, but Arcosanti hasn't quite achieved Soleri's original vision. It's still worth a stop to take a tour, have a bite at the café, and purchase one of the hand-cast bronze wind bells made on-site. ⊠ *Arcosanti ✦ 2 miles off I–17 and Exit 263 (Arcosanti Rd.)* ☎ *928/632–7135* ⊕ *www.arcosanti.org* 🎫 *Tour $15.*

Casa Grande Ruins National Monument

36 miles southeast of Downtown Phoenix.

Visitors have been fascinated by Casa Grande Ruins for more than 300 years, and it's no wonder. The buildings are a marvel of not just architecture, but also ancient astronomy.

GETTING HERE AND AROUND
Take U.S. 60 (Superstition Freeway) east to Florence Junction (U.S. 60 and AZ 89), and head south 16 miles on AZ 89 to Florence. Casa Grande is 9 miles west of Florence on AZ 287 or, from Interstate 10, 16 miles east on AZ 387 and AZ 87. Note: follow signs to the ruins, not to the town of Casa Grande. When leaving the ruins, take AZ 87 north 35 miles back to U.S. 60.

◉ Sights

Casa Grande Ruins National Monument
ARCHAEOLOGICAL SITE | This site, whose original purpose still eludes archaeologists, was unknown to European explorers until Father Kino, a Jesuit missionary, first recorded the site's existence in 1694. The area was set aside as federal land in 1892 and named a national monument in 1918. Although only a few prehistoric sites can be viewed, more than 60 are in the monument area, including the 35-foot-tall—that's four stories—Casa Grande (Big House). The tallest known Hohokam building, Casa Grande was built in the early 14th century and is believed by some to have been an ancient astronomical observatory or a center of government, religion, trade, or education. Allow an hour to explore the site, longer if park rangers are giving a talk or leading a tour. On your way out,

cross the parking lot by the covered picnic grounds and climb the platform for a view of a ball court and two platform mounds, said to date from the 1100s. ⊠ *1100 W. Ruins Dr., Coolidge* ☎ *520/723–3172* ⊕ *www.nps.gov/cagr* 🎫 *Free.*

The Apache Trail

President Theodore Roosevelt called this 150-mile drive "the most awe-inspiring and most sublimely beautiful panorama nature ever created." A stretch of winding highway, the AZ 88 portion of the Apache Trail closely follows the route forged through wilderness in 1906 to move construction supplies for building the Roosevelt Dam, which lies at the northernmost part of the loop.

PLANNING YOUR TIME
Although the complete 150-mile loop can easily be completed in less than a day, you could spend a night in Globe, continuing the loop back to Phoenix the following day.

GETTING HERE AND AROUND
From the town of Apache Junction you can choose to drive the trail in either direction; there are advantages to both. If you begin the loop going clockwise—heading eastward on AZ 88 to the Superstition Mountains, the Peralta Trail, Tonto National Monument, and Theodore Roosevelt Lake Reservoir and Dam—your drive might be more relaxing; you'll be on the farthest side of this narrow dirt road some refer to as the "white-knuckle route," with its switchbacks and drop-offs straight down into spectacular Fish Creek Canyon. ■ TIP→ **The 42-mile section of the drive on AZ 88 isn't for anyone afraid of heights.** You can choose to drive the whole 150-mile loop, from Apache Junction to Roosevelt Dam, south to Globe, and back east through Superior to return to Apache Junction.

Superstition Mountains

30 miles east of Downtown Phoenix.

Folklore abounds in the Superstition Mountains, where visitors have sought treasure from the Lost Dutchman Mine for generations.

GETTING HERE AND AROUND
From Phoenix, take Interstate 10 and then U.S. 60 (the Superstition Freeway) east through the suburbs of Tempe, Mesa, and Apache Junction.

◉ Sights

Goldfield Ghost Town
GHOST TOWN | FAMILY | Goldfield became an instant town of about 4,000 residents after a gold strike in 1892; it dried up five years later when the gold mine flooded. Today the Goldfield Ghost Town is an interesting place to grab a cool drink, pan for gold, go for a mine tour, or take a desert jeep ride or horseback tour of the area. The ghost town's shops and saloon are open daily and gunfights are held on weekends. ⊠ *4650 N. Mammoth Mine Rd., Goldfield ✛ 4 miles northeast of Apache Junction on AZ 188* ☎ *480/983–0333* ⊕ *goldfieldghosttown.com* ▨ *Free.*

Lost Dutchman State Park
MOUNTAIN—SIGHT | As the Phoenix metro area gives way to cactus- and creosote-dotted desert, the massive escarpment of the Superstition Mountains heaves into view and slides by to the north. The Superstitions are supposedly where the legendary Lost Dutchman Mine is, the location—not to mention the existence—of which has been hotly debated since pioneer days. ⊠ *5470 N. Apache Trail, Apache Junction* ⊕ *azstateparks.com/lost-dutchman* ▨ *$7 per vehicle.*

Superstition Mountain Museum
MUSEUM | FAMILY | The best place to learn about the "Dutchman" Jacob Waltz and the Lost Dutchman Mine is at Superstition Mountain Museum. Exhibits include

a collection of mining tools, historical maps, and artifacts relating to the "gold" age of the Superstition Mountains. ⊠ *4087 N. Apache Trail (AZ 188), Apache Junction* ☎ *480/983–4888* ⊕ *superstitionmountainmuseum.org* ▨ *$5.*

🏃 Activities

Peralta Trail
HIKING/WALKING | The 4-mile round-trip Peralta Trail winds 1,400 feet up a small valley for a spectacular view of **Weaver's Needle,** a monolithic rock formation that is one of Arizona's more famous sights. Allow a few hours for this rugged and challenging hike, bring plenty of water, sunscreen, a hat, and a snack or lunch. Don't hike it in the middle of the day in summer. *Moderate.* ⊠ *Goldfield.*

Boyce Thompson Arboretum

60 miles east of Downtown Phoenix, 30 miles southeast of the Peralta Trail.

If all that cacti get overwhelming, take a trip about an hour outside of Phoenix to the Boyce Thompson Arboretum, where you'll find a wonderland of exotic plants. Desert plants and tropical birds make this oasis worth the visit.

GETTING HERE AND AROUND
From Florence Junction, take U.S. 60 east for 12 miles.

◉ Sights

Boyce Thompson Arboretum
GARDEN | At the foot of Picketpost Mountain in Superior, the Boyce Thompson Arboretum is often called an oasis in the desert: the arid rocky expanse gives way to lush riparian glades home to 3,200 different desert plants and more than 230 bird and 72 terrestrial species. The arboretum offers a living album of the world's desert and semiarid region plants, including exotic species such as Canary Islands date

The Superstition Mountains are dotted with scrub as well as soaring saguaro cactus.

palms and Australian eucalyptus. Trails offer breathtaking scenery in the gardens and the exhibits, especially during the spring wildflower season. A variety of tours are offered year-round. Benches with built-in misters offer relief from the heat. Bring along a picnic and enjoy the beauty. ✉ *37615 U.S. 60, mile marker 223, Superior* ☎ *520/689–2723* ⊕ *www.btarboretum.org* ✉ *$15.*

Globe

90 miles east of Downtown Phoenix, 51 miles east of Apache Junction, 3 miles east of Claypool's AZ 188 turnoff, 30 miles east of Boyce Thompson Arboretum.

In the southern reaches of Tonto National Forest, Globe is the most modern of the area's dilapidated mining towns. Initially, it was gold and silver that brought miners here—the city allegedly got its name from a large, circular boulder of silver, with lines like continents, found by prospectors—although the region is now known for North America's richest copper deposits. ■TIP➔ **If you're driving the Apache Trail loop, stop in Globe to fill up the tank; it's the last chance to gas up until looping all the way back to U.S. 60 at Apache Junction.**

GETTING HERE AND AROUND

Globe is at the intersection of U.S. 60 and AZ 188.

◉ Sights

Besh-Ba Gowah Archaeological Park

ARCHAEOLOGICAL SITE | For a step 800 years back in time, tour the 2 acres of the excavated Salado Indian site at the Besh-Ba Gowah Archaeological Park on the southeastern side of town. After a trip through the small museum and a video introduction, view remnants of more than 200 rooms occupied by the Salado during the 13th and 14th centuries. Public areas include the central plaza (also the principal burial ground), roasting pits, and open patios. Besh-Ba Gowah is a name given by the Apaches, who, arriving in

The Lost Dutchman Mine

Not much is known about Jacob "the Dutchman" Waltz except that he was born around 1808 in Germany (he was "Deutsch," not "Dutch") and emigrated to the United States, where he spent several years at mining camps in the Southeast, in the West, and finally in Arizona. There's documentation that he did indeed have access to a large quantity of gold, though he never registered a claim for the mine that was attributed to him.

Golden Rumors

In 1868 Waltz appeared in the newly developing community of Pumpkin-ville, soon to become Phoenix. He kept to himself on his 160-acre homestead on the bank of the Salt River. From time to time he would disappear for a few weeks and return with enough high-quality ore to keep him in a wonderful fashion. Soon word was out that "Crazy Jake" had a vast gold mine in the Superstition Mountains, east of the city near the Apache Trail.

At the same time, stories about a rich gold mine discovered by the Peralta family of Mexico were circulat-ing. Local Apaches raided the mine, which was near their sacred Thunder Mountain. In what became known as the Peralta Massacre, the Peraltas and more than 100 people working for them at the mine were killed. Rumors soon spread that Waltz had saved the life of a young Mexican who was part of Peralta's group—one of few who had escaped—and was shown the Peraltas' mine as a reward.

Searching the Superstitions

As the legend of the Dutchman's mine grew, many opportunists attempted to follow Waltz into the Superstition Mountains. A crack marksman, Waltz quickly discouraged several who tried to track him. The flow of gold contin-ued for several years.

In 1891 the Salt River flooded, badly damaging Waltz's home. When the floodwaters receded, neighbors found Waltz there in a weakened condition. He was taken to the nearby home and boardinghouse of Julia Thomas, who nursed the Dutchman for months. When his death was imminent, he reportedly gave Julia the directions to his mine.

Julia and another boarder searched for the mine fruitlessly. In her later years she sold maps to the treasure, based upon her recollections of Waltz's description. Thousands have searched for the lost mine, many losing their lives in the process—either to the brutality of fellow searchers or that of the rugged desert—and more than a century later gold seekers are still trying to connect the puzzle pieces.

The Legend Today

There's no doubt that the Dutch-man had a source of extremely rich gold ore. But was it in the Supersti-tion Mountains, nearby Goldfield, or maybe even in the Four Peaks region? Wherever it was, it's still hidden. Perhaps the best-researched books on the subject are T. E. Glover's *The Lost Dutchman Mine of Jacob Waltz* and the companion book *The Holmes Manuscript*. The Feldman family runs O.K. Corral Stables (☎ 480/982–4040 ⊕ *www.okcorrals.com*) in Apache Junction. Experts on the subject, they lead adventurers on pack trips into the mysterious mountains to relive the lore and legends.

the 17th century, found the pueblo abandoned and moved in. Loosely translated, the name means "metal camp," and remains left on the site suggest it was part of an extensive commerce and trading network. ⊠ *1324 S. Jesse Hayes Rd.* ☎ *928/425–0320* ⊕ *www.globeaz.gov/ visitors/besh-ba-gowah* ⊠ *$5* ⊗ *Closed Mon. and Tues. July–Sept.*

Restaurants

Chalo's

$ | MEXICAN | A Globe mainstay, Chalo's offers just what you'd expect from a small-town Mexican restaurant: old-school dishes and very few frills. Fortunately, what Chalo's lacks in aesthetics is offset by its great food. **Known for:** serving the same dishes since opening in 1969; best refried beans in the area; good meal before driving to Eastern Arizona. ⓢ *Average main: $10* ⊠ *902 E. Ash St.* ☎ *928/425–0515* ⊗ *Closed Sun.*

🛏 Hotels

Noftsger Hill Inn

$ | B&B/INN | Built in 1907, this B&B was originally the North Globe Schoolhouse; now classrooms serve as guest rooms, filled with mining-era antiques and affording fantastic views of the Pinal Mountains and historic Old Dominion Mine. **Pros:** giant windows offer pleasant natural light; many rooms have original classroom chalkboards devoted to guest comments; unlike any hotel you've visited. **Cons:** city slickers might miss modern bath fixtures and amenities; high ceilings and wood floors make for noisy rooms; not much to do in Globe. ⓢ *Rooms from: $150* ⊠ *425 North St.* ☎ *928/425–2260* ⊕ *www.noftsgerhillinn.com* ⤴ *6 rooms* ⦿ *Free breakfast.*

Tonto National Monument

30 miles northwest of Globe.

One of the best-preserved examples of Salado cliff dwellings, Tonto National Monument offers visitors a peek at 13th-century life.

GETTING HERE AND AROUND

Tonto National Monument is located off AZ 188, approximately 25 miles north of U.S. 60. It's about a two-hour drive from the Phoenix area. If you feel like a real journey, take AZ 88, otherwise known as the Apache Trail, to Tonto National Monument. Almost half of the 47-mile trail is gravel, so be prepared for a very long and bumpy ride.

👁 Sights

Tonto National Monument

ARCHAEOLOGICAL SITE | You can visit a well-preserved complex of 13th-century Salado cliff dwellings at this site, which was nearly destroyed during a wildfire in 2019. A team of archaeologists and firefighters saved the site's two dwellings, but 88 percent of the Monument's almost 1,000 acres burned. You can visit the Lower Cliff Dwelling on your own, but must sign up for a ranger-led tour to see the Upper Cliff Dwelling. Tours are offered from Friday to Monday, from January to April. ⊠ *26260 N. AZ 188, Roosevelt* ☎ *928/467–2241* ⊕ *www.nps. gov/tont* ⊠ *$10.*

Theodore Roosevelt Lake Reservoir and Dam

5 miles northwest of Tonto National Monument on AZ 188, 125 miles north of Phoenix.

Water is a rarity in the desert, which is why Theodore Roosevelt Lake is one of the most popular recreation destinations in the area. Boaters, fishermen, and water-skiers flock here throughout the year.

GETTING HERE AND AROUND

Theodore Roosevelt Lake Reservoir and Dam is located off AZ 188, approximately 30 miles north of U.S. 60. It's on the same road as Tonto National Monument; the drive takes about two hours from Phoenix.

◉ Sights

Theodore Roosevelt Lake Reservoir and Dam

DAM | Flanked by the desolate Mazatzal and Sierra Anchas mountain ranges, Theodore Roosevelt Lake Reservoir and Dam is an aquatic recreational area—a favorite with bass anglers, water-skiers, and boaters. This is the largest masonry dam on the planet, and the massive bridge is the longest two-lane, single-span, steel-arch bridge in the nation. ✉ *Tonto Basin Ranger Station, Roosevelt* ☎ *602/225–5395.*

Tortilla Flat

18 miles southwest of Roosevelt Dam, 18 miles northeast of Apache Junction, 60 miles northeast of Phoenix.

Tortilla Flat might just be the closest thing to the end of the world you'll find. A sort of cowboy rest stop, it's a favorite for travelers who want to stretch their legs after a bumpy, desolate ride in the desert.

En Route ◉

West of the reservoir, AZ 88 is the most traveled stretch of the Apache Trail, a meandering dirt road that eventually winds its way back to Apache Junction. Along the drive, you can't miss the magnificent, bronze-hued volcanic cliff walls of **Fish Creek Canyon**, and its views of the sparkling lakes, towering saguaros, and, in the springtime, vast fields of wildflowers.

GETTING HERE AND AROUND

Tortilla Flat is located off AZ 88, the bumpy and historic Apache Trail. It's about 60 miles from Downtown Phoenix, but leave at least two hours for the journey. Take U.S. 60 east of Phoenix through Apache Junction, then take the Idaho exit and head north toward AZ 88 and drive for approximately 18 miles. Be prepared for a bumpy and gravelly ride on parts of AZ 88—it's historic for a reason.

◉ Sights

Tortilla Flat

STORE/MALL | Close to the end of the most commonly visited section of the Apache Trail, this old-time restaurant and country store are what is left of an authentic stagecoach stop at Tortilla Flat. This is a fun place for well-earned rest and refreshment—miner- and cowboy-style grub, of course—before heading back the last 18 miles to civilization. Enjoy a hearty bowl of killer chili and some prickly pear ice cream while sitting at the counter on a saddle bar stool. ☎ *480/984–1776* ⊕ *www.tortillaflataz.com.*

Chapter 4

GRAND CANYON NATIONAL PARK

4

Updated by
Mara Levin

⛺ Camping	🛏 Hotels	🏃 Activities	👁 Scenery	👥 Crowds
★★★★★	★★★★★	★★★★★	★★★★★	★★★★★

WELCOME TO GRAND CANYON NATIONAL PARK

TOP REASONS TO GO

★ **Its status:** This is one of those places about which you really want to say, "Been there, done that!"

★ **Awesome vistas:** The Painted Desert, sandstone canyon walls, pine and fir forests, mesas, plateaus, volcanic features, the Colorado River, streams, and waterfalls make for some jaw-dropping moments.

★ **Year-round adventure:** Outdoors enthusiasts can bike, boat, camp, fish, hike, ride mules, whitewater raft, watch birds and wildlife, cross-country ski, and snowshoe.

★ **Continuing education:** Adults and kids can have fun learning, thanks to free park-sponsored nature walks and interpretive programs.

★ **Sky-high and river-low experiences:** Experience the canyon via plane, train, and automobile, as well as by helicopter, row- or motorboat, bike, mule, or foot.

Grand Canyon National Park is a superstar—biologically, historically, and recreationally. One of the world's best examples of arid-land erosion, the canyon provides a record of three of the four eras of geological time. Almost 2 billion years' worth of Earth's history is written in the colored layers of rock stacked from the river bottom to the top of the plateau. In addition to its diverse fossil record, the park reveals long-ago traces of human adaptation to an unforgiving environment. It's also home to several major ecosystems, five of the world's seven life zones, three of North America's four desert types, and all kinds of rare, endemic, and protected plant and animal species.

1 South Rim. The South Rim is where the action is: Grand Canyon Village's lodging, camping, eateries, stores, and museums, plus plenty of trailheads into the canyon. Four free shuttle routes cover more than 35 stops, and visitors who'd rather relax than rough it can treat themselves to comfy hotel rooms and elegant restaurant meals (lodging and camping reservations are essential).

2 North Rim. Of the nearly 5 million people who visit the park annually, 90% enter at the South Rim, but many consider the North Rim even more gorgeous—and worth the extra effort. Open only from mid-May to the end of October (or the first good snowfall), the North Rim has legitimate bragging rights: at more than 8,000 feet above sea level (1,000 feet

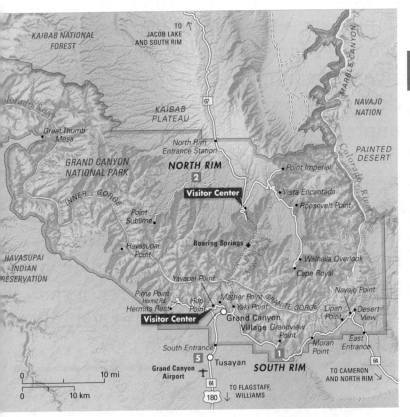

KAIBAB NATIONAL FOREST

TO JACOB LAKE AND SOUTH RIM

KAIBAB PLATEAU

67

NAVAJO NATION

MARBLE CANYON

Colorado River

Great Thumb Mesa

North Rim Entrance Station

PAINTED DESERT

GRAND CANYON NATIONAL PARK

NORTH RIM

2

Visitor Center

Point Imperial

Vista Encantada

Roosevelt Point

INNER GORGE

Point Sublime

Roaring Springs

Havasupai Point

Walhalla Overlook

Cape Royal

HAVASUPAI INDIAN RESERVATION

Yavapai Point

Pima Point
Hermit Rd.
Hermits Rest

Hopi Point

Mather Point GRANITE GORGE
Yaki Point

Navajo Point

Lipan Point

Desert View

Visitor Center

Grand Canyon Village

Grandview Point

South Entrance

East Entrance

64

0   10 mi
0   10 km

Grand Canyon Airport

Tusayan

5

Moran Point

1

SOUTH RIM

TO CAMERON AND NORTH RIM

64

TO FLAGSTAFF, WILLIAMS

180

higher than the South Rim), it has precious solitude and seven developed viewpoints. Rather than staring into the canyon's depths, you get a true sense of its expanse.

3 West Rim. Though not in Grand Canyon National Park, the far-off-the-beaten-path western end of the canyon has some spectacular scenery. At the West Rim, on the Hualapai Reservation, the Skywalk has become a major draw. This U-shape glass-floored deck juts out 3,600 feet above the Colorado River and isn't for the faint of heart.

4 Havasu Canyon. You can view some of the most stunning waterfalls in the United States in Havasu Canyon, a remote paradise on the Havasupai Reservation, but getting there requires making reservations far in advance.

5 Nearby Towns. Located just two miles from the park's south entrance, Tusayan is a good base for Grand Canyon adventures. Williams, an hour's drive south, offers lodging and dining along historic Route 66. The closest town to the North Rim is Jacob Lake.

When it comes to the Grand Canyon, there are statistics, and there are sensations. While the former are impressive—the canyon measures an average width of 10 miles, length of 277 river miles, and depth of 1 mile—they don't truly prepare you for that first impression. Viewing the canyon for the first time is an astounding experience. Actually, it's more than an experience: it's an emotion, one that only just begins to be captured with the word "Grand," the name bestowed upon the canyon by John Wesley Powell, an explorer of the American West, as he led his expedition down the Colorado River in 1869.

When President Teddy Roosevelt declared it a National Monument in 1908, he called it "the one great sight every American should see." Though many visitors do just that—stand at the rim and marvel in awe—there are manifold ways to soak up the canyon's magnificence. Hike or ride a trusty mule down into the canyon, bike or ramble along its rim, fly over, or raft through on the Colorado River.

Roughly 6 million visitors come to the park each year. You can access the canyon via two main points—the South Rim and the North Rim—but the South Rim is much easier to get to and therefore much more visited. The width from the North Rim to the South Rim varies from 600 feet to 18 miles, but traveling between rims by road requires a 215-mile drive. Hiking arduous trails from rim to rim is a steep and strenuous trek of at least 21 miles, but it's well worth the effort. You'll travel through five of North America's seven life zones. (To do this any other way, you'd have to journey from the Mexican desert to the Canadian woods.) West of Grand Canyon National Park, the tribal lands of the Hualapai and the Havasupai lie along the so-called West Rim of the canyon, where you'll find the impressive glass Skywalk.

Grand Canyon Planner

When to Go

There's no bad time to visit the canyon, though the busiest times of year are summer and spring break. Visiting the South Rim during these peak seasons, as well as holidays, requires patience and a tolerance for crowds. If you plan to hike into the canyon, be aware that temperatures rise as you descend; summer daytime highs at the bottom are often over 100° F. Fall and winter at the South Rim are spectacular and far less crowded. Note that weather changes on a whim in this exposed high-desert region. The North Rim shuts down mid-October through mid-May due to weather conditions and related road closures.

Planning Your Time

Plan ahead: Mule rides require at least a six-month advance reservation—longer for the busy season (most can be reserved up to 13 months in advance). Multiday rafting trips should be reserved at least a year in advance.

Once you arrive, pick up the free *Pocket Map and Services Guide*, a brochure with a detailed map and schedule of free programs, at the entrance gate or at any of the visitor centers. The free *Grand Canyon Accessibility Guide* is also available.

The park is most crowded on the South Rim, especially near the Visitor Center/Mather Point and in Grand Canyon Village, as well as on the scenic drives.

Getting Here and Around

SOUTH RIM
CAR
The best route into the park from the east or south is from Flagstaff. Take U.S. 180 northwest to the park's southern entrance and Grand Canyon Visitor Center. From the west on Interstate 40, the most direct route to the South Rim is taking Highway 64 from Williams to U.S. 180.

PARK SHUTTLE
The South Rim is open to car traffic year-round, though access to Hermits Rest is limited to shuttle buses during summer months. There are four free shuttle routes that run from one hour before sunrise until one hour after sunset, every 15 to 30 minutes: the **Hermits Rest Route** operates March through November, between Grand Canyon Village and Hermits Rest. The **Village Route** operates year-round in the village area, stopping at lodgings, the general store, and the Grand Canyon Visitor Center. The **Kaibab Rim Route** goes from the visitor center to five viewpoints, including the Yavapai Geology Museum and Yaki Point (where cars are not permitted). The **Tusayan Route** travels between the village and the town of Tusayan from March through September. A fifth route, the **Hiker's Express,** shuttles hikers from the village to the South Kaibab Trailhead twice each morning. ■TIP➔ In summer, South Rim roads are congested and it's easier, and sometimes required, to park your car and take the free shuttle.

TAXI AND SHUTTLE
Although there's no public transportation into the Grand Canyon, you can hire a taxi to take you to or from the Grand Canyon Village or any of the Tusayan hotels. Groome Transportation has frequent shuttle service between Flagstaff, Williams, Tusayan, and Grand Canyon Village (at Maswik Lodge); they also have connecting service from Phoenix and Sedona.

Grand Canyon Itineraries

Grand Canyon in 1 Day

Start early, pack a picnic lunch, and drive to the South Rim's **Grand Canyon Visitor Center**, just north of the south entrance, to pick up info and see your first incredible view at **Mather Point**. Continue east along **Desert View Drive** for about 2 miles to **Yaki Point**. Next, continue driving 7 miles east to **Grandview Point** for a good view of the buttes Krishna Shrine and Vishnu Temple. Go 4 miles east and catch the view at **Moran Point**, then 3 miles to the **Tusayan Ruin and Museum**, where a small display is devoted to the history of the Ancestral Puebloans. Continue another mile east to **Lipan Point** to view the Colorado River. In less than a mile, you'll arrive at **Navajo Point**, the highest elevation on the South Rim. **Desert View and Watchtower** is the final attraction along Desert View Drive.

On your return drive, stop off at any of the picnic areas if you've brought your own lunch; otherwise, there are choices ranging from food trucks to casual dining spots in Grand Canyon Village. After lunch, walk the paved **Rim Trail** west to **Maricopa Point**. Along the way, pick up souvenirs in the village and stop at the Kolb Studio and historic **El Tovar Hotel** (be sure to make reservations in advance if you want to eat dinner at El Tovar Dining Room). If you have time, drive or, during summer months, take the shuttle on **Hermit Road** to **Hermits Rest**, 7 miles away. Along that route, Hopi Point and Powell Point are excellent spots to watch the sunset.

Grand Canyon in 3 Days

On Day 1, follow the one-day itinerary for the morning, but spend more time exploring Desert View Drive and enjoy a leisurely picnic lunch. Later, drive 30 miles beyond Desert View to **Cameron Trading Post**, which has a good restaurant and is an interesting side trip. Travel Hermit Road on your second morning, by car, shuttle bus, or bicycle, and drive to Grand Canyon Airport for a late-morning small plane or helicopter tour. Have lunch in **Tusayan** and cool off at the IMAX film *Grand Canyon: The Hidden Secrets*. Back in the village, take a free ranger-led program. On your third day, hike partway down the canyon on **Bright Angel Trail**. It takes twice as long to hike back up, so plan accordingly. Get trail maps at **Grand Canyon Visitor Center**, and bring plenty of water.

Alternatively, spend Days 2 and 3 exploring the remote **West Rim**, 150 miles toward Nevada or California and far away from major highways. Fill the first day with a horseback ride along the rim, a helicopter ride into the canyon, or a walk on the Skywalk. The next day, raft the Class V–VII rapids near Peach Springs. Another option, but one that would require all three days, if not more, is to get a tribal permit for a visit to **Havasu Canyon**, a truly spiritual backcountry experience. You can opt to hike or take a helicopter 8 miles down to the small village of Supai and the Havasupai Lodge.

TAXI AND SHUTTLE CONTACTS Groome Transportation. ☎ *928/226–8060, 800/888–2749* ⊕ *www.groometransportation.com.* **Xanterra.** ☎ *928/638–2822, 888/297–2757* ⊕ *www.xanterra.com.*

TRAIN

Grand Canyon Railway

There's no need to deal with all of the other drivers racing to the South Rim. Sit back and relax in the comfy train cars of the Grand Canyon Railway. Live music, storytelling, and a pretend train robbery enliven the trip as you journey past the landscape through prairie, ranch, and national park land to the log-cabin train station in Grand Canyon Village. You won't see the Grand Canyon from the train, but you can walk (¼ mile) or catch the shuttle at the restored, historic Grand Canyon Railway Station. The vintage train departs from the Williams Depot every morning and makes the 65-mile journey in 2¼ hours. You can do the round-trip in a single day; however, it's a more relaxing and enjoyable strategy to stay for a night or two at the South Rim before returning to Williams. ☎ *800/843–8724* ⊕ *www. thetrain.com* ✉ *$82–$219 round-trip* ☞ *Rates do not include $35 park entry fee (for up to 9 persons).*

NORTH RIM

AIR

The nearest airport to the North Rim is **St. George Regional Airport** (☎ *435/627–4080* ⊕ *www.flysgu.com*) in Utah, 164 miles north, with regular service provided by American, Delta, and United airlines.

CAR

To reach the North Rim by car, take U.S. 89 north from Flagstaff past Cameron, turning left onto U.S. 89A at Bitter Springs. At Jacob Lake, take Highway 67 directly to the Grand Canyon North Rim. You can drive yourself to the scenic viewpoints and trailheads; the only transportation offered in the park is a shuttle twice each morning that brings eager hikers from Grand Canyon Lodge to the North Kaibab Trailhead (a 2-mile trip). Note that services on the North Rim shut down in mid-October, and the road closes after the first major snowfall (usually the end of October); Highway 67 south of Jacob Lake is closed.

SHUTTLE

From mid-May to mid-October, the **Trans Canyon Shuttle** (☎ *928/638–2820* ⊕ *www. trans-canyonshuttle.com*) travels daily between the South and North rims—the ride takes 4½ hours each way. The fare is $90 each way and reservations are required.

Park Essentials

PARK FEES AND PERMITS

A fee of $35 per vehicle or $20 per person for pedestrians and cyclists is good for one week's access at both rims.

The $70 Grand Canyon Pass gives unlimited access to the park for 12 months. The annual America the Beautiful **National Parks and Recreational Land Pass** (☎ *888/275–8747* ⊕ *store.usgs.gov/ pass, $80*) provides unlimited access to all national parks and federal recreation areas for 12 months.

No permits are needed for day hikers, but **backcountry permits** (☎ *928/638–7875* ⊕ *www.nps.gov/grca, $10, plus $8 per person per night*) are necessary for overnight hikers camping below the rim. Permits are limited, so make your reservation as far in advance as possible—they're taken by fax (☎ *928/638–2125*), by mail (✉ *1824 S. Thompson St., Suite 201, Flagstaff, AZ 86001*), or in person at the Backcountry Information centers (in the village on the South Rim and near the visitor center on the North Rim) up to four months prior to your arrival. A limited number of last-minute permits are available for Indian Garden, Bright Angel, and Cottonwood campgrounds each day. Camping on the North Rim and the South Rim is restricted to designated campgrounds (☎ *877/444–6777* ⊕ *www.recreation.gov*).

PARK HOURS

The South Rim is open continuously every day of the year (weather permitting), while the North Rim is open mid-May through October. Because Arizona does not observe daylight saving time, the park is in the same time zone as California and Nevada from mid-March to early November, and in the Mountain Standard Time zone the rest of the year. Just to the east of the park, the Navajo Nation observes daylight saving time.

CELL PHONE RECEPTION

Cell phone coverage can be spotty at both the South Rim and North Rim—though Verizon customers report better reception at the South Rim. Don't expect a strong signal anywhere in the park, but Grand Canyon Village is usually the best bet.

Hotels

The park's accommodations include three "historic-rustic" facilities and four motel-style lodges, all of which have undergone significant upgrades over the past decade. Of the 922 rooms, cabins, and suites, only 203 are at the North Rim, all at the Grand Canyon Lodge. Outside El Tovar Hotel, the canyon's architectural highlight, accommodations are relatively basic but comfortable, and the most sought-after rooms have canyon views. Rates vary widely, but most rooms fall in the $175 to $250 range, though the most basic units on the South Rim go for just $125. Yavapai Lodge, on the South Rim, is the only hotel in the park that allows pets.

Reservations are a must, especially during the busy summer season. ■TIP➔ If you want to get your first choice (especially Bright Angel Lodge or El Tovar), make reservations as far in advance as possible; they're taken up to 13 months ahead. You might find a last-minute cancellation, but

you shouldn't count on it. Although lodging at the South Rim will keep you close to the action, the frenetic activity and crowded facilities are off-putting to some. With short notice, the best time to find a room on the South Rim is in winter. And though the North Rim is less crowded than the South Rim, the only lodging available is at Grand Canyon Lodge.

Just south of the South Rim park boundary, Tusayan's hotels are in a convenient location but without bargains, while Williams (about an hour's drive) and Flagstaff (about 90 minutes away) can provide price breaks on food and lodging, as well as a respite from the crowds. Extra amenities (e.g., swimming pools and gyms) are also more abundant. Even outside the park, reservations are always a good idea.

LODGING CONTACTS Xanterra Parks & Resorts. ☎ 888/297-2757 ⊕ www. grandcanyonlodges.com. Delaware North. ☎ 877/404-4611 ⊕ www.visitgrandcan-yon.com.

Restaurants

Within the park on the South Rim, you can find everything from cafeteria food to casual café fare to creatively prepared, Western- and Southwestern-inspired American cuisine—there's even a coffeehouse with organic-joe. Reservations are accepted (and recommended) only for dinner at El Tovar Dining Room; they can be made up to six months in advance with El Tovar room reservations, 30 days in advance without. You should also make dinner reservations at the Grand Canyon Lodge Dining Room on the North Rim—as the only "upscale" dining option, the restaurant fills up quickly at dinner throughout the season (the other choice on the North Rim is a deli). The dress code is casual across the board, but El

Tovar is your best option if you're looking to dress up a bit and thumb through an extensive wine list. Options for picnic supplies at the South Rim include the general store in Market Plaza and healthy grab-and-go fare at Bright Angel Bicycles' café next to the Visitor Center. Drinking water and restrooms are only available at some picnic spots.

Bring your picnic basket and enjoy dining alfresco surrounded by some of the most beautiful backdrops in the country. Be sure to bring water, as it's unavailable at many of these spots, as are restrooms. **Buggeln,** 15 miles east of Grand Canyon Village on Desert View Drive, has some secluded, shady spots. **Grandview Point** has, as the name implies, grand vistas; it's 12 miles east of the village on Desert View Drive. **Cape Royal,** 23 miles south of the North Rim Visitor Center, at the end of Cape Royal Road, is the most popular designated picnic area on the North Rim due to its panoramic views. **Point Imperial,** 11 miles northeast of the North Rim Visitor Center, has shade and some privacy.

Eateries outside the park generally range from mediocre to terrible—you didn't come all the way to the Grand Canyon for the food, did you? Our selections highlight your best options. Of towns near the park, Flagstaff definitely has the leg up on culinary variety and quality, with Tusayan (near the South Rim) and Jacob Lake (the closest town to the North Rim) offering mostly either fast food or merely adequate sit-down restaurants. Near the park, even the priciest places welcome casual dress. On the Hualapai and Havasupai reservations in Havasu Canyon and on the West Rim, dining is limited and basic.

Hotel and restaurant reviews have been shortened. For full information, visit Fodors.com.

What it Costs

	$	$$	$$$	$$$$
RESTAURANTS				
	Under $12	$12–$20	$21–$30	Over $30
HOTELS				
	Under $120	$120–$175	$176–$250	Over $250

Tours

Grand Canyon Conservancy Field Institute
GUIDED TOURS | Instructors lead guided educational tours, hikes around the canyon, and weekend programs at the South Rim. With more than 200 classes a year, tour topics include everything from archaeology and backcountry medicine to photography and natural history. Contact GCC for a schedule and price list. Private hikes can be arranged. Discounted classes are available for members; annual dues are $35. ✉ *GCA Warehouse, 2–B Albright Ave., Grand Canyon Village* ☎ *928/638–7035, 866/471–4435* ⊕ *www.grandcanyon.org/fieldinstitute* ⊠ *From $235.*

Xanterra Motorcoach Tours
GUIDED TOURS | Narrated by knowledgeable guides, tours include the Hermits Rest Tour, which travels along the old wagon road built by the Santa Fe Railway; the Desert View Tour, which glimpses the Colorado River's rapids and stops at Lipan Point; Sunrise and Sunset Tours; and combination tours. ☎ *303/297–2757, 888/297–2757* ⊕ *www.grandcanyonlodges.com* ⊠ *From $40.*

Visitor Information

Grand Canyon National Park
Before you go, you can view and print the complimentary *Pocket Map and Service Guide,* updated regularly, from the Grand Canyon National Park website. You can also pick up a copy at the entrance stations

Tips for Avoiding Grand Canyon Crowds ◉

It's hard to commune with nature while you're searching for a parking place, dodging video cameras, and stepping away from strollers. However, this scenario is likely only during the peak summer months. One option is to bypass Grand Canyon National Park altogether and head to the West Rim of the canyon, tribal land of the Hualapai and Havasupai. If only the park itself will do, the following tips will help you to keep your distance and your cool.

Take Another Route

Avoid road rage by choosing a different route to the South Rim, forgoing traditional Highway 64 and U.S. 180 from Flagstaff. Take U.S. 89 north from Flagstaff instead, passing near Sunset Crater and Wupatki national monuments. When you reach the junction with Highway 64, take a break at Cameron Trading Post (1 mile north of the junction)—or stay overnight. This is a good place to shop for Native American artifacts, souvenirs, and the usual postcards, dream catchers, recordings, and T-shirts. There are also high-quality Navajo rugs, jewelry, and other authentic handicrafts, and you can sample Navajo tacos. U.S. 64 to the west takes you directly to the park's east entrance; the scenery along the Little Colorado River gorge en route is eye-popping. It's 23 miles from the east entrance to the main visitor center and Mather Point.

Explore the North Rim

Although the North Rim is just 10 miles across from the South Rim, the trip to get there by car is a five-hour drive of 215 miles. At first it might not sound like the trip would be worth it, but the payoff is huge. Along the way, you'll travel through some of the prettiest parts of the state and be granted even more stunning views than those on the more easily accessible South Rim. Those who make the North Rim trip often insist it has the canyon's most beautiful views and best hiking. To get to the North Rim from Flagstaff, take U.S. 89 north past Cameron, turning left onto U.S. 89A at Bitter Springs. En route you'll pass the area known as Vermilion Cliffs. At Jacob Lake, take Highway 67 directly to the Grand Canyon North Rim. North Rim services are closed from November through mid-May because of heavy snow, but in summer months and early fall, it's a wonderful way to beat the crowds at the South Rim.

and the visitor centers. ☎ 928/638–7888 ⊕ www.nps.gov/grca.

Grand Canyon South Rim

Visitors to the canyon converge mostly on the South Rim, and mostly in summer. Grand Canyon Village is here, with a majority of the park's lodging and camping, trailheads, restaurants, stores, and museums, along with a nearby airport and railroad depot. Believe it or not, the average stay in the park is a mere half day or so; this is not advised! You need to spend several days to truly appreciate this marvelous place, but at the very least, give it a full day. Hike down into the canyon, or along the rim, to get away from the crowds and experience nature at its finest.

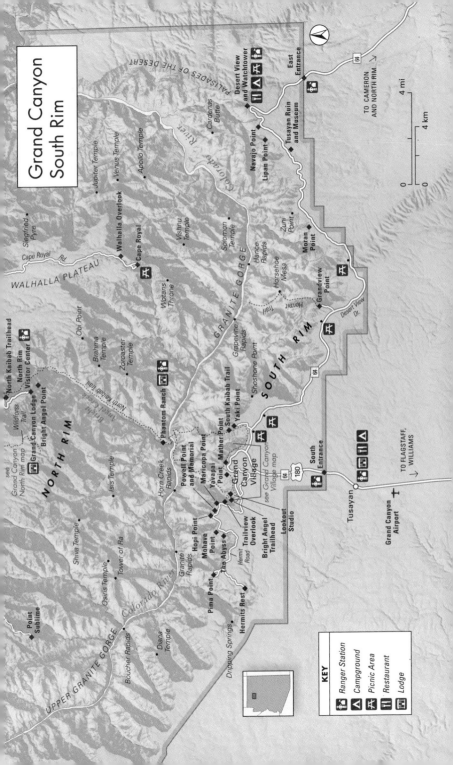

Grand Canyon
South Rim

PALISADES OF THE DESERT

Colorado River

Desert View
and Watchtower

East
Entrance

64

TO CAMERON
AND NORTH RIM

Cardenas
Butte

Tusayan Ruin
and Museum

Navajo Point

Lipan Point

4 mi

4 km

Jupiter Temple

Venus Temple

Apollo Temple

Walhalla Overlook

Vishnu
Temple

Solomon
Temple

Zuni
Point

Siegfried
Pyre

Cape Royal Rd.

Cape Royal

Walhalla Plateau

Wotans
Throne

Hance
Rapids

Horseshoe
Mesa

Moran
Point

Grandview
Point

Desert View
Dr.

Obi Point

Brahma
Temple

Zoroaster
Temple

Granite Gorge

Grapevine
Rapids

Hermit Trail

Shoshone Point

SOUTH RIM

North Kaibab Trailhead
North Rim
Visitor Center

Bright Angel Lodge

Bright Angel Point

North Kaibab Trail

Isis Temple

Phantom Ranch

Horn Creek
Rapids

South Kaibab Trail

Yaki Point

64

NORTH RIM

Shiva Temple

see
Grand Canyon
North Rim map

Osiris Temple

Tower of Ra

Point
Sublime

Colorado River

Diana
Temple

Bouchet Rapids

UPPER GRANITE GORGE

Powell Point
and Memorial

Maricopa Point

Yavapai
Point

Mather Point

Grand
Canyon
Village

see Grand Canyon
Village map

South
Entrance

180

64

Hopi Point

Mohave
Point

The Abyss

Trailview
Overlook

Bright Angel
Trailhead

Lookout
Studio

Granite
Rapids

Hermit
Road

Pima Point

Hermits Rest

Dripping Springs

Tusayan

TO FLAGSTAFF,
WILLIAMS

Grand Canyon
Airport

KEY

Ranger Station

Campground

Picnic Area

Restaurant

Lodge

Best Grand Canyon Views

The best time of day to see the canyon is before 10 and after 4, when the angle of the sun brings out the colors of the rock, and clouds and shadows add dimension. Colors deepen dramatically among the contrasting layers of the canyon walls just before and during sunrise and sunset.

Hopi Point is the top spot on the South Rim to watch the sun set; **Yaki** and **Pima** points also offer vivid views.

For a grand sunrise, try **Mather** or **Yaki Point.**

■TIP➔ Arrive at least 30 minutes early for sunrise views and as much as 90 minutes for sunset views at these points. For another point of view, take a leisurely stroll along the Rim Trail and watch the color change along with the views. Timetables are posted at park visitor centers.

◉ Sights

HISTORIC SIGHTS

Tusayan Ruin and Museum

ARCHAEOLOGICAL SITE | This museum offers a quick orientation to the prehistoric and modern indigenous populations of the Grand Canyon and the Colorado Plateau, including an excavation of an 800-year-old Pueblo site. Of special interest are split-twig figurines dating back 2,000 to 4,000 years and other artifacts left behind by ancient cultures. A ranger leads daily interpretive tours of the Ancestral Puebloan village. ⊠ *Grand Canyon National Park* ✛ *About 20 miles east of Grand Canyon Village on E. Rim Dr.* ☎ *928/638–7888* ⌨ *Free.*

PICNIC AREAS

Bring your picnic basket and enjoy dining alfresco surrounded by some of the most beautiful backdrops in the country. Be sure to bring water, as it's unavailable at many of these spots, as are restrooms.

Buggeln, 15 miles east of Grand Canyon Village on Desert View Drive, has some secluded, shady spots.

Grandview Point has, as the name implies, grand vistas; it's 12 miles east of the village on Desert View Drive.

SCENIC DRIVES

Desert View Drive

SCENIC DRIVE | This heavily traveled 25-mile stretch of road follows the rim from the east entrance to Grand Canyon Village. Starting from the less-congested entry near Desert View, road warriors can get their first glimpse of the canyon from the 70-foot-tall watchtower, the top of which provides the highest viewpoint on the South Rim. Six developed canyon viewpoints in addition to unmarked pullouts, the remains of an Ancestral Puebloan dwelling at the Tusayan Ruin and Museum, and the secluded and lovely Buggeln picnic area make for great stops along the South Rim. The Kaibab Rim Route shuttle bus travels a short section of Desert View Drive and takes 50 minutes to ride round-trip without getting off at any of the stops: Grand Canyon Visitor Center, South Kaibab Trailhead, Yaki Point, Pipe Creek Vista, Mather Point, and Yavapai Geology Museum. ⊠ *Grand Canyon National Park.*

Hermit Road

SCENIC DRIVE | The Santa Fe Company built Hermit Road, formerly known as West Rim Drive, in 1912 as a scenic tour route. Nine overlooks dot this 7-mile stretch, each worth a visit. The road is filled with hairpin turns, so make sure you adhere to posted speed limits. A 1.5-mile Greenway trail offers easy access to cyclists looking to enjoy the original 1912 Hermit Rim Road. From March through November, Hermit Road is closed to private auto traffic because of congestion; during this period, a free shuttle bus carries visitors to all the overlooks. Riding the bus round-trip without getting off at any of the viewpoints takes 80 minutes; the return trip stops only at Hermits Rest, Pima, Mohave, and Powell points. ⊠ *Grand Canyon National Park.*

SCENIC STOPS
The Abyss
VIEWPOINT | At an elevation of 6,720 feet, the Abyss is one of the most awesome stops on Hermit Road, revealing a sheer drop of 3,000 feet to the Tonto Platform, a wide terrace of Tapeats sandstone about two-thirds of the way down the canyon. From the Abyss you'll also see several isolated sandstone columns, the largest of which is called the Monument. ⊠ *Grand Canyon National Park ✛ About 5 miles west of Hermit Rd. Junction on Hermit Rd.*

Desert View and Watchtower
VIEWPOINT | From the top of the 70-foot stone-and-mortar watchtower with its 360-degree views, even the muted hues of the distant Painted Desert to the east and the Vermilion Cliffs rising from a high plateau near the Utah border are visible. In the chasm below, angling to the north toward Marble Canyon, an imposing stretch of the Colorado River reveals itself. Up several flights of stairs, the watchtower houses a glass-enclosed observatory with telescopes. ⊠ *Grand Canyon National Park ✛ Just north of East Entrance Station on Desert View Dr.* ☎ *928/638–7888* ⊕ *www.nps.gov/grca* ⌑ *Free.*

Grandview Point
VIEWPOINT | At an elevation of 7,399 feet, the view from here is one of the finest in the canyon. To the northeast is a group of dominant buttes, including Krishna Shrine, Vishnu Temple, Rama Shrine, and Sheba Temple. A short stretch of the Colorado River is also visible. Directly below the

point, and accessible by the steep and rugged Grandview Trail, is Horseshoe Mesa, where you can see remnants of Last Chance Copper Mine. ⊠ *Grand Canyon National Park ✛ About 12 miles east of Grand Canyon Village on Desert View Dr.*

Hermits Restare
VIEWPOINT | This westernmost viewpoint and Hermit Trail, which descends from it, were named for "hermit" Louis Boucher, a 19th-century French-Canadian prospector who had a number of mining claims and a roughly built home down in the canyon. The trail served as the original mule ride down to Hermit Camp beginning in 1914. Views from here include Hermit Rapids and the towering cliffs of the Supai and Redwall formations. You can buy curios and snacks in the stone building at Hermits Rest. ⊠ *Grand Canyon National Park ✛ About 8 miles west of Hermit Rd. Junction on Hermit Rd.*

★ Hopi Point
VIEWPOINT | From this elevation of 7,071 feet, you can see a large section of the Colorado River; although it appears as a thin line, the river is nearly 350 feet wide. The overlook extends farther into the canyon than any other point on Hermit Road. The incredible unobstructed views make this a popular place to watch the sunset.

Across the canyon to the north is Shiva Temple. In 1937 Harold Anthony of the American Museum of Natural History led an expedition to the rock formation in the belief that it supported life that had been cut off from the rest of the canyon. Imagine the expedition members' surprise when they found an empty Kodak film box on top of the temple—it had been left behind by Emery Kolb, who felt slighted for not having been invited to join Anthony's tour.

Directly below Hopi Point lies Dana Butte, named for a prominent 19th-century geologist. In 1919 an entrepreneur proposed connecting Hopi Point, Dana Butte, and the Tower of Set across the

Did You Know?

Grand Canyon National Park covers more than 1,900 square miles. That's bigger than the state of Rhode Island.

river with an aerial tramway, a technically feasible plan that fortunately has not been realized. ⊠ *Grand Canyon National Park* ✛ *About 4 miles west of Hermit Rd. Junction on Hermit Rd.*

Lipan Point

VIEWPOINT | Here, at the canyon's widest point, you can get an astonishing visual profile of the gorge's geologic history, with a view of every eroded layer of the canyon and one of the longest visible stretches of Colorado River. The spacious panorama stretches to the Vermilion Cliffs on the northeastern horizon and features a multitude of imaginatively named spires, buttes, and temples— intriguing rock formations named after their resemblance to ancient pyramids. You can also see Unkar Delta, where a creek joins the Colorado to form power-ful rapids and a broad beach. Ancestral Puebloan farmers worked the Unkar Del-ta for hundreds of years, growing corn, beans, and melons. ⊠ *Grand Canyon National Park* ✛ *About 25 miles east of Grand Canyon Village on Desert View Dr.*

★ Mather Point

VIEWPOINT | You'll likely get your first glimpse of the canyon from this view-point, one of the most impressive and accessible (next to the main visitor center plaza) on the South Rim. Named for the National Park Service's first director, Stephen Mather, this spot yields extraordinary views of the Grand Canyon, including deep into the inner gorge and numerous buttes: Wotans Throne, Brah-ma Temple, and Zoroaster Temple, among others. The Grand Canyon Lodge, on the North Rim, is almost directly north from Mather Point and only 10 miles away— yet you have to drive 215 miles to get from one spot to the other. ⊠ *Near Grand Canyon Visitor Center, Grand Canyon National Park* ☎ *928/638–7888* ⊕ *www. nps.gov/grca.*

Moran Point

VIEWPOINT | This point was named for American landscape artist Thomas Moran, who was especially fond of the play of light and shadows from this location. He first visited the canyon with John Wesley Powell in 1873. "Thomas Moran's name, more than any other, with the possible exception of Major Powell's, is to be associated with the Grand Can-yon," wrote noted canyon photographer Ellsworth Kolb. It's fitting that Moran Point is a favorite spot of photographers and painters. ⊠ *Grand Canyon National Park* ✛ *About 17 miles east of Grand Canyon Village on Desert View Dr.*

Trailview Overlook

VIEWPOINT | Look down on a dramatic view of the Bright Angel and Plateau Point trails as they zigzag down the canyon. In the deep gorge to the north flows Bright Angel Creek, one of the region's few permanent tributary streams of the Colorado River. Toward the south is an unobstructed view of the distant San Francisco Peaks, as well as Bill Williams Mountain (on the horizon) and Red Butte (about 15 miles south of the canyon rim). ⊠ *Grand Canyon National Park* ✛ *About 2 miles west of Hermit Rd. Junction on Hermit Rd.*

Yaki Point

VIEWPOINT | Stop here for an exceptional view of Wotans Throne, a flat-top butte named by François Matthes, a U.S. Geo-logical Survey scientist who developed the first topographical map of the Grand Canyon. The overlook juts out over the canyon, providing unobstructed views of inner-canyon rock formations, South Rim cliffs, and Clear Creek canyon. About a mile south of Yaki Point is the trailhead for the South Kaibab Trail. ■**TIP➔ The point is one of the best places on the South Rim to watch the sunrise and the sunset.** ⊠ *Grand Canyon National Park* ✛ *2 miles east of Grand Canyon Village on Desert View Dr.*

Mather Point is one of the most popular lookout points on the Grand Canyon's South Rim.

★ Yavapai Point

MUSEUM | Dominated by the Yavapai Geology Museum and Observation Station, this point displays panoramic views of the mighty gorge through a wall of windows. Exhibits at the museum include videos of the canyon floor and the Colorado River, a scaled diorama of the canyon with national park boundaries, fossils, and rock fragments used to re-create the complex layers of the canyon walls, and a display on the natural forces used to carve the chasm. Dig even deeper into Grand Canyon geology with free daily ranger programs. This point is also a good location to watch the sunset. ⊠ *Grand Canyon Village* ⊕ *1 mile east of Market Plaza.*

TRAILS

★ Bright Angel Trail

HIKING/WALKING | This well-maintained trail is one of the most scenic (and busiest) hiking paths from the South Rim to the bottom of the canyon (9.6 miles each way). Rest houses are equipped with water at the 1.5- and 3-mile points from May through September, and at Indian Garden (4 miles) year-round. Water is also available at Bright Angel Campground, 9¼ miles below the trailhead. Plateau Point, on a spur trail about 1.5 miles below Indian Garden, is as far as you should attempt to go on a day hike; the round-trip will take six to nine hours.

Bright Angel Trail is the easiest of all the footpaths into the canyon, but because the climb out from the bottom is an ascent of 5,510 feet, the trip should be attempted only by those in good physical condition and should be avoided in midsummer due to extreme heat. The top of the trail can be icy in winter. Originally a bighorn sheep path and later used by the Havasupai, the trail was widened late in the 19th century for prospectors and is now used for both mule and foot traffic. Also note that mule trains have the right-of-way—and sometimes leave unpleasant surprises in your path. *Moderate.* ⊠ *Grand Canyon National Park* ⊕ *Trailhead: Kolb Studio, Hermit Rd.*

Grandview Trail

HIKING/WALKING | Accessible from the parking area at Grandview Point, the trailhead is at 7,400 feet. The path heads steeply down into the canyon for 3 miles to the junction and campsite at East Horseshoe Mesa Trail. Classified as a wilderness trail, the route is aggressive and not as heavily traveled as some of the more well-known trails, such as Bright Angel and Hermit. There is no water available along the trail, which follows a steep descent to 4,800 feet at Horseshoe Mesa, where Hopi Indians once collected mineral paints. Hike 0.7 mile farther to Page Spring, a reliable water source year-round. Parts of this trail are icy in winter, and traction crampons are mandatory. *Difficult.* ⊠ *Grand Canyon National Park* ⊕ *Trailhead: Grandview Point, Desert View Dr.*

Hermit Trail

HIKING/WALKING | Beginning on the South Rim just west of Hermits Rest (and 7 miles west of Grand Canyon Village), this steep, unmaintained, 9.7-mile (one way) trail drops more than 5,000 feet to Hermit Creek, which usually flows year-round. It's a strenuous hike back up and is recommended for experienced long-distance hikers only; plan for six to nine hours. There's an abundance of lush growth and wildlife, including desert bighorn sheep, along this trail. The trail descends from the trailhead at 6,640 feet to the Colorado River at 2,300 feet. Day hikers should not go past Santa Maria Spring at 5,000 feet (a 5-mile round trip).

For much of the year, no water is available along the way; ask a park ranger about the availability of water at Santa Maria Spring and Hermit Creek before you set out. All water from these sources should be treated before drinking. The route leads down to the Colorado River and has inspiring views of Hermit Gorge and the Redwall and Supai formations. Six miles from the trailhead are the ruins of Hermit Camp, which the Santa Fe Railroad ran as a tourist camp from 1911 until 1930.

Difficult. ⊠ *Grand Canyon National Park* ⊕ *Trailhead: Hermits Rest, Hermits Rd.*

★ Rim Trail

HIKING/WALKING | The South Rim's most popular walking path is the 12-mile (one way) Rim Trail, which runs along the edge of the canyon from Pipe Creek Vista (the first overlook on Desert View Drive) to Hermits Rest. This walk, which is paved to Maricopa Point and for the last 1.5 miles to Hermits Rest, visits several of the South Rim's historic landmarks. Allow anywhere from 15 minutes to a full day, depending on how much of the trail you want to cover; the Rim Trail is an ideal day hike, as it varies only a few hundred feet in elevation from Mather Point (7,120 feet) to the trailhead at Hermits Rest (6,650 feet). The trail also can be accessed from several spots in Grand Canyon Village and from the major viewpoints along Hermit Road, which are serviced by shuttle buses during the busy summer months. On the Rim Trail, water is only available in the Grand Canyon Village area and at Hermits Rest. *Easy.* ⊠ *Grand Canyon National Park.*

South Kaibab Trail

HIKING/WALKING | This trail starts near Yaki Point, 4 miles east of Grand Canyon Village, and is accessible via the free shuttle bus.

Because the route is so steep (and sometimes icy in winter)—descending from the trailhead at 7,260 feet down to 2,480 feet at the Colorado River—and has no water, many hikers take this trail down, then ascend via the less-demanding Bright Angel Trail. Allow four to six hours to reach the Colorado River on this 6.4-mile trek. At the river, the trail crosses a suspension bridge and runs on to Phantom Ranch. Along the trail there is no water and little shade. There are no campgrounds, though there are portable toilets at Cedar Ridge (6,320 feet), 1.5 miles from the trailhead. An emergency phone is available at the Tipoff, 4.6 miles down the trail (3 miles past Cedar Ridge).

Grand Canyon History

The Grand Canyon's oldest layers date back to 1.8 billion years ago. The geological wonder is a prime example of arid-land erosion.

Indigenous groups inhabited the land much earlier than the first European explorers to "find" it in 1540. In fact, there's evidence of humans 12,000 years ago. Hualapai and Havasupai are among the tribes that still live in the area.

An explorer of the American West, John Wesley Powell, bestowed the name "Grand" to the canyon as he led his expedition down the Colorado River in 1869.

In 1903, train tracks were completed to Grand Canyon Village, enabling more visitors to see the Grand Canyon.

Teddy Roosevelt, a champion for protecting land with government funding, gave the Grand Canyon National Monument status in 1908.

The Grand Canyon became America's 17th National Park in 1919 under President Woodrow Wilson.

The trail corkscrews down through some spectacular geology. Look for (but don't remove) fossils in the limestone when taking water breaks. *Difficult.* ✉ *Grand Canyon National Park* ✣ *Trailhead: Yaki Point Rd., off Desert View Dr.*

VISITOR CENTERS

Desert View Information Center
Near the watchtower, at Desert View Point, this nonprofit Grand Canyon Association store and information center has a nice selection of books, park pamphlets, gifts, and educational materials. It's also a handy place to pick up maps and info if you enter the park at the Eastern entrance. All sales from the association stores go to support the park programs. ✉ *Eastern entrance, Grand Canyon National Park* ☎ *800/858–2808, 928/638–7888.*

Grand Canyon Verkamp's Visitor Center
This small visitor center is named for the Verkamp family, who operated a curios shop on the South Rim for more than a hundred years. The building serves as an official visitor center, ranger station (get your Junior Ranger badges here), bookstore, and museum, with compelling exhibits on the Verkamps and other pioneers in this region. ✉ *Desert View Dr., Grand Canyon Village* ✣ *Across from El Tovar Hotel* ☎ *928/638–7146.*

Grand Canyon Visitor Center
The park's main orientation center provides pamphlets and resources to help plan your visit. It also holds engaging interpretive exhibits on the park. Rangers are on hand to answer questions and aid in planning canyon excursions. A daily schedule of ranger-led hikes and evening lectures is available, and a 20-minute film about the history, geology, and wildlife of the canyon plays every 30 minutes in the theater. The bicycle rental office, a small café, and a huge gift store are also in this complex. It's a short walk from here to Mather Point, or a short ride on the shuttle bus, which can take you into Grand Canyon Village. The visitor center is also accessible from the village via a leisurely 1-mile walk on the Greenway Trail, a paved pathway that meanders through the forest. ✉ *East side of Grand Canyon Village, 450 Hwy. 64, Grand Canyon* ☎ *928/638–7888* ⊕ *www.explorethecanyon.com.*

Yavapai Geology Museum
Learn about the geology of the canyon at this Grand Canyon Association museum and bookstore. You can also catch the park shuttle bus or pick up information for the Rim Trail here. The views of the canyon and Phantom Ranch from inside this historic building are stupendous. ✉ *1 mile east of Market Plaza, Grand Canyon Village* ☎ *928/638–7888.*

🍴 Restaurants

Arizona Steakhouse
$$$ | **STEAKHOUSE** | The canyon views from this casual Southwestern-style steak house are the best of any restaurant at the South Rim. The dinner menu leans toward steak-house dishes while lunch is primarily salads and sandwiches with a Southwestern twist. **Known for:** views of the Grand Canyon; Southwest fare; local craft beers and wines. [$] *Average main: $28* ✉ *Bright Angel Lodge, Desert View Dr., Grand Canyon Village* ☎ *928/638–2631* 🌐 *www.grandcanyonlodges.com.*

★ El Tovar Dining Room
$$$ | **SOUTHWESTERN** | Even at the edge of the Grand Canyon it's possible to find gourmet dining. This cozy room of dark wood beams and stone, nestled in the historic El Tovar Lodge, dates to 1905. **Known for:** historic setting with canyon views; local and organic ingredients; fine dining that's worth the splurge. [$] *Average main: $28* ✉ *El Tovar Hotel, Desert View Dr., Grand Canyon Village* ☎ *928/638–2631* 🌐 *www.grandcanyonlodges.com.*

Fred Harvey Burger
$$ | **SOUTHWESTERN** | **FAMILY** | Open for breakfast, lunch, and dinner, this casual café at Bright Angel Lodge serves basics like pancakes, salads, sandwiches, pastas, burgers, and steaks. Or you can step it up a notch and order some of the same selections straight from the neighboring Arizona Steakhouse's menu, including prime rib, baby back ribs, and wild salmon. **Known for:** reasonably priced American fare; family-friendly menu and setting; some vegetarian and gluten-free options. [$] *Average main: $14* ✉ *Bright Angel Lodge, Desert View Dr., Grand Canyon Village* ☎ *928/638–2631* 🌐 *www.grandcanyonlodges.com.*

Maswik Food Court
$ | **AMERICAN** | **FAMILY** | You can get a burger, hot sandwich, pasta, or Mexican fare at this food court, as well as pizza by the slice and wine and beer in the adjacent Maswik Pizza Pub. This casual eatery is in Maswik Lodge, ¼ mile from the rim, and the Pizza Pub stays open until 11 pm (you can also order pizza to take out). **Known for:** good selection (something for everyone); later hours; pizza to go. [$] *Average main: $10* ✉ *Maswik Lodge, Desert View Dr., Grand Canyon Village* 🌐 *www.grandcanyonlodges.com.*

Yavapai Lodge Restaurant and Tavern
$$ | **AMERICAN** | If you don't have time for full-service, the restaurant in Yavapai Lodge offers cafeteria-style dining for breakfast, lunch, and dinner, including hot and cold sandwiches, pizza, barbecue ribs, and rotisserie chicken. Wine and beer, including craft brews from nearby Flagstaff, are also on the menu; or enjoy drinks on the patio at the adjacent Yavapai Tavern. **Known for:** quick bites or hearty meals; convenient dining in Market Plaza; patio with firepit at Yavapai Tavern. [$] *Average main: $19* ✉ *Yavapai Lodge, Desert View Dr., Grand Canyon Village* ☎ *928/638–4001* 🌐 *www.visitgrandcanyon.com.*

🛏 Hotels

Bright Angel Lodge
$ | **HOTEL** | Famed architect Mary Jane Colter designed this 1935 log-and-stone structure, which sits within a few yards of the canyon rim and blends superbly with the canyon walls; its location is similar to El Tovar's but for about half the price. **Pros:** good value for the amazing location; charming rooms and cabins steps from the rim; on-site Internet

Freebies at the Grand Canyon

While you're here, be sure to take advantage of the many complimentary services offered.

- The most useful is the system of free shuttle buses at the South Rim; it caters to the road-weary, with four routes winding through or just outside the park—Hermits Rest Route, Village Route, Kaibab Rim Route, and Tusayan Route. Of the bus routes, the Hermits Rest Route runs only March through November and the Tusayan Route only in summer; the other two run year-round, and the Kaibab Rim Route provides the only access to Yaki Point. Hikers coming or going from the South Kaibab Trailhead can catch the Hikers Express, which departs three times each morning from the Bright Angel Lodge, makes a quick stop at the Backcountry Information Center, and then heads out to the South Kaibab Trailhead.
- Ranger-led programs are always free and offered year-round, though more are scheduled during the busy spring and summer seasons. These programs might include activities such as stargazing and topics such as geology and the cultural history of prehistoric peoples. Some of the more in-depth programs may include a fossil walk or a condor talk. Check with the visitor center for seasonal programs including wildflower walks and fire ecology.
- Kids ages four and older can get involved with the park's Junior Ranger program, with ever-changing activities including hikes and hands-on experiments.
- Despite all of these options, rangers will tell you that the best free activity in the canyon is watching the magnificent splashes of color on the canyon walls during sunrise and sunset.

kiosks and transportation desk for the mule ride. **Cons:** popular lobby is always packed; parking is a bit of a hike; only some rooms have canyon views. [$] *Rooms from: $104* ✉ *Desert View Dr., Grand Canyon Village* ☎ *888/297–2757 reservations only, 928/638–2631* 🌐 *www.grandcanyonlodges.com* 🛏 *105 units* 🍴 *No meals.*

★ El Tovar Hotel

$$$$ | **HOTEL** | The hotel's proximity to all of the canyon's facilities, European hunting-lodge atmosphere, attractively updated rooms and tile baths, and renowned dining room make it the best place to stay on the South Rim. A registered National Historic Landmark, the "architectural crown jewel of the Grand Canyon" was built in 1905 of Oregon pine logs and native stone. **Pros:** historic lodging just steps from the South Rim; fabulous lounge with outdoor seating and canyon views; best in-park dining on-site. **Cons:** books up quickly; priciest lodging in the park; rooms are comfortable, not luxurious. [$] *Rooms from: $275* ✉ *Desert View Dr., Grand Canyon Village* ☎ *888/297–2757 reservations only, 928/638–2631* 🌐 *www.grandcanyonlodges.com* 🛏 *78 rooms* 🍴 *No meals.*

Kachina Lodge

$$$ | **HOTEL** | The well-appointed rooms at this motel-style lodge in Grand Canyon Village on the South Rim are a good bet for families and are within easy walking distance of dining facilities at nearby lodges. **Pros:** partial canyon views in half the rooms; family-friendly; steps from the best restaurants in the park. **Cons:** check-in at nearby El Tovar Hotel; limited parking; no air conditioning. [$] *Rooms from: $232* ✉ *Desert View Dr., Grand*

Canyon Village ☎ 888/297–2757 reservations only, 928/638–2631 🌐 www.grandcanyonlodges.com 🛏 49 rooms 🍴 No meals.

Maswik Lodge

$$ | **HOTEL** | **FAMILY** | Far from the noisy crowds, Maswik accommodations are in two-story, contemporary motel-style buildings nestled in a shady ponderosa pine forest. **Pros:** units are modern, spacious, and well equipped; good for families; affordable dining options. **Cons:** rooms lack historic charm; tucked away from the rim in the forest; no elevators for second-floor rooms. [$] *Rooms from: $159 ✉ Grand Canyon Village ☎ 888/297–2757 reservations only, 928/638–2631 🌐 www.grandcanyonlodges.com 🛏 278 rooms 🍴 No meals.*

Phantom Ranch

$ | **B&B/INN** | In a grove of cottonwood trees on the canyon floor, Phantom Ranch is accessible only to hikers, river rafters, and mule trekkers; there are 40 dormitory bunk beds and 14 beds in cabins, all with shared baths (though cabins have toilets and sinks). **Pros:** only inner-canyon lodging option; fabulous canyon views; remote access limits crowds. **Cons:** reservations are booked up to a year in advance; few amenities; shared bathrooms. [$] *Rooms from: $65 ✉ On canyon floor, Grand Canyon National Park ✣ At intersection of Bright Angel and Kaibab trails ☎ 303/297–2757, 888/297–2757 🌐 www.grandcanyonlodges.com 🛏 54 beds 🍴 No meals.*

Thunderbird Lodge

$$$$ | **HOTEL** | This motel with comfortable, simple rooms and partial canyon views has all the modern amenities you'd expect at a typical mid-price chain hotel—even pod coffeemakers. **Pros:** canyon views in some rooms; family-friendly; convenient to dining and activities in Grand Canyon Village. **Cons:** check-in at nearby Bright Angel Lodge; limited parking nearby; no air conditioning (but some rooms have effective evaporative coolers). [$] *Rooms from: $264 ✉ Desert View Dr., Grand Canyon Village ☎ 888/297–2757 reservations only, 928/638–2631 🌐 www.grandcanyonlodges.com 🛏 55 rooms 🍴 No meals.*

Yavapai Lodge

$$ | **HOTEL** | The largest motel-style lodge in the park is tucked in a pinyon-pine and juniper forest at the eastern end of Grand Canyon Village, across from Market Plaza. **Pros:** transportation-activities desk in the lobby; walk to Market Plaza in Grand Canyon Village; only pet-friendly lodging at South Rim. **Cons:** farthest lodging in park from the rim (1 mile); generic appearance. [$] *Rooms from: $154 ✉ 10 Yavapai Lodge Rd., Grand Canyon Village ☎ 877/404–4611 reservations only 🌐 www.visitgrandcanyon.com 🛏 358 rooms 🍴 No meals.*

Activities

BIKING

The South Rim's limited opportunities for off-road biking, narrow shoulders on park roads, and heavy traffic in summer may disappoint hard-core cyclists; for others, cycling is a fun and eco-friendly way to tour the park. Bicycles are permitted on all park roads and on the multiuse Greenway Trail System; visitors to the North Rim have Bridle Path and a 12-mile section of the Arizona Trail (⇨ *see Grand Canyon North Rim*). Bikes are prohibited on the paved portions of the Rim Trail between Mather Point and Bright Angel Trailhead. Some find Hermit Road a good biking option, especially from March through November when it's closed to cars. You can ride west 8 miles and then put your bike on the free shuttle bus back into the village (or vice versa). A shorter ride takes you east to Yaki Point (3.5 miles), a great place to stop and have a picnic. Bicyclists visiting the South Rim may also enjoy meandering through the ponderosa pine forest on the Greenway Trails or the Tusayan Bike Trail, a gentle uphill climb from Tusayan into the park.

Rentals and guided bicycling tours are available mid-March through October at the South Rim from Bright Angel Bicycles (☎ *928/638–3055* ⊕ *bikegrandcanyon.com*) at the visitor center complex. Bicycle camping sites ($6 per person per night) are available at Mather Campground.

BOATING AND RAFTING

The National Park Service restricts the number of visitors allowed on the Colorado River each season, and seats fill up fast. Due to the limited availability, reservations for multiday trips should be made a year or two in advance. Lots of people book trips for summer's peak period: June through August. If you're flexible, take advantage of the Arizona weather; May to early June and September are ideal rafting times in the Grand Canyon.

Most trips begin at Lees Ferry, a few miles below the Glen Canyon Dam near Page. There are tranquil half- and full-day float trips from the Glen Canyon Dam to Lees Ferry, as well as raft trips that run from 3 to 18 days. For outfitters, see the boating and rafting listings under Lees Ferry in ⇨ *Nearby Towns* of this chapter. The shorter three- and four-day voyages either begin or end at Phantom Ranch at the bottom of the Grand Canyon at river mile 87. On the longer trips, you'll encounter the best of the canyon's white water along the way, including Lava Falls, listed in the *Guinness Book of World Records* as "the fastest navigable white water stretch in North America." Life jackets, beverages, tents, sheets, tarps, sleeping bags, dry bags, first aid, and food are provided—but you'll still need to plan ahead by packing clothing, a rain suit, hats, sunscreen, toiletries, and other sundries. Commercial outfitters allow each river runner two waterproof bags to store items during the day. Just keep in mind that one of the bags will be filled up with the provided sleeping bag and tarp, which only leaves one for your personal belongings.

Arranging Tours ◉

Transportation-services desks are maintained at Bright Angel, Maswik Lodge, and Yavapai Lodge (closed in winter) in Grand Canyon Village. The desks provide information and handle bookings for sightseeing tours, taxi and bus services, and mule rides (but don't count on last-minute availability). There's also a concierge at El Tovar that can arrange most tours, with the exception of mule rides. On the North Rim, Grand Canyon Lodge has general information about local services.

CAMPING

Within the national park, there are two developed campgrounds on the South Rim and one on the North Rim. All campgrounds charge nightly camping fees in addition to the general park entrance fee; some accept reservations up to six months in advance (☎ *877/444–6777* ⊕ *www.recreation.gov*) and others are first-come first-served.

Camping anywhere outside a developed rim campground, including in the canyon, requires a permit from the Backcountry Information Center, which also serves as your reservation. Permits can be requested by mail or fax only; applying well in advance is recommended. Call ☎ *928/638–7875* between 1 pm and 5 pm weekdays for information.

Bright Angel Campground. This backcountry campground is near Phantom Ranch at the bottom of the canyon. There are toilet facilities and running water, but no showers.✉ *Intersection of South and North Kaibab trails, South Rim* ☎ *928/638–7875.*

Desert View Campground. Popular for spectacular views of the canyon from the nearby watchtower, this developed campground near the east entrance doesn't take reservations; show up before noon, as it fills up fast in summer. Open mid-May through mid-October, these sites have no hookups. ⊠ *Desert View Dr., 23 miles east of Grand Canyon Village off Hwy. 64, South Rim.*

Mather Campground. The largest developed campground in the park is set in a forested area near Grand Canyon Village. Open all year, Mather takes reservations from March to November and has water and toilet facilities, as well as showers and laundry (for an extra fee). There is a cofee bar/deli on-site, and the park shuttle stops here. ⊠ *Grand Canyon Village, South Rim* 📞 *877/444–6777* ⊕ *www. recreation.gov*

CROSS-COUNTRY SKIING
Tusayan Ranger District
SKIING/SNOWBOARDING | Although you can't schuss down into the Grand Canyon, you can cross-country ski in the woods near the rim when there's enough snow, usually mid-December through early March. The ungroomed trails, suitable for beginner and intermediate skiers, begin at the Grandview Lookout and travel through the Kaibab National Forest. For details, contact the Tusayan Ranger District. ⊠ *176 Lincoln Log Loop, Grand Canyon* 📞 *928/638–2443* ⊕ *www. fs.usda.gov/kaibab.*

HIKING
Although permits are not required for day hikes, you must have a backcountry permit for longer trips (⇨ *see Park Fees and Permits*). Some of the more popular trails are listed under ⇨ *Sights*, including **Bright Angel Trail, Rim Trail,** and **South Kaibab Trail;** more detailed information and maps can be obtained from the Backcountry Information centers. Also, rangers can help design a trip to suit your abilities.

Remember that the canyon has significant elevation changes and, in summer, extreme temperature ranges, which can pose problems for people who aren't in good shape or who have heart or respiratory problems. ■ **TIP→ Carry plenty of water and energy foods.** Listen to the podcast *Hiking Smart* on the Park's website to prepare for your trip. The majority of each year's 400 search-and-rescue incidents result from hikers underestimating the size of the canyon, hiking beyond their abilities, or not packing sufficient food and water.

■ **TIP→ Under no circumstances should you attempt a day hike from the rim to the river and back.** Remember that when it's 85°F on the South Rim, it's 110°F on the canyon floor. Allow two to four days if you want to hike rim to rim (it's easier to descend from the North Rim, as it's more than 1,000 feet higher than the South Rim). Hiking steep trails from rim to rim is a strenuous trek of at least 21 miles and should only be attempted by experienced canyon hikers.

HORSEBACK RIDING
Mule rides provide an intimate glimpse into the canyon for those who have the time, but not the stamina, to see the canyon on foot. ■ **TIP→ Reservations are essential and are accepted up to 13 months in advance.**

These trips have been conducted since the early 1900s. A comforting fact as you ride the narrow trail: no one's ever been killed while riding a mule that fell off a cliff. (Nevertheless, the treks are not for the faint of heart or people in questionable health.)

★ **Xanterra Parks & Resorts Mule Rides**
TOUR—SPORTS | These trips delve either into the canyon from the South Rim to Phantom Ranch, or east along the canyon's rim. Riders must be at least 9 years old and 57 inches tall, weigh less than 200 pounds for the Phantom Ranch ride or less than 225 pounds for the rim ride,

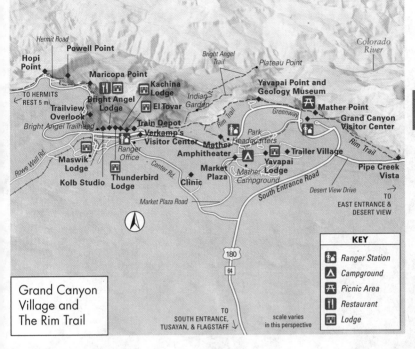

Grand Canyon Village and The Rim Trail

KEY

🧍 Ranger Station
△ Campground
🎪 Picnic Area
🍴 Restaurant
🏨 Lodge

scale varies
in this perspective

TO
SOUTH ENTRANCE,
TUSAYAN, & FLAGSTAFF

TO
EAST ENTRANCE &
DESERT VIEW

and understand English. Children under 18 must be accompanied by an adult. Riders must be in fairly good physical condition, and pregnant women are advised not to take these trips.

The two-hour ride along the rim costs $153. An overnight mule ride with a stay in a cabin at Phantom Ranch at the bottom of the canyon, with meals included, is $693 ($1,205 for two riders). Package prices vary since a cabin at Phantom Ranch can accommodate up to four people. From November through February, you can stay for up to two nights at Phantom Ranch. Reservations are a must, but you can check at the Bright Angel Transportation Desk to see if there's last-minute availability. ☎ 888/297–2757, 303/297–2757 ⊕ www.grandcanyonlodges.com ⚠ Reservations essential.

JEEP TOURS

Jeep rides can be rough; if you have had back injuries, check with your doctor before taking a 4X4 tour. It's a good idea to book a week or two ahead, and even longer if you're visiting in summer or on busy weekends.

Buck Wild Hummer Tours

DRIVING TOURS | With this tour company, you can see majestic rim views in Grand Canyon National Park and learn about the history, geology, and wildlife of the canyon from the comfort of a 13-passenger Hummer. Daily tours run either in the morning or at sunset. ✉ 469 AZ 64, Grand Canyon ☎ 928/362–5940 ⊕ buckwildhummertours.com 💲 From $99.

Grand Canyon Custom Tours

TOUR—SPORTS | This tour company offers a full-day off-road adventure to the bottom of the Grand Canyon West (rather than Grand Canyon National Park) year-round in comfortable cruisers (small luxury vans with heating and air-conditioning) rather than jeeps. Tours leave from either Flagstaff or Williams. ⊠ *Williams* ☎ *928/779–3163* ⊕ *grandcanyoncustomtours.com* 🖃 *From $269.*

Grand Canyon Jeep Tours & Safaris

TOUR—SPORTS | If you'd like to get off the pavement and see parts of the park that are accessible only by dirt road, a jeep tour can be just the ticket. From March through November, this tour operator leads daily three-hour off-road tours within the park, as well as jeep tours to a petroglyph site in Kaibab National Forest. Sunset tours to the canyon rim and combo tours adding helicopter or plane flights are also available. ⊠ *Grand Canyon National Park* ☎ *928/638–5337* ⊕ *grand-canyonjeeptours.com* 🖃 *From $79.*

SCENIC FLIGHTS

Flights by plane and helicopter over the canyon are offered by a number of companies, departing from the Grand Canyon Airport at the south end of Tusayan. Though the noise and disruption of so many aircraft buzzing around the canyon is controversial, flightseeing remains a popular, if expensive, option. You'll have more visibility from a helicopter, but they're louder and more expensive than the fixed-wing planes. Prices and lengths of tours vary, but you can expect to pay about $159 per adult for short plane trips and approximately $300 for helicopter tours (and about $550 for combination plane and helicopter tours leaving from Vegas). These companies often have significant discounts in winter—check the company websites to find the best deals.

Grand Canyon Airlines

FLYING/SKYDIVING/SOARING | This company offers a variety of plane tours, from a 45-minute fixed-wing tour of the eastern edge of the Grand Canyon, the North Rim, and the Kaibab Plateau to an all-day tour that combines "flightseeing" with four-wheel-drive tours of Antelope Canyon and float trips on the Colorado River. They also schedule combination tours that leave from Las Vegas (plane flight from Las Vegas to Grand Canyon Airport, then helicopter flight into the canyon). ⊠ *Grand Canyon Airport, Tusayan* ☎ *702/835–8484, 866/235–9422* ⊕ *www.grandcanyonairlines.com* 🖃 *From $159.*

Maverick Helicopters

FLYING/SKYDIVING/SOARING | This company offers 45-minute tours of the South Rim, North Rim, and Dragon Corridor of the Grand Canyon, as well as tours to the canyon out of Las Vegas. A landing tour option for those flying from Las Vegas to the West Rim sets you down in the canyon for champagne and a snack below the rim. ⊠ *Grand Canyon Airport, Grand Canyon* ☎ *928/638–2622* ⊕ *www.maverickhelicopter.com* 🖃 *From $299.*

⊖ Shopping

Nearly every lodging facility and retail store at the South Rim stocks arts and crafts made by Native American artists and Grand Canyon books and souvenirs. Prices are comparable to other souvenir outlets, though you may find some better deals in Williams. Nevertheless, a portion of the proceeds from items purchased at Kolb Studio, Tusayan Museum, and all the park visitor centers go to the nonprofit Grand Canyon Association.

Desert View Trading Post

GIFTS/SOUVENIRS | A mix of traditional Southwestern souvenirs and authentic Native American arts and crafts are for sale here. ⊠ *Desert View Dr., Grand Canyon National Park* ✛ *Near watchtower at Desert View* ☎ *928/638–3150.*

Hopi House

CRAFTS | This two-level shop near El Tovar and Verkamp's Visitor Center has the widest selection of Native American art and handicrafts in the vicinity. ⊠ *4 El Tovar Rd., Grand Canyon Village* ✛ *Across from El Tovar Hotel* ☎ *928/638–2631* ⊕ *www. grandcanyonlodges.com.*

Grand Canyon North Rim

The North Rim stands 1,000 feet higher than the South Rim and has a more alpine climate, with twice as much annual precipitation. Here, in the deep forests of the Kaibab Plateau, the crowds are thinner, the facilities fewer, and the views even more spectacular. Due to snow, the North Rim is off-limits in winter. The buildings and concessions are closed mid-October through mid-May. The road and entrance gate close when the snow makes them impassable—usually by the end of November.

Lodgings are limited in this more remote park, with only one historic lodge (with cabins and hotel-type rooms as well as a restaurant) and a single campground. Dining options have opened up a little with a deli and a coffeehouse/saloon next door to the lodge. Your best bet may be to pack your camping gear and hiking boots and take several days to explore the lush Kaibab Forest. The canyon's highest, most dramatic rim views can also be enjoyed on two wheels (via primitive dirt access roads) and on four legs (courtesy of a trusty mule).

◉ Sights

PICNIC AREAS

Cape Royal, 23 miles south of the North Rim Visitor Center, at the end of Cape Royal Road, is the most popular designated picnic area on the North Rim due to its panoramic views. **Point Imperial**, 11 miles northeast of the North Rim Visitor Center, has shade and some privacy.

SCENIC DRIVE

⭐ **Highway 67**

SCENIC DRIVE | Open mid-May to roughly mid-November (or the first big snowfall), this two-lane paved road climbs 1,400 feet in elevation as it passes through the Kaibab National Forest. Also called the North Rim Parkway, this scenic route crosses the limestone-capped Kaibab Plateau—passing broad meadows, sun-dappled forests, and small lakes and springs—before abruptly falling away at the abyss of the Grand Canyon. Wildlife abounds in the thick ponderosa pine forests and lush mountain meadows. It's common to see deer, turkeys, and coyotes as you drive through such a remote region. Point Imperial and Cape Royal branch off this scenic drive, which runs from Jacob Lake to Bright Angel Point. ⊠ *Hwy. 67, Grand Canyon National Park.*

HISTORIC SIGHTS

Grand Canyon Lodge

HISTORIC SITE | Built in 1937 by the Union Pacific Railroad (replacing the original 1928 building, which burned in a fire), this massive stone structure is listed on the National Register of Historic Places. Its huge sunroom has hardwood floors, high-beamed ceilings, and a marvelous view of the canyon through plate-glass windows. On warm days, visitors sit in the sun and drink in the surrounding beauty on an outdoor viewing deck, where National Park Service employees deliver free lectures on geology and history. The dining room serves breakfast, lunch, and dinner; the Roughrider Saloon is a bar by night and a coffee shop in the morning. ⊠ *Grand Canyon National Park* ✛ *Off Hwy. 67 near Bright Angel Point* ☎ *928/638–2611 May.– Oct.* ⊕ *www.grandcanyonforever.com* ⊘ *Closed Nov.–mid-May.*

SCENIC STOPS

⭐ **Bright Angel Point**

TRAIL | This trail, which leads to one of the most awe-inspiring overlooks on either rim, starts on the grounds of the Grand Canyon Lodge and runs along the crest of a point of rocks that juts into the canyon for several hundred yards. The walk is only 0.5 mile round-trip, but it's an exciting trek accented by sheer drops on each side of the trail. In a few spots where the route is extremely narrow, metal railings ensure visitors' safety. The temptation to clamber out on precarious perches to have your picture taken should be resisted at all costs. ⊠ *North Rim Dr., Grand Canyon National Park* ✛ *Near Grand Canyon Lodge.*

Cape Royal

TRAIL | A popular sunset destination, Cape Royal showcases the canyon's jagged landscape; you'll also get a glimpse of the Colorado River, framed by a natural stone arch called Angels Window. In autumn, the aspens turn a beautiful gold, adding even more color to an already magnificent scene of the forested surroundings. The easy and rewarding 1-mile round-trip hike along **Cliff Springs Trail** starts here; it takes you through a forested ravine and terminates at Cliff Springs, where the forest opens to another impressive view of the canyon walls. ⊠ *Cape Royal Scenic Dr., Grand Canyon National Park* ✛ *23 miles southeast of Grand Canyon Lodge.*

Point Imperial

VIEWPOINT | At 8,803 feet, Point Imperial has the highest vista point at either rim; it offers magnificent views of both the canyon and the distant country: the Vermilion Cliffs to the north, the 10,000-foot Navajo Mountain to the northeast in Utah, the Painted Desert to the east, and the Little Colorado River canyon to the southeast. Other prominent points of interest include views of Mount Hayden, Saddle Mountain, and Marble Canyon. ⊠ *Point Imperial Rd., Grand Canyon National Park* ✛ *11 miles northeast of Grand Canyon Lodge.*

★ Point Sublime

VIEWPOINT | You can camp within feet of the canyon's edge at this awe-inspiring site. Sunrises and sunsets are spectacular. The winding road, through gorgeous high country, is only 17 miles, but it will take you at least two hours one-way. The road is intended only for vehicles with high road clearance (pickups and four-wheel-drive vehicles). It is also necessary to be properly equipped for wilderness road travel. Check with a park ranger or at the information desk at Grand Canyon Lodge before taking this journey. You may camp here only with a permit from the Backcountry Information Center. ⊠ *North Rim Dr., Grand Canyon National Park* ✛ *About 20 miles west of North Rim Visitor Center.*

Roosevelt Point

VIEWPOINT | Named after the president who gave the Grand Canyon its national monument status in 1908 (it was upgraded to national park status in 1919), Roosevelt Point is the best place to see the confluence of the Little Colorado River and the Grand Canyon. The cliffs above the Colorado River south of the junction are known as the Palisades of the Desert. A short woodland loop trail leads to this eastern viewpoint. ⊠ *Cape Royal Rd., Grand Canyon National Park* ✛ *18 miles east of Grand Canyon Lodge.*

Vista Encantada

VIEWPOINT | This point on the Walhalla Plateau offers views of the upper drainage of Nankoweap Creek, a rock pinnacle known as Brady Peak, and the Painted Desert to the east. This is an enchanting place for a picnic lunch. ⊠ *Cape Royal Rd., Grand Canyon National Park* ✛ *16 miles southeast of Grand Canyon Lodge.*

Walhalla Overlook

VIEWPOINT | One of the lowest elevations on the North Rim, this overlook has views of the Unkar Delta, a fertile region used by Ancestral Puebloans as farmland. These ancient people also gathered food and hunted game on

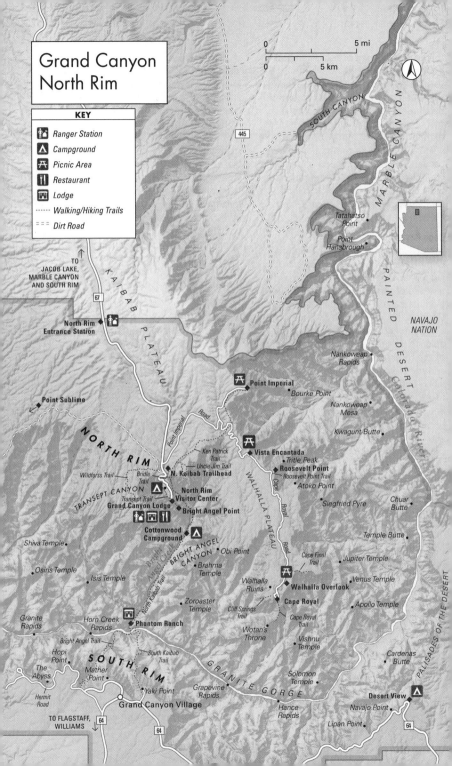

the North Rim. A flat path leads to the remains of the Walhalla Glades Pueblo, which was inhabited from 1050 to 1150. ⊠ *Cape Royal Rd., Grand Canyon National Park* ⊹ *22½ miles southeast of Grand Canyon Lodge.*

TRAILS

Cape Final Trail

HIKING/WALKING | This 4-mile (round-trip) gravel path follows an old jeep trail through a ponderosa pine forest to the canyon overlook at Cape Final with panoramic views of the northern canyon, the Palisades of the Desert, and the impressive spectacle of Juno Temple. *Easy.* ⊠ *Grand Canyon National Park* ⊹ *Trailhead: dirt parking lot 5 miles south of Roosevelt Point on Cape Royal Rd.*

Cape Royal Trail

HIKING/WALKING | **FAMILY** | Informative signs about vegetation, wildlife, and natural history add to this popular 0.6-mile, round-trip, paved path to Cape Royal; allow 30 minutes round-trip. At an elevation of 7,685 feet on the southern edge of the Walhalla Plateau, this popular viewpoint offers expansive views of Wotans Throne, Vishnu Temple, Freya Castle, Horseshoe Mesa, and the Colorado River. The trail also offers several nice views of Angels Window. *Easy.* ⊠ *Grand Canyon National Park* ⊹ *Trailhead: end of Cape Royal Rd.*

Cliff Springs Trail

HIKING/WALKING | An easy 1-mile (round-trip), one-hour walk near Cape Royal, Cliff Springs Trail leads through a forested ravine to an excellent view of the canyon. The trailhead begins at the Cape Royal parking lot, across from Angels Window Overlook. Narrow and precarious in spots, it passes ancient dwellings, winds beneath a limestone overhang, and ends at Cliff Springs. *Easy.* ⊠ *Grand Canyon National Park* ⊹ *Trailhead: end of Cape Royal Rd.*

Ken Patrick Trail

HIKING/WALKING | This primitive trail, one of the longest on the North Rim, travels 10 miles one-way (allow six hours each way) from the trailhead at 8,250 feet to Point Imperial at 8,803 feet. It crosses drainages and occasionally detours around fallen trees. The end of the road, at Point Imperial, brings the highest views from either rim. Note that there is no water along this trail. *Difficult.* ⊠ *Grand Canyon National Park* ⊹ *Trailhead: east side of North Kaibab trailhead parking lot.*

North Kaibab Trail

HIKING/WALKING | At 8,241 feet, this trail leads into the canyon and down to Phantom Ranch. It is recommended for experienced hikers only, who should allow four days for the round-trip hike. The long, steep path drops 5,840 feet over a distance of 14.5 miles to Phantom Ranch and the Colorado River, so the National Park Service suggests that day hikers not go farther than Roaring Springs (5,020 feet) before turning to hike back up out of the canyon. After about 7 miles, Cottonwood Campground (4,080 feet) has drinking water in summer, restrooms, shade trees, and a ranger. *Difficult.* ■TIP➔ **A free shuttle takes hikers to the North Kaibab trailhead twice daily from Grand Canyon Lodge; reserve a spot the day before.** ⊠ *Grand Canyon National Park* ⊹ *Trailhead: about 2 miles north of Grand Canyon Lodge.*

Roosevelt Point Trail

HIKING/WALKING | **FAMILY** | This easy 0.2-mile round-trip trail loops through the forest to the scenic viewpoint. Allow 20 minutes for this relaxed, secluded hike. *Easy.* ⊠ *Grand Canyon National Park* ⊹ *Trailhead: Cape Royal Rd.*

Transept Trail

HIKING/WALKING | **FAMILY** | This 3-mile-round-trip, 1½-hour trail begins near the Grand Canyon Lodge at 8,255 feet. Well-maintained and well-marked, it has little elevation change, sticking near the rim before reaching a dramatic view of a large stream through Bright

Perched on the North Rim's edge—1,000 feet higher than the South Rim—is the Grand Canyon Lodge.

Angel Canyon. The trail leads to Transept Canyon, which geologist Clarence Dutton named in 1882, declaring it "far grander than Yosemite." Check the posted schedule to find a ranger talk along this trail; it's also a great place to view fall foliage. Flash floods can occur any time of the year, especially June through September when thunderstorms develop rapidly. *Easy.* ☒ *Grand Canyon National Park* ✣ *Trailhead: near Grand Canyon Lodge east patio.*

Uncle Jim Trail

HIKING/WALKING | This 5-mile, three-hour loop starts at 8,300 feet and winds south through the forest, past Roaring Springs and Bright Angel canyons. The highlight of this rim hike is Uncle Jim Point, which, at 8,244 feet, overlooks the upper sections of the North Kaibab Trail. *Moderate.* ☒ *Grand Canyon National Park* ✣ *Trailhead: North Kaibab Trail parking lot.*

Widforss Trail

HIKING/WALKING | Round-trip, Widforss Trail is 9.8 miles, with an elevation change of only 200 feet. Allow five to six hours for the hike, which starts at 8,080 feet and passes through shady forests of pine, spruce, fir, and aspen on its way to Widforss Point, at 7,900 feet. Here you'll have good views of five temples: Zoroaster, Brahma, and Deva to the southeast, and Buddha and Manu to the southwest. You are likely to see wildflowers in summer, and this is a good trail for viewing fall foliage. It's named in honor of artist Gunnar M. Widforss, renowned for his paintings of national park landscapes. *Moderate.* ☒ *Grand Canyon National Park* ✣ *Trailhead: off dirt road about 2 miles north of Grand Canyon Lodge.*

VISITOR CENTER

North Rim Visitor Center

View exhibits, peruse the bookstore, and pick up useful maps and brochures at this visitor center. Interpretive programs are often scheduled in summer. If you're

Flora and Fauna of the Grand Canyon

Eighty-nine mammal species inhabit Grand Canyon National Park, as well as 355 species of birds, 56 kinds of reptiles and amphibians, and 17 kinds of fish. The rare Kaibab squirrel is found only on the North Rim—you can recognize them by their all-white tails and black undersides. The pink Grand Canyon rattlesnake lives at lower elevations within the canyon. Hawks and ravens are visible year-round. The endangered California condor has been reintroduced to the canyon region. Park rangers give daily talks on the magnificent birds, whose wingspan measures 9 feet. In spring, summer, and fall, mule deer, recognizable by their large ears, and elk are abundant at the South Rim. Don't be fooled by gentle appearances; these guys can be aggressive. It's illegal to feed them, as it'll disrupt their natural habitats and increase your risk of getting bitten or kicked.

The best times to see wildlife are early in the morning and late in the afternoon. Look for out-of-place shapes and motions, keeping in mind that animals occupy all layers in a natural habitat and not just at your eye level. Use binoculars for close-up views. While out and about try to fade into the woodwork by keeping your movements limited and noise at a minimum.

More than 1,700 species of plants color the park. The South Rim's Coconino Plateau is fairly flat, at an elevation of about 7,000 feet, and covered with stands of piñon and ponderosa pines, junipers, and Gambel's oak trees. On the Kaibab Plateau on the North Rim, Douglas fir, spruce, quaking aspen, and more ponderosas prevail. In spring you're likely to see asters, sunflowers, and lupine in bloom at both rims.

craving refreshments, it's a short walk from here to the Roughrider Saloon at the Grand Canyon Lodge. ✉ *Near Grand Canyon Lodge at North Rim, Grand Canyon National Park* ☎ *928/638–7864* 🌐 *www.nps.gov/grca.*

🍴 Restaurants

Deli in the Pines
$ | AMERICAN | Dining choices are limited on the North Rim, but this deli next to the lodge is your best bet for a meal on a budget or grabbing a premade sandwich on the go. Selections also include pizza (gluten-free or standard crust), salads, custom-made sandwiches, and soft-serve ice cream. **Known for:** convenient quick bite; sandwiches to take on the trail; outdoor seating. [$] *Average main: $9* ✉ *Grand Canyon Lodge, Bright Angel Point, North Rim* ☎ *928/638–2611* 🌐 *www.grandcanyonforever.com* 🕒 *Closed mid-Oct.–mid-May.*

★ Grand Canyon Lodge Dining Room
$$$ | SOUTHWESTERN | The high wood-beamed ceilings, stone walls, and spectacular views in this spacious, historic room are perhaps the biggest draw for the lodge's main restaurant. Dinner includes Southwestern steakhouse fare that would make any cowboy feel at home, including selections such as bison and elk. **Known for:** incredible views; charming, historic room; steaks, fish, game, and vegetarian selections. [$] *Average main: $25* ✉ *Grand Canyon Lodge, Bright Angel Point, North Rim* ☎ *928/638–2611* 🌐 *www.grandcanyonforever.com* 🕒 *Closed mid-Oct.–mid-May.*

Hotels

★ Grand Canyon Lodge

$$ | **HOTEL** | This historic property, constructed mainly in the 1920s and '30s, is the only lodging on the North Rim. The main building has locally quarried limestone walls and timbered ceilings. **Pros:** steps away from gorgeous North Rim views; close to several easy hiking trails; historic lodge building a national landmark. **Cons:** fills up fast; limited amenities; most cabins far from main lodge building. [$] *Rooms from: $146* ✉ *Hwy. 67, North Rim* ☎ *877/386–4383 reservations, 928/638–2611 May–Oct.* 🌐 *www.grandcanyonforever.com* 🕒 *Closed mid-Oct.–mid-May* 🛏 *218 rooms* 🍴 *No meals.*

Activities

BIKING

Mountain bikers can test the many dirt access roads found in this remote area. The 17-mile trek to Point Sublime is, well, sublime; though you'll share this road with high-clearance vehicles, it's rare to spot other people on most of these primitive pathways.

Bicycles and leashed pets are allowed on the well-maintained 1.2-mile (one way) **Bridle Trail,** which follows the road from Grand Canyon Lodge to the North Kaibab Trailhead. A 12-mile section of the **Arizona Trail** is also open to bicycles; it passes through pine forests within the park and continues north into Kaibab National Forest. Bikes are prohibited on all other national park trails.

CAMPING

North Rim Campground. The only designated campground at the North Rim of Grand Canyon National Park sits in a pine forest 3 miles north of the rim, and has 84 RV and tent sites (no hookups). Reserve in advance. ✉ *Hwy. 67, North Rim* ☎ *877/444–6777* 🌐 *www.recreation.gov.*

Duffel Service: Lighten Your Load

Hikers staying at either Phantom Ranch or Bright Angel Campground can take advantage of the ranch's duffel service: bags or packs weighing 30 pounds or less can be transported to or from the ranch by mule for a fee of $81 each way. As is true for many desirable things at the canyon, reservations are a must. ☎ *303/297–2757* 🌐 *www.grandcanyonlodges.com.*

EDUCATIONAL PROGRAMS

Interpretive Ranger Programs

TOUR—SIGHT | Daily guided hikes and talks may focus on any aspect of the canyon—from geology and flora and fauna to history and the canyon's early inhabitants. Schedules are available online. ☎ *928/638–7967* 🌐 *www.nps.gov/grca* 🎟 *Free.*

Junior Ranger Program

TOUR—SIGHT | **FAMILY** | In summer, children ages four and up can take part in hands-on educational programs and earn a Junior Ranger certificate and badge. Sign up at the North Rim Visitor Center for these independent and ranger-led activities. ☎ *928/638–7967* 🌐 *www.nps.gov/grca* 🎟 *Free.*

HORSEBACK RIDING

Canyon Trail Rides

TOUR—SPORTS | **FAMILY** | This company leads mule rides along the easier trails of the North Rim. Options include one- and three-hour rides along the rim or a three-hour ride down into the canyon (minimum age 7 for one-hour rides, 10 for three-hour rides). The one-hour ride is $45 and the three-hour rides are $90. Weight limits are 200 pounds for canyon rides and 220 pounds for the rim rides. Available daily from May 15 to

October 15, these excursions are popular, so make reservations in advance. ☏ *435/679–8665* ⊕ *www.canyonrides. com* ✉ *From $45.*

The West Rim and Havasu Canyon

Known as "The People" of the Grand Canyon, the indigenous Hualapai and Havasupai tribes have lived along the Colorado River and the vast Colorado Plateau for more than 1,000 years. Both tribes traditionally moved seasonally between the plateau and the canyon, alternately hunting game and planting crops. Today they rely on their tourism offerings outside the national park as an economic base.

Grand Canyon West

186 miles northwest of Williams, 70 miles north of Kingman.

The plateau-dwelling Hualapai ("people of the tall pines") acquired a larger chunk of traditional Pai lands with the creation of their reservation in 1883. Hualapai tribal lands include diverse habitats ranging from rolling grasslands to rugged canyons, and travel from elevations of 1,500 feet at the Colorado River to more than 7,300 feet at Aubrey Cliffs. In recent years, the Hualapai have been attempting to foster tourism on the West Rim—most notably with the spectacular Skywalk, a glass walkway suspended 70 feet over the edge of the canyon rim. Not hampered by the regulations in place at Grand Canyon National Park, Grand Canyon West offers helicopter flights down into the bottom of the canyon, horseback rides to rim viewpoints, ziplining, and rafting trips on the Colorado River.

The Hualapai Reservation encompasses a million acres in the Grand Canyon, along 108 miles of the Colorado River, with two main areas open to tourists. The West Rim has the Skywalk, Hualapai cultural exhibits and dancing, horseback riding, ziplining, and helicopter rides. Peach Springs, a two-hour drive from the West Rim on historic Route 66, is the tribal capital and the launch site for raft trips on this stretch of the river. Lodging is available both on the rim, at Hualapai Ranch, and in Peach Springs, at the Hualapai Lodge. Although increasingly popular, the West Rim is still relatively remote and visited by far fewer people than the South Rim—keep in mind that it's more than 120 miles away from the nearest interstate highways.

GETTING HERE AND AROUND

The West Rim is a five-hour drive from the South Rim of Grand Canyon National Park or a 2½-hour drive from Las Vegas. From Kingman, drive north 30 miles on U.S. 93, and then turn right onto Pierce Ferry Road and follow it for 28 miles. (A more scenic but slightly longer alternative is to drive 42 miles north on Stockton Hill Road, turning right onto Pierce Ferry Road for 7 miles.) Turn right (east) onto Diamond Bar Road and follow it for 21 miles to Grand Canyon West entrance.

Visitors aren't allowed to travel in their own vehicles to the viewpoints once they reach Grand Canyon West, and must purchase a tour package—which can range from day use to horseback or helicopter rides to lodging and meals—either online (⊕ *grandcanyonwest.com*) or in person from Hualapai Tourism.

TOURS

In addition to the exploring options provided by the Hualapai tribe, more than 30 tour and transportation companies service Grand Canyon West from Las Vegas, Phoenix, and Sedona by airplane, helicopter, coach, SUV, and Hummer. Perhaps the easiest way to visit the West Rim from Vegas is with a tour.

Bighorn Wild West Tours

GUIDED TOURS | This full-day tour takes you to Grand Canyon West in the comfort of a Hummer. Admission fees and lunch are included, as is a stop for photos at Hoover Dam. ☎ 702/385–4676 ⊕ www.bighorntours.com ✉ From $277.

VISITOR INFORMATION

CONTACTS Grand Canyon West. ☎ 888/868–9378, 928/769–2636 ⊕ www.grandcanyonwest.com.

 ## Sights

Grand Canyon Skywalk

VIEWPOINT | This cantilevered glass terrace is suspended nearly 4,000 feet above the Colorado River and extends 70 feet from the edge of the Grand Canyon. Approximately 10 feet wide, the bridge's deck, made of tempered glass several inches thick, has 5-foot glass railings on each side creating an unobstructed open-air platform. Admission to the skywalk is an add-on to the basic Grand Canyon West admission. Visitors must store personal items, including cameras, cell phones, and video cameras, in lockers before entering. A professional photographer takes photographs of visitors, which can be purchased from the gift shop. ⊕ www.grandcanyonwest.com ✉ $20.

Grand Canyon West

CANYON | FAMILY | Grand Canyon West, run by the Hualapai tribe, offers a basic admission ticket ($80 per person, including taxes and fees), which includes a Hualapai visitation permit and hop-on, hop-off shuttle transportation to three sites. The shuttle will take you to Eagle Point, where you can tour authentic dwellings at the Indian Village and view educational displays on the culture of five different Native American tribes (Havasupai, Plains, Hopi, Hualapai, and Navajo). Intertribal dance performances entertain visitors at the nearby amphitheater. The shuttle also goes to Hualapai Ranch, site

Visiting Tribal Lands

When visiting Native American reservations, respect tribal laws and customs. Remember you're a guest in a sovereign nation. Don't wander into residential areas or take photographs of residents without first asking permission. Possessing or consuming alcohol is illegal on tribal lands. In general, the Hualapai and Havasupai are quiet, private people. Offer respect and don't pursue conversations or personal interactions unless invited to do so.

of ziplining, horseback rides, and the only lodging on the West Rim, and Guano Point, where the "High Point Hike" offers panoramic views of the Colorado River. At all three areas, local Hualapai guides add a Native American perspective.

For extra fees, you can add meals (there are cafés at each of the three stops), overnight lodging at Hualapai Ranch, a helicopter trip into the canyon, ziplining, a rafting trip on the Colorado, a horseback ride along the canyon rim, or a walk on the Grand Canyon Skywalk. ⊠ Grand Canyon West ☎ 928/769–2636, 888/868–9378 ⊕ www.grandcanyonwest.com ✉ $80.

Hotels

Hualapai Lodge

$$$ | HOTEL | In Peach Springs on the longest stretch of the original historic Route 66, the hotel has clean, basic rooms and a comfortable lobby with a large fireplace that is welcoming on chilly nights. **Pros:** concierge desk arranges river trips with the Hualapai River Runners; good on-site restaurant with Native American

One of the best ways to see the Grand Canyon is by white-water rafting down the Colorado River.

dishes; Hualapai locals add a different perspective to the canyon experience. **Cons:** basic rooms lack historic charm; location off the beaten path. [$] *Rooms from: $199* ✉ *900 Rte. 66, Peach Springs* ☎ *928/769–2230, 888/868–9378* 🌐 *www.grandcanyonwest.com* 🛏 *60 rooms* 🍴 *Free breakfast.*

Hualapai Ranch

$$$ | **B&B/INN** | **FAMILY** | The only lodging on the West Rim, the comfortable cabins at Hualapai Ranch are clean and neat, but also small and unassuming. **Pros:** front porches with nice desert views; rustlers tell tall tales while you roast s'mores at the campfire; dining room and "saloon" serve all day long. **Cons:** no phones or TVs; no Internet; remote setting. [$] *Rooms from: $199* ✉ *Quartermaster Point Rd., Grand Canyon West* ☎ *928/769–2636, 888/868–9378* 🌐 *www.grandcanyonwest.com* 🛏 *26 cabins* 🍴 *Free breakfast.*

Activities

BOATING AND RAFTING

Hualapai River Runners

TOUR—SPORTS | One-, two- and five-day river trips are offered by the Hualapai Tribe through the Hualapai River Runners from mid-March through October. The trips leave from Peach Springs (a two-hour drive from the West Rim) and include rafting, hiking, and transport. Meals, snacks, and beverages are provided. Children must be at least eight to take the one-day trip and twelve for the overnight trips; the rapids here are rated as Class III–VII, depending on the river flow. ✉ *5001 Buck N Doe Rd., Peach Springs* ☎ *928/769–2636, 888/868–9378* 🌐 *www.grandcanyonwest.com* 🎟 *From $325.*

CAMPING

There's no camping on the West Rim, but you can pitch a tent at Diamond Creek near the Colorado River.

Diamond Creek. You can camp on the banks of the Colorado River, although this beach is a noisy launch point for river runners. You'll also need a four-wheel-drive vehicle to get here. The Hualapai permit camping on their tribal lands here, with an overnight camping permit of $27 per person per night, which can be purchased at the Hualapai Lodge. ☎ *928/769–2210, 888/255–9550* ⊕ *www. grandcanyonwest.com*

Havasu Canyon

141 miles northwest from Williams to the head of Hualapai Hilltop.

With the establishment of Grand Canyon National Park in 1919, the Havasupai ("people of the blue-green water") were confined to their summer village of Supai and the surrounding 518 acres in the 5-mile-wide and 12-mile-long Havasu Canyon. In 1975 the reservation was substantially enlarged but is still completely surrounded by national park lands on all but its southern border. Each year about 25,000 tourists fly, hike, or ride into Havasu Canyon to visit the Havasupai. Despite their economic reliance on tourism, the Havasupai take their guardianship of the Grand Canyon seriously and severely limit visitation in order to protect the fragile canyon habitats. Dubbed the "Shangri-la of the Grand Canyon," the waterfalls have drawn visitors to this remote reservation.

Major flooding in 2008 altered Havasu Canyon's famous landscape, and it was closed to visitors for almost 10 months. Supai reopened in 2009, but water and mud damage have changed some of the beautiful waterfalls, their streams and pools, and the amount of blue-green travertine. ■TIP➔ **Visiting Havasu Canyon requires preparation: Reservations and permits must be obtained well in advance. Camping reservations, which usually sell out in a few hours, can be made online only beginning Feb. 1 for the following year** (havasupaireservations.com); **Havasupai Lodge reservations can be made by phone only beginning June 1 for the following year** (928/448-2111).

GETTING HERE AND AROUND
Hualapai Hilltop is reached via Indian Route 18, which you follow about 65 miles north from historic Route 66 (34 miles west of Seligman and 50 miles east of Kingman). The total driving distance from the South Rim of the Grand Canyon is about 200 miles and takes about four hours. The closest lodging and services are in Peach Springs, a 90-minute drive, and Seligman, about 2 hours away.

The Havasupai restrict the number of visitors to the canyon; you must obtain entrance permits and make reservations well in advance. ■TIP➔ **You will be stopped and turned away if you don't have a reservation!**

The Hualapai Trail begins at Hualapai Hilltop. You can park your car here (the parking lot is patrolled), but there is no gas, lodging, or water available at the trailhead. From an elevation of 5,200 feet, the 8-mile trail travels down a moderate grade to Supai Village at 3,200 feet. Bring plenty of water and food, and avoid hiking during the middle of the day, when canyon temperatures can reach into the 100s. No day hiking is permitted; campers must pay for three nights. If you prefer to have a bed and plumbing, the Supai Lodge is in the village, along with a small grocery store and a café. The campground is 2 miles farther, closer to the waterfalls. Permits and camping reservations for the year ahead may be purchased online only beginning Feb. 1 ⊕ *havasupaireservations.com*; Supai Lodge reservations can be made by phone beginning June 1 ☎ *928/448–2111.*

Another option is a helicopter ride into the canyon with Air West Helicopters. Flights leave from Hualapai Hilltop four days a week during summer and two days a week during winter, and cost $85 per person each way. Reservations aren't accepted and visitors are transported on a first-come-first-served basis. Tribal members and supplies are boarded prior to tourists, so you are not guaranteed a ride down (or back up).

ESSENTIALS

TRANSPORTATION CONTACTS Air West Helicopters. ☎ *623/516–2790* 🌐 *www.airwesthelicopters.com.*

VISITOR INFORMATION Havasupai Tourist Enterprise. ☎ *928/448–2121* 🌐 *theofficialhavasupaitribe.com.*

Sights

Havasu Canyon

CANYON | South of the middle part of the Grand Canyon National Park's South Rim and away from the crowds, Havasu Canyon is the home of the Havasupai, a tribe that has lived in this isolated area for centuries. You'll discover why they are known as the "people of the blue-green waters" when you see the canyon's waterfalls—**Havasu Falls**, **Fiftyfoot Falls**, **Little Navajo Falls**, and (farther away from the campground) **Mooney Falls** and **Beaver Falls**. Accumulated travertine formations in some of the most popular pools were washed out in massive flooding decades ago and again in 2008 and 2010, but it's still a magical place.

The village of Supai, which currently has about 600 tribal residents, is accessed by the 8-mile-long **Hualapai Trail,** which drops 2,000 feet from the canyon rim to the tiny town.

To reach Havasu's waterfalls, you must hike downstream from the village of Supai. Pack adequate food and supplies. There is a café and a trading post in the village, but prices for food and sundries are more than double what they would be outside the reservation. The tribe does not allow alcohol, drugs, pets, or weapons. Reservations are necessary for camping or staying at the Havasupai Lodge. ✉ *Havasupai Tourist Enterprise, Supai* ☎ *928/448–2121 general info, 928/448–2201 lodging reservations* 🌐 *theofficialhavasupaitribe.com.*

Mail by Mule

Arguably the most remote mail route in the United States follows a steep 8-mile trail to the tiny town of Supai in Havasu Canyon. Havasupai tribal members living deep within the confines of the Grand Canyon rely on this route for the delivery of everything from food to furniture. During a typical week, more than a ton of mail is sent into the canyon by mule, with each animal carrying a cargo of about 130 pounds.

Hotels

Supai Lodge

$$$$ | **HOTEL** | Operated by the Havasupai Tribe at the bottom of Havasu Canyon, these are fairly spartan accommodations—each room has two double beds and a bathroom—but you won't mind much when you see the natural beauty surrounding you. **Pros:** sleep in a bed rather than a tent; Native American perspective on the natural and cultural history of the Grand Canyon; private bathroom. **Cons:** more than a 2-mile hike to the falls; plain and worn rooms; no phones, Internet, or TVs. [$] *Rooms from: $440* ✉ *159 Supai, Supai* ☎ *928/448–2111, 928/448–2201* 🌐 *theofficialhavasupaitribe.com* 🛏 *24 rooms* 🍴 *No meals.*

Activities

CAMPING

Havasu Canyon. You can stay in the primitive campgrounds in Havasu Canyon for $100 per person per night (a three-night stay is required and permits are included). Reservations are difficult to get here; they go on sale February 1 for the following year and sell out within a few hours. ☎ *928/448–2121, 928/448–2180* ⊕ *www.havasupaitribe.com.*

Kaibab National Forest. Both developed and undeveloped campsites are available either by reservation ⊕ *recreation.gov* or, space permitting, on a first-come first-served basis May through September at this forest that surrounds Williams and extends to the Grand Canyon National Park's South Rim. ☎ *928/699–1239* ⊕ *www.fs.usda.gov/kaibab.*

Nearby Towns

The northwest section of Arizona is geographically fascinating. In addition to the Grand Canyon, it's home to national forests, national monuments, and national recreation areas. Towns, however, are small and scattered. Many of them cater to visiting adventurers, and Native American reservations dot the map. Apart from Tusayan, located 2 miles from the South Rim, the closest town to the canyon's South Rim is Williams, the "Gateway to the Grand Canyon," 58 miles south.

The communities closest to the North Rim—all of them tiny and with limited services—include Fredonia, 76 miles north; Marble Canyon, 80 miles northeast; Lees Ferry, 85 miles east; and Jacob Lake, 45 miles north.

VISITOR INFORMATION
CONTACTS Kaibab National Forest, North Kaibab Ranger District. ⊠ *430 S. Main St., Fredonia* ☎ *928/643–7395* ⊕ *www. fs.usda.gov/kaibab.* **Kaibab National Forest, Tusayan Ranger District.** ⊠ *176 Lincoln Log Loop, Grand Canyon National Park* ☎ *928/638–2443* ⊕ *www.fs.usda.gov/kaibab.* **Kaibab Plateau Visitor Center.** ⊠ *U.S. 89A at Hwy. 67, Jacob Lake* ☎ *928/643–7298* ⊕ *www.fs.usda.gov/kaibab.*

Tusayan

57 miles north of Williams, 2 miles south of Grand Canyon National Park.

The small hamlet of Tusayan, incorporated as a town only in 2010, is little more than a place to sleep and eat when visiting the Grand Canyon's South Rim. The main attractions here are an IMAX theater and visitor center, where you can see a film about the canyon and purchase tickets for air and jeep tours, and the Grand Canyon Airport, the takeoff point for plane and helicopter tours.

GETTING HERE AND AROUND
Tusayan's quarter-mile strip of hotels, eateries, and services sits right on Highway 64, the road leading into Grand Canyon National Park. Parking lots are plentiful.

◉ Sights

Grand Canyon Visitor Center
INFO CENTER | Here you can get information about activities and tours, and buy a national park pass, which enables you to skip past some of the crowds and access the park by special entry lanes. Nevertheless, the biggest draw is the six-story IMAX screen that features the short movie *Grand Canyon: The Hidden Secrets.* You can learn about the geologic and natural history of the canyon, soar above stunning rock formations, and ride the rapids through the rocky gorge. The film is shown every hour on the half hour; the adjoining gift store is huge and well stocked. ⊠ *450 Hwy. 64/U.S. 180* ✛ *2 miles south of the Grand Canyon's south entrance* ☎ *928/638–2468* ⊕ *explorethecanyon.com* 🎞 *$13 for IMAX movies.*

🍴 Restaurants

Canyon Star Steakhouse and Saloon
$$$ | **AMERICAN** | **FAMILY** | Relax in the rustic timber-and-stone dining room at the Grand Hotel for reliable if uninspired American food, with an emphasis on steaks and barbecue at dinner. Popular options include

barbecue chicken and ribs, and Mexican fare. **Known for:** rollicking live music; better-than-average local dining; barbecue. $ *Average main: $26* ⊠ *Hwy. 64/U.S. 180* ☎ *928/638–3333* ⊕ *www.grandcanyon-lodges.com* ⊗ *No lunch.*

The Coronado Room

$$$ | AMERICAN | Inside the Best Western Grand Canyon Squire Inn is the most sophisticated cuisine in Tusayan. The menu includes well-prepared, hearty American food, with an emphasis on meat (steak, elk burgers, buffalo), plus grilled seafood, escargot, and oversize desserts. **Known for:** Tusayan's finest restaurant; splurge-worthy dining; splurge-worthy desserts. $ *Average main: $28* ⊠ *100 Hwy. 64/U.S. 180* ☎ *928/638–2681* ⊕ *www.grandcan-yonsquire.com* ⊗ *No lunch.*

🛏 Hotels

Best Western Grand Canyon Squire Inn

$$$$ | HOTEL | FAMILY | About 2 miles from the park's south entrance, this motel lacks the historic charm of the lodges at the canyon rim, but has more amenities, including pools, a bowling alley, a gym, a small cowboy museum, and one of the better restaurants in the region. **Pros:** cool pools in summer and a hot tub for cold winter nights; copious children's activities at the Family Fun Center; most rooms have refrigerators, microwaves, and coffeemakers. **Cons:** hall noise can be an issue with all of the in-hotel activities; very large (and bustling) property; rooms near pool can be especially noisy. $ *Rooms from: $269* ⊠ *100 Hwy. 64/U.S. 180, Grand Canyon* ☎ *928/638–2681, 800/622–6966* ⊕ *www.grandcanyonsquire.com* ⟿ *318 rooms* ❘○❘ *No meals.*

The Grand Hotel

$$$$ | HOTEL | FAMILY | At the south end of Tusayan, this popular hotel has bright, clean, and contemporary rooms, a cozy stone-and-timber lobby, and free Wi-Fi. **Pros:** Western entertainment at

restaurant; gift shop stocked with art, outdoor gear, and regional books; indoor pool and hot tub. **Cons:** somewhat generic property; on-site restaurant is uninspired and overpriced; indoor pool only. $ *Rooms from: $272* ⊠ *149 Hwy. 64/U.S. 180, Grand Canyon* ☎ *928/638–3333, 888/634–7263* ⊕ *www.grandcanyonlodg-es.com* ⟿ *121 rooms* ❘○❘ *No meals.*

★ Red Feather Lodge

$$ | HOTEL | About 6 miles from the canyon, this clean, family-run lodge has a two-story motel building and a newer, three-story hotel building, both a good value. **Pros:** lower-priced than most lodging close to park; pet-friendly; pool and hot tub. **Cons:** stairs only in the two-story motel (the three-story hotel building has an elevator); motel rooms have showers (hotel rooms have shower/tubs); only two devices per room allowed on Wi-Fi at a time. $ *Rooms from: $132* ⊠ *300 Hwy. 64/U.S. 180* ☎ *928/638–2414, 800/538–2345* ⊕ *www.redfeatherlodge.com* ⟿ *216 rooms* ❘○❘ *No meals.*

🏃 Activities

Apache Stables

HORSEBACK RIDING | FAMILY | There's nothing like a horseback ride to immerse you in the Western experience. From stables near Tusayan, these folks offer gentle horses and a ride through the forest. Choose from one- and two-hour trail rides (March–October) or the popular campfire rides and horse-drawn wagon excursions (late May–early September). ⊠ *Forest Service Rd. 328* ⊕ *1 mile north of Tusayan* ☎ *928/638–2891* ⊕ *www. apachestables.com* ▨ *From $59.*

Arizona Bike Trail

BICYCLING | Pedal the depths of the Kaibab National Forest on the Arizona Bike Trail–Tusayan Bike Trails System. Following linked loop trails at an elevation of 6,750 feet, you can bike as few as 3 miles or as many as 38 miles round-trip along old logging roads (some parts are paved) through ponderosa pine forest. Keep an eye out for elk, mule deer, hawks, eagles, pronghorn antelope, turkeys, coyote, and porcupines. Open for biking year-round (but most feasible March through October), the trail is accessed on the west side of Highway 64, a half mile north of Tusayan. ⊠ *Tusayan Ranger District* ☎ *928/638–2443* ⊕ *www.fs.usda.gov/recarea/kaibab.*

Williams

The cozy mountain town of Williams, founded in 1882 when the railroad passed through, was once a rough-and-tumble joint, replete with saloons and bordellos. Today it reflects a much milder side of the Wild West, with 3,300 residents and more than 25 motels and hotels. Wander along the main street—part of historic Route 66, but locally named, like the town, after trapper Bill Williams—and indulge in Route 66 nostalgia inside antiques shops or souvenir and T-shirt stores.

Fredonia

Fredonia, a small community of about 1,050, approximately an hour's drive north of the Grand Canyon, is often referred to as the gateway to the North Rim; it's also relatively close to Zion and Bryce Canyon national parks in Utah.

Lees Ferry

En route from the South Rim to the North Rim and about 5 miles northeast of the town of Marble Canyon, where Echo Cliffs and Vermilion Cliffs intersect, is Lees Ferry. Considered "mile zero" of the river—the point from which all distances on the rivers system in the Grand Canyon are measured—Lees Ferry is where most of the Grand Canyon river rafts put into the water. Huge trout lurk in the river near here, and there are several places in the area to pick up angling gear and a guide.

After Lees Ferry, there isn't another vehicle crossing point on the Colorado River until you reach the Hoover Dam (although two footbridges cross the river near Phantom Ranch). Lees Ferry, at the Pariah Canyon junction just 15 miles below Glen Canyon Dam, has for thousands of years offered one of the best places to cross the deep gash of the Grand Canyon. Today the town, the Lonely Dell Ranch Historic District, a small, sad cemetery, and a scattering of historic buildings offer a glimpse of frontier life. But most people journey to Lees Ferry to get onto the river. Commercial raft trips take off from the boat ramps, and fly-fishing guides regularly shuttle people upstream to the base of Glen Canyon Dam.

Marble Canyon

Marble Canyon marks the geographical beginning of the Grand Canyon at its northeastern tip. It's a good stopping point if you're driving U.S. 89 to the North Rim.

◉ Sights

SCENIC DRIVES
U.S. 89

SCENIC DRIVE | The route north from Cameron Trading Post (Cameron, Arizona) on U.S. 89 offers a stunning view of the **Painted Desert** to the right. The desert, which covers thousands of square miles stretching to the south and east, is a vision of subtle, almost harsh beauty, with windswept plains and mesas, isolated buttes, and barren valleys in pastel patterns. About 30 miles north of Cameron Trading Post, the Painted Desert country gives way to sandstone cliffs that run for miles. Brilliantly hued and ranging in color from light pink to deep orange, the **Echo Cliffs** rise to more than 1,000 feet in many places. They are essentially devoid of vegetation, but in a few high places, thick patches of tall cottonwood and poplar trees, nurtured by springs and water seepage from the rock escarpment, manage to thrive. ✉ *Grand Canyon.*

U.S. 89A

SCENIC DRIVE | At Bitter Springs, 60 miles north of Cameron, U.S. 89A branches off from U.S. 89, running north and providing views of **Marble Canyon,** the geographical beginning of the Grand Canyon. Like the Grand Canyon, Marble Canyon was formed by the Colorado River. Traversing a gorge nearly 500 feet deep is **Navajo Bridge,** a narrow steel span built in 1929 and listed on the National Register of Historic Places. Formerly used for car traffic, it now functions only as a pedestrian overpass. ✉ *Marble Canyon.*

SCENIC SPOTS

Vermilion Cliffs National Monument

NATURE SITE | West of the town of Marble Canyon are these spectacular cliffs, more than 3,000 feet high in many places. A four-wheel-drive vehicle is required here, as there are no paved roads and the sand is deep. Keep an eye out for condors; the giant endangered birds were reintroduced into the area in 1996. Reports suggest that the birds, once in captivity, are surviving well in the wilderness. ☎ *435/688–3200* 🌐 *www.blm.gov/node/10029.*

Hotels

Marble Canyon Lodge

$ | **HOTEL** | Popular with anglers and rafters, this lodge offers two types of accommodations: standard rooms in the original lodge building and two-bedroom apartments in a newer building. **Pros:** convenience store, restaurant, and trading post; great fishing on the Colorado River; some rooms have kitchens. **Cons:** no-frills rustic lodging; no Wi-Fi (one computer in lobby); apartments have evaporative coolers instead of AC. [$] *Rooms from: $87* ✉ *U.S. 89A, Marble Canyon* ✥ *¼ mile west of Navajo Bridge* ☎ *928/355–2225, 800/726–1789* 🌐 *www.marblecanyoncompany.com* 🛏 *54 rooms* 🍴 *No meals.*

Jacob Lake

The tiny town of Jacob Lake, nestled high in pine country at an elevation of 7,925 feet, was named after Mormon explorer Jacob Hamblin, also known as the "Buckskin Missionary." It has a hotel, café, campground, and lush mountain countryside.

Hotels

Jacob Lake Inn

$ | **HOTEL** | The bustling lodge at Jacob Lake Inn is a popular stop for those heading to the North Rim, 45 miles south. **Pros:** grocery store, bakery, and restaurant; quiet rooms; good base for exploring North Rim. **Cons:** only the newer rooms have TVs; no Internet; some rooms don't have AC. [$] *Rooms from: $114* ✉ *U.S. 89A and Hwy. 67, Jacob Lake* ☎ *928/643–7232* 🌐 *www.jacoblake.com* 🛏 *58 rooms* 🍴 *No meals.*

Activities

BOATING AND RAFTING

The National Park Service authorizes 16 concessionaires to run rafting trips through the canyon—you can view a full list at the park's website (🌐 *www.nps.gov/grca/planyourvisit/river-concessioners.htm*). Trips run from 3 to 18 days, depending on whether you opt for the upper canyon, lower canyon, or full canyon, and whether you ride in motorized or nonmotorized rafts. You can also experience a one-day rafting trip, either running a few rapids in the Grand Canyon West with the Hualapai tribe or floating through Glen Canyon near Page in Northeast Arizona.

Arizona Raft Adventures

WHITE-WATER RAFTING | This outfitter organizes 6- to 16-day paddle/oar and motor trips through the upper, lower, or full canyon, for all skill levels. Trips depart April through October. ✉ *4050 E. Huntington*

Continued on page 186

EXPLORING THE
COLORADO RIVER

High in Colorado's Rocky Mountains, the Colorado River begins as a catch-all for the snowmelt off the mountains west of the Continental Divide. By the time it reaches the Grand Canyon, the Colorado has been joined by multiple tributaries to become a raging river, red with silt as it sculpts spectacular landscapes. A network of dams can only partially tame this mighty river.

Snaking its way through five states, the Colorado River is an essential water source to the arid Southwest. Its natural course runs 1,450 miles from its origin in Colorado's La Poudre Pass Lake in Rocky Mountain National Park to its final destination in the Gulf of California, also called the Sea of Cortez. In northern Arizona, the Colorado River has been a powerful force in shaping the Grand Canyon, where it flows 4,000 to 6,000 feet below the rim. Beyond the canyon, the red river takes a lazy turn at the Arizona–Nevada border, where Hoover Dam creates the reservoir at Lake Mead. The Colorado continues at a relaxed pace along the Arizona–California border, providing energy and irrigation in Arizona, California, and Nevada before draining into northwestern Mexico.

A RIVER RUNS THROUGH IT

Stretching along 277 miles of the Colorado River is one of the seven natural wonders of the world: the Grand Canyon ranges in width from 4 to 18 miles, while the walls around it soar up to a mile high. Nearly 2 billion years of geologic history and majesty are revealed in exposed tiers of rock cut deep in the Colorado Plateau. What caused this incredible marvel of nature? Erosion by water coupled with driving wind are most likely the major culprits: under the sculpting power of wind and water, the shale layers eroded into slopes and the harder sandstone and limestone layers created terraced cliffs. Other forces that may have helped shape the canyon include ice, volcanic activity, continental drift, and earthquakes.

WHO LIVES HERE
Native tribes have lived in the canyon for thousands of years and continue to do so. The plateau-dwelling Hualapai ("people of the tall pines") live on a million acres along 108 miles of the Colorado River in the West Rim. The Havasupai ("people of the blue green water") live deep within the walls of the 12-mile-long Havasu Canyon—a major side canyon connected to the Grand Canyon.

ENVIRONMENTAL CONCERNS
When the Grand Canyon achieved national park status in 1919, only 44,173 people made the grueling overland trip to see it—quite a contrast from today's nearly 5 million annual visitors. The tremendous increase in visitation has greatly impacted the fragile ecosystems, as has Lake Powell's Glen Canyon Dam, which was constructed in the 1950s and '60s. The dam has changed the composition of the Colorado River, replacing warm water rich in sediments (nature's way of nourishing the riverbed and banks) with mostly cool, much clearer water. This has introduced nonnative plants and animals that threaten the extinction of several native species. Air pollution has also affected visibility and the constant buzz of aerial tours has disturbed the natural solitude.

Above and right, views of Colorado River in the Grand Canyon from Toroweap.

Did You Know?

The North Rim's isolated Toroweap overlook (also called Tuweep) is perched 3,000 feet above the canyon floor: a height equal to stacking the Sears Tower and Empire State Building on top of each other.

RIVER RAFTING THROUGH THE GRAND CANYON

Viewing the Colorado River from a canyon overlook is one thing, but looking up at the canyon from the middle of the river is quite another experience. If you're ready to tackle the churning white water of the Colorado River as it rumbles and hisses its way through the Grand Canyon, take a look at this map of what you might encounter along the way.

0 10 mi
0 10 km

KANAB PLATEAU

NEVADA / ARIZONA

GRAND CANYON

You'll hear the roar of **Lava Falls** before you see it—this large rapid is the fastest navigable white-water stretch in North America.

• Tuweep

Mile 179 ● Lava Falls

Lake Mead

Mile 296 ◆
South Cove

South Cove, on Lake Mead, is the final destination for many river trips.

GRAND CANYON NATIONAL PARK

● Kolb Rapid

Whitmore Wash

Many outfitters end their trips at **Diamond Creek**, where the river begins to slow down. One-day trips are operated by the Hualapai Tribe.

GRAND WASH CLIFFS

Colorado River

Dirt

Mile 225 ◆   **Diamond Creek**

Dirt

HUALAPAI INDIAN RES.

Peach Springs

COLORADO RIVER TRIPS

Time and Length	Entry and Exit points
1 day Float trip	Glen Canyon Dam to Lees Ferry (no rapids)
1 day Combo trip	Diamond Creek, then helicopter to West Rim
3–4 days	Lees Ferry to Phantom Ranch
6 days, 89 miles	Phantom Ranch to Diamond Creek
9–10 days, 136 miles	Lees Ferry to Diamond Creek
14–16 days, 225 miles	Lees Ferry to South Cove

*Trips either begin or end at Phantom Ranch/Bright Angel Beach at the bottom of the Grand Canyon, at river mile 87

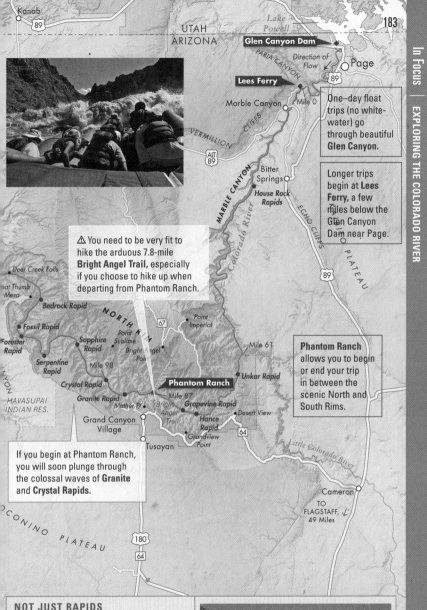

Kanab
89
Lake Powell
UTAH
ARIZONA
Glen Canyon Dam
Direction of Flow
Page
89
Lees Ferry
Marble Canyon
Mile 0

PARIA CANYON

VERMILION CLIFFS

AUT 89

MARBLE CANYON

Colorado River

Bitter Springs
House Rock Rapids

ECHO CLIFFS PLATEAU

89

One–day float trips (no white-water) go through beautiful **Glen Canyon.**

Longer trips begin at **Lees Ferry,** a few miles below the Glen Canyon Dam near Page.

⚠ You need to be very fit to hike the arduous 7.8-mile **Bright Angel Trail,** especially if you choose to hike up when departing from Phantom Ranch.

Deer Creek Falls
eat Thumb Mesa
Bedrock Rapid
Fossil Rapid
orester Rapid
Sapphire Rapid
Serpentine Rapid
Crystal Rapid
Granite Rapid
Mile 98

NORTH RIM

Point Sublime
Bright Angel Point
Mather Pt
Bright Angel Trail
Grand Canyon Village
Tusayan

67
Point Imperial
Mile 61
Unkar Rapid
Phantom Ranch
Mile 87
Grapevine Rapid
Hance Rapid
Grandview Point
Desert View
64

HAVASUPAI INDIAN RES.

Phantom Ranch allows you to begin or end your trip in between the scenic North and South Rims.

If you begin at Phantom Ranch, you will soon plunge through the colossal waves of **Granite** and **Crystal Rapids.**

Little Colorado River

Cameron
TO FLAGSTAFF, 49 Miles

OCONINO PLATEAU
180
64

NOT JUST RAPIDS

Don't think that your experience will be nonstop white-water adrenaline. Most of the Colorado River features long, relaxing stretches of water, where you drift amid grandiose rock formations. You might even spot a mountain goat or two. Multi-day trips include camping on the shore.

PLANNING YOUR RIVER RAFTING TRIP

OAR, MOTOR, OR HYBRID?

Base the type of trip you choose on the amount of effort you want to put in. Motor rafts, which are the roomiest of the choices, cover the most miles in less time and are the most comfortable. Guides do the rowing on oar boats and these smaller rafts offer a wilder ride. All-paddle trips are the most active and require the most involvement from guests. Hybrid trips are popular because they offer both the opportunity to paddle and to relax.

THE GEAR

Life jackets, beverages, tents, sheets, tarps, sleeping bags, dry bags, first aid, and food are provided—but you'll still need to plan ahead by packing clothing, hats, sunscreen, toiletries, and other sundries. Commercial outfitters allow each river runner two waterproof bags to store items during the day—just keep in mind that one of these will be filled up with the provided sleeping bag

and tarp. ■TIP➔ **Bring a rain suit: summer thunderstorms are frequent and chilly.**

WHEN TO GO

Lots of people book trips for summer's peak period: June through August. If you're flexible, take advantage of the Arizona weather and go from May to early June or in September. ■TIP➔ **Seats fill up quickly; make reservations for multiday trips a year or two in advance.**

TRIP LENGTH

Rafting options on the Colorado River range from one-day trips at either the east or west end of the Grand Canyon to leisurely, two-week paddle trips through the full length of Grand Canyon National Park. If you're short on time, take a one-day trip near Grand Canyon West, where you'll run several rapids and fly back to the West Rim by helicopter. Another action-packed choice is to raft the river for 3 or 4 days, disembark at Phantom Ranch, then hike up to the Grand Canyon South Rim. "Full Canyon" rafting trips can take 9 to 16 days.

Above, Getting wet—and loving it—on an oar boat.

Did You Know?

As you're hanging on for dear life, consider this: Civil War veteran John Wesley Powell chartered these treacherous rapids in 1869—not only were conditions more dangerous then, but he had only one arm.

Dr., Flagstaff ☎ *800/786–7238, 928/526–8200* ⊕ *azraft.com* ✉ *From $2400.*

Canyoneers

WHITE-WATER RAFTING | With a reputation for high quality and a roster of 4- to 14-day trips, Canyoneers is popular with those who want to do some hiking into side canyons as well. Motorized and oar trips are available mid-April through September. ✉ *7195 N. U.S. 89, Flagstaff* ☎ *928/526–0924, 800/525–0924* ⊕ *canyoneers.com* ✉ *From $1650.*

Grand Canyon Expeditions

WHITE-WATER RAFTING | You can count on Grand Canyon Expeditions to take you down the Colorado River safely and in style: evening meals might include filet mignon, pork chops, or shrimp. The 8- or 9-day motorized and 14-day Dory trips cover all 277 miles of the river, and some trips focus on special interests like archaeology and photography. Transportation from (and back to) Las Vegas is part of the package. ☎ *435/363–4443, 800/544–2691* ⊕ *www.gcex.com* ✉ *From $3050.*

Wilderness River Adventures

WHITE-WATER RAFTING | One of the canyon's larger rafting outfitters, Wilderness River Adventures by Aramark runs a wide variety of trips from 3 to 14 days, oar or motorized, from April to September. Their most popular trip is the seven-day motorized trip. ✉ *2040 E. Frontage Rd., Page* ☎ *928/645–3296, 800/992–8022* ⊕ *www.riveradventures.com* ✉ *From $1630.*

FISHING

The stretch of ice-cold, crystal clear water at Lees Ferry off the North Rim provides arguably the best trout fishing in the Southwest. Many rafters and anglers stay the night in a campground near the river or in nearby Marble Canyon before hitting the river at dawn.

Lees Ferry Anglers

FISHING | There are guides, state fishing licenses, and gear for sale at Lees Ferry Anglers. ✉ *Milepost 547, N. U.S. 89A, HC 67, Marble Canyon* ☎ *928/355–2261, 800/962–9755* ⊕ *www.leesferry.com.*

Marble Canyon Outfitters

FISHING | This company, based at Marble Canyon Lodge, sells Arizona fishing licenses and offers top-notch guided fishing trips. ✉ *Marble Canyon* ✛ *¼ mile west of Navajo Bridge on U.S. 89A* ☎ *800/533–7339* ⊕ *www.leesferryflyfishing.com.*

HIKING
Rainbow Rim Trail

BICYCLING | Rangers say the best bet for bikers heading to the North Rim—and only intermediate and experienced ones should attempt it—is the Rainbow Rim Trail, an 18-mile, one-way trail that begins at Parissawampitts Point at the end of Forest Road 214 and ends at Timp Point on Forest Road 271. This premier trail outside the park boundary includes three fantastic viewpoints of the Grand Canyon—Fence, Locust, and North Timp—and winds through a ponderosa pine forest, aspen groves, and pristine meadows. In the **Kaibab National Forest,** the trail is open to hikers, bikers, and horseback riders and stays within 200 feet of its 7,550 feet elevation. ✉ *Grand Canyon National Park* ☎ *928/643–7395* ⊕ *www.fs.usda.gov/kaibab.*

Chapter 5

NORTH-CENTRAL ARIZONA

WITH FLAGSTAFF AND SEDONA

Updated by
Mara Levin

⊙ Sights	🍴 Restaurants	🛏 Hotels	🛍 Shopping	🍸 Nightlife
★★★★★	★★★★☆	★★★★☆	★★★★★	★★★☆☆

WELCOME TO NORTH-CENTRAL ARIZONA

TOP REASONS TO GO

★ **Mother Nature:** Stunning red rocks, snowcapped mountains, and crisp country air rejuvenate the most cynical city dwellers. Nature lovers should visit either the Coconino or Prescott National Forest.

★ **Father Time:** Ancient Native American sites, such as Walnut Canyon and Montezuma's Castle, show life before Columbus "discovered" America. You can learn their history in the excellent national monument visitor centers.

★ **Main Street charm:** Jerome and Prescott exude small-town hospitality with turn-of-the-20th-century architecture and charming bed-and-breakfasts.

★ **Cool escapes:** Beat the heat in the high desert; temperatures throughout North-Central Arizona are typically 20°F cooler than in the Phoenix area.

★ **Free spirits:** The energy of Sedona is delightful; even skeptics might be tempted to get their aura read.

Nestled between the Grand Canyon and Phoenix, North-Central Arizona has enough natural beauty and sophisticated attractions to compete with its neighbors to the north and south. Most visitors flock to Sedona, world-renowned for red rocks and New Age energy. The surrounding area of the Verde Valley may not attract the same hordes, but this means welcome peace and quiet. Flagstaff is surrounded by the Coconino National Forest and wrapped around the base of the San Francisco Peaks, the tallest mountains in the state.

1 **Williams.** Take a historic train ride into the Grand Canyon from Williams, a cozy town along Route 66.

2 **Flagstaff.** College-town enthusiasm and high-country charm make this one of Arizona's most outdoors-friendly towns. Hiking, skiing, and climbing are local passions, and there are state and national parks to explore.

3 **East of Flagstaff.** East of Flagstaff are craters and volcanoes, Native American archaeology, and architecture.

4 **San Francisco Volcanic Field.** Hike around Sunset Crater or climb Humphreys Peak, the tallest in the state, both part of this dormant volcanic mountain range north of Flagstaff known as the San Francisco Peaks.

5 **Sedona and Oak Creek Canyon.** Surrounded by the Coconino National Forest, Sedona's residents call their home a museum without walls. You'll enjoy breathtaking red rock views, fantastic cuisine, and a dash of New Age whimsy.

6 **The Verde Valley.** Remote but still accessible, the towns of the Verde Valley embrace the life of yesteryear. You can take the Verde Canyon Railroad or visit Montezuma's Castle and see nature's untouched beauty and history.

7 **Jerome.** This tiny hilltop town, a hub for artisans, is brimming with shops, restaurants, mining history, and stunning vistas.

8 **Prescott.** Whiskey Row in Prescott still exudes turn-of-the-20th-century charm. Just outside of town are beautiful green areas to hike.

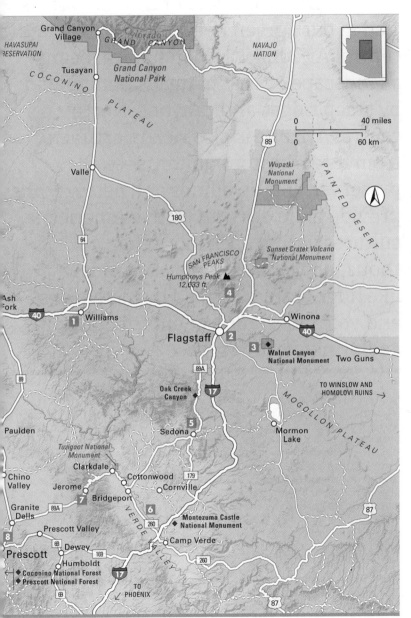

Red rock buttes ablaze in the light of late afternoon, majestic mountains tipped white from a fresh snowfall, pine forests clad in dark green needles—north-central Arizona is rich in natural beauty, a landscape of vast plateaus punctuated by steep ridges and canyons. North-central Arizona is also rich in artifacts from its earliest inhabitants—well-preserved cliff dwellings and petroglyphs provide glimpses into Native American cultures dating back more than a thousand years. Geological wonders, like huge craters formed by meteorites and volcanoes, add yet another layer to exploring in the region.

North of Flagstaff, the San Francisco Peaks, a string of tall volcanic mountains, rise more than 12,000 feet. To the south, ponderosa pines cover the Colorado Plateau before the terrain plunges dramatically into Oak Creek Canyon. The canyon then opens to reveal red buttes and mesas in the high-desert areas surrounding Sedona. The desert gradually descends to the Verde Valley, crossing the Verde River before reaching the 7,000-foot Black Range, over which lies the Prescott Valley.

Flagstaff, home to Northern Arizona University and the hub of this part of Arizona, was historically a way station en route to Southern California via the railroads and then Route 66. Many of those who were "just passing through" stayed and built a community, revitalizing downtown with cafés, an activity-filled square, eclectic shops, and festivals. The town's large network of bike paths and parks abuts hundreds of miles of trails and forest roads, an irresistible lure for outdoors enthusiasts. Not surprisingly, the typical resident of Flagstaff is outdoorsy, young, and has a large, friendly dog in tow.

Down in Sedona, the average age and income rises considerably. This was once a hidden hamlet used by Western filmmakers, but New Age enthusiasts flocked to the region in the 1980s, believing it was the center of spiritual powers. Well-off executives and retirees followed soon after. Sophisticated restaurants, upscale shops, luxe accommodations, and New Age entrepreneurs cater to both these populations and to the thriving tourist trade.

Pioneers and miners are now part of North-Central Arizona's past, but the wild and woolly days of the Old West aren't forgotten. The preserved fort at Camp Verde recalls frontier life, and the decrepit facades of the funky former mining town of Jerome have their own charm. The jumble of saloons and Victorian houses in temperate Prescott attests to the attempt to bring "civilization" to Arizona's territorial capital.

■TIP→ It's wise, especially if you're an outdoors enthusiast, to start in the relatively lowland areas of Prescott and the Verde Valley, climbing gradually to Sedona and Flagstaff—it can take several days to grow accustomed to the high elevation in Flagstaff.

North-Central Arizona Planner

When to Go

Autumn—when the wet season ends, the stifling desert temperatures are moderate (it's 20°F cooler than Phoenix), and the mountain aspens reach their full golden splendor—is a great time to visit this part of Arizona. During the summer months many Phoenix residents travel north to escape the heat, meaning excessive traffic along Interstate 17 just north of Phoenix on Friday and Sunday evenings. Hotels are less expensive in winter, but mountain temperatures dip below zero, and snowstorms can occur weekly, especially near Flagstaff.

Sedona has springlike temperatures even in January, when it's snowing in Flagstaff, but summer temperatures above 90°F are common.

FESTIVALS AND EVENTS

Historical Route 66 Car Show

FESTIVALS | Classic cars and trucks, from antiques to hot rods, are on display along Route 66 in downtown Williams for two days in mid-June. Outfit your own jalopy from the auto parts swap meet set up adjacent to the show. ⊠ *200 Railroad Ave., Williams* ⊕ *williamshistoricroute-66carshow.com.*

Festival of Science

CULTURAL FESTIVALS | FAMILY | This 10-day series of exhibits, activities, guided hikes, and talks in Flagstaff is a fun and interactive way to learn about current research in astronomy, geology, engineering, and biology. ☎ *800/842–7293* ⊕ *www.scifest. org.*

Planning Your Time

Sedona will probably occupy most of your time, so plan to spend at least two days there, hiking, shopping and soaking in the gorgeous views and the vortex energy. Oak Creek Canyon and Chapel of the Holy Cross are must-sees. Then, depending on your preferences, spend your time looking (window-shopping or stargazing) or doing (hiking, jeep-riding). If you can, plan to be in Sedona midweek, when the weekend crowds aren't around.

Outdoors enthusiasts should head to Flagstaff for a day to enjoy the Mount Elden Trail System or hit the slopes at Arizona Snowbowl. The evening can be spent enjoying dinner at one of downtown Flagstaff's many restaurants, followed by constellation viewing at the Lowell Observatory.

Prescott and Jerome can be combined for a day or less. You can check out the pulse of downtown Prescott's art and music scene on famous Whiskey Row, then spend a night in a historic hotel; Jerome has amazing vistas, several quaint B&Bs, and a shopping district with more affordable treasures than Sedona.

Getting Here and Around

Don't plan on flying into Flagstaff, Sedona, or Prescott; commercial flights are limited. Plus the scenery on the two-hour drive from Phoenix is gorgeous.

It makes sense to rent a car in this region, since trails and monuments stretch miles past city limits and many area towns can't be reached by the major bus companies. The major rental agencies have offices in Flagstaff, Prescott, and Sedona. Avoid interstates when possible; the back ways can be more direct and have the best views of the stunning landscape. Instead of Interstate 17, take AZ 89A through Verde Valley and Oak Creek Canyon. Weekend traffic around Sedona can be heavy, so leave early and allow extra time.

Hotels

Flagstaff and Prescott have the more affordable lodging options, with lots of comfortable motels and B&Bs, but no real luxury. The opposite is true in Sedona, which is filled with opulent resorts and hideaways, most offering solitude and spa services—just don't expect a bargain. Reservations are essential for Sedona and suggested for Flagstaff and Prescott in summer. Little Jerome has a few B&Bs, but call ahead if you think you might want to spend the night. If you're in for a thrill, many of the historic hotels have haunted rooms.

Restaurants

You'll find lots of American comfort food in this part of the country: barbecue restaurants, steak houses, and burger joints predominate. If you're looking for something different, Sedona and Flagstaff have the majority of good, multiethnic restaurants in the area, and if you're craving Mexican, you're sure to find something authentic and delicious (note that burritos are often called "burros" around here). Sedona is the best place in the area for fine dining, although Flagstaff and Prescott now boast a few upscale eateries. Some area restaurants close in the slower months of January and February, so call ahead. Reservations are suggested April through October.

Hotel and restaurant reviews have been shortened. For full information, visit Fodors.com.

What it Costs			
$	$$	$$$	$$$$
RESTAURANTS			
Under $13	$13–$20	$21–$30	Over $30
HOTELS			
Under $121	$121–$175	$176–$250	Over $250

Williams

59 miles south of Grand Canyon National Park, 36 miles west of Flagstaff.

If you are heading to the Grand Canyon from points west, Williams makes sense as a base, especially if you want to take the Grand Canyon Railway. The mountain town encompasses a nicely preserved half mile of Route 66, originally built to accommodate adventurous cross-country motorists. Sure, there are kitschy 1950s diners and souvenir shops, along with cowboys who enact staged gunfights on the streets, but you'll also find good restaurants, charming lodging, a few microbreweries, and outdoor activities like hiking, biking, and fishing.

GETTING HERE AND AROUND

From Flagstaff, you can take Exit 165 to reach the historic downtown area. You'll end up on Railroad Avenue, the one-way westbound street. If you're coming from points west, take Exit 163, Grand Canyon Boulevard, into the heart of town. Most shops and restaurants are along Route 66 (also called Main Street) and Railroad Avenue, which runs parallel. The Williams Visitor Center is on the corner of Railroad Avenue and Grand Canyon Boulevard, and there's a free parking lot next to it. The Grand Canyon Railway Depot is across the tracks.

ESSENTIALS

VISITOR INFORMATION Williams Visitor Center. ✉ *200 W. Railroad Ave., at Grand Canyon Blvd.* ☎ *928/635–4061* 🌐 *experiencewilliams.com.*

Sights

Bearizona Wildlife Park

ZOO | FAMILY | Drive through three miles of ponderosa pine forest in this wildlife park to observe black bears up close in their natural environment, all from the comfort of your car. You can also walk through a zoo setting to see animals including otters, beavers, reindeer, porcupines, wolves, and bobcats, more than half of which were rescued. It's a good stop for families who need a detour on the way to the Grand Canyon's South Rim, one hour away. ✉ *1500 E. Route 66* ☎ *928/635-2289* 🌐 *bearizona.com* 🎟 *$25.*

Planes of Fame Air Museum

LOCAL INTEREST | FAMILY | A good stop 30 miles north of Williams, at the junction of U.S. 180 and State Route 64 in Valle, is this satellite of the Air Museum Planes of Fame in Chino, California. The museum chronicles the history of aviation with an array of historic and modern aircraft. One of the featured pieces is a C-121A Constellation "Bataan," the personal aircraft General MacArthur used during the Korean War. Guided tours of this historic plane are offered for a $3 fee. ✉ *755 Mustang Way, Valle* ☎ *928/635–1000* 🌐 *planesoffame.org* 🎟 *$10* 🕒 *Closed Dec.–Mar.*

Restaurants

Cruisers Café 66

$$ | AMERICAN | FAMILY | Patterned after a '50s-style high-school hangout (but with cocktail service), this diner pleases kids and adults with a large menu of family-priced American classics—good burgers and fries, barbecue pork sandwiches, salads, and ribs. A large mural of the town's heyday along the "Mother Road" and historic cars out front make this a Route 66 favorite. **Known for:** burgers and barbecue; nice patio; craft beers from local brewery. [$] *Average main: $16* ✉ *233 W. Rte. 66* ☎ *928/635–2445* 🌐 *www.cruisers66.com.*

★ Red Raven Restaurant

$$$ | ECLECTIC | This dapper bistro in the heart of downtown Williams, with warm lighting and romantic booth seating, blends American, Italian, and Asian ingredients into creative and delicious fare. Specialties include a starter of crisp tempura shrimp salad with a ginger-sesame dressing and mains like charbroiled salmon with basil butter over cranberry–pine nut couscous. **Known for:** upscale dining in Williams; good wine list; continental and Italian specialties. [$] *Average main: $27* ✉ *135 W. Rte. 66* ☎ *928/635–4980* 🌐 *www.redravenrestaurant.com* 🕒 *Closed Sun.–Tues.*

Twisters

$ | AMERICAN | FAMILY | Kick up some Route 66 nostalgia at this old-fashioned soda fountain, bar, and kitschy gift shop built in 1926. Dine on burgers and hot dogs, a famous Twisters sundae (topped with raspberry sauce, nuts, and hot fudge), Route 66 beer float, or cherry phosphate—all to the sounds of '50s tunes. **Known for:** ice cream novelties; retro decor and above-average gift shop; burgers and brews. [$] *Average main: $9* ✉ *417 E. Rte. 66* ☎ *928/635–0266* 🌐 *www.route66place.com* ⏰ *Closed Sun. Closed Jan. and Feb.*

Hotels

Canyon Motel and RV Park

$ | **HOTEL** | **FAMILY** | Sleep in a historic railcar or a stone cottage from a 1938 motor lodge at this 13-acre property at the forest's edge on the outskirts of Williams. **Pros:** family-friendly property with train cars, horseshoes, playground, and indoor swimming pool; general store; friendly and helpful owners. **Cons:** short drive to restaurants and shops; RV-park traffic; rate for train car rooms much higher. [$] *Rooms from: $107* ✉ *1900 E. Rodeo Rd., Rte. 66* ☎ *928/635–9371* 🌐 *www.thecanyonmotel.com* 🛏 *23 units* 🍴 *No meals.*

Grand Canyon Railway Hotel

$$$$ | **HOTEL** | **FAMILY** | Designed to resemble the train depot's original Fray Marcos Hotel, this upscale place features attractive Southwestern-style accommodations with large bathrooms and comfy beds with upscale linens. **Pros:** railway package options and convenience; indoor pool and outdoor playground; short walk from historic downtown restaurants and bars. **Cons:** large-scale property; pricey for these parts; pets must be boarded at on-site kennel. [$] *Rooms from: $269* ✉ *233 N. Grand Canyon Blvd.* ☎ *928/635–4010, 800/843–8724* 🌐 *www.thetrain.com* 🛏 *298 rooms* 🍴 *No meals.*

The Red Garter

$$ | **B&B/INN** | This restored saloon and bordello from 1897 now houses a small, antiques-filled B&B. **Pros:** on-site coffeehouse and café; decorated in antiques and period pieces; steps from several restaurants and bars. **Cons:** all rooms are only accessible by stairs; parking is across the street; no children under 8. [$] *Rooms from: $165* ✉ *137 Railroad Ave.* ☎ *928/635–1484, 800/328–1484* 🌐 *www.redgarter.com* 🛏 *4 rooms* 🍴 *No meals.*

Sheridan House Inn

$$$ | **B&B/INN** | Nestled among 2 acres of pine trees a half mile uphill from Route 66, this upscale B&B has decks with good views and a flagstone patio with a hot tub. **Pros:** quiet location; scrumptious breakfasts; warm, helpful hosts. **Cons:** must drive to downtown Williams, where parking is scarce; no children under 16; some rooms are upstairs (no elevator). [$] *Rooms from: $185* ✉ *460 E. Sheridan Ave.* ☎ *928/814–2809* 🌐 *www.sheridanhouseinn.com* 🛏 *8 rooms* 🍴 *Free breakfast.*

Activities

Devil Dog Loop Trail

BICYCLING | Cyclists can enjoy the scenery along abandoned sections of Route 66 on this easy 5-mile trail. Maps of mountain bike trails are available at the Williams Visitor Center or on the Kaibab National Forest website. ✉ *Williams* 🌐 *www.fs.usda.gov/kaibab.*

Flagstaff

146 miles northwest of Phoenix, 27 miles north of Sedona via Oak Creek Canyon.

Few travelers slow down long enough to explore Flagstaff, a city of 72,000 known locally as "Flag"; most stop only to spend the night at one of the town's many motels before making the last leg of the trip to the Grand Canyon, 80 miles north. Flag makes a good base for day trips to ancient Native American sites and the Navajo and Hopi reservations, as well as to Petrified Forest National Park and the Painted Desert, but the city is a worthwhile destination in its own right. Set against a lovely backdrop of pine forests and the snowcapped San Francisco Peaks, Flagstaff is a laid-back college town with a frontier flavor.

The Arizona Snowbowl isn't just for winter; the chairlift has great views year-round.

In summer Phoenix residents head here seeking relief from the desert heat, because at any time of the year temperatures in Flagstaff are about 20°F cooler than in Phoenix. They also come to Flagstaff in winter to ski at the Arizona Snowbowl, about 15 miles northeast of town among the San Francisco Peaks.

GETTING HERE AND AROUND

Flagstaff lies at the intersection of Interstate 40 (east–west) and Interstate 17 (running south from Flagstaff), 146 miles north of Phoenix via Interstate 17. If you're driving from Sedona to Flagstaff or the Grand Canyon, head north on AZ 89A through the wooded Oak Creek Canyon: it's the most scenic route.

Flagstaff Airport is 3 miles south of town off Interstate 17 at Exit 337. American flies from Phoenix to Flagstaff, and United has direct flights to Denver and Dallas. A taxi from Flagstaff Airport to downtown should cost about $15. Cabs aren't regulated; some, but not all, have meters, so it's wise to agree on a rate before you leave for your destination.

Amtrak comes into the downtown Flagstaff station twice daily. There's no rail service into Prescott or Sedona, but Groome Transportation provides shuttle van service between Phoenix Sky Harbor Airport, Sedona, Flagstaff, Williams, and the Grand Canyon. Sun Taxi and Tours will take you around Flagstaff or to any place in northern Arizona.

A walking-tour map of the area is available at the visitor center in the Tudor Revival–style train depot, an excellent place to begin sightseeing.

PLANNING YOUR TIME

You can see much of Flagstaff in a day—especially if you visit the Lowell Observatory in the evening—but plan an extra day or two for outdoor adventures and nearby Native American sites.

Consult the schedule of tour times if you want to visit the Riordan Mansion State Historic Park. Devote at least an hour to the excellent Museum of Northern Arizona. The Historic Downtown District is a great place for lunch or dinner and

The tunnels of Lava River Cave were formed by lava flow hundreds of thousands of years ago.

shopping. If you're a skier, spend part of a winter's day at the Arizona Snowbowl; in summer and fall, you can ride the chairlift for a fantastic view at nearly 11,000 feet. Take your time enjoying the trails on Mount Elden, and remember to pace yourself in the higher elevations. The Lava River Cave is an easy—if dark—hike that can be done comfortably in an hour; Walnut Canyon, where you can walk through ancient cliff dwellings, is only 20 minutes east of town.

ESSENTIALS

TRANSPORTATION CONTACTS Groome Transportation. ☎ 928/350–8466 ⊕ *www. groometransportation.com.* **Sun Taxi and Tours.** ☎ *928/779–1111.*

VISITOR INFORMATION Flagstaff Visitor Center. ⊠ *Santa Fe Depot, 1 E. Rte. 66, Downtown* ☎ *928/774–9541, 800/842–7293* ⊕ *www.discoverflagstaff.com.*

💿 Sights

Arizona Snowbowl

VIEWPOINT | FAMILY | Although the Arizona Snowbowl is still one of Flagstaff's biggest attractions, snowy slopes can be a luxury in times of drought. Fortunately visitors can enjoy the beauty of the area year-round, with or without the fluffy white stuff. The chairlift climbs the San Francisco Peaks to a height of 10,800 feet, and doubles as a 30-minute scenic skyride in summer. From this vantage point you can see up to 70 miles; views may even include Sedona's red rocks and the Grand Canyon. There's a lodge at the base with a restaurant, bar, and ski school. To reach the ski area, take U.S. 180 north from Flagstaff; it's 7 miles from the Snowbowl exit to the skyride entrance. ⊠ *Snowbowl Rd., North Flagstaff* ☎ *928/779–1951* ⊕ *www.snowbowl.ski* ☒ *Skyride $19.*

Historic Downtown District

NEIGHBORHOOD | Storied Route 66 runs right through the heart of downtown Flagstaff. The late-Victorian, Tudor Revival, and early–art deco architecture in this district recall the town's heyday as a logging and railroad center. The **Santa Fe Depot** now houses the visitor center. The 1927 **Hotel Monte Vista**, built after a community drive raised $200,000 in 60 days, is one of the art-deco highlights of the district; today it houses a coffeehouse and cocktail bar. The 1888 **Babbitt Brothers Building** was constructed as a building-supply store and then turned into a department store by David Babbitt, the mastermind of the Babbitt empire. (The Babbitts are one of Flagstaff's wealthiest founding families.) The Weatherford Hotel, built in 1900, hosted many celebrities; Western author Zane Grey wrote *The Call of the Canyon* here. Most of the area's first businesses were saloons catering to railroad construction workers, which was the case with the 1888 **Vail Building**. Nowadays, downtown is a bustling dining and retail district, with restaurants, bakeries, and alluring shops. Across the railroad tracks, the revitalized Southside is home to popular eateries and craft breweries. ⊠ *Rte. 66 north to Birch Ave., and Beaver St. east to Agassiz St., Downtown.*

Lava River Cave

CAVE | FAMILY | Subterranean lava flow formed this mile-long cave roughly 700,000 years ago. Once you descend into its boulder-strewn maw, the cave is spacious, with 40-foot ceilings, but claustrophobes take heed: about halfway through, the cave tapers to a 4-foot-high squeeze that can be a bit unnerving. A 40°F chill pervades the cave throughout the year so take warm clothing.

To reach the turnoff for the cave, go approximately 9 miles north of Flagstaff on U.S. 180, then turn west onto Forest Road (FR) 245. Turn left at the intersection of FR 171 and look for the sign to the cave. Note: these forest roads are closed from mid-November to March due to snow. The trip is approximately 45 minutes from Flagstaff. Although the cave is on Coconino National Forest Service property, there are no rangers on-site; the only thing here is an interpretive sign, so it's definitely something you tackle at your own risk. ■ TIP→ **Pack a flashlight (or two).** ⊠ *FR 171B* ⊕ *fs.usda.gov/coconino.*

★ Lowell Observatory

OBSERVATORY | FAMILY | In 1894 Boston businessman, author, and scientist Percival Lowell founded this observatory from which he studied Mars. His theories of the existence of a ninth planet sowed the seeds for the discovery of Pluto at Lowell in 1930 by Clyde Tombaugh. The 6,500-square-foot Steele Visitor Center hosts exhibits and lectures and has a stellar gift shop. Several interactive exhibits—among them Pluto Walk, a scale model of the solar system—appeal to children. Visitors can peer through several telescopes at the Giovale Open Deck Observatory, including the 24-inch Clark telescope and the McAllister, a 16-inch reflector telescope. ■ TIP→ **The observatory is open and unheated, so dress for the outdoors.** ⊠ *1400 W. Mars Hill Rd., West Flagstaff* ☎ *928/774–3358, 928/233–3212 for recorded info* ⊕ *www.lowell.edu* ☑ *$15.*

Museum of Northern Arizona

MUSEUM | FAMILY | This institution, founded in 1928, is respected worldwide for its research and for its collections centering on the natural and cultural history of the Colorado Plateau. Among the permanent exhibitions are an extensive collection of Navajo rugs and a Hopi *kiva* (men's ceremonial chamber).

A gallery devoted to area geology is usually a hit with children: it includes a life-size model dilophosaurus, a carnivorous dinosaur that once roamed northern Arizona. Outdoors a life-zone exhibit shows the changing vegetation from the bottom of the Grand Canyon to the highest peak in Flagstaff. A nature trail, open only in summer, heads down across a small stream into a canyon and up into an aspen

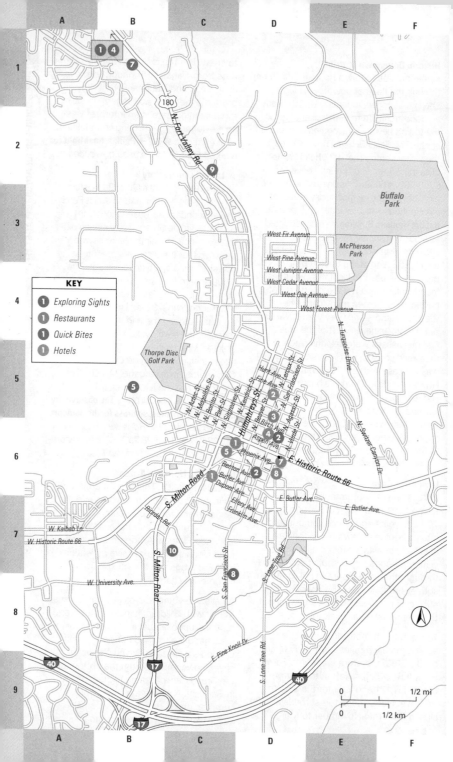

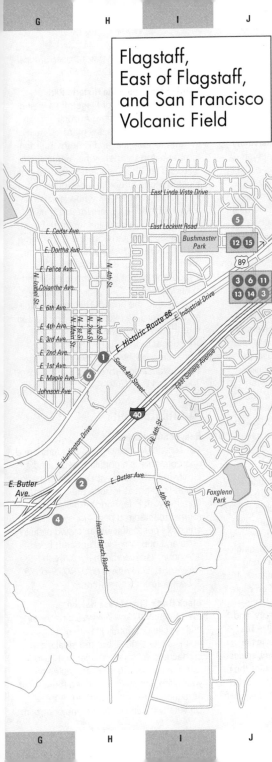

Flagstaff, East of Flagstaff, and San Francisco Volcanic Field

grove. Also in summer the museum hosts exhibits and the works of Native American artists, whose wares are sold in the well-stocked museum gift shop. ⊠ *3101 N. Fort Valley Rd., North Flagstaff* ☎ *928/774–5213* ⊕ *musnaz.org* 🖼 *$12.*

Northern Arizona University Observatory

OBSERVATORY | FAMILY | This observatory was built in 1952 by Dr. Arthur Adel, a scientist at Lowell Observatory whose study of infrared astronomy pioneered research into molecules that absorb light passing through Earth's atmosphere. Today's studies of Earth's shrinking ozone layer rely on some of Dr. Adel's early work. Visitors to the observatory—open only on Friday evenings for viewing through one of the largest research-grade telescopes that the public is allowed to move and manipulate—are hosted by friendly students and faculty members of the university's Department of Astronomy and Planetary Science. Dr. Adel's 24-inch telescope—the first infrared scope—is also on display. ⊠ *Dept. of Astronomy and Planetary Science, S. San Francisco St., Bldg. 47, University* ⊹ *Just north of Walkup Skydome, in front of the ROTC Building* ☎ *928/523–2661* ⊕ *www.physics.nau.edu* 🖼 *Free* ⊙ *Closed Sat.–Thurs.*

Pioneer Museum

MUSEUM | FAMILY | The Arizona Historical Society operates this museum in a volcanic-rock building constructed in 1908. The structure was Coconino County's first hospital for the poor, and the current displays include one of the depressingly small nurses' rooms, an old iron lung, and a reconstructed doctor's office. Most of the exhibits, however, touch on more cheerful aspects of Flagstaff history—like road signs, farming machinery, and pioneer children's games. ■TIP➔ **The museum holds folk-crafts festivals in the summer, with blacksmiths, weavers, spinners, quilters, and candle makers.** Some of their crafts are sold in the museum's gift shop. ⊠ *2340 N. Fort Valley Rd., North Flagstaff*

☎ *928/774–6272* ⊕ *www.arizonahistoricalsociety.org* 🖼 *$8* ⊙ *Closed Sun.*

Riordan Mansion State Historic Park

HOUSE | This artifact of Flagstaff's logging heyday is near Northern Arizona University. The centerpiece is a mansion built in 1904 for Michael and Timothy Riordan, lumber-baron brothers who married two sisters. The 13,300-square-foot, 40-room log-and-stone structure—designed by Charles Whittlesley, who was also responsible for El Tovar Hotel at the Grand Canyon—contains furniture by Gustav Stickley, father of the American Arts and Crafts design movement. One room holds "Paul Bunyan's shoes," a 2-foot-long pair of boots made by Timothy in his workshop. Everything on display is original to the house. The inside of the mansion may be explored only by guided tour (hourly on the hour); reservations are suggested. ⊠ *409 W. Riordan Rd., University* ☎ *928/779–4395* ⊕ *www.arizonahistoricalsociety.org* 🖼 *$12* ⊙ *Closed Tues. and Wed. Nov.–Apr.*

🍴 Restaurants

Beaver Street Brewery

$$ | AMERICAN | FAMILY | This restaurant and microbrewery is a popular, casual, and family-friendly place with a pleasant patio. Wood-fired pizzas include the Enchanted Forest—with Brie, Portobello mushrooms, roasted red peppers, spinach, and artichoke pesto. **Known for:** crowd-pleasing pizza and pub fare; excellent craft beers; late hours. $ *Average main: $16* ⊠ *11 S. Beaver St., Downtown* ☎ *928/779–0079* ⊕ *beaverstreetbrewery.com.*

Black Bart's Steakhouse Saloon

$$$ | AMERICAN | The Wild West decor at this rollicking, brightly lit barn of a restaurant is a bit cornball, but the steaks and barbecue chicken are tender and flavorful; just don't expect to see vegetables on your plate unless they're deep-fried. A big attraction here is the Northern Arizona University music students who entertain

while waiting tables, so don't be surprised when your server suddenly jumps onstage to belt out some show tunes. **Known for:** singing servers; good steaks; family-friendly entertainment. $ *Average main: $30* ⊠ *2760 E. Butler Ave., Downtown* ☎ *928/779–3142* ⊕ *www.blackbartssteakhouse.com* ⊘ *No lunch.*

★ Brix Restaurant & Wine Bar

$$$ | AMERICAN | A redbrick carriage house, built around 1910 as a garage for one of the first automobiles in Flagstaff, is home to one of the city's most sophisticated restaurants. With a seasonally updated menu, the chef pairs locally raised pork, beef, and roasted duck with wines from a list of almost 200 bottles (Brix refers to the sugar content of grapes at harvest). **Known for:** consistently delicious, locally sourced food; extensive wine list; commitment to sustainability. $ *Average main: $29* ⊠ *413 N. San Francisco St., Downtown* ☎ *928/213–1021* ⊕ *www.brixflagstaff. com* ⊘ *Closed Sun. and Mon. No lunch.*

Diablo Burger

$ | AMERICAN | With juicy burgers made from locally sourced, antibiotic- and hormone-free beef, this is arguably the best burger joint in the Southwest. Freshly cut french fries lightly dusted with herbs, veggie burgers, grilled cheese sandwiches, and organic salads round out the menu. **Known for:** best (and locally sourced) burgers; English muffin buns; crowds at lunchtime. $ *Average main: $12* ⊠ *Heritage Square, 120 Leroux St., Downtown* ☎ *928/774–3274* ⊕ *www. diabloburger.com.*

Pizzicletta

$$ | ITALIAN | When you take your first bite of any one of the five expertly crafted pizzas on the menu—like the simple tomato, basil, and mozzarella, or the mascarpone, pecorino, arugula, and prosciutto—you'll understand why this small eatery has developed a fierce following. Plates of paper-thin cured meats and olives and salads with chevre and pine nuts are

equally delicious. **Known for:** elevating pizza-making to an art; homemade gelato; cool vibe. $ *Average main: $15* ⊠ *203 W. Phoenix Ave., Downtown* ☎ *928/774–3242* ⊕ *pizzicletta.com* ⊘ *No lunch.*

Salsa Brava

$$ | MEXICAN | FAMILY | This cheerful Mexican restaurant, with light-wood booths and colorful designs, eschews heavy Sonoran-style fare in favor of the grilled dishes found in Guadalajara. It's considered the best Mexican food in town. **Known for:** unpretentious, fresh Mexican food; plenty of gluten-free dishes; happy hour tacos. $ *Average main: $14* ⊠ *2220 E. Rte. 66, East Flagstaff* ☎ *928/779–5293* ⊕ *www.salsabravaflagstaff.com.*

★ Tinderbox Kitchen

$$$ | MODERN AMERICAN | This deservedly popular downtown spot serves modern comfort food to local professionals and visiting foodies. Signature entrées include pesto-coated salmon and a grown-up, Southwestern take on mac 'n' cheese with spicy jalapeño and duck-leg confit. **Known for:** upscale comfort food; hip, sophisticated vibe; outstanding wine list. $ *Average main: $28* ⊠ *34 S. San Francisco St., Downtown* ☎ *928/226–8400* ⊕ *www.tinderboxkitchen.com* ⊘ *No lunch.*

Tourist Home All Day Cafe

$ | AMERICAN | FAMILY | The creative team that owns Tinderbox Kitchen and Annex Cocktail Lounge reclaimed the decaying building next door and turned it into the trendiest breakfast and lunch spot around. Breakfast burritos, eggs Benedict, salads, and sandwiches all get a modern spin, and the quinoa falafel makes a great burger or vegan "hash-bowl." Decadent desserts and a selection of daytime cocktails are equally alluring. **Known for:** breakfast served all day; fresh salads, sandwiches, and desserts; best patio dining. $ *Average main: $12* ⊠ *52 S. San Francisco St., Downtown* ☎ *928/779–2811* ⊕ *touristhomecafe.com* ⊘ *No dinner.*

☕ Coffee and Quick Bites

Eat n' Run

$ | **AMERICAN** | Breakfast, lunch, and coffee on the run has risen to new heights with the presence of this friendly café on Route 66, a few miles east of downtown Flagstaff. Exceptional smoothies, breakfast burritos, and five kinds of avocado toast, plus generous salads and sandwiches with house-made dressings and sauces accompany the coffee bar. **Known for:** great coffee; healthy (and delicious) breakfast and lunch; fast, friendly service. $ *Average main: $9* ⊠ *2400 W. Rte 66, East Flagstaff* ☎ *928/679–9818* ⊕ *flagstafflunchdelivery.com* ⊗ *Closed Sun. No dinner.*

★ Macy's European Coffee House and Bakery

$ | **VEGETARIAN** | Students, skiers, new and aging hippies, and just about everyone else who likes good coffee (and delicious vegetarian fare) jam into Macy's European Coffee House and Bakery for the best cup in town. **Known for:** best coffeehouse hangout in town; light vegetarian fare; breakfast pastries. $ *Average main: $8* ⊠ *14 S. Beaver St., Downtown* ☎ *928/774–2243* ⊕ *www. macyscoffee.net.*

🛏 Hotels

Trains pass through the downtown area along Route 66 about every 15 minutes throughout the day and night. Light sleepers may prefer to stay in the south or east section of town to avoid hearing trains rumbling through; at least the whistles are no longer blown within the downtown district.

Drury Inn & Suites

$$$ | **HOTEL** | So clean it sparkles, the Drury Inn sits at the edge of Northern Arizona University's campus and packs in the amenities, like happy hour dinner and drinks, an indoor pool, and comfy lounge areas with mountain views. **Pros:** plenty of extras; great location (walk to campus and historic district); spacious and well-equipped rooms. **Cons:** large-scale property; generic-looking rooms; the parking garage is a bit of a trek. $ *Rooms from: $179* ⊠ *300 S. Milton Rd., Downtown* ☎ *928/773–4900* ⊕ *www.druryhotels. com* ⇨ *160 rooms* ⊙ *Free breakfast.*

The Inn at 410

$$$ | **B&B/INN** | This downtown B&B in a beautifully restored 1907 residence—an inviting alternative to Flagstaff's chain motels—has spacious suites with private baths and fireplaces, some with two-person Jacuzzi tubs. **Pros:** convenient downtown location; romantic; complimentary cookies and cocktails every afternoon. **Cons:** some rooms are upstairs (no elevator); no children allowed; two-night minimum stay during high season. $ *Rooms from: $199* ⊠ *410 N. Leroux St., Downtown* ☎ *928/774–0088, 800/774–2008* ⊕ *www.inn410.com* ⇨ *10 suites* ⊙ *Free breakfast.*

Little America Hotel Flagstaff

$$$ | **HOTEL** | **FAMILY** | This deservedly popular hotel is a little distance from the roar of the trains, the grounds are surrounded by evergreen forests, and it's one of the few places in Flagstaff with room service. **Pros:** large, clean rooms; many amenities, including restaurant, gym, pool, and store; walking trails through the forested grounds. **Cons:** large-scale property; a few miles east of the shopping and dining district; some highway noise outside (but rooms are quiet). $ *Rooms from: $214* ⊠ *2515 E. Butler Ave., Downtown* ☎ *928/779–7900, 800/352–4386* ⊕ *flagstaff.littleamerica. com* ⇨ *247 rooms* ⊙ *No meals.*

Starlight Pines Bed and Breakfast

$$ | **B&B/INN** | If you prefer the clean lines of 1920s design to Victorian froufrou, consider staying at this stylish B&B on the city's quieter, residential east side. **Pros:** pretty, immaculate rooms, all with claw-foot tubs; hospitable hosts and lavish breakfasts; one room has a balcony

with a view of San Francisco Peaks. **Cons:** a 10-minute drive from downtown; no elevator; two-night minimum in summer. [$] *Rooms from: $169* ✉ *3380 E. Lockett Rd., East Flagstaff* ☎ *928/527–1912* 🌐 *www.starlightpinesbb.com* 🛏 *4 rooms* 🍴 *Free breakfast.*

Nightlife

Flagstaff's large college contingent has plenty of places to gather after dark; most are in historic downtown and charge little or no cover. It's easy to walk from one rowdy spot to the next. Use the Brewery Trail Map (🌐 *www.flagstaffale-trail.com*) to guide you to six breweries within a 1-mile radius. During the summer months, catch free, family-friendly performances (music, theater, and dance) and movies Thursday to Saturday evening outdoors at Heritage Square. For information on what's going on, pick up the free *Flagstaff Live*.

Annex Cocktail Lounge

BARS/PUBS | The hip crowd here tends to be post-college and more affluent; the cocktails are creative, the food is great, and there's often live music on the wraparound patio. ✉ *50 S. San Francisco St., Downtown* ☎ *928/226–8400* 🌐 *www.annexcocktaillounge.com.*

Monte Vista Lounge

MUSIC CLUBS | This lounge in the historic Hotel Monte Vista packs 'em in most nights with live blues, jazz, classic rock, and punk. ✉ *Hotel Monte Vista, 100 N. San Francisco St., Downtown* ☎ *928/779–6971* 🌐 *www.hotelmontevista.com.*

Museum Club Roadhouse and Danceclub

MUSIC CLUBS | Fondly known as the Zoo, this Flagstaff institution once housed an extensive taxidermy collection in the 1930s and is now a popular country-and-western club (a few owls still perch above the dance floor). A gigantic log cabin constructed around five trees, with a huge, wishbone-shape pine as the entryway, the venue offers a taste of Route 66 color along with live music and other events. ✉ *3404 E. Rte. 66, Downtown* ☎ *928/440–5214* 🌐 *www.museumclub.net.*

★ Weatherford Hotel

MUSIC CLUBS | You'll find four bars here: Charly's Pub & Grill hosts late-night jazz and blues bands, while the smaller Exchange Pub tends to attract folksy ensembles. In the basement, the Gopher Hole has a game room and live music on Friday and Saturday nights. The Zane Grey Ballroom upstairs affords a great view of the city. Good food and historical charm enhance the experience. ✉ *23 N. Leroux St., Downtown* ☎ *928/779–1919* 🌐 *weatherfordhotel.com.*

Performing Arts

There's no shortage of cultural entertainment in Flagstaff, including several summer festivals.

A Celebration of Native American Art

CULTURAL FESTIVALS | During the summer months, art festivals highlighting the Zuni (May), Hopi (July), and Navajo (August) cultures take place at the Museum of Northern Arizona. ✉ *3101 N. Fort Valley Rd., North Flagstaff* ☎ *928/774–5213* 🌐 *musnaz.org.*

Flagstaff Arts Council/Coconino Center for the Arts

ARTS CENTERS | Many excellent art exhibitions, theatrical productions, and music performances take place at Coconino Center for the Arts under the direction of the Flagstaff Arts Council. ✉ *2300 N. Fort Valley Rd., North Flagstaff* ☎ *928/779–2300* 🌐 *www.flagartscouncil.org.*

Flagstaff Symphony Orchestra

MUSIC | Classical concerts from September to April, mostly held in Ardrey Auditorium on the NAU campus, are given by the Flagstaff Symphony Orchestra. ☎ *928/774–5107, 888/520–7214 for NAU ticket office* 🌐 *www.flagstaffsymphony.org.*

Orpheum Theater

FILM | The 1917 Orpheum Theater, in the heart of the historic district, features music acts, films, lectures, and plays. ⊠ *15 W. Aspen Ave., Downtown* ☎ *928/556–1580* ⊕ *www.orpheumflagstaff.com.*

Theatrikos Theatre Company

THEATER | This highly regarded performance-art group produces five mainstage productions annually using a diverse base of local talent. ⊠ *11 W. Cherry Ave., Downtown* ☎ *928/774–1662* ⊕ *theatrikos.com.*

🛍 Shopping

The Artists' Gallery

CRAFTS | For fine arts and crafts— everything from ceramics and stained glass to weaving and painting—visit the Artists' Gallery, a local artists' cooperative. ⊠ *17 N. San Francisco St., Downtown* ☎ *928/773–0958* ⊕ *www.flagstaffartistsgallery.com.*

Babbitt's Backcountry Outfitters

SPORTING GOODS | Just about all your sporting-goods needs can be met at Babbitt's Backcountry Outfitters. ⊠ *12 E. Aspen Ave., Downtown* ☎ *928/774–4775* ⊕ *babbittsbackcountry.com.*

Bookmans

BOOKS/STATIONERY | Packed solid with used books, music, musical instruments, and movies, Bookmans is also a laid-back café where you can munch on pastries, surf the Internet, and hear live folk music. ⊠ *1520 S. Riordan Ranch St., University* ☎ *928/774–0005* ⊕ *bookmans.com.*

Museum of Northern Arizona Gift Shop

GIFTS/SOUVENIRS | High-quality Native American art, jewelry, and crafts can be found at the Museum of Northern Arizona Gift Shop. ⊠ *3101 N. Fort Valley Rd., North Flagstaff* ☎ *928/774–5213* ⊕ *musnaz.org.*

Winter Sun Trading Company

GIFTS/SOUVENIRS | This company sells medicinal herbs, unique fragrances, and Native American jewelry and crafts. ⊠ *107 N. San Francisco St., Suite 1, Downtown* ☎ *928/774–2884* ⊕ *www.wintersun.com.*

Zani Cards and Gifts

BOOKS/STATIONERY | An excellent selection of artisan jewelry, pottery, gifts, handmade paper, and greeting cards is stocked here, just south of the railroad tracks. ⊠ *107 W. Phoenix Ave., Downtown* ☎ *928/774–9409* ⊕ *www.zanigifts.com.*

🏃 Activities

HIKING

You can explore Arizona's alpine tundra in the San Francisco Peaks, part of the Coconino National Forest, where more than 80 species of plants grow on the upper elevations. The habitat is fragile, so hikers are asked to stay on established trails (there are lots of them). ■**TIP→ Flatlanders should give themselves a day or two to adjust to the altitude before lengthy or strenuous hiking.** The altitude here will make even the hardiest hikers breathe a little harder, so anyone with cardiac or respiratory problems should be cautious about overexertion. Note that most of the forest trails aren't accessible during winter due to snow.

Coconino National Forest–Flagstaff Ranger District

HIKING/WALKING | The rangers of the Coconino National Forest maintain many of the region's trails and can provide you with details on hiking in the area. Excellent maps of the Flagstaff trails are sold here for $12. Both the forest's main office in West Flagstaff and the ranger station in East Flagstaff (5075 N. U.S 89) are open weekdays 8–4. ⊠ *1824 S. Thompson St., West Flagstaff* ☎ *928/527–3600 for main office, West Flagstaff, 928/526–0866 for East Flagstaff office* ⊕ *fs.usda.gov/coconino.*

Elden Lookout Trail

HIKING/WALKING | The most challenging trail in the Mount Elden trail system, which happens to be the route with the most rewarding views, is along the steep switchbacks of the Elden Lookout Trail. If you traverse the full 3 miles to the top, keep your focus on the landscape rather than the tangle of antennae and satellite dishes that greets you at the end. *Difficult.* ✉ *Flagstaff* ✛ *Trailhead: Off U.S. 89, 3 miles east of downtown Flagstaff.*

★ Humphreys Peak Trail

HIKING/WALKING | Climbing Arizona's highest peak is on many a hiker's bucket list, and this 10-mile round-trip to the 12,600-foot summit will satisfy and delight experienced hikers. You'll travel the first few miles through meadows and pine forest; then it's a rocky, steep ascent to the top, where 360-degree views of the Grand Canyon, the Painted Desert and the Verde Valley await. Beware of the thin air at this altitude—the trail starts at 8,800 feet—and set aside a whole day. *Difficult.* ✉ *Trailhead: North end of Snowbowl's lower parking lot; Snowbowl Rd., off AZ 180.*

Kachina Trail

HIKING/WALKING | Those who don't want a long hike can do just the first mile or 2 of the 5-mile-long Kachina Trail; gently rolling, this route is surrounded by huge stands of aspen and offers fantastic vistas. In fall, changing leaves paint the landscape shades of yellow, russet, and amber. *Moderate.* ✉ *Flagstaff* ✛ *Trailhead: Snowbowl Rd., 7 miles north of U.S. 180.*

MOUNTAIN BIKING

With more than 50 miles of urban bike trails and more than 30 miles of challenging forest and mountain trails a short ride from town, it was inevitable that one of Flagstaff's best-kept secrets would leak out. The mountain biking on Mount Elden is on par with that of more celebrated trails in Colorado and Utah. Although there isn't a concise loop trail such as those in Moab, Utah, experienced bikers can create one by connecting Schultz Creek Trail, Sunset Trail, and Elden Lookout Road. Beginners (as well as those looking for rewarding scenery with less of an incline) may want to start with Lower Fort Valley and Campbell Mesa. Local bike-shop staff can help with advice and planning. Pick up a FUTS (Flagstaff Urban Trails System) map at the visitor center detailing low- and no-traffic bike routes around town.

Arizona Nordic Village

BICYCLING | From mid-June through mid-October, the Arizona Nordic Village opens its cross-country trails for mountain biking—good for families and beginners, because they're scenic and not technically challenging. During winter you can rent snow bikes here. ✉ *16848 U.S. 180, North Flagstaff* ✛ *16 miles north of Flagstaff* 🕾 *928/220–0550* ⊕ *www.arizonanordicvillage.com.*

★ Lower Oldham Trail

BICYCLING | Originating on the north end of Buffalo Park in Flagstaff, the Lower Oldham Trail is steep in some sections but rewarding. The terrain rolls, climbing about 800 feet in 3 miles, and the trail is difficult in spots but easy enough to test your tolerance of the elevation. Many fun trails spur off this one; it's best to stop in at the local bike shop to get trail maps and discuss rides with staff who know the area. ✉ *North Flagstaff* ✛ *Trailhead: Buffalo Park, 2400 N. Gemini Rd.*

Schultz Creek Trail

BICYCLING | The popular Schultz Creek Trail is fun and suitable for strong beginners, although seasoned experts will be thrilled as well. Most opt to start at the top of the 600-foot-high hill and swoop down the smooth, twisting path through groves of wildflowers and stands of ponderosa pines and aspens, ending at the trailhead 4 giddy miles later. ✉ *Flagstaff* ✛ *Trailhead: Schultz Pass Rd., near intersection with U.S. 180.*

Sunset Trail

BICYCLING | Near the summit of Mount Elden, Sunset Trail has amazing views off the ridge rendered barren by a 1977 fire. The trail narrows into the aptly nick-named "Catwalk," with precipitous drops a few feet on either side. Fear—either from the 9,000-foot elevation or the sheer exposure—is not an option. You need to be at least a moderately experienced mountain biker to attempt this trail. When combined with Elden Lookout Road and Schultz Creek Trail, the usual loop, the trail totals 15 miles and climbs almost 2,000 feet. You can avoid the slog up Mount Elden by parking one vehicle at the top of Elden Lookout Road, at the trailhead, and a friend's vehicle at the bottom. ⊠ *Flagstaff* ✛ *Trailhead: Elden Lookout Rd., 7 miles from intersection with Schultz Pass Rd.*

EQUIPMENT AND RENTALS
Absolute Bikes

BICYCLING | You can rent mountain bikes, get good advice and gear, and purchase trail maps here. ⊠ *202 E. Rte. 66, Downtown* ☎ *928/779–5969* ⊕ *www.absolutebikes.net.*

ROCK CLIMBING
Flagstaff Climbing Center

CLIMBING/MOUNTAINEERING | The tallest indoor climbing walls in the Southwest can be found at this rock-climbing gym, which also offers guided climbing excursions around the Flagstaff area. ⊠ *205 S. San Francisco St., Downtown* ☎ *928/556–9909* ⊕ *flagstaffclimbing.com.*

SKIING AND SNOWBOARDING

The ski season usually starts in mid-December and ends in mid-April.

Arizona Nordic Village

SKIING/SNOWBOARDING | FAMILY | Nine miles north of Snowbowl Road, the Flagstaff Nordic Center has 25 miles of well-groomed cross-country trails here that are open Thursday through Monday (when there's enough snow). Coffee, hot chocolate, and snacks are served at the lodge. Lessons, equipment rental (with or without lessons), and snow bikes ("fat tires") are available as full-day or half-day packages. ⊠ *16848 U.S. 180, Flagstaff* ✛ *16 miles north of Flagstaff* ☎ *928/220–0550* ⊕ *www.arizonanordicvillage.com.*

Arizona Snowbowl

SKIING/SNOWBOARDING | FAMILY | Seven miles north of Flagstaff off U.S. 180, the Arizona Snowbowl, on the western slope of Mount Humphreys, has 55 downhill runs, eight lifts, and a vertical drop of 2,800 feet. The eight-person Agassiz Lift gondolas whisk skiers 2,000 feet up in seven minutes, affording a fabulous view of the Grand Canyon in the distance. There are two restaurants, an equipment-rental and retail shop, and a SKIwee center for ages four to seven.

All-day adult lift tickets are $99, and children 10 and under can ski for free all season. The closest lodging to the ski area is Snowbowl's Ski Lift Lodge, with cabins and a restaurant at the base of the mountain. Some Flagstaff motels have ski packages that include transportation to Snowbowl. ⊠ *Snowbowl Rd., North Flagstaff* ☎ *928/779–1951, 928/779–4577 for snow report* ⊕ *www.snowbowl.ski.*

TOURS
Ventures

TOUR—SPORTS | The Ventures program, run by the education department of the Museum of Northern Arizona, offers day trips and multiday tours of the area led by local scientists, artists, and historians. Trips might include rafting excursions down the San Juan River, treks into the Grand Canyon or Colorado Plateau backcountry, or bus tours into the Navajo Reservation to visit with Native American artists. Prices start at about $100 for day trips and go up to $1,500 for outdoor adventures. ☎ *928/774–5211* ⊕ *musnaz.org/ventures* ⊠ *From $100.*

East of Flagstaff

Within an hour's drive east of Flagstaff, you'll find plenty of natural and cultural attractions, from craters and volcanoes to Native American art and architecture. After exploring sites like Walnut Canyon and Homolovi State Park, you can take a break by "standing on a corner in Winslow, Arizona," and then tour the beautifully restored La Posada Hotel.

GETTING HERE AND AROUND

From Flagstaff, follow Interstate 40 a few miles east to Exit 204 for Walnut Canyon National Monument. Continue east along the highway for Meteor Crater off Exit 233, a 45-minute drive. Continue east on Interstate 40, to the town of Winslow, about 50 miles from Flagstaff; head 4 miles northeast to see the Hopi pueblos at Homolovi State Park.

◉ Sights

Homolovi State Park

ARCHAEOLOGICAL SITE | *Homolovi* is a Hopi word meaning "place of the little hills." The pueblo sites here are thought to have been occupied between AD 1200 and 1425, and include 40 ceremonial kivas and two pueblos containing more than 1,000 rooms each. The Hopi believe their immediate ancestors inhabited this place, and they consider the site sacred. Many rooms have been excavated and recovered for protection. The Homolovi Visitor Center has a small museum with Hopi pottery and Ancestral Puebloan artifacts; it also hosts workshops on native art, ethnobotany, and traditional foods. Campsites with water and hookups are nearby. ⊠ *AZ 87, Winslow* ✛ *4 miles northeast of Winslow* ☎ *928/289–4106, 877/697–2757 for camping reservations* ⊕ *azstateparks.com/homolovi* ⊠ *$7 per vehicle.*

Meteor Crater

NATURE SITE | FAMILY | A natural phenomenon in a privately owned park 43 miles east of Flagstaff, Meteor Crater is impressive if for no other reason than its sheer size. A hole in the ground 600 feet deep, nearly 1 mile across, and more than 3 miles in circumference, Meteor Crater is large enough to accommodate the Washington Monument or 20 football fields. It was created by a meteorite crash 49,000 years ago.

You can't descend into the crater because of the efforts of its owners to maintain its condition—scientists consider this to be the best-preserved crater on Earth—but guided rim tours give useful background information, and telescopes along the rim offer you a closer look. There's a restaurant on-site, and the gift shop sells specimens from the area and jewelry made from native stones. ⊠ *I–40, Exit 233, Winslow* ☎ *928/289–5898* ⊕ *meteorcrater.com* ⊠ *$22.*

Rock Art Ranch

ARCHAEOLOGICAL SITE | The 3,000 Ancestral Puebloan petroglyphs on this working cattle ranch in Chevelon Canyon are startlingly vivid after more than 1,000 years. Ranch owner Brantly Baird and family will guide you down to the canyon, explaining Western and archaeological history. It's mostly an easy driving and walking tour, except for the climb in and out of Chevelon Canyon, where there are handrails. Baird houses his Native American artifacts and pioneer farming implements in his own private museum. It's out of the way and on a dirt road, but you'll see some of the best rock art in northern Arizona. Reservations are required. ⊠ *Off AZ 99, Winslow* ✛ *15 miles southeast of Winslow* ☎ *928/386–5047* ⊠ *From $35 per person* ⊗ *Closed Sun. Closed Feb.–Apr.*

★ Walnut Canyon National Monument
ARCHAEOLOGICAL SITE | The group of cliff dwellings that make up Walnut Canyon National Monument were constructed by the Sinagua people, who lived and farmed in and around the canyon starting around AD 700. The more than 300 dwellings here were built between 1080 and 1250, and abandoned, like those at so many other settlements in Arizona and New Mexico, around 1300. The Sinagua traded far and wide with other indigenous groups, including people at Wupatki. Even macaw feathers, which would have come from tribes in what is now Mexico, have been excavated in the canyon. Early Flagstaff settlers looted the site for pots and "treasure"; Woodrow Wilson declared this a national monument in 1915, which began a 30-year process of stabilizing the site.

Part of the fascination of Walnut Canyon is the opportunity to enter the dwellings, stepping back in time to an ancient way of life. Some of the Sinagua homes are in near-perfect condition in spite of all the looting, because of the dry, hot climate and the protection of overhanging cliffs. You can reach them by descending 185 feet on the 1-mile, 240-stair, stepped **Island Trail,** which starts at the visitor center. As you follow the trail, look across the canyon for other dwellings not accessible on the path. Island Trail takes about an hour to complete at a normal pace. Those with health concerns should opt for the easier 0.5-mile **Rim Trail,** which has overlooks from which dwellings, as well as an excavated, reconstructed pit house, can be viewed. **■ TIP→ Do not rely on GPS to get here; stick to Interstate 40.** ✉ *Walnut Canyon Rd., Winona* ✣ *3 miles south of I–40, Exit 204* ☎ *928/526–3367* 🌐 *www.nps.gov/waca* 🎟 *$15.*

Winslow
TOWN | Frequent flooding on the Little Colorado River frustrated the attempts of Mormon pioneers to settle here, but with the coming of the railroad the town roared to life. Later Route 66 sustained the community until Interstate 40 passed north of town. New motels and restaurants sprouted near the interstate exits, and the downtown was all but abandoned. Still, visitors wishing to find themselves "standing on a corner in Winslow, Arizona" abound thanks to a song by The Eagles; and the historic masterpiece, La Posada, remains one of the best places to sleep and dine in the state. The town is 58 miles east of Flagstaff on Interstate 40. ✉ *Winslow.*

🛏 Hotels

Pick a historic hotel or site of significance built in the late 19th or early 20th century in northern or eastern Arizona, and there's a good chance architect Mary Jane Colter was part of it. A student of Frank Lloyd Wright, Colter designed La Posada in Winslow, the Painted Desert Inn, and several structures at the Grand Canyon, including the Hopi House. She also decorated the canyon's El Tovar Hotel.

★ La Posada Hotel
$$ | **HOTEL** | One of the great railroad hotels, La Posada ("resting place") exudes the charm of an 18th-century Spanish hacienda, and its restoration has been a labor of love. **Pros:** historic charm; unique architecture; impressive restaurant. **Cons:** mazes of staircases aren't wheelchair-friendly (but ground floor rooms and restaurant are); an hour's drive from Flagstaff; little to do in the town of Winslow. [$] *Rooms from: $129* ✉ *303 E. 2nd St., Winslow* ☎ *928/289–4366* 🌐 *www.laposada.org* 🛏 *51 rooms* 🍴 *No meals.*

A visit to Meteor Crater complements Arizona's many observatories for a different look at the impact of the heavens.

San Francisco Volcanic Field

The San Francisco Volcanic Field north of Flagstaff encompasses 2,000 square miles of fascinating geological phenomena, including ancient volcanoes, cinder cones, valleys carved by water and ice, and the San Francisco Peaks themselves, some of which soar to almost 13,000 feet. Some of the most extensive Native American dwellings in the Southwest are also here: don't miss Sunset Crater and Wupatki. These national monuments can be explored in relative solitude during much of the year.
■ TIP→ **The area is short on services, so fill up on gas and consider taking a picnic.**

GETTING HERE AND AROUND

To get to both Sunset Crater and Wupatki national monuments, take U.S. 89 north out of Flagstaff. After 12 miles, turn right for Sunset Crater. Wupatki National Monument is another 19 miles north on this road.

◉ Sights

Sunset Crater Volcano National Monument
NATURE SITE | Sunset Crater, a cinder cone that rises 1,000 feet, was an active volcano 900 years ago. Its final eruption contained iron and sulfur, which give the rim of the crater its glow and thus its name. You can walk around the base, but you can't descend into the huge, fragile cone. The **Lava Flow Trail,** a half-hour, mile-long, self-guided walk, provides a good view of the evidence of the volcano's fiery power: lava formations and holes in the rock where volcanic gases vented to the surface.

If you're interested in hiking a volcano, head to **Lenox Crater,** about 1 mile east of the visitor center, and climb the 280 feet to the top of the cinder cone. The cinder is soft and crumbly, so wear sturdy, closed-toe shoes. From **O'Leary Peak,** a 5-mile hike from the visitor center on Forest Route 545A, enjoy great views of the San Francisco Peaks, the Painted Desert, and beyond. The trail is an unpaved, rutted road (closed during winter), with a steep 2½-mile hike to the top. To get to the area from Flagstaff, take Santa Fe Avenue east to U.S. 89, and head north for 12 miles; turn right onto the road marked Sunset Crater and go another 2 miles to the visitor center. ✉ *6082 Sunset Crater Rd., Flagstaff ✢ 14 miles northeast of Flagstaff* ☎ *928/526–0502* ⊕ *www.nps.gov/sucr* ✍ *$25 per vehicle, including Wupatki National Monument.*

Wupatki National Monument

ARCHAEOLOGICAL SITE | Families from the Sinagua and other Ancestral Puebloans are believed to have lived together in harmony on the site that is now Wupatki National Monument, farming and trading with one another and with those who passed through. The eruption of Sunset Crater may have influenced migration to this area a century after the event, as freshly laid volcanic cinders held in moisture needed for crops. Although there's evidence of earlier habitation, most of the settlers moved here around 1100 and left the pueblo by about 1250. The 2,700 identified sites contain archaeological evidence of a Native American settlement.

The national monument was named for the Wupatki (meaning "tall house" in Hopi) site, which was originally three stories high, built above an unexplored system of underground fissures. The structure had almost 100 rooms and an open ball court—evidence of Southwestern trade with Mesoamerican tribes for whom ball games were a central ritual. Next to the ball court is a blowhole, a geologic phenomenon in which air is forced upward by underground pressure.

Other sites to visit are Wukoki, Lomaki, and the Citadel, a pueblo on a knoll above a limestone sink. Although the largest remnants of Native American settlements at Wupatki National Monument are open to the public, other sites are off-limits. On Saturdays November through April, free guided 3-mile hikes to backcountry pueblos and petroglyphs are

The Sinagua People ◉

The achievements of the Sinagua people, who lived in north-central Arizona from the 8th through the 15th century, reached their height in the 12th and 13th centuries, when related groups occupied the San Francisco Volcanic Field and Verde Valley. The Sinagua sites around modern-day Camp Verde, Clarkdale, and Flagstaff provide a window onto this remarkable culture. Some of the best examples of surviving Sinagua architecture can be found at Walnut Canyon and Wupatki National Monument, northeast of Flagstaff.

offered (reservations required). Between the Wupatki and Citadel ruins, **Doney Mountain** affords 360-degree views of the Painted Desert and the San Francisco Volcanic Field. It's a perfect spot for a sunset picnic. In summer rangers give lectures. ✉ *Sunset Crater–Wupatki Loop Rd. ✢ 19 miles north of Sunset Crater visitor center* ☎ *928/679–2365* ⊕ *www. nps.gov/wupa* ✍ *$25 per vehicle, including Sunset Crater National Monument.*

Sedona and Oak Creek Canyon

27 miles south of Flagstaff on AZ 89A; 114 miles north of Phoenix, I–17 to AZ 179 to AZ 89A; 60 miles northeast of Prescott, U.S. 89 to AZ 89A.

It's easy to see what draws so many people to Sedona. Red rock buttes—Cathedral Rock, Bear Mountain, Courthouse Rock, and Bell Rock, among others—reach up into an almost-always blue sky, and both colors are intensified by dark-green pine forests. Surrealist Max Ernst, writer Zane Grey, and many filmmakers drew inspiration from these vistas—more than 80 Westerns were shot in the area in the 1940s and '50s alone. .

These days, Sedona lures enterprising restaurateurs and gallery owners from the East and West coasts. New Age followers, who believe that the area contains some of Earth's more important vortexes (energy centers), also come in great numbers, seeking a "vibe" that confers a sense of balance and well-being and enhances creativity.

Expansion since the early 1980s has been rapid, and lack of planning has taken its toll in the form of unattractive developments and increased traffic.

The city of Sedona is young, and there are few historic sites; as many visitors conclude, you don't come to Sedona to tour the town itself. The main downtown activity is shopping, mostly for Southwestern-style paintings, clothing, rugs, and jewelry. Just beyond the shops and restaurants, however, canyons, creeks, ancient dwellings, and the red rocks beckon. The area is relatively easy to hike and bike, or you can take a jeep tour into the hills.

GETTING HERE AND AROUND

Sedona stretches along AZ 89A, its main east-west thoroughfare, and AZ 179, which winds south to the Village of Oak Creek. Uptown, the section with most of the shops and restaurants, is at the east end of AZ 89A. There is metered parking here, or park all day in the free public lot off Jordan Road. Free parking is much more plentiful in West Sedona and the Village of Oak Creek.

The most scenic route into town from Phoenix is taking Interstate 17 to AZ 260 toward Cottonwood, then going northeast on AZ 89A. To reach Sedona a little faster from Phoenix, take Interstate 17 north until you come to AZ 179; it's another winding 7½ miles on that road,

past the Village of Oak Creek, into town. The trip should take about 2 hours. The 27-mile drive north from Sedona to Flagstaff on AZ 89A, which winds its way through Oak Creek Canyon, is breathtaking.

Sedona Airport, in West Sedona, is a base for several air tours but has no regularly scheduled flights.

Groome Transportation makes 16 trips daily between Sedona and Phoenix. You can also get on or off at Camp Verde, Cottonwood, or the Village of Oak Creek. Reservations are required.

Weekend traffic near Sedona, especially during summer months, can approach gridlock on the narrow highways. Leave for your destination at first light to bypass the day-trippers, late risers, and midday heat.

Sedona is roughly divided into three neighborhoods: Uptown, which is a walkable shopping district that encompasses the areas just north and south of the "Y" (where AZ 179 and AZ 89A intersect); West Sedona, which is a 4-mile-long commercial strip chock-full of restaurants and hotels; and the Village of Oak Creek, which lies a few miles south of the "Y" along AZ 179. The Verde Lynx provides bus transportation (and has wheelchair lifts) east and west along AZ 89A and south on AZ 179 until midnight.

Sedona Trolley offers two types of daily orientation tours, both departing from the main bus stop in Uptown and lasting less than an hour. One goes along AZ 179 to the Chapel of the Holy Cross; the other passes through West Sedona to Boynton Canyon (Enchantment Resort). Rates are $20 for one or $30 for both.

If you want to explore the red rocks of Sedona on your own, you can rent a four-wheel-drive vehicle from an agency such as Barlow Adventures; most visitors opt for a jeep tour.

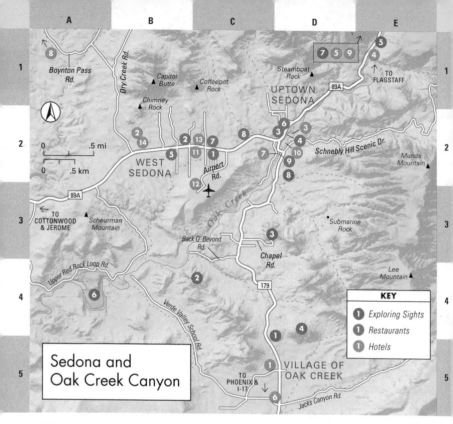

Sedona and Oak Creek Canyon

Sedona Vortex Tour

What is a vortex? The word *vortex* comes from the Latin *vertere*, which means "to turn or whirl." In Sedona a vortex is a funnel created by the motion of spiraling energy. Sedona has long been believed to be a center for spiritual power because of the vortexes of subtle energy in the area. This energy isn't described as electricity or magnetism, though it's said to leave a slight residual magnetism in the places where it's strongest.

New Agers believe there are four major vortexes in Sedona: Airport, Cathedral Rock, Boynton Canyon, and Bell Rock. Each manifests a different kind of energy, and this energy interacts with the individual in its presence. People come from all over the world to experience these energy forms, hoping for guidance in spiritual matters, health, and relationships.

Juniper trees, which are all over the Sedona area, are said to respond to vortex energy in a way that reveals where this energy is strongest. The stronger the energy, the more axial twist the junipers bear in their branches.

Airport Vortex is said to strengthen one's "masculine" side, aiding in self-confidence and focus. **Cathedral Rock Vortex** nurtures one's "feminine" aspects, such as patience and kindness. You'll be directed to **Boynton Canyon Vortex** if you're seeking balance between the masculine and feminine. And finally **Bell Rock Vortex**, the most powerful of all, strengthens all three aspects: masculine, feminine, and balance.

These energy centers are easily accessed, and vortex maps are available at crystal shops all over Sedona.

PLANNING YOUR TIME

In warmer months visit air-conditioned shops at midday and do hiking and jeep tours in the early morning or late afternoon, when the light is softer and the heat less oppressive. Many of the most memorable spots in Sedona are considered energy centers; pick up a vortex map of the area at the visitor center.

The vistas of Sedona from Airport Mesa at sunset can't be beat. The Upper Red Rock Loop has great photo opportunities.

ESSENTIALS

TRANSPORTATION CONTACTS Groome Transportation. ☎ 800/448–7988 in Arizona ⊕ www.groometransportation.com. **Barlow Adventures.** ☎ 928/282–8700 ⊕ barlows.us. **Sedona Trolley.** ☎ 928/282–4211 ⊕ www.sedonatrolley.com. **Verde Lynx.** ☎ 928/634–2287 ⊕ www.ride-cat.com.

VISITOR INFORMATION Sedona Visitor Center. ✉ 331 Forest Rd., Uptown ✛ Just off AZ 89A ☎ 928/282–7722, 800/288–7336 ⊕ visitsedona.com.

👁 Sights

Bell Rock

NATURE SITE | With its distinctive shape right out of your favorite Western film and its proximity to the main drag, this popular butte ensures a steady flow of admirers, so you may want to arrive early in the day. The parking lot next to the Bell Rock Pathway often fills by midmorning, even midweek. The views from here are good, but an easy and fairly accessible path follows mostly gentle terrain for 1 mile to the base of the butte. Mountain bikers, parents with all-terrain baby strollers, and not-so-avid hikers should have little problem getting there. No official

In addition to panoramic views, the Airport Vortex is said to have spirals of energy that strengthen focus.

paths climb the rock itself, but many forge their own routes (at their own risk). ⊠ AZ 179, Big Park ✛ *Several hundred yards north of Bell Rock Blvd.*

Cathedral Rock

NATURE SITE | It's almost impossible not to be drawn to this butte's towering, variegated spires. The approximately 1,200-foot-high Cathedral Rock looms dramatically over town. When you emerge from the narrow gorge of Oak Creek Canyon, this is the first recognizable formation you'll spot. The butte is best seen toward dusk from a distance. Hikers may want to drive to the Airport Mesa and then hike the rugged but generally flat path that loops around the airfield. The trail is ½ mile up Airport Road off AZ 89A in West Sedona; the reward is a panoramic view of Cathedral Rock without the crowds. ■TIP→ **Those not hiking should drive through the Village of Oak Creek and 5 miles west on Verde Valley School Road to its end, where you can view Cathedral Rock from a beautiful streamside vantage point and take a dip in Oak Creek if you wish.** ⊠ *Big Park* ✛ *5 miles to end of Verde Valley School Rd., west off AZ 179.*

Chapel of the Holy Cross

RELIGIOUS SITE | You needn't be religious to be inspired by the setting and the architecture here. Built in 1956 by Marguerite Brunwige Staude, a student of Frank Lloyd Wright, this modern landmark, with a huge cross on the facade, rises between two red rock peaks. Vistas of the town and the surrounding area are spectacular. Though there is only one regular service—a beautiful Taizé service of prayer and song on Monday at 5 pm—all are welcome for quiet meditation.

A small gift shop sells religious artifacts and books. A trail east of the chapel leads you—after a 20-minute walk over occasional loose-rock surfaces—to a seat surrounded by voluptuous red-limestone walls, worlds away from the bustle and commerce around the chapel. ⊠ *Chapel Rd., off AZ 179, Big Park* ☎ *928/282–4069* ⊕ *www.chapeloftheholycross.com* 🖅 *Free.*

Courthouse Butte

NATURE SITE | Toward sunset, when this monolith is free of shadow, the red sandstone seems to catch on fire. From the highway, Courthouse Butte sits in back of Bell Rock and can be viewed without any additional hiking or driving. ⊠ *AZ 179, Central.*

Oak Creek Canyon

CANYON | Whether you want to swim, hike, picnic, or enjoy beautiful scenery framed through a car window, head north through the wooded Oak Creek Canyon. It's the most scenic route to Flagstaff and the Grand Canyon, and worth a drive-through even if you're not heading north. The road winds through a steep-walled canyon, where you crane your neck for views of the dramatic rock formations above. Although the forest is primarily evergreen, the fall foliage is glorious. Oak Creek, which runs along the bottom, is lined with tent campgrounds, fishing camps, cabins, motels, and restaurants. ⊠ *AZ 89A, Oak Creek Canyon* ✛ *Beginning 1 mile north of Sedona.*

Red Rock State Park

NATIONAL/STATE PARK | Two miles west of Sedona via AZ 89A is the turnoff for this 286-acre state park, a less crowded alternative to Slide Rock State Park, though without the possibility of swimming. The 5 miles of interconnected trails are well marked and provide beautiful red rock vistas. There are daily naturalist-led walks and bird-watching excursions on Wednesday and Saturday. ⊠ *4050 Red Rock Loop Rd., West* ☎ *928/282–6907* ⊕ *azstateparks.com/red-rock* ✉ *$7.*

Slide Rock State Park

NATIONAL/STATE PARK | **FAMILY** | A good place for a picnic, Slide Rock is 7 miles north of Sedona. On a hot day you can plunge down a natural rock slide into a swimming hole (bring an extra pair of jeans or a sturdy bathing suit and river shoes to wear on the slide). The site started as an early-20th-century apple orchard, and the natural beauty attracted Hollywood—a number of John Wayne and Jimmy Stewart movies were filmed here.

A few easy hikes run along the rim of the gorge. One downside is the traffic, particularly on summer weekends; you might have to wait to get into the park after midmorning. Unfortunately the popularity of the stream has led to the occasional midsummer closing due to *E. coli*–bacteria infestations; the water is tested daily, and there is a water-quality hotline at ☎ *602/542–0202.* ⊠ *6871 N. AZ 89A, Oak Creek Canyon* ☎ *928/282–3034* ⊕ *azstateparks.com/slide-rock* ✉ *Mid-May–Oct.: $20 per vehicle Mon.–Thurs., $30 per vehicle Fri.–Sun. Mar.–mid-May: $20 per vehicle. Nov.–Feb.: $10 per vehicle.*

Snoopy Rock

NATURE SITE | **FAMILY** | Kids love this butte that looks uncannily like the famed *Peanuts* beagle lying atop red rock instead of his doghouse. You can distinguish the formation from several places around town, including the mall in Uptown Sedona, but to get a clear view, venture up Schnebly Hill Road. Park by the trailhead on the left immediately before the paved road deteriorates to dirt. Marg's Draw, one of several trails originating here, is worthwhile, gently meandering 100 feet down-canyon, through the tortured desert flora to Morgan Road. Backtrack to the parking lot for close to a 3-mile hike. ⊠ *Schnebly Hill Rd., off AZ 179, Central.*

🍴 Restaurants

Some Sedona restaurants close in January and February, so call before you go; if you're planning a visit in high season (April through October), make reservations.

ChocolaTree Organic Oasis

$ | **VEGETARIAN** | The word "oasis" is apt here; you will feel worlds away from everything stressful when you taste their lovingly made vegetarian dishes

Red Rock Geology

It's hard to imagine that the landlocked desert surrounding Sedona was, for much of prehistoric time, an area of dunes and swamps on the shore of an ancient sea. The ebb and flow of this sea shaped the land. When the sea rose, it planed the dunes before dropping more sediment on top. The process continued for a few hundred million years. Eventually the sediment hardened into gray layers of limestone on top of the red sandstone. When North America collided with another continental plate, the land buckled and lifted, forming the Rocky Mountains and raising northern Arizona thousands of feet. Volcanoes erupted in the area, capping some of the rock with erosion-resistant basalt.

Oak Creek started flowing at this time, eroding through the layers of sandstone and limestone. Along with other forces of erosion, the creek carved out the canyons and shaped the buttes. Sedona's buttes stayed intact because a resilient layer of lava had hardened on top and slowed the erosion process considerably. As iron minerals in the sandstone were gradually exposed to the elements, they turned red in a process similar to rusting. The iron minerals, in turn, stained the surrounding colorless quartz and grains of sand—it only takes 2% red-iron material to give the sandstone its red color.

Like the rings of a tree, the striations in the rock document the passage of time and the events: limestone marking the rise of the sea, sandstone indicating when the region was coastline.

while soft, relaxing music plays in the background. Sit indoors, outside on their dog-friendly patio, or in the junglelike rear garden. **Known for:** vegetarian, vegan, and raw selections; heavenly house-made chocolates; organic, locally sourced food. [$] *Average main: $12* ✉ *1595 W. AZ 89A, West* ☎ *928/282–2997* 🌐 *www.chocolatree.com.*

Coffee Pot Restaurant

$ | **AMERICANAMERICAN** | Locals and tourists alike swarm to this spacious, old-school eatery for scrumptious breakfast (served all day) and lunch, served by a friendly waitstaff. One hundred and one omelet options are the stars of the show and include such concoctions as a basic ham and cheese and the quirky peanut butter, jelly, and banana, purportedly Elvis Presley's order back in the day. **Known for:** big omelets; unpretentious all-day breakfast and lunch; family-friendly place. [$] *Average main: $10* ✉ *2050 W. AZ 89A, West* ☎ *928/282–6626* 🌐 *www.coffeepotsedona.com* 🕒 *No dinner.*

Cowboy Club

$$$ | **STEAKHOUSE** | At this restaurant catering to carnivores, you can hang out in the casual Cowboy Club or dine in the more formal Silver Saddle Room, where suede booths are surrounded by cowboy art and a pair of large cattle horns. High-quality cuts of beef are the specialty, but the burgers, grilled trout, and vegetable pot pies are delicious, too. **Known for:** steaks, burgers, and even rattlesnake; old-fashioned Western ambience; institution status. [$] *Average main: $25* ✉ *241 N. AZ 89A, Uptown* ☎ *928/282–4200* 🌐 *www.cowboyclub.com.*

Cress on Oak Creek

$$$$ | **FRENCH** | On the L'Auberge de Sedona resort property, Sedona's most formal—and most expensive—dining room promises a quiet, civilized evening

Did You Know?

Sedona's striking red rocks are often named after their shape, such as Coffee Pot Rock, shown here on the far right.

of indulgence. The menu, a fusion of American cuisine with French influences, is offered as a seven-course meal, and can be paired with selections from the resort's 1,200-bottle wine cellar. **Known for:** elegant creekside dining; filet mignon and coq au vin; pricey prix-fixe menu. $ *Average main: $145* ✉ *L'Auberge de Sedona, 301 L'Auberge La., Uptown* ☎ *928/282–1661* ⊕ *www.lauberge.com.*

Dahl & Di Luca Ristorante Italiano

$$$ | ITALIAN | At this popular Italian restaurant, owned by top-rated chef Lisa Dahl, expect to find delicious home-made soups and specialties like potato gnocchi with a vodka sauce and *pollo piccata* (chicken in a lemon, capers, and Chardonnay sauce). Any pasta dish can be made gluten-free with corn fusilli. **Known for:** excellent Italian; romantic dining; special-occasion setting. $ *Average main: $27* ✉ *2321 W. AZ 89A, West* ☎ *928/282–5219* ⊕ *dahlanddiluca.com* ⊗ *No lunch.*

★ Elote Café

$$$ | MEXICAN | Traditional Mexican recipes get a creative and tasty update at this deservedly popular restaurant. Start with the namesake *elote,* roasted corn on a stick; this Mexican street-food favorite is transformed into an addictive dip of grilled corn kernels, Cotija cheese, lime, and chiles. **Known for:** great creative Mexican food; being one of Sedona's top restaurants; taking reservations. $ *Average main: $27* ✉ *350 Jordan Rd., Uptown* ☎ *928/203–0105* ⊕ *www.elotecafe.com* ⊗ *Closed Sun. and Mon. No lunch.*

Heartline Café

$$$ | EUROPEAN | Fresh flowers and innovative cuisine that even the staff struggle to characterize are this attractive café's hallmarks. Local ingredients pepper the menu, giving a Sedona twist to Continental fare; favorites include pecan-crusted, Sedona-raised trout with Dijon sauce and mesquite-crusted rack of lamb. **Known for:** tasty, creative cooking; intimate setting; stellar desserts. $ *Average main: $29* ✉ *1610 W. AZ 89A, West* ☎ *928/282–3365* ⊕ *www.heartlinecafe. com* ⊗ *Closed Tues. and Wed. No lunch.*

★ Mariposa

$$$$ | LATIN AMERICAN | At this Latin-inspired restaurant in one of Sedona's most picturesque spots, chef-owner Lisa Dahl proves her fourth restaurant in town is another culinary masterpiece. Enjoy tapas, empanadas, and grilled selections with your view, either on the expansive patio or in the more formal, romantic dining room; the experience is worth the splurge. **Known for:** tapas and South American dishes; outstanding wine list; stunning red rock views. $ *Average main: $36* ✉ *700 AZ 89A, West* ☎ *928/862–4444* ⊕ *mariposasedona.com* ⊗ *Closed Tues. and Wed.*

René at Tlaquepaque

$$$$ | EUROPEAN | Ease into plush banquettes at this quiet, lace-curtained restaurant for classic French and Southwest-inspired dishes. Rack of lamb is the house specialty, and the Dover sole is a real find, far from the white cliffs. **Known for:** fine French cooking; flaming desserts; special-occasion splurge. $ *Average main: $35* ✉ *Tlaquepaque Arts & Crafts Village, AZ 179, Unit B–117, Central* ☎ *928/282–9225* ⊕ *renerestaurantsedona.com.*

🛏 Hotels

Adobe Village Inn

$$$ | B&B/INN | All the rooms at this inn south of Sedona have either wood-burning or gas fireplaces, and some of them also have Jacuzzi tubs and balconies that look out onto the red rocks. **Pros:** above-average hospitality; variety of accommodations; close to hiking and biking trails. **Cons:** no elevators; children are not permitted in some rooms and suites; it's a drive to the shopping and dining district. $ *Rooms from: $229* ✉ *150 Canyon Circle Dr., Sedona* ☎ *928/284–1425* ⊕ *www.adobevillageinn.com* ⇆ *15 units* ❢❢ *Free breakfast.*

Alma de Sedona Bed and Breakfast Inn

$$$ | **B&B/INN** | This romantic B&B with spectacular views and ultracomfortable beds was built well off the main drag and in the shadow of the buttes for views and privacy. **Pros:** spacious and private rooms; all rooms have deck or patio with excellent views; peaceful vibe. **Cons:** most rooms only accommodate two; some rooms require climbing stairs; decor could use updating in some rooms. [$] *Rooms from: $199* ✉ *50 Hozoni Dr., West* ☎ *928/282–2737* 🌐 *www.almadesedona.com* 🛏 *12 rooms* 🍴 *Free breakfast.*

Amara Resort and Spa

$$$$ | **RESORT** | The sleek rooms at this boutique property next to gurgling Oak Creek but convenient to town come with many extras, including yoga classes, access to a spa and fitness center, complimentary mountain bikes, and a shuttle to nearby shops and restaurants. **Pros:** good spa and restaurant; walk (or take complimentary shuttle) to Uptown; expansive views. **Cons:** city-chic feels somewhat incongruous with natural setting; 2- and 3-night minimum stay in high season; resort fee raises the already high cost. [$] *Rooms from: $300* ✉ *100 Amara La., Uptown* ☎ *928/282–4828* 🌐 *www.amararesort.com* 🛏 *100 rooms* 🍴 *No meals.*

Briar Patch Inn

$$$$ | **B&B/INN** | This B&B in verdant Oak Creek Canyon exudes rustic elegance in its Southwestern-themed rooms in charming wooden cabins, many with full kitchens and decks overlooking the creek. **Pros:** private and quiet; tranquil creekside setting with beautiful gardens; lavish breakfasts. **Cons:** pricey; some cabins can be dark; two-night minimum stay required some weekends. [$] *Rooms from: $295* ✉ *3190 N. AZ 89A, Oak Creek Canyon* ☎ *928/282–2342, 888/809–3030* 🌐 *www.briarpatchinn.com* 🛏 *19 cottages* 🍴 *Free breakfast.*

The Canyon Wren

$$ | **B&B/INN** | The best value in the Oak Creek Canyon area, this small and serene B&B across the road from the creek has four private cabins, all with kitchens, decks, and views of the canyon walls. **Pros:** romantic yet homey; wonderful hosts and breakfast; foresty feel, with private decks. **Cons:** some cabins close to road; added cleaning fee per stay; some may find the space a little too cozy. [$] *Rooms from: $165* ✉ *6425 N. AZ 89A, Oak Creek Canyon* ☎ *928/282–6900, 800/437–9736* 🌐 *www.canyonwrencabins.com* 🛏 *4 cabins* 🍴 *Free breakfast.*

Desert Quail Inn

$ | **HOTEL** | Close to the lion's share of the trailheads in the Village of Oak Creek, this clean, older property is a good base for outdoor adventures, and the front desk has plenty of maps and advice on offer. **Pros:** large, clean rooms; good value; pool. **Cons:** older two-story roadside motel; no elevators for second-floor rooms; some rooms are closer to road (noise). [$] *Rooms from: $110* ✉ *6626 AZ 179, Sedona* ☎ *928/284–1433, 800/385–0927* 🌐 *www.desertquailinn.com* 🛏 *40 rooms* 🍴 *No meals.*

★ El Portal Sedona Hotel

$$$$ | **B&B/INN** | This stunning hacienda, one of the most beautifully designed boutique hotels in the Southwest, has decor accents including authentic Tiffany and Roycroft pieces, French doors leading to balconies or a grassy central courtyard, stained-glass windows and ceiling panels, river-rock or tile fireplaces, and huge custom-designed beds. **Pros:** attractive rooms and grounds; next to Tlaquepaque shops and restaurants; pet-friendly rooms have private outdoor spaces and no extra fee. **Cons:** location not as secluded as some; pricey (but luxurious); fewer amenities than a resort. [$] *Rooms from: $299* ✉ *95 Portal La., Central* ☎ *928/203–9405, 800/313–0017* 🌐 *www.elportalsedona.com* 🛏 *12 rooms* 🍴 *No meals.*

★ Enchantment Resort

$$$$ | RESORT | A few miles outside town, gorgeous Boynton Canyon is the setting for this luxurious resort and its world-class destination spa, Mii amo. **Pros:** gorgeous setting next to great hiking trails; state-of-the-art spa; numerous on-site activities. **Cons:** 20-minute drive into town; world-class luxury comes at a price; property is spread out. $ *Rooms from: $425* ✉ *525 Boynton Canyon Rd., West* ☏ *928/282–2900, 888/250–1699* ⊕ *www.enchantmentresort.com* ⬎ *118 rooms* ¶❍¶ *No meals.*

Junipine Resort

$$$$ | RESORT | These one- and two-bedroom cabins nestled in a juniper and pine forest (hence the name) are spacious and airy, with vaulted ceilings, wood-burning fireplaces, and large decks overlooking either the creek or the canyon. **Pros:** huge, well-equipped cabins with decks (some with hot tubs); trailheads on-site; wood-burning fireplaces. **Cons:** creek views and hot tubs push up the cost; the group appeal can mean some partying neighbors; 8 miles to Sedona. $ *Rooms from: $360* ✉ *8351 N. AZ 89A, Oak Creek Canyon* ☏ *928/852–4589, 800/742–7463* ⊕ *www.junipine.com* ⬎ *50 cabins* ¶❍¶ *No meals.*

★ L'Auberge de Sedona

$$$$ | RESORT | This elegant resort consists of private hillside units with spectacular views and cozy cottages in the woods along Oak Creek. **Pros:** luxurious rooms and cabins; secluded setting yet close to town; excellent restaurant and bar for romantic creekside dining. **Cons:** in-house restaurant is the most expensive in Sedona; at the upper price point for Sedona lodging; may feel too exclusive for some. $ *Rooms from: $499* ✉ *301 L'Auberge La., Uptown* ☏ *928/282–1661, 855/905–5745* ⊕ *www.lauberge.com* ⬎ *89 units* ¶❍¶ *No meals.*

Lodge at Sedona

$$$ | B&B/INN | Rooms in this rambling wood-and-stone Craftsman house have a refined rustic style; most have fireplaces, and some have jetted tubs, redwood decks, or hot tubs. **Pros:** tranquil setting yet short walk from West Sedona; friendly staff; garden and labyrinth for solitude. **Cons:** limited views; no TV in some rooms; two-night minimum stay on weekends. $ *Rooms from: $229* ✉ *125 Kallof Pl., West* ☏ *928/204–1942, 800/619–4467* ⊕ *www.lodgeatsedona. com* ⬎ *14 rooms* ¶❍¶ *Free breakfast.*

Sky Ranch Lodge

$$$ | HOTEL | There may be no better vantage point in town from which to view Sedona's red rock canyons and sunsets than the private patios and balconies at Sky Ranch Lodge, near the top of Airport Mesa. **Pros:** good value; spectacular views; family- and pet-friendly. **Cons:** driving up and down the hill into town; popular wedding venue means a bit more traffic; no on-site restaurant (patio bar only). $ *Rooms from: $199* ✉ *1105 Airport Rd., West* ☏ *928/282–6400, 888/708–6400* ⊕ *skyranchlodge.com* ⬎ *94 rooms* ¶❍¶ *No meals.*

Sugar Loaf Lodge

$ | HOTEL | Though it may be hard to believe, there are still bargains in Sedona, and this one-story, no-frills, family-run motel delivers. **Pros:** cheap and clean; walk to restaurants and shops in West Sedona; pool and hot tub. **Cons:** older, basic furnishings; smallish rooms; some traffic noise in rooms closer to the road. $ *Rooms from: $105* ✉ *1870 W. AZ 89A, West* ☏ *928/282–9451, 877/282–0632* ⊕ *www.sedonasugarloaf.com* ⬎ *15 rooms* ¶❍¶ *Free breakfast.*

The Suites at Sedona

$$$$ | B&B/INN | At this quiet inn tucked behind the main street in West Sedona, the romantic rooms are exquisitely decorated in an upscale Western motif, complete with genuine cowboy artifacts. **Pros:** hosts go the extra mile to pamper and advise; private decks and hot tubs in most rooms; walking distance to West Sedona restaurants and galleries. **Cons:** first-floor rooms may get noise from upstairs guests; some rooms upstairs (no elevator); no children permitted. [$] *Rooms from: $280* ✉ *2900 Hopi Dr., West* ☎ *928/282–1944, 800/201–1944* 🌐 *www.oldwestbb.com* 🛏 *6 rooms* 🍴 *Free breakfast.*

Nightlife

Nightlife in Sedona tends to be sedate, although on high-season weekends there's usually live music at the Enchantment Resort and the Amara Resort. You can also hear local musicians almost every night at Reds, the restaurant at Sedona Rouge Hotel. Options vary from jazz to rock and pop; in all cases, call ahead. The region's weekly newspaper, *Kudos,* comes out on Wednesday, and provides a comprehensive listing of local entertainment.

Relics Restaurant & Lounge at Rainbow's End

BARS/PUBS | The closest thing to a rollicking cowboy bar in Sedona is Relics Restaurant & Lounge at Rainbow's End, a steak house with a wooden dance floor and live rock or country-and-western music most nights. ✉ *3235 W. AZ 89A, West* ☎ *928/282–1593* 🌐 *relicsrestaurant.com.*

Sound Bites Grill

BARS/PUBS | This casual restaurant and bar offers live music, mostly jazz, on Wednesday through Sunday nights. It also has reasonably priced appetizers and cocktails, and excellent views of the sun setting over the red rocks if you're lucky enough to grab a table by the window or on the outside deck. ✉ *101 N. AZ 89A, Uptown* ☎ *928/282–2713* 🌐 *soundbites-grill.com.*

Performing Arts

Chamber Music Sedona

CONCERTS | From October through May, Chamber Music Sedona hosts a classical concert series. They also host the "Met Live in HD" opera performances and a JazzFest in April. ✉ *Sedona* ☎ *928/204–2415* 🌐 *chambermusicsedona.org.*

Sedona Arts Center

ARTS CENTERS | In addition to offering classes and workshops in all media, this center hosts the Plein Air Festival for a week in October and has a retail gallery selling works of local and regional artists. There's no sales tax, since it's a nonprofit. ✉ *15 Art Barn Rd., Uptown* ☎ *928/282–3809* 🌐 *www.sedonaartscenter.com.*

Sedona International Film Festival

ARTS FESTIVALS | This nine-day festival takes place in late February and features independent films from all over the world. ✉ *2030 W. AZ 89A, West* ☎ *928/282–1177* 🌐 *www.sedonafilmfestival.org.*

Shopping

With a few exceptions, most of the stores in Uptown Sedona north of the "Y" (running along AZ 89A to the east of its intersection with AZ 179) cater to the tour-bus trade with New Age souvenirs and jewelry made by Native American artists. If this isn't your style, the largest concentration of stores and galleries is along AZ 179, just south of the "Y," with plenty of offerings for serious shoppers.

ARTS AND CRAFTS

Esteban's

CRAFTS | Native American crafts and a wide array of ceramics are the focus at Esteban's. ✉ *Tlaquepaque, 336 AZ 179, No. 103, Bldg. B, Uptown* ☎ *928/282–4686* 🌐 *www.estebanssedona.com.*

Garland's Navajo Rugs

HOUSEHOLD ITEMS/FURNITURE | There's a huge collection of new and antique rugs here, as well as Native American kachina dolls, pottery, and baskets. ✉ *411 AZ 179, Uptown* ☎ *928/282–4070* ⊕ *www. garlandsrugs.com.*

James Ratliff Gallery

ART GALLERIES | Fun and functional pieces by up-and-coming artists are exhibited here. ✉ *Hillside Sedona, 671 AZ 179, A1 and A2, Uptown* ☎ *928/282–1404* ⊕ *www.jamesratliffgallery.com.*

Kuivato Glass Gallery

CERAMICS/GLASSWARE | In line with its name, this gallery has gorgeous glass art pieces, including chandeliers, sculptures, bowls, and jewelry. ✉ *Tlaquepaque, 336 AZ 179, No. 125, Bldg. B, Uptown* ☎ *928/282–1212* ⊕ *creativegateways.com.*

JEWELRY

Crystal Magic

BOOKS/STATIONERY | This shop dabbles in the metaphysical, with crystals, jewelry, aromatherapy items, and books for the New Age. ✉ *2978 W. AZ 89A, West* ☎ *928/282–1622* ⊕ *www.crystalmagic.com.*

SHOPPING CENTERS

There are three main art-gallery complexes in Sedona—Hozho, Tlaquepaque, and Hillside, all located just south of the "Y." Each has smaller galleries within the larger complex.

Hillside Sedona

ART GALLERIES | Half a dozen galleries and two popular restaurants, The Hudson and Javelina Cantina, are housed in the Hillside Sedona complex. ✉ *671 AZ 179, Uptown* ☎ *928/282–4500* ⊕ *www. hillsidesedona.net.*

Hozho Center

SHOPPING CENTERS/MALLS | Next door to Hillside Sedona shopping complex on AZ 179, the Hozho Center is a small, upscale complex in a beige Santa Fe–style building, with galleries and fine-art souvenirs. ✉ *431 AZ 179, Uptown.*

★ Tlaquepaque Arts & Crafts Village

SHOPPING CENTERS/MALLS | Home to more than 55 shops and galleries and several restaurants, Tlaquepaque Arts & Crafts Village remains one of the best places for travelers to find mementos from their trip to Sedona. The complex of clay tile–roofed buildings arranged around a series of courtyards shares its name and architectural style with a crafts village just outside Guadalajara. It's a lovely place to browse, but beware: prices tend to be high, and locals joke that it's pronounced "to-lock-your-pocket." ✉ *AZ 179, just south of "Y," Uptown* ☎ *928/282–4838* ⊕ *www.tlaq.com.*

SPORTING GOODS

Canyon Outfitters

SPORTING GOODS | This shop in West Sedona is good for gearing up with maps, clothing, and camping equipment before your outdoor adventures. ✉ *2701 W. AZ 89A, West* ☎ *928/282–5294* ⊕ *www. canyonoutfitterssedona.com.*

★ The Hike House

SPORTING GOODS | A unique shopping experience, The Hike House can not only outfit you from head to toe, they can also match you with a suitable and satisfying hiking itinerary through their interactive Trail Finder service. If you'd rather go on a guided hike, staff can arrange that as well. Grab some cookies, a smoothie, or some strong coffee at the coffee bar before hitting the trail. ✉ *Hozho Center, 431 AZ 179, Uptown* ☎ *928/282–5820* ⊕ *www.thehikehouse.com.*

🏃 Activities

A Red Rock Pass is required to park in the Coconino National Forest from Oak Creek Canyon through Sedona and the Village of Oak Creek. Passes cost $5 for the day, $15 for the week, or $20 for an entire year, and can be purchased online and at the **Coconino Forest Service Red Rock Ranger Station** (✉ *8375 AZ 179, just south of Village of Oak Creek*

Jeep tours get you close to Sedona's red rocks while someone else does the driving.

☎ 928/203–7500 ⊕ www.redrockcoun-
try.org), which is open daily and has
copious information on regional outdoor
activities. Passes are also available from
vending machines at popular trailheads—including Boynton Canyon and
Bell Rock—and at the Sedona Chamber
of Commerce, Circle K stores, grocery
stores, and many Sedona hotels.

BALLOONING

Northern Light Balloon Expeditions

BALLOONING | One of only two companies
with permits to fly over Sedona, Northern
Light Balloon Expeditions offers sunrise
flights, in either 6- or 12-passenger
balloons, that include a postflight champagne breakfast picnic. ☎ 928/282–2274,
800/230–6222 ⊕ www.northernlightbal-
loon.com ☞ $250 per person.

Red Rock Balloon Adventures

BALLOONING | Fly over the red rocks for
about an hour with a Red Rock Balloon
Adventures tour; you'll be served a picnic
upon landing, along with a souvenir DVD.
☎ 800/258–3754, 928/284–0040 ⊕ www.
redrockballoons.com ☞ $225 per person.

GOLF

Oak Creek Country Club

GOLF | This semiprivate 18-hole, par-72
course was designed by the father-son
team of Robert Trent Jones Sr. and
Robert Trent Jones Jr. It is a traditional,
rather than desert, course with long,
tree-lined fairways and slightly elevated greens amid lovely red rock views.
Providing challenges for beginner
through advanced golfers, this course
is described as "player-friendly." It's
budget-friendly, too, in the afternoons:
tee off after 3 pm and the greens fee is
only $81. ✉ 690 Bell Rock Blvd., Sedona
☎ 888/284–1660, 928/295–6400 ⊕ www.
oakcreekcc.com ☜ $139; $104 after 1
pm; $81 after 3 pm ⚲ 18 holes, 6824
yards, par 72.

★ Sedona Golf Resort

GOLF | A gorgeous course, Sedona Golf
Resort was designed by Gary Panks to
take advantage of the many changes
in elevation and scenery. Golf courses
are a dime a dozen in Arizona, but this
one is regarded as one of the best in

the state. Don't let the stunning views around every bend distract your focus from the undulating greens and fairways. The restaurant—with panoramic red rock vistas—serves breakfast and lunch daily. ⊠ *35 Ridge Trail Dr., Big Park* ☎ *928/284–9355* ⊕ *www.sedonagolfresort.com* ☎ *$125; $99 after 12; $80 after 2* ⚘ *18 holes, 6646 yards, par 71.*

HIKING AND BACKPACKING

Among the most popular hikes in Sedona are West Fork Trail (traversing Oak Creek Canyon), Doe Mountain Trail (an easy ascent with many switchbacks), and Cathedral Rock Trail (with panoramic views). Backpacking in the **Red Rock–Secret Mountain Wilderness** near Sedona guarantees stunning vistas, otherworldly rock formations, and Zen-like serenity, but little water, so pack a good supply. ■ **TIP→ Plan your trip for spring or fall: summer brings 100°F heat and sudden thunderstorms that flood canyons without warning.** Most individual trails in the wilderness are too short for anything longer than an overnighter, but several trails can be linked up to form a memorable multiday trip. Contact Coconino National Forest's Red Rock Ranger District in Sedona for hiking and backpacking details.

Cathedral Rock Trail

TRAIL | A vigorous but nontechnical 1½-mile scramble up the slickrock (smooth, rather than slippery, sandstone), this path leads to a nearly 360-degree view of red rock country. Follow the cairns (rock piles marking the trail) and look for the footholds in the rock. Carry plenty of water: though short, the trail offers little shade and the pitch is steep. You can see the Verde Valley and Mingus Mountain in the distance. Look for the barely discernible "J" etched on the hillside marking the former ghost town of Jerome 30 miles away. ⊠ *Sedona* ✛ *Trailhead: about ½ mile down Back O' Beyond Rd. off AZ 179, 3 miles south of Uptown.*

Coconino National Forest–Red Rock Ranger District

HIKING/WALKING | For free detailed maps, hiking advice, and information on campgrounds, contact the rangers of the Coconino National Forest in Sedona. ⊠ *8375 AZ 179, Big Park* ☎ *928/203–7500* ⊕ *www.fs.usda.gov/coconino.*

HORSEBACK RIDING

M Diamond Ranch

HORSEBACK RIDING | Ride on horseback through varied terrain for views of red rocks and the Verde Valley with wranglers at the M Diamond Ranch. One- and two-hour trail rides, as well as cowboy cookouts, are offered, starting at $75. ⊠ *3255 FR 618, Verde* ☎ *928/300–6466* ⊕ *www.sedonahorsebackrides.com.*

Trail Horse Adventures

HORSEBACK RIDING | Among the tour options at Trail Horse Adventures are a midday ride with picnic and a ride along the Verde River to Native American cliff dwellings. Rides range from $65 for an hour to $135 for a three-hour ride with lunch. Pony rides for the youngest wranglers are also available. ⊠ *Dead Horse Ranch State Park, 675 Dead Horse Ranch Rd., Cottonwood* ☎ *928/634–5276* ⊕ *www.trailhorseadventures.com.*

JEEP TOURS

Several jeep-tour operators headquartered along Sedona's main Uptown drag conduct excursions, some focusing on geology, some on astronomy, some on vortexes, some on all three. You can even find a combination jeep tour and horseback ride. Prices start at about $60 per person for two hours and go upward of $100 per person for four hours. Although all the excursions are safe, many aren't for those who dislike heights or bumps.

A Day in the West

TOUR—SPORTS | With this tour operator, you can go to all the prime spots and combine a jeep tour with a horseback ride or local wine tasting. ☎ 928/282–4320, 800/973–3662 ⊕ www.adayinthewest.com ☞ From $75.

Pink Adventure Tours

TOUR—SPORTS | The ubiquitous Pink jeeps are a popular choice for driving through the red rocks. Off-road tours range from 1 to 4 hours; paved-road tours are offered for those seeking a smoother adventure. ✉ 204 N. AZ 89A, Uptown ☎ 800/873–3662, 928/282–5000 ⊕ www.pinkadventuretours.com ☞ From $65.

Red Rock Western Jeep Tours

TOUR—SPORTS | This reliable operator spins some good cowboy tales on its private two-hour jeep tours. ✉ 2900 W. AZ 89A, West ☎ 928/282–6667 ⊕ www.redrockjeep.com ☞ From $249 (for 2–5 people).

MOUNTAIN BIKING

Given the red rock splendor, challenging terrain, miles of single track, and mild weather, you might think Sedona would be a mountain-biking destination on the order of Moab or Durango. Inexplicably you won't find the Lycra-clad throngs · patronizing pasta bars or throwing back microbrews on the Uptown mall, but all the better for you: the mountain-biking culture remains fervent but low-key. A few excellent, strategically located bike shops can outfit you and give advice.

As a general rule, mountain bikes are allowed on all trails and jeep paths unless designated as wilderness or private property. The rolling terrain, which switches between serpentine trails of buff red clay and mounds of slickrock, has few sustained climbs, but be careful of blind drop-offs that often step down several feet in unexpected places. The thorny trailside flora makes carrying extra inner tubes a must, and an inner-tube sealant is a good idea, too. If you plan to ride for

Boynton Canyon ◉

You might want to drive out to Boynton Canyon, sacred to the Yavapai Apache, who believe it was their ancient birthplace. This is also the site of Enchantment Resort, where all are welcome to hike the canyon and stop in for lunch or a late-afternoon drink on the terrace.

several hours, pack a gallon of water and start early in the morning on hot days. Shade is rare, and with the exception of (nonpotable) Oak Creek, water is nonexistent.

Bell Rock Pathway

BICYCLING | For the casual rider, Bell Rock Pathway is a scenic and easy ride traveling 3 miles through some of the most breathtaking scenery in red rock country. Several single-track trails spur off this one, making it a good starting point for many other rides in Sedona. Two bike shops, offering rentals, gear, and info, are a stone's throw from the trailhead. ✉ Sedona ⊹ Trailhead: 5 miles south of Sedona on AZ 179.

★ Broken Arrow–Submarine Rock Trail

BICYCLING | There's good reason why the Broken Arrow–Submarine Rock Trail is perhaps the most popular single-track loop in the area. The 10-mile trail is a heady mixture of prime terrain and scenery following slickrock and twisty trails up to Chicken Point, a sandstone terrace overlooking colorful buttes. The trail continues as a bumpy romp through washes, almost all downhill. Be wary of blind drop-offs in this section. It wouldn't be overly cautious to scout any parts of the trail that look sketchy. ✉ Sedona ⊹ Trailhead: 2 miles south of Sedona, off AZ 179; take Morgan Rd. to Broken Arrow Trail parking lot.

TOURS AND OUTFITTERS

Absolute Bikes

BICYCLING | Close to several biking trails, Absolute Bikes is a good source for rentals, equipment, and advice on trails and conditions. ⊠ *6101 AZ 179, Big Park* ☎ *928/284–1242* ⊕ *www.absolutebikes.net.*

Sedona Bike and Bean

BICYCLING | About a block south of Bell Rock Pathway, the friendly folks at Bike and Bean offer rentals, equipment, trail maps, and their own blend of coffee. ⊠ *30 Bell Rock Plaza, at AZ 179, Big Park* ☎ *928/284–0210* ⊕ *www.bike-bean.com.*

SPAS

While some prefer to harness Sedona's rejuvenating energy at a vortex site, others seek renewal at one of the many spas in town. From all-inclusive spa retreats nestled in red rock canyons to inexpensive bodywork performed by healing-arts students, Sedona has relaxing options for every budget and preference.

With its history of Native American traditions, Sedona is thought of as one of the most sacred healing spots on Earth. Spas incorporate indigenous materials, like red rock clay, into their spa services—and choosing your treatments is part of the pleasure. Some of Sedona's spas are destinations in themselves, offering experiences tailored to individual needs and desires.

★ Mii amo Spa

FITNESS/HEALTH CLUBS | Set in spectacular Boynton Canyon, Mii amo is a state-of-the-art facility with indoor and outdoor pools and treatment rooms. Meditate in the sand-floor crystal grotto before your Watsu water therapy or deep-tissue massage. Take a guided hike or try a yoga, pilates, or photography class. Afterward, dine in the spa's healthful and tasty café (no egg yolks in these omelets), wearing only your spa robe if you like. ⊠ *Enchantment Resort, 525 Boynton Canyon Rd., West* ☎ *928/203–8500, 844/993–9518* ⊕ *www.miiamo.com.*

NAMTI

FITNESS/HEALTH CLUBS | Students and faculty at the Northern Arizona Massage Therapy Institute, NAMTI, offer quality one-hour and 90-minute massage, acupuncture, and facial treatments at lower prices than you'll pay at resort spas in the area. Discounts are given for multiple treatments, such as a facial and a massage, or a seawater crystal body scrub, massage, and hot spot foot treatment. ⊠ *60 Tortilla Dr., West* ☎ *928/282–7737* ⊕ *namti.com.*

Sedona's New Day Spa

FITNESS/HEALTH CLUBS | The popular Sedona's New Day Spa uses local ingredients for their massage oils, exfoliation scrubs and body wraps. Their signature treatments, called Native Wisdom "Soul Journeys," include a psychic reading of your chakras along with a massage. For couples, they have several luxurious packages. ⊠ *3004 W. AZ 89A, West* ☎ *928/282–7502* ⊕ *www.sedonanewday-spa.com.*

The Spa at L'Auberge

FITNESS/HEALTH CLUBS | As one of Sedona's upscale resorts, L'Auberge offers an array of spa amenities for both resort guests and those lodging elsewhere. Here you can indulge in an outdoor massage on the bank of gurgling Oak Creek, or restore balance to your being with an Energy Healing Therapy such as Reiki. Their signature service is the 90-minute Sedona Dreams, which incorporates a ginger-lime exfoliating scrub, aromatherapy, and a hot-stone massage. The spa is intimate, with a rustic yet elegant vibe. ⊠ *L'Auberge de Sedona, 301 L'Auberge La., Uptown* ☎ *800/905–5745, 928/204–4321* ⊕ *www.lauberge.com.*

★ The Spa at Sedona Rouge

FITNESS/HEALTH CLUBS | This spa is like an understated healing environment. Deepak Chopra chooses this simple and tranquil setting for his weeklong "SynchroDestiny" workshop each year. Skilled spa therapists meet with clients first to

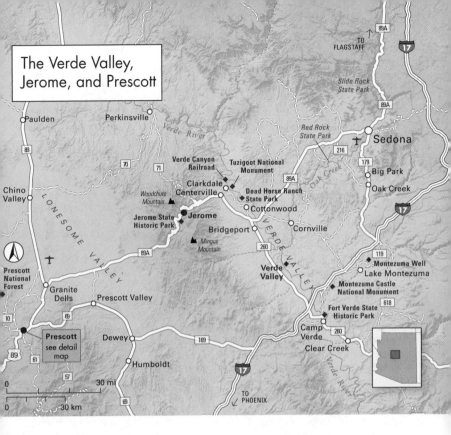

The Verde Valley, Jerome, and Prescott

discuss individual goals before embarking on treatments like the Seven Sacred Pools Massage, which brings balance to the body's seven energy centers, or chakras. Mind-body coaching services and ayurvedic treatments are also popular. The gardens and interior lounges contribute to the overall nourishing experience. Yoga classes ($10) meet daily at 8 am. ⊠ *Sedona Rouge Hotel and Spa, 2250 W. AZ 89A, West* ☎ *866/312–4111, 928/203–4111* ⊕ *www.sedonarouge.com.*

Verde Valley

18 miles southwest of Sedona on AZ 89A, 94 miles north of Phoenix on I–17.

About 90 miles north of Phoenix, as you round a curve approaching Exit 285 off Interstate 17, the valley of the Verde River suddenly unfolds in a panorama of grayish-white cliffs, tinted red in the distance and dotted with desert scrub, cottonwood, and pine.

Often overlooked by travelers on trips to Sedona or Flagstaff, the Verde Valley offers several enjoyable diversions, including wine tasting in Cornville and Cottonwood, as well as the historical wonders at Montezuma Castle and Tuzigoot. And if you're tired of the car, the Verde Canyon Railroad in Clarkdale is a great way to get off-road without doing the driving.

GETTING HERE AND AROUND

From Phoenix, it's a leisurely and picturesque route through Verde Valley. Follow Interstate 17 north 25 miles past Cordes Junction until you see the turnoff for AZ 260, which will take you to Cottonwood in 12 miles. Here you can pick up AZ 89A, which leads southwest to Prescott (41 miles) or northeast to Sedona (19 miles).

◉ Sights

Dead Horse Ranch State Park

NATIONAL/STATE PARK | The 423-acre spread of Dead Horse Ranch State Park, which combines high-desert and wetland habitats, is a pleasant place to while away the day. You can fish in the Verde River or the well-stocked Park Lagoon, or hike on some 6 miles of trails that begin in a shaded picnic area and wind along the river; adjoining forest service pathways are available for hikers and mountain bikers who enjoy longer journeys. Birders can check off more than 100 species from the Arizona Audubon Society lists provided by the rangers. Bald eagles perch along the Verde River in winter, and the common black hawks—a misnomer for these threatened birds—nest here in summer. The park is 1 mile north of Cottonwood, off Main Street. ⊠ *675 Dead Horse Ranch Rd., Cottonwood* ☎ *928/634–5283* ⊕ *azstateparks.com/dead-horse* 🎫 *$7 per car for up to four people.*

Fort Verde State Historic Park

MILITARY SITE | The military post for which Fort Verde State Historic Park is named was built between 1871 and 1873 as the third of three fortifications in this part of the Arizona Territory. To protect the Verde Valley's farmers and miners from Tonto Apache and Yavapai raids, the fort's administrators oversaw the removal of nearly 1,500 Native Americans to the San Carlos and Fort Apache reservations. A museum details the history of the area's military installations, and three furnished officers' quarters show the day-to-day living conditions of the top brass. It's a good break from the interstate if you've been driving for too long. ⊠ *125 E. Hollamon St., Camp Verde* ☎ *928/567–3275* ⊕ *azstateparks.com/fort-verde* 🎫 *$7.*

Did Someone ◉ Say Dead Horses?

In the late 1940s, when Calvin "Cap" Ireys asked his family to help him choose between the ranches he was thinking about buying in the Verde Valley, his son immediately picked "the one with the dead horse on it." Ireys sold the land to the state in 1973 at one-third of its value, with the stipulation that the park into which it was to be converted retain the ranch's colorful name.

Montezuma Castle National Monument

ARCHAEOLOGICAL SITE | The five-story, 20-room cliff dwelling at Montezuma Castle National Monument was named by explorers who believed it had been erected by the Aztecs. Southern Sinagua Native Americans actually built the roughly 600-year-old structure, which is one of the best-preserved prehistoric dwellings in North America—and one of the most accessible. An easy, paved trail (0.3 mile round-trip) leads to the dwelling and to the adjacent Castle A, a badly deteriorated six-story living space with about 45 rooms. No one is permitted to enter the site, but a viewing area is close by. From Interstate 17, take Exit 289 and follow signs to Montezuma Castle Road. ⊠ *Montezuma Castle Rd., Camp Verde* ⊹ *7 miles northeast of Camp Verde* ☎ *928/567–3322* ⊕ *www.nps. gov/moca* 🎫 *$10 (includes admission to Tuzigoot National Monument).*

Montezuma Well

BODY OF WATER | A limestone sinkhole with a limpid blue-green pool lying in the middle of the desert, Montezuma Well is 11 miles north of Montezuma Castle National Monument and equally striking. This cavity—55 feet deep and 365 feet across—is all that's left of an ancient subterranean cavern; the water remains at a constant 76°F year-round. It's a short

Cliff dwellings of the Sinagua people have been preserved for about 600 years at Montezuma Castle.

hike, but the peace, quiet, and views of the Verde Valley reward the effort. There are some Sinagua and Hohokam sites here, too. ✉ *Montezuma Well Rd., Camp Verde* ✛ *Off I–17 at Exit 293, 4 miles east of freeway* ⊕ *www.nps.gov/moca.*

Tuzigoot National Monument

NATIVE SITE | Impressive in scope, Tuzigoot National Monument is a complex of the Sinagua people, who lived on this land overlooking the Verde Valley from about AD 1000 to 1400. The pueblo, constructed of limestone and sandstone blocks, once rose three stories and incorporated 110 rooms. Inhabitants were skilled dry farmers and traded with peoples hundreds of miles away. Implements used for food preparation, as well as jewelry, weapons, and farming tools excavated from the site, are displayed in the visitor center. Within the site, you can step into a reconstructed room. ✉ *25 W. Tuzigoot Rd., Clarkdale* ✛ *3 miles north of Cottonwood* ☎ *928/634–5564* ⊕ *www.nps.gov/ tuzi* ✉ *$10 (includes admission to Montezuma Castle National Monument).*

★ Verde Canyon Railroad

TOUR—SIGHT | Train buffs come to the Verde Valley to catch the 22-mile Verde Canyon Railroad, which follows a dramatic route through the Verde Canyon, the remains of a copper smelter, and much unspoiled desert that is inaccessible by car. The destination—the city of Clarkdale—might not be that impressive, but the ride is undeniably scenic. Knowledgeable announcers regale riders with the area's colorful history and point out natural attractions along the way—in winter you're likely to see bald eagles.

This four-hour trip is especially popular in fall-foliage season and in spring, when the desert wildflowers bloom; book well in advance. Upgrade to more comfortable, living-room-like first-class cars, where hors d'oeuvres and a champagne toast are included in the price (a cash bar is also available) for $99. Reservations are required. ✉ *Arizona Central Railroad, 300 N. Broadway, Clarkdale* ☎ *800/582–7245* ⊕ *www.verdecanyonrr.com* ✉ *$74.*

Getting there is half the fun with a classic train ride on the Verde Canyon Railroad.

WINERIES

Almost a dozen vineyards are nestled in the Verde Valley, and most offer daily wine tastings. Three notable vineyards are along Page Springs Road in Cornville. In Old Town Cottonwood's tasting rooms, you can sample wines from this area as well as from Willcox in the southern part of the state. Download a Verde Valley wine trail map at ⊕ *vvwinetrail.com.*

Javelina Leap Vineyard & Winery

WINERY/DISTILLERY | Predominantly red wines with bold, dry flavors are produced by Javelina Leap Vineyard. Taste a few here and you'll be welcomed by the owners as if you were family. ⊠ *1565 Page Springs Rd., Cornville* ☎ *928/649–2681* ⊕ *www.javelinaleapwinery.com.*

Oak Creek Vineyards & Winery

WINERY/DISTILLERY | This winery offers Syrah, Merlot, Chardonnay, and dessert wines. You can also munch on panini here or pick up fixings for a picnic—salami, cheeses, crackers, and chocolates. ⊠ *1555 N. Page Springs Rd., Cornville* ☎ *928/649–0290* ⊕ *oakcreekvineyards.net.*

★ Page Springs Cellars

WINERY/DISTILLERY | The award-winning wines at Page Springs Cellars focus on grapes popular in the Rhône wine region of France. Sit outside on the deck overlooking Oak Creek and enjoy the wines, as well as antipasti plates and pizzas. There's live music on some evenings, and you can take a tour Friday–Sunday ($34 includes wine tasting). ⊠ *1500 N. Page Springs Rd., Cornville* ☎ *928/639–3004* ⊕ *pagespringscellars.com.*

🍴 Restaurants

Manzanita Restaurant

$$$ | EUROPEAN | You might not expect to find sophisticated cooking in Cornville, 6 miles east of Cottonwood, but the German fare here, made using organic produce whenever possible, proves it can be done. Game like elk and bison, plus recipes such as Trout Almondine and lamb chops with demi-glace are all beautifully presented, and the sauerbraten and Wiener schnitzel don't disappoint. **Known for:** well-prepared German dishes;

gracious service; wild game. $ *Average main: $27* ⊠ *11425 E. Cornville Rd., Cornville* ☏ *928/634–8851* ⊕ *www. themanzanitarestaurant.com* ⊘ *Closed Mon. and Tues.*

⚡ Activities

Black Canyon Trail

HIKING/WALKING | This trail is a bit of a slog, rising more than 2,200 feet in 6 miles, but the reward is grand views from the gray cliffs of Verde Valley to the red buttes of Sedona to the blue range of the San Francisco Peaks. *Difficult.* ⊠ *AZ 260, Camp Verde* ✛ *4 miles south of Cottonwood, then 4½ miles east on FR 359.*

Prescott National Forest-Verde Ranger District

BOATING | The Verde Ranger District office of the Prescott National Forest is a good resource for places to hike, fish, and boat along the Verde River. ⊠ *300 E. AZ 260, Camp Verde* ☏ *928/567–4121* ⊕ *www. fs.usda.gov/prescott.*

Jerome

20 miles northwest of Camp Verde, 3½ miles southwest of Clarkdale, 33 miles northeast of Prescott, 25 miles southwest of Sedona on AZ 89A.

Jerome was once known as the Billion Dollar Copper Camp, but after the last mines closed in 1953, the booming population of 15,000 dwindled to 50 determined souls. Although its population has risen back to almost 500, Jerome still holds on to its "ghost town" designation, and several B&Bs and eateries regularly report spirit sightings. It's hard to imagine that this town was once the location of Arizona's largest JCPenney store and one of the state's first Safeway supermarkets. Jerome saw its first revival during the mid-1960s, when hippies arrived and turned it into an arts colony of sorts, and it has since become a tourist attraction. In addition to its shops and historic sites, Jerome is worth visiting for its scenery: it's built into the side of Cleopatra Hill, and from here you can see Sedona's red rocks, Flagstaff's San Francisco Peaks, and even Eastern Arizona's Mogollon Rim country.

Jerome is about a mile above sea level, but structures within town sit at elevations that vary by as much as 1,500 feet, depending on whether they're on Cleopatra Hill or at its foot. Blasting at the United Verde (later Phelps Dodge) mine regularly shook buildings off their foundations—the town's jail slid across a road and down a hillside, where it sits today. And that's not all that was unsteady about Jerome. In 1903 a reporter from a New York newspaper called Jerome "the wickedest town in America," due to its abundance of drinking and gambling establishments—town records from 1880 list 24 saloons. Whether by divine retribution or drunken accidents, the town burned down several times.

GETTING HERE AND AROUND

You can get a map of the town's shops and its attractions at the visitor-information trailer on AZ 89A (which becomes Hull Street). The three streets in the main shopping area—Hull, Main, and Hill—run parallel to each other on the hillside. Street parking is easy to come by, but be prepared for some steep climbing up and down Cleopatra Hill when you're exploring by foot.

PLANNING YOUR TIME

The town can easily be explored in an afternoon with a stop for lunch, but the historic charm and shopping opportunities entice some visitors to stay overnight. Jerome currently has around 50 retail establishments (that's more than one for every 10 residents). Attractions and businesses don't always stay open as long as their stated hours if things are slow.

At the top of the idyllic mountain town of Jerome sits a hotel that is said to be haunted.

ESSENTIALS

VISITOR INFORMATION Jerome Chamber of Commerce & Visitor Center. ✉ *310 Hull Ave., off AZ 89A* ☏ *928/634–2900* ⊕ *jeromechamber.com.*

⊙ Sights

Jerome State Historic Park

MUSEUM | Of the three mining museums in town, the most inclusive is part of Jerome State Historic Park. At the edge of town, signs on AZ 89A will direct you to the turnoff for the park, reached by a short, precipitous road. The museum occupies the 1917 mansion of Jerome's mining king, Dr. James "Rawhide Jimmy" Douglas Jr., who purchased Little Daisy Mine in 1912. You can tour the mansion and see tools and heavy equipment used to grind ore; some minerals are on display, but accounts of the town's wilder elements—such as the House of Joy brothel—are not so prominently featured. Just outside the mansion/park gates is Audrey Head Frame Park, where you can peer 1,900 feet down into the

Daisy Mineshaft. ✉ *100 Douglas Rd.* ☏ *928/634–5381* ⊕ *azstateparks.com/jerome* 🎟 *$7.*

Mine Museum

MUSEUM | Run by the Jerome Historical Society, the Mine Museum in downtown Jerome focuses on the social history of miners in the area. The museum's collection of mining stock certificates alone is worth the (small) price of admission—the amount of money that changed hands in this town 100 years ago boggles the mind. ✉ *200 Main St.* ☏ *928/634–5477* ⊕ *jeromehistoricalsociety.com* 🎟 *$2.*

🍴 Restaurants

★ The Asylum Restaurant

$$$ | **AMERICAN** | Don't be put off by the name, a tribute to its past identity—this charming restaurant inside the Jerome Grand Hotel is the standout choice in town for fine dining, good wines, and wonderful vistas. Burgundy interior walls hung with local artists' work create a warm and romantic setting for creative

Southwest fare. **Known for:** fine dining in Jerome; stellar views; excellent wine list. [$] *Average main: $28 ⌧ 200 Hill St. ☎ 928/639–3197 ⊕ www.asyluminjerome.com.*

Haunted Hamburger

$$ | AMERICAN | After the climb up the stairs from Main Street to this former boardinghouse, you'll be ready for the hearty burgers, chili, cheese steaks, and ribs that dominate the menu. Lighter fare, including salads and veggie wraps, are also available. **Known for:** burgers and shakes; deluxe views from the patio; a resident ghost. [$] *Average main: $13 ⌧ 410 Clark St. ☎ 928/634–0554 ⊕ www. thehauntedhamburger.com.*

Coffee and Quick Bites

The Flatiron

$ | AMERICAN | Ask where to have breakfast, lunch, or a coffee, and nearly every Main Street shop owner will direct you to this tiny eatery at the fork in the road. The menu includes egg dishes, healthful salads and sandwiches, gluten-free pastries, and many coffee drinks. **Known for:** favorite daytime hangout for locals; good coffee; breakfast. [$] *Average main: $12 ⌧ 416 Main St. ☎ 928/634–2733 ⊕ www. theflatironjerome.com ⊗ Closed Tues. and Wed. No dinner.*

Hotels

Ghost City Inn

$ | B&B/INN | The outdoor veranda at this 1898 B&B affords sweeping views of the Verde Valley and Sedona. **Pros:** authentic historic charm; fabulous views; walking distance to restaurants and shops. **Cons:** some rooms are small; climbing stairs is required for both first and second-floor rooms; no children under 14. [$] *Rooms from: $105 ⌧ 541 N. Main St. ☎ 928/634–4678, 888/634–4678 ⊕ www. ghostcityinn.com ⇱ 6 rooms ⭤ Free breakfast.*

Jerome Grand Hotel

$$ | HOTEL | This full-service hotel at the highest point in town, housed in Jerome's 1927 former hospital, has comfy rooms with homey furnishings that part with the institutional past, and many have splendid views. **Pros:** historic property with knockout views; great restaurant; great ghost-hunting. **Cons:** a little creaky (and possibly haunted); steep walk down hill to shops; close-by parking is limited. [$] *Rooms from: $165 ⌧ 200 Hill St. ☎ 928/634–8200, 888/817–6788 ⊕ jeromegrandhotel.net ⇱ 29 rooms ⭤ Free breakfast.*

★ The Surgeon's House

$$$ | B&B/INN | Plants, knickknacks, bright colors, and plenty of sunlight make this beautiful Mediterranean-style home a welcoming place to stay. **Pros:** friendly host and fabulous breakfast; beautiful vistas; private patios and unique gardens. **Cons:** rigid breakfast time; climbing some stairs is required; children under 15 permitted only with prior approval. [$] *Rooms from: $210 ⌧ 101 Hill St. ☎ 928/639–1452 ⊕ www.surgeonshouse.com ⇱ 4 rooms ⭤ Free breakfast.*

Nightlife

Jerome's a ghost town, so don't expect a hopping nightlife—although there are some places to have fun.

Paul & Jerry's Saloon

BARS/PUBS | The two pool tables and old wooden bar at Paul & Jerry's Saloon attract a regular crowd (relatively speaking). ⌧ *206 Main St. ☎ 928/634–2603.*

Spirit Room

BARS/PUBS | On weekends there's live music and a lively scene at the Spirit Room. The mural over the bar harks back to the days when it was a dining spot for the prostitutes of the red-light district. ⌧ *166 Main St. ☎ 928/634–8809 ⊕ www. spiritroom.com.*

🛍 Shopping

Jerome has its share of art galleries (some perched precariously on Cleopatra Hill), along with boutiques, and they're funkier than those in Sedona. Main Street and just around the bend Hull Avenue are Jerome's two primary shopping streets. Your eyes may begin to glaze over after browsing through one boutique after another, most offering tasteful Southwestern paraphernalia.

Jerome Artists Cooperative Gallery

ART GALLERIES | The focus at this gallery is on jewelry, sculpture, painting, and pottery by local artists. ✉ 502 Main St. ☎ 928/639–4276 ⊕ www.jeromecoop. com.

★ Nellie Bly Kaleidoscopes and Art Glass

CERAMICS/GLASSWARE | This shop specializes in art glass and beautiful, hand-made kaleidoscopes—they claim to have the world's largest collection of them—made by artists from around the country. ✉ 136 Main St. ☎ 928/634–0255 ⊕ www. nellieblyscopes.com.

Pura Vida Gallery

ART GALLERIES | Step into this lovely shop filled with handmade jewelry, ceramics, glass, and fiber art, and you're sure to find gifts for yourself and as many friends as your wallet will allow. ✉ 501 School St. ☎ 928/634–0937 ⊕ puravidagalleryjerome.com.

Raku Gallery

HOUSEHOLD ITEMS/FURNITURE | You'll find wrought-iron furniture, free-blown glass, jewelry, and textiles at Raku Gallery, which stocks the work of about 300 artists. ✉ 250 Hull Ave. ☎ 928/639–0239 ⊕ www.facebook.com/ RakuGalleryJeromeAZ.

Prescott

33 miles southwest of Jerome on AZ 89A to U.S. 89, 100 miles northwest of Phoenix via I–17 to AZ 69.

In a forested bowl 5,300 feet above sea level, Prescott is a prime summer refuge for Phoenix-area dwellers. It was proclaimed the first capital of the Arizona Territory in 1864 and settled by Yankees to ensure that gold-rich northern Arizona would remain a Union resource. (Tucson and Southern Arizona were strongly pro-Confederacy.) Although early territorial settlers thought that the area's original inhabitants were of Aztec origin, today it's believed that they were ancestors of the Yavapai, whose reservation is on the outskirts of town. The Aztec theory—inspired by *The History and Conquest of Mexico,* a popular book by historian William Hickling Prescott, for whom the town was named—has left its mark on such street names as Montezuma, Cortez, and Alarcon.

Despite a devastating downtown fire in 1900, Prescott remains the "West's most Eastern town," with a rich trove of late-19th-century New England–style architecture. The cowboy spirit endures, though, especially in the shops, museums, and saloons in the downtown district. With two institutions of higher education, Yavapai College and Prescott College, Prescott could be called a college town, but it doesn't really feel like one, perhaps because so many retirees have also moved here, drawn by the temperate climate and low cost of living.

The 1916 Yavapai County Courthouse stands in the heart of Prescott, bounded by Gurley, Goodwin, Cortez, and Montezuma streets, and guarded by an equestrian bronze of turn-of-the-20th-century journalist and lawmaker Bucky O'Neill, who died while charging San Juan Hill in Cuba with Teddy Roosevelt during the Spanish-American War. Those interested in architecture will enjoy the Victorian neighborhoods. Many Queen Annes have been beautifully restored, and a number are now B&Bs. The town takes great pride in its pioneer heritage and hosts two popular events: the Cowboy Poets Gathering in August, and Frontier Days—including the world's oldest rodeo—over July 4.

GETTING HERE AND AROUND

The most direct route to Prescott from Phoenix is to take Interstate 17 north for 60 miles to Cordes Junction and then drive northwest on AZ 69 for 36 miles into town. Interstate 17, a four-lane divided highway, has several steep inclines and descents (complete with a number of runaway-truck ramps), but it's generally an easy and scenic thoroughfare.

Prescott Municipal Airport is 8 miles north of town on U.S. 89. United Airlines affiliate Skywest offers service to and from Los Angeles and Denver.

The city's main drag is Gurley Street, which AZ 69 turns into from the east. You can usually find street parking along Gurley or on the side streets as you approach town, or use the free public garage on Granite Street, between Gurley and Goodwin. Most of the town's Victorian neighborhoods, shops, and restaurants, best explored on foot, are within walking distance of the Courthouse Plaza, sitting just off Gurley Street on Montezuma. Art galleries and saloons line Cortez and Montezuma Streets to the north and west of the courthouse. The Prescott Chamber of Commerce & Visitor Center is on Goodwin Street, across from the courthouse and next to the post office.

ESSENTIALS

TRANSPORTATION CONTACT Prescott Regional Airport. ☎ *928/777–1114* ⊕ *www. prcairport.com.*

VISITOR INFORMATION Prescott Chamber of Commerce & Visitor Center. ✉ *117 W. Goodwin St., across from courthouse* ☎ *928/445–2000, 800/266–7534* ⊕ *www. prescott.org.*

⊙ Sights

Museum of Indigenous People

MUSEUM | The 1935 stone-and-log building, which resembles a pueblo, is almost as interesting as the Native American artifacts and exhibits inside. Baskets, kachinas, pottery, rugs, and beadwork make up the collection, which represents indigenous cultures from the pre-Columbian period to the present. ✉ *147 N. Arizona Ave., Downtown* ☎ *928/445–1230* ⊕ *www.museumofindigenouspeople. org* ✉ *$8.*

Phippen Museum

MUSEUM | The paintings and bronze sculptures of George Phippen, along with works by other artists of the West, form the permanent collection of this museum about 5 miles north of downtown. Phippen met with a group of prominent cowboy artists in 1965 to form the Cowboy Artists of America, a group dedicated to preserving the Old West as they saw it. He became the president but died the next year. A memorial foundation set up in his name opened the doors of this museum in 1984. ✉ *4701 AZ 89 N* ☎ *928/778–1385* ⊕ *www.phippenartmuseum.org* ✉ *$10* ⊙ *Closed Mon.*

Prescott National Forest

SCENIC DRIVE | The drive down a mountainous section of AZ 89A from Jerome to Prescott is gorgeous (if somewhat harrowing in bad weather), filled with twists and turns through Prescott National Forest. A scenic turnoff near Jerome provides one last vista and a place to apply chains during surprise snowstorms. There's camping, picnicking, and hiking at the crest of Mingus Mountain. If you're coming to Prescott from Phoenix, the route that crosses the Mogollon Rim, overlooking the Verde Valley, has nice views of rolling hills and is less precipitous. ✉ *Prescott* ⊕ *www.fs.usda.gov/ prescott.*

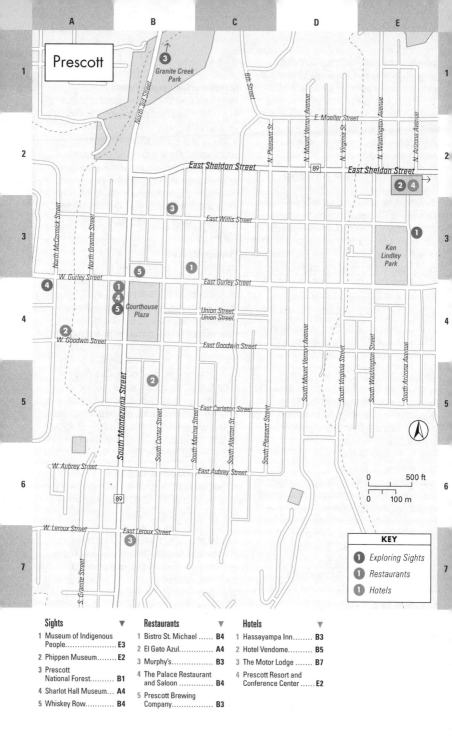

Prescott

Granite Creek Park

Sights ▼

1 Museum of Indigenous People.................... **E3**
2 Phippen Museum........ **E2**
3 Prescott National Forest.......... **B1**
4 Sharlot Hall Museum... **A4**
5 Whiskey Row............ **B4**

Restaurants ▼

1 Bistro St. Michael **B4**
2 El Gato Azul............. **A4**
3 Murphy's................. **B3**
4 The Palace Restaurant and Saloon **B4**
5 Prescott Brewing Company................ **B3**

Hotels ▼

1 Hassayampa Inn........ **B3**
2 Hotel Vendome.......... **B5**
3 The Motor Lodge **B7**
4 Prescott Resort and Conference Center **E2**

KEY

1 Exploring Sights
1 Restaurants
1 Hotels

0   500 ft
0   100 m

Sharlot Hall Museum

MUSEUM | **FAMILY** | Local pioneer history is documented at this remarkable museum, the creative vision of historian and poet Sharlot Hall. Along with an original 1863 ponderosa pine log cabin and the mansion which housed the territorial governor in 1864, the parklike museum contains several additional restored period homes and a transportation exhibit housed in a former auto repair shop circa 1937. Territorial times are the focus, but natural history and artifacts of the area's prehistoric peoples are also on display. ✉ *415 W. Gurley St., Downtown* ✣ *2 blocks west of Courthouse Plaza* ☎ *928/445–3122* 🌐 *www.sharlothallmuseum.org* 🎫 *$12* 🕒 *Closed Mon.*

Whiskey Row

HISTORIC SITE | Twenty saloons and bordellos once lined this stretch of Montezuma Street, along the west side of Courthouse Plaza. Social activity is more subdued these days, although live music pulses every evening, and the buildings have been beautifully restored. The historical bars provide an escape from the street's many boutiques. ✉ *Montezuma St., Downtown.*

🍴 Restaurants

Bistro St. Michael

$ | **AMERICAN** | This is a great place to enjoy a coffee, eggs Benedict, or a burger while people-watching on Whiskey Row. The café/bar, which serves breakfast, lunch, and dinner, has been restored to its original 1901 style. **Known for:** tasty, reasonably priced American fare; historical charm; in the heart of downtown. [$] *Average main: $12* ✉ *Hotel St. Michael, 205 W. Gurley St., Downtown* ☎ *928/776–1999* 🌐 *www.stmichaelhotel.com.*

★ **El Gato Azul**

$$ | **SPANISH** | Come for the tapas; stay for the Southwestern entrees, such as chicken with cilantro pecan pesto or poblano shrimp with polenta, at this cheery, popular restaurant a few blocks off bustling Whiskey Row. The lovely creekside patio affords a casual ambiance where top-notch service matches the superb cuisine. **Known for:** tapas and drinks; favorite spot of locals (and visitors); creekside patio. [$] *Average main: $18* ✉ *316 W. Goodwin St.* ☎ *928/445–1070* 🌐 *elgatoazulprescott.com.*

Murphy's

$$$ | **AMERICAN** | Mesquite-grilled meats and beer brewed exclusively for the restaurant are the specialties at this classy bar and grill, a sort of local institution set in a restored, polished-up 1890 mercantile building. The baby back ribs, prime rib, and fresh fried catfish are standouts. **Known for:** good steaks and ribs; well-preserved historical building; happy hour and Sunday brunch. [$] *Average main: $29* ✉ *201 N. Cortez St., Downtown* ☎ *928/445–4044* 🌐 *www.murphysprescott.com.*

The Palace Restaurant and Saloon

$$$ | **AMERICAN** | Legend has it that the patrons who saved the Palace's ornately carved 1880s Brunswick bar from a Whiskey Row fire in 1900 continued drinking at it while the row burned across the street. Whatever the case, the bar remains the centerpiece of the beautifully restored turn-of-the-20th-century structure, with a high, pressed-tin ceiling. **Known for:** lively frontier pub feel; steaks and burgers; corn chowder. [$] *Average main: $29* ✉ *120 S. Montezuma St., Downtown* ☎ *928/541–1996* 🌐 *www.whiskeyrowpalace.com.*

Prescott Brewing Company

$$ | **AMERICAN** | Good beer, good food, good service, and good prices—for a casual meal, it's hard to beat this cheerful restaurant on the town square. In addition to burgers, chili, fish-and-chips, and British-style bangers and mash, pizzas and salads are also on the menu. **Known for:** crowd-pleasing menu (with beer-infused dishes); excellent happy hour; award-winning craft beers.

$ *Average main: $14* ✉ *130 W. Gurley St., Downtown* ☎ *928/771–2795* 🌐 *www.prescottbrewingcompany.com.*

Hotels

Hassayampa Inn
$$$ | **HOTEL** | Built in 1927 for early automobile travelers, the Hassayampa Inn has a lot of character; the ceiling in the lobby is hand-painted, and some rooms still have the original furnishings. **Pros:** central location; historical charm; live music in cocktail bar. **Cons:** thin walls; small bathrooms; on-site restaurant is pricey. $ *Rooms from: $199* ✉ *122 E. Gurley St., Downtown* ☎ *928/778–9434, 800/322–1927* 🌐 *www.hassayampainn.com* 🛏 *68 rooms* 🍴 *No meals.*

Hotel Vendome
$$ | **B&B/INN** | This World War I–era hostelry, tastefully restored, has seen miners, health seekers, and celebrities walk through its doors. **Pros:** central location; historical charm with modern amenities; wine bar. **Cons:** creaky floors raise noise factor; no elevator; only a few suites have an additional sofa sleeper. $ *Rooms from: $169* ✉ *230 S. Cortez St., Downtown* ☎ *928/776–0900* 🌐 *www.vendomehotel.com* 🛏 *20 rooms* 🍴 *No meals.*

★ **The Motor Lodge**
$$ | **HOTEL** | Impeccably renovated to reflect its heyday as a circa-1960 motor hotel, this boutique property delivers comfort and great value as well as a fun blast from the past. **Pros:** comfy beds and cheery '60s decor; most rooms have fireplaces, kitchenettes, and private patios; bicycles to borrow. **Cons:** a long-ish walk to downtown; small showers in some rooms; small bathrooms. $ *Rooms from: $139* ✉ *503 S. Montezuma St.* ☎ *928/717–0157* 🌐 *www.themotorlodge.com* 🛏 *13 rooms* 🍴 *No meals.*

Prescott Resort and Conference Center
$$$ | **RESORT** | On a hill on the outskirts of town, this upscale property run by the Yavapai tribe has views of the mountain ranges surrounding Prescott and the valley, although many guests hardly notice, so riveted are they by the poker machines and slots in Prescott's only hotel casino. **Pros:** comfortable, nicely updated rooms; great views on the higher floors; pool and full-service spa. **Cons:** large-scale property; drive to town center; draws conference groups. $ *Rooms from: $209* ✉ *1500 AZ 69* ☎ *928/227–2313, 885/957–4637* 🌐 *www.prescottresort.com* 🛏 *160 rooms* 🍴 *No meals.*

Nightlife

Montezuma Street's Whiskey Row, off Courthouse Plaza, is nowhere near as wild as it was in its historic heyday, but most bars have live music—with no cover charge—on weekends.

Jersey Lilly Saloon
DANCE CLUBS | Located above the Palace, the Jersey Lilly Saloon is a former brothel with live entertainment, a great patio, and a dance floor. ✉ *116 S. Montezuma St., Downtown* ☎ *928/541–7854* 🌐 *www.jerseylillysaloon.com.*

LazyG Brewhouse
BREWPUBS/BEER GARDENS | **FAMILY** | This lively place serves up tasty pub fare and plenty of beer, with twenty-four of their own brews on tap, plus a few "guests." There's live music to accompany cornhole games on the family- and pet-friendly patio most weekends. ✉ *220 W. Leroux St.* ☎ *928/445–2994* 🌐 *lazygbrewhouse.com.*

Matt's Saloon
MUSIC CLUBS | For live country-and-western music and two-stepping on the dance floor, mosey on over to Matt's Saloon. ✉ *112 S. Montezuma St., Downtown* ☎ *928/776–2974* 🌐 *www.mattssaloon.com.*

Hikers climb the Granite Dells for views over the verdant Prescott Valley.

★ Raven Cafe

CAFES—NIGHTLIFE | A contemporary and attractive coffeehouse and bar, Raven Cafe serves excellent organically grown food from morning to night and hosts live music on Friday and Saturday evenings. ✉ *142 N. Cortez St., Downtown* ☎ *928/717–0009* ⊕ *www.ravencafe.com.*

👜 Shopping

Shops selling antiques and collectibles line Cortez Street, just north of Courthouse Plaza. You'll find fun stuff—Western kitsch abounds—as well as some good buys on valuable pieces. Courthouse Plaza, especially along Montezuma Street, is lined with artist cooperatives, specialty stores, and gift shops. Many match those in Sedona for quality.

Arts Prescott Gallery

ART GALLERIES | Be sure to check out Arts Prescott, a cooperative gallery of talented local artisans. ✉ *134 S. Montezuma St., Downtown* ☎ *928/776–7717* ⊕ *www. artsprescott.com.*

Merchandise Mart Antique Mall

ANTIQUES/COLLECTIBLES | At 14,000 square feet, the Merchandise Mart Antique Mall houses the largest array of antiques dealers in the district along Cortez Street, informally dubbed Antique Row. ✉ *205 N. Cortez St., Downtown* ☎ *928/776–1728.*

★ Van Gogh's Ear

ART GALLERIES | Exquisite work by local and national artists is beautifully displayed at Van Gogh's Ear. ✉ *156 S. Montezuma St., Downtown* ☎ *928/776–1080* ⊕ *www.vgegallery.com.*

🏃 Activities

HIKING

With hundreds of miles of hiking trails just outside of town, the Prescott National Forest's mountains and lakes are beautiful in an understated way. Many trails are open to mountain bikes, and all permit dogs (on leash). Pick up a hiking trail map ($1) at the Prescott Chamber of Commerce & Visitor Center ⊕ *www.*

prescott.org or contact the ranger district of Prescott National Forest ⊕ *www. fs.usda.gov/prescott*.

The Granite Dells

HIKING/WALKING | Granite rock formations, lakes, and miles of hiking and biking trails overlooking the green Prescott Valley are the big draw to this outdoor recreation spot about 4 miles north of Prescott's downtown. The Dells' two parks, Watson Lake Park and Willow Lake Park, are open year-round. ⊠ *Watson Lake Park, 3101 Watson Lake Rd* ✛ *4 miles north of downtown Prescott* ⊕ *www.prescott-az. gov* ☞ *$3 parking*.

Prescott National Forest–Bradshaw Ranger District

CAMPING—SPORTS-OUTDOORS | Contact the Bradshaw Ranger District for information about hiking trails and campgrounds in the Prescott National Forest south of town. ⊠ *344 S. Cortez St.* ☎ *928/443-8000* ⊕ *www.fs.usda.gov/prescott*.

Thumb Butte Loop Trail

HIKING/WALKING | A 2-mile trek on a paved yet steep loop, the Thumb Butte Loop Trail takes you 600 feet up near the crest of its namesake. The vistas are large, but you won't be alone on this popular trail. *Easy–Moderate.* ⊠ *Prescott* ✛ *Trailhead: Thumb Butte Rd., 3 miles west of Prescott on Gurley St., which turns into Thumb Butte Rd.*

Chapter 6

NORTHEAST ARIZONA

6

Updated by
Teresa Bitler

 Sights	🍴 Restaurants	🛏 Hotels	🛍 Shopping	🍸 Nightlife
★★★★★	★★☆☆☆	★★☆☆☆	★★★☆☆	★☆☆☆☆

WELCOME TO NORTHEAST ARIZONA

TOP REASONS TO GO

★ **See Canyon de Chelly and Antelope Canyon:** Visit two of the most spectacular natural wonders in the Southwest—rivaling even the Grand Canyon for jaw-dropping views, although on a much smaller scale. Both are musts for photography buffs.

★ **Go boating at Glen Canyon:** Get to know this stunning, mammoth reservoir by taking a boat out amid Lake Powell's towering cliffs.

★ **Explore Hubbell Trading Post:** Take the self-guided tour to experience the relationship between early traders and the Navajo.

★ **Shop for handmade crafts on the Hopi Mesas:** Pick up crafts by some of Arizona's leading Hopi artisans, who sustain their culture through continuous occupation of the ancient villages on these mesas.

★ **Take a jeep tour through Monument Valley:** See firsthand the landscape depicted in such iconic Western films as *Stagecoach* and *The Searchers*.

The vast, sweeping northeast quadrant of Arizona is mostly Navajo Nation and Hopi Reservation land. Both areas have beautiful scenery and a chance to learn about some of the world's most vibrant indigenous communities.

1 Window Rock. The governmental and cultural hub of the Navajo people.

2 Canyon de Chelly. National Monument with some of the most spectacular panoramas in the Southwest.

3 Hubbell Trading Post National Historic Site. Well-preserved Navajo trading post.

4 Keams Canyon Trading Post. Trading post specializing in Hopi arts and crafts.

5 The Hopi Mesas. An artistically rich tribal land home to the Hopi Arts Trail, the 1,000-year-old village of Oraibi, trading posts, and more.

6 Tuba City. Half Navajo, half Hopi community and entrance to Hopi lands.

7 Cameron Trading Post. A turnoff point for the South Rim of the Grand Canyon.

8 Kayenta. Southern gateway to Monument Valley.

9 Monument Valley Navajo Tribal Park. These ancient lands appear in everything from classic Western movies to Ansel Adams photos; you can explore this sweeping valley on a variety of Navajo-led tours.

10 Goulding's Trading Post. Old Western filming location, campground, and trading post in Monument Valley.

11 Navajo National Monument. Ancestral Puebloan sandstone cliff dwellings.

12 Goosenecks Region, Utah. Scenic area dominated by red rocks and the San Juan River.

13 Glen Canyon Dam and Lake Powell. A geological wonderland of waterways, arches, and slot canyons best explored by boat.

14 Page. Practical base for Lake Powell adventures, Antelope Canyon tours, and trips to Horseshoe Bend Trail.

15 Antelope Canyon. Slot canyon known for its dramatic red walls.

16 Wahweap. Lake Powell marina, resort, and campground.

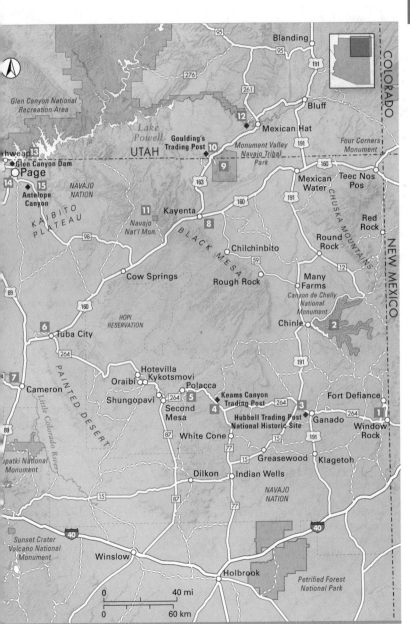

NATIVE AMERICAN EXPERIENCE

A member of the Navajo Nation performs a traditional ritual.

More than 296,000 Native American people reside in sovereign nations within Arizona's state borders, as they have for thousands of years. Alongside ancient cliff dwellings and stunning natural monuments, the reality of the 22 tribes' cultures is best experienced on the reservations.

Arizona's tribes, all of which are culturally and spiritually distinct, live on reservations that comprise more than a quarter of the state's lands. Many tribal lands enable them to derive income from natural resources, such as coal, but most rely to some extent on tourism for revenue. Some tribes, such as the Navajo, open up much of their culture to visitors. Native American artisans are famed for handmade items popular with tourists, but casinos are increasingly vital to tribal economies.

RESERVATION REALITIES

For all their richness in culture, reservations are places where poverty is often prevalent. Panhandlers often cluster at shopping centers and viewpoints. Visitors should respond to them with a polite but firm *no*. If you wish to help, make a donation to a legitimate organization.

NAVAJO NATION AND HOPI RESERVATION RULES

Alcohol and drugs: The possession and consumption of alcoholic beverages or illicit drugs is illegal on Hopi and Navajo land.

Camping: No open fires are allowed in reservation campgrounds; you must use grills or fireplaces, and you may not gather firewood. Camping areas have quiet hours from 11 pm to 6 am. Pets must be kept on a leash or confined.

Hopi shrines: Hopi spirituality is intertwined with daily life, and objects that seem ordinary to you may have deeper significance. If you see a collection of objects at or near the Hopi Mesas, do not disturb them.

Permits and permissions: No off-trail hiking, rock climbing, or off-road travel is allowed unless you're accompanied by a local guide. A tribal permit is required for fishing, and hunting and fishing violations are punishable by heavy fines, imprisonment, or both.

Photography: Always ask permission before taking photos of locals. Even if no money is requested, consider offering a dollar or two to the person whose photo you've taken. The Navajo are very open about photographs; the Hopi don't

A Navajo flag waves in the sun.

allow photographs at all, including video and tape recordings.

Religious ceremonies: Should you see a ceremony, look for posted signs indicating who is welcome or check with local shops or the village community. Unless you're invited, stay out of *kivas* (ceremonial rooms) and stay on the periphery of dances or processions.

Respect for the land: Do not wander through residential areas or disturb property. Do not disturb or remove animals, plants, rocks, petrified wood, or artifacts.

CULTURE

Heritage flavors: Native American food staples are well adapted to living in Arizona's arid lands. Corn is a universal ingredient—ground into flour to make tortillas, included in stew, or simply steamed and left on the cob. The fruits of the saguaro, prickly pear, and other cacti are commonly harvested by tribes as well as tepary beans grown from seeds handed down over generations. Fry bread—pillow-shaped fried dough—is the basis of the popular Navajo taco, usually topped with beans, ground beef, and shredded cheese.

A Navajo woman prepares to weave.

Most Hopi ceremonies take place in village plazas and kivas; observers are sometimes invited.

Song and dance: Ceremonies involving music and dance are central to Native American culture. Not every ceremony is accessible to visitors. Cultural centers and museums, such as the Heard Museum in Phoenix, frequently hold powwows and other festivals that often celebrate more than one tribe.

Sacred spaces: The Hopi kivas are square- or circular-walled, mostly underground structures that are used exclusively for religious ceremonies, and often accessed by a ladder from above. Most kivas, including ruins, are off-limits to tourists. The hogan is the traditional dwelling of the Navajo, and the door always faces east to welcome the rising sun. Hogans play an important part in Navajo spirituality and represent the universe and all things in it.

Arts and crafts: Many of the craftspeople on the reservations sell their wares, with specialties that include pottery, turquoise and sterling-silver jewelry, handwoven baskets, and Navajo wool rugs. As the Spanish ventured northward from Mexico in the late 1500s and early 1600s, they taught the Native Americans their silver-crafting skills, while tribes specializing in pottery and weaving carry on a tradition that began hundreds of years ago. Native beadwork traces its origins to trade beads from early explorers.

ON THE GROUND

Visiting the Navajo: Always ask for permission before taking someone's picture. If you aren't asked for a gratuity, consider giving one. Canyon de Chelly, Chaco Canyon, Monument Valley Navajo Tribal Park, and Navajo National Monument offer glimpses into the past and present of Native American life and culture.

Visiting the Hopi: Recordings, including photographs, are prohibited in the Hopi Reservation, except in limited cases by permit. Central to the reservation are Hopi Mesas that contain two of the oldest continually inhabited villages in North America. Though Hopi villages offer visitors limited access, visitors can buy handicrafts from Hopi artisans at many shops, or book a studio tour through the Moenkopi Legacy Inn in Tuba City.

THE NAVAJO AND THE HOPI PEOPLE

The **Navajo** use few words and have a subtle sense of humor that can pass you by if you're not a good listener. They're taught not to talk too much, be loud, or show off. Eye contact is considered impolite; if you're conversing with Navajos, some may look down or away even though they're paying attention to you. Likewise touching is seen differently; a handshake may be the only physical contact that you see. When shaking hands a light touch is preferred to a firm grip, which is considered overbearing. Some of these traits are changing with younger generations, especially as technology and travel lead to less insular communities.

Although most Navajos speak English, listen closely to the language of the Diné. Stemming from the Athabascan family of languages, it's difficult for outsiders to learn because of subtle accentuation. The famous Marine Corps Navajo code talkers of World War II saved thousands of lives in the South Pacific by creating a code within their native Navajo language.

The **Hopi** Reservation is surrounded by the far larger Navajo Nation and has begun to open up a bit more to visitors, who can now book guided tours of artists' studios. Over the years the proximity of the two tribes has been the cause of contention, often involving the assistance of the United States government in settling land claims, yet the spirituality of the Hopi—"the peaceful ones"—is decidedly antiwar. In fact, Hopi mythology holds that a white-skinned people will save the tribe from its difficult life. Long ago, however, in the face of brutal treatment by whites, most Hopi became convinced that salvation would originate elsewhere.

TRIBAL TIMELINE

950 The first settlements are built at Keet Seel.

1120–1210 Ancestral Puebloans occupy Wupatki Pueblo.

1150 The Hopi build the village of Old Orabi.

1250 Ancestral Puebloans are living at Keet Seel.

1276–1300 Tribes abandon northern Arizona during the "big drought."

1540–1542 Francisco Vásquez de Coronado leads an expedition in search of gold.

1863 Congress creates the Arizona Territory.

1864 Navajos forced to march 300 miles to Fort Sumner during the "Long Walk."

1868 The Navajo and the United States sign a treaty.

1886 Geronimo surrenders after evading U.S. troops for over a year.

1907 Arizona outlaws gambling.

1912 Arizona becomes 48th state.

1993 Sixteen Arizona tribes sign gambling compacts with the state.

Hopi mural

Northeast Arizona is a vast and magnificent land of lofty buttes, towering cliffs, and turquoise skies. Most of the land in the area belongs to the Navajo and Hopi, who adhere to ancient traditions based on spiritual values, kinship, and an affinity for nature. Spend time at some of the region's most spectacular sites, such as Canyon de Chelly, Lake Powell and surrounding Glen Canyon, and Monument Valley, and you'll quickly come to appreciate why indigenous locals so revere the landscape.

Life here has changed little during the last two centuries, and visiting this land can feel like traveling to a foreign country or going back in time, although a handful of distinctive, inviting hotels have opened in the region in recent years, helping to entice overnight visitors aiming to venture off the beaten path without necessarily foregoing creature comforts.

In such towns as Tuba City and Window Rock, it's not uncommon to hear the gliding vowels and soft consonants of the Navajo language, a tongue as different from Hopi as English is from Japanese. As you drive in the vicinity, tune your radio to KTNN 660 AM (⊕ *www.ktnnonline.com*), the Voice of the Navajo Nation since 1985. You'll quickly understand why the U.S. Marine Navajo code talkers

communicating in their native tongue were able to devise a code within their language that was never broken by opposing forces.

In the Navajo Nation's approximate center sits the nearly 2,350-square-mile Hopi Reservation, a series of adobe villages built on high mesas overlooking the cultivated land. On Arizona's borders, where the Navajo Nation continues into Utah and New Mexico, the Navajo and Canyon de Chelly national monuments contain haunting cliff dwellings of ancient people who lived in the area some 1,500 years ago. Glen Canyon Dam, which abuts the northwestern corner of the reservation, holds back 185 miles of emerald waters known as Lake Powell.

Most of Northeast Arizona is high desert, but it's far from monochromatic: eerie and spectacular rock formations as colorful as desert sunsets highlight immense mesas, canyons, and cliffs; towering stands of ponderosa pine cover the Chuska Mountains to the north and east of Canyon de Chelly. Navajo Mountain to the north and west in Utah soars more than 10,000 feet, and the San Francisco Peaks climb to similar heights to the south and west by Flagstaff. According to the Navajo creation myth, these are two of the four mountainous boundaries of the sacred land where the Navajo first emerged from Earth's interior.

MAJOR REGIONS

The sweeping northeast quadrant of Arizona, which comprises the Navajo and Hopi reservations, has relatively few visitors but offers both stunning scenery and the chance to learn about some of the world's most vibrant indigenous communities. It can be broken into a few distinct regions, starting with **Navajo Nation East,** home to Canyon de Chelly and Window Rock.

Another is the minimally developed **Hopi Mesas,** a region that can be thought of as a doughnut hole surrounded by the Navajo Nation. The dramatically situated tribal land rises above the high-desert floor, and is rife with trading posts and art studios selling fine weavings, jewelry, and crafts. The Hopis' 12 villages in First Mesa, Second Mesa, and Third Mesa have very few services, even relative to the rest of Northeast Arizona.

Just 80 miles east of the Grand Canyon's South Rim, the community of Tuba City anchors **Navajo Nation West** and Hopi tribal lands—it's an excellent base for checking out the region's painted-desert landscapes and Navajo trading posts.

Monument Valley spans the Arizona and Utah borders, extending northeast from Kayenta, Arizona, nearly to Bluff, Utah. You've probably seen images of these ancient lands in Western movies and can explore the valley on a Navajo-led tour.

The one section of Northeast Arizona not set on tribal lands is dominated by the nation's second-largest man-made body of water, **Lake Powell,** and 710-foot-tall **Glen Canyon Dam.** It's a boating paradise, and the town of Page has the region's greatest number of hotels, restaurants, and bars. It's a good base for day trips to nearby Antelope Canyon, on Navajo Nation land, and Horseshoe Bend Trail.

Northeast Arizona Planner

When to Go

FESTIVALS AND EVENTS

Bluff International Balloon Festival

FESTIVALS | Held the weekend before Martin Luther King Jr. Day, this three-day ballooning festival includes concerts, a taco supper, an ice cream social, a "night glow," and flights over Valley of the Gods and Monument Valley. ⊕ *bluffutah.org.*

Navajo Nation Annual Tribal Fair

CULTURAL FESTIVALS | The world's largest Native American fair includes a rodeo, traditional Navajo music and dances, food booths and fry-bread competitions, a Miss Navajo Nation Pageant, and an intertribal powwow during the first week of September, at Window Rock. ☎ *928/871–6478* ⊕ *www.facebook.com/ NavajoNationFair.*

Planning Your Time

Northeast Arizona encompasses an enormous area but relatively few key attractions, so it's best to use one or two primary communities (Page or Tuba City on the west side, Kayenta on the north, and Chinle or Window Rock on the east) as bases for day trips to outlying attractions.

If your time is limited, put Canyon de Chelly and Monument Valley at the top of your list—if you're ambitious, you could explore these two sites on consecutive days, spending the night in Chinle, Kayenta, or in Monument Valley itself. Focus on the South Rim Drive at Canyon de Chelly, and in Monument Valley book a jeep tour with the highly respected Sacred Monument Tours. On travel days from one base community to another, plan a scenic drive, such as AZ 264 from Tuba City to Window Rock (don't miss the great crafts shopping at Second Mesa) or AZ 98 to U.S. 160 to U.S. 191 from Page to Chinle. Give yourself at least two days to get to know any one part of the region, and as much as a week to fully explore all of it.

■TIP➡ Unlike the rest of Arizona (including the Hopi Reservation), the Navajo Reservation observes daylight saving time. Thus for half the year—mid-March to early November—it's an hour later on the Navajo Reservation than everywhere else in the state.

Getting Here and Around

CAR

It's virtually impossible to see much of Northeast Arizona without a car—this is your best bet not only for getting here, but also for visiting attractions and communities throughout the region.

Many visitors see Northeast Arizona as part of a road-tripping adventure through the Four Corners Region, perhaps combining their visit with trips to the national parks of southern Utah and southwestern Colorado. This "en route" road-tripping strategy makes the most sense, especially given the region's stunningly scenic drives.

ROAD CONDITIONS AND SERVICES

Most of the 27,400 square miles of the Navajo Reservation and other areas of Northeast Arizona are off the beaten track. It's prudent to stay on the well-maintained paved thoroughfares. If you don't have the equipment for wilderness travel—including a four-wheel-drive vehicle and provisions—and lack backcountry experience, stay off dirt roads unless they're signed and graded and the skies are clear. Be on the lookout for ominous rain clouds in summer or signs of snow in winter. Never drive into dips or low-lying areas during a heavy rainstorm, and be vigilant for both wildlife and livestock (the Navajo Nation is open range, meaning cattle roam freely). If you heed these simple precautions, car travel through the region is as safe as anywhere else in the Southwest.

■TIP➡ While driving around the Navajo Nation, tune in to KTNN 660 AM for local news and weather.

A tour of Navajo-Hopi country can involve driving significant distances between widely scattered communities, so a detailed, up-to-date road map is essential (relying on smartphone GPS isn't a great idea, as cell coverage is spotty). Gas stations are in all major towns, but distances between them can be considerable—it's best to service your vehicle before venturing into the Navajo and Hopi reservations, and to carry emergency equipment and supplies.

Hotels

Page has the area's greatest concentration of lodgings, most of them fairly standard chain motels and hotels, but this base camp for exploring Lake Powell also has a few bed-and-breakfasts as well as houseboat rentals, and just over the border in Utah is the ultraluxurious Amangiri resort. You'll find a handful of well-maintained chains in the Navajo

Nation, in Kayenta, Chinle, Tuba City, and Window Rock. Additionally the Navajo's View Hotel in Monument Valley and the Hopi's Moenkopi Legacy Inn in Tuba City are beautifully designed, contemporary hotels. This is a popular area for both tent and RV camping—you can obtain a list of campgrounds from the Page/Lake Powell Tourism Bureau and the Navajo Nation Tourism Office.

Restaurants

Northeast Arizona is a vast area with small hamlets and towns scattered miles apart, and there are few stores or restaurants. With the exception of Page, which has slightly more culinary variety, the region's restaurants mostly serve basic but tasty Native American, South-western, and frontier-inspired American (steaks, burgers) cuisine. Navajo and Hopi favorites include mutton stew, Hopi *piki* (paper-thin, blue-corn bread), and Navajo fry bread.

Hotel and restaurant reviews have been shortened. For full information, visit Fodors.com.

What it Costs			
$	$$	$$$	$$$$
RESTAURANTS			
Under $12	$12–$20	$21–$30	Over $30
HOTELS			
Under $121	$121–$175	$176–$250	Over $250

Activities

Some of the best hikes in this region are in Canyon de Chelly, up the streambed between the soaring vermilion, orange, and white sandstone cliffs, with the remains of the ancient Ancestral Pueb-loan communities frequently in view. The Navajo National Monument offers impressive hikes to Betatakin, a settle-ment dating back to AD 1250, and Keet Seel, which dates back as far as AD 950. Both are in alcoves at the base of gigan-tic overhanging cliffs. Remember you can't hike or camp on private property or tribal land without a backcountry permit.

Window Rock

192 miles from Flagstaff, 26 miles from Gallup, New Mexico.

Named for the immense arch-shaped "window" in a massive sandstone ridge above the city, Window Rock is the capi-tal of the Navajo Nation and the center of its tribal government. With a population of around 2,950, this community serves as the business and social center for Navajo families throughout the reser-vation. Window Rock is a good place to stop for food, supplies, and gas.

GETTING HERE AND AROUND

From Flagstaff follow Interstate 40 east for 160 miles, then Highway 12 north. From Gallup, New Mexico, follow U.S. 491 north and then NM 264 west (which becomes AZ 264). Window Rock lies on the border between the two states, with most businesses on the Arizona side.

VISITOR INFORMATION

CONTACTS Navajo Nation Tourism Office. ☎ 928/810–8501 ⊕ *www.discovernavajo. com.*

◎ Sights

Navajo Nation Council Chambers
NATIVE SITE | The murals on the walls of this handsome structure, built to resemble a large ceremonial hogan, depict scenes from the history of the tribe, and the bell beside the entrance was a gift to the tribe by the Santa Fe Railroad to commemorate the thousands of Navajos who built the railroad. Visitors can observe sessions of the council, where 24 delegates representing 110

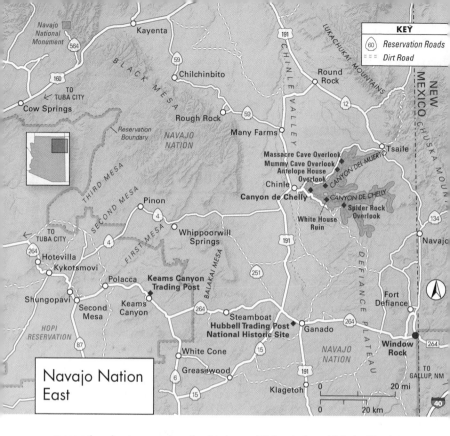

Navajo Nation East

---

reservation chapters meet on the third Monday of January, April, July, and October. ■ TIP→ **Be aware that when the council is not in session, the building is locked, but the exterior still makes for a nice stop.** Turn east off Indian Highway 12, about ½ mile north of AZ 264, to reach the Council Chambers. Nearby **Window Rock Navajo Tribal Park & Veteran's Memorial** is a memorial park honoring Navajo veterans, including the famous World War II code talkers. ⊠ AZ 264 ☎ 928/871–7160 ⊕ www.navajonationcouncil.org. .

Navajo Nation Museum
MUSEUM | FAMILY | Devoted to the art, culture, and history of the Navajo people, this museum also has an excellent library on the Navajo Nation. Each season brings new exhibitions by native artists; call for a list of current shows. There are also permanent exhibits on the Long

Walk—during which the Navajo were tragically and temporarily relocated to Fort Sumner, New Mexico—and on the culture and philosophies of the Navajo people. In the same building is the Navajo Nation Visitor Center, a great resource for all sorts of information on reservation activities. ⊠ AZ 264 and Loop Rd. ✛ Next to Quality Inn Navajo Nation Capital ☎ 928/871–7941 ⊕ www.facebook.com/NavajoNationMuseum ⊠ Free ⊗ Closed Sun.

The Navajo Nation Zoological and Botanical Park
ZOO | FAMILY | Amid the sandstone monoliths on the border between Arizona and New Mexico, the Navajo Nation Zoological and Botanical Park displays about 50 species of domestic and wild animals, birds, and amphibians that figure in Navajo legends, as well as

Navajo Nation East

Land has always been central to the history of the Navajo people: it's embedded in their very name. The Tewa were the first to call them *Navahu*, which means "large area of cultivated land," but according to the Navajo creation myth, they were given the name *ni'hookaa diyan diné* ("holy earth people") by their creators. Today tribal members call themselves the Diné (pronounced din- *eh*), "the people." The eastern portion of the Arizona Navajo Nation (in Navajo, *diné bikéyah*) is a dry but often surprisingly green land, especially in the vicinity of the aptly named Beautiful Valley, south of Canyon de Chelly along U.S. 191. A landscape of rolling hills, wide arroyos, and small canyons, the area is dotted with traditional Navajo hogans, sheepfolds, cattle tanks, and wood racks. The region's easternmost portion is marked by tall mountains and towering sandstone cliffs cut by primitive roads that are generally accessible only on horseback or with four-wheel-drive vehicles.

examples of plants used by traditional people. Most of the animals here were brought in as orphans or after sustaining injuries—they include black bears, mountain lions, Mexican gray wolves, bobcats, cougars, golden eagles, Gila monsters, and prairie rattlesnakes. It's the nation's only Native American–owned zoo. ✉ *AZ 264* ✥ *Just east of Quality Inn; shares parking lot with Navajo Nation Museum* ☎ *928/871–6574* 🌐 *www.navajozoo.org* 🎟 *Free* 🕒 *Closed Sun.*

🍴 Restaurants

Blake's Lotaburger

$ | AMERICAN | The westernmost branch of the beloved New Mexico chain of old-school burger joints is technically in the Land of Enchantment (i.e., New Mexico) but just a few hundred feet over the Arizona state line, and within walking distance of the Quality Inn and Window Rock museums. Blake's began in 1952 in Albuquerque and enjoys a cult following for its Angus-beef green-chile cheeseburgers, seasoned fries, breakfast burritos, and milkshakes. **Known for:** cheeseburger made with Hatch green chiles; meals that are made fresh to order; flavorful cherry milkshakes. [$] *Average main: $5* ✉ *NM 264, at Alma Dr., Gallup* ☎ *505/371–5400* 🌐 *www.lotaburger.com.*

Cocina de Dominguez

$ | SOUTHWESTERN | FAMILY | One of the few dining options in Window Rock that isn't fast food, this bare-bones, family-owed restaurant with TVs broadcasting soccer games and Spanish-speaking soap operas is usually packed, especially during lunch. Devour burritos, burgers, and New Mexican specialties like *carne adovada* (New Mexican–style pork with chiles). **Known for:** homestyle Mexican and New Mexican dishes; friendly service; spaghetti and lasagna after 5 pm. [$] *Average main: $10* ✉ *Rte. 12, Suite 16* ✥ *In shopping center on northeast corner of Rte. 12 and Hwy. 264* ☎ *928/810–3777* 🌐 *www.cocinadedominguez nm.com* 🕒 *Closed weekends.*

🛏 Hotels

Quality Inn Navajo Nation Capital

$ | HOTEL | Rooms in this two-story beam-and-stucco hotel near the Navajo Museum are decorated with an earthy Navajo-inspired palette that complements the dark wood furnishings. **Pros:** within walking distance of Navajo Museum; decent on-site restaurant; surprisingly bright and attractively furnished rooms. **Cons:** on busy road; dull setting; bland exterior. [$] *Rooms from: $100* ✉ *48 W. AZ 264, at Hwy. 12* ☎ *928/871–4108* 🌐 *www.choicehotels.com* 🛏 *56 rooms* 🍴 *Free breakfast.*

Shopping

★ **Navajo Arts and Crafts Enterprises**
CRAFTS | This outlet of the Navajo Arts and Crafts Enterprises stocks tribal art purchased from craftspeople across Navajo Nation, including stunning silverwork and traditional Navajo dolls, pottery, and rugs. Local artisans are occasionally at work here. There are six other outlets: four are in Northeast Arizona (Cameron, Chinle, Kayenta, Navajo National Monument), and one is in northwestern New Mexico (Shiprock). Major credit cards are accepted. ✉ *AZ 264 at Hwy. 12* ✥ *Next to Quality Inn Navajo Nation Capital* ☎ *928/871–4090, 888/831–7384* 🌐 *www.gonavajo.com.*

Canyon de Chelly

30 miles west of Window Rock on AZ 264, then 25 miles north on U.S. 191.

Comprising two long canyons, each one more than 1,000 feet deep, Canyon de Chelly is one of the major sites in the Four Corners region. It's somewhat overshadowed by the Grand Canyon and some of southern Utah's national parks, and you can only venture into the canyons with an authorized guide, but visitors with just a little time can experience Canyon de Chelly's dramatic viewing areas along two park roads (there's no admission fee) that snake along the canyon rims.

GETTING HERE AND AROUND

U.S. 191 runs north–south through Chinle, the closest town to the Canyon de Chelly entrance.

Guided tours allow visits directly into the canyons, not just the park drives high above them; jeep tours even have the option of camping overnight. Each kind of tour has its pros and cons: you'll cover the most ground in a jeep; horseback trips get you close to one of the park's most notable geological formations, Spider Rock; and guided walks provide the most leisurely pace and an excellent opportunity to interact with your guide and ask questions. You can also plan custom treks lasting several days.

PLANNING YOUR TIME

To get even a basic sense of the park's scope and history, spend at least a full day here. If time is short, the best strategy is to stop into the visitor center, where you can watch an informative 23-minute video about the canyons, and then drive the most magnificent of the two park roads, South Rim Drive. You could, if you're ambitious, drive both park roads in one day, but it's better to set aside a second day for North Rim Drive, or take the North Rim Drive as an alternative route to Kayenta, by way of Tsaile. From the different overlooks along the park roads you'll be treated to amazing photo ops of the valley floors below, and you can also access certain dwellings. For a more in-depth experience, book one of the guided hiking, jeep, or horseback tours into the canyon.

Both Canyon de Chelly and Canyon del Muerto have a paved rim drive with turnoffs and parking areas. Each drive takes a minimum of two hours—allow more if you plan to hike to White House Ruin, picnic, or spend time photographing the sites. Overlooks along the rim drives provide incredible views of the canyon; be sure to stay on trails and away from the canyon edge, and to control children and pets at all times.

Who Were the Cliff Dwellers?

The first inhabitants of the canyons arrived more than 2,000 years ago—anthropologists call them the basket makers, because baskets were the predominant artifacts they left behind. By AD 750, however, the basket makers had disappeared—their reason for leaving the region is unknown, but some speculate they were forced to leave because of encroaching cultures or climatic changes—and they were replaced by Pueblo tribes who constructed stone cliff dwellings. The departure of the Pueblo people around AD 1300 is widely believed to have resulted from changing climatic conditions,

soil erosion, dwindling local resources, disease, and internal conflict. Present-day Hopi see these people as their ancestors. Beginning around AD 780, Hopi farmers settled here, followed by the Navajo around 1300. Evidence indicates that the Navajo migrated from far northern Canada, although the timing of their initial voyage south isn't clear. Despite evidence to the contrary, most Navajos hold that their people have always lived here and that the Diné passed through three previous underworlds before emerging into this, the fourth or "Glittering World."

The visitor center has exhibits on the history of the cliff dwellers and provides information on scheduled hikes, tours, and National Park Service programs offered throughout the summer months.

VISITOR INFORMATION

CONTACTS Canyon de Chelly Visitor Center. ⊠ *Indian Hwy. 7, Chinle* ✛ *3 miles east of U.S. 191* ☎ *928/674–5500* ⊕ *www.nps. gov/cach.*

◉ Sights

★ Canyon de Chelly

ARCHAEOLOGICAL SITE | Home to Ancestral Puebloans from AD 350 to 1300, the nearly 84,000-acre Canyon de Chelly (pronounced d'*shay*) is one of the most spectacular natural wonders in the Southwest. On a smaller scale, it rivals the Grand Canyon for beauty. Its main gorges—the 26-mile-long Canyon de Chelly ("canyon in the rock") and the adjoining 35-mile-long Canyon del Muerto ("canyon of the dead")—comprise sheer, heavily eroded sandstone walls that rise to 1,100 feet over dramatic valleys. Ancient pictographs and petroglyphs

decorate some of the cliffs, and within the canyon complex there are more than 7,000 archaeological sites. Stone walls rise hundreds of feet above streams, hogans, tilled fields, and sheep-grazing lands.

You can view prehistoric sites near the base of cliffs and perched on high, sheltering ledges, some of which you can access from the park's two main drives along the canyon rims. The dwellings and cultivated fields of the present-day Navajo lie in the flatlands between the cliffs, and those who inhabit the canyon today farm much the way their ancestors did. Most residents leave the canyon in winter but return in early spring to farm.

Canyon de Chelly's South Rim Drive (37 miles round-trip with seven overlooks) starts at the visitor center and ends at **Spider Rock Overlook,** where cliffs plunge nearly 1,000 feet to the canyon floor. The view here is of two pinnacles, Speaking Rock and Spider Rock. Other highlights on the South Rim Drive are Junction Overlook, where Canyon del Muerto joins Canyon de Chelly; White House

Best Northeast Arizona Campgrounds 🛏

Cottonwood Campground. This sometimes cramped and noisy campground has RV and tent sites right in Canyon de Chelly.⊠ *Indian Hwy. 7, near Canyon de Chelly Visitor Center, Chinle* ☎ 928/674–2106 ⊕ *www. nps.gov/cach.*

Goulding's Good Sam Campground. Views of Monument Valley are the draw at this clean, modern campground.⊠ *Monument Valley Rd., off U.S. 163 just north of Utah/Arizona border, 24 miles north of Kayenta, Monument Valley Navajo Tribal Park* ☎ 435/727–3231 ⊕ *www.gouldings.com.*

Mitten View Campground. Sites are crowded together, but most offer spectacular views of Monument Valley.⊠ *Monument Valley Navajo Tribal Park, near visitor center, Monument Valley Rd., off U.S. 163 just north of Utah/Arizona border, 24 miles north of Kayenta* ☎ 435/727–5870 ⊕ *www.navajonationparks.org.*

Navajo National Monument Campground. Beautiful and serene with no fee, this campground with RV and tent sites has no hookups, and open fires aren't allowed (you must use camp stoves).⊠ *AZ 564, Shonto* ☎ 928/672–2700 ⊕ *www.nps.gov/nava.*

Spider Rock Campground. Cordial Navajo owner Howard Smith makes everyone feel comfortable at this informal campground nestled in low piñons within a few hundred yards of the canyon.⊠ *Indian Hwy. 7, 10 miles east of Canyon de Chelly Visitor Center* ☎ 928/781–2016 ⊕ *www.spiderrock-campground.com.*

Wahweap/Lake Powell RV & Campground. This campground in the Wahweap Marina complex, which is run by the National Park Service concessionaire, has views of the lake and serves both RVers and tent campers.⊠ *U.S. 89, 5 miles north of Page near shore of Lake Powell, Wahweap* ☎ 888/896–3829 ⊕ *www. lakepowell.com.*

Overlook, from which a 2½-mile round-trip trail leads to the **White House Ruin,** with remains of nearly 60 rooms and several kivas; and Sliding House Overlook, where you can see dwellings on a narrow, sloped ledge across the canyon. The carved and sometimes narrow trail down the canyon side to White House Ruin is the only access into Canyon de Chelly without a guide—if you have a fear of heights, this may not be the hike for you.

The only slightly less breathtaking **North Rim Drive** (34 miles round-trip with three overlooks) of Canyon del Muerto also begins at the visitor center and continues

northeast on Indian Highway 64 toward the town of Tsaile. Major stops include **Antelope House Overlook,** a large site named for the animals painted on an adjacent cliff; **Mummy Cave Overlook,** where two mummies were found inside a remarkably unspoiled pueblo dwelling; and **Massacre Case Overlook,** which marks the spot where an estimated 115 Navajo were killed by the Spanish in 1805. (The rock walls of the cave are still pock-marked by the Spaniards' ricocheting bullets.) ⊠ *Indian Hwy. 7, Chinle ✛ 3 miles east of U.S. 191* ☎ 928/674–5500 *visitor center* ⊕ *www.nps.gov/cach* ⧉ *Free.*

🍴 Restaurants

Chinle is the closest town to Canyon de Chelly. There are lodgings with basic restaurants, as well as a supermarket and a campground. Be aware that you may be approached by panhandlers in the grocery store parking lot.

Garcia's Restaurant
$$ | **AMERICAN** | The lobby restaurant at Chinle's Holiday Inn is low-key, a bit lacking in natural light, and rather ordinary, but people come here because it is one of the area's only non–fast food dining options. You can count on well-prepared Navajo and American fare, such as fry bread topped with chili and cheese, but be prepared for slow service and no alcohol. **Known for:** reliable food; Southwestern decor; limited hours in the winter. [$] *Average main: $13* ✉ *Indian Hwy. 7, Chinle* ☎ *928/674–5000 hotel* 🌐 *www.holidayinn.com* 🕒 *No lunch Nov.–Mar.*

The Junction
$ | **AMERICAN** | Across the parking lot from the Best Western Canyon de Chelly Inn, this sun-filled, airy dining room with cream-color walls, a long granite counter, and a mix of attractive booths and tables has a cheerier feel than any other restaurant in town. Specialties include posole and sheepherder's sandwiches (a tortilla or fry bread stuffed with steak, Swiss cheese, grilled onions, chiles, and tomatoes). **Known for:** American, Southwestern, and Chinese dishes; vegetarian options; bright, open dining space. [$] *Average main: $10* ✉ *100 Main St., Chinle* ☎ *928/674–8443* 🌐 *www.bestwestern.com.*

🛏 Hotels

Best Western Canyon de Chelly Inn
$ | **HOTEL** | This two-story motel about 3 miles from Canyon de Chelly but close to the junction with U.S. 191 has cheerful rooms with modern, no-frills oak furnishings and coffeemakers. **Pros:** affordable; fun retro-motel exterior; indoor pool with hot tub and sauna. **Cons:** not within walking distance of the park; ordinary rooms; no elevator to second floor. [$] *Rooms from: $110* ✉ *100 Main St., Chinle* ☎ *928/674–5875 hotel direct, 800/780–7234 reservations* 🌐 *www.bestwestern.com* 🔑 *104 rooms* 🍽 *No meals.*

Holiday Inn Canyon de Chelly
$$ | **HOTEL** | Once called Garcia's Trading Post, this well-kept hotel near Canyon de Chelly is less generic than you might expect: the exterior is "territorial fort" in style and the rooms have been updated with jewel tones and minimalist artwork. **Pros:** attractive adobe-style building; nice pool and fitness center; a short drive from park entrance. **Cons:** slightly pricier than other options in town; dull roadside setting; older hotel with occasional maintenance issues. [$] *Rooms from: $127* ✉ *Indian Hwy. 7, Chinle* ☎ *928/674–5000, 888/465–4329* 🌐 *www.holidayinn.com* 🔑 *108 rooms* 🍽 *No meals.*

Thunderbird Lodge
$ | **HOTEL** | **FAMILY** | Ideally located within the national monument's borders, this pleasant, if basic, establishment owned by the Navajo Nation hosts Native American dance performances weekends August through October. **Pros:** only hotel inside park borders; summer performances by Native American dancers; tours offered right from hotel. **Cons:** small, rustic rooms not for everyone; spotty area cell phone service; a distance from other

restaurants and services. [$] *Rooms from: $99* ✉ *Indian Hwy. 7, Chinle* ☎ *928/674–5842, 800/679–2473* 🌐 *thunderbirdlodge.com* 🛏 *70 rooms* 🍴 *No meals.*

Shopping

Navajo Arts and Crafts Enterprises
CRAFTS | This branch of the respected Navajo gallery carries an excellent selection of locally made crafts and works of art. ✉ *Hwy. 191 and Indian Rte. 12, Chinle* ☎ *928/ 674–5343* 🌐 *www.gonavajo.com.*

Activities

HIKING

From about late May through early September, free three-hour ranger hikes depart most weekend mornings from the Canyon de Chelly Visitor Center—call ahead for times and to reserve a spot. Only one hike within Canyon de Chelly National Monument—the **White House Ruin Trail** on the South Rim Drive—can be undertaken without an authorized guide. The trail starts near White House Overlook and runs along sheer walls that drop about 550 feet. If you have concerns about heights, be aware that the path gets narrow and requires careful footing. The hike is 2½ miles round-trip, and hikers should carry their own drinking water.

TOURS

Ancient Canyon Tours
TOUR—SPORTS | This Navajo-owned tour company offers both day-hiking and overnight-camping excursions into the park's two canyons, de Chelly and del Muerto. The moderately difficult day hikes venture into some of the park's most spectacular backcountry and can last from three to four hours, if covering the lower parts of the canyons, and as long as nine hours for excursions into the higher terrain. The cost is $40 per hour (three-hour minimum) for up to 10 hikers; there are additional $30 per guide and $50 per night land-use fees for overnight trips. Private 4X4 tours into the canyons are also available. ✉ *Chinle* ☎ *928/349–6185* 🌐 *www.ancientcanyontours.com* 🎫 *From $40/hr.*

Canyon de Chelly Tours
TOUR—SPORTS | Book a private jeep tour into Canyon de Chelly or choose from group tours, late-afternoon and evening tours, and bus tours along South Rim Drive. Entertainment such as storytellers, music, and Navajo legends can be arranged with an advance reservation. ✉ *Best Western Canyon de Chelly Inn, 100 Main St., Chinle* ☎ *928/349–1600* 🌐 *www.canyondechellytours.com* 🎫 *From $88.*

Thunderbird Lodge Canyon Tours
TOUR—SPORTS | Treks in six-wheel-drive Pinzgauer army troop vehicles are available from late spring to late fall. Choose a half-day tour or an all-day tour with lunch. ✉ *Indian Hwy. 7, Chinle* ☎ *928/674–5842, 800/679–2473* 🌐 *www.thunderbirdlodge.com/tours* 🎫 *From $70.*

Justin's Horse Rental
HORSEBACK RIDING | **FAMILY** | Located just past the visitor center on Indian Route 7, this outfitter guides riders on horseback tours, ranging from a 2-hour, round-trip ride to First Ruins to a 10-hour journey to Massacre Cave. Overnight adventures are available as well. ✉ *Indian Rte. 7, Chinle* ☎ *928/675–5575* 🌐 *www.justinshorserental.com.*

WALKING TOURS

Footpath Journeys
HIKING/WALKING | Hoof it into Canyon de Chelly on a scheduled six-hour hike or custom multiday trek. ✉ *Chinle* ☎ *928/401–0430* 🌐 *www.footpathjourneys.com* 🎫 *From $100 per person.*

Hubbell Trading Post National Historic Site

40 miles south of Canyon de Chelly, off AZ 264, 30 miles west of Window Rock.

Administered by the National Park Service, this well-preserved Navajo trading post provides a glimpse into the region's legacy as a trading hub of fine weavings. High-quality, handmade rugs are still sold in the park store.

GETTING HERE AND AROUND
The site is just off AZ 264, well marked from the road, and easily explored on foot once you arrive. The National Park Service Visitor Center exhibits illustrate the post's history, and you can take a self-guided tour of the grounds and Hubbell home, and visit the Hubbell Trading Post, which contains a fine display of Native American artistry. The visitor center has a fairly comprehensive bookstore specializing in Navajo history, art, and culture; local weavers often demonstrate their craft on-site.

👁 Sights

★ Hubbell Trading Post National Historic Site

HISTORIC SITE | Merchant John Lorenzo Hubbell established this trading post in 1876. In addition to trading goods, Hubbell taught, translated letters, settled family quarrels, and explained government policy to the Navajo, and during an 1886 smallpox epidemic he turned his home into a hospital and ministered to the sick and dying. He died in 1930 and is buried near the trading post. Visitors today can tour the historic home and explore the grounds and outbuildings.

The Hubbell Trading Post National Historic Site is famous for "Ganado red" Navajo rugs, which are sold at the store here. Rugs can cost anywhere from $100 to more than $30,000, but considering the quality and time that goes into weaving each one, the prices are quite reasonable. Documents of authenticity are provided for all works. Note: when photographing weavers, ask permission first. They expect a few dollars in return. ⊠ *AZ 264, Ganado* ✛ *1 mile west of U.S. 191* ☎ *928/755–3475* ⊕ *www.nps.gov/hutr* 🎫 *Free, including Hubbell home tour.*

Keams Canyon Trading Post

43 miles west of Hubbell Trading Post on AZ 264.

The trading post established by Thomas Keam in 1875 to do business with local tribes is now the area's main tourist attraction, offering a primitive campground, restaurant, service station, and shopping center, all set in a dramatic rocky canyon. An administrative center for the Bureau of Indian Affairs, Keams Canyon also has a number of government buildings. A road, accessible by passenger car, winds northeast 3 miles into the 8-mile wooded canyon. At **Inscription Rock,** about 2 miles down the road, frontiersman Kit Carson engraved his name in stone. There are several picnic spots in the canyon.

GETTING HERE AND AROUND
Keams Canyon is along AZ 264, the main route between Window Rock and Tuba City.

🍴 Restaurants

Keams Canyon Cafe

$ | AMERICAN | This typical no-frills roadside diner with Formica tabletops offers both American and Native American dishes, including Navajo tacos heaped with ground beef, chili, beans, lettuce, and grated cheese. Daily specials may include anything from barbecued ribs to lamb chops to crab legs. **Known for:**

amazing fry bread; early closing hours; daily specials. $ *Average main: $10* ✉ *Keams Canyon Shopping Center, AZ 264, Keams Canyon* ☎ *928/738–2296* ✆ *Closed Sun. No dinner Sat.*

🛍 Shopping

McGee's Indian Art

CRAFTS | Head upstairs from the Keams Canyon Restaurant to peruse first-rate, high-quality Hopi crafts such as hand-crafted jewelry, pottery, beautiful carvings, basketry, and artwork. ✉ *AZ 264, Keams Canyon* ☎ *928/738–2295* ⊕ *www.hopiart.com.*

The Hopi Mesas

The Hopi occupy 12 villages in regions referred to as First Mesa, Second Mesa, and Third Mesa. Although these areas have similar languages and traditions, each has its own individual features. Generations of Hopitu, "the peaceful people," much like their Puebloan ancestors, have lived in these largely agrarian settlements of stone-and-adobe houses, which blend in with the earth so well that they appear to be natural formations. Television antennae, satellite dishes, and automobiles notwithstanding, these Hopi villages still exude the air of another time.

Descendants of the ancient Hisatsinom, the number of Hopi living among the villages today is about 7,000. Their culture can be traced back more than 2,000 years, making them one of the oldest known tribes in North America. They successfully developed "dry farming," and grow many kinds of vegetables and corn (called maize) as their basic food—in fact the Hopi are often called the "corn people." They incorporate nature's cycles into most of their religious rituals. In the celebrated Snake Dance ceremony, dancers carry venomous snakes in their mouths to appease the gods and to bring rain. In addition to farming the land, the Hopi create fine pottery and basketwork and excel at carving wooden kachina dolls.

First Mesa

11 miles west of Keams Canyon, on AZ 264.

The easternmost of the three main Hopi Mesas, First Mesa comprises several centuries-old communities acclaimed for polychrome pottery and kachina-doll carving. Hano, Sichomovi, and Walpi—with its dramatic setting beneath sheer cliffs—are the key communities at First Mesa.

GETTING HERE AND AROUND

The first village that you approach is Polacca; the older and more impressive villages of Hano, Sichomovi, and Walpi are at the top of the sweeping mesa. From Polacca, a paved road (off AZ 264) angles up to a parking lot near the village of Sichomovi and to the Punsi Hall Visitor Center. ■**TIP→ You must get permission to take the guided walking tour of Hano, Sichomovi, and Walpi. Tour times vary; call ahead to the Moenkopi Legacy Inn in Tuba City for more information.**

VISITOR INFORMATION
Hopi Tribe
Staff at the Hopi Tribe offices can answer basic questions and provide guidance for visiting the Hopi Mesas. ☎ *928/734–3202* ⊕ *www.hopi-nsn.gov.*

Moenkopi Legacy Inn
Although the Hopi Tribe offices can provide basic information to travelers, the staff at the Moenkopi Legacy Inn in Tuba City has become the tribe's de facto visitor information center and best overall tourism resource. The staff here can also arrange tours led by Hopi-certified guides. ✉ *AZ 164 at U.S. 160, Tuba City* ☎ *928/283–4500* ⊕ *www.experiencehopi.com.*

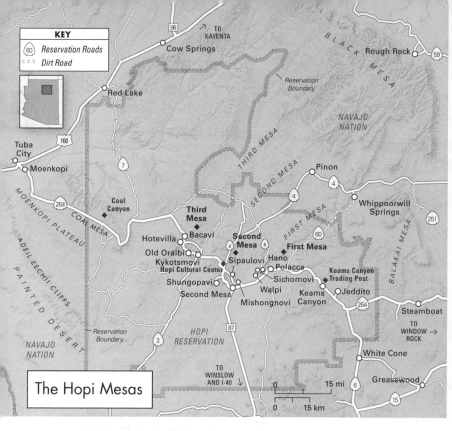

The Hopi Mesas

◎ Sights

★ First Mesa

TOWN | First Mesa villages are renowned for their polychrome pottery and kachina-doll carvings. The older Hopi villages have structures built of rock and adobe mortar in simple architectural style. **Hano** actually belongs to the Tewa, a New Mexico Pueblo tribe. In 1696 the Tewa sought refuge with the Hopi on First Mesa after an unsuccessful rebellion against the Spanish in the Rio Grande Valley. Today the Tewa live close to the Hopi but maintain their own language and ceremonies. **Sichomovi** is built so close to Hano that only the residents can tell where one ends and the other begins. Constructed in the mid-1600s, this village is believed to have been built to ease overcrowding

at Walpi, the highest point on the mesa. **Walpi,** built on solid rock and surrounded by steep cliffs, frequently hosts ceremonial dances. It's the most pristine of the Hopi villages, with cliff-edge houses and vast scenic vistas. Inhabited for more than 1,100 years (dating back to 900 AD), Walpi's cliff-edge houses seem to grow out of the nearby terrain. Today only about 10 residents occupy this settlement, which has neither electricity nor running water; one-hour guided tours of the village are available daily, except when certain ceremonies are taking place (call for hours). Note that Walpi's steep terrain makes it a less than ideal destination for acrophobes. ⊠ *Punsi Hall Visitor Center, AZ 264, at milepost 392* ☏ *928/737–2670* ⊕ *www.experiencehopi. com/walpi-village* ⌖ *Guided tours $20.*

Second Mesa

8 miles southwest of First Mesa, on AZ 264.

Dubbed the "Center of the Universe" of Hopi culture, Second Mesa contains the communities of Shungopavi and Mishongnovi; in the former, you'll find the Hopi Cultural Center, which contains a museum, trading post, and no-frills hotel and restaurant.

GETTING HERE AND AROUND

The Second Mesa communities are reached via the main highway (AZ 264) through the Hopi Reservation.

TOURS

★ Experience Hopi Tour

GUIDED TOURS | Led by authorized Hopi guides, this tour spends a good part of the day on the Second Mesa, where you'll visit an art gallery, watch a silversmith at work, and have lunch at the Hopi Cultural Center. Other stops include the 1,000-year-old village of Old Oraibi, Coalmine Canyon, and the petroglyphs at Prophecy Rock and in Dawa Park. Tours depart from Moenkopi Legacy Inn at 8:30 am and end at approximately 4 pm. ⊠ *AZ 164 at U.S. 160, Tuba City* 🖀 *928/283–4500 schedule through front desk* ⊕ *experiencehopi.com/tours* 🖾 *$145 per person, two person minimum.*

Hopi Arts Trail and Tours

GUIDED TOURS | These Hopi-authorized tours, arranged by and run out of Tuba City's Moenkopi Legacy Inn, specialize in studio tours of the Hopi Villages, including Second Mesa's artists as well as those in nearby villages, such as Walpi and Sipaulovi. The tours are led by knowledgeable guides and are a great way to undertake an arts-shopping adventure, especially given that many of the individual galleries keep irregular hours and can be hard to find. At the hotel, you can alternatively pick up a copy of the Hopi Arts Trail brochure and passport, which lists several galleries and a dozen artists in the Hopi Villages with studios open to the public; present the brochure when visiting these establishments for discounts. ⊠ *AZ 164 at U.S. 160, Tuba City* 🖀 *928/283–4500* ⊕ *www. hopiartstrail.com.*

◉ Sights

Hopi Cultural Center

INFO CENTER | Here you can stop for the night, learn about the people and their communities, and eat authentic Hopi cuisine. The center's museum is dedicated to preserving Hopi traditions and to presenting those traditions to non-Hopi visitors; hours vary. A gift shop sells works by local Hopi artisans at reasonable prices, and a modest picnic area on the west side of the building is a pleasant spot for lunch with a view of the San Francisco Peaks. ⊠ *AZ 264* 🖀 *928/734–2401* 🖾 *Museum $3.*

Second Mesa

TOWN | The Mesas are the Hopi universe, and Second Mesa is the "Center of the Universe." **Shungopavi,** the largest and oldest village on Second Mesa, which was founded by the Bear Clan, is reached by a paved road angling south off AZ 264, between the junction of AZ 87 and the Hopi Cultural Center. The villagers here make silver overlay jewelry and coil plaques. Coil plaques are woven from galleta grass and yucca and are adorned with designs of kachinas, animals, and corn. The art of making the plaques has been passed from mother to daughter for generations, and fine coil plaques have become highly sought-after collector's items. The famous Hopi snake dances (closed to the public) are held here in August during even-numbered years. Two smaller villages are off a paved road that runs north from AZ 264, about 2 miles east of the Hopi Cultural Center. **Mishongnovi,** the easternmost settlement, was established in the late 1600s. ⊠ *Second Mesa.*

🍴 Restaurants

Hopi Cultural Center Restaurant
$ | **SOUTHWESTERN** | The restaurant at the Hopi Cultural Center is an attractive, light-filled room where you can sample traditional tribal fare. Authentic dishes include traditional tacos, Hopi blue-corn pancakes, *piki* (paper-thin, blue-corn bread), fry bread (delicious with honey or salsa), and *nok qui vi* (a tasty stew made with tender bits of lamb, hominy, and mild green chiles). **Known for:** Hopi crafts for sale in the gift shop; authentic Hopi dishes; one of the few Hopi restaurants on tribal lands. [$] *Average main: $11* ✉ *AZ 264* ✣ *5 miles west of AZ 87* ☎ *928/734–2401* 🌐 *hopiculturalcenter.com.*

🛏 Hotels

Hopi Cultural Center Inn
$ | **HOTEL** | This small Hopi-run motel, the only place to eat or sleep in the immediate area, occupies an attractive adobe building with a reddish-brown exterior. **Pros:** adjacent to cultural center; only place to stay for miles in either direction; peaceful setting. **Cons:** remote unless you are here to explore Hopi culture; Wi-Fi in rooms can be slow and unreliable; basic accommodations are not for everybody. [$] *Rooms from: $115* ✉ *AZ 264* ✣ *5 miles west of AZ 87* ☎ *928/734–2401* 🛏 *34 rooms* 🍽 *No meals.*

👜 Shopping

Hopi Cultural Center
CRAFTS | This collection of shops carries work by local artists and artisans, including pottery, baskets, and dolls. ✉ *AZ 264* ☎ *928/734–2401.*

Tsa-Kursh-Ovi
CRAFTS | At this small shop, 1½ miles east of the Hopi Cultural Center, Hopi come to buy bundles of sweetgrass and sage, deer hooves with which to make rattles, and ceremonial belts adorned with seashells. Proprietors Joseph and Janice Day (she is a renowned Hopi basket maker) are a font of information on local artwork, and the shop has one of the largest collections of Hopi baskets in the Southwest. It's also where you'll find the popular "Don't Worry Be Hopi" novelty T-shirts. ✉ *AZ 264* ☎ *928/734–2478* 🕒 *Closed Sun.*

Third Mesa

12 miles northwest of Second Mesa, on AZ 264.

Home to a number of studios in which artisans create weavings, wicker baskets, and jewelry, the Hopi tribe's Third Mesa has four main communities: Kykotsmovi, Old Oraibi, Hotevilla, and Bacavi.

GETTING HERE AND AROUND

The Third Mesa communities are the closest to Tuba City, about 50 miles away along AZ 264.

TOURS

Ancient Pathways Tours
GUIDED TOURS | A knowledgeable guide and member of a Hopi clan from Old Oraibi, Bertram "Tsaava" Tsavadawa leads one-, three-, and six-hour tours of the Third Mesa area, including trips to see the Taawa petroglyphs, symbols of the people who have resided here for more than 1,000 years. ☎ *928/797–8145* 🎟 *From $15.*

👁 Sights

Third Mesa
TOWN | Third Mesa villages are known for their agricultural accomplishments, textile weaving, wicker baskets, silver overlay, and plaques. You'll find crafts shops and art galleries, as well as occasional roadside vendors, along AZ 264.

At the eastern base of Third Mesa, **Kykotsmovi,** literally "ruins on the hills," is named for the sites on the valley floor

Off the Beaten Path: Coal Canyon

Coal Canyon. Beyond Hotevilla, AZ 264 descends from Third Mesa, exits the Hopi Reservation, and crosses into Navajo territory, past Coal Canyon, where Native Americans have long mined coal from the dark seam just below the rim. The colorful mudstone, dark lines of coal, and bleached white rock have an eerie appearance, especially by the light of the moon. Due to the very rough and narrow road, visiting the canyon with a guide, who can be booked through the Moenkopi Legacy Inn & Suites, is strongly recommended. Twenty miles west of the canyon, at the junction of AZ 264 and U.S. 160, is the town of Moenkopi, the last Hopi outpost. Established as a farming community, it was settled by the descendants of former Oraibi residents.

and in the surrounding hills. Present-day Kykotsmovi was established by Hopi people from nearby Oraibi who either converted to Christianity or wished to attend school and be educated. Kykotsmovi is the seat of the Hopi Tribal Government.

Old Oraibi, a few miles west and on top of Third Mesa at about 7,200 feet in elevation, is believed to be the oldest continuously inhabited community in the United States, dating from around AD 1150. It was also the site of a rare, bloodless conflict between two groups of the Hopi people; in 1906, a dispute, settled uniquely by a "push of war" (a pushing contest), sent the losers off to establish the town of Hotevilla. Oraibi is a dusty spot and, as a courtesy, tourists are asked to park their cars outside and approach the village on foot.

Hotevilla and **Bacavi** are about 4 miles west of Oraibi, and their inhabitants are descended from the former residents of that village. The men of Hotevilla continue to plant crops and beautiful gardens along the mesa slopes. ⊠ *Moenkopi Legacy Inn & Suites, U.S. 160, at AZ 264, Tuba City* ☎ *928/283–4500* ⊕ *www. experiencehopi.com.*

Tuba City

52 miles northwest of Third Mesa on AZ 264.

Tuba City, believed to be named after a Hopi chief, "Tsuve," has about 8,600 permanent residents and is the administrative center for the western portion of the Navajo Nation. Most of the population are Navajo, but there's also a small Hopi community—this is where you'll find the Moenkopi Legacy Inn, which acts as something of a general information center and tour desk for the Hopi tribe. In addition to two hotels and a few restaurants, this small town has a hospital, a bank, a trading post, and a movie theater. In mid- to late October Tuba City hosts the Western Navajo Fair, a celebration combining traditional Navajo song and dance with a parade, pageant, and countless arts-and-crafts exhibits.

GETTING HERE AND AROUND

Tuba City is one of the main base communities in the Navajo and Hopi region as well as a potential base for exploring either rim of the Grand Canyon from the east. The town lies about midway between Flagstaff and Page (80 miles from each) via U.S. 89 and U.S. 160, and 60 miles from the eastern entrance to the South Rim of the Grand Canyon via AZ 64, U.S. 89, and U.S. 160.

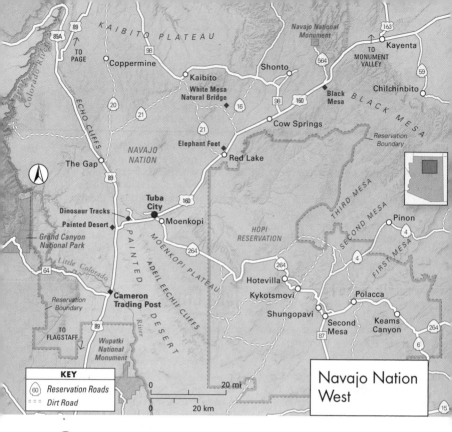

KEY
- 🛣 (60) Reservation Roads
- = = = Dirt Road

Navajo Nation West

0 ———— 20 mi
0 ———— 20 km

◉ Sights

Dinosaur Tracks

ARCHAEOLOGICAL SITE | FAMILY | About 5½ miles west of Tuba City, between mileposts 316 and 317 on U.S. 160, is a small sign for the Dinosaur Tracks. It's free to see these tracks that a dilophosaurus—a carnivorous bipedal reptile over 10 feet tall—left in mud that turned to sandstone, but Navajo guides will often greet you as you arrive and insist on taking you around the site. They're very friendly and helpful, but if you take them up on their offer, they expect to be tipped, usually at least $20. Ask them about guiding you to the nearby petroglyphs and freshwater springs. ⊠ *U.S. 160, between mile markers 316 and 317* 🆓 *Free.*

★ Explore Navajo Interactive Museum

MUSEUM | The tribe operates this enlightening 7,000-square-foot museum, which is set inside a geodesic dome–shaped structure that is meant to recall a traditional Navajo hogan. Inside the dome is a vast trove of artifacts, photos, artwork, and memorabilia. One of the more poignant exhibits tells of the infamous "Long Walk" of 1864, when the U.S. military forced the Navajo to leave their native lands and march to an encampment at Fort Sumner, New Mexico, where they were confined for more than four years. Admission also includes entry to the small **Navajo Code Talkers Memorial Museum** in the back of the Tuba City Trading Post next door. Both facilities are adjacent to the Quality Inn Navajo

Nation. ✉ *10 N. Main St., at Moenave St.* ☎ *928/412-0297, 928/283–4545 Quality Inn* 🌐 *www.explorenavajo.com* 🎟 *$5* 🕒 *Seasonal. Closed weekends.*

Painted Desert
VIEWPOINT | The junction of U.S. 160 with U.S. 89, 4 miles west of the Dinosaur Tracks, is one of the most colorful regions of the Painted Desert, with amphitheaters of maroon, orange, and red rocks facing west—it's especially glorious at sunset. ✉ *Tuba City.*

Tuba City Trading Post
HISTORIC SITE | The octagonal store, founded in the early 1870s, sells groceries and authentic, reasonably priced Navajo rugs, pottery, baskets, and jewelry—it's adjacent to the Quality Inn Navajo Nation and Explore Navajo Interactive Museum. ✉ *Main St. and Moenave Rd.* ☎ *928/283–5441.*

🍴 Restaurants

Hogan's Restaurant
$$ | **SOUTHWESTERN** | The fare at this spot attached to the Quality Inn Navajo Nation is mostly Southwestern and American, but the kitchen also serves a few basic Mexican and Navajo dishes. Highlights include tasty barbecue ribs, mutton stew, and honey-dipped fried chicken. **Known for:** reasonable, non–fast food; tasty Navajo tacos and fry bread; soup and salad bar. [$] *Average main: $15* ✉ *Quality Inn Navajo Nation, 10 Main St.* ☎ *928/283–5260* 🌐 *www.qualityinntubacity.com.*

🛏 Hotels

★ **Moenkopi Legacy Inn & Suites**
$$ | **HOTEL** | **FAMILY** | Operated by the Hopi tribe and situated across from the Tuuvi Travel Center, this striking, contemporary hotel contains light-filled, boldly colored rooms with flat-screen TVs, work desks, and coffeemakers. **Pros:** high-quality furnishings and linens; pool perfect after a day of hiking; guided tours to nearby Hopi villages offered. **Cons:** no restaurant on-site (there's a Denny's next door); at a busy intersection; pricier than most accommodations on Hopi and Navajo lands. [$] *Rooms from: $150* ✉ *U.S. 160, at AZ 264* ☎ *928/283–4500* 🌐 *www.experiencehopi.com* 🛏 *100 rooms* 🍴 *Free breakfast.*

Quality Inn Navajo Nation
$$ | **HOTEL** | Tuba City's longest-running hotel has upgraded its rooms in an effort to better compete with the snazzy Moenkopi Legacy Inn down the street, but it's still a pretty run-of-the-mill property. **Pros:** rooms have attractive Navajo-style prints and art; Navajo museum and trading post are across parking lot; dining on-site plus Navajo fry bread offered in the lobby. **Cons:** rates are a little high for what you get; an older property; beds aren't the most comfortable. [$] *Rooms from: $137* ✉ *10 N. Main St., at Moenave Rd.* ☎ *928/283–4545* 🌐 *www.qualityinn.com* 🛏 *80 rooms* 🍴 *Free breakfast.*

Cameron Trading Post

25 miles southwest of Tuba City on U.S. 89.

Cameron Trading Post and Motel, established in 1916 overlooking a spectacular gorge and vintage suspension bridge, is one of the few remaining authentic trading posts in the Southwest. A convenient stop if you're driving from the Hopi Mesas to the Grand Canyon, it has reasonably priced dining, lodging, camping, and shopping.

GETTING HERE AND AROUND

The trading post is along the main highway (U.S. 89) between Flagstaff and Page and just 30 miles from the eastern entrance to the South Rim of the Grand Canyon.

En Route to Kayenta

As you proceed toward Kayenta, 22 miles northeast of Tuba City on U.S. 160, you'll come to the tiny community of Red Lake. Off to the left of the highway is a geologic phenomenon known as **Elephant Feet.** These massive eroded-sandstone buttes offer a great family photo opportunity to pose under the enormous columns. Northwest of here at the end of a graded dirt road in Navajo backcountry is the **White Mesa Natural Bridge**, a massive arch of white sandstone that extends from the edge of White Mesa. The long **Black Mesa** plateau runs for about 15 miles along U.S. 160. Above the prominent escarpments of this land formation, mining operations—a major source of revenue for the Navajo Nation—delve into the more than 20 billion tons of coal deposited there.

Hotels

Cameron Trading Post

$$ | HOTEL | At the turnoff for the western entrance to the Grand Canyon's South Rim, this trading post dates back to 1916 and contains handsome Southwestern-style rooms with carved-oak furniture, tile baths, and balconies overlooking the Colorado River. **Pros:** impressive collection of Southwestern art in the trading post gallery and gift shop; restaurant serving Native American specialties and American favorites; historic lodging with campground next door. **Cons:** high traffic volume; occasional highway noise; somewhat remote. [$] *Rooms from: $139* ✉ *466 U.S. 89, Cameron* ☎ *800/338–7385* 🌐 *www.camerontradingpost.com* 🛏 *66 rooms* 🍴 *No meals.*

Shopping

Navajo Arts and Crafts Enterprises

CRAFTS | Fine authentic Navajo products are sold at this outlet of the Navajo Arts and Crafts Enterprises, open since 1941. ✉ *U.S. 89, at AZ 64, Cameron* ☎ *928/679–2244* 🌐 *www.gonavajo.com.*

Kayenta

75 miles northeast of Tuba City, on U.S. 160, 22 miles south of Monument Valley.

Kayenta, a small and rather dusty town with a couple of convenience stores, three hotels, and a hospital, is a good base for exploring nearby Monument Valley Navajo Tribal Park and the Navajo National Monument. The Burger King in town has an excellent "Navajo Code Talker" exhibit, with lots of memorabilia relating to this heroic World War II marine group.

GETTING HERE AND AROUND

Kayenta is the first sizable Arizona community you reach if driving to the Navajo Nation via the Four Corners on U.S. 160 or U.S. 163.

Sights

Navajo Cultural Center of Kayenta

MUSEUM | FAMILY | Take a self-guided walking tour through the Navajo Cultural Center of Kayenta, which includes the small Shadehouse Museum and a 2-acre outdoor cultural park. The museum is designed to resemble an authentic shadehouse (these wood-frame, rather crude structures are used to shelter sheepherders in the region's often

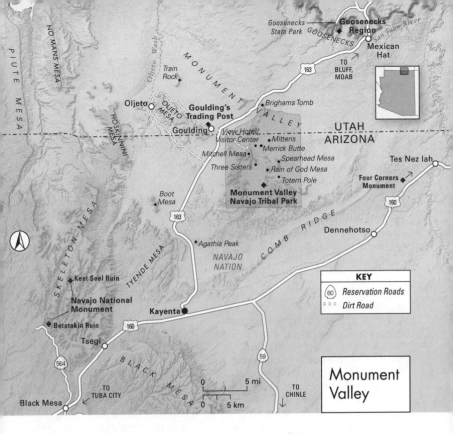

Monument Valley

unforgiving high-desert sun). Inside, visitors will find an extensive collection of Navajo code talkers memorabilia and local artwork, as well as exhibits on the beliefs and traditions that have shaped North America's largest Native American tribe. As you walk through the grounds of the cultural park, note the different types of traditional hogans and sweat lodges. ⊠ *U.S. 160* ✛ *Between Hampton Inn and Burger King* ☎ *928/697–3170 Hampton Inn* 🖾 *Free* ☾ *Museum closed Nov.–Feb.*

🍴 Restaurants

Amigo Cafe
$ | SOUTHWESTERN | The tables are packed with locals who frequent this small establishment, where everything is made from scratch. The delicious fry bread is the real draw. **Known for:** made-from-scratch Mexican dishes; some of the best fry bread in northeast Arizona; adobe-walled patio. $ *Average main: $10* ⊠ *U.S. 163, just north of U.S. 160* ☎ *928/697–8448* ⊕ *www.amigocafekayenta.com* ☾ *Closed Sun.*

Reuben Heflin Restaurant
$$ | AMERICAN | Hampton Inn hotels aren't known for their restaurants, but this attractive spot just off the lobby serves the best food in town. Upholstered Navajo-print chairs with rustic lodge-pole frames, hammered-tin sconces, a wood-beamed ceiling, and a mammoth adobe fireplace set an inviting mood for the American fare with a regional bent. **Known for:** yummy selections from pizza to steak to Navajo specialties; nightly dinner specials; nicest restaurant in the area. $ *Average main: $17* ⊠ *Hampton Inn of Kayenta, U.S. 160* ☎ *928/697–3170* ☾ *No lunch mid-Oct.–mid-Mar.*

Hotels

★ Hampton Inn of Kayenta
$$ | **HOTEL** | **FAMILY** | This warm and inviting hotel is the best accommodation in Kayenta, although it's much like any other hotel in the chain except for its unusually good restaurant and Navajo-inspired design. **Pros:** clean, updated rooms; welcoming staff; excellent restaurant and quality gift shop. **Cons:** books up many weeks in advance in summer; Internet can be spotty; on busy, unattractive stretch of road. [$] *Rooms from: $169* ✉ *U.S. 160* ☎ *928/697–3170* 🌐 *www.hamptoninn.hilton.com* 🛏 *73 rooms* 🍴 *Free breakfast.*

Wetherill Inn
$$ | **HOTEL** | This clean but very basic two-story, red-tile-roofed motel, located in an area with few lodging options, has Southwestern decor and plain but new furnishings. **Pros:** a little closer to Monument Valley than other properties in Kayenta; well-kept guest rooms; curio shop on-site. **Cons:** bland setting; rates a little high for such basic accommodations; thin walls. [$] *Rooms from: $140* ✉ *1000 U.S. 163* ☎ *928/697–3231* 🌐 *www.wetherill-inn.com* 🛏 *54 rooms* 🍴 *Free breakfast.*

Monument Valley Navajo Tribal Park

24 miles northeast of Kayenta, off U.S. 163.

The magnificent Monument Valley stretches to the northeast of Kayenta into Utah. At a base altitude of about 5,500 feet, the sprawling, arid expanse was once populated by Ancestral Puebloan people (more popularly known by the Navajo word "Anasazi," which means both "ancient ones" and "ancient enemies") and in the last few centuries has been home to generations of Navajo farmers. The soaring red buttes, eroded mesas, deep canyons, and naturally sculpted rock formations of Monument Valley are easy to enjoy on a leisurely drive.

Even first-time visitors to Monument Valley typically recognize the otherworldly landscape—it has appeared in countless Hollywood feature films. Straddling the Arizona/Utah border, the Monument Valley Navajo Tribal Park contains a 17-mile drive through this dramatic scenery as well as one of the most beautifully situated hotels in Arizona.

GETTING HERE AND AROUND

The park is just off U.S. 163 north of the Arizona/Utah border and very well marked. At the entrance is a street of disheveled buildings called Vendor Village. Here you can purchase trinkets and souvenirs; bartering is perfectly acceptable and expected.

It's impossible not to drive slowly on this park's bumpy roads, which are best conquered with an SUV or all-wheel-drive vehicle (especially during rainy times of year), but if you take your time and exercise caution, you can make the entire drive in a conventional car. If in doubt, inquire at the drive's entrance gate. Call ahead for road conditions in winter.

Sights

★ Monument Valley Navajo Tribal Park
NATIONAL/STATE PARK | **FAMILY** | For generations, the Navajo have grown crops and herded sheep in Monument Valley, considered to be one of the most scenic and mesmerizing destinations in the Navajo Nation. Within Monument Valley lies the 30,000-acre Monument Valley Navajo Tribal Park, home as well to the View Hotel, where eons of wind and rain have carved the mammoth red-sandstone monoliths into memorable formations. The monoliths, which jut hundreds of feet above the desert floor, stand on the horizon like sentinels, frozen in time and

unencumbered by electric wires, telephone poles, or fences—a scene virtually unchanged for centuries. These are the very same nostalgic images so familiar to movie buffs who recall the early Western films of John Wayne. A 17-mile self-guided driving tour on an extremely rough dirt road (there's only one road, so you can't get lost) passes the memorable **Mittens** and **Totem Pole** formations, among others. ■ **TIP→ Be sure to walk (15 minutes round-trip) from North Window around the end of Cly Butte for the views.** ✉ *Monument Valley Rd., Monument Valley* ✣ *Off U.S. 163, just north of Arizona/Utah border* ☎ *435/727–5874 visitor center* 🌐 *navajonationparks.org* 🎟 *$10 per person or $20 per vehicle (up to 4 people).*

Monument Valley Visitor Center
INFO CENTER | FAMILY | The handsome center contains an extensive crafts shop and exhibits devoted to ancient and modern Native American history, including a display on the World War II Navajo code talkers. Most of the independent guided group tours, necessary to go deep into the valley, leave from the center. You can generally find Navajo guides—who will escort you to places that you are not allowed to visit on your own—in the center or at the booths in the parking lot. The center adjoins the stunning View Hotel (and restaurant), which sits on a gradual rise overlooking the valley and its magnificent red rock monoliths, with big-sky views in every direction. ✉ *Monument Valley Rd., off U.S. 163, Monument Valley* ☎ *435/727–5874* 🌐 *navajonationparks.org.*

🍴 Restaurants

View Restaurant
$$ | **SOUTHWESTERN** | Connected to the View Hotel through a second-floor breezeway, this airy space comprises a few high-ceilinged rooms with massive plate-glass windows framing mesmerizing views of the valley—in warm weather you can dine outside on a terrace, awed by the same panorama. Navajo rugs and local art hang on the walls above the light-wood tables and chairs, and the tribal visitor center's extensive curio shop is attached. **Known for:** massive plate-glass windows framing the iconic Monument Valley landscape; huge portions; good selection of Navajo dishes. [$] *Average main: $15* ✉ *Monument Valley Rd., off U.S. 163* ☎ *435/727–5555* 🌐 *monumentvalleyview.com* ⏲ *No lunch mid-Jan.–Feb. Dinner for hotel guests only.*

🛏 Hotels

★ View Hotel
$$$ | **HOTEL** | The Navajo tribe operates this sleek pink-stucco hotel, the only lodging inside Monument Valley Navajo Tribal Park and one of the most spectacularly situated hotels in the Southwest, with astounding vistas that lend the hotel its name. **Pros:** only hotel in the park; design reflects the surroundings and Navajo culture; unbelievable panoramas from every room; eco-conscious bath products, appliances, and buildings standards; rates are similar to or less than run-of-the-mill hotels nearby. **Cons:** books up weeks in advance in summer; Wi-Fi doesn't reach all rooms; on-site dining is mediocre. [$] *Rooms from: $219* ✉ *Monument Valley Rd., off U.S. 163* ☎ *435/727–5555* 🌐 *monumentvalleyview.com* 🛏 *96 rooms* 🍴 *No meals.*

Activities

Monument Valley Tours
TOUR—SPORTS | Some of the jeep tours on offer include entertainment and outdoor barbecues, and custom hikes into the valley as well. The all-day, 60-mile Monument Valley and Mystery Valley tour, which includes lunch, is especially

Did You Know?

If Monument Valley looks familiar, it probably should. Scenes from many films and shows, including *How the West Was Won*, *Forrest Gump*, *Stagecoach*, *2001: A Space Odyssey*, and HBO's *Westworld*, have been filmed here.

Off the Beaten Path: Four Corners

Four Corners Monument. An inlaid brass plaque marks the only point in the United States where four states meet: Arizona, New Mexico, Colorado, and Utah. Despite the Native American wares and booths selling greasy food, there's not much else to do here but pay a fee and stay long enough to snap a photo; you'll see many a twisted tourist trying to get an arm or a leg in each state. The monument is a 75-mile drive from Kayenta and is administered by the Navajo Nation Parks and Recreation Department. The entry fee is cash only. ⊠ *4 Corners Rd., Teec Nos Pos ✛ 7 miles northwest of U.S. 160 and U.S. 64 junction* ☎ *928/206–2540 Navajo Parks & Recreation Dept.* ⊕ *navajonationparks.org* 🔁 *$5 per person Oct.– Feb.; $10 per person Mar.–Sept.*

popular. ☎ *435/727–3313* ⊕ *www.monumentvalleytours.net* 🔁 *From $70.*

Roy Black's Guided Tours

TOUR—SPORTS | A wide variety of tour options—from jeep and horseback adventures to hiking—are available with this respected tour operator. You can also book an overnight stay in a Navajo hogan. ⊠ *Monument Valley* ☎ *505/701–9609* ⊕ *royblacksguidedtours.com* 🔁 *From $85.*

Sacred Monument Tours

TOUR—SPORTS | Native guides lead hiking, jeep, and horseback-riding tours into Monument Valley. ⊠ *Monument Valley* ☎ *435/727–3218, 435/459–2501 mobile/ text* ⊕ *toursacred.com* 🔁 *From $65.*

Simpson's Trailhandler Tours

TOUR—SPORTS | This operator offers four-wheel-drive jeep trips, photography tours, and guided hikes, plus the chance to stay overnight in a traditional Navajo hogan. If you don't have time or interest in one of the several-hour hiking tours, Simpson's can also customize a fairly easy hour-long guided hike, tailored to your interest and skill level. ⊠ *Monument Valley* ☎ *435/727–3362, 888/723–6236* ⊕ *emonumentvalley.com* 🔁 *From $75.*

Goulding's Trading Post

2 miles west of entrance road to Monument Valley Navajo Tribal Park, off U.S. 163 on Indian Hwy. 42.

Established in 1924 by Harry Goulding and his wife "Mike," this trading post provided a place where Navajos could exchange livestock and handmade goods for necessities. Goulding's is probably best known, though, for being used as a headquarters by director John Ford when he filmed the Western classic *Stagecoach*. Today the compound has a lodge, restaurant, museum, gift shop, grocery store, and campground. The Goulding Museum displays Native American artifacts and Goulding family memorabilia, as well as an excellent multimedia show about Monument Valley.

🛏 Hotels

★ Goulding's Lodge

$$$ | **HOTEL** | Nestled beneath a massive red rock monolith, this two-level property affords spectacular views of Monument Valley from each room's private balcony. **Pros:** incredible views; very peaceful; indoor pool open all year. **Cons:** remote location; not cheap; books up weeks in advance in summer. 💲 *Rooms from:*

$222 ✉ 1000 Gouldings Trading Post Rd., Monument Valley ⊹ U.S. 163 to Monument Valley Rd. (24 miles north of Kayenta), left on Gouldings Trading Post Rd. ☎ 866/313-9769 ⊕ www.gouldings. com ⤳ 159 rooms ⦿ No meals.

Navajo National Monument

53 miles southwest of Goulding's Trading Post, 21 miles west of Kayenta.

It takes a little effort to reach this remote national monument designated on the site of two prominent, 13th-century pueblos, each with well over 100 rooms. You can sign up for a guided ranger-led hike to both ruins or set out on a handful of shorter treks on your own.

GETTING HERE AND AROUND

From Kayenta, take U.S. 160 southwest to AZ 564 and follow signs 9 miles north to the monument. AZ 564 turns north off U.S. 160 at the Black Mesa gas station and convenience store, and leads to the visitor center. No food, gasoline, or hotel lodging is available at the monument, but Kayenta is about a 40-minute drive.

The visitor center houses a small museum, exhibits of prehistoric pottery, and a good crafts shop. Free campground and picnic areas are nearby, and rangers sometimes present campfire programs in summer.

◉ Sights

★ Navajo National Monument

ARCHAEOLOGICAL SITE | Two unoccupied 13th-century cliff pueblos, Betatakin and Keet Seel, stand under the overhanging cliffs of Tsegi Canyon. The largest ancient dwellings in Arizona, these stone-and-mortar complexes were built by Ancestral Puebloans, obviously for permanent occupancy, but abandoned after less than half a century.

The well-preserved, 135-room **Betatakin** (Navajo for "ledge house") is a cluster of cliff dwellings from AD 1250 that seem to hang in midair before a sheer sandstone wall. When discovered in 1907 by a passing American rancher, the apartments were full of baskets, pottery, and preserved grains and ears of corn—as if the occupants had been chased away in the middle of a meal. For an impressive view of Betatakin, walk to the rim overlook about ½ mile from the visitor center. Ranger-led tours (a 5-mile, four-hour, strenuous round-trip hike including a 700-foot descent into the canyon) leave once or twice a day from late May to early September, and on weekends (weather permitting) the rest of the year. No reservations are accepted; groups of no more than 25 form on a first-come-first-serve basis.

Keet Seel (Navajo for "broken pottery") is also in good condition in a serene location, with 160 rooms and 5 kivas dating from AD 950. Explorations of Keet Seel, which lies at an elevation of 7,000 feet and is 8½ miles from the visitor center on foot, are restricted: only 20 people are allowed to visit per day, and only between late May and early September, when a ranger is present at the site. A permit—which also allows campers to stay overnight nearby—is required. To get the permit, all visitors hiking to Keet Seel must attend a mandatory meeting the day before the scheduled hike. ■TIP➔ **Trips to Keet Seel are very popular, so reservations are taken up to two months in advance.** Anyone who suffers from vertigo might want to avoid this trip: the trail leads down a 1,100-foot, near-vertical rock face. ✉ AZ 564, Shonto ⊹ 10 miles north of junction with U.S. 160 ☎ 928/672–2700 ⊕ www.nps.gov/nava ▨ Free.

Ancestral Puebloans' construction methods and their mysterious fate are worth pondering during a visit to Navajo National Monument.

Activities

Navajo National Monument Hiking Trails

HIKING/WALKING | Hiking is the best way for adventurous souls to see the Navajo National Monument. It's a fairly strenuous 5-mile hike to the Betatakin sites, permissible only with a guide from the visitor center, but if you're fit, it's well worth it to visit one of the best-preserved ancient dwellings in the Southwest. It's free, but the trail is open daily only during the summer months (May through September), and on weekends the rest of the year, when weather permits (call ahead to confirm if you are planning to hike October through April); there are two Betatakin hikes each morning. Call ahead to make a reservation—it's a good idea to reserve at least four weeks in advance. There are also three shorter self-guided hikes, open year-round, leaving from the visitor center. All are between a half mile and a full mile round-trip. The Sandal Trail leads to a viewpoint overlooking the Betatakin/ Talastima cliff dwellings, and the Canyon Trail ends at a historic ranger station and

takes in expansive views of Tsegi Canyon. ✉ Shonto ☎ 928/672–2700 ⊕ www.nps. gov/nava 🎫 Free.

Goosenecks Region, Utah

33 miles north of Monument Valley Navajo Tribal Park, on U.S. 163.

Monument Valley's scenic route, U.S. 163, continues from Arizona into Utah, where the land is crossed, east to west, by a stretch of the San Juan River known as the Goosenecks—named for its myriad twists and curves. This barren, erosion-blasted gorge has a stark beauty and is a well-known take-out point for white-water runners on the San Juan, a river that vacationing sleuths will recognize as the setting of many of Tony Hillerman's Jim Chee mystery novels. The small village of Bluff (population 245), which lies at the northeastern end of the region, has an excellent hotel and restaurant, and is a good base for exploring Goosenecks and the northern reaches of Monument Valley.

GETTING HERE AND AROUND

The scenic overlook for the Goosenecks is reached by turning west from U.S. 163 onto UT 261, 4 miles north of the tiny community of **Mexican Hat,** then proceeding on UT 261 for 1 mile to a directional sign at the road's junction with UT 316. Turn left onto UT 316 and proceed 4 miles to the vista-point parking lot. To take in spectacular scenery, drive northeast on U.S. 163 from Kayenta through Monument Valley all the way past Mexican Hat to Bluff, then turn south on U.S. 191 back into Arizona, and then turn west onto U.S. 160 back to Kayenta; the 140-mile loop takes three hours without stops, but allow a full day for breaks and lunch in Bluff.

Sights

Goosenecks State Park

NATIONAL/STATE PARK | From the overlook you can peer down on what geologists claim is the best example of an "entrenched meander" in the world. The river's serpentine course resembles the necks of geese in spectacular 1,000-foot-deep chasms. Although the Goosenecks of the San Juan River is a state park, no facilities other than pit toilets are provided, and no fee is charged. You'll find it 10 miles northwest of Mexican Hat off Highway 261. ✉ *Hwy. 316, Mexican Hat.*

Restaurants

★ Twin Rocks Cafe

$$ | **ECLECTIC** | It's hard to miss this low-slung, roadhouse-style restaurant in Bluffs—it's tucked beneath a sandstone ridge crowned by two rock pillars that look as though they might topple in a bad storm. Here you'll find the most varied menu in the region with everything from country fried steak to a Navajo burger using fry bread. **Known for:** outdoor patio surrounded by breathtaking sandstone landscape; picnic lunches to go for a day of exploring; breakfast served all day. [$] *Average main: $13* ✉ *913 E. Navajo Twins Dr., off U.S. 191, Bluff* ☎ *435/672–2341* 🌐 *www.twinrockscafe.com.*

Hotels

★ Desert Rose Inn and Cabins

$$ | **HOTEL** | This nicely maintained motel with a handsome timber-frame facade and panoramic views of the surrounding red rocks is in Bluff, 25 miles northeast of Mexican Hat; it's an excellent base for exploring Goosenecks State Park, the northern end of Monument Valley, and even Canyonlands National Park, to the north. **Pros:** family-owned and run by a great staff; scenic setting; good base if you're coming from points north or east; indoor pool. **Cons:** a 40-minute (beautiful) drive to Monument Valley Tribal Park; no alcohol at on-site restaurant. [$] *Rooms from: $170* ✉ *701 W. U.S. 191, Bluff* ☎ *435/672–2303, 888/475–7673* 🌐 *www.desertroseinn.com* 🛏 *53 rooms* 🍴 *No meals.*

San Juan Inn & Trading Post

$ | **HOTEL** | This quirky motel's well-maintained, Southwestern-style, rustic rooms overlook the San Juan River in Mexican Hat, Utah, and the setting, against the red rocks, is quite inspiring, even if accommodations have few frills. **Pros:** magnificent setting; affordable rooms; parking right outside your room; three yurts available for glamping; restaurant with a liquor license. **Cons:** basic room decor—it's all about the setting; nothing much in Mexican Hat; no Internet. [$] *Rooms from: $100* ✉ *U.S. 163, at San Juan River, Mexican Hat* ☎ *435/683–2220* 🌐 *www.sanjuaninn.net* 🛏 *45 rooms* 🍴 *No meals.*

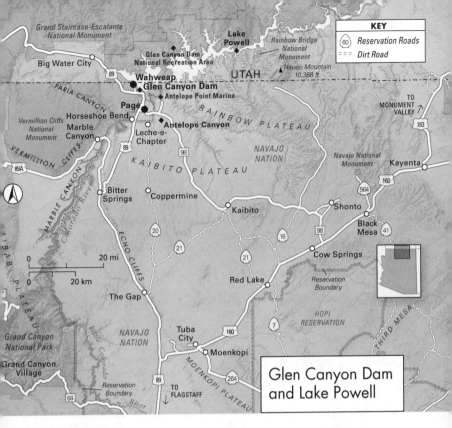

KEY

🛣 60 Reservation Roads
═══ Dirt Road

Glen Canyon Dam and Lake Powell

Glen Canyon Dam and Lake Powell

1 mile north of Page on U.S. 89.

Lake Powell is the heart of the huge Glen Canyon National Recreation Area, which at about 1.25 million acres is roughly the size of Grand Canyon National Park. Created by the barrier of Glen Canyon Dam in the Colorado River, Lake Powell is ringed by red cliffs that twist off into 96 major canyons and countless inlets (most accessible only by boat) with huge, red-sandstone buttes randomly jutting from the sapphire waters. It extends through terrain so rugged it was the last major area of the United States to be mapped. In the 1990s, the Sierra Club and Glen Canyon Institute started a movement to drain the lake to restore water-filled Glen Canyon, which some believe was more spectacular than the Grand Canyon, but these efforts failed to gain significant momentum, and the lake is likely to be around for years to come. The remote lakefront and rock formations are best visited by tour boat or houseboat.

■ **TIP →** **For restaurants and hotels near Glen Canyon Dam and Lake Powell, see Page or Wahweap marina, the area's closest access points.**

GETTING HERE AND AROUND
Just off the highway at the north end of the bridge is the **Carl Hayden Visitor Center,** where you can learn about the controversial creation of Glen Canyon Dam and Lake Powell, enjoy panoramic views of both, and take guided tours of the dam ($5).

👁 Sights

★ Glen Canyon Dam National Recreation Area

DAM | FAMILY | Once you leave the Page business district heading northwest, the Glen Canyon Dam National Recreation Area and Lake Powell behind it immediately become visible. This concrete-arch dam—all 5 million cubic feet of it—was completed in September 1963, its power plant an engineering feat that rivaled the Hoover Dam. The dam's crest is 1,560 feet across and rises 710 feet from bedrock and 583 feet above the waters of the Colorado River. When Lake Powell is full, it's 560 feet deep at the dam. The plant generates some 1.3 million kilowatts of electricity when each generator's 40-ton shaft is producing nearly 200,000 horsepower. Power from the dam serves a five-state grid consisting of Colorado, Arizona, Utah, California, and New Mexico, and provides energy for more than 1.5 million users.

With only 8 inches of annual rainfall, the Lake Powell area enjoys blue skies nearly year-round. Summer temperatures range from the 60s to the 90s. Fall and spring are usually balmy, with daytime temperatures often in the 70s and 80s, but chilly weather can set in. Nights are cool even in summer, and in winter the risk of a cold spell increases, but all-weather houseboats and tour boats make for year-round cruising. Boaters and campers should note that regulations require the use of portable toilets on the lake and lakeshore to prevent water pollution. ✉ *U.S. 89, Page ✛ 2 miles northwest of town* ☎ *928/608–6200* ⊕ *www.nps.gov/ glca* 🎫 *$30 per vehicle or $15 per person (entering on foot or by bicycle), good for up to 7 days; boating fee $30 up to 7 days.*

Lake Powell

BODY OF WATER | You could spend 30 years exploring the lake's 2,000 miles of shoreline within Glen Canyon National Recreation Area and still not experience everything there is to see. Most of us have only a few days or a week, but that's still plenty of time for recreation in the second-largest reservoir in the nation. Every water sport imaginable awaits you, from waterskiing to fishing. Renting a houseboat and camping are popular within Lake Powell, though small communities around marinas in Page and Wahweap have hotels, restaurants, and shops where you can restock vital supplies.

South of Lake Powell the landscape gives way to **Echo Cliffs,** orange-sand-stone formations rising 1,000 feet and more above the highway in places. At **Bitter Springs** the road ascends the cliffs and provides a spectacular view of the 9,000-square-mile Arizona Strip to the west and the 3,000-foot Vermilion Cliffs to the northwest. ✉ *Page ✛ 2 miles northwest of Page via S Lake Powell Blvd. and US-89* ⊕ *www.lakepowell.com.*

🏃 Activities

For water sports on Lake Powell, see Wahweap. For Horseshoe Bend Trail, see Page.

Dam Overlook

HIKING/WALKING | This hike, a short walk from the parking lot down a flight of uneven rock steps, takes you to a viewpoint on the canyon rim high above the Colorado River, and provides fantastic views of the Colorado as it flows through Glen Canyon. *Easy.* ✉ *Off U.S. 89, Page ✛ To reach parking lot, turn west on Scenic View Dr., 1½ miles south of Carl Hayden Visitor Center.*

Page

90 miles west of the Navajo National Monument, 136 miles north of Flagstaff on U.S. 89.

Built in 1957 as a Glen Canyon Dam construction camp, Page is now a tourist spot and a popular base for day trips to Lake Powell; it's also become a major point of entry to Horseshoe Bend Trail and Navajo Nation's Antelope Canyon. At the nearby Vermilion Cliffs, the endangered California condor has been successfully reintroduced into the wild. The town's human population of about 7,600 makes it the largest community in far-northern Arizona, and each year more than 3 million people come to play at Lake Powell.

GETTING HERE AND AROUND

Most of the motels, restaurants, and shopping centers are concentrated along Lake Powell Boulevard, the name given to U.S. 89 as it loops through the business district.

The only airline that offers service directly to Northeast Arizona is Contour Airlines, which flies into Page Municipal Airport (PGA) from Phoenix Sky Harbor International Airport (PHX).

CONTACTS Contour Airlines. ☎ *888/332–6686 reservations* 🌐 *www.contourairlines.com.* **Page Municipal Airport.** ✉ *238 10th Ave.* ☎ *928/645–4240* 🌐 *www.cityofpage.org.*

VISITOR INFORMATION

CONTACTS Page/Lake Powell Tourism Bureau. ✉ *Powell Museum, 6 N. Lake Powell Blvd.* ☎ *928/645–9496* 🌐 *www.visitpagelakepowell.com.*

Sights

Powell Museum

MUSEUM | At the corner of North Navajo Drive and Lake Powell Boulevard is the Powell Museum, whose namesake, John Wesley Powell, led the first known expeditions down the Green River and the rapids-choked Colorado through the Grand Canyon between 1869 and 1872. Powell mapped and kept detailed records of his trips, naming the Grand Canyon and many other geographic points of interest in northern Arizona. Artifacts from his expeditions are displayed in the museum. The museum also doubles as the town's visitor information center. A travel desk dispenses information and allows you to book boating tours, raft trips, scenic flights, accommodations in Page, or Antelope Canyon tours. When you sign up for tours here, concessionaires give a donation to the nonprofit museum with no extra charge to you. ✉ *6 N. Lake Powell Blvd.* ☎ *928/640–3900* 🌐 *www.powellmuseum.org* 🎟 *Free, donations accepted.*

Restaurants

Big John's Texas BBQ

$$ | **BARBECUE** | Hungry carnivores queue under a blanket of smoke for fall-off-the-bone-tender pork ribs, Texas-style low-and-slow-cooked brisket, and hot corn bread muffins drizzled with honey. Seating is inside a repurposed gas station or at picnic tables under the covered space where the pumps used to be. **Known for:** some of the best Texas-style barbecue in the state; live country music and line dancing; covered outdoor patio. [$] *Average main: $15* ✉ *153 S. Lake Powell Blvd.* ☎ *928/645–3300* 🌐 *www.bigjohnstexasbbq.com* 🕒 *Closed Dec. and Jan.*

BirdHouse

$ | **FAST FOOD** | Fried chicken is elevated to an art form at this repurposed Sonic Drive-In with a walk-up counter and covered patio dining. Choose from three crispy coating flavors (original, very spicy, or honey butter) and sides like crinkle-cut fries and broccoli salad. **Known for:** fast fried chicken; outdoor dining; Arizona-brewed beer. $ *Average main: $10* ⌧ *707 N. Navajo Dr.* ☎ *928/645-4087* ⊕ *www.birdhouseaz.com* ⊗ *Closed Wed.*

El Tapatio

$$ | **MEXICAN** | This small, colorful cantina inside a modest-looking former fast-food restaurant is part of an affordable and consistently good chain. Spend any time waiting for a table perusing the astoundingly long menu's mix of Americanized and authentic Mexican dishes, including charcoal-grilled carne asada and *mariscada a la diabla* (real crab legs, tilapia, scallops, octopus, and jumbo shrimp cooked in a spicy sauce). **Known for:** 10-page menu; more than 125 tequilas; south-of-the-border seafood. $ *Average main: $18* ⌧ *25 Lake Powell Blvd.* ☎ *928/645–4055* ⊕ *www.tapatiorestaurants.com.*

🛏 Hotels

Best Western View of Lake Powell

$$ | **HOTEL** | On a bluff at the northern end of Page, this ordinary though reliable motel has large rooms with beige and burnt-orange walls, queen-size beds, and simple furnishings, not to mention some of the best views of Lake Powell, just 2 miles away, in the area. **Pros:** panoramic views with lake in the distance; renovated rooms; fine dining restaurant next door. **Cons:** pricey for what you get; few amenities; mediocre breakfast. $ *Rooms from: $150* ⌧ *716 Rimview Dr.* ☎ *928/645–8868, 800/780–7234* ⊕ *www. bestwestern.com* ⇗ *102 rooms* ⫶⊙⫶ *Free breakfast.*

Lake Powell Fast Facts

■ Lake Powell is 185 miles long with nearly 2,000 miles of shoreline—longer than America's Pacific coast.

■ It is the second-largest man-made lake in the nation, and it took 17 years to fill.

■ The Glen Canyon Dam is a 710-foot-tall wall of concrete.

Days Inn & Suites by Wyndham Page Lake Powell

$$ | **HOTEL** | It may be part of a budget chain, but this particular Days Inn—an attractive Southwest-style building atop a plateau with expansive views—is the best among value-oriented accommodations in the region. **Pros:** many rooms have balconies; superfriendly staff; panoramic views. **Cons:** need a car to get to downtown shopping and restaurants; on a busy road at the edge of town; better rates than competitors but can still be pricey in summer. $ *Rooms from: $154* ⌧ *961 N. U.S. 89* ☎ *928/645–2800, 800/329–1992 reservations* ⊕ *www.wyndhamhotels.com* ⇗ *82 rooms* ⫶⊙⫶ *Free breakfast.*

Hampton Inn and Suites Page–Lake Powell

$$$ | **HOTEL** | Conveniently located right off Highway 89, this comfortable and exceedingly clean Hampton Inn, one of the newest hotels in Page, has bright, larger-than-expected rooms with TVs and work space. **Pros:** one of the newest hotels in Page; good value for the area; indoor pool with outdoor sundeck. **Cons:** farther from restaurants and shopping than other area hotels; can be noisy; Internet can be spotty. $ *Rooms from: $200* ⌧ *294 Sandhill Rd.* ☎ *928/645–0075, 855/605–0317* ⊕ *www.hamptoninn.com* ⇗ *102 rooms* ⫶⊙⫶ *Free breakfast.*

Houseboats are a unique lodging option; they're also great for exploring Lake Powell's almost 2,000 miles of shoreline.

🏃 Activities

For water sports on Lake Powell, see Wahweap.

Glen Canyon Recreation Area

BOATING | Check out the park website to help plan your Glen Canyon trip. ☎ 928/608–6200 ⊕ www.nps.gov/glca.

BOATING

★ Colorado River Discovery

TOUR—SPORTS | FAMILY | This respected outfitter offers waterborne tours, including a 4½-hour guided rafting excursion down a calm portion of the Colorado River on comfortable, motorized pontoon boats. The scenery—multicolor-sandstone cliffs adorned with Native American petroglyphs—is spectacular. The company also offers full-day rowing trips along the river, using smaller boats maneuvered by well-trained guides. These trips are quieter and more low-key, and provide a more intimate brush with this magnificent body of water. ✉ 6900 Townsend Winona Rd., Flagstaff ☎ 800/637–7238 ⊕ outdoorsunlimited.com/colorado-river-discovery.html ✉ From $87.

GOLF

Lake Powell National Golf Course

GOLF | Wide fairways, tiered greens with some of the steepest holes in the Southwest, and a generous lack of hazards make for a pleasant golfing experience. From the fairways you can enjoy spectacular vistas of Glen Canyon Dam and Lake Powell. ✉ 400 Clubhouse Dr., off U.S. 89 ☎ 928/645–2023 ⊕ lakepowellnationalgolfcourse.com ✉ $65 ⚑ 18 holes, 7064 yards, par 72.

HIKING

★ Horseshoe Bend Trail

HIKING/WALKING | The views along this hike are well worth the steep up-and-down paths and the bit of deep sand to maneuver. The trail leads up to a bird's-eye view of Glen Canyon and the Colorado River downstream from Glen Canyon Dam. There are some sheer drop-offs here, so watch children. To reach the trail, drive 4 miles south of Page on U.S. 89 and turn west (right) onto a blacktop

Midday light on Antelope Canyon's sandstone walls is a favorite shot for many photographers.

road just south of mile marker 545. It's a ¾-mile hike from the parking area to the top of the canyon, and the entire round-trip hike can easily be done in an hour. ■TIP➡ **No parking on U.S. 89.** *Difficult.* ✉ *Off U.S. 89* ⊕ *cityofpage.org/hsb* 🖃 *$10 per car.*

Antelope Canyon

4 miles east of Page in the Navajo Nation, on AZ 98.

It's saying a lot that in the beautiful swath of Northeast Arizona, Antelope Canyon is arguably the favorite destination of both professional and amateur photographers. Accessible only if accompanied by a licensed Navajo guide, Antelope Canyon is a narrow, red-sandstone slot canyon famous for the mesmerizing way sunlight filters through it.

GETTING HERE AND AROUND

Access to Antelope Canyon is restricted by the Navajo tribe to licensed tour operators. The tribe charges an $8 per-person fee,

included in the price of tours offered by the licensed concessionaires in Page. The easiest way to book a tour is in town at the John Wesley Powell Memorial Museum Visitor Center. Most companies offer 1- to 1½-hour sightseeing tours for about $60 to $80. ■TIP➡ **The best time to see the canyon is between 8 am and 2 pm. Note that photography tours of Upper Antelope Canyon (the most popular one) are no longer allowed due to crowds. You are allowed to take photos on a regular tour but without a monopod or tripod.**

TOURS

Antelope Canyon Navajo Tours

GUIDED TOURS | One-hour sightseeing tours are available at Antelope Canyon. The canyon's $8 admission fee is included. ☎ *928/310–9458, 928/691–0244* ⊕ *navajotours.com* 🖃 *$80.*

Antelope Canyon Tours

GUIDED TOURS | Several tours are offered daily, from 8 am to 4:30 pm, each running 90 minutes. The company also offers all-day Vermilion Cliff tour options. ✉ *22 S. Lake Powell Blvd., Page* ☎ *855/574–9102* ⊕ *www.antelopecanyon.com* 🖃 *From $57.*

Sights

★ Antelope Canyon

CANYON | You've probably seen dozens of photographs of Antelope Canyon, a narrow, red-sandstone slot canyon with convoluted corkscrew formations, dramatically illuminated by light streaming down from above. And you're likely to see assorted shutterbugs waiting patiently for just the right shot of these colorful, photogenic rocks, which are actually petrified sand dunes. The best photos are taken at high noon, when light filters through the slot in the canyon surface. Be prepared to protect your camera equipment against blowing dust and leave your tripod and monopod at home. Navajo Nation and Recreation no longer permits photography tours of the canyon, and while regular tours permit you to take photos, you won't be able to set up your tripod or monopod during your visit. ✉ *AZ 98, Page* ✣ *3 miles east of Page* ☎ *928/871–6647* 🌐 *navajonationparks.org* 🎟 *$8.*

Restaurants

Ja'di' To'oh at Antelope Point Marina

$$$ | **AMERICAN** | The floating, sandstone restaurant and lounge at the Navajo-operated Antelope Point Marina serves decent American food with contemporary accents—wood-fired pizzas, fish tacos, Angus burgers, and rib eye steak with garlic-herb butter—and has one of the region's better wine lists. It's a long walk from the parking area to the front door, but staff whisk visitors to and fro in golf carts. **Known for:** dramatic dining room with soaring windows overlooking Lake Powell; proximity to Antelope Canyon, so popular spot to catch lunch after a tour; vegetarian options. [$] *Average main: $22* ✉ *537 Marina Pkwy., end of Indian Rte. N22B, off AZ 98, Page* ✣ *9 miles northeast of Page* ☎ *928/645–5900* 🌐 *www.antelopepointlakepowell.com* 🕑 *Closed Jan. and Feb.*

Activities

Antelope Point Marina

BOATING | **FAMILY** | About 5 miles north of AZ 98, opposite the turnoff for Antelope Canyon, the Navajo Nation built Antelope Point Marina in the early 2000s on a scenic canyon of Lake Powell. This impressive 27,000-square-foot floating village has 300 wet slips for houseboats and watercraft, a variety of boat and houseboat rentals, the Ja'di' To'oh restaurant and lounge, a seasonal ice-cream stand, a fishing dock, and a market. ✉ *537 Marina Pkwy. Hwy. N22B, off AZ 98, Page* ✣ *9 miles northeast of Page* ☎ *928/645–5900* 🌐 *www.antelopepointlakepowell.com.*

Wahweap

5 miles north of Glen Canyon Dam on U.S. 89.

Most waterborne recreational activity on the Arizona side of Lake Powell is centered on this vacation village, where everything needed for a lakeside holiday is available: tour boats, fishing, boat rentals, dinner cruises, and more. The Lake Powell Resorts have excellent views of the lake area, and you can take a boat tour from the Wahweap Marina.

GETTING HERE AND AROUND

Wahweap has two well-marked entrance roads off U.S. 89, one just north of Glen Canyon Dam, and the other about 3½ miles north and more direct if arriving from Utah. Keep in mind that you must pay the Glen Canyon National Recreation Area entry fee on entering Wahweap—this is true even if you're just passing through or having a meal at Lake Powell Resorts (although the fee collection stations are often closed in winter, meaning you can pass through freely).

Sights

Rainbow Bridge National Monument

NATURE SITE | The 290-foot red-sandstone arch is the world's largest natural bridge; it can be reached by boat or strenuous hike and can also be viewed by air. A boat tour to the monument ($126) is a great way to see not only the monument but also the enormity of the lake and its incredible, rugged beauty. The lake level is down, however, due to the prolonged drought throughout the region, so expect a 1-mile (or more) hike from the boat dock to the monument. To the Navajos this is a sacred area with deep religious and spiritual significance, so outsiders are asked not to hike underneath the arch itself. ✉ *Wahweap* ☎ *928/608–6200, 888/896-3829 boat tour info* 🌐 *www.nps.gov/rabr* 🎟 *Free.*

Slot Canyons

Slot canyons are unique to the Southwest. Carved through sandstone by wind and water, they're narrow at the top—some are only a foot wide on the surface—and wider at the bottom, which can be more than 100 feet below ground level. The play of light as it filters down through the slot onto the sandstone walls makes them remarkable subjects for photographs, but they're dangerous, particularly during the summer rainy season when flash floods can rush through them and sweep away an unwary hiker. Before hiking, consult with locals and check the weather.

Hotels

★ Amangiri

$$$$ | **RESORT** | One of just two U.S. properties operated by the famously luxurious Aman resort company, this ultraplush and ultraexpensive 34-suite compound lies just a few miles north of Lake Powell on a 600-acre plot of rugged high desert, soaring red rock cliffs, and jagged mesas. **Pros:** stunning accommodations inside and out; exceedingly gracious and professional staff; world-class restaurant and spa; endless activities. **Cons:** many times more expensive than most accommodations in the area; extremely remote; airy, super-sleek rooms are gorgeous but not everyone's idea of cozy. [$] *Rooms from: $3500* ✉ *1 Kayenta Rd., Canyon Point* ✣ *15 miles northwest of Page, off U.S. 89* ☎ *435/675–3999, 877/695–3999 reservations* 🌐 *www.aman.com* 🛏 *34 suites* 🍴 *All meals.*

Dreamkatchers Lake Powell Bed and Breakfast

$$ | **B&B/INN** | This sleek, contemporary Southwestern-style home sits on a bluff just a few miles northwest of Lake Powell and 15 miles from Page. **Pros:** peaceful and secluded location perfect for stargazing; delicious breakfasts; laid-back, friendly hosts. **Cons:** often booked months in advance; few services in the remote surrounding area; late check-in not available. [$] *Rooms from: $175* ✉ *1055 S. American Way, Big Water* ☎ *435/675–5828* 🌐 *www.dreamkatchers-lakepowell.com* 🕒 *Closed mid-Nov.–mid-Mar.* 🛏 *3 rooms* 🍴 *Free breakfast.*

Lake Powell Resorts & Marinas

$$$ | **RESORT** | **FAMILY** | This sprawling property consisting of several one- and two-story buildings, run by Aramark, sits on a promontory above Lake Powell and serves as the center for recreational activities in the area—guests can relax beside two seasonal swimming pools. **Pros:** stunning lake setting; couldn't be closer to the water; all rooms have patios or balconies. **Cons:** can be a long way from your room to the restaurant and lobby; property in need of a refresh; only reliable Internet is in the lobby. [$] *Rooms from: $225* ✉ *100 Lake Shore Dr., off U.S. 89, Page* ✣ *7 miles north of Page* ☎ *888/896–3829* 🌐 *www.lakepowell.com* 🛏 *348 rooms* 🍴 *No meals.*

HOUSEBOATS

Without a doubt, the most popular and fun way to vacation on Lake Powell is to rent a houseboat. Houseboats, ranging in size from 46 to 75 feet and sleeping 6 to 16 people, come complete with marine radios, fully equipped kitchens, and bathrooms with hot showers; you need only bring sheets and towels. The larger, luxury boats are a good choice in hot summer months, since they have air-conditioning.

Lake Powell Resorts & Marinas

Houseboat rentals at this marina—the only concessionaire that rents boats on Lake Powell—range widely in size, amenities, and price, depending on season. A smaller, more basic houseboat that sleeps up to 12 runs from $3,800 for a week in winter to about $6,000 for a week during the summer peak. At the other end of the spectrum, 75-foot luxury houseboats, some of which can sleep up to 16, cost as much as $15,000 in high season for seven nights. You receive hands-on instruction before you leave the marina. You may want to rent a powerboat or personal watercraft along with a houseboat to explore the many narrow canyons and waterways on the lake. A 19-foot powerboat for eight passengers starts at $360 and goes to $500 per day from June through mid-August. Kayaks rent for $50 per day, and wakeboards, water skis, stand-up paddleboards, and Jet Skis are also available. There are many vacation packages available. ✉ *100 Lakeshore Dr.* ☎ *928/645–2433, 888/896–3829* 🌐 *www.lakepowell.com.*

Activities

BOATING

One of the most scenic lakes of the American West, Lake Powell has 185 miles of clear sapphire waters edged with vast canyons of red and orange rock. Ninety-six major side canyons intricately twist and turn into the main channel of Lake Powell, into what was once the main artery of the Colorado River through Glen Canyon. In some places the lake is 500 feet deep, and by June the lake's waters begin to warm and stay that way well into October.

Lake Powell Resort

TOUR—SPORTS | **FAMILY** | Excursions on double-decker scenic cruisers piloted by experienced guides leave from the dock of Lake Powell Resort. The most popular tour is the full-day trip to Rainbow Bridge National Monument. Other options include two-hour sunset dinner cruises, two-hour Antelope Canyon cruises, and Canyon Adventure tour that visits both Antelope Canyon and Navajo Canyon. Tours generally run spring through early fall. ✉ *100 Lake Shore Dr., Page* ☎ *928/645–2433, 888/896–3829* 🌐 *www.lakepowell.com* 🎟 *From $48.*

Wahweap Marina

BOATING | The largest and most impressive of the five full-service Lake Powell marinas run by Aramark's Lake Powell Resorts & Marinas has more than 900 slips and the most facilities, including a floating restaurant, public launch ramp, camping, extensive docks, fishing guide and private tour services, and a marina store, where you can buy fishing licenses and other necessities. It's the only full-service marina on the Arizona side of the lake. ✉ *100 Lake Shore Dr., Page* ☎ *888/896–3829* 🌐 *www.lakepowell.com/executive-marina.aspx.*

CAMPING

Beautiful campsites are abundant on Lake Powell, from large beaches to secluded coves, with the most desirable areas accessible only by boat. You're allowed to camp anywhere along the shores of the lake unless it's restricted by the National Park Service; however, camping within ¼ mile of the shoreline requires a portable toilet or bathroom facilities on your boat. Campfires are allowed on the shoreline, but since there's little firewood available around the lake you'll need to bring your own.

The **Wahweap Campground,** run by the National Park Service concessionaire, has views of the lake and serves both RVers and tent campers. There are showers and coin-laundry services at the nearby grocery store, and it's convenient to restaurants and marina. Some sites even pick up campground Wi-Fi.

FISHING

Marina Store at Wahweap Marina

FISHING | Anglers delight in the world-class bass fishing on Lake Powell. You'll hear over and over how the big fish are "biting in the canyons," so you'll need a small vessel if you plan on fishing for the big one. Landing a 20-pound striper isn't unusual (the locals' secret is to use anchovies for bait). Fishing licenses for both Arizona and Utah are available at the Marina Store at Wahweap Marina. Afterwards, catch a bite to eat at Latitude 37, the marina's floating restaurant, from Memorial Day through Labor Day. ✉ *100 Lake Shore Dr., Page* ☎ *888/896–3829* ⊕ *www.lakepowell.com/executive-marina.aspx.*

Stix Liquor & Sporting Goods

FISHING | Come to Stix for supplies and fishing-guide recommendations. ✉ *5 S. Lake Powell Blvd., Page* ☎ *928/645–2891.*

HIKING

Bring plenty of water when hiking at Lake Powell and drink often. It's important to remember to watch the sky for storms: it may not be raining where you are, but flooding can occur in downstream canyons—particularly slot canyons—from a storm miles away.

Lake Powell Navajo Tribal Park Office

HIKING/WALKING | At this office near Page Hospital, you can purchase backcountry permits ($12 per person per 24-hour period), which are required before hiking to Rainbow Bridge or elsewhere on wilderness lands in the Navajo Nation. The office is open weekdays 8 to 5 and only accepts exact cash. ■TIP→ **Purchasing permits online is a simpler option.** ✉ *337 N. Navajo Dr., Page* ☎ *928/645–0268* ⊕ *navajonationparks.org.*

Rainbow Bridge

HIKING/WALKING | Only seasoned hikers in good physical condition will want to try either of the trails leading to Rainbow Bridge; both are about 35 miles round-trip through challenging and rugged terrain with few trail signs. This site is considered sacred by the Navajo; visitors are asked to show respect by not walking under the bridge and backcountry hiking permits are required. Take Indian Highway 16 north toward the Utah state border. At the fork in the road, take either direction for about 5 miles to the trailhead leading to Rainbow Bridge. Excursion boats pull in at the dock near the arch, but no supplies are sold there. *Difficult.* ✉ *Page* ⊕ *www.nps.gov/rabr.*

Chapter 7

EASTERN ARIZONA

WITH THE PETRIFIED FOREST

Updated by
Elise Riley

7

⊙ Sights	🍴 Restaurants	🛏 Hotels	🛍 Shopping	🍸 Nightlife
★★★☆☆	★★☆☆☆	★★☆☆☆	★★☆☆☆	★★☆☆☆

WELCOME TO EASTERN ARIZONA

TOP REASONS TO GO

★ **Get outside:** No place for couch potatoes, Eastern Arizona is home to some of the state's best recreation areas for skiing, fishing, camping, and exploring. If you love the outdoor life, you might fall in love with this place.

★ **Be petrified:** Marvel at huge fossilized logs and the dazzling colors of nature at Petrified Forest National Park.

★ **View nature's handiwork at Salt River Canyon:** Watch the desert cacti disappear as the country's pines delight your senses. U.S. 60 dramatically switchbacks down—and back up—2,000 feet of eroded canyon.

★ **Hit the road:** Whether you're traveling the Coronado Trail National Scenic Byway or getting your kicks on Route 66, these roads were made for travelers.

★ **Discover native traditions:** The rich culture and heritage of Native American tribes permeates this area.

This large region is made up of small towns and historic sites along the Mogollon Rim, where the topography is markedly different than the rest of the state. In the White Mountains, forests of towering pine trees replace the desert and provide great opportunities for camping and outdoor adventures. It's also home to Petrified Forest National Park and its beautiful Painted Desert.

1 Salt River Canyon. Watch the desert cacti disappear and the ponderosa pines emerge at this geological marvel.

2 Show Low. A central base from which to explore eastern Arizona, Show Low got its name from the turn of a playing card.

3 Pinetop-Lakeside. Home to the largest stand of ponderosa pines in the world, Pinetop-Lakeside is a haven for outdoors enthusiasts.

4 Snowflake-Taylor. One of Arizona's quintessential small towns, Snowflake-Taylor celebrates Arizona's pioneers.

5 Coronado Trail. This winding, 123-mile stretch of state highway boasts some of the most scenic views in the state, including those at Blue Vista and Rose Peak.

6 Springerville-Eagar. A favorite place for road-trippers to enjoy an overnight rest, Springerville-Eagar is also a place to admire petroglyphs.

7 Petrified Forest National Park. The Petrified Forest takes you back in time, with fossils that help you see the plant and animal life of a former ecosystem. One of Arizona's most unusual sites, the park has yielded animal fossils, some even as large as nearly 200 feet. It's worth the trip just to see the park's beautiful Painted Desert—especially if you catch the brilliant colors of the landscape at midday.

8 Holbrook. Famous for Route 66 and the historic Wigwam Motel, Holbrook awakens the feeling of nostalgia in all travelers.

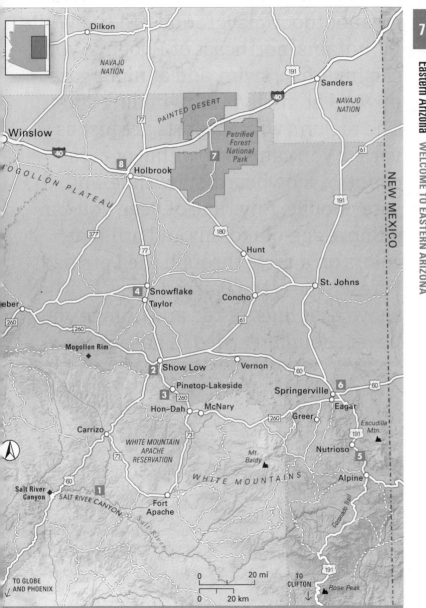

Dilkon

NAVAJO
NATION

191

Sanders

NAVAJO
NATION

40

PAINTED DESERT

77

Winslow

40

61

MOGOLLON PLATEAU

8 Holbrook

7 Petrified
Forest
National
Park

191

377

180

77

Hunt

NEW MEXICO

4 Snowflake
Taylor

Concho

St. Johns

61

eber

260

260

Mogollon Rim

2 Show Low

Vernon

60

6 Springerville

3 Pinetop-Lakeside

260

Eagar

Hon–Dah

McNary

260

Greer

60

Carrizo

WHITE MOUNTAIN
APACHE
RESERVATION

73

Mt.
Baldy

Escudilla
Mtn.

191

Nutrioso 5

Salt River
Canyon

60

SALT RIVER CANYON

73

1

WHITE MOUNTAINS

Alpine

Fort
Apache

Salt River

Coronado Trail

191

TO GLOBE
AND PHOENIX

0   20 mi

0   20 km

TO
CLIFTON

191

Rose Peak

In a state of dramatic natural wonders, Eastern Arizona is often overlooked. This is unfortunate, as it's one of Arizona's great outdoor playgrounds. In the White Mountains, northeast of Phoenix, you can hike, fish, swim, and at night gaze upward at millions of twinkling stars. The region's winter sports are just as varied: you can ski downhill or cross-country, snowboard, snowshoe, and snowmobile. Any time of year, you can glimpse age-old fossils and brilliant colors on a drive through the Petrified Forest, where the Painted Desert showcases hues of red and orange you never thought existed in nature.

The White Mountains are unspoiled high country at its best. In vast tracts of preserved primitive wilderness, the air is punctuated with piercing cries of hawks and eagles, and majestic herds of elk graze in verdant, wildflower-laden meadows. Past volcanic activity has left the land strewn with cinder cones, and the whole region is bounded by the Mogollon Rim—a 200-mile geologic upthrust that splits the state—made famous as the "Tonto Rim" in the books of the best-selling Western author Zane Grey. Much of the plant life is unique to this region; this is one of the few places in the country where such desert plants as juniper and manzanita grow intermixed with mountain pines and aspen.

Volcanic activity also gave us the Petrified Forest and the Painted Desert. Once a great steamy swampland, the area experienced seismic activity that forced the swamp's decaying plant matter underground, where it eventually turned to stone. The Painted Desert, which cuts through Petrified Forest National Park, is famous for its multihued sedimentary layers. The human aspects of the landscape here are equally appealing, from prehistoric sites that are reminders of the native cultures that once flourished here to historic Route 66.

MAJOR REGIONS

Eastern Arizona is a large, somewhat loosely defined series of small towns and historic sites along the Mogollon Rim. Pronounced "*muh*-gee-on," the rim is a 200-mile-long area of volcanic and sedimentary rock that marks a distinct change in the topography of the state. Say goodbye to cacti and desert, and hello to forests of towering trees. Visitors searching for an escape from the desert heat head for **the White Mountains** and their majestic vistas of ponderosa pines. Locations include Salt River Canyon, Show Low, Pinetop-Lakeside, and Snowflake-Taylor.

To the east, **the Round Valley and Coronado Trail** is considered one of the most scenic drives in the country—though not for the faint of heart. The 123-mile stretch of highway takes you through terrifying switchbacks and majestic pine forests, unveiling the beauty of Arizona. Fill up your gas tank in Springerville, head south toward Clifton, and enjoy the ride. Along the way, you'll find quaint towns, charming inns, and plenty of reasons to marvel at what Mother Nature created.

Only about 1½ hours northeast from Show Low and the lush, verdant forests of the White Mountains, Arizona's diverse and dramatic landscape changes from pine-crested mountains to sunbaked terrain. Inside the lunar landscape of the Painted Desert is the fossil-filled **Petrified Forest.**

Eastern Arizona Planner

When to Go

If you're not a winter-sports enthusiast, it's best to plan your trip to Eastern Arizona for the high season (May–October). You'll be joined by residents of Phoenix and Tucson, who flock here in summer to escape the unbearably hot temperatures

in their hometowns, but you can find some solitude if you rent a cabin or stay at a bed-and-breakfast.

If you're a skier, winter is the time to tour the White Mountains. Sunrise Park Resort has 10 lifts, 68 trails, and a private snowboarders' park. ■TIP➔ **Eastern Arizona is enjoyable year-round, but many lodging facilities, restaurants, and tourist attractions are closed in autumn and winter.** It's wise to call ahead November through April, as the opening and closing dates of many seasonal properties are dependent on when the snow starts (and when it melts). Snowstorms can close the highways that lead into the area, so if you plan on making the trip from Phoenix or even Flagstaff, make sure you have an alternative plan.

Planning Your Time

The Petrified Forest is the main attraction for most of Eastern Arizona's visitors; it's easy to see the fossils and petroglyphs in just a few hours. Plan to reserve a day for the park and the surrounding Painted Desert. Depending on your preferences, you can add day trips and excursions to nearby towns.

Pinetop-Lakeside, with its wide range of lodging facilities and amenities, might be the best base for your trip. Neighboring area towns, such as Snowflake-Taylor, have memorable motels and B&Bs. If solitude is your goal, consider staying at a lodge surrounded by private forest.

Getting Here and Around

CAR TRAVEL

There isn't much choice: you'll be driving to and around Eastern Arizona. Amtrak runs limited service, but it isn't that helpful for travelers. Part of the experience in Eastern Arizona is the drive. Rent a car in Phoenix, Tucson, or even Flagstaff, and enjoy the open road.

If you're arriving from points west via Flagstaff, Interstate 40 leads directly to Holbrook, where drivers can take AZ 77 south into Show Low or U.S. 180 southeast to Springerville-Eagar. From Phoenix, take the scenic drive northeast on U.S. 60, or the slightly faster (and less curvy) AZ 87 north to AZ 260 east, both of which lead to Show Low. From Tucson, AZ 77 north connects with U.S. 60 at Globe, and continues through Show Low up to Holbrook. For those who want to drive the Coronado Trail south-to-north, U.S. 70 and AZ 78 link up with U.S. 191 from Globe to the west and New Mexico to the east, respectively.

WINTER ROAD CONDITIONS

Weather conditions change rapidly in Eastern Arizona. Before heading out on a daylong excursion—particularly in winter—be sure to call the Arizona Department of Transportation's Traveler Information Service (☎ 511).

Hotels

Most places supply clean rooms without many frills. These aren't the world-class resorts and spas of Phoenix, but that isn't necessarily a bad thing. "Resort" in this area means you'll probably have a room with a kitchenette and occasional (but not daily) maid service in a picturesque, woodsy setting. Plan on bringing your own toiletries and the like (there's a reason some of these prices are so affordable).

Restaurants

Luxury travel this is not. Fine dining is difficult to find; homestyle cooking, steak houses, and the occasional authentic Mexican joint pepper most towns. Casual is the norm—a pair of jeans will gain you entrance to just about any eatery in the area—anything dressier and you'd be out of place. Reservations are helpful during the busy summer months, and

remember that some places are closed from November to April.

Hotel and restaurant reviews have been shortened. For full information, visit Fodors.com.

What it Costs			
$	$$	$$$	$$$$
RESTAURANTS			
Under $12	$12–$20	$21–$30	Over $30
HOTELS			
Under $121	$121–$175	$176–$250	Over $250

Salt River Canyon

40 miles north of Globe on U.S. 60.

Carved from years of erosion, the multi-color spires, buttes, mesas, and walls of the Salt River Canyon—which dramatically drop 2,000 feet—have inspired this marvel's nickname, the Mini-Grand Canyon. But you don't need mules (or your feet) to get to the canyon floor. From Phoenix, U.S. 60 climbs through rolling hills as it approaches the Salt River Canyon, and the terrain changes from high desert with cactus and mesquite trees to forests of ponderosa pine. After entering the San Carlos Reservation, the highway descends sharply into the canyon, making a series of hairpin turns to reach the Salt River. **Hieroglyphic Point** is just one of the viewpoints along the scenic drive. Stop to stretch your legs at the viewing and interpretive display area before crossing the bridge. Wander along the banks below and enjoy the rock-strewn rapids. On hot days slip your shoes off and dip your feet into the chilly water. ■ TIP➔ **The river and canyon are open to hiking, fishing, and white-water rafting, but you need a permit, as this is tribal land. For information and recreational**

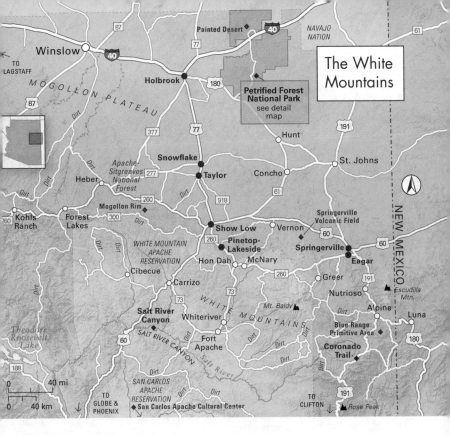

permits, contact the San Carlos Apache (Nde) and White Mountain Apache tribes.

The Apache people migrated to the Southwest around the 10th century. Divided into individual bands instead of functioning as a unified tribe, they were a hunting and gathering culture, moving with the seasons to gather food, and their crafts—baskets, beadwork, and cradleboards (traditional baby-carriers)—were compatible with their mobile lifestyle. The U.S. government didn't understand that different Apache bands might be hostile to each other and tried to gather separate tribes on one reservation, compounding relocation problems. Eventually, the government established the San Carlos Apache Reservation in 1871 and the Fort Apache Reservation in 1897. Both tribes hold on fiercely to their cultures. The native language is still spoken and taught in schools, and tribal ceremonies continue to be held. Both tribes have highly acclaimed "hot-shot" crews that immediately respond to forest fires throughout the West. The Salt River forms the boundary between these two large Apache reservations in Eastern Arizona.

WHEN TO GO
As with most of Eastern Arizona, it's best to visit Salt River Canyon in summer, when there are no worries about winter storms.

GETTING HERE AND AROUND
From the Phoenix area, take U.S. 60 east through Globe, and then continue north for 40 miles. From rim to rim, the road into the canyon is only 9 miles, but allow plenty of time for slowing down for the tight turns—and for enjoying the views. It's a three-hour drive from Phoenix through Globe.

U.S. 60 descends 2,000 feet into the Salt River Canyon on a series of tight switchbacks with great views.

PERMITS AND INFORMATION
CONTACTS San Carlos Apache Tribe.
☎ 928/475–1600 ⊕ www.sancarlosapache.com. **White Mountain Apache Tribe.**
☎ 928/338–4346 ⊕ whitemountainapache.org.

👁 Sights

Fort Apache Historical Park
NATIVE SITE | One entrance price buys access to three great places to visit on the Fort Apache Reservation. The **Fort Apache Historical Park** harks back to cavalry days with horse barns, parade grounds, log cabins, and officers' homes. The **Apache Cultural Center** museum explains the history, culture, and artistic traditions of the Apaches, and sells local crafts and books. **Kinishba Ruins** is a partly restored sandstone pueblo, and the only Native American ruin on the reservation open to visitors. ✉ 127 Scout St. ✛ ½ mile east of AZ 73 and 4 miles south of Whiteriver ☎ 928/338–4346 ⊕ whitemountainapache.org/fortapache

🎫 $5 🕙 Closed Sun. May–Oct. Closed weekends Nov.–Apr.

San Carlos Apache Cultural Center
MUSEUM | Exhibits on Apache history and culture are displayed at the San Carlos Apache Cultural Center, along with explanations of cultural traditions, such as the Changing Women Ceremony, a girls' puberty rite. Crafts are sold here as well. ✉ U.S. 70, mile marker 272 ☎ 928/475–2894 ⊕ www.sancarlosapache.com/San_Carlos_Culture_Center.htm 🎫 $4 🕙 Closed weekends.

Show Low

60 miles north of the Salt River Canyon on U.S. 60.

Show Low has little of the charm of its neighboring White Mountains communities, but it's the main commercial center for the high country. The city is also a crossing point for east–west traffic along the Mogollon Rim and traffic headed for Holbrook and points north. If you're heading up to the Painted Desert and Petrified Forest from Phoenix, you might want to spend the night here.

WHEN TO GO

You'll have to pass through the Salt River Canyon to reach Show Low (or take highways 87 and 260 through Payson). Either way, it means you'll be driving through mountains; be prepared in winter for storms and cold weather.

GETTING HERE AND AROUND

Show Low is a fairly good central location from which to explore Eastern Arizona by car. You can take AZ 260 south to reach Pinetop-Lakeside, or travel north on AZ 77 to Snowflake-Taylor and, eventually, Petrified Forest National Park.

🍴 Restaurants

Licano's Mexican Food and Steakhouse

$$ | **MEXICAN** | Along with what locals claim are the best enchiladas on the mountain, Licano's serves shrimp tacos, prime rib, and Alaskan salmon, making for a fairly broad menu. The spacious lounge, with a weekday happy hour from 4:30 to 6:30, stays open to 9 nightly. **Known for:** traditional, quality Mexican food; diverse menu; secret, family-recipe marinade. [$] *Average main: $15* ✉ *573 W. Deuce of Clubs* ☎ *928/537–8220* 🌐 *licanos.net.*

Native Grill & Wings

$$ | **AMERICAN** | With dozens of TVs in the dining room and the adjacent sports bar, this regional chain restaurant is a good place to keep tabs on your favorite team. It's known for its wings and bar food, but it also has the area's closest thing to a late-night scene: the bar stays open on weekends until 10 pm. **Known for:** dependable sports bar fare; bar open until 10 pm; one of the liveliest spots in town. [$] *Average main: $12* ✉ *391 W. Deuce of Clubs* ☎ *928/532–5100* 🌐 *nativegrillandwings.com* 🕓 *Closed Mon.*

En Route

The road out of the Salt River Canyon climbs along the canyon's northern cliffs, providing views of this truly spectacular chasm, unfairly overlooked in a state full of world-famous gorges. The highway continues some 50 miles northward to the **Mogollon Rim**—a huge geologic ledge that bisects much of Arizona—and its cool upland pinewoods.

🛏 Hotels

Best Western Paint Pony Lodge

$$ | **HOTEL** | Spacious rooms have wood accents and picture windows overlooking the pine-studded high country. **Pros:** affordable, large rooms; some rooms have fireplaces; modern conveniences. **Cons:** no frills; spotty Wi-Fi; rooms could be maintained a bit more thoroughly. [$] *Rooms from: $140* ✉ *581 W. Deuce of Clubs* ☎ *928/537–5773* 🌐 *www.bestwestern.com* 🛏 *50 rooms* 🍴 *Free breakfast.*

Holiday Inn Express

$$ | **HOTEL** | Larger rooms and more conveniences than much of its competition make for a comfortable night's rest. **Pros:** the closest thing to a "big-city" hotel in Show Low; everything you expect from a brand-name property; complimentary parking and Wi-Fi. **Cons:** limited sightseeing nearby means this is a better pit stop than vacation base; inconsistent housekeeping standards; rooms need refreshing. [$] *Rooms from: $149* ✉ *151 W. Deuce of Clubs* ☎ *928/537–5115* 🌐 *www.hiexpress.com* 🛏 *71 rooms* 🍴 *Free breakfast.*

The White Mountains

With elevations climbing to more than 11,000 feet, the White Mountains area of east-central Arizona is a winter wonderland and a summer haven from the desert heat. In the 1870s, the U.S. soldier John Gregory Bourke wrote in his diary that the White Mountains region was "a strange upheaval, a freak of nature, a mountain canted up on one side; one rides along the edge and looks down two or three thousand feet ... into a weird scene of grandeur and rugged beauty." The area, although much less remote than in Bourke's time, is still grand and rugged, carved by deep river canyons and tall cliffs covered with ponderosa pine. Towns in the area include Pinetop-Lakeside, Show Low, and Snowflake-Taylor, great spots for outdoor adventures such as camping, hiking, and skiing.

KC Motel

$ | **HOTEL** | Victorian decorating and large rooms help this not-so-typical two-story motel stand out. **Pros:** good value; continental breakfast included; style is original. **Cons:** few frills; style not for everyone; unreliable air conditioning. [$] *Rooms from: $95* ✉ *60 W. Deuce of Clubs* ☎ *928/537–4433* 🌐 *www.kcmotelshowlow.com* 🛏 *35 rooms* 🍴 *Free breakfast.*

Activities

FISHING

Fool Hollow Lake Recreational Area

BOATING | In addition to fishing, this year-round park is popular for boating, camping, and wildlife-viewing. Set amid a piney 800 acres, the lake is stocked with rainbow trout, walleye, and bass. There are five fishing platforms available, plus two fish-cleaning stations at the park. ✉ *1500 N. Fool Hollow Lake Rd.* ✥ *2 miles north of U.S. 60 off AZ 260* ☎ *928/537–3680* 🌐 *azstateparks.com/fool-hollow* 🎟 *$7 Mon.–Thurs., $10 Fri.–Sun.*

GOLF

Bison Golf

GOLF | Designed by Billy Mayfair, Bison Golf has a back nine in the pines and a front nine in a more open meadow. The course is open year-round, but expect closings throughout the winter. The club also has a fitness center. ✉ *860 N. 36th Dr., at AZ 260* ☎ *928/537–4564* 🌐 *bisongolf.net* 🎟 *$59* ⛳ *18 holes, 5916 yards, par 70.*

Silver Creek Golf Club

GOLF | This championship course has been voted by the PGA as one of the top 10 golf courses in Arizona—no small feat in a state that lives and breathes golf. It's also one of the more affordable options in the area. Given its lower elevation, this course is usually a few degrees warmer than Show Low and stays open year-round. ✉ *2051 Silver Lake Blvd.* ☎ *928/537–2744* 🌐 *www.silvercreekgolfaz.com* 🎟 *$59* ⛳ *18 holes, 6813 yards, par 72.*

Did You Know?

With 68 ski runs, 10 chair lifts, plus trails for cross-country skiing, Sunrise Park is Arizona's most popular ski resort in the White Mountains.

Eastern Arizona attracts outdoors lovers for fishing, hiking, camping, and skiing.

Pinetop-Lakeside

15 miles southeast of Show Low on AZ 260.

At 7,200 feet, the community of Pinetop-Lakeside borders the world's largest stand of ponderosa pine. Two towns, Pinetop and Lakeside, were incorporated in 1984 to form this municipality—although they still retain separate post offices. The year-round population is just 4,400, but in summer months it can jump to as high as 30,000. Once popular only with retirees and those with summerhouses, the city now lures thousands of "flatlanders" up from the Valley of the Sun with gorgeous scenery, excellent multiuse trails, premier golf courses, and temperatures that rarely exceed 85°F.

WHEN TO GO

Desert dwellers flock to Pinetop-Lakeside in summer to escape the heat. In winter, it's a wonderland of snow and mountains, but be prepared, as U.S. 60 and Interstate 40 are routinely closed and impassable during snowstorms.

GETTING HERE AND AROUND

A 15-minute drive from Show Low, Pinetop-Lakeside is ideal for exploring by car. The main drag is known as both AZ 260 and White Mountain Boulevard.

🍴 Restaurants

Charlie Clark's Steak House

$$$ | **STEAKHOUSE** | Attracting golfers relishing a successful day on the links as well as locals in search of good food, Charlie Clark's has been the meeting place of the White Mountains since it opened in 1938. Prime rib is the house specialty, and make sure to try a cup of the French onion soup. **Known for:** prime rib; hearty portions; one of the few fine dining options in the area. [$] *Average main: $22* ✉ *1701 E. White Mountain Blvd., Pinetop* ☎ *928/367–4900* 🌐 *charlieclarks.com.*

Los Corrales

$$ | **MEXICAN** | Locals come to this family-style Mexican eatery for the enchiladas and lunch specials. Dessert specialties include fried ice cream and apple chimichangas. **Known for:** classic Mexican food; combo plates with big portions; family-friendly atmosphere. $ *Average main: $12* ✉ *845 E. White Mountain Blvd., Lakeside* ☎ *928/367–5585.*

🛏 Hotels

Hon-Dah Resort Casino and Conference Center

$$ | **HOTEL** | Stuffed high-country animals atop a mountain of boulders welcome you to Hon-Dah, operated by the White Mountain Apache Tribe (the name means "Welcome to my home" in Apache). **Pros:** best destination for travelers who aren't interested in roughing it; big draw for the casino crowd; employees are locals who take pride in their community. **Cons:** can get noisy in the evening; the term "resort" can be misleading; spartan furnishings. $ *Rooms from: $129* ✉ *777 AZ 260, Pinetop* ☎ *928/369–0299, 800/929–8744* ⊕ *hondah.com* ⬎ *128 rooms* ❍ *No meals.*

Lake of the Woods Resort

$$ | **RESORT** | **FAMILY** | Whether you're looking for a modern cabin with most of the creature comforts or something a little more cozy and rustic, this resort can satisfy both cravings. **Pros:** rural atmosphere on Lakeside's main street; stocked private lake; great for families. **Cons:** some cabins can feel cramped, especially with six people sharing a single bathroom; spotty Wi-Fi; rooms closest to the road can hear traffic. $ *Rooms from: $149* ✉ *2244 W. White Mountain Blvd., Lakeside* ☎ *928/368–5353* ⊕ *lakeofthewoodsaz.com* ⬎ *33 cabins* ❍ *No meals.*

Northwoods Cabins

$ | **RESORT** | **FAMILY** | Each of the 14 fully furnished cottages at this mountain retreat has its own covered porch and a grill, and inside, the fully electric

Camping Resources 🛏

Apache-Sitgreaves National Forests has a listing of all public camping facilities in the region, most of which operate from April to November. ☎ *928/368–2100* ⊕ *www.fs.usda.gov/asnf.*

To reserve a site, use the **National Recreation Reservation Service.** ☎ *877/444–6777* ⊕ *www.recreation.gov.*

Book your campground site well in advance with the Game and Fish Department of the **White Mountain Apache Tribe.** ☎ *928/338–4385* ⊕ *whitemountainapache.org.*

kitchens have refrigerators, ovens, microwaves, and adjacent dinette sets. **Pros:** no highway noise; ideal for a family vacation; Wi-Fi available. **Cons:** close-set cabins mean little privacy; treads the line between rustic and outdated; unless you go off property, you're cooking your own dinner. $ *Rooms from: $119* ✉ *Mile marker 352, AZ 260* ☎ *928/367–2966, 800/813–2966* ⊕ *northwoodsaz.com* ⬎ *14 cabins* ❍ *No meals.*

Whispering Pines Resort

$ | **RESORT** | **FAMILY** | On 12 acres bordering the Apache-Sitgreaves National Forest, these well-maintained cabins are in walking distance of Woodland Lake and Walnut Creek. **Pros:** great accommodations for large parties; extremely private; some cabins have luxury touches such as whirlpool baths. **Cons:** older furnishings in rooms; icy roads in the resort can be difficult to navigate in winter; lots and lots of wood paneling. $ *Rooms from: $99* ✉ *237 E. White Mountain Blvd. (AZ 260)* ⊹ *Just beyond mile marker 352* ☎ *928/367–4386, 800/840–3867* ⊕ *www.whisperingpinesaz.com* ⬎ *38 cabins* ❍ *No meals.*

Top Outdoor Activities

Hiking: Hikers and mountain bikers of all abilities enjoy the White Mountains' 225 miles of interconnecting loop trails, open to visitors on foot or on nonmotorized wheels. Ranger stations have maps. Allow an hour for every 2 miles of trail, plus an additional hour for every 1,000 feet gained in altitude. Carry water, wear sunscreen, and watch out for poison ivy.

Fishing: Anglers flock to the more than 65 lakes, streams, and reservoirs in the White Mountains. Artificial lures and flies are permitted in winter only. An Arizona fishing license is required; on tribal land you'll also need a White Mountain Apache fishing license. Want an easier catch? Some lodges have private lakes stocked with trout.

Golfing: The high country's links draw golfers from all over, and these mountain fairways angle through lush forests and past lakes and springs.

Skiing: The 11,000-foot White Mountains have hilly, wooded landscapes that invite downhill and cross-country skiing adventurers. No matter where you stay in the White Mountains, Sunrise Park Resort is never more than an hour's drive away.

Activities

BICYCLING AND HIKING

Listed in the American Hiking Society's "Trail Town Hall of Fame," Pinetop-Lakeside is the primary trailhead for the White Mountains Trails System, which includes roughly 200 miles of interconnecting multiuse loop trails that span the White Mountains. All these trails are open to mountain bikers, horseback riders, and hikers.

Apache-Sitgreaves National Forests

BICYCLING | You can get trail brochures or other information from the Apache-Sitgreaves National Forests, including a booklet on the White Mountains Trail System. ⊠ Lakeside Ranger Station, 2022 W. White Mountain Blvd., Lakeside ☎ 928/368–2100 ⊕ www.fs.usda.gov/asnf.

SKIING AND SNOW SPORTS
The Skier's Edge

SKIING/SNOWBOARDING | Rent cross-country and downhill skis as well as snowboards and boots. They close in the summer and open when the first snowfall of the year is expected. ⊠ 560 W. White Mountain Blvd., Pinetop ☎ 928/367–6200 ⊕ www.facebook.com/skiersedgepinetop.

Snowflake-Taylor

30 miles north of Pinetop-Lakeside on Rte. 260 and AZ 77.

Snowflake and Taylor are a good jumping-off point for exploring Eastern Arizona, especially if you want to get away from the crowds during summer trips into the nearby White Mountains. Most Phoenix weekenders head for the higher towns of Pinetop and Lakeside, so Snowflake and Taylor don't get the crush of summer visitors that results in higher prices at hotels and restaurants. Yet, because they're sandwiched between the White Mountains and the Colorado Plateau, the communities enjoy year-round pleasant weather, with summer highs in the 90s. Yes, as the name suggests, it snows in Snowflake, but it seldom lasts more than a day. It's also an easy day trip to the Petrified Forest.

Snowflake and Taylor were settled by Mormons in the 1870s and named for Mormon church leaders. Snowflake's unusual name is a combination of Erastus Snow, an apostle in the early Mormon church of Salt Lake City, and William Flake, one of the town founders. The towns still have a large Mormon contingent in their combined population of 10,000. You can take a walking tour of Snowflake's historical district, which has pioneer homes and antiques stores.

WHEN TO GO

Because Snowflake-Taylor isn't as far into the White Mountains as other communities, it's somewhat easier to reach in winter. Still, most visitors explore this area in summer.

GETTING HERE AND AROUND

From Show Low off AZ 77, Snowflake-Taylor is about one-third of the way to Interstate 40.

Restaurants

La Cocina de Eva

$ | **MEXICAN** | Any trip to Arizona should become a tour of different styles of Mexican food, and if you like trying different interpretations of Sonoran cuisine, stop here. Portions are large, and the service is friendly at this popular spot. **Known for:** green chile dishes with extra spice; very casual atmosphere; loyal clientele. [$] *Average main: $10* ✉ *201 N. Main St., Snowflake* ☎ *928/536–7683* 🕒 *Closed Sun.*

Trapper's Cafe

$ | **AMERICAN** | Opened in 1973 by "Trapper" Hatch, this family-owned diner is decorated with Hatch's old trapping equipment and animal paintings by local artists. Chicken-fried steak and homemade barbecue sauce draw a loyal crowd. **Known for:** homemade pie; relaxing atmosphere for sipping a cup of coffee; friendly staff. [$] *Average main: $10* ✉ *9 S. Main St., Taylor* ☎ *928/536–7758* 🕒 *Closed Sun.*

Hotels

★ Heritage Inn Bed & Breakfast

$ | **B&B/INN** | Elegantly furnished with Victorian antiques and decorated pioneer style, this popular redbrick B&B has charm to spare. **Pros:** quiet B&B setting; great breakfast; exceptional service. **Cons:** some rooms only have a Jacuzzi tub with no shower; not much going on in town; bathroom fixtures could use some maintenance. [$] *Rooms from: $105* ✉ *161 N. Main St., Snowflake* ☎ *928/536–3322* 🌐 *www.heritage-inn.net* 🛏 *10 rooms* 🍴 *Free breakfast.*

Rodeway Inn Silver Creek Inn

$ | **HOTEL** | Simply furnished, clean, and handy to fast-food restaurants, Silver Creek Inn attracts regulars who travel through the area often. **Pros:** convenient town location; inexpensive; free Wi-Fi. **Cons:** intended for travelers just passing through; no on-site restaurant; zero frills. [$] *Rooms from: $99* ✉ *825 N. Main St., Taylor* ☎ *928/536–2600* 🌐 *www.choicehotels.com* 🛏 *42 rooms* 🍴 *Free breakfast.*

Coronado Trail

The 123-mile stretch of U.S. 191 from Springerville to Clifton.

One of the most picturesque drives in Arizona—and one of the curviest, too—the Coronado Trail is a 123-mile stretch of off-the-beaten-path road, where you'll find quaint inns, wandering meadows, steep cliffs, and a feast for the eyes. Start the journey with a full tank of gas, and don't be shy about turning around if the curves become too much.

WHEN TO GO

It's best to drive in summer. The majority of the road is anything but straight—it was once called the Devil's Highway for a reason. Don't drive on it in snow or ice.

Skiing Sunrise Park

One of Arizona's favorite locations for snow play, Sunrise Park Resort is a prime destination for desert dwellers looking to ski or snowboard—or build a snowman. In summer it's a great place to ride horses or just take in the beauty of the ponderosa pines. But in winter the place really shines: in addition to downhill and cross-country skiing there's snowboarding, snowmobiling, snowshoeing, ice fishing, and sleigh rides. The resort has 10 lifts and 68 trails on three mountains rising to 11,000 feet. The large majority of the downhill runs are for beginning or intermediate skiers, and many less intense trails begin at the top, so skiers of varying skill levels can ride the chairlifts together. Kids have their own hill to get comfy on the slopes, and snowboarders do, too. Additionally, cross-country skiers can enjoy 13½ miles of trails. Equipment rental is available at the ski shop, and an on-site hotel offers basic accommodations with quick access to the slopes. ☎ *(855) 735-7669* ✉ *200 Hwy. 273, Greer, AZ 85927* ⊕ *www.sunriseskipark. com*

GETTING HERE AND AROUND

Take U.S. 191 for 123 miles from Springerville to Clifton, and be prepared for an eye-opening ride. Allow a good four hours to make the steep, winding drive, more if you plan on making stops and having a leisurely trip.

◉ Sights

Blue Range Primitive Area

NATURE PRESERVE | Lovingly referred to by locals as "the Blue," these unspoiled 170,000 acres about 60 miles south of Springerville-Eagar are the last designated primitive area in the United States. The diverse terrain surrounds the Blue River and is crossed by the Mogollon Rim from east to west. No motorized or mechanized equipment is allowed, and that includes mountain bikes; passage is restricted to foot or horseback. Many trails interlace the Blue: prehistoric paths of the ancient native peoples, cowboy trails to move livestock between pastures and water sources, access routes to lookout towers and fire trails. Avid backpackers and campers may want to spend a few days exploring the dozens of hiking trails. Even though trail access is fairly good, hikers need to remember that this is primitive, rough country, and it's essential to carry adequate water and other supplies. Access it off U.S. 191; get directions and instructions from the Alpine Ranger District. ✉ *Alpine Ranger District, Alpine* ☎ *928/339–5000.*

Coronado Trail

SCENIC DRIVE | Surely one of the world's curviest roads, the twisting Coronado Trail portion of U.S. 191 was referred to as the Devil's Highway in its prior incarnation as U.S. 666. The route parallels the one allegedly followed more than 450 years ago by Spanish explorer Francisco Vásquez de Coronado on his search for the legendary Seven Cities of Cibola, where he'd heard that the streets were paved with gold and jewels.

This 123-mile stretch of highway is renowned for the transitions of its spectacular scenery over a dramatic 5,000-foot elevation change—from rolling meadows to spruce- and ponderosa pine–covered mountains, down into the Sonoran Desert's piñon pine, grassland savannas, juniper stands, and cacti. A trip down the Coronado Trail crosses through the Apache-Sitgreaves National Forests,

If you're driving the Coronado Trail, stop at Hannagan Meadow for scenery and solitude.

as well as the Fort Apache and San Carlos Apache reservations.

Pause at **Blue Vista,** perched on the edge of the Mogollon Rim, about 54 miles south of Springerville-Eagar, to take in views of the Blue Range Mountains to the east and the succession of tiered valleys dropping some 4,000 feet back down into the Sonoran Desert. Still above the rim, this is one of your last opportunities to enjoy the blue spruce, ponderosa pine, and high-country mountain meadows.

About 17 miles south of Blue Vista, the Coronado Trail continues to twist and turn, eventually crossing under 8,786-foot **Rose Peak.** Named for the wild roses growing on its mountainside, Rose Peak is also home to a fire lookout tower from which peaks more than 100 miles away can be seen on a clear day. This is a great picnic-lunch stop.

After Rose Peak, enjoy the remaining scenery some 70 more miles until you reach the less scenic towns of Clifton

and Morenci, homes to a massive copper mine. U.S. 191 then swings back west, links up with U.S. 70, and provides a fairly straight shot to Globe. ✉ *From Springerville to Globe.*

Hannagan Meadow

VIEWPOINT | Remote even for Eastern Arizona standards, Hannagan Meadow is located along the picturesque Coronado Trail. Stop and have a bite to eat at the lodge, fill up your gas tank (bring cash), or linger a bit and rest your head for the night. The lush, isolated, and mesmerizing spot at 9,500 feet is home to elk, deer, and range cattle, as well as blue grouse, wild turkeys, and the occasional eagle. Adjacent to the meadow is the Blue Range Primitive Area, which provides access to miles of untouched wilderness and some stunning rugged terrain. It's a designated recovery area for the endangered Mexican gray wolf. Francisco Vásquez de Coronado and his party may have come through the meadow on their famed expedition in 1540 to find the Seven Cities of Cibola.

✉ *Alpine Ranger District, Hannagan Meadow* ⊕ *Drive south on US 191 for 22 mi.* ☎ *928/339–5000.*

Hotels

Hannagan Meadow Lodge

$ | **RESORT** | **FAMILY** | Located about 50 miles south of Springerville along the picturesque Coronado Trail, Hannagan Meadow is considered remote—even by Eastern Arizona standards. **Pros:** gorgeous surroundings; fantastic service; absolute solitude. **Cons:** don't rely on daily room cleaning; more lodge than hotel; 30–60 minute drive to next restaurant, gas, and hotel. [$] *Rooms from: $85* ✉ *23150 U.S. 191, HC 61, Hannagan Meadow* ⊕ *22 miles south of Alpine* ☎ *928/339–4370* 🌐 *www.hannaganmeadow.com* 💳 *No credit cards* 🛏 *15 rooms* 🍴 *No meals.*

Springerville-Eagar

45 miles east of Pinetop-Lakeside on AZ 260, 67 miles southeast of Petrified Forest National Park on U.S. 180.

Sister cities Springerville and Eagar are the self-proclaimed "Gateway to the White Mountains." Insulated by the unique geography of the Round Valley where they sit, Springerville and Eagar have less-severe winter temperatures and lighter snowfall than in neighboring mountain towns.

WHEN TO GO

The Round Valley is the favorite of skiers in the know, who appreciate the location as they commute to the lifts at Sunrise with the sun always at their back—important when you consider the glare off those blanketed snowscapes between the resort and Pinetop-Lakeside. There's also a lot less traffic on this less-icy stretch of AZ 260.

Although Springerville-Eagar doesn't get as much snow as other parts of the region, it remains a very remote area. It can be hard to reach—and leave—in winter.

GETTING HERE AND AROUND

It's about an hour's drive from Pinetop-Lakeside to this isolated area.

Sights

Casa Malpais Archaeological Park

ARCHAEOLOGICAL SITE | Built in the 13th century, the pueblo complex at 14½-acre Casa Malpais Archaeological Park has a series of narrow terraces lining eroded edges of basalt (hardened lava flow) cliff, as well as an extensive system of subterranean rooms nestled within Earth's fissures underneath. Strategically designed gateways in the walls of the "House of the Badlands," as Spanish settlers called it, allow streams of sunlight to illuminate significant petroglyphs prior to the setting equinox or solstice sun. Casa Malpais's Great Kiva (any kiva larger than 30 feet is considered great) is square-cornered instead of round, consistent with Ancestral Puebloan practice. Some archaeologists believe the pueblo served as a regional ceremonial center for the Mogollon people. Both the Hopi and Zuni tribes trace their history to Casa Malpais. Start your visit at the Springerville Heritage Center, home of the Casa Malpais Museum. Two-hour tours leave at 9 and 1. ✉ *418 E. Main St., Springerville* ☎ *928/333–5375* 🌐 *www.casamalpais.org* 🎟 *$10* 🕒 *Museum closed Sun. No tours Dec.–Feb.*

Springerville Volcanic Field

NATURE SITE | The junction of U.S. 180/191 and U.S. 60, just north of Springerville, is the perfect jumping-off spot for a driving tour of the Springerville Volcanic Field, which covers an area larger than the state of Rhode Island. On the

The White Mountains' elevation makes the area a great place to stay cool in summer.

southern edge of the Colorado Plateau, it's spread across a high-elevation plain similar to the Tibetan Plateau. Six miles north of Springerville on U.S. 180/191 are sweeping westward views of the double volcanoes **Twin Knolls.** As you travel west on U.S. 60, Green's Peak Road and various south-winding Forest Service roads make for a leisurely, hour-long drive past **St. Peter's Dome** and a stop for impressive views from **Green's Peak,** the topographic high point of the Springerville Field. Stop by the **Springerville-Eagar Regional Chamber of Commerce** (*418 Main St., Springerville* ☎ *928/333–2123* 🌐 *www.springervilleeagarchamber.com*) for a map and more information on the Volcanic Field. ✉ *Springerville.*

🍴 Restaurants

Booga Reds

$$ | **MEXICAN** | This family-owned restaurant prides itself on serving comfort food with a kick: most of the wide-ranging menu is devoted to Mexican dishes that feature hot hatch chiles. If you're not in the mood for spice, you can opt for a burger, sandwich, or salad. **Known for:** spicy dishes made with hatch chiles; breakfast enchiladas; loyal clientele. [$] *Average main: $13* ✉ *521 E. Main St., Springerville* ☎ *928/333–2640.*

🛏 Hotels

Reed's Lodge

$ | **HOTEL** | **FAMILY** | This is an older motel but a town favorite, thanks to the helpful staff and a handful of perks such as free bikes to borrow and use of a rec room with pool table, video games, and a pinball machine, as well as coffee, tea, cocoa, or cider every morning. **Pros:** well priced; fantastic service; gift shop on-site. **Cons:** modest accommodations; few frills; some rooms in need of updating. [$] *Rooms from: $75* ✉ *514 E. Main St., Springerville* ☎ *928/333–4323, 800/814–6451* 🌐 *www.k5reeds.com* 🛏 *50 rooms* 🍽 *No meals.*

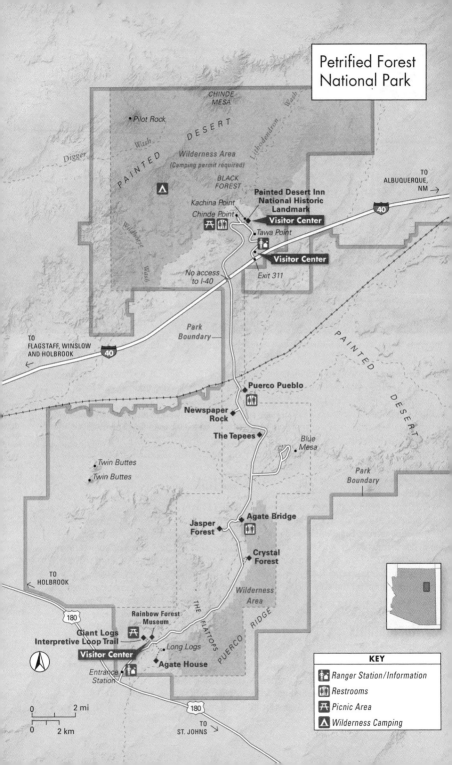

X Diamond Ranch

$$ | RESORT | This magnificent ranch has log cabins complete with porches, fireplaces, and full kitchens, and a slew of activities—fly-fishing, horseback riding, and tours of Little Bear archaeological site among them. **Pros:** one of the best-known and most picturesque spots in the area; real working-ranch experience; feels frozen-in-time, in the best way. **Cons:** no on-site restaurant; total relaxation is hard to come by at a working ranch; remote location. $ *Rooms from: $125* ⊠ *S. Fork Rd., Springerville* ✛ *10 miles southwest of Eagar, off AZ 260* ☎ *928/333–2286* ⊕ *www.xdiamondranch.net* ⤵ *6 cabins* ⦿| *No meals.*

🛍 Shopping

Western Drug & General Store

FISHING | Open 365 days a year, Western Drug has a well-stocked sporting-goods and outdoor-equipment section, as well as a replacement for anything you forgot to pack for your vacation. As one of the only drugstores within a 50-to-75-mile radius, it's a good spot to know about in this remote neck of the woods. ⊠ *105 E. Main St., Springerville* ☎ *928/333–4321.*

Petrified Forest National Park

Northern Entrance: 110 miles northwest of Springerville-Eagar on U.S. 191 and I–40, 27 miles east of Holbrook on I–40. Southern Entrance: 66 miles northwest of Springerville-Eagar on U.S. 191 and U.S. 180, 18 miles east of Holbrook on U.S. 180.

Only about 1½ hours from Show Low and the lush, verdant forests of the White Mountains, Arizona's diverse and dramatic landscape changes from pine-crested mountains to sunbaked terrain. Inside the lunar landscape of the Painted Desert is the Petrified Forest.

There are few places where the span of geologic and human history is as wide or apparent as it is at Petrified Forest National Park. Fossilized trees and countless other fossils date back to the Triassic Period, while a stretch of the famed Route 66 of more modern lore is protected within park boundaries. Ancestors of the Hopi, Zuni, and Navajo left petroglyphs, pottery, and even structures built of petrified wood. Nine park sites are on the National Register of Historic Places; one, the Painted Desert Inn, is one of only 3% of such sites that are also listed as National Historic Landmarks.

The good thing is that most of Petrified Forest's treasures can easily be viewed without a great amount of athletic conditioning. Much can be seen by driving along the main road, from which historic sites are readily accessible. By combining a drive along the park road with a short hike here and there and a visit to one of the park's landmarks, you can see most of the sights in as little as half a day.

WHEN TO GO

The park is rarely crowded. Weatherwise, the best time to visit is autumn, when nights are chilly but daytime temperatures hover near 70°F. Half of all yearly rain falls between June and August, so it's a good time to spot blooming wildflowers. The park is least crowded in winter because of cold winds and occasional snow, though daytime temperatures are in the 50s and 60s.

GETTING HERE AND AROUND

Holbrook, the nearest large town with services such as gas or food, is on U.S. 40, 27 miles from the park's north entrance and 18 miles from its south entrance.

Parking is free, and there's ample space at all trailheads, as well as at the visitor center and the museum. The main park road extends 28 miles from the Painted Desert Visitor Center (north entrance)

Petrified Forest in One Day

A nonstop drive through the park (28 miles) takes only 45 minutes, but you can spend half a day or more exploring if you stop along the way. From almost any vantage point you can see the multicolor rocks and hills, where small Triassic dinosaurs once roamed (a few of their fossils have been unearthed here).

Entering from the north, stop at **Painted Desert Visitor Center** for a 20-minute introductory film. Two miles in, the **Painted Desert Inn National Historic Landmark** provides guided ranger tours. Drive south 8 miles to reach **Puerco Pueblo**, a 100-room pueblo built before 1400. Continuing south, you'll encounter **Newspaper Rock**, marked with Puebloan petroglyphs, and, just beyond, **the Tepees**, cone-shaped rock formations.

Blue Mesa is roughly the midpoint of the drive, and the start of a 1-mile, moderately steep loop hike that leads you around badland hills made of bentonite clay. Drive on for 5 miles until you come to **Jasper Forest**, just past **Agate Bridge**, with views of the landscape strewn with petrified logs. **Crystal Forest**, about 20 miles south of the north entrance, is named for the smoky quartz, amethyst, and citrine along the 0.8-mile loop trail. **Rainbow Forest Museum**, at the park's south entrance, has restrooms, a bookstore, and exhibits. Just behind Rainbow Forest Museum is **Giant Logs**, a 0.4-mile loop that takes you to "Old Faithful," the largest log in the park, estimated to weigh 44 tons.

to the Rainbow Forest Museum (south entrance). For park road conditions, call ☏ *928/524–6228*.

PARK ESSENTIALS
ACCESSIBILITY
The visitor center, museum, and overlooks on the scenic drive are wheelchair accessible. All trails are paved, although they are uneven, rough, and sometimes steep. Check the park website (⊕ *nps.gov/pefo*) for information on accessibility. The park's visitor centers, as well as some picnic areas, have accessible restrooms.

PARK FEES AND PERMITS
Entrance fees are $25 per car for seven consecutive days or $15 per person on foot or bicycle, or $20 per motorcycle. Backcountry hiking and camping permits are free (15-day limit) at the Painted Desert Visitor Center or the Rainbow Forest Museum before 4 pm.

PARK HOURS
It's a good idea to call ahead or check the website, because the park's hours vary so much; as a rule of thumb, the park is open daily from sunrise to sunset or approximately 8 am–5 pm. Keep in mind that the area does not observe daylight saving time.

VISITOR INFORMATION
CONTACTS Petrified Forest National Park. ✉ *1 Park Rd.* ☏ *928/524–6228* ⊕ *www.nps.gov/pefo*.

Sights

HISTORIC SIGHTS
Agate House
ARCHAEOLOGICAL SITE | This eight-room pueblo is thought to have been built entirely of petrified wood 700 years ago. Researchers believe it might have been used as a temporary dwelling by

seasonal farmers or traders from one of the area tribes. ⊠ *Rainbow Forest Museum parking area.*

Newspaper Rock

ARCHAEOLOGICAL SITE | See huge boulders covered with petroglyphs believed to have been carved by the Pueblo people more than 500 years ago. ■ **TIP➔ Look through the binoculars that are provided here—you'll be surprised at what the naked eye misses.** ⊠ *Main park road ✛ 6 miles south of Painted Desert Visitor Center.*

Painted Desert Inn
National Historic Landmark

MUSEUM | A nice place to stop and rest in the shade, this site offers vast views of the Painted Desert from several lookouts. Inside, cultural history exhibits, murals, and Native American crafts are on display. ⊠ *Main park road ✛ 2 miles north of Painted Desert Visitor Center.*

Puerco Pueblo

ARCHAEOLOGICAL SITE | This is a 100-room pueblo, built before 1400 and said to have housed Ancestral Puebloan people. Many visitors come to see the petroglyphs, as well as a solar calendar. ⊠ *Main park road ✛ 10 miles south of Painted Desert Visitor Center.*

SCENIC DRIVES

Painted Desert Scenic Drive

SCENIC DRIVE | A 28-mile scenic drive takes you through the park from one entrance to the other. If you begin at the north end, the first 5 miles take you along the edge of a high mesa, with spectacular views of the Painted Desert. Beyond lies the desolate Painted Desert Wilderness Area. After the 5-mile point, the road crosses Interstate 40, then swings south toward the Puerco River across a landscape covered with sagebrush, saltbrush, sunflowers, and Apache plume. Past the river, the road climbs onto a narrow mesa leading to Newspaper Rock, a panel of Pueblo rock art. Then the road bends southeast, enters a barren stretch, and passes teepee-shaped

buttes in the distance. Next you come to Blue Mesa, roughly the park's midpoint and a good place to stop for views of petrified logs. The next stop on the drive is Agate Bridge, really a 100-foot log over a wide wash. The remaining overlooks are Jasper and Crystal forests, where you can get further glimpses of the accumulated petrified wood. On your way out of the park, stop at the Rainbow Forest Museum for a rest and to shop for a memento. ⊠ *Begins at Painted Desert Visitor Center.*

SCENIC SPOTS

Agate Bridge

NATURE SITE | Here you'll see a 100-foot log spanning a 40-foot-wide wash. ⊠ *Main park road ✛ 19 miles south of Painted Desert Visitor Center.*

Crystal Forest

NATURE SITE | The fragments of petrified wood strewn here once held clear quartz and amethyst crystals. ⊠ *Main park road ✛ 20 miles south of Painted Desert Visitor Center.*

Giant Logs Interpretive Loop Trail

NATURE SITE | A short walk leads you past the park's largest log, known as Old Faithful. It's considered the largest because of its diameter (9 feet 9 inches), as well as how tall it once was. ⊠ *Main park road ✛ 28 miles south of Painted Desert Visitor Center.*

Petroglyphs: The Writing on the Wall 👁

The rock art of early Native Americans is carved or painted on basalt boulders, on canyon walls, and on the underside of overhangs throughout the area. No one knows the exact meaning of these signs, and interpretations vary; they've been seen as elements in shamanistic or hunting rituals, as clan signs, maps, or even indications of visits by extraterrestrials.

Where to Find Them
Susceptible to (and often already damaged by) vandalism, many rock-art sites aren't open to the public. Two good petroglyphs to check out at **Petrified Forest National Park** are Newspaper Rock, an overlook near mile marker 12, and Puerco Pueblo, near mile marker 11. Other sites in Arizona include **Hieroglyphic Point** in Salt River Canyon and **Deer Valley Petroglyph Preserve** north of Phoenix.

Determining Its Age
It's just as difficult to date a "glyph" as it is to understand it. Archaeologists try to determine a general time frame by judging the style, the date of the ruins and pottery in the vicinity, the amount of patination (formation of minerals) on the design, or the superimposition of newer images on top of older ones. Most of Eastern Arizona's rock art is estimated to be at least 1,000 years old, and many of the glyphs were created even earlier.

Varied Images
Some glyphs depict animals like bighorn sheep, deer, bear, and mountain lions; others are geometric patterns. The most unusual are the anthropomorphs, strange humanlike figures with elaborate headdresses. Concentric circles are a common design. A few of these circles served as solstice signs, indicating the summer and winter solstices and other important dates. At the solstice, when the angle of the sun is just right, a shaft of light shines through a crack in a nearby rock, illuminating the center of the circle. Archaeologists believe that these solar calendars helped determine the time for ceremonies and planting.

Many solstice signs are in remote regions, but you can visit Petrified Forest National Park around June 20 to see a concentric circle illuminated during the summer solstice. The glyph, reached by a paved trail just a few hundred yards from the parking area, is visible year-round, but light shines directly in the center during the week of the solstice. The phenomenon occurs at 9 am.

■ TIP→ **Do not touch petroglyphs or pictographs—the oil from your hands can damage the images.**

7

Eastern Arizona PETRIFIED FOREST NATIONAL PARK

Jasper Forest
VIEWPOINT | More of an overlook than a forest, this spot has a large concentration of petrified trees in jasper or red. ⊠ *Main park road ⊹ 17 miles south of Painted Desert Visitor Center.*

The Tepees
NATURE SITE | Witness the effects of time on these cone-shape rock formations colored by iron, manganese, and other minerals. ⊠ *Main park road ⊹ 8 miles south of Painted Desert Visitor Center.*

Flora and Fauna

Engelmann's asters and sunflowers are among the blooms in the park each summer. Juniper trees, cottonwoods, and willows grow along Puerco River wash, providing shelter for all manner of wildlife. You might spot mule deer, coyotes, prairie dogs, and foxes, though other inhabitants, like porcupines and bobcats, tend to hide. Bird-watchers should keep an eye out for mockingbirds, red-tailed and Swainson's hawks, roadrunners, swallows, and hummingbirds. Look for all three kinds of lizards—collared, side-blotched, and southern prairie—in rocks.

Beware of rattlesnakes. They're common but can generally be easily avoided: watch where you step, and don't step anywhere you can't see. If you do come across a rattler, give it plenty of space, and let it go its way before you continue on yours. Other reptiles are just as common but not as dangerous. The gopher snake looks similar to a rattlesnake, but is nonvenomous. The collared lizard, with its yellow head, can be seen scurrying out of your way in bursts measured at up to 15 mph. They aren't venomous, but they will bite if caught.

TRAILS

Agate House

HIKING/WALKING | A fairly flat 1-mile trip takes you to an eight-room pueblo sitting high on a knoll. *Moderate.* ⊠ *Petrified Forest National Park* ⊹ *Trailhead: 26 miles south of Painted Desert Visitor Center.*

★ Blue Mesa

HIKING/WALKING | Although it's only 1 mile long and significantly steeper than the rest, this trail at the park's midway point is one of the most popular and worth the effort. *Moderate.* ⊠ *Petrified Forest National Park* ⊹ *Trailhead: 14 miles south of Painted Desert Visitor Center.*

Crystal Forest Trail

HIKING/WALKING | This easy ¾-mile loop leads you past petrified wood that once held quartz crystals and amethyst chips. *Easy.* ⊠ *Petrified Forest National Park* ⊹ *Trailhead: 20 miles south of Painted Desert Visitor Center.*

Giant Logs Trail

HIKING/WALKING | At 0.4 mile, Giant Logs is the park's shortest trail. The loop leads you to Old Faithful, the park's largest petrified log—9 feet, 9 inches at its base, weighing an estimated 44 tons. *Easy.* ⊠ *Petrified Forest National Park* ⊹ *Trailhead: directly behind Rainbow Forest Museum, 28 miles south of Painted Desert Visitor Center.*

Kachina Point

HIKING/WALKING | This is the trailhead for wilderness hiking at Petrified Forest National Park. A 1-mile trail leads to the Wilderness Area, but from there you're on your own. There are no developed trails, so hiking here is cross-country style. Expect to see strange formations, beautifully colored landscapes, and maybe, just maybe, a pronghorn antelope. *Difficult.* ⊠ *Petrified Forest National Park* ⊹ *Trailhead: on northwest side of Painted Desert Inn National Historic Landmark.*

For max Route 66 kitsch, book a stay in the iconic teepees of the Wigwam Motel.

Long Logs Trail

HIKING/WALKING | Although barren, this easy 1.6-mile loop passes the largest concentration of wood in the park. *Easy.* ⊠ *Petrified Forest National Park* ⊹ *Trailhead: 26 miles south of Painted Desert Visitor Center.*

Painted Desert Rim

HIKING/WALKING | The 1-mile trail is at its best in early morning or late afternoon, when the sun accentuates the brilliant red, blue, purple, and other hues of the desert and petrified forest landscape. *Moderate.* ⊠ *Petrified Forest National Park* ⊹ *Trail runs between Tawa Point and Kachina Point, 1 mile north of Painted Desert Visitor Center; drive to either point from visitor center.*

Puerco Pueblo Trail

HIKING/WALKING | **FAMILY** | A relatively flat and interesting 0.3-mile trail takes you past remains of a home of the Ancestral Puebloan people, built before 1400. The trail is paved and wheelchair accessible. *Easy.* ⊠ *Petrified Forest National Park*

⊹ *Trailhead: 10 miles south of Painted Desert Visitor Center.*

VISITOR CENTERS

Painted Desert Inn National Historic Landmark

INFO CENTER | This visitor center isn't as large as the other two, but here you can get information as well as view cultural history exhibits. ⊠ *Main park road* ⊹ *2 miles north of Painted Desert Visitor Center* ☎ *928/524-6228.*

Painted Desert Visitor Center

INFO CENTER | This is the place to go for general park information and an informative 20-minute film. Proceeds from books purchased here will fund continued research and interpretive activities for the park. ⊠ *North entrance* ⊹ *Off I–40, 27 miles east of Holbrook* ☎ *928/524-6228.*

Rainbow Forest Museum and Visitor Center

INFO CENTER | View displays of prehistoric animals, watch an orientation video, and—perhaps most important—use the restroom facilities at this visitor center at the southern end of the park. ✉ *South entrance* ✥ *Off U.S. 180, 18 miles southeast of Holbrook* ☎ *928/524–6228.*

🍴 Restaurants

Dining in the park is limited to a cafeteria in the Painted Desert Visitor Center and snacks in the Rainbow Forest Museum. You may want to pack a lunch and eat at one of the park's picnic areas.

🛏 Hotels

There's no lodging or campgrounds within the Petrified Forest. Backcountry camping is allowed if you obtain a free permit at the visitor center or museum; the only camping allowed is minimal-impact camping in a designated zone in the wilderness area. Group size is limited to eight. RVs aren't allowed. There are no fire pits, nor is any shade available. Also note that if it rains, that pretty Painted Desert rock formation turns to sticky clay.

🏃 Activities

Because the park goes to great pains to maintain the integrity of the fossil- and artifact-strewn landscape, activities in the park are limited to on-trail hiking.

All trails begin off the main road, and restrooms can be found at visitor centers and picnic areas. Most maintained trails are relatively short, paved, clearly marked, and, with a few exceptions, easy to moderate in difficulty. Hikers with greater stamina can make their own trails in the Wilderness Area, located just north of the Painted Desert Visitor Center. The area's most popular trails include **Blue Mesa**, **Giant Logs Trail**, and **Painted Desert Rim.** Watch your step for rattlesnakes, which are common in the park—if left alone and given a wide berth, they're passed easily enough.

Holbrook

27 miles west of Petrified Forest National Park via I–40.

Holbrook, the largest town close to Petrified Forest National Park, is a monument to Route 66 kitsch. The famous "Mother Road" traveled through the center of Holbrook before Interstate 40 replaced it as the area's major east–west artery, and remnants of the "good ol' days" can be found all over town. It's probably not worth staying overnight in Holbrook, although the town's iconic Wigwam Motel is a quirky and iconic option if you do find yourself here.

GETTING HERE AND AROUND

Holbrook is on Interstate 40, approximately 90 miles east of Flagstaff and 30 miles west of Petrified Forest National Park. You can access AZ 77, en route to Snowflake, Taylor, and other Eastern Arizona recreation towns, directly from Interstate 40 in Holbrook.

🛏 Hotels

Wigwam Motel
$ | HOTEL | On the National Register of Historic Places, the iconic Wigwam consists of 15 bright-white concrete teepees. **Pros:** impeccably kitschy; one of the signature spots along Route 66; a travel bucket-list item. **Cons:** very sparse accommodations that can fit no more than two; awkward bathroom configuration; spotty Wi-Fi. [$] *Rooms from: $79* ✉ *811 West Hopi Dr.* ☎ *928/524–3048* 🌐 *www.sleepinawigwam.com* 🔑 *15 rooms* 🍽 *No meals.*

Chapter 8

TUCSON

Updated by
Mara Levin

◉ Sights	🍴 Restaurants	🛏 Hotels	🛍 Shopping	🍸 Nightlife
★★★★☆	★★★★☆	★★★★★	★★★☆☆	★★★☆☆

WELCOME TO TUCSON

TOP REASONS TO GO

★ **Get close to the cacti:** Unique to this region, the saguaro is the quintessential symbol of the Southwest. See them at Sabino Canyon and Saguaro National Park.

★ **Enjoy Mexican food:** Tucson boasts that it's the "Mexican Food Capital," and you won't be disappointed at any of the authentic restaurants.

★ **Explore the Arizona–Sonora Desert Museum:** Anyone who thinks that museums are boring hasn't been here, where you can learn about the region's animals, plants, and geology up close in a gorgeous, mostly outdoor setting.

★ **Tour Mission San Xavier del Bac:** The "White Dove of the Desert" is the oldest building in Tucson. Ornate carvings and frescoes inside add to the mystical quality of this active parish on the Tohono O'odham Reservation.

★ **Stroll the U of A campus:** Stop in at one of the five museums, then walk University Boulevard and 4th Avenue for a taste of Tucson's hipper element.

1 Downtown Tucson. Three historic districts—Barrio Historico, El Presidio, and Armory Park—make up the Downtown area, and Congress Street is the hub of Tucson nightlife.

2 The University of Arizona. The 353-acre campus, classified as an arboretum, has several top-rated museums. At the west entrance, University Boulevard is lined with boutiques, cafés, and bookstores.

3 Central Tucson. Restaurants, businesses, and residential neighborhoods coexist in this dense part of town, also home to the city zoo and a top-rated public golf course.

4 Eastside. Mostly residential, Tucson's Eastside has a large indoor shopping mall and the Pima Air & Space Museum.

5 Catalina Foothills. North of River Road the streets wind up to beautiful homes and resorts. At the east end, Sabino Canyon is a must for hikers.

6 Northwest Tucson. Suburban sprawl at its finest, the Northwest part of town just keeps growing. The area is home to several spas and resorts as well as parks and a fascinating earth science center.

7 Westside. In this area, the untamed Tucson Mountains region embraces miles of saguaro forests, the Arizona–Sonora Desert Museum, and Mission San Xavier del Bac.

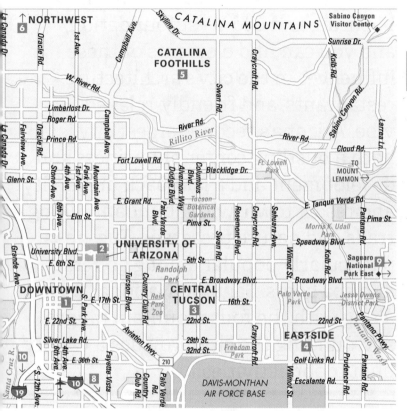

8 South Tucson. This largely Hispanic city-within-a-city is home to many Mexican restaurants and colorful outdoor murals.

9 Saguaro National Park. Hillsides of stately saguaro cacti dominate the land in the East and West sections of this National Park; the West district also has petroglyphs.

10 Side Trips Near Tucson. The ASARCO Mineral Discovery Center, Titan Missile Museum, artist colony of Tubac, Madera Canyon, and Tumacacori National Historic Park are easy excursions.

The "Old Pueblo," as Tucson is affectionately known, is built upon a deep Native American, Spanish, Mexican, and Old West foundation, and you can find elements of these influences in the city's architecture, restaurants, and friendly, relaxed vibe. Arizona's second-largest city is both a bustling center of business and development and a laid-back university and resort town, with abundant hiking trails and nature preserves. Tucson is particularly popular among golfers and spa goers. Saguaro National Park, along with the four mountain ranges surrounding the city, provides a variety of outdoor activities.

Metropolitan Tucson has more than 850,000 residents, including thousands of snowbirds who flee colder climes to enjoy the sun that shines on the city more than 340 days out of 365. The city's tricultural population (Hispanic, Anglo, Native American) offers visitors the chance to see how these cultures interact and to sample their flavorful cuisine.

The city also has a youthful energy, largely due to the population of students attending the University of Arizona. Although high-tech industries have moved into the area, the economy still relies heavily on the university and tourism. Come summer, though, you'd never guess; when the snowbirds and students depart, Tucson can be a sleepy place.

The metropolitan area covers more than 500 square miles in a valley ringed by mountains—the Santa Catalinas to the north, the Santa Ritas to the south, the Rincons to the east, and the Tucson Mountains to the west. Saguaro National Park bookends Tucson, with one section on the far east side and the other out west near the Arizona–Sonora Desert Museum. The central portion of the city has most of the shops, restaurants, and businesses, but not many tourist sites. Downtown's historic district and the neighboring university area are much smaller and easily navigated on foot. Up north in the Catalina Foothills are first-class resorts, restaurants, and hiking trails, most with spectacular views of the entire valley.

Tucson Planner

When to Go

Summer lodging rates (late May to September) are hugely discounted, even at many of the resorts, but there's a good reason: summer in Tucson is hot! Swimming and indoor activities like visiting museums (and spa treatments) are doable; but only the hardiest hikers and golfers stay out past noon in summer.

Tucson averages only 12 inches of rain a year. Winter temperatures hover around 65°F during the day and 38°F at night. Summers are unquestionably hot—July averages 104°F during the day and 75°F at night—but, as Tucsonans are fond of saying, "It's a dry heat."

The International Gem and Mineral Show descends on Tucson the first two weeks in February; book your hotel room in advance or you'll be hard-pressed to find a vacancy.

FESTIVALS AND EVENTS
4th Avenue Street Fair

FESTIVALS | Feeling casual and eclectic? Hit Tucson's 4th Avenue Street Fair, usually held in May and December, where you can buy handcrafted wares and hear local bands while munching on every kind of festival food imaginable. ⊠ *Tucson* ☎ *520/624–5004* ⊕ *www. fourthavenue.org.*

La Fiesta de los Vaqueros

FESTIVALS | FAMILY | America's largest outdoor midwinter rodeo is at the Tucson Rodeo Grounds the third weekend in February. ☎ *520/294–8896* ⊕ *www. tucsonrodeo.com.*

Tubac Festival of the Arts

ARTS FESTIVALS | Every February this rural artisan extravaganza brings artists from around the country to exhibit their eclectic, fine, and tourist-oriented art in the charming village of Tubac, about 45 miles south of Tucson. ⊠ *Tubac Plaza, Tubac* ☎ *520/398–2704* ⊕ *www.tubacaz. com/festival.*

★ **Tucson Gem, Mineral & Fossil Showcase**

FESTIVALS | This huge two-week trade show in February, comprising nearly 40 different shows at venues in and around Downtown, is the largest of its kind in the world. Most vendors sell to the public as well as to wholesalers. Admission to the shows is free, except for the prestigious Gem and Mineral Show held at the Tucson Convention Center during the last four days of the two-week period. The Tucson Visitor Center is the best source of information about the event. ☎ *520/624–1817* ⊕ *www.visittucson.org/ events/gem-show.*

Tucson Originals World Margarita Championship

FESTIVALS | In October, Tucson Originals, a group of independent local restaurants, hosts the World Margarita Championship. Sample foods, wines, and killer margaritas prepared by more than 40 local indie chefs and mixologists, and then cast your votes for your favorites. ⊠ *Tucson* ☎ *520/477–7950* ⊕ *tucsonoriginals.com.*

Planning Your Time

Even if you have only one day, you can experience both the wild and developed parts of Tucson. You can visit the Arizona–Sonora Desert Museum in the morning and combine it with a stop at Mission

San Xavier del Bac or Old Tucson Studios. On the way back to town, stop in Downtown's Barrio Historico and El Presidio neighborhoods to meander through the adobe-lined streets, then have dinner at one of the outstanding Mexican restaurants in Downtown or South Tucson.

Another option is spending a half day in Saguaro National Park. ■TIP→ **Set out for a desert visit in the early morning when it's cooler and the liveliest time for wildlife.** If you're based in the Foothills, you can choose Sabino Canyon instead; the saguaros are almost as plentiful and the vistas are equally rewarding. Nature in the morning can be combined with an afternoon in the university area: visit any of the five campus museums, then stroll University Boulevard and 4th Avenue for ethnic eats and vintage boutiques.

If you have another day for exploring and like to shop, head south toward the Mexican border. If you haven't seen Mission San Xavier yet, it's directly en route to Tubac, an artists' colony with historic sights as well as galleries. You can then head back toward Tucson, stopping at the Titan Missile Museum or at one of the casinos.

Getting Here and Around

You can fly to Tucson International Airport (TUS), which is 8½ miles south of Downtown, off the Valencia exit of Interstate 10, but cheaper, nonstop flights into Phoenix—a two-hour drive away on Interstate 10—are often easier to find. Once in town, a car is essential to get to the outlying tourist sights.

AIR
CONTACTS Tucson International Airport (TUS). ✉ 7250 S. Tucson Blvd., South ☎ 520/573–8100 ⊕ www.flytucson.com.

GROUND TRANSPORTATION
Many hotels have a courtesy airport shuttle; inquire when making reservations. Taxis are abundant at the airport.

The Tucson Stagecoach Express shuttle will carry you between the airport and all parts of Tucson and outlying areas including Marana, Sierra Vista, and Green Valley for $15 to $60, depending on the location. Ride-share services such as Uber and Lyft drop off and pick up here.

CONTACTS Tucson Stagecoach Express. ☎ 520/889–1000 ⊕ www.stagecoachexpressshuttle.com.

BUS
Within the city limits, public transportation, which is geared primarily to commuters, is available through Sun Tran, Tucson's bus system. The electric streetcar, Sun Link, is a fun and convenient way to travel between Downtown, 4th Avenue, and the University area. Before you board, buy a ticket at any of the streetcar stops ($4.50 for 24 hours) and hop on. Ticket machines take exact change or credit cards.

CONTACTS Sun Link Streetcar. ☎ 520/792–9222 ⊕ www.sunlinkstreetcar.com. **Sun Tran.** ☎ 520/792–9222 ⊕ www.suntran.com.

CAR
You'll need a car to get around Tucson and the surrounding area, and it makes sense to rent at the airport; all the major car-rental agencies are represented. A few rental agencies have additional locations in Central Tucson, and the larger resorts arrange rental-car pickups on-site.

Driving time from the airport to the center of town varies, but it's usually less than a half hour; add 15 minutes to any destination during rush hours (7:30 to 9 am and 4:30 to 6 pm). Parking isn't a problem in most parts of town, except near the university and downtown, where there are multiple pay lots and parking garages as well as meters.

TAXI
Taxi rates vary because they're unregulated, but the taxi companies listed here charge around $2.00 per mile plus an

initial pickup fee of $2.75 ($4.50 from the airport). It's always wise to inquire about the cost before getting into a cab. It should be about $30 from the airport to Central Tucson. Ride-share services Uber and Lyft are also available.

CONTACTS VIP Taxi. ☎ 520/798–1111 ⊕ viptaxi.com. **Yellow Cab.** ☎ 520/624–6611, 520/300–0000 ⊕ www.yellow-cabaz.com.

TRAIN

Amtrak serves the city with westbound trains (to Los Angeles, CA) and eastbound trains daily. The train station is in the downtown district.

CONTACTS Amtrak. ✉ 400 N. Toole Ave., Downtown ☎ 800/872–7245 ⊕ www. amtrak.com.

Sights

Central Tucson—which has most of the shops, restaurants, and businesses—is roughly bounded by Craycroft Road to the east, Oracle Road to the west, River Road to the north, and 22nd Street to the south. The Downtown section, east of Interstate 10 off the Broadway-Congress exit, is smaller and easy to navigate on foot. Downtown streets don't run on any sort of grid, however, and many are one way, so it's best to get a good, detailed map. The city's Westside area is the vast region west of interstates 10 and 19, which includes the western section of Saguaro National Park and the San Xavier Mission.

Hotels

If you like being able to walk to sights, shops, and restaurants, plan on staying in either the Downtown or University neighborhood. For a quieter but equally convenient base, opt for one of the charming B&Bs near the U of A campus.

The posh resorts, primarily situated in the Catalina Foothills and Northwest areas, although farther away from town, have many activities on-site, as well as some of Tucson's top-rated restaurants, golf courses, and spas; resort staff can arrange transportation to shopping and sights.

For a unique experience, you can check into one of several Southwestern-style dude ranches on the outskirts of town. If you're seeking accommodations that can change your life, book a stay at one of Tucson's world-class health spas for pampering, serenity, and guidance for attaining an improved sense of well-being.

Summer rates (late May through September) are up to 60% lower than those in winter. Note that unless you book months in advance, you'll be hard-pressed to find a Tucson hotel room at any price the week before and during the huge gem and mineral show, which is held the first two weeks in February. (⇨ See "Festivals and Events" in Tucson Planner.) Also, resorts typically charge an additional daily fee for "use of facilities," such as pools, tennis courts, and exercise classes and equipment, so be sure to ask what's included when you book a room.

What it Costs			
$	$$	$$$	$$$$
FOR TWO PEOPLE			
Under $151	$151–$225	$226–$350	Over $350

Hotel reviews have been shortened. For full information, visit Fodors.com.

8

Tucson TUCSON PLANNER

Restaurants

Tucson boldly proclaims itself to be the "Mexican Food Capital of the United States," and most of the Mexican food in town is Sonoran-style. This means prolific use of cheese, mild peppers, corn tortillas, pinto beans, and beef or chicken. It's the birthplace of the *chimichanga* (Spanish for "whatchamacallit"), a flour tortilla filled with meat or cheese, rolled, and deep-fried.

The best Mexican restaurants are concentrated in South Tucson and Downtown, although some favorites have additional locations around town. If Mexican's not your thing, there are plenty of other options: you won't have any trouble finding excellent sushi, Thai, Italian, and Ethiopian food at reasonable prices.

For sampling regional flavors, upscale Southwestern cuisine flourishes at several resorts in the Foothills, most notably the Grill at Hacienda del Sol and Flying V Grill at Loews Ventana Canyon. A recent trend in Tucson dining is combining hip restaurants with chic shopping locations. Choose from sushi, steak, Italian, or Mexican at La Encantada in the Foothills. Casas Adobes Plaza, in the Northwest, is home to upscale shops alongside Wildflower Grill and trendy, thin-crust pizza at Sauce—and the gelato shop, Frost, is handy for dessert. Downtown has recently exploded with first-rate dining and drinking establishments, from modern comfort food and homemade ice cream to gourmet pizzas, craft beers, and contemporary Mexico City cuisine.

Tasty fare as varied as Indian, Chinese, and Middle Eastern can be enjoyed on the west side of U of A's campus, along University Boulevard and 4th Avenue—another great area for people-watching and barhopping as well as quelling hunger pangs.

On Friday and Saturday nights and during the Gem Show (first two weeks of February), reservations are usually a good idea at upscale and popular restaurants.

What it Costs			
$	$$	$$$	$$$$
AT DINNER			
Under $13	$13–$20	$21–$30	Over $30

Nightlife

The majority of Tucson's bars and clubs, many with live music or a DJ, are clustered along Congress Street Downtown and on or near 4th Avenue. A proliferation of craft breweries and gastropubs pour local brews in this district. In addition, most of the major resorts have late spots for drinks or dancing. The Westward Look Resort's Lookout Bar, with its expansive view and classic rock band on Friday and Saturday nights, is popular for dancing. The bars at Westin La Paloma, Hacienda del Sol, and Loews Ventana have live acoustic music on weekends.

Performing Arts

For a city of its size, Tucson is abuzz with cultural activity. It's one of only 14 cities in the United States with a symphony as well as opera, theater, and ballet companies. Wintertime, when Tucson's population swells with vacationers, is the high season, but the arts are alive and well year-round. The low cost of Tucson's cultural events comes as a pleasant surprise to those accustomed to paying East or West Coast prices: concert tickets are as little as $20 for some performances, and touring Broadway musicals can often be seen for $45. Parking is plentiful and frequently free.

The free *Tucson Weekly* (⊕ *www.tucson-weekly.com*) and the "Caliente" section of the *Arizona Daily Star* ⊕ *www.azstarnet.com*) both hit the stands on Thursday, and have listings of what's going on in town.

Shopping

Much of Tucson's retail activity is focused around malls, but shops with more character and some unique wares can be found in the city's open plazas: Old Town Artisans (Meyer Avenue and Washington Street), St. Philip's Plaza (River Road and Campbell Avenue), Casas Adobes Plaza (Oracle and Ina roads), and La Encantada (Skyline Drive and Campbell Avenue).

The 4th Avenue neighborhood near the University of Arizona—especially between 5th and 9th streets—is fertile ground for unusual items in the artsy boutiques, galleries, and second-hand-clothing stores.

If you're seeking work by regional artists, there are excellent galleries Downtown and in the Catalina Foothills; or you might want to drive down to Tubac, a community 45 miles south of Tucson (⇨ *see Side Trips Near Tucson*).

San Xavier Plaza, across from San Xavier Mission and also part of the Tohono O'odham Reservation, is a good place to find vendors and stores selling the work of this and other area tribes.

Activities

Fall, winter, and spring in Tucson are mild with little rainfall, making the Tucson area wonderful for outdoor sports. The city has miles of bike paths (shared by joggers and walkers), plenty of open spaces with memorable desert views, and some of the best golf courses in the country. Hikers enjoy the desert trails in Saguaro National Park, Sabino Canyon, and Catalina State Park—all within 20 minutes of

Central Tucson. In summer there are cooler treks in nearby mountain ranges—Mount Lemmon to the north and Madera Canyon to the south. Equestrians can find scenic trails at one of the many area stables or dude ranches.

BICYCLING
Tucson is one of America's top bicycling cities and has well-maintained bikeways, routes, lanes, and paths all over the city. Download a map of the Loop Pathway System, 100 miles of connecting bike trails encircling the city, from the city's website (⊕ *www.tucsonaz.gov/bicycle/maps*). Scenic-loop roads in both sections of Saguaro National Park are rewarding rides for all levels of cyclists, though the West district's road is unpaved.

BIRD-WATCHING
The naturalist and illustrator Roger Tory Peterson (1908–96) considered Tucson one of the country's top birding spots, and avid "life listers"—birders who keep a list of all the birds they've sighted and identified—soon see why. In the early morning and early evening Sabino Canyon is alive with cactus and canyon wrens, hawks, and quail. Spring and summer, when species of migrants come in from Mexico, are great hummingbird seasons. In the nearby Santa Rita Mountains and Madera Canyon you can see elegant trogons nesting in early spring. The area also supports species usually found only in higher elevations.

GOLF
One of Tucson's best-kept secrets is that the city's five low-priced municipal courses are maintained to standards usually found only at the best country clubs. All five have pro shops, driving ranges and putting greens, snack bars, and rental clubs. The greens fees listed include a cart; walking will save a few more dollars. To reserve a tee time, call the main reservation number ☏ *520/791–4653* or go online at ⊕ *www.tucsoncitygolf.com*.

The resort courses listed in this chapter are open to the public, but resort guests pay slightly lower greens fees. All have complete country-club facilities. Those who don't mind getting up early to beat the heat will find some excellent golf packages at these places in summer. The city's public courses also have lower fees Monday through Thursday.

HIKING

For hiking inside Tucson's city limits, you can test your skills climbing up the popular Tumamoc Hill, a paved, steep but moderately easy trail with excellent views (across from St. Mary's Hospital, off Anklam Road). The Santa Catalina Mountains, Sabino Canyon, and Saguaro National Park East and West beckon hikers with waterfalls, birds, critters, and huge saguaro cacti.

SPAS

From day spas to top-rated destination spas to a multitude of posh resorts, the array of wellness treatments in Tucson is wide. Many Tucson spas feature treatments that incorporate Native American traditions and desert plants. Most of the resorts and destination spas—including Canyon Ranch—lie in the Foothills or Northwest, while popular day spas are located around town.

Tours

Southwest Trekking

GUIDED TOURS | This outfitter arranges top-notch guided mountain biking, hiking, rock climbing, and camping outings. Custom-designed tours, based on the groups' interests and abilities, might consist of a four-hour bike ride (bicycles provided) or an all-day hike among the spectacular boulders of the Cochise Stronghold (includes breakfast in Tombstone). ⊠ *Tucson* ☎ *520/296–9661* ⊕ *www.swtrekking.com* ✉ *From $150.*

Trail Dust Adventures

GUIDED TOURS | This company runs three-hour open-air jeep tours that explore the flora and fauna in the Sonoran Desert and mountains outside the city. Cookout dinners (for groups of 25 or more) can be added. ☎ *520/747–0323* ⊕ *traildustof-froadtoursinc.com* ✉ *Call for pricing.*

Visitor Information

CONTACTS Southern Arizona Heritage and Visitor Center. ⊠ *115 N. Church Ave., Suite 200, Downtown* ☎ *800/638–8350* ⊕ *www.visittucson.org.*

Downtown Tucson

The area bordered by Franklin Street on the north, Cushing Street on the south, Church Avenue on the east, and Main Avenue on the west contains more than two centuries of Tucson's history, dating from the original walled fortress, El Presidio de Tucson, built by the Spanish in 1776, when Arizona was still part of New Spain. A good deal of the city's history was destroyed in the 1960s, when large sections of Downtown's barrio were bulldozed to make way for the Tucson Convention Center, high-rises, and parking lots.

Nevertheless, within the area's three small historic districts it's still possible to explore Tucson's cultural and architectural past. Adobe—brick made of mud and straw, cured in the hot sun—was used widely as a building material in early Tucson because it provides natural insulation from the heat and cold and because it's durable in Tucson's dry climate. When these buildings are properly made and maintained, they can last for centuries. Driving around Downtown Tucson, you'll see adobe houses painted in vibrant hues such as bright pink and canary yellow.

Revitalization is in full swing Downtown, especially along Congress Street, where multiple restaurants and bars are now

Downtown Tucson is known for its colorful adobe houses and shops.

thriving, and a streetcar line shuttles riders between Downtown and the 4th Avenue–University areas.

GETTING HERE AND AROUND

Downtown only approaches "bustling" on weekdays at lunchtime and weekend evenings. It's possible to find metered street parking (free after 6 pm); otherwise, there is ample parking in several parking garages all within a few blocks of Congress Street.

◉ Sights

"A" Mountain

MOUNTAIN—SIGHT | The original name of this mountain, Sentinel Peak, west of Downtown, came from its function as a lookout point for the Spanish, though the Pima village and cultivated fields that once lay at the base of the peak are long gone. In 1915 fans of the University of Arizona football team whitewashed a large "A" on its side to celebrate a victory, and the tradition has been kept up ever since—the permanent "A" is now red,

white, and blue. During the day, the peak's a great place to get an overview of the town's layout; at night the city lights below form a dazzling carpet, but the teenage hangout scene may make some uncomfortable. ⊠ *Congress St. on Sentinel Peak Rd., Downtown.*

Children's Museum Tucson

MUSEUM | FAMILY | Youngsters are encouraged to touch and explore the science, language, and history exhibits here. They can examine a patient in the Bodyology Center and care for (stuffed) doggies at the PetVet exhibit. Investigation Station has air-pressure tubes where balls and scarves whiz around, and there's a Discovery Garden for all ages to climb, slide, and burn off steam. ⊠ *200 S. 6th Ave., Downtown* ☎ *520/792–9985* ⊕ *www.childrensmuseumtucson.org* 🎫 *$9* ⊗ *Closed Mon.*

Downtown Historic Districts

HISTORIC SITE | North of the Convention Center and the government buildings, **El Presidio Historic District** is an architectural thumbnail of the city's former self. The north–south streets Court, Meyer,

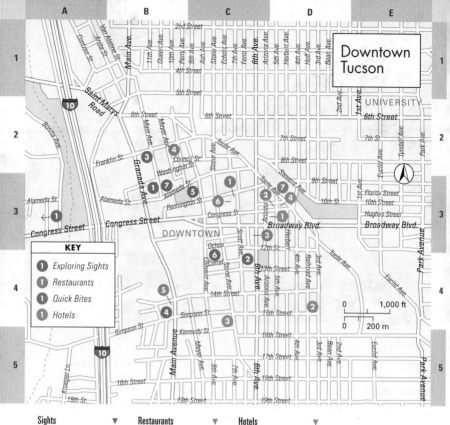

Downtown Tucson

KEY

1 Exploring Sights
1 Restaurants
1 Quick Bites
1 Hotels

and Main are sprinkled with traditional Mexican adobe houses sitting cheek by jowl with Territorial-style houses with wide attics and porches. Paseo Redondo, once called Snob Hollow, is the wide road along which wealthy merchants built their homes.

The area most closely resembling 19th-century Tucson is the **Barrio Historico,** also known as Barrio Viejo. The narrow streets of this neighborhood, including Convent Avenue, have a good sampling of thick-walled adobe houses. The colorfully painted houses are close to the street, hiding the yards and gardens within.

To the east of the Barrio Historico, across Stone Avenue, is the **Armory Park** neighborhood, mostly constructed by and for the railroad workers who settled here after the 1880s. The brick or wood Territorial-style homes here were the Victorian era's adaptation to the desert climate. ⊠ *Downtown.*

El Tiradito (The Castaway)

MEMORIAL | No one seems to know the details of the story behind this little shrine, but everyone agrees a tragic love triangle was involved. A bronze plaque indicates only that it's dedicated to a sinner who is buried here on unconsecrated ground. The candles that line the cactus-shrouded spot attest to its continuing importance in local Catholic lore. People light candles and leave *milagros* ("miracles," or little icons used in prayers for healing) for loved ones. A modern-day miracle: the shrine's inclusion on the National Register of Historic Places helped prevent a freeway from plowing through this section of the Barrio Historico. ⊠ *Main Ave., south of Cushing St., Downtown.*

Pima County Courthouse

GOVERNMENT BUILDING | This pink Spanish colonial–style building with a mosaic-tile dome is among Tucson's most beautiful historic structures. Still in use, it was built in 1927 on the site of the original single-story adobe court of 1869; a portion of the old presidio wall can be seen in the south wing of the courthouse's second floor. The first floor now houses the Tucson Visitor Center and the University of Arizona Gem and Mineral Museum. At the side of the building is a diorama depicting the area's early days. ⊠ *115 N. Church Ave., Downtown* ⊹ *Between Alameda and Pennington Sts.* ⊕ *www. sc.pima.gov* ⊠ *Free* ⊙ *Closed Sun.*

St. Augustine Cathedral

RELIGIOUS SITE | Although the imposing white-and-beige, late-19th-century, Spanish-style building was modeled after the Cathedral of Queretaro in Mexico, a number of its details reflect the desert setting. For instance, above the entryway, next to a bronze statue of St. Augustine, are carvings of local desert scenes with saguaro cacti, yucca, and prickly pears—look closely and you'll find the horned toad. Compared with the magnificent facade, the modernized interior is a bit disappointing. ■TIP→ For a **distinctly Southwestern experience, attend the mariachi Mass celebrated Sunday at 8 am.** ⊠ *192 S. Stone Ave., Downtown* ☎ *520/623–6351* ⊕ *cathedral-staugustine.org* ⊠ *Free.*

Tucson Museum of Art and Historic Block

MUSEUM | The museum consists of a modern building housing superb collections of Latin American Art and Western Art, and five adjacent historic buildings on Main Avenue that are listed in the National Register of Historic Places. You can tour four of the historic houses, La Casa Cordova, the Stevens Home, the J. Knox Corbett House, and the Edward Nye Fish House, though each have different hours. The fifth, the Romero House, believed to incorporate a section of the presidio wall, is now used for the museum's ceramics education program. Visitors enter through the main museum on Alameda Street. The Latin American Art wing includes ancient Andean and Incan sculpture and Spanish-Colonial art as well as contemporary Latin works. The Art of the American

West exhibits showcase Western and indigenous Southwestern art.

La Casa Cordova, one of the oldest buildings in Tucson and one of the best local examples of a Sonoran row house has a Spanish-style design adapted to adobe construction. The oldest section of La Casa Cordova, constructed around 1848, is only open November to January to display El Nacimiento, the largest nativity scene in the Southwest.

The **Stevens Home** was where the wealthy politician and cattle rancher Hiram Stevens and his wife, Petra Santa Cruz, entertained many of Tucson's leaders during the 1800s. A drought brought the Stevens' cattle ranching to a halt in 1893, and Stevens killed himself in despair after unsuccessfully attempting to shoot his wife (the bullet was deflected by the comb she wore in her hair). The 1865 house was restored in 1980 and now houses Café à la C'Art, a delightful restaurant.

The **J. Knox Corbett House** was built in 1906–07 and occupied by members of the Corbett family until 1963. J. Knox Corbett was a successful businessman, postmaster, and mayor of Tucson, and his wife, Elizabeth Hughes Corbett, an accomplished musician and daughter of Tucson pioneer Sam Hughes. The two-story, Mission Revival–style residence has been furnished with Arts and Crafts pieces. It's open only on weekends.

The **Edward Nye Fish House,** an 1868 adobe that belonged to an early merchant, entrepreneur, and politician and his wife, is notable for its 15-foot beamed ceilings and saguaro cactus–rib supports.

Admission to the museum and all four homes is free on the second Sunday and the first Thursday evening of every month, and there are free docent tours daily. ⊠ *140 N. Main Ave., Downtown* ☎ *520/624–2333* ⊕ *www.tucsonmuseumofart.org* 🎫 *$12* ⊘ *Closed Mon.*

🍴 Restaurants

★ Café Poca Cosa

$$ | **MEXICAN** | At what is arguably Tucson's most creative Mexican restaurant, the chef prepares recipes inspired by different regions of her native country in a modern, vibrant setting. The menu, which changes daily, is listed on a chalkboard brought around to each table. **Known for:** innovative Mexican cooking; generous portions; lively energy. $ *Average main: $19* ⊠ *110 E. Pennington St., Downtown* ☎ *520/622–6400* ⊕ *www.cafepocacosatucson.com* ⊘ *Closed Sun. and Mon.*

Cup Café

$$ | **AMERICAN** | This charming spot off the lobby of Hotel Congress is at the epicenter of Tucson's hippest scene, but it also serves up excellent food from breakfast through late night. Try the cast-iron baked eggs or huevos rancheros for breakfast, and the ahi poke bowl or "Queer Steer" (veggie burger) later in the day. **Known for:** weekend brunch; late-night dining; cool vibe to match the great food. $ *Average main: $18* ⊠ *Hotel Congress, 311 E. Congress St., Downtown* ☎ *520/798–1618* ⊕ *hotelcongress.com.*

Downtown Kitchen & Cocktails

$$$ | **MODERN AMERICAN** | Ever-evolving maverick and master chef Janos Wilder draws inspiration from warm-weather regions around the world as he fuses French technique and Southwestern flavors. His emphasis on locally grown, organic foods informs the seasonally changing menu, but you can always get his signature J Dawg, a Sonoran hot dog with black beans, bacon, and smoked–poblano chile crema. **Known for:** award-winning chef; inventive dishes; locally sourced foods. $ *Average main: $25* ⊠ *135 S. 6th Ave., Downtown* ☎ *520/623–7700* ⊕ *downtownkitchen.com* ⊘ *No lunch.*

El Charro Café

$$ | **MEXICAN** | Started by Monica Flin in 1922, the oldest Mexican restaurant in town still serves splendid versions of the Mexican-American staples Flin claims to have originated, most notably chimichangas and cheese crisps. Located in an old stone house in El Presidio Historic District, the colorful restaurant and bar exude a festive, if slightly touristy, vibe. **Known for:** carne seca (beef air-dried on the roof); crowd-pleasing menu; fun ambience. $ *Average main: $17* ⊠ *311 N. Court Ave., Downtown* ☎ *520/622–1922* ⊕ *www.elcharrocafe.com.*

El Minuto Café

$ | **MEXICAN** | Popular with local families and the business crowd at lunch, this bustling restaurant in Tucson's Barrio Historico neighborhood has been serving *topopo* salads (a crispy tortilla shell heaped with beans, guacamole, and many other ingredients), huge burritos, and green-corn tamales (in season) made just right for over 50 years. The spicy *menudo* (tripe soup) is reputed to be a great hangover remedy. **Known for:** consistent, tasty Sonoran food; good value; cheese crisps (cheese and veggies melted on tortillas). $ *Average main: $12* ⊠ *354 S. Main Ave., Downtown* ☎ *520/882–4145* ⊕ *www. elminutotucson.com* ⊗ *Closed Mon.*

47 Scott

$$$ | **MODERN AMERICAN** | Hip in an under-stated way, this classy bistro and bar is firmly ensconced at the top of local "best of Tucson" lists, and its cocktails have garnered national attention. The minimalist setting—walnut banquettes, exposed pipes, and bare-bulb lighting—contrasts with the great care taken in preparing entrées like phyllo-wrapped chicken stuffed with spinach and goat cheese or steamed mussels with andouille sausage and pommes frites. **Known for:** top-rated food and drink; creative cocktails; excellent happy hour. $ *Average main: $23* ⊠ *47 N. Scott Ave., Downtown* ☎ *520/624–4747* ⊕ *www.47scott.com* ⊗ *No lunch.*

★ Maynards

$$$ | **FRENCH** | An anchor in the downtown district, this French-inspired bistro, bar, and gourmet market takes up part of Tucson's historic train depot. Clever thematic touches—a dining room fashioned long and narrow like a train car, with wheel-like divider walls and lamps made from rail spikes—and the attentive yet relaxed service evoke the romance of a largely bygone era. **Known for:** romantic dining; great patio (especially for train-watching); one of the city's best restaurants. $ *Average main: $27* ⊠ *400 N. Toole Ave., Downtown* ☎ *520/545–0577* ⊕ *www. maynardstucson.com* ⊗ *No lunch Mon.–Sat. in restaurant (only at The Market).*

☕ Coffee and Quick Bites

★ Café à la C'Art

$ | **CAFÉ** | Tucked inside the Stevens Home, part of the Tucson Museum of Art and Historic Block, this gem of a café serves breakfast frittatas, burritos, and pancakes as well as delightful salads, soups, and sandwiches daily from 8 to 4, and is open for happy hour and dinner Wednesday through Saturday until 9. **Known for:** delectable desserts; lovely garden patio; popular breakfast and lunch spot for locals. $ *Average main: $12* ⊠ *150 N. Main Ave., Downtown* ☎ *520/628–8533* ⊕ *www.cafealacarttucson.com* ⊗ *No dinner Sun.–Tues.*

🛏 Hotels

AC Hotel Tucson Downtown

$$$ | **HOTEL** | If you're seeking the convenience of Downtown with ultramodern style, vibe, and amenities, this Marriott boutique hotel fits the bill nicely. **Pros:** a stone's throw from Downtown restaurants, galleries, and nightlife; rooftop pool; complimentary cocktails at 5 pm. **Cons:** parking costs extra; no microwaves or room service; no restaurant. $ *Rooms from: $256* ⊠ *151 E. Broadway Blvd., Downtown*

The iconic Hotel Congress is more than just a hotel—it's a destination for concerts and nightlife, too.

☎ 520/385–7111 🌐 www.marriott.com 🛏 136 rooms 🍴 No meals.

Armory Park Inn

$$$ | **B&B/INN** | Historic charm meets modern luxury in this beautifully renovated 1875 adobe home, walking distance to Downtown sights, dining, and nightlife. **Pros:** gorgeous historic property; plentiful common spaces for relaxing; full breakfasts and evening cocktails. **Cons:** pricey; street parking; some rooms are on second floor (stairs only). [$] *Rooms from: $259 ✉ 438 S. 3rd Ave., Downtown ☎ 520/838–0535 🌐 armoryparkinn.com 🛏 7 rooms 🍴 Free breakfast.*

The Downtown Clifton

$ | **HOTEL** | A hidden gem in the Downtown district, the Clifton exudes cool retro energy and delivers with spacious, attractive rooms that won't bust your budget. **Pros:** comfortable, affordable rooms; great restaurant and bar; cool vibe with warm hospitality. **Cons:** longish (10-minute) walk to downtown hub; no elevator to second-floor rooms; breakfast is continental. [$] *Rooms from: $149 ✉ 485 S. Stone Ave., Downtown ☎ 520/623-3163 🌐 downtowntucsonhotel.com 🛏 30 rooms 🍴 Free breakfast.*

★ Hotel Congress

$ | **HOTEL** | This hotel, built in 1919, has been artfully restored to its original Western version of art deco; it's now the center of Tucson's hippest scene and a great place for younger and adventurous travelers to stay. **Pros:** prime location; good restaurant and bars; historic, funky, and fun. **Cons:** no elevator to guest rooms; no TVs in rooms (only in common areas); noise from nightclub in some rooms. [$] *Rooms from: $119 ✉ 311 E. Congress St., Downtown ☎ 520/622–8848, 800/722–8848 🌐 www.hotelcongress.com 🛏 40 rooms 🍴 No meals.*

Nightlife

BARS AND CLUBS

Club Congress

MUSIC CLUBS | The city's main venue for cutting-edge bands and singer-songwriters, Club Congress has a mixed-bag crowd of alternative rockers, international travelers, young professionals, and college kids. There is live indie rock and folk/roots during the week, while Friday and Saturday nights bring more rock and dance parties. ⊠ *Hotel Congress, 311 E. Congress St., Downtown* ☎ *520/622–8848* ⊕ *www.hotelcongress.com.*

La Cocina

MUSIC CLUBS | Hear some of the best local talent play folk-rock, blues, and jazz Wednesday to Saturday nights and during weekend brunch hours at this eclectic restaurant and bar in the courtyard of Old Town Artisans. Sit under the stars and order from the late-night menu until midnight on Friday and Saturday. If you feel like performing as well as listening, head indoors to the adjacent Dusty Monk, where you can belt out your favorite tunes at the piano bar. ⊠ *Old Town Artisans, 201 N. Court Ave., Downtown* ☎ *520/622–0351* ⊕ *www. lacocinatucson.com.*

Playground

BARS/PUBS | Four distinct spaces at this popular bar offer something for everyone—everyone who likes a modern, urban vibe, that is. The spacious rooftop deck has a DJ and dancing most nights. Downstairs, the sleek, minimalist bar, with large-screen TVs and happy-hour specials, has occasional live music. Check out the intimate covered rear patio for quieter conversation, or see and be seen on the front patio along Congress Street. ⊠ *278 E. Congress St., Downtown* ☎ *520/396–3691* ⊕ *playgroundtucson.com.*

🎭 Performing Arts

Arizona Friends of Chamber Music

MUSIC | A Wednesday-night chamber-music series is hosted by the Arizona Friends of Chamber Music at the Leo Rich Theater in the Tucson Convention Center from October through April. There's also a music festival the first week of March. ⊠ *260 S. Church St., Downtown* ☎ *520/577–3769* ⊕ *arizonachambermusic.org.*

Arizona Opera Company

MUSIC | This Phoenix-based company puts on five major productions each year at the Tucson Convention Center's Music Hall. ⊠ *260 S. Church St., Downtown* ☎ *520/293–4336* ⊕ *www.azopera.org.*

Arizona Theatre Company

THEATER | From September through May, Arizona's state theater performs classical pieces, contemporary drama, and musical comedy at the historic Temple of Music and Art. It's worth coming just to see the beautifully restored historic Spanish colonial–Moorish-style theater; dinner at the adjoining Temple Lounge is a tasty prelude. ⊠ *Temple of Music and Art, 330 S. Scott Ave., Downtown* ☎ *520/622–2823 for box office* ⊕ *www. arizonatheatre.org.*

Borderlands Theater

THEATER | This company presents new stories of the Southwest border region—often multicultural and bilingual—at venues throughout Tucson, usually from September through April. ⊠ *151 S. Granada Ave., Downtown* ☎ *520/276–9598* ⊕ *www.borderlandstheater.org.*

Fox Tucson Theatre

MUSIC | A beautifully refurbished old movie palace, the art deco Fox Theatre hosts film festivals and mostly folk-rock concerts. ⊠ *17 W. Congress St., Downtown* ☎ *520/547–3040* ⊕ *foxtucson.com.*

Rialto Theatre

MUSIC | One of Tucson's hottest venues, the Rialto Theatre, once a silent-movie theater, now reverberates with the sounds of hard rock, jazz, folk, and world-music concerts. You can experience great musicians up close for reasonable ticket prices. ⊠ *318 E. Congress St., Downtown* ☎ *520/740–1000* ⊕ *www. rialtotheatre.com.*

Tucson Convention Center

ARTS CENTERS | Much of the city's cultural activity, including opera, touring Broadway shows, and Tucson Symphony concerts, as well as the international gem and mineral show, takes place at the Tucson Convention Center. Within this complex are the Arena, the Music Hall, and the smaller Leo Rich Theater. ⊠ 260 S. Church Ave., Downtown ☎ 520/791–4101 ⊕ tucsonconventioncenter.com.

Tucson Poetry Festival

FESTIVALS | The first weekend in April brings the Tucson Poetry Festival and its four days of readings and related events, including workshops, panel discussions, and a poetry slam. Such internationally acclaimed poets as Jorie Graham and Sherman Alexie have participated. ⊠ Hotel Congress, 311 E. Congress St. ⊕ www.tucsonpoetryfestival.org.

Tucson Symphony Orchestra

MUSIC | Part of Tuscon's cultural scene since 1929, this orchestra performs at the Tucson Convention Center and at sites in the Foothills and the Northwest from October through May. ⊠ Box Office, 2175 N. 6th Ave., Downtown ☎ 520/882–8585 box office ⊕ www.tucsonsymphony.org.

🛍 Shopping

Davis-Dominguez Gallery

ART GALLERIES | This highly regarded Downtown gallery exhibits and sells contemporary paintings, drawings, and sculpture of leading regional artists. ⊠ 154 E. 6th St., Downtown ☎ 520/629–9759 ⊕ davisdominguez.com ☞ Closed Sun. and Mon.

★ Etherton Gallery

ART GALLERIES | This gallery specializes in vintage, classic, and contemporary photography but also represents artists in other media. ⊠ 135 S. 6th Ave., Downtown ☎ 520/624–7370 ⊕ www.ethertongallery.com ⊙ Closed Sun. and Mon.

Old Town Artisans Complex

SHOPPING CENTERS/MALLS | Across from the Tucson Museum of Art, the Old Town Artisans complex of adobe buildings dating back to the 1850s has a large selection of Southwestern wares, including Native American jewelry, baskets, Mexican handicrafts, pottery, and textiles, as well as La Cocina Restaurant and bar. ⊠ 201 N. Court Ave., Downtown ☎ 520/622–0351 ⊕ www.oldtownartisans.com.

★ Philabaum Glass Gallery and Studio

CERAMICS/GLASSWARE | Magnificent hand-blown glass pieces by Tom Philabaum and others, including vases, artwork, table settings, and jewelry, are sold at this gallery at the southern edge of Downtown. ⊠ 711 S. 6th Ave., Downtown ☎ 520/884–7404 ⊕ www.philabaumglass.com.

The University of Arizona

The U of A (as opposed to rival ASU, in Tempe) is a major economic influence in Tucson, with a student population of more than 40,000. The land for the university was "donated" by a couple of gamblers and a saloon owner in 1891—their benevolence reputedly inspired by a bad hand of cards—and $25,000 of territorial money (Arizona was still a territory back then) was used to build Old Main, the original building, and to hire six faculty members. Money ran out before Old Main's roof was placed, but a few enlightened citizens pitched in funds to finish it. Most of the city's populace was less than enthusiastic about the institution. They were disgruntled when the 13th Territorial Legislature granted the University of Arizona to Tucson and awarded Phoenix what was considered the real prize: an insane asylum and a prison.

The university's flora is impressive—it represents a collection of plants from arid and semiarid regions around the world. An extremely rare mutated, or "crested," saguaro grows at the northeast corner of the Old Main building. The long, grassy mall in the heart of campus—itself once a vast cactus garden—sits atop a huge underground student activity center, and makes for a pleasant stroll on a balmy evening.

GETTING HERE AND AROUND

If you drive, leave your car in a university garage or lot, free on weekends and holidays. Metered street parking is difficult to find. Both the campus and the shopping/dining district just west along University Boulevard are best explored on foot. The streetcar route runs from the Banner-University Medical Center through the north and west portions of campus (with stops near the museums), then goes west along University Boulevard, down 4th Avenue and into Downtown.

PLANNING YOUR TIME

Call ahead to verify hours for the university's museums, or visit the University of Arizona website (⊕ *www.arizona.edu*) for parking maps and the latest visitor information.

Sights

Arizona History Museum

MUSEUM | FAMILY | The museum has exhibits exploring the history of Southern Arizona, starting with the indigenous Hohokam Tribe and the Spanish explorers. The harrowing "Life on the Edge: A History of Medicine in Arizona" exhibit promotes a new appreciation of modern drugstores in present-day Tucson. Children enjoy the exhibit on copper mining (with an atmospheric replica of a mine shaft and camp) and the stagecoaches in the transportation area.

The library has an extensive collection of historic Arizona photographs and sells inexpensive reprints. Park in the garage at the corner of 2nd and Euclid streets and get a free parking pass in the museum. ⊠ *949 E. 2nd St.,*

University 🕾 *520/628–5774* ⊕ *www.arizonahistoricalsociety.org/tucson* 🎫 *$10* 🕙 *Closed Sun. and Mon.*

Arizona State Museum

MUSEUM | FAMILY | Inside the main gate of the university is Arizona's oldest museum, dating from territorial days (1893) and a preeminent resource for the study of Southwestern cultures. Exhibits include the largest collections of Southwest Native American pottery and basketry, as well as *Paths of Life: American Indians of the Southwest*—a permanent exhibit that explores the cultural traditions, origins, and contemporary lives of 10 native tribes of Arizona and Sonora, Mexico. ⊠ *1013 E. University Blvd., at Park Ave., University* 🕾 *520/621–6302* ⊕ *www.statemuseum.arizona.edu* 🎫 *$8* 🕙 *Closed Sun.*

Center for Creative Photography

MUSEUM | Ansel Adams conceived the idea of a photographer's archive and donated the majority of his negatives to this museum. In addition to its superb collection of his work, the center houses the David Hume Kennerly Archive and works by other major photographers, including Paul Strand, W. Eugene Smith, Edward Weston, and Louise Dahl-Wolfe. Changing exhibits in the main gallery display selected pieces from the collection. ⊠ *1030 N. Olive Rd., north of 2nd St., University* 🕾 *520/621–7968* ⊕ *ccp.arizona.edu* 🎫 *Free* 🕙 *Closed Sun. and Mon.*

Flandrau Science Center and Planetarium

MUSEUM | FAMILY | Attractions at the university's science museum include a 16-inch public telescope for evening stargazing, hands-on science exhibits, and planetarium shows. ⊠ *1601 E. University Blvd., at Cherry Ave., University* 🕾 *520/621–4516, 520/621–7827 for recorded info* ⊕ *flandrau.org* 🎫 *$8 for museum, $8 for planetarium/laser show, telescope viewing free.*

The University of Arizona

0 — 1,000 ft
0 — 200 m

Sights ▼

1 Arizona History
   Museum **B3**
2 Arizona State
   Museum **C3**
3 Center for
   Creative Photography... **C2**
4 Flandrau
   Science Center
   and Planetarium **D3**
5 4th Avenue **A4**
6 University of Arizona
   Museum of Art........... **C2**
7 University of Arizona
   Richard F. Caris
   Mirror Lab **D4**

Restaurants ▼

1 Arizona Inn
   Restaurant................ **E1**
2 The B Line **A4**
3 Boca Tacos y
   Tequila **A4**

Quick Bites ▼

1 Gentle Ben's
   Brewing Company...... **B3**
2 Kababeque **B3**
3 Time Market............. **A3**

Hotels ▼

1 Adobe Rose
   Bed and Breakfast....... **E3**
2 Arizona Inn **E1**
3 Catalina Park Inn
   Bed & Breakfast........ **A3**
4 Tucson Marriott
   University Park.......... **B3**

4th Avenue

NEIGHBORHOOD | Students and counterculturists favor the ½-mile strip of 4th Avenue between University Boulevard and 8th Street, where vintage-clothing stores rub shoulders with eclectic gift shops and eateries. After dark, 4th Avenue bars pulse with live and recorded music. ✉ *University* ☎ *520/624–5004* 🌐 *www.fourthavenue.org.*

University of Arizona Museum of Art

MUSEUM | This small campus museum houses a collection of more than 6,000 artworks, mainly European and American paintings from the Renaissance through modern day, including works by Georgia O'Keeffe and Jackson Pollock. A highlight is the Kress Collection's *retablo* from Ciudad Rodrigo: 26 panels of an altarpiece made in the 1490s by Fernando Gallego. ✉ *Fine Arts Complex, 1031 N. Olive Rd., University* ✣ *North of 2nd St.* ☎ *520/621–7567* 🌐 *www.artmuseum.arizona.edu* 🎟 *$8* 🕒 *Closed Mon.*

University of Arizona Richard F. Caris Mirror Lab

COLLEGE | The giant mirrors used in the world's most advanced telescopes take about five years to create, and on this guided 90-minute tour you can view them in the different stages of the production process: glass melting, casting, grinding, and polishing. Reservations for the tours, offered weekdays for ages 10 and older, must be made in advance, and closed-toe, flat shoes are a must. ✉ *527 National Championship Dr., University* ✣ *east side of football stadium* ☎ *520/626–8792* 🌐 *mirrorlab.arizona.edu* 🎟 *$20* 🕒 *Closed weekends.*

🍴 Restaurants

Arizona Inn Restaurant

$$$$ | **EUROPEAN** | At one of Tucson's oldest and most elegant restaurants, dine on the patio overlooking the lush grounds or enjoy the view from the dining room, which has Southwestern details from the 1930s. The culinary range here is broad, from roasted duck in a tart cherry demi-glace to a vegetarian tomato and mushroom cannelloni. **Known for:** special-occasion meals, including Sunday Brunch; beautiful setting; classy piano bar for late-night dining. [$] *Average main: $34* ✉ *Arizona Inn, 2200 E. Elm St., University* ☎ *520/325–1541* 🌐 *www.arizonainn.com.*

The B Line

$ | **AMERICAN** | In the heart of 4th Avenue's amalgam of antique clothing stores and pubs, this casual café in a converted 1920s bungalow attracts a mix of students, professors, downtown professionals, and artists with its simple but refined meals and desserts. Homemade biscuit sandwiches and excellent coffee start the day; the lunch–dinner menu features soups, salads, pastas, burritos, and 13 brews on tap. **Known for:** fresh food with plenty of vegan options; yummy pastries and desserts; great people-watching. [$] *Average main: $10* ✉ *621 N. 4th Ave., University* ☎ *520/882–7575* 🌐 *www.thebline.xyz.*

Boca Tacos y Tequila

$ | **MEXICAN** | Maria Mazon, the award-winning chef and owner of Boca, has elevated tacos to an art form at this restaurant and bar in the center of the 4th Avenue district. Creative fillings of meats, veggies, and seafood are topped with cabbage and guacamole in either flour or corn tortillas. **Known for:** best restaurant on 4th Ave.; inventive tacos and house-made tortilla chips; huge selection of beers and tequilas. [$] *Average main: $12* ✉ *533 N. 4th Ave., University* ☎ *520/777–8134* 🌐 *bocatacos.com.*

☕ Coffee and Quick Bites

Gentle Ben's Brewing Company

$ | **BURGER** | Beer lovers should head to Gentle Ben's, a friendly, laid-back burger-and-brew pub that also makes a scrumptious veggie burger. The deck upstairs offers a good view of the sunset. **Known**

The University of Arizona's lush campus and museums are worth a visit.

for: craft beers; laid-back, college vibe; crowd-pleasing menu. $ *Average main: $10* ✉ *865 E. University Blvd., University* ☎ *520/624–4177* ⊕ *www.gentlebens.com.*

Kababeque

$ | **INDIAN** | From curry to kebab, the tasty and plentiful dishes at Kababeque satisfy for a quick bite Indian-style. **Known for:** tasty Indian food; proximity to campus; fast service and affordable prices. $ *Average main: $8* ✉ *845 E. University Blvd., University* ☎ *520/388–4500* ⊕ *kababeque.net.*

★ Time Market

$ | **AMERICAN** | The term "market" is slightly misleading for this neighborhood gathering spot serving delectable pizzas, creative sandwiches on freshly baked breads, pastries, espresso, and craft beers. Sit a while or take it to go, along with all the wonderful local and imported treats you've loaded into your shopping basket. **Known for:** amazing pizza; great sandwiches and desserts; specialty grocery (including wines and chocolates). $ *Average main: $10* ✉ *444 E. University Blvd., University* ☎ *520/622–0761* ⊕ *timemarket.xyz.*

🛏 Hotels

Adobe Rose Bed and Breakfast

$$ | **B&B/INN** | In the historic, residential Sam Hughes neighborhood, this well-maintained inn just east of the university is within easy walking distance of shops and restaurants. **Pros:** sumptuous breakfasts that can be prepared vegan, gluten-free, and dairy-free; homelike yet private; attentive hosts. **Cons:** some rooms are small; it's about a mile walk to University Blvd. and 4th Ave. sights; no kids under 12. $ *Rooms from: $165* ✉ *940 N. Olsen Ave., University* ☎ *520/318–4644* ⊕ *adoberoseinn.com* 🛏 *6 rooms* ⦿ *Free breakfast.*

★ Arizona Inn

$$$$ | **HOTEL** | Although near the university and many sights, the beautifully landscaped lawns and gardens of this 1930 inn seem far from the hustle and bustle. **Pros:** unique historical property; emphasis on service; gorgeous gardens and common areas. **Cons:** rooms may not be modern enough for some; close

to University Medical Center but long walk (1½ miles) from the main campus; too sedate and posh for some. 🛈 *Rooms from: $359* ⊠ *2200 E. Elm St., University* ☎ *520/325–1541, 800/933–1093* ⊕ *www.arizonainn.com* ⬩ *94 rooms* ⦿ *No meals.*

★ Catalina Park Inn Bed & Breakfast

$ | B&B/INN | Classical music plays softly in the living room of this beautifully restored 1927 neoclassical house in the University of Arizona vicinity, an easy walk to restaurants and the streetcar line. **Pros:** large and quiet rooms with comfortable beds; convenient to University, 4th Avenue, and Downtown; charming hosts. **Cons:** West University location not quite as bucolic as east of campus; closed in summer; some rooms have exterior entrances. 🛈 *Rooms from: $125* ⊠ *309 E. 1st St., University* ☎ *520/792–4541* ⊕ *www.catalinaparkinn.com* ⊙ *Closed mid-May–Sept.* ⬩ *5 rooms* ⦿ *Free breakfast.*

Tucson Marriott University Park

$$$ | HOTEL | With the University of Arizona less than a block from the front door, this clean, contemporary hotel is an ideal place to stay when visiting the campus. **Pros:** excellent location near campus; many rooms have mountain views; on-site gym. **Cons:** generic property; uninspired restaurant; fee for parking. 🛈 *Rooms from: $250* ⊠ *880 E. 2nd St., University* ☎ *520/792–4100* ⊕ *www.marriott.com* ⬩ *250 rooms* ⦿ *No meals.*

Nightlife

IBT's (It's 'Bout Time)

BARS/PUBS | Tucson's most popular gay bar, IBT's has rock and disco DJs, karaoke, live music, or drag shows nightly. ⊠ *616 N. 4th Ave., University* ☎ *520/882–3053* ⊕ *www.ibtstucson.com.*

Tap and Bottle

BARS/PUBS | Known for its huge selection of beers—especially local craft beers—and convivial atmosphere, this popular pub sits two blocks off 4th Avenue. It's

a pleasant alternative to the rowdier college hangouts and dive bars nearby. ⊠ *403 N. 6th Ave., University* ☎ *520/344–8999* ⊕ *thetapandbottle.com.*

Performing Arts

Arizona Repertory Theatre

THEATER | Outstanding performances by students occur throughout the academic year at this University of Arizona theater. ⊠ *1025 N. Olive St., University* ☎ *520/621–1162* ⊕ *theatre.arizona.edu.*

Centennial Hall

ARTS CENTERS | Dance, music, musical theater, and other performances take place at the University of Arizona's Centennial Hall. The UA Presents series is held here during the academic year (September through May). ⊠ *1020 E. University Blvd., University* ☎ *520/621–3341* ⊕ *uapresents.org.*

University of Arizona Poetry Center

ARTS CENTERS | A free series of readings and classes open to the public is run by the University of Arizona in its beautiful Poetry Center. Check online or call during fall and spring semesters for schedules. ⊠ *1508 E. Helen St., University* ☎ *520/626–3765* ⊕ *poetry.arizona.edu.*

Shopping

Antigone Books

BOOKS/STATIONERY | This lovely independent bookstore on 4th Avenue specializes in books by and about women, and sells creative cards, gifts, and T-shirts as well as a broad range of books. ⊠ *411 N. 4th Ave., University* ☎ *520/792–3715* ⊕ *www.antigonebooks.com.*

Book Stop

BOOKS/STATIONERY | This is a wonderful browsing place for used, rare, and out-of-print books. ⊠ *214 N. 4th Ave., University* ☎ *520/326–6661* ⊕ *www.bookstoptucson.com.*

Colorful murals can be seen all over Tucson, especially Downtown and South Tucson.

Del Sol

CRAFTS | This shop specializes in Mexican folk art, jewelry, and Southwest-style clothing. ✉ *435 N. 4th Ave., University* ☎ *520/628–8765* ⊕ *www. delsolstores.com.*

★ Popcycle

CRAFTS | This unique and fun store sells affordable art and gifts, ranging from the funky to the divine, all made by local artists using recycled materials. ✉ *422 N. 4th Ave., University* ☎ *520/622–3297* ⊕ *www.popcycleshop.com.*

🏃 Activities

Fair Wheel Bikes

BICYCLING | Mountain bikes and road bikes can be rented by the day or week here. The company also organizes group rides of varying difficulty. ✉ *1110 E. 6th St., University* ☎ *520/884–9018* ⊕ *fair-wheelbikes.com.*

Sierra Club

HIKING/WALKING | The club's local chapter, the Rincon Group, welcomes out-of-towners on weekend hikes, ranging in level of difficulty. ✉ *738 N. 5th Ave., University* ☎ *520/620–6401* ⊕ *www. sierraclub.org/arizona/rincon.*

Tucson Audubon Society and Nature Shop

BIRD WATCHING | You can get the latest birding word on the local Audubon Society's 24-hour line; sightings of rare or interesting birds in the area are recorded regularly. The society's shop carries field guides, bird feeders, binoculars, and natural-history books. ✉ *300 E. University Blvd., Suite 120, University* ☎ *520/629–0510* ⊕ *tucsonaudubon.org* ⊘ *Closed Sun.*

Central Tucson

Tucson expanded north and east from the university during the 1950s and '60s, and currently continues to spread southeast. The east–west thoroughfares of Broadway, Speedway, and Grant are lined with small and large businesses and eateries, mostly in unattractive strip malls. Sights worth seeing in this area include the Reid Park Zoo, the Tucson Botanical Gardens, and a couple of eccentric museums.

PLANNING YOUR TIME

If it's warm, visit outdoor attractions such as the zoo or Tucson Botanical Gardens in the morning; the museums and shopping malls are cooler options for the afternoon.

⊙ Sights

Fort Lowell Park and Museum

MUSEUM | FAMILY | Fertile soil and proximity to the Rillito River once enticed the Hohokam to construct a village on this site. Centuries later, a fort (in operation from 1873 to 1891) was built here to protect the fledgling city of Tucson against the Apaches. The former commanding officer's quarters at this quirky fort museum has artifacts from military life in territorial days. The park has a playground, ball fields, tennis courts, and a duck pond. ⊠ 2900 N. Craycroft Rd., Central ☎ 520/885–3832 ⊕ www.arizonahistorical-society.org ⊠ Free ⊘ Closed Sun.–Wed.

The Mini Time Machine Museum of Miniatures

MUSEUM | FAMILY | When Pat Arnell began collecting miniatures in the late 1970s, she probably didn't imagine that her hobby would eventually outgrow her house and become an offbeat but effective vehicle for people of all ages to explore history and culture. The modern museum displays more than 275 doll houses and room boxes, antique through contemporary, from the United States, Europe, and Asia. There are also plenty of wee folk, like fairies, wizards, and kewpie dolls, and even tiny appliance "samples" that were carried door-to-door by traveling salesmen. ⊠ 4455 E. Camp Lowell Dr., Central ☎ 520/881–0606 ⊕ theminitimemachine. org ⊠ $10 ⊘ Closed Sun. and Mon.

Reid Park Zoo

ZOO | FAMILY | This small but well-designed zoo won't tax your patience. There are plenty of shady places to sit, a well-stocked gift shop, and a snack bar to rev you up when your energy flags. You can feed carrots to the zoo's friendly giraffes each morning at 10 (9:30 June–Sept., $3). At the African elephants habitat, you might view a training session (look for posted times at the entrance). If you're visiting in summer, go early in the day when the animals are active. ⊠ Reid Park, 1100 S. Randolph Way, off 22nd St., Central ☎ 520/791–3204 ⊕ reidparkzoo.org ⊠ $11.

Tucson Botanical Gardens

GARDEN | Five acres of gardens are home to a variety of experiences: a tropical greenhouse; a sensory garden, where you can touch and smell the plants and listen to the abundant bird life; historical gardens that display the Mediterranean landscaping the property's original owners planted in the 1930s; a garden designed to attract birds; and a cactus garden. Other gardens showcase wildflowers, Australian plants, and Native American crops and herbs. From October through April, interact with butterflies from all over the world in their own greenhouse. A delightful café is open for breakfast and lunch daily. All paths are wheelchair accessible. ⊠ 2150 N. Alvernon Way, Central ☎ 520/326–9686 ⊕ www.tucsonbotanical.org ⊠ $15.

🍴 Restaurants

Bangkok Cafe

$$ | THAI | Easily the best Thai food in town, this bright, spacious café serves favorite Thai dishes and has pleasant service. The Thoong Tong appetizer of fried veggie-filled pouches is blissfully good, as are the curries and soups. **Known for:** top-notch Thai; weekend crowds; lunch specials. $ *Average main: $15* ✉ *2511 E. Speedway Blvd., Central* ☎ *520/323–6555* ⊕ *www.bangkokcafe.net* ⊘ *No lunch Sun.*

Beyond Bread

$ | **CAFÉ** | Twenty-seven varieties of bread are made at this bustling bakery with Central, Eastside, and Northwest locations, and highlights from the menu of generous sandwiches include Annie's Addiction (hummus, tomato, sprouts, red onion, and cucumber) and Brad's Beef (roast beef, provolone, onion, green chiles, and Russian dressing); soups, salads, and desserts are equally scrumptious. Eat inside or on the patio, or order takeout, but either way, splurge on one of the incredible desserts. **Known for:** stellar breads and pastries; large portions; friendliness. $ *Average main: $10* ✉ *3026 N. Campbell Ave., Central* ☎ *520/322–9965* ⊕ *www.beyondbread. com* ⊘ *No dinner Sun.*

Feast

$$$ | **ECLECTIC** | One of Tucson's most popular upscale bistros, Feast has a contemporary setting that is bright, cheerful, and conducive to conversation. The eclectic menu, which changes monthly, is filled with interesting combinations of flavors such as rosemary–goat cheese risotto with artichoke hearts and tomatoes, and orange-glazed chicken breast with roasted beets on sesame-cream noodles. **Known for:** eclectic, locally sourced menu; extensive wine list; sophisticated dining. $ *Average main: $25* ✉ *3719 E. Speedway, Central* ☎ *520/326–9363* ⊕ *www. eatatfeast.com* ⊘ *Closed Mon.*

Kingfisher Bar and Grill

$$$ | **AMERICAN** | A standout for classic American cuisine, Kingfisher has an emphasis on fresh seafood, especially oysters and mussels, but the kitchen does baby back ribs and steak with equal success. Try the delicately battered fish-and-chips or the clam chowder on the late-night menu, served from 10 pm

to midnight nightly. **Known for:** fabulous seafood; late-night dining; dynamic vibe. $ *Average main: $24* ✉ *2564 E. Grant Rd., Central* ☎ *520/323–7739* ⊕ *www.kingfishertucson.com* ⊘ *No lunch weekends.*

Zemam's

$ | **ETHIOPIANETHIOPIAN** | This small, friendly eatery with a loyal following prepares classic Ethiopian dishes, served on a communal platter with *injera,* a spongy bread, and eaten with the hands. Sampler plates of any three items allow you to try dishes like *yesimir wat* (a spicy lentil dish) and *lega tibs* (a milder beef dish with a tomato sauce). **Known for:** inexpensive, authentic Ethiopian cuisine; many vegan selections; warm hospitality. $ *Average main: $12* ✉ *2731 E. Broadway Blvd., Central* ☎ *520/323–9928* ⊕ *www.zemams.com* ⊘ *Closed Mon.*

🛏 Hotels

Doubletree by Hilton Tucson–Reid Park

$ | **HOTEL** | **FAMILY** | A sprawling, 1970s-era hotel and conference center, the Doubletree sits directly across the street from Randolph Park, Tucson's best municipal golf course, and Reid Park, which houses the city zoo, a lake with paddleboats, and numerous play areas. **Pros:** free shuttle service within a 4-mile radius; close to recreation and restaurants; sceney restaurant and bar. **Cons:** older property; smallish rooms; some second-floor rooms are accessible only by stairs. $ *Rooms from: $149* ✉ *445 S. Alvernon Way, Central* ☎ *520/881–4200, 800/222–8733* ⊕ *doubletree3.hilton.com* ⤴ *295 rooms* ⧇ *No meals.*

Lodge on the Desert

$$ | **HOTEL** | A charming hacienda-style hotel built in the 1930s offers modern comfort in an old-world setting. **Pros:** quiet, garden setting with attractive pool area; central location; excellent breakfast included. **Cons:** short drive but long walk to shops and restaurants; located just off busy thoroughfare; some plumbing issues

Tucson Food: North of the Border

Although Tucson ensures that authentic south-of-the-border culinary and cultural influences aren't lost in translation, it also cooks up plenty of cross-border sway. The growing University metropolis boasts eats from around the world and mixes these tastes with more local flavors.

Emerging from an era of meat and potatoes and carne and frijoles—all of which it still does exceptionally well—Tucson has become a foodie tour de force. You can indulge in authentic chicken mole and *carne seca* (dried beef); fill up on some local/global fusion food; or get good and greasy with a Sonoran hot dog.

Start with some classic Mexican dishes such as tamales or enchiladas. But today even Mexican-American foods are evolving into a new generation of creations. Do you prefer the chimichangas that purportedly originated at El Charro Café or the mango-filled ones at Mi Nidito for dessert? Taste and decide for yourself.

Say Cheese

Many identify Mexican food by bright, glistening layers of cheddar that render the entrée below it unrecognizable. Not that there's anything wrong with that, but true Mexico-style meals are untouched by orange cheese. Authentic dishes are served with much smaller rations of white cheese, usually *queso blanco* or *panela*—mild cheeses that become soft and creamy when heated, but don't melt—and Cotija, a Mexican-style Parmesan.

Pick a Pepper

Another key to authentic Mexican food is its heat source: fresh peppers. These heat-tolerant plants were once a south-of-the-border specialty; increased demand has led to their being raised in the southern United States, where they've had a growing impact on regional cuisine. There are endless varieties of the spicy fruit, but here are some more commonly seen on local menus.

Green and Red: Often roasted and peeled for stews and broths, sauces, rubs, marinades, confectionery, chili, and chiles rellenos. Green chiles are unripe, with mild to medium-high heat. Red chiles are ripe, with maximum heat.

Jalapeño: These flavorful green peppers can range from mild to hot and are served pickled, canned, deep-fried for "poppers," or as a garnish for everything from salads to nachos.

Chipotle: When select jalapeños mature from green to a deep red, they're prime for the wood-smoking process that creates chipotle peppers. Their distinct flavor is popular in sauces, marinades, and salsas.

Habañero: This thumb-shape pepper is one of the hottest. A little goes a long way in cooking. It's most often found in chili recipes and hot sauces.

Poblano: This green pepper, aka *pasilla*, is usually mild, but can sometimes pack a punch. Dried, it's an ancho chile. The poblano is used for moles.

in older historic rooms. $ *Rooms from: $195* ⊠ *306 N. Alvernon Way, Central* ☎ *520/320–2000* ⊕ *www.lodgeonthedesert.com* ⤴ *103 rooms* ⦿| *Free breakfast.*

Nightlife

The Shelter

MUSIC CLUBS | Sip a martini or a local brew and go totally retro at the Shelter, a former bomb shelter decked out in plastic 1960s kitsch, lava lamps, and JFK memorabilia. Watch Elvis videos and listen to the music of Burt Bacharach, as well as current alternative rock. ⊠ *4155 E. Grant Rd., Central* ☎ *520/326–1345.*

Performing Arts

Ballet Tucson

DANCE | The city's professional ballet company performs classics like *The Nutcracker* in December, as well as contemporary works throughout the year. ⊠ *200 S. Tucson Blvd., Central* ☎ *520/903–1445* ⊕ *www.ballettucson.org.*

Invisible Theatre

THEATER | Contemporary plays and musicals, as well as classics, are presented in an intimate 80-seat theater by this highly regarded nonprofit company. ⊠ *1400 N. 1st Ave., Central* ☎ *520/882–9721* ⊕ *www.invisibletheatre.com.*

Tucson Jazz Society

MUSIC | The small but vibrant jazz scene in Tucson encompasses everything from afternoon jam sessions in the park to Sunday jazz brunches at resorts in the Foothills. The Tucson Jazz Festival brings national and international artists to town for 10 days in mid-January; call for information. ☎ *520/903–1265* ⊕ *www.tucsonjazz.org.*

Tucson Pops Orchestra

MUSIC | FAMILY | In May, June, and September the Tucson Pops Orchestra gives outstanding free concerts on Sunday evenings at the DeMeester Outdoor Performance Center in Reid Park. Arrive about an hour before the music starts (usually at 7 pm) to stake your claim on a viewing spot. ⊠ *Tucson* ☎ *520/722–5853* ⊕ *www.tucsonpops.org.*

Shopping

Arizona Hatters

CLOTHING | For that Stetson you've always wanted, Arizona Hatters is your best bet. ⊠ *2790 N. Campbell Ave., Central* ☎ *520/292–1320* ⊕ *www.arizonahatters.com.*

Bookmans Entertainment Exchange

BOOKS/STATIONERY | A Tucson institution, Bookmans carries an enormous and eclectic selection of used and new books, movies, music, magazines, games, and musical instruments in three spacious locations. ⊠ *3330 E. Speedway Blvd., Central* ☎ *520/325–5767* ⊕ *bookmans.com.*

The Lost Barrio Tucson

SHOPPING CENTERS/MALLS | Located in an old warehouse district southeast of Downtown, the Lost Barrio is a cluster of shops with Southwestern art, furniture, and funky gifts (both antique and modern). ⊠ *228 S. Park Ave., south of Broadway, Central* ☎ *520/628–4764* ⊕ *www.thelostbarrio.com.*

Madaras Gallery

ART GALLERIES | Bright watercolor prints of cacti, desert scenes, and animals by the popular local artist Diana Madaras can be found at this gallery. ⊠ *3035 N. Swan Rd., Central* ☎ *520/615–3001* ⊕ *www.madaras.com.*

★ Native Seeds/SEARCH

LOCAL SPECIALTIES | Dedicated to preserving native crops and traditional farming methods, Native Seeds/SEARCH sells 350 kinds of seeds as well as an excellent selection of Native American foods, baking mixes, woven baskets, and other regional crafts. ⊠ *3061 N. Campbell Ave., Central* ☎ *520/622–5561* ⊕ *www.nativeseeds.org.*

Activities

Gadabout

FITNESS/HEALTH CLUBS | Pampering from head to toe is what awaits at this popular day spa with five locations around town. Hair stylists and "nail therapists" are friendly and skilled; massages, facials, waxing, and makeup lessons are also on the menu, at lower prices than you'll pay at a resort. Each 50-minute facial includes a soothing neck, shoulder, hand, and foot moisturizing massage. ⊠ 3207 E. Speedway, Central ☎ 520/325–0000 ⊕ www.gadabout.com.

Randolph-Dell Urich Golf Course

GOLF | This pretty, centrally located 18-hole course, one of two at Randolph Park, has dramatic elevation changes and beautiful mountain views from every hole. ⊠ 600 S. Alvernon Way, Central ☎ 520/791–4653 ⊕ www.tucsoncitygolf. com ⛳ $36 for 9 holes, $56 for 18 holes ⅄ 18 holes, 6633 yards, par 70.

★ Randolph-North Course

GOLF | A longtime LPGA Tour host and the flagship of Tucson's municipal courses, Randolph North is also the longest municipal course, with great mountain views and tall trees lining the fairways. ⊠ 600 S. Alvernon Way, Central ☎ 520/791–4653 ⊕ www.tucsoncitygolf. com ⛳ $36 for 9 holes, $56 for 18 holes ⅄ 18 holes, 6863 yards, par 72.

Wild Bird Store

BIRD WATCHING | This shop is an excellent resource for birding information, feeders, books, and trail guides. Free bird walks are offered most Sundays October–May. ⊠ 3160 E. Fort Lowell Rd., Central ☎ 520/322–9466 ⊕ www.wildbirdsonline.com.

Eastside

The sprawling Eastside of Tucson is mostly residential, but there are a few gems on the southeastern outskirts that are well worth the journey: the Pima Air and Space Museum, Colossal Cave, and Saguaro National Park's east district.

PLANNING YOUR TIME

Because of copious traffic lights, it's a 30- to 45-minute drive across town to the far Eastside. Because this area is not particularly scenic, you can take I–10 instead to reach sights like Pima Air and Space Museum, Colossal Cave, or Saguaro National Park East (if you're starting from Downtown or the Westside/Northwest). During the summer months, plan the outdoor sights for the morning. Note that Colossal Cave stays at a constant cool temperature, which makes it a good option on a warm afternoon.

Sights

Colossal Cave Mountain Park

CAVE | **FAMILY** | This limestone grotto 20 miles southeast of Tucson is the largest dry cavern in the world. Guides discuss the fascinating crystal formations and relate the many romantic tales surrounding the cave, including the legend that an enormous sum of money stolen in a stagecoach robbery is hidden here.

Forty-five-minute cave tours begin every hour on the hour and require a ½-mile walk and a climb of 363 steps. The park includes a ranch area with trail rides through saguaro forests (from $38), hiking trails, a gemstone-sluicing area, a petting zoo, a gift shop, and a café. ⊠ 16721 E. Old Spanish Trail, Eastside ☎ 520/647–7275 ⊕ www.colossalcave.com ⛳ $18.

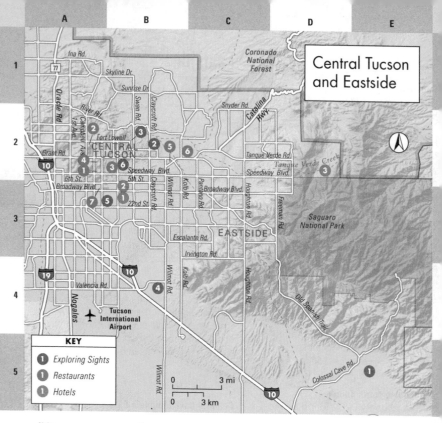

Central Tucson and Eastside

KEY

- **1** Exploring Sights
- **1** Restaurants
- **1** Hotels

Pima Air and Space Museum

MUSEUM | FAMILY | This huge facility ranks among the largest private collections of aircraft in the world. More than 300 airplanes are on display in hangars and outside, including a presidential plane used by both John F. Kennedy and Lyndon B. Johnson; a full-scale replica of the Wright brothers' 1903 Wright Flyer; the SR-71 reconnaissance jet; and a mock-up of the X-15, the world's fastest aircraft. World War II planes are particularly well represented.

Meander on your own (even leashed pets are allowed) or take a free walking tour led by volunteer docents. The open-air tram tour (an additional $6 fee) narrates all outside aircraft. A two-hour tour of Aerospace Maintenance and Regeneration Group (AMARG)—affectionately nicknamed "The Boneyard"—provides an eerie glimpse of hundreds of mothballed aircraft lined up in rows on a vast tract of desert. This $10 AMARG tour, available only on weekdays by reservation, is a photographer's delight. An on-site restaurant, The Flight Grill, is open daily. ✉ *6000 E. Valencia Rd., Eastside* ✣ *Off I–10, Exit 267* ☎ *520/574–0462* 🌐 *www.pimaair.org* 🎟 *$17.*

🍴 Restaurants

Pinnacle Peak Steakhouse

$$ | STEAKHOUSE | FAMILY | Anybody caught eating newfangled foods like fish tacos here would probably get a glare, and city slickers' ties would be snipped. This cowboy steak house is part of the family-friendly Trail Dust Town, a re-creation of a turn-of-the-20th-century town, complete with a working antique carousel, a narrow-gauge train, and Western stunt shows staged outside Wednesday through Sunday at 7 and 8 ($5). **Known for:** basic steaks and ribs; kitschy cowboy fun; good for large groups. [$] *Average main: $20* ✉ *6541 E. Tanque Verde Rd., Eastside* ☎ *520/296–0911* 🌐 *www.trail-dusttown.com* ⏲ *No lunch.*

Tucson Tamale Company

$ | MODERN MEXICAN | A good homemade tamale is special, and a restaurant that prepares and serves them fresh every day with all sorts of creative fillings is a find indeed. Carnivores can indulge in beef, pork, or chicken tamales, while vegetarians can opt for traditional, cheese-filled green-corn tamales or numerous vegan choices like the Austin, with a spinach and mushroom filling. **Known for:** tamales with creative fillings; an abundance of gluten-free fare; tasty vegan options. [$] *Average main: $9* ✉ *7159 E. Tanque Verde Rd., Eastside* ☎ *520/298–8404* 🌐 *tucsontamale.com* ⏲ *Closed Mon.*

🛏 Hotels

Tanque Verde Ranch

$$$ | RESORT | FAMILY | The most upscale of Tucson's guest ranches and one of the oldest in the country, the Tanque Verde sits on 640 beautiful acres in the Rincon Mountains next to Saguaro National Park East. **Pros:** authentic Western experience, including great riding; loads of all-inclusive activities; bed-and-breakfast-only is an economical option. **Cons:** at the eastern edge of town; all-inclusive package excludes alcohol. [$] *Rooms from: $250* ✉ *14301 E. Speedway Blvd., Eastside* ☎ *520/296–6275, 800/234–3833* 🌐 *www.tanqueverderanch.com* 🛏 *74 rooms* 🍴 *Free breakfast.*

🍸 Nightlife

The Maverick

MUSIC CLUBS | An excellent house band gets the crowd two-stepping Tuesday through Saturday nights at this country Western club. Dance lessons and dinner are also offered. ✉ *6622 E. Tanque Verde Rd., Eastside* ☎ *520/298–0430* 🌐 *www.tucsonmaverick.com.*

🎭 Performing Arts

Arizona Symphonic Winds

MUSIC | FAMILY | In winter the Arizona Symphonic Winds performs a series of free indoor concerts and then goes outdoors with a spring–summer concert schedule at Udall Park in Northeast Tucson. Performances in the park are Saturday at 7 pm; arrive at least an hour early for a good spot on the grass. ✉ *László Veres Amphitheater, Udall Park, 7200 E. Tanque Verde Rd., Tusayan* ☎ *520/722–5853* ⊕ *www.facebook.com/ArizonaSymphonicWinds.*

Gaslight Theatre

THEATER | FAMILY | Children of all ages love the clever, original melodramas at the Gaslight Theatre, where hissing at the villain and cheering the hero are part of the audience's duty. ✉ *7010 E. Broadway, Eastside* ☎ *520/886–9428* ⊕ *thegaslighttheatre.com.*

🛍 Shopping

B&B Cactus Farm

LOCAL SPECIALTIES | You'll pass this cactus farm en route to Saguaro National Park East. There's a huge selection of cacti and succulents, and they'll ship anywhere in the country. ✉ *11550 E. Speedway Blvd., Eastside* ☎ *520/721–4687* ⊕ *www.bandbcactus.com.*

Park Place

SHOPPING CENTERS/MALLS | This busy enclosed mall has an extensive food court, a 20-screen cineplex, and more than 120 stores, including Dillard's department store. Round 1 Bowling & Amusement, offering bowling, billiards, karaoke, and arcade games, is also here. ✉ *5870 E. Broadway Blvd., Eastside* ☎ *520/747–7575* ⊕ *www.parkplacemall.com.*

🏃 Activities

Arizona National Golf Club

GOLF | This is a gorgeous Robert Trent Jones Jr.–designed course at the base of the Santa Catalina Mountains on the northeastern edge of town. You won't need to go to Saguaro National Park after playing here—the saguaro-studded hillsides around the course are as magnificent and plentiful. ✉ *9777 E. Sabino Greens Dr., Eastside* ☎ *520/749–4089* ⊕ *www.arizonanationalgolfclub.com* 🏌 *$65* ⚐ *18 holes, 6776 yards, par 71.*

Balloon America

BALLOONING | Passengers can soar above Sabino Canyon and the Santa Catalinas in a hot-air balloon. Two-hour tours (includes a film of your flight and a champagne breakfast) depart from the Eastside of Tucson, October through mid-May. ✉ *1501 N. Houghton Rd.* ☎ *520/299–7744* ⊕ *balloonrideusa.com* 🏌 *From $249.*

Dorado Golf Course

GOLF | A good choice for those who want to play just a few short rounds, Dorado's executive course has a putting green and a chipping green but no driving range or lessons. ✉ *6601 E. Speedway Blvd., Eastside* ☎ *520/885–6751* ⊕ *doradogolfcourse.com* 🏌 *$25 for 9 holes, $32 for 18 holes* ⚐ *18 holes, 3751 yards, par 62.*

Fred Enke Golf Course

GOLF | This hilly, semiarid (less grass and more native vegetation) course is in the southeastern part of town. ✉ *8251 E. Irvington, Eastside* ☎ *520/791–4653* ⊕ *www.tucsoncitygolf* 🏌 *$23 for 9 holes, $43 for 18 holes* ⚐ *18 holes, 6567 yards, par 72.*

Saguaro Stables

HORSEBACK RIDING | This reliable operator offers one-hour and longer rides into Saguaro National Park East. ✉ *7151 S. Camino Loma Alta, Eastside* ☎ *520/298–8980* ⊕ *www.allaroundtrailhorses.com/saguaro-stables.*

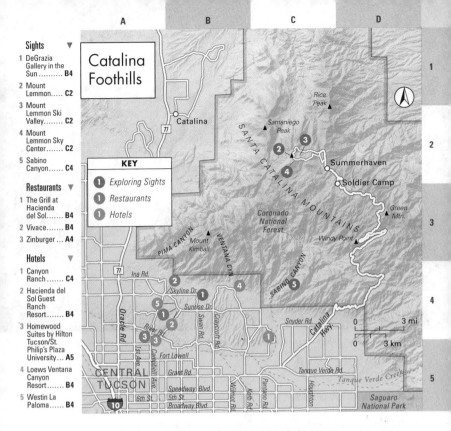

KEY

1 *Exploring Sights*

1 *Restaurants*

1 *Hotels*

★ Summit Hut

HIKING/WALKING | For hiking on your own, this store has an excellent collection of hiking reference materials, supplies, and a friendly staff who will help you plan your trip. Packs, tents, bags, and climbing shoes can be rented and purchased here. The other store branch is located in the Northwest at 7745 North Oracle Road. ⊠ *5251 E. Speedway Blvd., Eastside* ☎ *520/325–1554* ⊕ *www. summithut.com.*

Catalina Foothills

Considered by some to be the "Beverly Hills of Tucson," the Catalina Foothills area is home to posh resorts and upscale shopping. Because the neighborhood abuts the beautiful Santa Catalina Mountains, it also has an abundance of hiking trails.

PLANNING YOUR TIME

It may be hard to choose from the shopping, hiking, golf, and spa options along the Skyline Drive/Sunrise Drive corridor, but you can plan to spend at least a few hours strolling, hiking, or taking the tram through Sabino Canyon. Shopping and dining at La Encantada or the smaller complexes across the road can easily fill the other half of a day. If you want to venture farther into the mountains, head northeast up to Mount Lemmon. It's time-consuming (a one-hour drive each way), but the higher elevation and cooler temperatures make it an excellent destination in summer.

Sabino Canyon, with its inviting swimming holes and trails, is one of Tucson's most popular hiking areas.

👁 Sights

DeGrazia Gallery in the Sun

MUSEUM | Arizonan artist Ted DeGrazia, who depicted Southwest Native American and Mexican life in a manner some find kitschy and others adore, built this sprawling, spacious, single-story museum with the assistance of Native American friends, using only natural material from the surrounding desert. You can visit DeGrazia's workshop, former home, tranquil chapel, and grave. Although the original works are not for sale, the museum's gift shop has a wide selection of prints, ceramics, and books by and about the colorful artist. ✉ *6300 N. Swan Rd., Foothills* ☎ *520/299–9191* 🌐 *www.degrazia.org* 💲 *$8.*

Mount Lemmon

MOUNTAIN—SIGHT | Part of the Santa Catalina range, Mount Lemmon—named for Sara Lemmon, the first woman to reach the peak of this mountain, in 1881—is the southernmost ski slope in the continental United States, but you don't have to be a skier to enjoy the area: in summer, it's a popular place for picnicking, and there are 150 miles of marked and well-maintained trails for hiking. The mountain's 9,157-foot elevation brings relief from summer heat (temperatures are typically 25 degrees lower than in Tucson).

Mount Lemmon Highway twists for 28 miles up the mountainside; driving time from midtown is about an hour. Every 1,000-foot climb in elevation is equivalent, in terms of climate, to traveling 300 miles north: you'll move from typical Sonoran Desert plants in the foothills to vegetation similar to that found in southern Canada at the top. Rock formations along the way look as though they were carefully balanced against each other by sculptors from another planet.

Even if you don't make it to the top of the mountain, you'll find stunning views of Tucson at Windy Point, about halfway up. Look for a road on your left between the Windy Point and San Pedro lookouts; it leads to Rose Canyon lake, a lovely reservoir.

Just before you reach the ski area, you'll pass through the tiny alpine-style village of **Summerhaven,** which has some casual restaurants and gift shops.

■ TIP→ There are no gas stations on Mount Lemmon Highway, so gas up before you leave town and check the road conditions in winter. To reach the highway, take Tanque Verde Road to Catalina Highway, which becomes Mount Lemmon Highway. ✉ *Mount Lemmon Hwy., Northeast* ☎ *520/576–1400 for recorded snow report, 520/547–7510 for winter road conditions* 🎟 *Free.*

Mount Lemmon Ski Valley
RESORT—SIGHT | Follow Mount Lemmon Highway to its end and you're at Mount Lemmon Ski Valley. Skiing and snowboarding here depend on natural conditions; there's no artificial snow, so call ahead. There are 21 runs, ranging from beginner to advanced. Lift tickets cost $57 for an all-day pass and $50 for a half-day pass starting at 12:30 pm. Equipment rentals and instruction are available.

Off-season you can take a ride on the chairlift ($15), which whisks you to the top of the slope—some 9,100 feet above sea level. Many ride the lift, then hike on one of several trails that crisscross the summit. The Iron Door Restaurant, across the road, serves sandwiches, soups, and homemade pies, which you can enjoy with gorgeous views. ✉ *10300 Ski Run Rd., Mount Lemmon* ☎ *520/576–1321* 🌐 *www.skithelemmon.com* 🕒 *Closed Tues. and Wed.*

★ **Mount Lemmon Sky Center**
OBSERVATORY | **FAMILY** | At the University of Arizona's research observatory on Mount Lemmon, visitors can plumb the night sky on the highest mountain in the area using the largest public-viewing telescope in the Southwest. A five-hour stargazing program is offered nightly (weather permitting), and includes an interactive astronomy presentation, telescope viewing, and a light dinner. ✉ *Ski Run Rd., Mount Lemmon* ☎ *520/626–8122* 🌐 *www.skycenter.arizona.edu* 🎟 *$65* 🕒 *Closed Mon. and Tues.*

★ **Sabino Canyon**
NATURE PRESERVE | Year-round, but especially in summer, locals flock to Coronado National Forest to hike, picnic, and enjoy the waterfalls, streams, swimming holes, saguaros, and shade trees. No cars are allowed, but a narrated tram ride (about 45 minutes round-trip) takes you up a WPA-built road to the top of the canyon; you can hop off and on at any of the nine stops or hike any of the numerous trails.

There's also a shorter tram ride (or you can walk) to adjacent Bear Canyon, where a rigorous but rewarding hike leads to the popular Seven Falls (it'll take about 1½ to 2 hours each way from the drop-off point, so carry plenty of water). **■ TIP→ If you're in Tucson near a full moon between April and November, take the special night tram and watch the desert come alive with nocturnal critters.** ✉ *Sabino Canyon Rd. at Sunrise Dr., Foothills* ☎ *520/749–8700 for visitor center and recorded tram info* 🌐 *www.fs.usda.gov/coronado* 🎟 *$8 per vehicle, tram $6–$12.*

🍴 Restaurants

The Grill at Hacienda del Sol
$$$$ | **SOUTHWESTERN** | Tucked into the foothills and surrounded by spectacular flowers and cactus gardens, this special-occasion restaurant, a favorite among locals hosting out-of-town visitors, provides an alternative to the chili-laden dishes of most nouvelle Southwestern cuisine. Wild-mushroom bisque, grilled buffalo in dark-chocolate mole, and pan-seared sea bass are among the menu choices at this luxurious guest ranch resort. **Known for:** romantic dining; outstanding wine list; beautiful setting. [$] *Average main: $32* ✉ *Hacienda del Sol Guest Ranch Resort, 5501 N. Hacienda Del Sol Rd., Foothills* ☎ *520/529–3500* 🌐 *www.haciendadelsol.com/dining/the-grill.*

Vivace

$$$ | **ITALIAN** | A modern Italian bistro in a lovely Foothills setting, Vivace has long been a favorite with Tucsonans. Wild mushrooms and goat cheese in puff pastry is hard to resist as a starter, and the fettuccine with grilled salmon is a nice, lighter alternative to such entrées as a rich osso buco. **Known for:** Italian fine dining; lovely patios with mountain and city views; a popular spot (reservations are a must on weekends). [$] *Average main: $30* ✉ *6440 N. Campbell Ave., Foothills* ☎ *520/795–7221* 🌐 *www.vivacetucson.com* 🕒 *Closed Sun.*

Zinburger

$ | **AMERICAN** | Have a glass of wine or a cocktail with your gourmet burger and fries at this high-energy, somewhat noisy, and unquestionably hip burger joint. Zinburger delivers tempting burgers—try the Kobe beef with cheddar and wild mushrooms—and decadent milkshakes made of creative combinations like dates and honey or melted chocolate with praline flakes. **Known for:** gourmet burgers and fries; innovative shakes; lively atmosphere. [$] *Average main: $12* ✉ *1865 E. River Rd., Foothills* ☎ *520/299–7799* 🌐 *www.zinburgeraz.com.*

🛏 Hotels

★ Canyon Ranch

$$$$ | **RESORT** | This award-winning resort draws an international crowd of well-to-do health seekers to its superb spa facilities on 70 acres in the desert foothills. **Pros:** a stay here can be a life-changing experience; gorgeous setting; all-inclusive activities are varied and engaging. **Cons:** very pricey; not family-friendly; vast property means greater distances between activities. [$] *Rooms from: $1050* ✉ *8600 E. Rockcliff Rd., Foothills* ☎ *520/749–9000, 855/376–1056* 🌐 *www.canyonranch.com* 🛏 *240 rooms* 🍴 *All-inclusive.*

Hacienda del Sol Guest Ranch Resort

$$ | **RESORT** | This 32-acre hideaway in the Santa Catalina Foothills is a charming and more intimate alternative to the larger resorts, combining luxury with Southwestern character. **Pros:** outstanding restaurant and bar; historic and stunningly beautiful property; quieter than the larger resorts. **Cons:** golfers must be shuttled to a nearby course; some historic rooms are smaller; may feel too posh for some. [$] *Rooms from: $225* ✉ *5501 N. Hacienda Del Sol Rd., Foothills* ☎ *520/299–1501, 800/728–6514* 🌐 *www.haciendadelsol.com* 🛏 *59 rooms* 🍴 *No meals.*

Homewood Suites by Hilton Tucson/St. Philip's Plaza University

$$ | **HOTEL** | **FAMILY** | Set in a chic shopping plaza filled with boutiques, galleries, good restaurants, and a weekend farmers' market, this all-suites hotel provides a range of amenities, including a complimentary hot breakfast daily and a complimentary light dinner buffet (including wine and beer) Monday through Thursday. **Pros:** free happy hour snacks on weekdays; good value, especially for location; walk to shops, restaurants, and the adjacent Rillito River Path. **Cons:** it's a suite, but both rooms are on the small side; some rooms have views of parking lot; weekend farmers' market brings traffic. [$] *Rooms from: $169* ✉ *4250 N. Campbell Ave., Foothills* ☎ *520/577–0007* 🌐 *homewoodsuites3.hilton.com* 🛏 *122 suites* 🍴 *Free breakfast.*

★ Loews Ventana Canyon Resort

$$$ | **RESORT** | **FAMILY** | This is one of the most luxurious and prettiest of the big resorts, with dramatic stone architecture and an 80-foot waterfall cascading down the mountains. **Pros:** many activities including great golf; excellent full spa and amenities; spectacular setting close to hiking. **Cons:** some rooms overlook the parking lot; not for those who don't like a posh atmosphere; at the eastern edge of the foothills. [$] *Rooms from: $269* ✉ *7000 N. Resort Dr., Foothills*

☎ 520/299–2020, 800/234–5117 🌐 www.loewshotels.com/Ventana-Canyon 🛏 398 rooms 🍴 No meals.

Westin La Paloma
$$$ | RESORT | FAMILY | Popular with business travelers and families, this sprawling resort, with grand views of the Santa Catalina Mountains and the city below, specializes in relaxation, with an emphasis on fun. **Pros:** top-notch golf, tennis, and spa; huge pool complex with swim-up bar and waterslide; kids' programs. **Cons:** so big it can feel mazelike; long walk to parking; pool areas can be crowded at times. [$] *Rooms from: $239 ✉ 3800 E. Sunrise Dr., Foothills ☎ 520/742–6000 🌐 westinlapalomaresort.com 🛏 487 rooms 🍴 No meals.*

Shopping

Bahti Indian Arts
CRAFTS | This shop is owned and run by the knowledgeable Mark Bahti, whose father, Tom, literally wrote the book on Native American art, including an early definitive work on katsinas. The store sells high-quality jewelry, pottery, rugs, art, and more. *✉ St. Philip's Plaza, 4330 N. Campbell Ave., Foothills ☎ 520/577–0290 🌐 mark-bahti-btof.squarespace.com.*

La Encantada
SHOPPING CENTERS/MALLS | FAMILY | This beautiful outdoor mall has close to 50 stores (and six restaurants) decidedly aimed at affluent consumers. North Italia, a nouvelle Italian bistro, and Ra Sushi are the standout eateries. Trendy tenants include Crate & Barrel, Pottery Barn, Apple, and Tiffany & Co., plus AJs, a gourmet grocery that also serves casual meals. *✉ Skyline Dr. and Campbell Ave., Foothills ☎ 520/615–2561 🌐 www.laencantadashoppingcenter.com.*

St. Philip's Plaza
SHOPPING CENTERS/MALLS | More than a dozen chic boutiques and galleries are arranged around Spanish-style outdoor courtyards at St. Philip's Plaza. Union Public House, serving food and drink into the wee hours, and Reforma Cocina y Cantina are located here, as is a farmers' market on weekend mornings. *✉ 4280 N. Campbell Ave., at River Rd., Foothills 🌐 stphilipsplaza.com.*

Tucson Mall
SHOPPING CENTERS/MALLS | FAMILY | This indoor mall has Dillard's, Macy's, H&M, and more than 200 specialty shops. For tasteful Southwestern-style T-shirts, belts, jewelry, and prickly pear candies, check out the shops on "Arizona Avenue," a section on the first floor that's devoted to regional items. *✉ 4500 N. Oracle Rd., at Wetmore Rd., Central ☎ 520/293–7330 🌐 www.tucsonmall.com.*

Activities

★ Bear Canyon Trail
HIKING/WALKING | FAMILY | Also known as Seven Falls Trail, this favorite route in Sabino Canyon is a three- to four-hour, 7.8-mile round-trip that is moderate and fun, crossing the stream several times on the way up the canyon. Kids enjoy the boulder-hopping, and all hikers are rewarded with pools and waterfalls as well as views at the top. The trailhead can be reached from the parking area by either taking a five-minute Bear Canyon Tram ride ($6) or walking the 1.8-mile tram route. *Moderate. ✉ Sabino Canyon Rd., at Sunrise Dr., Foothills ☎ 520/749–2861 🌐 www.fs.usda.gov/coronado.*

Lakeside Spa at Loews Ventana Canyon Resort
FITNESS/HEALTH CLUBS | At the quiet and unassuming Lakeside Spa, take in the sweeping desert views along the trail on the daily 7-mile guided power walk or from the serene pool area during an aqua fitness class. Fortify your skin for the dry climate by choosing a signature spa treatment like the Sedona Sacred Ritual, which begins with an Arizona red-clay wrap, adds a face-and-scalp massage, and finishes with an ultrahydrating body

massage using jojoba lotion. ⊠ *7000 N. Resort Dr., Foothills* ☎ *520/529–7830* ⊕ *www.loewshotels.com/ventana-canyon/discover/lakeside-spa.*

★ Lodge at Ventana Canyon

GOLF | There are two beautiful Tom Fazio–designed courses here. The signature hole, No. 3 on the mountain course, is a favorite of golf photographers for its panoramic views and majestic saguaros. Guests staying up the road at Loews Ventana Canyon Resort have member privileges here (and one course is always open to the public). ⊠ *6200 N. Clubhouse La., Foothills* ☎ *520/577–1400* ⊕ *www.thelodgeatventanacanyon.com* ☒ *$159* ⚸ *Canyon Course: 18 holes, 6819 yards, par 72; Mountain Course: 18 holes, 6898 yards, par 72.*

Spanish Trail Outfitters

HORSEBACK RIDING | **FAMILY** | This stable, based at Westward Look Resort, saddles up for one- and two-hour rides, including sunset rides, in the Foothills. They'll also lead your little darlin' around a ring if too young (or too timid) to hit the trail. ⊠ *Westward Look Wyndham Grand Resort, 245 E. Ina Rd., Foothills* ☎ *520/631–3787* ⊕ *spanishtrailoutfitters.com.*

Northwest Tucson

Once a vast, open space dotted with horse ranches, Northwest Tucson is now a rapidly growing residential area encompassing the townships of Oro Valley and Marana. Families and retirees are moving here in droves, and the traffic congestion proves the point. You'll also find first-rate golf resorts and restaurants, a popular outlet store mall, and the oases of Tohono Chul Park and Catalina State Park, which calm the senses.

PLANNING YOUR TIME

Most activities in the northwest are spread out. Biosphere 2 is 24 miles north along Oracle Road (you'll drive through the city of Oro Valley); plan for a half-hour drive and at least two hours for the tour. You can enjoy golfing, horseback riding, a hot air balloon ride or a hike at Catalina State Park in the morning. A warm afternoon can be spent shopping at Tucson Premium Outlets in Marana or strolling through the shaded paths and greenhouses at Tohono Chul Park. Plenty of restaurants are clustered here, near the intersection of Oracle and Ina Roads, when you're ready for a bite.

Sights

Biosphere 2

GARDEN | In the town of Oracle, about 30 minutes northwest of Tucson, this unique, self-contained cluster of ecosystems opened in 1991 as a facility to test nature technology and human interaction with it. Now managed by the University of Arizona, the biomes include tropical rain forest, savanna, desert, thorn scrub, marsh, and ocean areas. The newest biome, the Landscape Evolutionary Observatory, tracks rainfall in simulated desert environments to study the effects of climate change on water sources and plant life in this region.

Guided walking tours take you inside the biomes, and a brief film gives an overview of Biosphere projects, from the original "human missions"—where scientists literally ate, slept, and breathed their work in a closed system—to current research. A snack bar overlooks the Santa Catalina Mountains. ⊠ *32540 S. Biosphere Rd., Northwest* ✛ *Off AZ 77 at mile marker 96.5* ☎ *520/838–6200* ⊕ *www.biosphere2.org* ☒ *$20.*

Tohono Chul Park

NATIONAL/STATE PARK | A 48-acre desert garden retreat designed to promote the conservation of arid regions, Tohono Chul—"desert corner" in the language of the Tohono O'odham—uses demonstration gardens, a greenhouse, and a geology wall to explain this unique desert area. Nature trails, a small art gallery, gift shops (including folk art, prickly pear products, and a great selection of desert

Walk through rain forest, savanna, and desert habitats at Biosphere 2, an Earth Science research center north of Tucson.

plants), and a bistro can all be found at this peaceful spot. ■ **TIP→ You can visit the restaurant and outstanding gift shops without paying admission.** ✉ *7366 N. Paseo del Norte, Northwest* ☎ *520/742–6455* 🌐 *tohonochulpark.org* 🎟 *$15.*

🍴 Restaurants

Saffron Indian Bistro

$$ | **INDIAN** | Quality Indian cooking is hard to find in Tucson, but this sophisticated eatery holds its own with the best anywhere. Delicious samosas, tandoori, and chicken tikka masala can be enjoyed in a casual yet refined dining room. **Known for:** excellent Indian food; pleasant, quiet ambience; lunch buffet. [$] *Average main: $15* ✉ *7607 N. Oracle Rd., Northwest* ☎ *520/742–9100* 🌐 *tucsonindianrestaurant.com.*

Sauce

$ | **ITALIAN** | **FAMILY** | Modern Italian fuses with fast food at this lively, family-friendly eatery in Casas Adobes Plaza. Delicious thin-crust pizzas, chopped salads, pastas, and panini are ordered at the counter; the restaurant is brightly decorated in a contemporary twist on the colors of Italy's flag—green, white, and tomato-red. **Known for:** casual Italian; huge chopped salads; dog-friendly patio. [$] *Average main: $10* ✉ *Casas Adobes Plaza, 7117 N. Oracle Rd., Northwest* ☎ *520/297–8575* 🌐 *www.saucepizzaandwine.com.*

Tohono Chul Garden Bistro

$$ | **SOUTHWESTERN** | **FAMILY** | The food at Tohono Chul Garden Bistro is fine, but what many come for is the location inside a wildlife sanctuary, surrounded by flowering desert gardens. The Southwestern interior has Mexican tile, light wood, and a cobblestone courtyard, but the back patio, where you can watch hummingbirds and butterflies, is the place to be. **Known for:** beautiful patio dining; popular weekend brunch; prickly pear chicken salad. [$] *Average main: $15* ✉ *Tohono Chul Park, 7366 N. Paseo del Norte, Northwest* ☎ *520/742–6455* 🌐 *www.tohonochulpark.org* 🕒 *No dinner; Closed Mon.–Wed.*

Wildflower

$$ | **AMERICAN** | Well known—and loved—for its creative American fare and stunning presentation, Wildflower has compelling choices like a salmon and seafood bouillabaise; bow-tie pasta with grilled chicken, tomatoes, spinach, and pine nuts; and red wine–braised short ribs. The decadently huge desserts are equally top-notch. **Known for:** upscale comfort food; giant desserts; patio seating. $ *Average main: $20* ⊠ *Casa Adobes Plaza, 7037 N. Oracle Rd., Northwest* ☎ *520/219–4230* ⊕ *www.wildflowertucson.com.*

🛏 Hotels

Hilton Tucson El Conquistador

$$$ | **RESORT** | **FAMILY** | A huge copper mural of cowboys and cacti and a wide view of the Santa Catalina Mountains grace the lobby of this friendly upscale golf and tennis resort. **Pros:** exceptional variety of on-site activities, including horseback riding; good restaurant on-site; kids' program. **Cons:** huge place; farther from in-town sights; golf course is a few miles away. $ *Rooms from: $299* ⊠ *10000 N. Oracle Rd., Northwest* ☎ *520/544–5000* ⊕ *www.hiltonelconquistador.com* ⇌ *428 rooms* �‖ *No meals.*

La Posada Lodge and Casitas

$ | **HOTEL** | This 1960s motor lodge has been reborn as a Santa Fe–style boutique hotel with a Latin theme. **Pros:** good location; Southwestern restaurant on-site (where your breakfast is served); attractive grounds. **Cons:** busy road means front-facing rooms not as tranquil; smallish rooms; older property. $ *Rooms from: $150* ⊠ *5900 N. Oracle Rd., Northwest* ☎ *520/887–4800* ⊕ *www.laposadalodge.com* ⇌ *72 rooms* �‖ *Free breakfast.*

Miraval

$$$$ | **RESORT** | This New Age health spa 30 miles north of Tucson, popular with celebrities, has a secluded desert setting and beautiful Southwestern rooms. **Pros:** very high-end getaway in the middle of nowhere; tranquil; abundant wellness activities. **Cons:** posh attitude makes some uncomfortable; very expensive; far, far away from town. $ *Rooms from: $1258* ⊠ *5000 E. Via Estancia Miraval, Catalina* ☎ *520/825–4000, 800/232–3969* ⊕ *www.miravalresorts.com* ⇌ *117 rooms* �‖ *All-inclusive.*

Omni Tucson National Golf Resort & Spa

$$ | **RESORT** | Perfect for groups or couples with differing ideas on how to spend a vacation, the friendly Omni Tucson National is both a premier golf resort and a full-service European-style spa, where you can be coiffed, waxed, and wrapped to your heart's content. **Pros:** outstanding golf (two 18-hole courses); relaxed yet luxurious; convenient to Northwest shopping and restaurants. **Cons:** far-flung from central Tucson sights; too sedate for some; emphasis on golf may turn off those who aren't interested. $ *Rooms from: $190* ⊠ *2727 W. Club Dr., Northwest* ☎ *520/297–2271, 800/843–6664* ⊕ *www.omnihotels.com* ⇌ *128 rooms* �‖ *No meals.*

The Ritz-Carlton, Dove Mountain

$$$$ | **RESORT** | The most elegant and exclusive of Tucson's golf and tennis resorts is the ever-posh Ritz-Carlton, set in the rolling hills of Marana, about 20 miles northwest of Central Tucson. **Pros:** great golf, spa, and dining; top-notch service; beautiful desert setting. **Cons:** somewhat isolated location in the far Northwest; priciest resort in town; may feel too opulent for some. $ *Rooms from: $399* ⊠ *15000 N. Secret Springs Dr., Marana* ☎ *520/572–3000, 800/241–3333* ⊕ *www.ritzcarlton.com/dovemountain* ⇌ *250 rooms* �‖ *No meals.*

Westward Look Wyndham Grand Resort

$$ | **RESORT** | **FAMILY** | Originally the 1912 homestead of William and Mary Watson, this laid-back lodging with gorgeous city views and desert gardens has Southwestern character and all the amenities you expect at a major resort. **Pros:** great tennis, horseback riding, and nature trails; convenient yet feels like a retreat; you can

actually park near your room. **Cons:** no golf (privileges at private club 4 miles away); rather plain pool areas; less plush than neighboring resorts. ⑤ *Rooms from: $159* ✉ *245 E. Ina Rd., Northwest* ☎ *520/297–1151, 800/722–2500* ⊕ *www.westward-look.com* ⮐ *244 rooms* ⦿*No meals.*

★ White Stallion Ranch

$$$$ | **RESORT** | **FAMILY** | A 3,000-acre working cattle ranch run by the hospitable True family since 1965, this place is the real deal, satisfying for families as well as singles or couples. **Pros:** solid dude-ranch experience with exceptional riding program; plentiful ranch activities and evening entertainment; charming hosts. **Cons:** no TV in rooms; alcohol not included in the rate—pay extra or bring your own; rustic, rather than luxurious. ⑤ *Rooms from: $468* ✉ *9251 W. Twin Peaks Rd., Northwest* ☎ *520/297–0252* ⊕ *www.whitestallion.com* ⮐ *41 rooms, 1 house* ⦿*All-inclusive.*

🛍 Shopping

Casas Adobes Plaza

SHOPPING CENTERS/MALLS | This outdoor, Mediterranean-style shopping center originally served the ranchers and orange-grove owners in this once remote part of town, now the city's fastest-growing area. There's a Whole Foods grocery store, the popular Wildflower restaurant, a gelato shop, upscale pizzas at Sauce, Starbucks, and diverse boutiques and gift shops. ✉ *7001–7153 N. Oracle Rd., Northwest* ⊕ *www.casasadobesplaza.com.*

Tucson Premium Outlets

OUTLET/DISCOUNT STORES | Find good deals on athletic wear from Nike, Adidas, and Under Armour; designer brands like Kate Spade and Michael Kors; and children's wear from OshKosh and Carter's at this large outdoor outlet mall in Marana. A play area, a few eateries, and a Disney outlet store will keep kids happy. ✉ *6401 W. Marana Center Blvd., Northeast* ☎ *520/385–7726* ⊕ *premiumoutlets.com/tucson.*

🏃 Activities

Catalina State Park

HIKING/WALKING | This park is criss-crossed by hiking trails. One of them, the moderately easy, two-hour, 5½-mile round-trip **Romero Canyon Trail**, leads to Romero Pools, a series of natural *tinajas,* or stone "jars," filled with water much of the year. The trailhead is on the park's entrance road, past the restrooms on the right side. *Moderate.* ✉ *11570 N. Oracle Rd., Northwest* ☎ *520/628–5798* ⊕ *azstateparks.com/catalina.*

El Conquistador

GOLF | Tucked into the Santa Catalina Foothills, this golf club, in partnership with the nearby Hilton El Conquistador Resort, has panoramic views of the city. You'll pay less to play here, without sacrificing any of the resort or clubhouse amenities. ✉ *10555 N. La Canada Dr., Northwest* ☎ *520/544–1800* ⊕ *www.elcongolf.com* 🏌 *$75 for 18 holes* ⓧ *Cañada Course: 18 holes, 6713 yards, par 72; Conquistador Course: 18 holes, 6801 yards, par 71.*

Fleur de Tucson Balloon Tours

BALLOONING | Operating out of Northwest Tucson from October through April, this company flies over the Tucson Mountains and Saguaro National Park West. Flights include photos as well as a continental champagne brunch after you arrive back on the ground. ✉ *Northwest* ☎ *520/403–8547* ⊕ *www.fleurdetucson.net* 🏌 *From $250.*

Omni Tucson National Golf Resort

GOLF | Cohost of an annual PGA winter open, this resort offers two courses: the desert Sonoran Course and the Catalina Course. Designed by Robert Van Hagge and Bruce Devlin, the Catalina has eight lakes and gorgeous, long par 4s. ✉ *2727 W. Club Dr., Northwest* ☎ *520/297–2271* ⊕ *www.tucsonnational.com* 🏌 *$200* ⓧ *Catalina Course: 18 holes, 6610 yards, par 73; Sonoran Course: 18 holes, 6065 yards, par 70.*

The Ritz-Carlton Spa, Dove Mountain

FITNESS/HEALTH CLUBS | Ancient civilizations supposedly used gemstones to treat various ailments of mind and body. With the "Desert Gemstone Ritual," a signature service at the luxurious 17,000-square-foot Dove Mountain Spa, amethyst and citrine stones help heal sore muscles and increase energy flow in a rejuvenating 100-minute massage, exfoliation, and aromatherapy treatment. Before and after, relax indoors in the men's, ladies', or co-ed lounge areas or by the secluded infinity pool. ⊠ *15000 N. Secret Springs Dr., Marana* ☎ *520/572–3030, 800/542–8680* ⊕ *www.ritzcarlton.com/en/hotels/arizona/dove-mountain/spa.*

Silverbell Golf Course

GOLF | With spacious fairways and ample greens, this course along the Santa Cruz River northwest of town has two large lakes. ■TIP→ **The greens fee includes a cart here.** ⊠ *3600 N. Silverbell Rd., Northwest* ☎ *520/791–4653* ⊕ *www.tucsoncitygolf.com* ⌕ *$27 for 9 holes, $47 for 18 holes* ⌗ *18 holes, 6936 yards, par 70.*

Westside

The Westside is far less developed than other areas of Tucson, and beautiful vistas of saguaro-studded hills are around every bend. Saguaro National Park West, the Arizona–Sonora Desert Museum, Old Tucson Studios, and the San Xavier Mission are all in this section of town. If you're interested in the flora and fauna of the Sonoran Desert—as well as some of its appearances in the cinema—heed the same advice given the pioneers: go west.

PLANNING YOUR TIME

A good idea is to start the morning at Saguaro National Park West and then head over to the Arizona–Sonora Desert Museum, where you can lunch at Ironwood Terrace or the more upscale Ocotillo Café. How long you spend at Saguaro National Park depends on whether you

choose a short walk to see petroglyphs at Signal Hill on the Loop Drive (an hour should suffice) or hike a longer mountain trail, but leave yourself at least two hours for your visit at the desert museum. The hottest part of an afternoon can be spent enjoying the indoor sanctuary of San Xavier Mission, although the mission is also a good stop if you're heading out of town to Tubac or Tumacácori.

◉ Sights

★ Arizona–Sonora Desert Museum

MUSEUM | FAMILY | The name "museum" is a bit misleading, since this delightful site is actually a zoo, aquarium, and botanical garden featuring the animals, plants, and even fish of the Sonoran Desert. Hummingbirds, coatis, rattlesnakes, scorpions, bighorn sheep, bobcats, and Mexican wolves all busy themselves in ingeniously designed habitats.

An Earth Sciences Center has an artificial limestone cave to climb through and an excellent mineral display. The coyote and javelina (a wild, piglike mammal with an oddly oversize head) exhibits have "invisible" fencing that separates humans from animals, and at the Raptor Free Flight show (October through April, daily at 10 and 2), you can see the powerful birds soar and dive, untethered, inches above your head.

The restaurants are above average, and the gift shop, which carries books, jewelry, and crafts, is outstanding. ■TIP→ **June through August, the museum stays open until 10 pm every Saturday, which provides a great opportunity to see nocturnal critters.** ⊠ *2021 N. Kinney Rd., Westside* ☎ *520/883–2702* ⊕ *www.desertmuseum.org* ⌕ *$22.*

★ Mission San Xavier del Bac

RELIGIOUS SITE | The oldest Catholic church in the United States still serving the community for which it was built, San Xavier was founded in 1692 by Father Eusebio Francisco Kino, who established 22 missions in northern Mexico and Southern

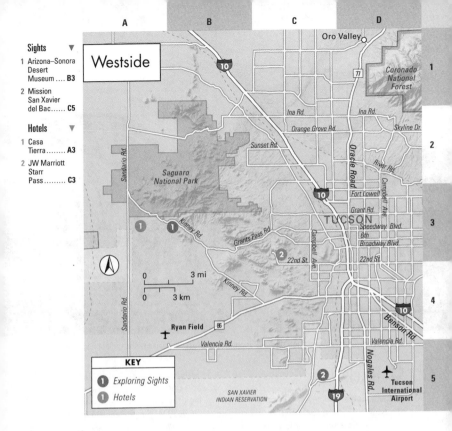

Westside

KEY

1 Exploring Sights

1 Hotels

Arizona. The current structure was made out of native materials by Franciscan missionaries between 1777 and 1797, and is owned by the Tohono O'odham tribe.

The beauty of the mission, with elements of Spanish, baroque, and Moorish architectural styles, is highlighted by the stark landscape against which it is set, inspiring an early-20th-century poet to dub it the White Dove of the Desert.

Inside, there's a wealth of painted statues, carvings, and frescoes. Paul Schwartzbaum, who helped restore Michelangelo's masterwork in Rome, supervised Tohono O'odham artisans in the restoration of the mission's artwork, completed in 1997; Schwartzbaum has called the mission the Sistine Chapel of the United States.

Across the parking lot from the mission, San Xavier Plaza has a couple of crafts shops selling the handiwork of the Tohono O'odham tribe, including jewelry, pottery, friendship bowls, and woven baskets with man-in-the-maze designs. ⊠ 1950 W. San Xavier Rd., Westside ⊕ 9 miles southwest of Tucson on I–19 ☎ 520/294–2624 ⊕ www.sanxaviermission.org ⊠ Free.

🍽 Restaurants

Except for a few fast food joints and taquerias, the Westside restaurant selection is slim. However, the area's Arizona–Sonora Desert Museum and JW Marriott Starr Pass both have good options if you're not up for a short drive to Downtown.

Don't let the name fool you: the Arizona–Sonora Desert Museum is also a zoo and botanical garden.

🛏 Hotels

★ Casa Tierra

$$ | B&B/INN | For a real desert experience, head to this lovely B&B on 5 acres near the Desert Museum and Saguaro National Park West, the last 1½ miles on a dirt road. **Pros:** serene Southwest getaway; hot tub; copious complimentary snacks. **Cons:** far from town (30-minute drive); two-night minimum stay; no TV in some rooms. $ *Rooms from: $225* ✉ *11155 W. Calle Pima, Westside* ☎ *520/578–3009* ⊕ *www.casatierratuc-son.com* ⤴ *3 rooms* ⋈ *Free breakfast.*

★ JW Marriott Starr Pass

$$$ | RESORT | Set amid saguaro forests and mesquite groves in the Tucson Mountains (yet only 15 minutes from Downtown), the city's largest resort has massive sun-bleached stone walls that blend rather than compete with the natural surroundings and stunning views from the interior dining areas and lounges. **Pros:** posh and beautiful; excellent spa and golf; great walking/hiking paths. **Cons:**

expensive; parking is far from lobby areas and guest rooms; setting may feel too isolated for some. $ *Rooms from: $339* ✉ *3800 W. Starr Pass Blvd., Westside* ☎ *520/792–3500* ⊕ *www.jwmarriottstarr-pass.com* ⤴ *575 rooms* ⋈ *No meals.*

🏃 Activities

El Rio Golf Course

GOLF | On fairly flat terrain west of Downtown, this course has tight fairways, small greens, two lakes, and nice views of the nearby Tucson Mountains. ✉ *1400 W. Speedway Blvd., Westside* ☎ *520/791–4653* ⊕ *www.tucsoncitygolf. com* 🖾 *$25 for 9 holes, $43 for 18 holes* ⅄. *18 holes, 6936 yards, par 70.*

★ Hashani Spa at JW Marriott Starr Pass

FITNESS/HEALTH CLUBS | The trilevel modern Hashani Spa, built on a hillside just east of the JW Marriott, connects to the main resort via a walkway above a wildlife area, but it feels a world away. The top level houses the salon and a shop selling activewear and high-end skin and beauty products. Sleek, Asian-inspired indoor/outdoor lounge areas, a gym, and a dance/yoga studio occupy the middle level; the lower floor is for heavenly treatments like the hot desert-stone massage and the signature creosote body wrap. After your spa service, lie out or lunch poolside. ✉ *3800 W. Starr Pass Blvd., Southwest* ☎ *520/791–6117* 🌐 *www.hashanispa.com.*

★ Starr Pass Golf Club

GOLF | With 27 magnificent holes in the Tucson Mountains, Starr Pass has become a favorite of visiting pros; playing its No. 15 signature hole has been likened to threading a moving needle. Guests at the JW Marriott Starr Pass Resort have privileges (and pay lower greens fees) here. ✉ *3645 W. Starr Pass Blvd., Westside* ☎ *520/791–6270* 🌐 *www.jwmarriottstarrpass.com* 🎫 *$100 for 9 holes, $179 for 18 holes* ⛳ *27 holes, 6731 yards, par 71.*

South Tucson

This 1-square-mile district directly south of Downtown is a city in its own right, with its own mayor, close-knit neighborhoods, and abundance of Mexican eateries, ranging from legendary restaurants to tiny taquerias. Everyone you ask will have their own favorite spot to recommend, but you really can't go wrong at any of them.

PLANNING YOUR TIME

The main streets of South Tucson, 6th Avenue and 4th Avenue, run parallel to each other. You can drive down 6th Avenue to see some classic mid-century modern buildings like the KY Market; then you'll probably want to head over to 4th Avenue, between 22nd Street and 36th Street, where most restaurants are located.

🍴 Restaurants

★ El Guero Canelo

$ | **MEXICAN** | Talk about fusion. Take the American tradition of ballpark franks, give it a Mexican spin, and you'll have a Sonoran hot dog, created by and sold in El Guero Canelo restaurants and their strategically placed taco stands. **Known for:** Sonoran hot dogs; cheap, casual Mexican food; local favorite. [$] *Average main:* ✉ *5201 S. 12th Ave., South* ☎ *520/295–9005* 🌐 *www.elguerocanelo.com* 🕒 *Closed Mon.*

★ Mi Nidito

$ | **MEXICAN** | A perennial favorite among locals (the wait is worth it), Mi Nidito ("my little nest") has also hosted its share of visiting celebrities: following President Clinton's lunch here, the rather hefty Presidential Plate (bean tostada, taco with barbecued meat, chiles rellenos, chicken enchilada, and beef tamale with rice and beans) was added to the menu. Top that off with the mango chimichangas for dessert, and you're talkin' executive privilege. **Known for:** reliably delicious Mexican food; festive atmosphere; great margaritas. [$] *Average main: $12* ✉ *1813 S. 4th Ave., South* ☎ *520/622–5081* 🌐 *www.miniditorestaurant.com* 🕒 *Closed Mon. and Tues.*

🍸 Nightlife

CASINOS

Two tribes operate casinos on their Tucson-area reservations west of the airport. They're quite unlike their distant and much grander cousins in Las Vegas and Atlantic City. Don't expect much glamour, ersatz or otherwise: these casinos are more like glorified video arcades, though you can lose money much faster. You'll be greeted by a wall of cigarette smoke (the reservation is exempt from antismoking laws) and the wail of slot machines, video poker, blackjack,

Tucson's Native Cultures

The Tohono O'odham and the Pascua Yaqui tribes have a strong presence in Tucson. In fact, the name "Tucson" came from the Native American word *stjukshon* (pronounced *stook*-shahn), meaning "spring at the foot of a black mountain." The springs at the foot of Sentinel Peak, made of black volcanic rock, are now dry. The name was pronounced "*tuk*-son" by the Spanish explorers who built a wall around the city in 1776 to keep Native Americans from reclaiming it. A good spot to learn about the indigenous cultures and their intersection with the settlers who came later, experience religious festivals and sample fry bread, a snack on many menus here, is Mission San Xavier del Bac, a thriving reservation parish.

roulette, and craps machines. The only "live" gaming is keno, bingo, blackjack, and certain types of poker. No one under age 21 is permitted.

Casino del Sol

CASINOS | The Pascua Yaqui tribe's main facility, Casino del Sol Resort has live poker and blackjack, bingo, and slots. The excellent PY Steakhouse, an Asian-fusion restaurant, and several casual eateries provide multiple dining options. Attached to the casino are a 215-room hotel and conference center, a golf course, and the 4,600-seat outdoor amphitheater AVA, which books entertainers as varied as Flo Rida, Toby Keith, and James Taylor. ⊠ *5655 W. Valencia Rd., Southwest* ☎ *520/838–6506, 855/765–7829* ⊕ *casinodelsol.com.*

Casino of the Sun

CASINOS | The Pascua Yaqui tribe's original gaming venture has slot and video-gambling machines only, and one casual restaurant. ⊠ *7406 S. Camino de Oeste, off W. Valencia Rd. about 5 miles west of I-19, Southwest* ☎ *520/838–6506, 855/765–7829* ⊕ *casinodelsol.com.*

Desert Diamond Casinos Tucson

CASINOS | The Tohono O'odham tribe operates the Desert Diamond Casinos, which has an indoor concert venue, a hotel and conference center, several restaurants, and plenty of one-armed bandits and

video poker in addition to live blackjack, poker, and bingo. ⊠ *7350 S. Old Nogales Hwy., South* ✛ *1 mile south of Valencia, just west of airport* ☎ *520/294–7777, 866/332–9467* ⊕ *ddcaz.com.*

Activities

San Ignacio Golf Club

GOLF | Designed by renowned architect Arthur Hills, San Ignacio's challenging and picturesque course winds through mesquite groves. Set in Green Valley, a 40-minute drive south of Tucson, it has nice mountain views and low greens fees. ⊠ *4201 S. Camino del Sol, Green Valley* ☎ *520/822–8313* ⊕ *www.sanignaciogolf.com* ⊲ *$25 for 9 holes, $55 for 18 holes* ⅃ *18 holes, 5875 yards, par 72.*

Tucson Rodeo

RODEO | FAMILY | In late February, Tucson hosts **Fiesta de Los Vaqueros,** the largest annual winter rodeo in the United States, a nine-day extravaganza with more than 600 events and a crowd of more than 44,000 spectators a day at the Tucson Rodeo Grounds. The rodeo kicks off with a 2-mile parade of Western and fancy-dress Mexican *charros,* wagons, stagecoaches, and horse-drawn floats, touted as the largest nonmotorized parade in the world. ⊠ *4823 S. 6th Ave., South* ☎ *520/741–2233* ⊕ *www.tucsonrodeo.com.*

Saguaro in One Day

Before setting off, choose which section of the park to visit and pack a lunch (there's no food service in either park district).

In the western section, start out by watching the 15-minute video at the **Red Hills Visitor Center**, then stroll the ½-mile-long **Desert Discovery Trail**. Drive north along Kinney Road, then turn right onto the graded dirt **Bajada Loop Drive**. Before long you'll see a turnoff for the **Hugh Norris Trail** on your right. If you're game for a steep 45-minute hike uphill, this trail leads to a perfect spot for a picnic. Hike back down and drive along the Bajada Loop Drive until you reach the turnoff for **Signal Hill**. From here it's a short walk to the **Hohokam petroglyphs.**

Alternatively, in the eastern section, pick up a free map of the hiking trails at the **Rincon Mountain Visitor Center.** Drive south along the paved **Cactus Forest Drive** to the Javelina picnic area, where you'll see signs for the **Freeman Homestead Trail,** an easy 1-mile loop that winds through a stand of mesquite as interpretive signs describe early inhabitants in the Tucson basin. If you're up for more difficult hiking, you might want to tackle part of the **Tanque Verde Ridge Trail,** which affords excellent views of saguaro-studded hillsides. Along the northern loop of Cactus Forest Drive is **Cactus Forest Trail**, which branches off into several fairly level paths. You can easily spend the rest of the afternoon strolling among the saguaros.

8

Tucson SAGUARO NATIONAL PARK

Saguaro National Park

Saguaro National Park West: 14 miles west of Central Tucson; Saguaro National Park East: 12 miles east of Central Tucson.

Saguaro National Park's two distinct sections flank the city of Tucson. Perhaps the most familiar emblem of the Southwest, the towering saguaros are found only in the Sonoran Desert. Saguaro National Park preserves some of the densest stands of these massive cacti.

Known for their height (often 50 feet) and arms reaching out in weird configurations, these slow-growing giants can take 15 years to grow a foot high and up to 75 years to grow their first arm. The cacti can live up to 200 years and weigh up to 2 tons. In late spring (usually May), the succulent's top is covered with tiny white blooms—the Arizona state flower. The cacti are protected by state and federal laws, so don't disturb them.

ORIENTATION

Saguaro East. Also called the Rincon Mountain District, this area encompasses 57,930 acres of designated wilderness area, an easily accessible scenic loop drive, several easy and intermediate trails through the cactus forest, and opportunities for adventure and backcountry camping at six rustic campgrounds.

Saguaro West. Also called the Tucson Mountain District, this is the park's smaller, more-visited section. At the visitor center is a video about saguaros; also in the park's western part are hiking trails, an ancient Hohokam petroglyph site at Signal Hill, and a scenic drive through the park's densest desert growth. This section is near the Arizona–Sonora Desert Museum in Tucson's Westside, and many visitors combine these sights.

WHEN TO GO

Saguaro never gets crowded. Nevertheless, most people visit in milder weather, October through May. December through February can be cool and are likely to see gentle rain showers. The spring days of March through May are bright and sunny with wildflowers and cacti in bloom. Because of high temperatures, from June through September it's best to visit the park in the early morning or late afternoon. Cooler temperatures return in October and November, providing perfect weather for hiking and camping throughout the park.

GETTING HERE AND AROUND

Both districts are about a half-hour drive from Central Tucson. To reach the Rincon Mountain District (East section) from Interstate 10, take Exit 275, then go north on Houghton Road for 10 miles. Turn right on Escalante and left onto Old Spanish Trail, and the park will be on the right side. If you're coming from town, go east on Speedway Boulevard to Houghton Road. Turn right on Houghton and left onto Old Spanish Trail.

To reach the Tucson Mountain District (West section) from Interstate 10, take Exit 242 or Exit 257, then go west on Speedway Boulevard (the name will change to Gates Pass Road), follow it to Kinney Road, and turn right.

As there's no public transportation to or within Saguaro, a car is a necessity. In the western section, Bajada Loop Drive takes you through the park and to various trailheads; Cactus Forest Drive does the same for the eastern section.

PARK ESSENTIALS
ACCESSIBILITY

In the western section, the Red Hills Visitor Center and two nearby nature trails are wheelchair accessible. The eastern district's visitor center is accessible, as are the paved Desert Ecology and Cactus Garden Trails.

PARK FEES AND PERMITS

Admission to Saguaro is $25 per vehicle and $15 for individuals on foot or bicycle; it's good for seven days from purchase at both park districts. Annual passes cost $45. For hike-in camping at one of the primitive campsites in the eastern district (the closest campsite is 6 miles from the trailhead), obtain a required backcountry permit ($8 per night) up to three months in advance. ⊕ *www.recreation.gov*

VISITOR INFORMATION

PARK CONTACT INFORMATION Saguaro National Park. ✉ *3693 S. Old Spanish Trail, Tucson* ☎ *520/733–5158 for Saguaro West, 520/733–5153 for Saguaro East* ⊕ *www.nps.gov/sagu.*

⊙ Sights

HISTORIC SIGHTS
Manning Camp

HOUSE | The summer home of Levi Manning, onetime Tucson mayor, was a popular gathering spot for the city's elite in the early 1900s. The cabin can be reached only on foot or horseback via one of several challenging high-country trails: Douglas Spring Trail to Cow Head Saddle Trail (12 miles), Turkey Creek Trail (7.5 miles), or Tanque Verde Ridge Trail (15.4 miles). The cabin itself is not open for viewing. ✉ *Saguaro East ⊹ Douglas Spring Trail (6 miles) to Cow Head Saddle Trail (6 miles).*

SCENIC DRIVES

Unless you're ready to lace up your hiking boots for a long desert hike, the best way to see Saguaro National Park is from the comfort of your car.

★ Bajada Loop Drive

SCENIC DRIVE | This 6-mile drive winds through thick stands of saguaros and past two picnic areas and trailheads to a few short hikes, including one to a petroglyph site. Although the road is unpaved and somewhat bumpy, it's a worthwhile trade-off for access to some of the park's

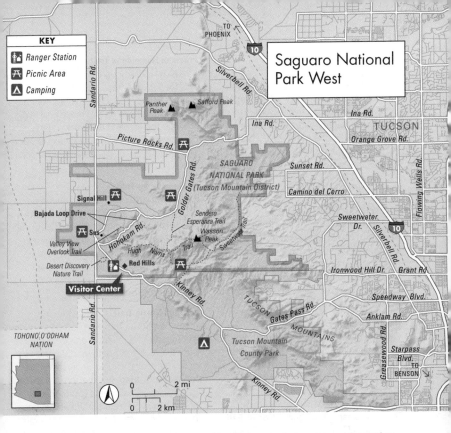

KEY
- Ranger Station
- Picnic Area
- Camping

TO PHOENIX

Saguaro National Park West

Silverbell Rd.

Panther Peak | Safford Peak

Picture Rocks Rd.

Ina Rd.

Ina Rd.

TUCSON

Orange Grove Rd.

SAGUARO NATIONAL PARK (Tucson Mountain District)

Sunset Rd.

Signal Hill

Camino del Cerro

Bajada Loop Drive

Golden Gates Rd.

Sendero Esperanza Trail

Wasson Peak

Sweetwater Dr.

Sweetwater Trail

Valley View Overlook Trail

Hohokam Rd.

Hugh Norris Trail

Desert Discovery Nature Trail

Red Hills

Ironwood Hill Dr. | Grant Rd.

Visitor Center

Kinney Rd.

Speedway Blvd.

TUCSON

Gates Pass Rd.

Anklam Rd.

Flowing Wells Rd.

Silverbell Rd.

TOHONO O'ODHAM NATION

Sandario Rd.

MOUNTAINS

Tucson Mountain County Park

Greasewood Rd.

Starpass Blvd. TO BENSON

Kinney Rd.

0   2 mi

0   2 km

densest desert growth. It's one-way between Hugh Norris Trail and Golden Gate Road, so if you want to make the complete circuit, travel counterclockwise. The road is susceptible to flash floods during the monsoon season (July and August), so check road conditions at the visitor center before proceeding. This loop route is also popular among bicyclists, and dogs on leash are permitted along the road. ⊠ *Saguaro West.*

★ **Cactus Forest Drive**
SCENIC DRIVE | This paved 8-mile drive provides a great overview of all Saguaro East has to offer. The one-way road, which circles clockwise, has several turnouts with roadside displays that make it easy to pull over and admire the scenery; you can also stop at two picnic areas and three easy nature trails. This is a good

bicycling route, but watch out for snakes and javelinas crossing in front of you. ⊠ *Cactus Forest Dr., Saguaro East.*

SCENIC STOPS
Signal Hill
ARCHAEOLOGICAL SITE | FAMILY | The most impressive petroglyphs, and the only ones with explanatory signs, are on the Bajada Loop Drive in Saguaro West. An easy five-minute stroll from the signposted parking area takes you to one of the largest concentrations of rock carvings in the Southwest. You'll have a close-up view of the designs left by the Hohokam people between AD 900 and 1200, including large spirals some believe are astronomical markers. ⊠ *Bajada Loop Dr., Saguaro West* ✛ *4½ miles north of visitor center.*

TRAILS

Cactus Forest Trail

HIKING/WALKING | This 2.5-mile one-way loop is a moderately easy walk along a dirt path that passes historic lime kilns and a wide variety of Sonoran Desert vegetation. It's one of the only off-road trails for bicyclists. *Moderate.* ⊠ *Saguaro East ✛ Trailhead: 2 miles south of Rincon Mountain Visitor Center, off Cactus Forest Dr.*

Cactus Garden Trail

HIKING/WALKING | This 100-yard paved trail in front of the Rincon Mountain Visitor Center is wheelchair accessible and has resting benches and interpretive signs about common desert plants. *Easy.* ⊠ *Saguaro East ✛ Trailhead: next to Rincon Mountain Visitor Center.*

Desert Discovery Trail

HIKING/WALKING | **FAMILY** | Learn about plants and animals native to the region on this paved path in Saguaro West. The 0.5-mile loop is wheelchair accessible, and has resting benches and ramadas (wooden shelters that supply shade). Dogs on leash are permitted here. *Easy.* ⊠ *Saguaro West ✛ Trailhead: 1 mile north of Red Hills Visitor Center.*

Desert Ecology Trail

HIKING/WALKING | **FAMILY** | Exhibits on this ¼-mile loop near the Mica View picnic area explain how local plants and animals subsist on limited water. Dogs on leash are permitted. *Easy.* ⊠ *Saguaro East ✛ Trailhead: 2 miles north of Rincon Mountain Visitor Center.*

Douglas Spring Trail

HIKING/WALKING | This challenging 6-mile trail, steep in some parts, leads almost due east into the Rincon Mountains. After a half mile through a dense concentration of saguaros, you reach the open desert. About 3 miles in is Bridal Wreath Falls, worth a slight detour in spring when melting snow creates a larger cascade. *Moderate.* ⊠ *Saguaro East ✛ Trailhead: eastern end of Speedway Blvd.*

Freeman Homestead Trail

HIKING/WALKING | Learn a bit about the history of homesteading in the region on this 1-mile loop. Look for owls living in the cliffs above as you make your way through the lowland vegetation. *Easy.* ⊠ *Saguaro East ✛ Trailhead: next to Javelina picnic area, 2 miles south of Rincon Mountain Visitor Center.*

★ Hope Camp Trail

HIKING/WALKING | Well worth the 5-mile round-trip trek, this Rincon Valley route rewards hikers with gorgeous views of the Tanque Verde Ridge and Rincon Peak. The trail is also open to mountain bicyclists. *Moderate.* ⊠ *Saguaro East ✛ Trailhead: from Camino Loma Alta trailhead to Hope Camp.*

★ Hugh Norris Trail

HIKING/WALKING | This 10-mile trail through the Tucson Mountains is one of the most impressive in the Southwest. It's full of switchbacks, and some sections are moderately steep, but the top of 4,687-foot Wasson Peak treats you to views of the saguaro forest spread across the *bajada* (the gently rolling hills at the base of taller mountains). *Difficult.* ⊠ *Saguaro West ✛ Trailhead: 2½ miles north of Red Hills Visitor Center on Bajada Loop Dr.*

King Canyon Trail

HIKING/WALKING | This 3.5-mile trail is the shortest, but steepest, route to the top of Wasson Peak in Saguaro West. It meets the Hugh Norris Trail less than half a mile from the summit. The trail, which begins across from the Arizona–Sonora Desert Museum, is named after the Copper King Mine. It leads past many scars from the search for mineral wealth. ■**TIP**→ **Look for petroglyphs in this area.** *Difficult.* ⊠ *Saguaro West ✛ Trailhead: 2 miles south of Red Hills Visitor Center.*

Sendero Esperanza Trail

HIKING/WALKING | Follow a sandy mine road for the first section of this 6-mile trail in Saguaro West, then ascend via a series of switchbacks to the top of a

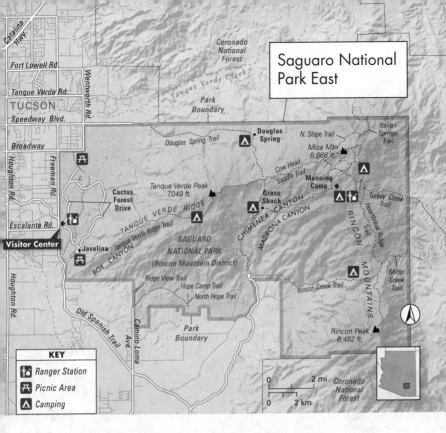

Saguaro National
Park East

Coronado National Forest

Tanque Verde Creek

Park Boundary

Catalina Hwy.

Fort Lowell Rd.

Tanque Verde Rd.

TUCSON

Speedway Blvd.

Broadway

Wentworth Rd.

Houghton Rd.

Freeman Rd.

Escalante Rd.

Visitor Center

Houghton Rd.

Cactus Forest Drive

Javelina

Douglas Spring Trail

Douglas Spring

N. Slope Trail

Italian Springs Trail

Mica Mtn. 8,666 ft.

Cow Head Saddle Trail

Manning Camp

Tanque Verde Peak 7,049 ft.

Grass Shack

Turkey Creek Trail

TANQUE VERDE RIDGE

CHIMENEA CANYON

MADRONA CANYON

RINCON

Tanque Verde Ridge Trail

BOX CANYON

SAGUARO NATIONAL PARK
(Rincon Mountain District)

MOUNTAINS

Heartbreak Ridge Trail

Miller Creek Trail

Ridge View Trail

Hope Camp Trail

North Hope Trail

Rincon Creek Trail

Camino Loma Alta

Old Spanish Trail

Park Boundary

Rincon Peak 8,482 ft.

Coronado National Forest

0   2 mi
0   2 km

KEY

- 👥 Ranger Station
- 🏕 Picnic Area
- ⛺ Camping

ridge and cross the Hugh Norris Trail. Descending on the other side, you'll meet up with the King Canyon Trail. The Esperanza ("Hope") Trail is often rocky and sometimes steep, but rewards include ruins of the Gould Mine, dating back to 1907. *Moderate.* ✉ *Saguaro West* ⊹ *Trailhead: 1½ miles east of the intersection of Bajada Loop Dr. and Golden Gate Rd.*

★ Signal Hill Trail

HIKING/WALKING | FAMILY | This ¼-mile trail in Saguaro West is a simple, rewarding ascent to ancient petroglyphs carved a millennium ago by the Hohokam people. *Easy.* ✉ *Saguaro West* ⊹ *Trailhead: 4½ miles north of Red Hills Visitor Center on Bajada Loop Dr.*

Sweetwater Trail

HIKING/WALKING | Though technically within Saguaro West, this trail is on the eastern edge of the district, and affords access to Wasson Peak from the eastern side of the Tucson Mountains. After gradually climbing 3.4 miles, it ends at King Canyon Trail (which would then take you on a fairly steep 1.2-mile climb to Wasson Peak). Long and meandering, this little-used trail allows more privacy to enjoy the natural surroundings than some of the more frequently used trails. *Moderate.* ✉ *Saguaro West* ⊹ *Trailhead: western end of El Camino del Cerro Rd.*

Tanque Verde Ridge Trail

HIKING/WALKING | Be rewarded with spectacular scenery on this 18-mile round-trip trail that takes you through desert scrub, oak, alligator juniper, and pinyon pine

Continued on page 372

TIPS FOR STARGAZING
IN THE NATIONAL PARKS

If your typical view of the night sky consists of a handful of stars dimly twinkling through a hazy light-polluted sky, get ready for a treat. In most of the national parks, the night sky blazes with starlight—and with a little practice, you can give your family a memorable astronomical tour.

Constellations

Constellations are stories in the sky—many depict animals or figures from Greek mythology. Brush up on a few of these tales before your trip, and you'll be an instant source of nighttime entertainment.

The stars in the Northern Hemisphere appear to rotate around Polaris, the North Star, in fixed positions relative to one another. To get your celestial bearings, first find the bright stars of the Big Dipper. An imaginary line drawn through the two stars that form the outside edge of the cup (away from the handle) will point straight to Polaris (which also serves as the last star in the handle of the Little Dipper). Once you've identified Polaris, you should be able to find the other stars on our chart. Myriad astronomy books and Web sites have additional star charts; *National Geographic* has a cool interactive version with images from the Hubble Space Telescope (⊕ *www. nationalgeographic.com/science*).

Planets

Stars twinkle, planets don't (because they're so much closer to Earth, the atmosphere doesn't distort their light as much). Planets are also bright, which makes them fairly easy to spot. Unfortunately, we can't show their positions on this star chart because planets orbit the sun and move in relation to the stars.

The easiest planet to spot is Venus, the brightest object in the night sky besides the moon and the Earth's closest planetary neighbor. Look for it just before sunrise or just after sunset; it'll be near the point where the sun is rising or setting. (Venus and Earth orbit the sun at different speeds; when Venus is moving away from Earth, we see it in the morning, and when it's moving toward us, we see it in the evening.) Like the moon, Venus goes through phases—check it out through a pair of binoculars. You can also spot Mars, Jupiter, Saturn, and Mercury, with or without the aid of binoculars.

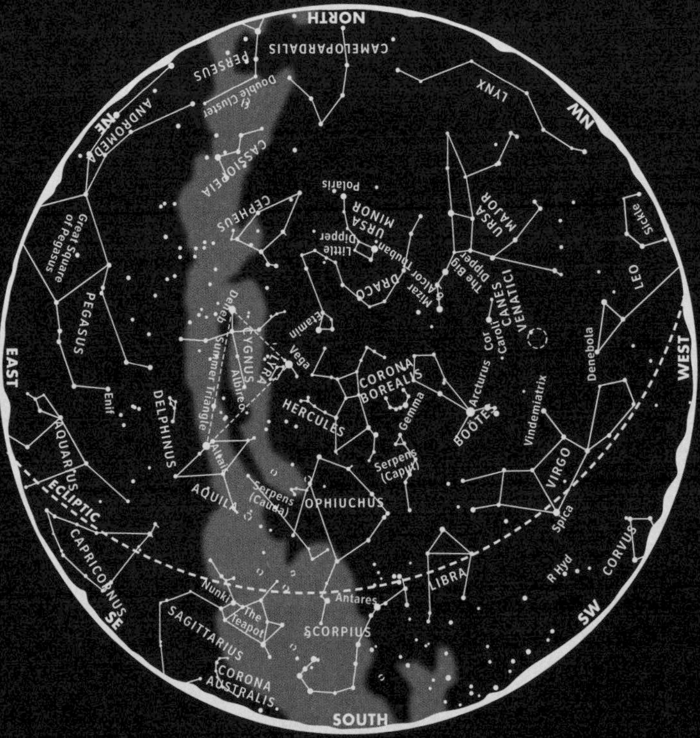

Meteors

It's hard to match the magic of a meteor shower, the natural fireworks display that occurs as Earth passes through a cloud of debris called meteoroids. These pieces of space junk—most the size of a pebble—hit our atmosphere at high speeds, and the intense friction produces brief but brilliant streaks of light. Single meteors are often called "shooting stars" or "falling stars."

Because our planet passes through the same patches of interstellar refuse each year, it's easy to roughly predict when the major meteor showers will occur. Notable ones include the Perseids (mid-August), the Orionids (late October), the Leonids (mid-November), and the Geminids (mid-December). Each shower is named after the point in the sky where meteors appear to originate. If you're not visiting during a shower, don't worry—you can spot individual meteors any time of the year.

Satellites

Right now, according to NASA, there are about 2,700 operative man-made satellites (along with many more pieces of space junk) orbiting the Earth—and you can catch a glimpse of one with a little practice. Satellites look like fast-moving, non-blinking points of light; the best way to spot one is to lie on your back and scan the sky for movement. Be on the lookout for satellites an hour or two before or after sunset (though you may see them at other times as well).

You can take the guesswork out of the search with a few cool online tools (*🌐 www.nasa.gov or www.heavens-above.com*). Select your location, and these Web sites will help you predict—down to the minute—when certain objects will be streaking overhead. It's especially worthwhile to use these sites to look for the two brightest satellites: the International Space Station and the space shuttle.

Saguaro National Park Flora and Fauna ◉

The saguaro may be the centerpiece of Saguaro National Park, but more than 1,200 plant species, including 50 types of cactus, thrive in the park. Among the most common cacti here are the prickly pear, barrel cactus, and teddy bear cholla—so named because it appears cuddly, but rangers advise packing a comb to pull its barbed hooks from unwary fingers.

For many of the desert fauna, the saguaro functions as a high-rise hotel. Each spring the Gila woodpecker and gilded flicker create holes in the cactus and then nest there. When they give up their temporary digs, elf owls, cactus wrens, sparrow hawks, and other birds move in, as do dangerous Africanized honeybees.

You may not encounter any of the park's six species of rattlesnake or the Gila monster, a venomous lizard, but avoid sticking your hands or feet under rocks or into crevices. Look where you're walking; if you do get bitten, get to a clinic or hospital as soon as possible. Not all snakes pass on venom; 50% of the time the bite is "dry" (nonvenomous).

Wildlife, from bobcats to jackrabbits, is most active in early morning and at dusk. In spring and summer, lizards and snakes are out and about but tend to keep a low profile during the midday heat.

at the 6,000-foot peak, where views of the surrounding mountain ranges from both sides of the ridge delight. *Difficult.* ✉ *Saguaro East ⚑ Trailhead: Javelina picnic area, 2 miles south of Red Hills Visitor Center.*

★ Valley View Overlook Trail

HIKING/WALKING | On clear days you can spot the distinctive slope of Picacho Peak from this relatively easy 1.5-mile trail with a gentle ascent in Saguaro West. There are splendid vistas of Avra Valley and signs describing the flora along the way. *Moderate.* ✉ *Saguaro West ⚑ Trailhead: 3 miles north of Red Hills Visitor Center on Bajada Loop Dr.*

VISITOR CENTERS

Red Hills Visitor Center

INFO CENTER | Take in gorgeous views of nearby mountains and the surrounding desert from the center's large windows and shaded outdoor terrace. A spacious gallery is filled with educational exhibits, and a lifelike display simulates the flora and fauna of the region. A 15-minute slide show, "Voices of the Desert," provides a poetic, Native American perspective on the Saguaro. Park rangers and volunteers hand out maps and suggest hikes to suit your interests. The bookstore sells books, trinkets, a few local items like honey and prickly pear jellies, and reusable water bottles that you can fill at water stations outside. ✉ *2700 N. Kinney Rd., Saguaro West* ☎ *520/733–5158* ⊕ *www.nps.gov/sagu.*

Rincon Mountain Visitor Center

INFO CENTER | Stop here to pick up free maps and printed materials on various aspects of the park, including maps of hiking trails and backcountry camping permits. Exhibits at the center are comprehensive, and a relief map of the park lays out the complexities of this protected landscape. Two 20-minute slide shows explain the botanical and cultural history of the region, and there is a short self-guided nature walk along the paved Cactus Garden Trail. A select variety of books and other gift items, along with energy bars, beef jerky, and

A massive, open-pit copper mine lies just south of Tucson at the ASARCO Mineral Discovery Center.

refillable water bottles, are sold here.
✉ *3693 S. Old Spanish Trail, Saguaro East*
☏ *520/733–5153* ⊕ *www.nps.gov/sagu.*

🏃 Activities

BIKING

Scenic drives in the park—Bajada Loop in the West and Cactus Forest Drive in the East section—are popular among cyclists, though you'll have to share the roads with cars. Bajada Loop Drive is a gravel and dirt road, so it's quite bumpy and only suitable for mountain bikers; Cactus Forest Drive is paved. In the East section, Cactus Forest Trail (2.5 miles) is a great unpaved path for both beginning and experienced mountain bikers who don't mind sharing the trail with hikers and the occasional horse; Hope Camp Trail is also open to mountain bikes.

BIRD-WATCHING

To check out the more than 200 species of birds living in or migrating through the park, begin by focusing your binoculars on the limbs of the saguaros, where many birds make their home. In general, early morning and early evening are the best times for sightings. In winter and spring, volunteer-led birding hikes begin at the visitor centers.

The finest areas to flock to in Saguaro East (the Rincon Mountain District) are the Desert Ecology Trail, where you may find rufous-winged sparrows, verdins, and Cooper's hawks along the washes, and the Javelina picnic area, where you'll most likely spot canyon wrens and black-chinned sparrows. At Saguaro West (the Tucson Mountain District), sit down on one of the visitor center benches and look for ash-throated flycatchers, Say's phoebes, curve-billed thrashers, and Gila woodpeckers. During the cooler months, keep a lookout for wintering neotropical migrants such as hummingbirds, swallows, orioles, and warblers.

CAMPING

You can slumber amid saguaros, just down the road from Saguaro National Park West inside Tucson Mountain Park, at **Gilbert Ray Campground** about 13 miles

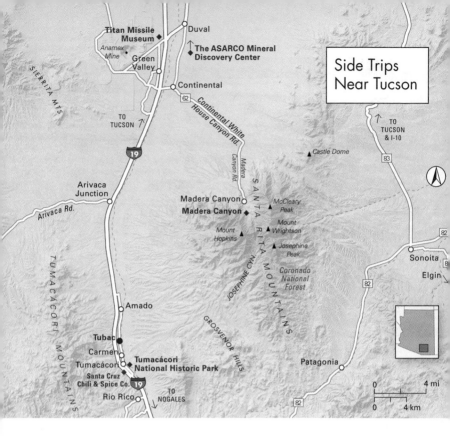

Side Trips Near Tucson

Titan Missile Museum
Duval
Anamex Mine
Green Valley
The ASARCO Mineral Discovery Center

Continental
62
Continental White House Canyon Rd.

TO TUCSON

TO TUCSON & I-10

Madera Canyon Rd.

Castle Dome
83

Arivaca Junction
Arivaca Rd.

Madera Canyon
Madera Canyon

McCleary Peak
Mount Wrightson

Mount Hopkins
Josephine Peak

Coronado National Forest

Sonoita
82

Elgin

82

JOSEPHINE CYN
SANTA RITA MOUNTAINS

82

Amado

GROSVENOR HILLS

Tubac
Carmen
Tumacácori
Tumacácori National Historic Park
Santa Cruz Chili & Spice Co.
19
Rio Rico
TO NOGALES

Patagonia

82

0   4 mi
0   4 km

---

west of Tucson. This campground has drinking water, flush toilets (but no showers), and 130 sites with tables, grills, and electricity. Sites cost $20 for RVs and $10 for tents; you can make reservations online, and there's a seven-day stay limit. ✉ *8451 W. McCain Loop* ☎ *520/403–8116* ⊕ *webcms.pima.gov*

HIKING
The park has more than 100 miles of trails. The shorter hikes, such as the **Desert Discovery** and **Desert Ecology** trails, are perfect for those looking to learn about the desert ecosystem without expending too much energy. The **Hope Camp Trail**, **Hugh Norris Trail**, and **Signal Hill Trail** are also excellent for hiking. For more information see the trail listings under ⇨ *Sights*.

■ **TIP**→ Rattlesnakes are commonly seen on trails; so are coyotes, javelinas, roadrunners, Gambel's quail, and desert spiny lizards. Hikers should keep their distance from all wildlife.

Side Trips Near Tucson

Interstate 19 heads south from Tucson through Tubac to Nogales at the border of Mexico, carrying with it history buffs, bird-watchers, hikers, art enthusiasts, duffers, and shoppers. The road roughly follows the Camino Real (King's Road), which the conquistadors and missionaries traveled from Mexico up to what was once the northernmost portion of New Spain.

The ASARCO Mineral Discovery Center

15 miles south of Tucson off I–19.

The American Smelting and Refining Company (abbreviated as ASARCO) gives visitors a glimpse not only of a vast, open-pit mine but also of the complex processes involved in extracting minerals like copper from the earth.

GETTING HERE AND AROUND

From Interstate 19 south take Exit 80. Turn right (west) onto Pima Mine Road, and the entrance will be almost immediately on your left.

Sights

ASARCO Mineral Discovery Center

MINE | This mining operations center elucidates the importance of mining to everyday life. Indoor exhibits include a walk-through model of an ore crusher, video stations that explain refining processes, and a film about how minerals are actually extracted. Outside, you can see some of the actual equipment, including a few gargantuan trucks used for hauling the stuff. The big draw, though, is the yawning open pit of the Mission Mine, some 2 miles long and 1¾ miles wide because so much earth has to be torn up to extract the 1% that is copper. It's impressive, but doesn't bolster the case the center tries to make about how environmentally conscious mining has become. Tours of the pit take a little over an hour; the last one starts at 3:30. From May to September, pit mine tours are only offered on Saturday. ✉ *1421 W. Pima Mine Rd.* ☎ *520/625–7513* ⊕ *www.asarco.com* 🎫 *Mine tour $10 (Discovery Center is free)* ⊗ *Closed Sun. and Mon.*

Titan Missile Museum

25 miles south of Tucson.

The Titan Missile Museum houses one of the 54 missile silos built around the country during the Cold War in case the United States needed to deploy nuclear bombs. A guided tour gives you a sense of the military mindset during this era.

GETTING HERE AND AROUND

From Interstate 19, take Exit 69 (Duval Mine Road) approximately 1 mile west to the museum.

⊙ Sights

Titan Missile Museum

MILITARY SITE | Now a National Historic Landmark, the Titan Missile Museum makes for a sobering visit. During the Cold War, Tucson was ringed by 18 of the 54 Titan II missiles maintained in the United States. After the SALT II treaty with the Soviet Union was signed in 1979, this was the only missile-launch site left intact.

Guided one-hour tours, which must be reserved in advance, take you down 55 steps into the command post, where a ground crew of four lived and waited. Among the sights is the 103-foot, 165-ton, two-stage liquid-fuel rocket. Now empty, it originally held a nuclear warhead with 214 times the explosive power of the bomb that destroyed Hiroshima. ✉ *1580 W. Duval Mine Rd., off I–19, Exit 69, Green Valley* ☎ *520/625–7736* ⊕ *www.titanmissilemuseum.org* 🎫 *$13.*

Madera Canyon

61½ miles southeast of Tucson.

This prime hiking and birding area south of Tucson is where the Coronado National Forest meets the Santa Rita Mountains. Higher elevations and thick pine cover make it especially popular with Tucsonans looking to escape the summer heat.

Colorful ceramic pottery is sold at local markets in the artist colony of Tubac.

GETTING HERE AND AROUND

From Interstate 19, take Exit 63 (Continental Road) east for about a mile, then turn right (southeast) on White House Canyon Road for 12½ miles (it turns into Madera Canyon Road).

⊙ Sights

Madera Canyon

NATURE PRESERVE | With approximately 200 miles of scenic trails, the recreation area of Madera Canyon—which includes Mount Wrightson, the highest peak in Southern Arizona, at 9,453 feet—is a haven for hikers and birders. Trails vary from a steep trek up Mount Baldy to a paved, wheelchair-accessible path along the creek. Birders flock here year-round; about 400 avian species have been spotted in the area.

There are picnic tables and ramadas near the parking areas, and camping is available. The Santa Rita Lodge (⊕ *santaritalodge.com*), with charming cabins, has numerous bird feeders and a gift shop.

Friends of Madera Canyon (⊕ *friendsofmaderacanyon.org*) operates an information station here on the weekends. ✉ *Madera Canyon Rd.* ☎ *520/281–2296 for Nogales Ranger District office* ⊕ *www.fs.usda.gov/coronado* ☒ *$8.*

Tubac

45 miles south of Tucson at Exit 40 off I–19.

Established in 1726, Tubac is the site of the first European settlement in Arizona. A year after the Pima uprising in 1751, a military garrison was established here to protect Spanish settlers, missionaries, and peaceful Native American converts of the nearby Tumacácori Mission. It was from here that Juan Bautista de Anza led 240 colonists across the desert—the expedition resulted in the founding of San Francisco in 1776. In 1860 Tubac was the largest town in Arizona. Today the quiet little town is a popular art colony. More than 80 shops sell such crafts as carved wooden furniture, hand-thrown pottery, delicately painted tiles, and silkscreen fabrics (many shops are closed Monday). You can also find Mexican pottery and trinkets without having to cross the border. The annual **Tubac Festival of the Arts** has been held in February for more than 50 years.

GETTING HERE AND AROUND

When you exit Interstate 19 at Tubac Road, signs will point you east into Tubac village. There's plenty of free parking, and you can pick up a free map of the village at most of the shops.

ESSENTIALS

VISITOR INFORMATION Tubac Chamber of Commerce. ☎ *520/398–2704* 🌐 *tubacaz.com.*

Sights

Tubac Presidio State Historic Park

NATIONAL/STATE PARK | There's an archaeological display of portions of the original 1752 fort at this museum, as well as artifacts and detailed exhibits on the history of the early colony. The park includes picnic areas, gardens, an adobe rowhouse built in 1897, and Tubac's well-preserved 1885 schoolhouse. ✉ *1 Burruel St.* ☎ *520/398–2252* 🌐 *www.tubacpresidio.org* 🎟 *$7* 🕓 *Closed Mon. and Tues.*

Restaurants

★ Elvira's

$$ | **MEXICAN** | This colorful and deservedly popular restaurant serves delicious Sonoran classics in Tubac village. Try one of the five chicken moles, ranging from sweet to nutty to spicy, and you'll know why chef Ruben has such a devoted following. **Known for:** delicious Sonoran classics with a contemporary twist; weekend nightlife; striking dining room. [$] *Average main: $19* ✉ *2221 E. Frontage Rd.* ☎ *520/398–9421* 🌐 *elvirasrestaurant.com* 🕓 *Closed Mon. No dinner Sun.*

Tubac Deli & Coffee Co.

$ | **AMERICAN** | With freshly roasted coffee, breakfast pastries, and generous sandwiches, salads, and soups, this pleasant little eatery smack in the middle of Tubac village is a very convenient and friendly place to "set awhile" with the locals. **Known for:** homemade breads and pastries; inexpensive lunch break while shopping; hearty breakfasts. [$] *Average main: $9* ✉ *6 Plaza Rd.* ☎ *520/398–3330* 🌐 *tubacdeli.com.*

Hotels

Amado Territory Inn

$ | **B&B/INN** | Although this quiet, friendly B&B is directly off the highway frontage road, it feels worlds away. **Pros:** good breakfast; pleasant porches and garden areas; friendly hosts. **Cons:** no TV in some rooms; a short drive to Tubac village; room decor a bit dated. [$] *Rooms from: $149* ✉ *3001 E. Frontage Rd., Amado* ✣ *Off I–19, Exit 48* ☎ *520/398–8684* 🌐 *www.amadoterritory-inn.com* 🛏 *10 rooms* 🍴 *Free breakfast.*

Tubac Country Inn

$$ | **B&B/INN** | Down the lane from the shops and eateries of Tubac village is this charming two-story inn, tastefully decorated in contemporary Southwest style. **Pros:** spacious, comfortably furnished rooms with separate entrances; in Tubac village; kitchenettes. **Cons:** no B&B camaraderie here—it feels more like you're staying in someone's guest cottage; continental-type breakfast; stairs only to second-floor rooms. [$] *Rooms from: $155* ✉ *13 Burruel St.* ☎ *520/398–3178* 🌐 *www.tubaccountry-inn.com* 🛏 *5 rooms* 🍴 *Free breakfast.*

Activities

Juan Bautista de Anza National Historic Trail

HIKING/WALKING | **FAMILY** | You can tread the same road as the conquistadors: the first 4½ miles of the Juan Bautista de Anza National Historic Trail—which stretches all the way from Nogales, Arizona, to Bautista's end point in San

Francisco—lead from Tumacácori to Tubac. You'll have to cross the Santa Cruz River—which is usually low—three times to complete the hike, and the path is rather sandy, but it's a pleasant journey along the tree-shaded banks of the river. *Moderate.* ☎ *415/623–2344* ⊕ *www. anzahistorictrail.org, www.nps.gov/juba.*

Tubac Golf Resort

GOLF | The rolling hills and pastoral land surrounding these 27 holes in the lovely town of Tubac, 45 minutes south of Tucson, are a change from desert golf environs. This resort has an on-site pro shop, excellent restaurant, and a cantina. ✉ *1 Ave. De Otero Rd.* ☎ *520/398–2211* ⊕ *www.tubacgolfresort.com* ▨ *$46 for 9 holes, $99 for 18 holes* ⚑. *27 holes, 6375 yards, par 71.*

Tumacácori National Historic Park

3 miles south of Tubac.

Father Kino established the Tumacácori Mission in 1791, but the Jesuits didn't build a church here until 60 years later. Walk through the mission ruins and visit the main attraction, the pretty Mission of San José de Tumacácori, built by the Franciscans around 1799–1803. The historic Anza Trail runs through the park.

GETTING HERE AND AROUND

Take Exit 29 off Interstate 19 and follow signs half a mile to the park (from Tucson, go under the highway to East Frontage Road and turn left).

◉ Sights

Santa Cruz Chili & Spice Co.

STORE/MALL | Across the street from the Tumacácori National Historic Park, the Santa Cruz Spice Factory packs and sells 240 varieties of herbs and spices, including the owner's home-grown chili powders and pastes. A little museum, tasting area, and store are open Monday through Saturday. ✉ *1868 E. Frontage Rd., Tumacácori* ☎ *520/398–2591* ⊕ *www. santacruzchili.com* ⊘ *Closed Sun.*

Tumacácori National Historic Park

NATIONAL/STATE PARK | **FAMILY** | Encompassing mission ruins, the church of San José de Tumacácori, and a portion of the Juan Bautista de Anza National Historic Trail, this park became a national monument in 1908. Guided tours of the beautiful church and grounds are available daily at 11 and 2, January through March, and information on both the mission and the historic trail is available at the visitor center. A small museum displays some of the mission's artifacts, and often during winter and spring months fresh tortillas are made on a wood-fire stove in the courtyard. Creative educational programs, such as full-moon tours, bird walks, and a Junior Ranger Program, are offered throughout the year. An annual fiesta the first weekend of December has arts and crafts and food booths. ✉ *1891 E. Frontage Rd., Tumacácori* ✛ *Off I–19, Exit 29* ☎ *520/377–5060* ⊕ *www.nps. gov/tuma* ▨ *$10.*

Chapter 9

SOUTHERN ARIZONA

Updated by
Mara Levin

◉ Sights	🍴 Restaurants	🛏 Hotels	🛍 Shopping	🍸 Nightlife
★★★★☆	★★☆☆☆	★★☆☆☆	★★★☆☆	★★☆☆☆

WELCOME TO SOUTHERN ARIZONA

TOP REASONS TO GO

★ **Tour Kartchner Caverns:** The underground world of a living "wet" cave system is a rare and wonderful sensory experience. You'll see a multicolor limestone kingdom.and probably feel "cave kiss" droplets grace your head; just don't touch anything.

★ **Hike in the Chiricahuas:** Stunning "upside-down" rock formations, flourishing wildlife, and relatively easy trails make for great hiking in this unspoiled region. The 3½-mile Echo Canyon Loop Trail is a winner.

★ **Explore Bisbee:** Board the Queen Mine Train and venture into the life of a copper miner at the turn of the last century. Afterward check out the narrow, hilly town's Victorian houses and thriving shops.

★ **Stargaze at Kitt Peak:** Clear skies and dry air provide ideal conditions for stargazing; the evening observation program, with top-notch telescopes and enthusiastic guides, is an excellent introduction to astronomy.

1 Tombstone. Channel your inner cowboy in this well-preserved western town with saloons, stagecoach rides, and a courthouse.

2 Bisbee. A picturesque mining town-turned-artist-colony, Bisbee is brimming with history and architecture, as well as shopping and nightlife.

3 Sonoita. Vineyards, tasting rooms, and horse ranches dot the gently rolling hills and grasslands less than an hour's drive from Tucson.

4 Patagonia. There is ample opportunity for birding, hiking, and boating around Patagonia and Patagonia Lake.

5 Sierra Vista. This military town, home of Fort Huachuca, is a gateway to some of the best birding in the state.

6 Chiricahua National Monument. Stunning rock formations and abundant wildlife are a draw for hikers and birders in this remote southeast region.

7 Fort Bowie National Historic Site. This historic military site, where soldiers were stationed to protect settlers traveling west, also has scenic hiking trails.

8 Willcox. An unassuming farming town, known for fresh-picked apples

and veggies, Willcox is now a burgeoning wine-tasting destination.

9 Texas Canyon. These rocky hillsides, where the Apaches and their leader, Cochise, reigned, can be explored by foot or on horseback.

10 Kartchner Caverns State Park. Touring one of the only living cave systems in the world is a unique experience.

11 Buenos Aires National Wildlife Refuge. You won't have much human company while birding and hiking in this tranquil spot.

12 Kitt Peak National Observatory. Stargaze with telescopes used by top astronomers on this isolated peak on the Tohono O'odham nation.

13 Ajo. This friendly, former mining town serves as a stopover for travelers to Rocky Point, Mexico, and Organ Pipe Cactus National Monument.

14 Organ Pipe Cactus National Monument. Rare and beautiful Organ Pipe cacti are copious in this isolated area near the Mexican border.

15 Yuma. Halfway between the Phoenix-Tucson area and the California coast, Yuma (aka "The Lettuce Capital") is a pleasant city on the Colorado River.

16 Imperial National Wildlife Refuge. Hiking, birding, fishing, and hunting are popular in this refuge north of Yuma.

EXPERIENCE THE WILD WEST

You can still ride a stagecoach in Tombstone.

Arizona's identity was forged like horseshoes by cattle, copper, and the men who chased both. The "Old West" stretches as long as a cowboy's yarn and as broad as a 19th-century cattle drive. Follow the echoes of gunslingers like Wyatt Earp, or drink in majestic landscapes popularized on the silver screen.

In 1862, when Arizona became a U.S. territory, it began to fill immediately with fortune seekers. In towns like Bisbee (copper) and Tombstone (silver), the discovery of a single ore begot legendary boom-and-bust mining cycles. Precious metal brought miners, then speculators, real wealth, and services such as saloons and brothels. Just as quickly, the ore ran out, and envy, shoot-outs, and desolation followed. With the arrival of railroads in 1880, Arizona's stock grew from a few thousand to a million-plus in less than 20 years—but ranchers were also shortsighted and the "boom" subsided just as fast. Still, cowboy life is one of the most enduring icons of Americana.

TOURISM BONANZA

Movies like *Gunfight at the O.K. Corral* started a renaissance in many ghost towns, and the modern "boom" is tourism. Main Street's drinking and gambling establishments have given way to B&Bs (try **School House Inn** in Bisbee), historic bars (visit **Crystal Palace Saloon** in Tombstone), and boutiques (**55 Main Gallery** in Bisbee).

SOUTHERN ARIZONA WILD WEST ROAD TRIP

Southeast Arizona may be the most dense and interesting corner in which to explore various aspects of the Old West. The Apache tribe, led by Cochise and later Geronimo, held out for decades against U.S. troops and settlers amid the 12 ranges of the Coronado National Forest, before surrendering in 1886. You can hike through the remains of the Butterfield stagecoach stop at **Fort Bowie**. Imagine warrior-tribes in the canyons and rock formations of the **Chiricahua National Monument,** where jaguar, rare deer, and flora are treasures in their own right.

Also in the southeast, the colorful towns of Tombstone and Bisbee were centers of mining (silver and copper, respectively) and wealth, larger-than-life characters, and movie depictions that came with them. **Tombstone** is touristy, but the historic Allen Street buildings and the re-creation of the gunfight at the O.K. Corral are so steeped in Old West history (Wyatt Earp and Doc Holliday walked away, but three of the notorious Clanton gang weren't so lucky) that it's worth a visit. Take a stagecoach ride and mosey through town in the morning; then head south where more authentic experiences await in **Bisbee.** Don a hard hat and yellow rain slicker when you take the 75-minute underground tour of the **Copper Queen Mine,** or if you're prone to claustrophobia, stick to the **Bisbee Mining and Historical Museum,** which served as the company's offices.

Western watchers will find Canyon de Chelly familiar.

ELSEWHERE IN ARIZONA

In North-Central Arizona, **Jerome** and **Prescott** are two other boomtowns worth a half-day's exploration. Jerome was once known as the Billion Dollar Copper Camp, but its 15,000-person population dwindled to 50 before rebounding to today's 500 or so. Stop for a hearty burger in the **Haunted Hamburger/Jerome Palace,** where the resident ghost purportedly hangs out upstairs. Thirty miles away, Prescott is home to the world's oldest rodeo during July's **Frontier Days** and has regular live music at the historic bars on **Whiskey Row.**

Thanks to Hollywood, the wide-open vistas of the West are some of the most recurring images of a bygone era. Fortunately for you, **Monument Valley** and **Canyon de Chelly** in Northeast Arizona remain virtually unchanged from the way that cowboys and Native Americans experienced them in the 19th century.

Tours go deep into the Copper Queen Mine.

Southern Arizona can do little to escape its cliché-ridden image as a landscape of cow skulls, tumbleweeds, dried-up riverbeds, and mother lodes—but it doesn't need to. Abandoned mining towns, sleepy Western hamlets, rugged rock formations, and deep pine forests beckon visitors for birding, hiking, and horseback riding, as well as more tame adventures like wine-tasting, stargazing, and shopping on historic main streets. This diverse range of activities, along with the feel of stepping back in time, affords a rich and satisfying tour.

In 1540, 80 years before the pilgrims landed at Plymouth Rock, Spanish conquistador Don Francisco Vásquez de Coronado led one of Spain's largest expeditions from Mexico along the fertile San Pedro River valley, where the little towns of Benson and St. David are found today. They'd come north to seek the legendary Seven Cities of Cibola, where Native American pueblos were rumored to have doors of polished turquoise and streets of solid gold. The wealth of the region, however, lay in its rich veins of copper and silver, not tapped until more than 300 years after the Spanish marched on in disappointment. Once word of this cache spread, these parts of the West quickly became much wilder: fortune seekers who rushed in came face-to-face with the Chiricahua Apaches, led by Cochise

and Geronimo, while warriors battled encroaching settlers and the U.S. Cavalry was sent to protect them.

The western side of the state wasn't untouched by the search for mineral booty and the rage to plunder. Interest in going for the gold in California gave rise to the town of Yuma. The Colorado River had to be crossed to get to the West Coast, and Fort Yuma was established in part to protect the Anglo ferry business at a good fording point from Indian competitors. The Yuma Tribe lost that battle, but another group of Native Americans, the Tohono O'odham, fared better in this part of the state. Known for a long time as the Papago, or "bean eaters," they were deeded a large portion of their ancestral homeland by the U.S. Bureau of Indian Affairs, and you'll traverse their vast reservation if you travel to Organ Pipe Cactus National Monument and Kitt Peak Observatory.

MAJOR REGIONS

Southern Arizona ranges from the searing deserts surrounding Organ Pipe Cactus National Monument and the town of Yuma in the southwest to the soaring "Sky Islands"—steep hills that rise from the desert floor into the clouds—and rolling grasslands in the southeast.

From the rugged mountain forests to the desert grasslands of Sierra Vista, **Southeast Arizona** is one of the state's most scenic regions. Much of this area is part of Cochise County, dotted with small towns and encompassing six, and part of the seventh, of the 12 mountain ranges that compose the 1.7-million-acre Coronado National Forest.

In the valleys between southeastern Arizona's jagged mountain ranges, you'll discover the 19th-century charm of Bisbee—Queen of the Copper Camps. You can explore the eerie hoodoos and spires of Chiricahua National Monument and walk in the footsteps of the legendary Apaches, who valiantly stood against the U.S. Army until Geronimo's final surrender in 1886. This is also where you can travel through the grassy plains surrounding Sonoita and Elgin—the heart of Arizona's wine country.

A trip to this historically and ecologically important corner of the state will also take you to Fort Huachuca, the oldest continuously operating military installation in the American Southwest; to southeastern Arizona's "Sky Islands," the lush microclimates in the Huachuca mountains, where jaguars roam and migratory tropical birds flit through the canopy; and to historic mining and military towns, the tenacious survivors of the Old West—including Sierra Vista and Tombstone.

The turbulent history of the West is writ large in now-sleepy **Southwest Arizona.** It's home to the Tohono O'odham Reservation—the second-largest in the country, after the Navajo Nation's—and towns such as Ajo, created (and almost undone) by the copper-mining industry, and Nogales, along the U.S.–Mexico border. Yuma, abutting the California border, was a major crossing point of the Colorado River as far back as the time of the conquistadors.

These days people mostly travel *through* Sells, Ajo, and Yuma en route to the closest beaches. During the school year, especially on warm weekends and semester breaks, the 130-mile route from Tucson to Ajo is busy with traffic headed southwest to Puerto Penasco (Rocky Point), Mexico, the closest access to the sea for Arizonans. All summer long, Interstate 8 takes heat-weary Tucsonans and Phoenicians to San Diego, California; Yuma is the midpoint.

Natural attractions are a lure in this starkly scenic region: Organ Pipe Cactus National Monument provides trails for desert hikers and birders, and Buenos Aires and Imperial wildlife refuges—homes to many unusual species—are important destinations for birders and other nature-watchers. Much of the time, however, your only companions will be the low-lying scrub and cactus, and the mesquite, ironwood, and palo verde trees.

Southern Arizona Planner

When to Go

As you might expect, the desert areas are popular in winter, and the cooler mountain areas are more heavily visited in summer. If you're seeking outdoor adventure, spring and fall are the best times to visit this part of the state. The region is in full bloom by late March and early April, and spring and fall are the peaks of birding season.

FESTIVALS AND EVENTS

Cochise Cowboy Poetry and Music Gathering

CULTURAL FESTIVALS | In Sierra Vista, this two-day festival in early February showcases Western culture, history, and folklore through poetry readings, storytelling, and musical performances. Most of the programs are held at Buena High School Performing Arts Center. ☏ 520/417–6960 ⊕ www.cowboypoets.com.

Helldorado Days

FESTIVALS | The third weekend of October, history comes alive in Tombstone with gunfights in the streets, a parade, and an 1880s fashion show. ☏ 520/457–3929 ⊕ www.tombstonehelldoradodays.com.

The Rex Allen Days

FESTIVALS | A rodeo, a country fair (turtle races, anyone?), and Western music and dance fill the first weekend of October each year in Willcox. Watch the parade in historic downtown on Saturday. Rodeo events are held at the Willcox Rodeo Arena, while the fair and evening films and concerts take place at Keiller Park and Willcox Historic Theater, respectively, both in downtown Willcox. ☏ 520/312–9332 ⊕ www.rexallendays.org.

Wings Over Willcox

FESTIVALS | This four-day birding extravaganza the third week in January is highlighted by the morning flights of thousands of wintering sandhill cranes lifting off from the Willcox Playa. ☏ 800/200–2272, 520/384–2272 ⊕ www.wingsoverwillcox.com.

Planning Your Time

The diverse geography of the region and the driving distances between sights require that you strategize when planning your trip. With Tucson as a starting point, the rolling hills and grasslands of Sonoita

and Patagonia are little more than an hour away, as are the underground marvels in Kartchner Caverns (to the southeast) and the starry skies above Kitt Peak Observatory (to the southwest). You can explore the Old West of Tombstone, Bisbee, and the surrounding ghost towns in one day, or at a more leisurely pace in two. If you're heading to the cactus-studded hillsides at Organ Pipe Cactus National Monument, leave yourself at least a full day to explore the monument and the nearby town of Ajo. A trek through the stunning Chiricahua rock formations calls for an overnight stay, since the area is a 2½-hour drive southeast of Tucson.

Getting Here and Around

Tucson is the major starting point for exploring both the southwest region and the southeast corner of the state. Yuma's remote location on the California–Arizona border makes it a destination in itself, or a convenient halfway point on a road trip from Phoenix or Tucson to San Diego, California. Although it can be reached on a lengthy three-hour drive from Tucson or Phoenix, Yuma is also easily accessed through Yuma International Airport.

CAR

A car is essential in Southern Arizona. In fact, the best way to explore southeastern Arizona is on a leisurely road trip. The intricate network of highways in the San Pedro Valley provides looping access to the many scenic vistas and Old West communities, which makes the drive an integral part of the adventure. In stark contrast, a drive through the southwestern portion of the state is filled with long stretches of desert broken infrequently with tiny towns and intermittent gas stations. If you're heading west, pack a lunch, a few games, and plenty of music for entertainment along the way.

The best plan is to fly into Tucson, which is the hub of the area, or Phoenix, which has the most flights. You can rent a car from most national companies at the Tucson or Phoenix airports, and several at Yuma International Airport.

To get to southeastern Arizona from Tucson, take Interstate 10 east; AZ 90 is the turnoff for Kartchner Caverns and Sierra Vista. One mile farther east brings you to the town of Benson, where you can take AZ 80 south to reach Tombstone, Bisbee, and Douglas. If you want to go to Sonoita and Patagonia, or just take a pretty drive, turn off Interstate 10 earlier, at the exit for AZ 83 south; you'll come to Sonoita where the road intersects AZ 82. From here you can either continue southeast to Sierra Vista, head southwest on AZ 82 to Patagonia, or head east to Tombstone. If you're driving to southwestern Arizona, Ajo lies on AZ 85 (north–south) and Yuma is at the junction of Interstate 8 and U.S. 95. For a scenic route to Ajo from Tucson (126 miles), take AZ 86 west to Why and turn north on AZ 85. Yuma is 170 miles from San Diego on Interstate 8 and 300 miles from Las Vegas on U.S. 95.

TRAIN

Amtrak trains run three times a week from Tucson to Benson and Yuma.

Hotels

There are chain hotels throughout the southern region of Arizona, especially along the interstate highways, but why settle for boring basics in this beautiful and historic corner of the state? For the best experience, seek out an old-fashioned room in a historic hotel, a rustic casita at a working cattle ranch, or a spacious suite in a homey bed-and-breakfast. There are a few scattered dude ranches in the sweeping grasslands to the south. It's usually not hard to find a room any time of the year, but keep in mind that prices tend to go up in high season (winter and spring) and down in low season (summer through early fall).

Restaurants

In Southern Arizona, cowboy fare is more common than haute cuisine. There are exceptions, though, especially in the wine region of Sonoita and in the artsy town of Bisbee, both popular for weekend outings from Tucson. And, as one would expect, Mexican food dominates menus.

Hotel and restaurant reviews have been shortened. For full information, visit Fodors.com.

What it Costs			
$	$$	$$$	$$$$
RESTAURANTS			
Under $12	$12–$20	$21–$30	Over $30
HOTELS			
Under $121	$121–$175	$176–$250	Over $250

Tombstone

70 miles southeast of Tucson, 24 miles south of Benson via AZ 80, 28 miles northeast of Sierra Vista via AZ 90.

When prospector Ed Schieffelin headed out in 1877 to seek his fortune along the arid washes of San Pedro Valley, a patrolling soldier warned that all he'd find was his tombstone. Against all odds, his luck held out: he evaded bands of Apaches, braved the harsh desert terrain, and eventually stumbled across a ledge of silver ore. The town of Tombstone was named after the soldier's offhand comment.

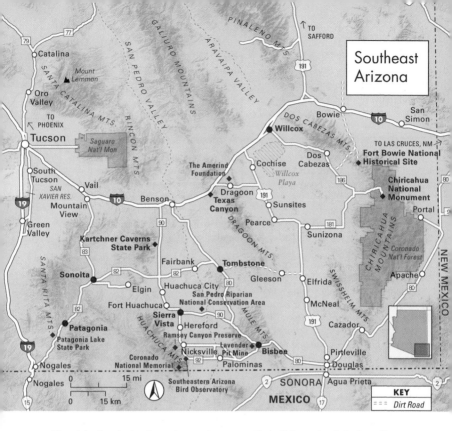

The rich silver lodes from the area's mines attracted a wide mix of fortune seekers ranging from prospectors to prostitutes and gamblers to gunmen. But as the riches continued to pour in, wealthy citizens began importing the best entertainment and culture that silver could purchase. Even though saloons and gambling halls made up two out of every three businesses on Allen Street, the town also claimed the Cochise County seat, a cultural center, and fancy French restaurants. By the early 1880s the noto-rious boomtown was touted as the most cultivated city west of the Mississippi.

In 1881 a shoot-out between the Earp brothers and the Clanton gang ended with three of the "cowboys" (Billy Clan-ton and Tom and Frank McLaury) dead and two of the Earps (Virgil and Morgan) and Doc Holliday wounded. The infamous "gunfight at the O.K. Corral" and the ensuing feud between the Earp brothers and the Clanton gang firmly cemented Tombstone's place in the Wild West— even though the actual course of events is still debated by historians.

All in all, Tombstone's heyday lasted only a decade, but the colorful characters attached to the town's history live on— immortalized on the silver screen in such famous flicks as *Gunfight at the O.K. Corral, Tombstone,* and *Wyatt Earp.* The town's tourist industry parallels Holly-wood hype. As a result, the main drag on Allen Street looks and feels like a movie set (even though most of the buildings are original), complete with gunning des-perados, satin-bedecked saloon girls, and leather-clad cowboys. Today the kitschy "Town Too Tough to Die" attracts a mix of rough-and-tumble bikers, European tourists, and pulp-fiction thrill seekers looking to walk the boardwalks of Tombstone's infamous past.

GETTING HERE AND AROUND

Start your tour of this tiny town and pick up a free map at the visitor center. As you drive into Tombstone on U.S. 80, historic Allen Street, closed to cars, parallels the highway one block west. The visitor center sits in the middle, on the corner of Allen and 4th streets. Park along any side street or at the free lot on 6th Street.

TOURS

Old Tombstone Tours

CARRIAGE TOURS | FAMILY | There's a self-guided walking tour, but the best way to get the lay of the land is to take the 20-minute stagecoach ride around downtown with Old Tombstone Tours. Drivers, dressed in cowboy attire, relate a condensed version of Tombstone's notorious past. The tour also passes by the Tombstone Courthouse and down Toughnut Street, once called Rotten Row because of the lawyers who lived there. ⊠ *429 E. Allen St.* ☏ *520/457–3018* ⊕ *www.oldtombstonetours.net* ⊠ *From $10.*

VISITOR INFORMATION

CONTACTS City of Tombstone Visitor Center. ⊠ *395 E. Allen St., at 4th St.* ☏ *520/457–3929.*

⊙ Sights

The Bird Cage Theater

LOCAL INTEREST | A Tombstone institution, known as the wildest, wickedest night spot between Basin Street and the Barbary Coast, the Bird Cage Theater is a former music hall where Enrico Caruso, Sarah Bernhardt, and Lillian Russell, among others, performed. It was also the site of the longest continuous poker game recorded: the game started when the Bird Cage opened in 1881 and lasted eight years, five months, and three days. Some of the better-known players included Diamond Jim Brady, Adolphus Busch (of brewery fame), and William

Randolph Hearst's father. The cards were dealt round the clock; players had to give a 20-minute notice when they were planning to vacate their seats, because there was always a waiting list of at least 10 people ready to shell out $1,000 (the equivalent of about $30,000 today) to get in. In all, some $10 million changed hands.

When the mines closed in 1889, the Bird Cage was abandoned, but the building has remained in the hands of the same family, who threw nothing out. You can walk on the stage visited by some of the top traveling performers of the time, see the faro table once touched by the legendary gambler Doc Holliday, and pass by the hearse that carried Tombstone's deceased to Boot Hill. The basement, which served as an upscale bordello and gambling hall, still has all the original furnishings and fixtures intact, and you can see the personal belongings left behind by the ladies of the night when the mines closed and they, and their clients, headed for California. Nightly 90-minute ghost tours ($25) are also popular. ⊠ *535 E. Allen St., at 6th St.* ☏ *520/457–3421* ⊕ *www.tombstonebirdcage.com* ⊠ *$14.*

Boot Hill Graveyard

CEMETERY | This graveyard, where the victims of the O.K. Corral shoot-out are buried, is on the northwest corner of town, facing U.S. 80. Chinese names in one section of the "bone orchard" bear testament to the laundry and restaurant workers who came from San Francisco during the height of Tombstone's mining fever. One of the more amusing epitaphs at the cemetery, however, is engraved on the headstone of Wells Fargo agent Lester Moore; it poetically lists the cause of his untimely demise: "Here lies Lester Moore, four slugs from a .44, no les [sic], no more." If you're put off by the commercialism of the place—you enter through a gift shop that sells novelty items in the shape of tombstones—remember that Tombstone itself is the

The Legend of Wyatt Earp

Popularized in dime novels and on the silver screen, the legend of Wyatt Earp follows the American tradition of the tall tale. This larger-than-life hero of the Wild West is cloaked with romance and derring-do. Stripped of the glamour, though, Earp emerges as a man with a checkered past who switched from fugitive to lawman several times during his long life.

Born in 1848, Wyatt Berry Stapp Earp earned renown as the assistant city marshal of Dodge City. Wyatt and his brothers James, Virgil, and Morgan moved to Tombstone in 1879, and it was here that they, along with Wyatt's friend Doc Holliday, made their mark in history. Wyatt ran a gambling concession at the Oriental Saloon, and Virgil became Tombstone's city marshal. When trouble began to brew with the Clanton gang, Virgil recruited Wyatt and Morgan as deputy policemen. The escalating animosity between the "cowboys" and the Earps peaked on October 26, 1881, at the O.K. Corral—a 30-second gunfight that left three of the Clanton gang dead and Morgan and Virgil wounded. Doc Holliday was grazed, but Wyatt walked away from the fight uninjured. And then the real trouble for the Earps began.

In December Virgil was shot and crippled by unknown assailants, and on March 18, 1882, Morgan was shot to death in a pool hall. In retribution, Wyatt went on a bloody vendetta. After the smoke settled, the remaining "cowboys" were dead and Wyatt had left Tombstone for good. He made the rounds of mining camps in the West and up into Alaska, and then settled in California. He died on January 13, 1929. His legend lives on in movies such as *Tombstone* and *Wyatt Earp*.

result of crass acquisition. ✉ *408 U.S. 80* ☎ *520/457–2540* ⊕ *tombstoneboothillgiftshop.com* 🎫 *$3, no credit cards.*

O.K. Corral and Tombstone Historama

MUSEUM | FAMILY | Vincent Price narrates the dramatic version of the town's fascinating past in the "Historama"—a 26-minute multimedia presentation that provides a solid overview. At the adjoining, authentic **O.K. Corral,** the actual spot where the 1881 shootout took place, a recorded voiceover details the gunfight, while life-size figures of the participants stand poised to shoot. A reenactment of the gunfight at the O.K. Corral is held daily at 11, noon, 2, and 3:30. Photographer C. S. Fly, whose studio was next door to the corral, didn't record this bit of history, but Geronimo and his pursuers were among the historic figures he did capture with his camera. Many of his fascinating Old West images and his equipment may be viewed at the **Fly Exhibition Gallery & Studio.** ✉ *326 Allen St., between 3rd and 4th Sts.* ☎ *520/457–3456* ⊕ *www. ok-corral.com* 🎫 *$10 ($6 without gunfight reenactment).*

Rose Tree Inn Museum

MUSEUM | The museum might not look like much from the outside, but the collectibles and tree make this one of the best places to visit in town. Originally a boardinghouse for the Vizina Mining Company and later a popular hotel, the Rose Tree Inn Museum has 1880s period rooms and—its main attraction—a humongous rose tree (hence the name). Covering more than 8,600 square feet, the Lady Banksia rose tree, planted by a homesick bride in 1885, is reported to be the largest of its kind in the world. The best time to see the tree is from

A visit to Tombstone isn't complete without witnessing the re-created gunfight at the O.K. Corral.

mid-March to May, when its tiny white roses bloom. Romantics can purchase a healthy clipping from the tree to plant in their own yards. ⊠ *118 S. 4th St., at Toughnut St.* ☎ *520/457–3326* ⊕ *tombstonerosetree.com* ✉ *$5.*

★ Tombstone Courthouse State Historic Park

MUSEUM | For an introduction to the town's—and the area's—past, visit the Tombstone Courthouse State Historic Park. This redbrick 1882 county courthouse offers exhibits on the area's mining and ranching history and a collection of Wyatt Earp's letters; you can also see the restored 1904 courtroom and district attorney's office. The two-story building housed the Cochise County jail, a courtroom, and public offices until the county seat was moved to Bisbee in 1929. The stately building became the cornerstone of Tombstone's historic-preservation efforts in the 1950s, and was Arizona's first operational state park. ⊠ *219 E. Toughnut St., at 3rd St.* ☎ *520/457–3311* ⊕ *azstateparks.com/tombstone* ✉ *$7.*

Tombstone Epitaph Museum

MUSEUM | You can see the original printing presses for the town's newspaper and watch a video about the production process at the Tombstone Epitaph Museum. The newspaper was founded in 1880 by John P. Clum, a colorful character in his own right, and is still publishing today. You can purchase one of the newspaper's special editions—*The Life and Times of Wyatt Earp, The Life and Times of Doc Holliday,* or *Tombstone's Pioneering Prostitutes.* ⊠ *11 S. 5th St.* ☎ *520/457–2211* ⊕ *www.tombstoneepitaph.com* ✉ *Free.*

🍴 Restaurants

Crystal Palace Saloon

$$ | AMERICAN | If you're looking to wet your whistle or fill up on satisfying portions of steak, salmon, or pizza, stop by the Crystal Palace, where a beautiful mirrored mahogany bar, wrought-iron chandeliers, and tinwork ceilings date back to Tombstone's heyday. Locals come here on weekends to dance to live country-and-western music. **Known for:** historic building; somewhat bawdy saloon atmosphere; burgers and milkshakes. [$] *Average main: $12* ✉ *436 E. Allen St., at 5th St.* ☎ *520/457–3611* 🌐 *www.crystalpalacesaloon.com.*

Longhorn Restaurant
$$ | **AMERICAN** | **FAMILY** | You won't find anything fancy at this friendly eatery just down the street from Big Nose Kate's Saloon, but you will find generous helpings of basic American and Mexican food at decent prices. The menu covers everything from breakfast to dinner with such entrées as omelets, burgers, steaks, tacos, and enchiladas. **Known for:** American and Mexican favorites; kid-friendly menu; hearty breakfasts. [$] *Average main: $12* ✉ *501 E. Allen St.* ☎ *520/457–3405* 🌐 *thelonghornrestaurant.com.*

Hotels

The Tombstone Grand Hotel
$ | **HOTEL** | Nestled into a hill just outside town, this modern two-story property offsets basic rooms with spectacular views of the mountains and desert valley. **Pros:** clean; modern; pool and hot tub. **Cons:** long walk (or three-minute drive) into town; no elevator (request a ground-floor room if you don't want to climb stairs); generic property. [$] *Rooms from: $119* ✉ *580 W. Randolph Way* ☎ *520/457–9507* 🌐 *www.facebook.com/TombstoneGrand* 🛏 *60 rooms* 🍴 *Free breakfast.*

Nightlife

★ **Big Nose Kate's Saloon**
BARS/PUBS | This popular pub was once part of the original Grand Hotel, built in 1881. Saloon girls dressed in red-feather boas encourage visitors to get into the 1880s spirit. Live music and a well-stocked gift shop make this a fun spot for food, drinks, and Wild West amusement. ✉ *417 E. Allen St., between 4th and 5th Sts.* ☎ *520/457–3107* 🌐 *bignosekatestombstone.com.*

Shopping

Several souvenir shops and old-time photo emporiums await in the kitschy collection of stores lining Allen Street.

Silver Hills Trading Co
GIFTS/SOUVENIRS | This store offers everything from Native American jewelry to Southwestern and Old West souvenirs, including replica guns and Tombstone sheriff badges. ✉ *504 E. Allen St.* ☎ *520/457–3335* 🌐 *www.silverhillstrading.com.*

T. Miller's Tombstone Mercantile
ANTIQUES/COLLECTIBLES | Get into the spirit of the Old West by purchasing high-quality, 1880s-style clothing and jewelry, as well as Western art, cowboy hats, and spurs. Refuel for more shopping or shoot-outs with a root beer float from their adjoining ice cream and sandwich shop. ✉ *530 E. Allen St.* ☎ *520/457–2405* 🌐 *www.tombstonemercantileco.com.*

Bisbee

24 miles southeast of Tombstone on AZ 80.

Like Tombstone, Bisbee was a mining boomtown, but its wealth was in copper, not silver, and its success continued much longer. The gnarled Mule Mountains aren't as impressive as some of the other mountain ranges in Southern Arizona, but their rocky canyons concealed one of the richest mineral sites in the world.

Jack Dunn, a scout with Company C from Fort Huachuca, first discovered an outcropping of rich ore here while chasing the Apaches in 1877. By 1900 more than 20,000 people lived in the crowded canyons around the Bisbee mines. Phelps Dodge purchased all the major mines by the Great Depression, and mining continued until 1975, when the mines were closed for good. In less than 100 years of mining, the area surrounding Bisbee yielded more than $6.1 billion of mineral wealth.

Once known as the Queen of the Copper Camps, Bisbee was rediscovered in the 1980s by burned-out city dwellers, and the cool but scruffy vibe, hilly terrain, and Victorian architecture conjure up a sort of 1960s San Francisco scene. The locals are an interesting mix of retired miners and their families, aging hippie jewelry makers, and enterprising restaurateurs and boutique owners from all over the country. Milder temperatures (about 10 to 15 degrees lower than Tucson), plentiful lodging (quaint inns, cottage rentals, and vintage trailers), and the town's history and natural beauty make for a rewarding visit.

GETTING HERE AND AROUND

If you want to head straight into town from AZ 80, get off at the Brewery Gulch interchange. You can cross under the highway, taking Main, Commerce, or Brewery Gulch streets, all of which intersect at the large, free public parking lot. Most restaurants and shops are in an easily navigated 4-to 5-block area. This includes Main Street, lined with appealing art galleries, antiques stores, crafts shops, boutiques, and restaurants—many in well-preserved turn-of-the-20th-century brick buildings. To reach the Lavender Pit Mine, drive a half mile south on AZ 80. A little farther south, at the roundabout, take the turnoff for the Warren district to see where the mining managers built beautiful mansions.

TOURS

Lavender Jeep Tours

DRIVING TOURS | Run by Bisbee natives, these tours range from a one-hour ride around greater Bisbee to a six-hour tour that includes neighboring ghost towns. Driver guides regale visitors with fascinating tales while winding through the hills of historic Bisbee and the surrounding region. ⊠ *Copper Queen Hotel, 11 Howell Ave.* ☏ *520/432–5369* ⊕ *www. lavenderjeeptours.com* ✉ *From $50.*

VISITOR INFORMATION

CONTACTS **Bisbee Visitor Center.** ⊠ *5 Copper Queen Plaza* ✢ *south side of the Bisbee Mining and Historical Museum* ☏ *520/432–3554* ⊕ *www.discoverbisbee.com.*

⊙ Sights

Bisbee Mining and Historical Museum

MUSEUM | The redbrick structure this museum is housed in was built in 1897 to serve as the Copper Queen Consolidated Mining Offices. The rooms today are filled with colorful exhibits, photographs, and artifacts that offer a glimpse into the everyday life of Bisbee's early mining community. The exhibit *Bisbee: Urban Outpost on the Frontier* paints a fascinating portrait of how this "Shady Lady" of a mining town transformed into a true mini urban center. Upstairs, the *Digging In* exhibit shows you everything you ever wanted to know about copper mining, including what it felt and sounded like in a mining car. This was the first rural museum in the United States to become a member of the Smithsonian Institution Affiliations Program, and it tells a story you can take with you as you wander through Bisbee's funky streets. ⊠ *5 Copper Queen Plaza* ☏ *520/432–7071* ⊕ *bisbeemuseum.org* ✉ *$8.*

Brewery Gulch

HISTORIC SITE | A short street running north–south, Brewery Gulch is adjacent to the Copper Queen Hotel. In the old days the brewery housed here allowed the dregs of the beer that was being brewed to flow down the street and into the gutter. Nowadays this narrow road is home to Bisbee's nightlife. ⊠ *Bisbee.*

Copper Queen Hotel

BUILDING | Built a century ago and still in operation, the Copper Queen Hotel has hosted some famous people over the years; General John "Black Jack" Pershing, John Wayne, Theodore Roosevelt, and mining executives from all over the world made this their home away from home. Though the restaurant fare is basic, the outdoor bar area is a great spot for enjoying a margarita and people-watching. The hotel also allegedly hosts three resident ghosts; the journal at the front desk contains descriptions of guests' encounters. ⊠ *11 Howell Ave.* ⚓ *behind the Mining and Historical Museum* ☎ *520/432–2216* ⊕ *www. copperqueen.com.*

Copper Queen Mine Underground Tour

MINE | FAMILY | For a lesson in mining history, take a tour led by Bisbee's retired copper miners, who are wont to embellish their spiel with tales from their mining days. The 60-minute tours (you can't enter the mine at any other time) go into the shaft via a small open train, like those the miners rode when the mine was active. Before you climb aboard, you're outfitted in miner's garb—a safety vest and a hard hat with a light that runs off a battery pack. You'll travel thousands of feet into the mine, up a grade of 30 feet (not down, as many visitors expect). The mine is less than ½ mile to the east of the Lavender Pit, across AZ 80 from downtown at the Brewery Gulch interchange. Reservations are suggested. ⊠ *478 N. Dart Rd.* ☎ *520/432–2071, 866/432–2071* ⊕ *www.queenminetour. com* ☕ *$14.*

Lavender Pit Mine

MINE | About ¼ mile after AZ 80 intersects with AZ 92, you can pull off the highway into a gravel parking lot for a view of the Lavender Pit Mine, a huge hole left by the copper miners. Though the piles of "tailings," or waste, are lavender-hued, the pit's namesake is actually Harrison (Harry) Lavender, the engineer largely responsible for transforming Bisbee's rock into commercial copper ore. Arizona's largest pit mine yielded some 94 million tons of ore before mining activity came to a halt. ⊠ *AZ 80.*

🍴 Restaurants

Bisbee's Table

$$ | AMERICAN | You might not expect diversity at a place with a reputation for having the best burger in town, but this restaurant delivers with salads, sandwiches, pasta, salmon, steaks, and ribs. The dining room, built to resemble an old train depot, fills up fast on weekends. **Known for:** healthy comfort food; gluten-free options; vibrant atmosphere. $ *Average main: $17* ⊠ *2 Copper Queen Plaza* ☎ *520/432–6788* ⊕ *www.bisbeetable.com.*

★ Café Roka

$$$ | MODERN AMERICAN | This is the deserved darling of both the hip Bisbee crowd and foodies from all over. The constantly changing, locally sourced evening menu is not extensive, but whatever you order—wild yellow fin tuna, roasted duck, rack of lamb—will be wonderful. **Known for:** best dining in the region; excellent wine list; sophisticated yet relaxed vibe. $ *Average main: $26* ⊠ *35 Main St.* ☎ *520/432–5153* ⊕ *caferoka.com* ☾ *Closed Mon.–Wed. No lunch.*

☕ Coffee and Quick Bites

★ Patisserie Jacqui

$ | FRENCH | What's a nice little Parisian bakery doing in southeastern Arizona? Churning out perfect sweet and savory croissants, eclairs, tarts, and cookies every Friday and Saturday for the lucky folks who know about the petite pink shop at the upper end of Main Street. **Known for:** fancy French pastries; flaky croissants; quick stop for breakfast, picnics, and dessert. $ *Average main: $5* ⊠ *91 Main St.* ☎ *612/770-4247* ⊕ *patisserie-jacqui.square.site* ☾ *Closed Sun.–Thurs.*

🛏 Hotels

Canyon Rose Suites

$$ | HOTEL | Steps from the heart of downtown, this all-suites inn includes seven pretty and spacious units of varying size, all with hardwood floors, 10-foot ceilings, and fully equipped kitchens. **Pros:** quiet, yet just off Main Street; well-equipped, attractive suites; easy parking behind building. **Cons:** no common area; no elevator (guest rooms are on second floor); some street noise. **$** *Rooms from: $129* ✉ *27 Subway St.* ☎ *520/432–5098* ⊕ *www.canyonrose.com* ⇨ *7 rooms* ⦿ *No meals.*

Letson Loft Hotel

$$ | B&B/INN | This beautifully restored boutique hotel is perched above the galleries and shops of Main Street and well appointed with upscale comforts. **Pros:** luxurious amenities; comfy, pillow-top mattresses; elegant breakfasts. **Cons:** some noise from Main Street below in front rooms; no elevator (all guest rooms are upstairs); no children under age 12. **$** *Rooms from: $150* ✉ *26 Main St.* ☎ *520/432–3210* ⊕ *www.letsonlofthotel. com* ⇨ *8 rooms* ⦿ *Free breakfast.*

School House Inn B&B

$ | B&B/INN | Each of the rooms at this quirky 1918 schoolhouse-turned-B&B is brimming with character and themed in a different "subject"—history, music, library, reading, arithmetic, art, geography, and the principal's office—reflected in the decor. **Pros:** historic property; great views; hearty vegetarian breakfast. **Cons:** a mile walk or short drive into town; children under 10 only with owner's permission; somewhat worn. **$** *Rooms from: $89* ✉ *818 Tombstone Canyon Rd.* ☎ *520/432–2996* ⊕ *www.schoolhouseinnbb.com* ⇨ *9 rooms* ⦿ *Free breakfast.*

★ Shady Dell Trailer Court

$ | RENTAL | For a blast from the past, stay in one of the funky vintage aluminum trailers at this trailer park south of town, where accommodations range from a 1952 10-foot homemade unit to a 1951 33-foot Royal Mansion. **Pros:** unique and fun (how many hip vintage trailer-park hotels are there?); cheap; Dot's Diner (on-site) is great for a quick bite. **Cons:** no children under 12, except with prior approval; walking to the public restrooms in the middle of the night (some units don't have a toilet; some have toilet but no shower); drive into town. **$** *Rooms from: $75* ✉ *1 Douglas Rd.* ☎ *520/432–3567* ⊕ *www.theshadydell.com* ⇨ *10 trailers* ⦿ *No meals.*

🍸 Nightlife

St. Elmo Bar

BARS/PUBS | Established in 1902, the St. Elmo Bar is decorated with an assortment of the past and present, including a 1922 official map of Cochise County that hangs next to a neon beer sign. Locals and tourists hang out here beginning at lunchtime. The jukebox plays during the week, but on weekends live bands rock the house with sounds ranging from rock to rhythm-and-blues. ✉ *36 Brewery Ave.* ☎ *520/432–5578.*

Stock Exchange Saloon

BARS/PUBS | Located in the historic Muheim building, the beautifully renovated Stock Exchange Saloon serves food along with libations, and has a pool table, shuffleboard, and—on many nights—live music ranging from local jazz, rock and blues to national acts (the place has great acoustics). The 1914 stock board still hangs on the wall. ✉ *15 Brewery Ave.* ☎ *520/432–1333* ⊕ *stockexchangesaloon. com.*

🛍 Shopping

Belleza Gallery

ART GALLERIES | This fine-art gallery is owned and operated by Bisbee's Women's Transition Project, which aids homeless women and their children. Belleza features the work of local and national artists, as well as a line of wood

Does southern Arizona look familiar? The TV series *Little House on the Prairie* was filmed near the area.

Adirondack furniture made by women receiving assistance from the program. The gallery's commission from furniture sales goes directly into funding the Transition Project. ⊠ *23 Main St.* ☏ *520/432–5877* ⊕ *bellezagallery.org.*

55 Main Gallery

ART GALLERIES | Although many artist studios, galleries, and boutiques in historic buildings line Main Street, which runs though Tombstone Canyon, 55 Main Gallery is one of several noteworthy galleries selling contemporary work at a range of prices along the main drag. ⊠ *55 Main St.* ☏ *520/432–4694.*

Killer Bee Guy

FOOD/CANDY | A trip to Bisbee wouldn't be complete without a stop at the tiny shop of beekeeper Reed Booth. Sample his amazing array of honeys, honey butters, and mustards, and pick up some killer honey recipes. ⊠ *20 Main St.* ☏ *520/432–8016* ⊕ *www.killerbeeguy.com.*

Old Bisbee Roasters

FOOD/CANDY | In Peddlers Alley, grab a free cup of freshly brewed espresso from Old Bisbee Roasters, then buy some equally fresh-roasted, organic beans, bought in small batches from small, sustainable farms, at their shop down the road. ⊠ *7 Naco Rd.* ☏ *866/432–5063* ⊕ *oldbisbeeroasters.com.*

★ Óptimo Custom Panama Hatworks

JEWELRY/ACCESSORIES | Custom, hand-woven Panama hats, as well as works of beaver, hare, and rabbit fur-felt, are what this nationally renowned shop is known for. It's also where people get their historical hats cleaned and restored. ⊠ *47 Main St.* ☏ *520/432–4544* ⊕ *www.optimohatworks.com.*

Sonoita

55 miles northwest of Bisbee on AZ 90 to AZ 82, 34 miles southeast of Tucson on I–10 to AZ 83, 57 miles west of Tombstone on AZ 82.

The grasslands surrounding modern-day Sonoita captured the attention of early Spanish explorers, including Father Eusebio Francisco Kino, who mapped and claimed the area in 1701. The Tuscan-like beauty of the rolling, often green hills framed by jutting mountain ranges has been noticed by Hollywood filmmakers. As you drive along AZ 83 and AZ 82 you might recognize the scenery from movies filmed here, including *Oklahoma* and *Tin Cup*.

Today this region is known for its family-run vineyards and wineries, as well as for its ranching history.

Sonoita's "town," at the junction of AZ 83 and AZ 82 (known by locals as "the crossroads"), consists of just a few restaurants, an inn, and a gas station; it's the dozen or so wineries nearby that draw the crowds. There are often weekend events at the wineries, including live jazz concerts and the Blessing of the Vines in spring. Harvest time—late summer and early fall—is also a good time to visit, when you can escape the heat of Tucson and enjoy the countryside, sample some of Arizona's vintages, and chat with local vintners.

GETTING HERE AND AROUND

To explore the wineries of Southern Arizona, head either south on AZ 83 from Sonoita or east on Elgin Road. Many of the growers are in and around the tiny village of Elgin, a few miles southeast of Sonoita. The best times to visit the vineyards are Friday through Sunday, when most are open for tastings (though a few are open daily). To plot your course through this section of Arizona's wine country, check out the Sonoita map from Arizona Wine Growers Association (⊕ *azwinegrowersassociation.com*).

◉ Sights

★ AZ Hops & Vines

WINERY/DISTILLERY | FAMILY | With interesting varietals and sangrias, a hip vibe, and bottomless bowls of Cheetos to accompany tastings, AZ Hops & Vines rocks the Sonoita wine-tour scene. This spunky, women-owned and family-friendly winery boasts outdoor seating, games, and a petting zoo. ⊠ *3450 AZ 82* ☎ *301/237–6556* ⊕ *azhopsandvines.com.*

★ Callaghan Vineyards

WINERY/DISTILLERY | This vineyard produces some of the best wine in Arizona. Its Buena Suerte 2015 ("good luck" in Spanish) is a favorite, and Caitlin's is considered one of the top wines in the United States. ⊠ *336 Elgin Rd., Elgin* ☎ *520/455–5322* ⊕ *callaghanvineyards. com* ⊙ *Closed Mon.–Wed.*

Dos Cabezas WineWorks

WINERY/DISTILLERY | Award-winning reds and whites (and a sparkling rosé) can be sampled here. They also rent a couple of suites to stay in after your tasting tour. ⊠ *3248 AZ 82, near AZ 83* ☎ *520/455–5141* ⊕ *www.doscabezas.com* ⊙ *Closed Mon.–Wed.*

Kief-Joshua Vineyards

WINERY/DISTILLERY | Winemaker Kief Manning uses the traditional methods of open fermentation and barrel aging he learned in Australia. You can get a tour of the vineyards or a private, in-depth tasting if you call ahead. ⊠ *370 Elgin Rd., Elgin* ☎ *520/455–5582* ⊕ *kj-vineyards. com* ⊙ *Closed Mon.–Wed.*

Lightning Ridge Cellars

WINERY/DISTILLERY | You might think you're in Italy when you visit this Tuscan-style building perched on a pretty hillside. The wide porch with Adirondack chairs and a bocce ball court invite you to linger awhile after sampling Italian varietals like Sangiovese and Primitivo. ⊠ *2368 AZ 83, Elgin* ☎ *520/455–5383* ⊕ *lightningridge-cellars.com* ⊙ *Closed Mon.–Thurs.*

Arizona Wineries: A Grape Escape

"Arizona wine country" may sound odd, but the soil and climate in the Santa Cruz Valley, southeast of Tucson, are ideal for growing grapes. Wine grapes first took root in the region 400 years ago, when the Spanish missionaries planted the first vines of "mission" grapes for the production of sacramental wine. But it wasn't until the 1970s that the first commercial *Vitis vinifera* grapes were planted here as part of an agricultural experiment. The hardier vines, such as Syrah, Grenache, and Malvasia, seem to tolerate the summer heat and retain good acidity.

Connoisseurs have debated the merits of the wines produced in this area since 1974, but tour some of the region's wineries and decide for yourself. **AZ Hops & Vines, Callaghan Vineyards, Dos Cabezas Wineworks, Flying Leap Vineyards, Kief-Joshua Vineyards, Lightning Ridge Cellars, Rune Wines, Sonoita Vineyards,** and **Hannah's Hill Vineyard** all have something

to tantalize the taste buds. Some vintners proudly feature estate wines, which means they grow the grapes, process them, and bottle the wine at the vineyard. You can purchase a wine glass with tastings ($10–$15) at the first tasting room you choose, then take it with you to any of the other wineries for a reduced tasting fee.

Farther east, notable vineyards have sprung up around Willcox, which now has several tasting rooms as well as the region's only grape-crushing facility. Actually, most of the grapes grown for Arizona wines are grown just south of Willcox. Elsewhere in the state, a few vineyards near Sedona, along lower Oak Creek and in the neighboring town of Cottonwood, are garnering attention as well. ⇨ *See the listings in this chapter and Chapter 5, North-Central Arizona, for contact info.* Maps of the tasting rooms are available from ⊕ *azwinegrowersasso-ciation.com.*

Sonoita Vineyards

WINERY/DISTILLERY | This vineyard, known for its high-quality reds, was the first commercial vineyard in Arizona, planted in the early 1970s as an experiment by Dr. Gordon Dutt, former agriculture professor at the University of Arizona. It's still going strong with Gordon's granddaughter, Lori, at the helm. ⊠ *290 Elgin-Canelo Rd., Elgin* ☎ *520/455–5893* ⊕ *www.sonoitavineyards.com.*

Village of Elgin Winery

WINERY/DISTILLERY | One of the largest producers of wines in the state is home to Four Monkeys wines and Tombstone Red, which the winemaker claims is "great with scorpion, tarantula, and rattlesnake meat." Sample craft spirits (rum, whiskey,

and brandy) next door at Elgin Distillery. ⊠ *471 Elgin Rd., Elgin* ☎ *520/455–9309* ⊕ *www.elginwines.com.*

Wilhelm Family Vineyards

WINERY/DISTILLERY | This producer of seven red varietals, including a homegrown Syrah and Tempranillo, offers tastings Friday–Sunday 11–4 and by appointment. ⊠ *21 Mountain Ranch Dr., Elgin* ☎ *520/455–9291* ⊕ *wilhelmvineyards.com.*

🍴 Restaurants

Copper Brothel Brewery

$$ | AMERICAN | If you're looking for a lively place to grab a bite when touring the wineries—or if you prefer sampling craft beers to wines—you can find it at

the Copper Brothel. The bar fare, such as fish-and-chips, tacos, and pulled pork sandwiches (smoked on-site), is way above average; enjoy it as you watch sports on TV or sit on the patio and drink in the scenery. **Known for:** craft beers; excellent barbecue; friendly pub atmosphere. $ *Average main: $14* ✉ *3112 AZ 83* ☎ *520/405-6721* ⊕ *copperbrothel-brewery.com.*

Steak Out Restaurant & Saloon

$$ | **AMERICAN** | A frontier-style design and a weathered-wood exterior help to create the mood at this Western restaurant and bar known for its tasty margaritas and live country music played on weekend evenings. Built and owned by the family that operates the Sonoita Inn next door, the restaurant serves mesquite-grilled steaks, ribs, chicken, and fish. **Known for:** good-quality cowboy fare; the only nightlife in town (pool tables and live music some nights). $ *Average main: $20* ✉ *3235 AZ 82* ☎ *520/455–5205* ⊕ *www. azsteakout.com* ⊘ *No lunch weekdays.*

🛏 Hotels

La Hacienda de Sonoita

$$ | **B&B/INN** | Down a private dirt road just a stone's throw from the wineries of Sonoita sits this charming bed-and-breakfast designed in contemporary Southwest style. **Pros:** convenient to wineries; full breakfast (including homemade biscuits); friendly hosts. **Cons:** smaller rooms; may be too sedate for some. $ *Rooms from: $125* ✉ *34 Swanson Rd.* ☎ *520/455–5308* ⊕ *haciendasonoita.com* ⮑ *4 rooms* ⦿*| Free breakfast.*

Sonoita Inn

$$ | **B&B/INN** | The former owner of this small hotel also owned the Triple Crown–winning racehorse Secretariat, and the inn, built to resemble a huge barn, celebrates the horse's career with photos, racing programs, and press clippings. **Pros:** cheery equestrian decor; walking distance to restaurants; some

rooms have mountain views. **Cons:** some road noise; no elevator (but some ground-floor and accessible rooms); handy but less scenic location. $ *Rooms from: $129* ✉ *3243 AZ 82, near AZ 83* ☎ *520/455–5935* ⊕ *www.sonoitainn.com* ⮑ *18 rooms* ⦿*| Free breakfast.*

Patagonia

12 miles southwest of Sonoita via AZ 82, 18 miles northeast of Nogales via AZ 82.

Served by a spur of the Atchison, Topeka, and Santa Fe Railroad, Patagonia was a shipping center for cattle and ore. The town declined after the railroad departed in 1962, and the old depot is now the town hall. Today, with the recent migration of artists and health-conscious urban refugees, art galleries, natural food stores, and yoga/Pilates studios coexist with real Western saloons in this tiny, tree-lined village in the Patagonia Mountains. The surrounding region is a prime birding destination, with more than 275 species of birds found around Sonoita Creek.

GETTING HERE AND AROUND

As you approach Patagonia on AZ 82 from either direction, the galleries and restaurants are along the highway (called Naugle Avenue through town) and one block south on McKeown Avenue. There's plenty of street parking.

VISITOR INFORMATION

CONTACTS Patagonia Visitor Center. ✉ *317 McKeown Ave., at 3rd Ave.* ☎ *520/394–7750* ⊕ *www.visitskyislands.com.*

⊙ Sights

Nature Conservancy Patagonia–Sonoita Creek Preserve

NATURE PRESERVE | At this 1,350-acre preserve, cottonwood-willow riparian habitat is protected along the Patagonia–Sonoita Creek watershed. More than 275 bird species have been sighted here, along with white-tailed deer, javelina, coatimundi (raccoonlike animals native to the region), desert tortoise, and snakes. There's a self-guided nature trail, and guided walks are occasionally offered. The admission fee is good for seven days. ✉ *Blue Haven Rd.* ✣ *From Patagonia, make right on 4th Ave.; at stop sign, turn left onto Blue Haven Rd.* ☎ *520/394–2400* 🌐 *www.nature.org/arizona* 🎟 *$8* ⏲ *Closed Mon. and Tues.*

Patagonia Lake State Park

NATIONAL/STATE PARK | **FAMILY** | Five miles south of town, this is the spot for water sports, birding, picnicking, and camping. Formed by the damming of Sonoita Creek, the 265-acre reservoir lures anglers with its largemouth bass, crappie, bluegill, and catfish; it's stocked with rainbow trout in the wintertime. You can rent rowboats, paddleboats, canoes, and fishing gear at the marina. Most swimmers head for Boulder Beach. The adjoining Sonoita Creek State Natural Area is home to giant cottonwoods, willows, sycamores, and mesquites; nesting black hawks; and endangered species. From mid-October to mid-April, rangers offer guided birding and discovery tours by pontoon boat ($7) on weekends at 9, 10:15, and 11:30 (call visitor center to sign up) and free guided bird walks during the week. ✉ *400 Lake Patagonia Rd.* ☎ *520/287–6965, 520/287–2791 for visitor center* 🌐 *azstateparks.com/patagonia-lake* 🎟 *$15 per vehicle weekdays, $20 weekends.*

🍴 Restaurants

Gathering Grounds

$ | **CAFÉ** | This colorful café and espresso bar, which also doubles as an art gallery featuring local artists, serves healthful breakfasts and soups, salads, and sandwiches through the late afternoon. Vegetarian options, like vegan burritos and spinach pesto wraps, are plentiful. **Known for:** good coffee; veggie and gluten-free items; ice cream. [$] *Average main: $10* ✉ *319 McKeown Ave.* ☎ *520/394–2009* 🌐 *www.gatheringgroundsaz.com* ⏲ *No dinner.*

Velvet Elvis Pizza Company

$$ | **PIZZA** | There aren't too many places where you can enjoy a pizza heaped with organic veggies; a crisp salad of organic greens tossed with homemade dressing; freshly pressed juice (try the beet-, apple-, and lime-juice concoction); and creative cocktails while surrounded by images of Elvis *and* the Virgin Mary. The owner uses a 1930s dough recipe for the pizza's delightful whole wheat crust; a gluten-free, almond-based pizza crust and bountiful salads entice those who may seek a low-carb alternative. **Known for:** excellent pizzas; lively atmosphere; best dinner in town. [$] *Average main: $14* ✉ *292 Naugle Ave.* ☎ *520/394–0069* 🌐 *velvetelvispizzapatagonia.com* ⏲ *Closed Mon.–Wed.*

🛏 Hotels

Circle Z Ranch

$$$$ | **RESORT** | **FAMILY** | Rimmed by giant sycamore, ash, and cottonwood trees and surrounded by the Patagonia–Sonoita Creek Preserve, this seasonal guest ranch with plenty of activities served as a setting in the movie *Red River* and in several episodes of *Gunsmoke*. Rooms in the adobe-style buildings have hardwood floors, area rugs, and antique Monterey pine chests. **Pros:** excellent dude-ranch experience in a lush (rather than desert) setting; friendly staff and guests; satisfying for beginner through advanced riders. **Cons:** four-night minimum stay; no transportation provided from airport; BYOB. [$] *Rooms from: $355* ✉ *1476 AZ 82* ✣ *4 miles southwest of town* ☎ *520/394–2525, 888/854–2525* 🌐 *circlez.com* ⏲ *Closed May–Oct.* 🛏 *24 rooms* 🍽 *All-inclusive.*

Duquesne House Bed & Breakfast/Gallery

$$ | **B&B/INN** | Built as a miners' boardinghouse at the turn of the 20th century, this adobe home has rooms painted in pastel Southwest colors, lovingly and whimsically detailed by a local artist, and decorated with hand-stitched quilts and

Did You Know?

Patagonia Lake is a picturesque place to fish, camp, water ski, and picnic in Southeastern Arizona.

Mexican folk art. **Pros:** quiet location only a couple of blocks from town; cheerful, contemporary interior; large suites. **Cons:** breakfast isn't served Tuesday–Thursday (but rates are lower); historic home means older plumbing; some may prefer a countryside setting. [$] *Rooms from: $140* ✉ *357 Duquesne Ave.* ☎ *520/394–2732* 🌐 *www.theduquesnehouse.com* 🛏 *4 rooms* 🍴 *Free breakfast.*

Shopping

Global Arts Gallery
ART GALLERIES | Everything from Native American jewelry and local art and antiques to Middle Eastern rugs and musical instruments is showcased at Global Arts. ✉ *315 McKeown Ave.* ☎ *520/394–0077* 🌐 *www.globalartsgallery.com.*

★ High Spirits Flutes
MUSIC STORES | Odell Borg's Native American–style flutes can be admired, and purchased, at his factory store; just call first to make sure someone's there to open the showroom. In addition to being beautiful, the flutes' five-note pentatonic scale makes them easy to learn to play. ✉ *714 Red Rock Ave., off Harshaw Rd.* ☎ *520/394–2900* 🌐 *highspirits.com.*

Mesquite Grove Gallery
ART GALLERIES | Regina Medley, a talented local painter, weaver, and jewelry maker, markets her lovely wares here, along with the work of other regional artists. ✉ *375 McKeown Ave.* ☎ *520/400–7230* 🌐 *www.reginamedley.com* 🕒 *Closed Sun. and Mon.*

Patagonia Trading Post
ART GALLERIES | This gallery features a thoughtful selection of jewelry, paintings, photography, quilts, and pottery by more than 60 local artists. High Spirits wooden flutes are also sold here. ✉ *317 McKeown Ave.* ☎ *520/394–2100* 🌐 *www.patagoniatradingpost.com* 🕒 *Closed Tues.–Thurs.*

Sierra Vista

42 miles east of Patagonia, 70 miles southeast of Tucson, 30 miles southeast of Sonoita, via AZ 82 to AZ 90.

A characterless military town on the outskirts of Fort Huachuca, Sierra Vista is nonetheless a good base from which to explore the more scenic areas that surround it—and at 4,620 feet above sea level, the whole area has a year-round temperate climate. There are quite a few fast-food and chain restaurants for your basic dining needs, and more than 1,100 rooms in area hotels, motels, and B&Bs offer shelter for the night.

Fort Huachuca, headquarters of the army's Global Information Systems Command, is the last of the great Western forts still in operation. It dates back to 1877, when the Buffalo Soldiers (yes, Bob Marley fans—*those* Buffalo Soldiers), the first all-Black regiment in the U.S. forces, came to aid settlers battling invaders from Mexico, indigenous tribes reluctant to give up their homelands, and assorted American desperadoes on the lam from the law back East.

GETTING HERE AND AROUND

The most direct route to Sierra Vista from Interstate 10 is a straight shot south on AZ 90 (about 30 miles). If you're not going to Fort Huachuca, take a left on the Route 90 bypass to reach the shopping centers, most of the chain motels, and the intersection of AZ 92, which takes you to Ramsey Canyon and Coronado National Memorial. If you're going to the fort, stay on AZ 90 and the fort will be on your right. From here, Fry Boulevard will lead you west through town to the AZ 92.

Sights

Coronado National Memorial

NATIONAL/STATE PARK | FAMILY | Those driving to Coronado National Memorial, dedicated to Francisco Vásquez de Coronado, will see many of the same stunning vistas of Arizona and Mexico the conquistador saw when he trod this route in 1540 seeking the mythical Seven Cities of Cibola. Hikers come here for both the excellent views and the opportunity to walk the 1-mile Yaqui Trail, the southernmost leg of the 800-mile Arizona Trail, that ends at the Mexico border. The views are excellent atop the nearly 7,000-foot Coronado Peak; to get there you drive (or walk) a little more than 3 miles up a dirt road from the visitor center to Montezuma Pass Overlook, and then go another ½ mile on foot only. There's also Crest Trail, a difficult but rewarding 12-mile round trip to Miller Peak, the highest point in the Huachuca Mountains (9,466 feet).

Kids ages 5 to 12 can participate in the memorial's Junior Ranger program, explore Coronado Cave, and dress up in replica Spanish armor.

The turnoff for the monument is 16 miles south of Sierra Vista on AZ 92; the visitor center is 5 miles farther. ⊠ *4101 E. Montezuma Canyon Rd., Hereford* ☎ *520/366–5515* ⊕ *www.nps.gov/coro* ◻ *Free.*

Fort Huachuca Museum

MUSEUM | Three miles from the fort's main gate are the Fort Huachuca museums. The late-19th-century bachelor officers' quarters and the annex across the street provide a record of military life on the frontier and the Buffalo Soldiers regiments, most of whom were based here. More often than not, you'll be sharing space with new cadets learning about the history of this far-flung outpost. Motion sensors activate odd little sound bites in the multimedia experience. Another half block south, the **U.S. Army Intelligence Museum** focuses on American intelligence operations from the Apache Scouts through Desert Storm. Code machines, codebooks, decoding devices, and other intelligence-gathering equipment are on display. You need a driver's license or other photo identification to get on base. ■ TIP→ **International visitors need to call at least 3 weeks in advance to arrange for a military escort.** ⊠ *Grierson Ave. and Boyd St., off AZ 90, Fort Huachuca* ✛ *West of Sierra Vista* ☎ *520/533–3638* ⊕ *www.army.mil* ◻ *Free* ☉ *Closed Sun. and Mon.*

★ Ramsey Canyon Preserve

NATURE PRESERVE | Managed by the Nature Conservancy, Ramsey Canyon Preserve marks the convergence of two mountain and desert systems: this spot is the northernmost limit of the Sierra Madre and the southernmost limit of the Rockies, and it's at the edge of the Chihuahuan and Sonoran deserts. Visitors to this world-famous bird-watching hot spot train their binoculars skyward hoping to catch a glimpse of some of the preserve's most notable inhabitants. Painted redstarts nest here, and 14 magnificent species of hummingbird, the jewels of this pristine habitat, congregate from spring through autumn. Even for nonbirders, the beauty of the canyon makes this a destination in its own right. The rare stream-fed, sycamore-maple riparian corridor provides a lush contrast to the desert highlands at the base of the mountains. Guided hikes along the half-mile trail begin at 9 Monday, Thursday, and Saturday from March through November. Stop at the visitor center for maps and books on the area's natural history, flora, and fauna. Admission is good for one week. ⊠ *27 Ramsey Canyon Rd., Hereford* ☎ *520/335–8740* ⊕ *www.nature.org/arizona* ◻ *$8* ☉ *Closed Tues. and Wed.*

Ramsey Canyon Preserve is known for its lush landscape, hiking trails, and variety of flora and fauna.

San Pedro Riparian
National Conservation Area

NATURE PRESERVE | The San Pedro River, partially rerouted underground by an 1887 earthquake, may not look like much, but it sustains an impressive array of flora and fauna and makes for great hiking and birding. To maintain this fragile creekside ecosystem, 56,000 acres along the river were designated a protected riparian area in 1988. More than 350 species of birds come here, as well as 82 mammal species and 45 reptiles and amphibians. Animals from long ago—including woolly mammoths and mastodons—also make their former presence here known through the area's massive fossil pits; in fact, many of the huge skeletons in Washington's Smithsonian Institute and New York's Museum of Natural History came from here. As evidenced by a number of small, unexcavated ruins, the migratory tribes who passed through thousands of years later also found this valley hospitable, in part because of its many useful plants.

Information, guided tours and bird walks, books, and gifts are available from the volunteer staff at San Pedro House, a visitor center operated by Friends of the San Pedro River (⊕ *sanpedroriver.org/ wpfspr*). ⊠ *San Pedro House, 9800 E. AZ 90* ☎ *520/508–4445, 520/439–6400 Sierra Vista BLM office* ⊕ *www.blm.gov/ visit/san-pedro* ✉ *Free.*

★ Southeastern Arizona Bird Observatory

ECOTOURISM | This nonprofit organization offers guided birding tours, educational programs, and detailed information about birding in the region. Tours range from morning walks and evening "owl prowls" to one-week hummingbird trips. Get up close at feeding stations for hummingbirds and many other species at their Ash Canyon Bird Sanctuary. Sign up to observe a hummingbird banding session April–September. ⊠ *Ash Canyon Bird Sanctuary, 5255 E. Spring Rd., Hereford* ⊹ *off AZ 92* ☎ *520/432–1388* ⊕ *www. sabo.org.*

🍴 Restaurants

Tandem
$$$ | **AMERICAN** | Locals and visitors head to this unpretentious yet sophisticated bistro, where Chef Patrick serves French-inspired comfort food for the American palette at lunch, dinner, and Sunday brunch. The lunch menu, featuring lower-priced soups, salads, burgers, and fried chicken with waffles, and the dinner menu, featuring steak and seafood, are both served all day. **Known for:** upscale but casual dining; best restaurant in these parts; Sunday brunch. *[$] Average main: $25 ✉ Windemere Hotel, 2047 S. AZ 92 ☎ 520/685–9061 🌐 www.tandemaz.com 🕒 Closed Mon.; No dinner Sun.*

🛏 Hotels

★ Casa de San Pedro
$$ | **B&B/INN** | Bird-watchers are drawn to this contemporary hacienda-style B&B abutting the San Pedro Riparian National Conservation Area. **Pros:** gracious hosts; tranquil and wildlife-rich setting; guided birding tours can be arranged. **Cons:** some may feel too isolated; not in town (midway between Bisbee and Sierra Vista). *[$] Rooms from: $175 ✉ 8933 S. Yell La., Hereford ☎ 520/366–1300, 888/257–2050 🌐 www.bedandbirds.com 🔑 11 rooms 🍽 Free breakfast.*

Garden Place Suites
$ | **HOTEL** | Though not technically suites, all the rooms at this convenient hotel have kitchenettes, sitting areas with pull-out sofa beds, and king-size beds (the bedroom and sitting room are separated by a half-wall). **Pros:** pool and hot tub; happy-hour drinks daily; free dinner Monday–Thursday. **Cons:** bland decor; located on business corridor. *[$] Rooms from: $105 ✉ 100 N. Garden Ave. ☎ 520/439–3300 🌐 www.gardenplacesuites.com 🔑 96 rooms 🍽 Free breakfast.*

Ramsey Canyon Inn Bed & Breakfast
$$ | **B&B/INN** | The Ramsey Canyon Preserve is an internationally renowned bird haven, and the neighboring Ramsey Canyon Inn is a bird-watcher's delight. **Pros:** perfect base for birding and hiking; comfortable rooms; fresh-baked pie in the afternoon. **Cons:** a little dull for nonbirders; no TV; breakfast is included for main inn but not creekside suites. *[$] Rooms from: $150 ✉ 29 Ramsey Canyon Rd., Hereford ☎ 520/378–3010 🌐 www.ramseycanyoninn.com 🔑 8 rooms 🍽 Free breakfast.*

Chiricahua National Monument

65 miles northeast of Sierra Vista on AZ 90 to I–10 to AZ 186, 58 miles northeast of Douglas on U.S. 191 to AZ 181, 36 miles southeast of Willcox.

With its "upside-down" rock formations and abundant wildlife, the Chiricahua National Monument is well worth the two-hour drive from Tucson. You'll be rewarded with unique, stunning scenery and unspoiled wilderness for birding, hiking, and camping.

GETTING HERE AND AROUND

Though a little more remote than other sights in southeastern Arizona, Chiricahua National Monument is just more than a half-hour drive from Willcox. You might combine a trip to this area with a Willcox wine tasting. The nearest gas stations are in Willcox or Sunizona, so be sure to fill your tank first.

👁 Sights

★ Chiricahua National Monument
NATIONAL/STATE PARK | **FAMILY** | Vast fields of desert grass are suddenly transformed into a landscape of forest, mountains, and striking rock formations as you enter the 12,000-acre Chiricahua National

Geronimo: No Bullet Shall Pass

The fearless Apache war shaman Geronimo, known among his people as "the one who yawns," fought to the very end in the Apache Wars. His surrender to General Nelson Miles on September 5, 1886, marked the end of the Indian Wars in the West. Geronimo's fleetness in evading the massed troops of the U.S. Army and his legendary immunity to bullets made him the darling of sensationalistic journalists, and he became the most famous outlaw in America.

When the combined forces of the U.S. Army and Mexican troops failed to rout the powerful shaman from his territory straddling Arizona and Mexico, General Miles sent his officer Lieutenant Gatewood and relatives of Geronimo's renegade band of warriors to persuade Geronimo to parley with Miles near the mouth of Skeleton Canyon, at the edge of the Peloncillo Mountains. After several days of talks, Geronimo and his warriors agreed to the presented treaty and surrendered their arms.

Geronimo related the scene years later: "We stood between his troopers and my warriors. We placed a large stone on the blanket before us. Our treaty was made by this stone, as it was to last until the stone should crumble to dust; so we made the treaty, and bound each other with an oath." Nevertheless, the political promises quickly unraveled, and the most feared among Apache medicine men spent his next 23 years in exile as a prisoner of war. He died on February 17, 1909, never having returned to his beloved homeland, and was buried in the Apache cemetery in Fort Sill, Oklahoma.

In 1934 a stone monument was built on State Route 80 in Apache, Arizona, as a reminder of Geronimo's surrender in 1886. The 16-foot-tall monument lies 10 miles northwest of the actual surrender site in Skeleton Canyon, where an unobtrusive sign and a pile of rocks mark the place where the last stone was cast.

Monument. The Chiricahua Apache—who lived in the mountains for centuries and, led by Cochise and Geronimo, tried for 25 years to prevent white pioneers from settling here—dubbed it "the Land of the Standing-Up Rocks." Enormous outcroppings of volcanic rock have been worn by erosion and fractured by uplift into strange pinnacles and spires. Because of the particular balance of sunshine and rain in the area, April and May see brown, yellow, and red leaves coexisting with new green foliage. Summer in Chiricahua National Monument is exceptionally wet: from July through September there are thunderstorms nearly every afternoon. Few other areas in the United States have such varied plant, bird, and animal life. Deer, coatimundi, peccaries, and lizards live among the aspen, ponderosa pine, Douglas fir, oak, and cypress trees—to name just a few.

Chiricahua National Monument is an excellent area for bird-watchers, and hikers have more than 17 miles of scenic trails. Hiking-trail maps and advice are available at the visitor center. A popular and rewarding hike is the moderately easy **Echo Canyon Loop Trail**, a 3½-mile path that winds through cavelike grottos, brilliant rock formations, and a wooded canyon. Birds and other wildlife are abundant. ⊠ *AZ 181* ✛ *36 miles southeast of Willcox* ☎ *520/824–3560* ⊕ *www.nps. gov/chir* ▨ *Free.*

Chiricahua National Monument is filled with dramatic "upside-down" or "standing-up" volcanic rocks.

Hotels

Lodging is a bit of a challenge in this remote area. Campsites in Bonita Canyon Campground, within the monument, can be reserved in advance (☎ *877/444–6777* or 🌐 *www.recreation.gov*). For those preferring to sleep indoors, the closest accommodations are about a half-hour drive, either north to one of several decent chain hotels in Willcox or to a B&B south of the monument.

Dreamcatcher Bed and Breakfast
$ | **B&B/INN** | Twelve miles south of Chiricahua National Monument, this 27-acre property has plenty of wildlife, from deer to Mexican blue jays, and a U-shaped hacienda with five rooms, all with large walk-in showers, ceiling fans, and private entrances that open onto a flower-filled courtyard. **Pros:** excellent value; tranquil; convenient to Chiricahuas. **Cons:** isolated; no services nearby (though dinner is offered for an extra charge). [$] *Rooms from: $105* ✉ *13097 S. AZ 181, Pearce* ☎ *520/824–3127* 🌐 *www.dreamcatcherbnb.com* 🛏 *5 rooms* 🍴 *Free breakfast.*

Portal Peak Lodge
$ | **HOTEL** | With a lodge and a few cottages on the eastern side of Chiricahua National Monument, this humble structure near the New Mexico border is notable less for its rooms (clean and pleasant but nondescript) than for its winged visitors: the elegant trogon, 14 types of hummingbird, and 10 species of owl are among the 330 varieties of birds that flock to nearby Cave Creek canyon. **Pros:** inexpensive; great deck; on-site restaurant and store. **Cons:** remote setting; no king-size beds; limited hours for restaurant and store. [$] *Rooms from: $95* ✉ *2358 S. Rock House Rd., Portal* ☎ *520/558–2223* 🌐 *www.portallodge.com* 🛏 *16 rooms* 🍴 *No meals.*

Fort Bowie National Historical Site

8 miles northwest of Chiricahua National Monument.

Fort Bowie was built in 1882 to protect this important travel route for wagon trains. Historic sites, including the fort ruins and the stagecoach stop, and sweeping mountain vistas are accessible by moderately easy trails.

GETTING HERE AND AROUND

From Chiricahua National Monument, take AZ 186 west (about a 30-minute drive); 5 miles north of the junction with AZ 181, signs direct you to an unpaved road leading to the fort. At the site's entrance there's a winding gravel road to the parking area, where a moderately easy walking trail leads 1½ miles to the visitor center and ruins. For those unable to hike to the visitor center, arrangements can be made to drive in (call ahead).

◉ Sights

Fort Bowie National Historical Site

ARCHAEOLOGICAL SITE | It's a bit of an outing to get to the site of Arizona's last battle between Native Americans and U.S. troops in the Dos Cabezas (Two-Headed) Mountains, but history buffs will find it an interesting hike with the added benefit of high-desert scenic beauty. Once a focal point for military operations—the fort was built here because Apache Pass was an important travel route for Native Americans and wagon trains—it now serves as a sobering reminder of the brutal clashes between the two cultures. The fort itself is virtually in ruins, but there's a small ranger-staffed visitor center with historical displays, restrooms, and books for sale.

A 1½-mile historic trail, moderately easy but rocky in some areas, leads to the visitor center and ruins. (Those with mobility issues can drive up to the visitor center.) Points of interest along the way include the remnants of an Apache *wickiup* (hut), the fort cemetery, Apache Springs (their water source), and the **Butterfield stage stop,** a crucial link in the journey from east to west in the mid-19th century that happened to be in the heart of Chiricahua Apache land. The alternate trail, looping back to the parking area, is higher and affords nice views of the ruins and surrounding hills. ✉ *3327 S. Old Fort Bowie Rd., Bowie* ✛ *26 miles southeast of Willcox* ☎ *520/847–2500* ⊕ *www.nps. gov/fobo* 🗓 *Free.*

Willcox

26 miles northwest of Fort Bowie National Historical Site on AZ 186.

The small town of Willcox, in the heart of Arizona ranching country, began in the late 1870s as a railroad construction camp called Maley. When the Southern Pacific Railroad line arrived in 1880, the town was renamed in honor of the highly regarded Fort Bowie commander, General Orlando B. Willcox. Once a major shipping center for cattle ranchers and mining companies, the town's rustic charm is in the process of renewal; the downtown area looks like it did in the 1930s. An elevation of 4,167 feet means moderate summers and chilly winters, ideal for growing apples, and apple pie fans from as far away as Phoenix make pilgrimages to sample the harvest. The climate also seems favorable for growing grapes, and Willcox has sprouted several vineyards and tasting rooms, as well as a premier grape-crushing facility, in the last few years. Pick up a map of the tasting rooms at the Willcox Visitor Center or online ⊕ *www.willcoxwinecountry.org.*

GETTING HERE AND AROUND

The small, historic downtown area of Willcox is just a few blocks south of Interstate 10 from Exit 340. Take Rex Allen Drive south, turn right on Haskell Avenue, then left on Maley Street, and left onto Railroad Avenue for an authentic glimpse of southern Arizona circa 1912, including mercantile stores, banks, and the railroad depot. Museums, a few wine-tasting rooms, and a couple of restaurants are here. To reach Willcox Playa and the vineyards off Kansas Settlement Road, continue down Maley Street, which turns into AZ 186 heading southeast.

VISITOR INFORMATION

CONTACTS Willcox Visitor Center. ⊠ *1500 N. Circle I Rd.* ☏ *520/384–2272* ⊕ *www. willcoxchamber.com.* **Willcox Wineries.** ⊕ *www.willcoxwinecountry.org.*

⊙ Sights

Apple Annie's Orchards and Country Store

FARM/RANCH | From August to October, you can pick your own apples just outside town at Apple Annie's Orchards. Peaches are ready July through September; veggies ripen midsummer through fall. If you'd rather enjoy the fruits of someone else's labor, Apple Annie's in-town country store, next to the Willcox Visitor Center, carries delicious homemade pies, fudge, and fruit butters. ⊠ *1510 N. Circle I Rd.* ☏ *520/384–2084 orchards, 520/766–2084 country store* ⊕ *www. appleannies.com.*

Chiricahua Regional Museum and Research Center

MUSEUM | Learn about the fierce Chiricahua Apaches and the fearless leaders Cochise and Geronimo at this research center, located in downtown Willcox. Other interesting tidbits about the area can be found in displays featuring the U.S. Cavalry, a nice collection of rocks and minerals, and relics of the famed Butterfield Overland Stage Route. One oddity the museum points out is that the memoirs of Civil War general Orlando Willcox, for whom the town was named, don't even mention a visit to Arizona. ⊠ *127 E. Maley St.* ☏ *520/384–3971* ⊠ *Free* ⊙ *Closed Sun.*

Rex Allen Arizona Cowboy Museum

MUSEUM | FAMILY | This museum in the historic district is a tribute to Willcox's most famous native son, cowboy singer Rex Allen. He starred in several rather average "singing cowboy" movies during the 1940s and '50s for Republic Pictures, but he's probably most famous as the friendly voice that narrated Walt Disney nature films of the 1960s. Check out the glittery suits the star wore on tour—they'd do Liberace proud. ⊠ *150 N. Railroad Ave.* ☏ *520/384–4583* ⊕ *www. rexallenmuseum.org* ⊠ *$3* ⊙ *Closed Sun.*

Willcox Playa

NATURE PRESERVE | If you visit in winter, you can see some of the more than 10,000 sandhill cranes that roost at the Willcox Playa, a 37,000-acre area resembling a dry lake bed 10 miles south of town. They migrate in late fall and head north to nesting sites in February, and bird-watchers migrate to Willcox the third week in January for the annual Wings over Willcox bird-watching event held in their honor. ⊠ *Kansas Settlement Rd., Cochise* ✥ *3 miles south of AZ 186.*

Zarpara Vineyard

WINERY/DISTILLERY | One of the original vineyards planted in the Willcox region, Zarpara makes outstanding wines, from Sauvignon Blanc to Syrah, and has enough grapes left over to sell to vintners elsewhere in Arizona. Taste five wines in a souvenir glass ($9) or a disposable one ($6), while you stroll through the vineyards or enjoy views of the Dos Cabezas Mountains from the patio (open Friday–Sunday and by appointment). ⊠ *6777 S. Zarpara Ln.* ☏ *520/222–7114* ⊕ *zarpara.com.*

🍴 Restaurants

La Unica

$ | **MEXICAN** | With reasonably priced Mexican favorites from morning 'til night, this humble eatery is a welcome surprise for anyone passing through. Don't let the weather-beaten exterior keep you from sampling tacos, burritos, tamales, and "shrimp cocktail" (served in a gazpacho-like soup)—they are all winners. **Known for:** inexpensive Mexican classics; generous portions; house-made tortillas. *[$] Average main: $11 ✉ 142 N. Haskell Ave. ☎ 520/384–0010.*

🛏 Hotels

Holiday Inn Express & Suites Willcox

$ | **HOTEL** | The pickings for hotels are slim in cowboy country, so the Holiday Inn Express, with clean and well-furnished rooms and full breakfast buffet, is a welcome option. **Pros:** clean; comfortable; cheap. **Cons:** generic hotel off the highway; short drive to historic downtown. *[$] Rooms from: $109 ✉ 1251 N. Virginia Ave. ☎ 520/384–3333 🌐 www.ihg.com 🛏 100 rooms 🍴 Free breakfast.*

Texas Canyon

16 miles southwest of Willcox off I–10.

A dramatic change of scenery along Interstate 10 will signal that you're entering Texas Canyon. The rock formations here are exceptional—huge boulders appear to be delicately balanced against each other. It's worth a stop for a picnic, a short hike, and some photo opportunities.

GETTING HERE AND AROUND

Get off Interstate 10 at Exit 318, and then turn right onto Dragoon Road. The Amerind Foundation is a mile down on the left, and Triangle T Guest Ranch, with lodging and a restaurant, is next door.

👁 Sights

The Amerind Foundation

MUSEUM | Texas Canyon is the home of the Amerind Foundation (a contraction of "American" and "Indian"), founded by amateur archaeologist William Fulton in 1937 to foster understanding about Native American cultures. The research facility and museum are housed in a Spanish colonial–style structure designed by noted Tucson architect H. M. Starkweather. The museum's rotating displays of archaeological materials, crafts, and photographs give an overview of Native American cultures of the Southwest and Mexico.

The adjacent Fulton–Hayden Memorial Art Gallery displays an assortment of art collected by William Fulton. Permanent exhibits include the work of Tohono O'odham women potters, an exquisite collection of Hopi kachina dolls, prized paintings by acclaimed Hopi artists, Pueblo pottery ranging from prehistoric pieces to modern ceramics, and archaeological exhibits on the indigenous cultures of the prehistoric Southwest. The museum's gift shop has a superlative selection of Native American art, crafts, and jewelry. Beautiful picnic areas among the boulders can accommodate large and small groups. *✉ 2100 N. Amerind Rd., Dragoon ✥ 1 mile southeast of I–10, Exit 318 ☎ 520/586–3666 🌐 www.amerind.org 🎟 $10 🕑 Closed Mon.*

🛏 Hotels

Triangle T Guest Ranch

$$$ | **B&B/INN** | Enjoy the romance of the Old West at this historic ranch on 160 acres of prime real estate in Texas Canyon. **Pros:** horseback riding (fee) and hiking trails; restaurant and bar with live country and Western music; good base for exploring the region. **Cons:** isolated; rustic; less authentic feel than some guest ranches. *[$] Rooms from: $179 ✉ 4190 Dragoon Rd., off I–10, Exit 318, Dragoon ☎ 520/586–7533 🌐 www.azretreatcenter.com 🛏 11 casitas 🍴 Free breakfast.*

Lined with stalactites and stalagmites, Kartchner Caverns is a wet cave system with 13,000 feet of passages.

Kartchner Caverns State Park

9 miles south of Benson on AZ 90.

Kartchner Caverns is a large and beautifully maintained cave system where visitors can walk through the fantastic stalactites and stalagmites while learning about the unique and fragile ecosystem. It's a wet, "live" cave, meaning that water still rises up from the surface to continually add to the multicolor calcium carbonate formations already visible. Amateur cavers discovered Kartchner Caverns in 1974, and it opened to the public in 1999.

GETTING HERE AND AROUND
From Exit 302 off Interstate 10, take AZ 90 for 9 miles.

The closest place to stay to the caverns is Benson, a small town 12 miles west of Texas Canyon and 50 miles southeast of Tucson via I–10. Amtrak runs trains from Tucson to Benson three times a week. You likely won't linger in Benson on your way to the caverns, but it's a good place to grab a meal and fill your gas tank.

◉ Sights

★ Kartchner Caverns
CAVE | FAMILY | The publicity that surrounded the official opening of Kartchner Caverns in 1999 was in marked contrast to the secrecy that shrouded their discovery 25 years earlier and concealed their existence for 14 years. The two young spelunkers, Gary Tenen and Randy Tufts, who stumbled into what is now considered one of the most spectacular cave systems anywhere, played a fundamental role in its protection and eventual development. Great precautions have been taken to protect the wet-cave system—which comprises 13,000 feet of passages and two chambers as long as football fields—from damage by light and dryness.

The Discovery Center introduces visitors to the cave and its formations, and guided Rotunda/Throne Room tours take small groups into the upper cave. Spectacular formations include the longest soda straw stalactite in the United States at 21 feet and 2 inches. The Big Room is viewed on a separate tour for ages 7 and up: it holds the world's most extensive formation of brushite moonmilk, the first reported occurrence of turnip shields, and the first noted occurrence of birds-nest needle formations. Other funky and fabulous formations include brilliant red flowstone, rippling multihued stalactites, delicate white helictites, translucent orange bacon, and expansive mudflats. It's also the nursery roost for female cave myotis bats from mid-April through mid-October, during which time this lower cave is closed.

The total cavern size is 2.4 miles long, but the explored areas cover only 1,600 feet by 1,100 feet. The average relative humidity inside is 99%, so visitors are often graced with "cave kisses," water droplets from above. Because the climate outside the caves is so dry, it is estimated that if air got inside, it could deplete the moisture in only a few days, halting the growth of the speleothems that decorate its walls. To prevent this, there are 22 environmental monitoring stations that measure air and soil temperature, relative humidity, evaporation rates, air trace gases, and airflow inside the caverns. ■ **TIP→ Tour reservations are strongly recommended, especially during winter months. If you're here and didn't make a reservation, go ahead and check: sometimes same-day reservations are available (call or arrive early in the day for these).** Hiking trails, picnic areas, and campsites are available on the park's 550 acres, and the Bat Cave Café, open daily, serves pizza, hot dogs, salads, and sandwiches. ✉ *AZ 90, Benson* ✣ *9 miles south of I–10, Exit 302* ☎ *520/586–4100 info and tour reservations* 🌐 *azstateparks.com/kartchner* 🎟 *Park admission $7 per vehicle up to 4 people, $3 each additional person (fees waived for those with cave tour reservations). Rotunda/Throne Room tour or Big Room tour $23.*

Hotels

Comfort Inn Benson

$ | HOTEL | The closest lodging to Kartchner Caverns State Park, this modern motel just off Interstate 10 at the "Kartchner Corridor," a few miles west of Benson, has the comfort and amenities you'd expect, but with a bit of Southwestern elegance rarely found in properties around the area. **Pros:** convenient location; friendly; bountiful breakfast included. **Cons:** just off the highway; not particularly serene or scenic; generic. [$] *Rooms from: $105* ✉ *630 S. Village Loop, Benson* ☎ *520/586–8800* 🌐 *www.choicehotels.com* 🛏 *62 rooms* 🍴 *Free breakfast.*

Buenos Aires National Wildlife Refuge

66 miles southwest of Tucson.

Encircled by seven mountain ranges in the Altar Valley, remote Buenos Aires National Wildlife Refuge is the only place in the United States where the Sonoran-savanna grasslands that once pervaded this region can still be seen. The U.S. Fish and Wildlife Service oversees this 115,000-acre preserve, managing programs to restore native grasses and protect endangered species such as the masked bobwhite quail. Birding and wildlife-viewing are popular here.

GETTING HERE AND AROUND

From Tucson, take AZ 86 west 22 miles to AZ 286; go south 40 miles to mile marker 8, and it's another 3 miles east to the preserve headquarters.

Southwest Arizona

Sights

Buenos Aires National Wildlife Refuge

NATURE PRESERVE | Bird-watchers consider Buenos Aires National Wildlife Refuge unique because it's the only place in the United States where they can see a "grand slam" (four species) of quail: Montezuma quail, Gambel's quail, scaled quail, and masked bobwhite. If it rains, the 100-acre Aguirre Lake, 1½ miles north of the headquarters, attracts wading birds, shorebirds, and waterfowl—in all, more than 320 avian species have been spotted here. The quail share the turf with deer, coati, badgers, bobcats, and mountain lions. Touring options include a 10-mile auto tour; nature trails; a 3¾-mile guided hike in Brown Canyon (second and fourth Saturdays, November–April, or call to arrange other dates for private groups); a boardwalk through the marshes at Arivaca

Cienega; and guided bird walks, also at Arivaca Cienega (November–April, first Saturday at 8). Admission and guided bird walks are free; Brown Canyon hikes cost $5. Pick up maps at the visitor center. ⊠ AZ 286, at mile marker 7.5, Sasabe ⊕ Turn off AZ 286 at mile marker 7.5, and drive into the refuge for 3 miles to Refuge Headquarters and Visitor Center ☎ 520/823–4251 ⊕ www.fws.gov/refuge/buenos_aires ☜ Free ⊙ Visitor center open limited hours Apr.–Oct. (call ahead).

Hotels

Rancho de la Osa

$$ | **ALL-INCLUSIVE** | **FAMILY** | Set on 250 eucalyptus-shaded acres near the Mexican border and Buenos Aires Wildlife Refuge, this tranquil late 19th-century ranch with adobe buildings offers guests plenty of activities like horseback riding, hiking,

Border Town Safety: Nogales, Mexico [◉]

Nogales used to draw tourists and locals who would park on the American side and walk across the border. Though shopping bargains and cheap bars are enticing, safety issues have changed in recent years.

■ **TIP→ Drug-related violence in Mexico—especially near the U.S. border—has increased to the point that the U.S. government strongly discourages travel in and around Mexico border towns. Check 🌐 www.state.gov/travel for updates and details.**

If you decide to cross, bring your passport (it's required), remain alert, and stay in the central area on Avenida Obregón, which begins a few blocks west of the border entrance and runs north–south.

biking, and archery. **Pros:** excellent ranch activities; good food and extensive wine list; historic setting. **Cons:** somewhat isolated; about an hour and a half drive from Tucson. [$] *Rooms from: $169* ✉ *41480 S. Sasabe Hwy., Sasabe* ☎ *520/339–1086* 🌐 *www.ranchodelaosa.com* 🛏 *18 rooms* 🍴 *Free breakfast.*

Kitt Peak National Observatory

70 miles northwest of Buenos Aires National Wildlife Refuge on AZ 286 to AZ 86, 56 miles southwest of Tucson.

Funded by the National Science Foundation and managed by a group of more than 20 universities, Kitt Peak National Observatory is on the Tohono O'odham Reservation. Kitt Peak scientists use the high-powered telescopes here to conduct vital solar research and observe distant galaxies; visitors can tour the facilities by day and view stellar happenings at the evening observation program.

GETTING HERE AND AROUND

To reach Kitt Peak from Tucson, take Interstate 10 to Interstate 19 south, and then AZ 86. After 44 miles on AZ 86, turn left at the AZ 386 junction and follow the winding mountain road 12 miles up to the observatory. In inclement weather, contact the highway department to confirm that the road is open. To get to Sells (for the nearest food and gas) from the base of the mountain, it's 20 miles west on AZ 86.

[◉] Sights

Kitt Peak National Observatory
OBSERVATORY | After much discussion back in the late 1950s, tribal leaders of the Tohono O'odham nation agreed to share a small section of their 4,400-square-mile reservation with the National Science Foundation to house sophisticated research telescopes. Among these is the McMath-Pierce, the world's largest solar telescope, which uses piped-in liquid coolant. From the visitors' gallery you can see into the telescope's light-path tunnel, which goes down hundreds of feet into the mountain.

The visitor center has exhibits on astronomy, information about the telescopes, and hour-long guided tours ($11 per person) that depart daily at 10, 11:30, and 1:30. Complimentary brochures enable you to take self-guided tours of the grounds, and there are picnic areas outside and below the observatory. The observatory sells snacks and drinks, which is good to know, because there are no restaurants (or gas stations, for that matter) within 20 miles of Kitt Peak. The observatory offers an outstanding nightly program for ages eight and older ($55 per person); reservations are necessary. ⊠ AZ 386, Pan Tak ☎ 520/318–8726 ⊕ www.noao.edu/kpno ☎ Free; tours and observatory programs extra.

Ajo

135 miles west of Tucson on AZ 86.

"Ajo" (pronounced *ah-ho*) is Spanish for garlic, and some say the town got its name from the wild garlic that grows in the area. Others claim the word comes from the Native American word *au-auho*, referring to red paint derived from a local pigment.

For many years Ajo, like Bisbee, was a thriving Phelps Dodge company town. Copper mining had been attempted in the area in the late 19th century, but it wasn't until the 1911 arrival of the Calumet & Arizona Mining Company that the region began to be developed profitably. Calumet and Phelps Dodge merged in 1935, and the huge pit mine produced millions of tons of copper until it closed in 1985. Nowadays Ajo is pretty sleepy: the town's population of less than 4,000 has a median age of 50, and most visitors are on their way to or from Rocky Point, Mexico, or Organ Pipe National Monument. At the center of town is a sparkling white Spanish-style plaza with a few modest shops and restaurants. Unlike Bisbee, Ajo hasn't yet drawn an artistic crowd—although mural projects and an artists-in-residence program evidence the town's desire to encourage and attract creative folks.

GETTING HERE AND AROUND
As you drive into Ajo on AZ 85, you'll see the small historical plaza, with a few shops, a library, and the visitor center immediately on your right. After jogging west for several blocks and changing its name three times,

the highway turns north again, becomes 2nd Avenue, and takes you out of town, past the Cabeza Prieta Wildlife Refuge and north to Gila Bend.

VISITOR INFORMATION
CONTACTS Ajo Visitor Center. ⊠ 1 W. Plaza St. ☎ 520/387–7742 ⊕ ajochamber.com.

◉ Sights

Cabeza Prieta National Wildlife Refuge
NATURE PRESERVE | This 860,000-acre national wildlife refuge, about 5 miles (a 10-minute drive) from Ajo, was established in 1939 as a preserve for endangered bighorn sheep and other Sonoran Desert wildlife, including the long-nosed bat and the Sonoran pronghorn deer, the fastest mammal in North America. People come here for hiking, photography, and primitive desert camping. ■ TIP→ A free permit, essentially a "hold-harmless" agreement, is required to enter, and only those with four-wheel drive, high-clearance vehicles, or all-terrain vehicles—needed to traverse the rugged terrain—can obtain one. Pick up a permit from the refuge's visitor center in Ajo, about a mile north of the downtown plaza. ⊠ 1611 N. 2nd Ave., at North St. ☎ 520/387–6483 ⊕ www. fws.gov/refuge/cabeza_prieta ☎ Free.

New Cornelia Open Pit Mine Lookout Point
MINE | You get an expansive view of Ajo's ugly gash of an open-pit mine, almost 2 miles wide, from the New Cornelia Open Pit Mine Lookout Point. Some of the abandoned equipment remains in the pit, and mining operations are diagrammed at the volunteer-run visitor center, where there's a 30-minute film about mining. The lookout point is always "open," but the visitor center's hours are sporadic. The mine is about a mile southwest of the plaza; take La Mina Road or Estrella Road to Indian Village Road. ⊠ Indian Village Rd. ☎ 520/387–7742 ☎ Free.

Organ Pipe Cactus National Monument's namesake cacti stand tall alongside desert flora.

🛏 Hotels

Sonoran Desert Inn and Conference Center
$ | **B&B/INN** | Part hotel, part affordable live and work space for artists, this not-for-profit inn has spacious, comfortable rooms with 8-foot windows and mountain views. **Pros:** chic and comfortable; on-site gallery sells work of resident artists; walk to town plaza. **Cons:** no dining service; its history as a schoolhouse means it can feel somewhat institutional. [$] *Rooms from: $95* ✉ *55 Orilla Ave.* ☎ *520/373–0804* 🌐 *www.sonorancc.com* 🛏 *21 rooms* 🍴 *No meals.*

Organ Pipe Cactus National Monument

32 miles southwest of Ajo on AZ 86 to AZ 85.

The largest habitat north of the border for organ pipe cacti (the beautiful multi-armed cousins of the saguaro) is off the beaten path unless you're driving to Puerto Penasco, Mexico. But it's a worthwhile destination to view large groves of this desert flora, fairly common in Mexico but rare in the United States.

GETTING HERE AND AROUND

From Ajo, drive to Why and take AZ 85 south for 22 miles to reach the visitor center.

SAFETY AND PRECAUTIONS

Be aware that Organ Pipe continues to be an illegal-border-crossing hot spot where some people cross from Mexico under the cover of darkness. You probably won't encounter this type of situation, but it is possible, even with the copious fencing along the U.S.–Mexico border. Park officials emphasize that tourists only occasionally have been the victims of isolated property crimes—primarily theft of personal items from parked cars. Visitors are advised by rangers to keep valuables locked and out of plain view and not to initiate contact with groups of strangers whom they may encounter on hiking trails.

◉ Sights

Organ Pipe Cactus National Monument
NATIONAL/STATE PARK | This designated part of the Sonoran Desert preserves more than two dozen species of cacti, including the park's namesake, as well as other desert plants and animals. Because organ pipe cactus tend to grow on the warmer, usually south-facing slopes, you'll get the best views by taking either the 21-mile scenic loop **Ajo Mountain Drive** (a one-way, partly dirt road) or **Puerto Blanco Drive,** a 45-mile loop road (4-wheel drive vehicles are recommended). Ranger-led talks and guided van tours are offered January through April. Check with rangers for the schedule of "trailhead drops," which enable hikers to leave their cars in more populated areas. ⊠ *10 Organ Pipe Dr., Ajo* ☎ *520/387–6849* ⊕ *www. nps.gov/orpi* ⊡ *$25 per vehicle.*

Yuma

232 miles northwest of Organ Pipe Cactus National Monument, 170 miles northwest of Ajo.

Today many people think of Yuma as a convenient stop for gas and a meal between Phoenix or Tucson and San Diego. Although this is surely true, the town boasts some historical sites and agricultural tours (Yuma is the lettuce capital of the U.S.) that may prompt you to pause here a bit longer.

It's difficult to imagine the lower Colorado River, now dammed and bridged, as either a barrier or a means of transportation, but until the early part of the 20th century this section of the great waterway was a force to contend with. Records show that since at least 1540 the Spanish were using Yuma (then the home of the indigenous Quechan tribe) as a ford across a relatively shallow stretch of the Colorado.

Three centuries later, the advent of the shallow-draft steamboat made the settlement a point of entry for fortune seekers heading through the Gulf of California to mining sites in Eastern Arizona. Fort Yuma was established in 1850 to guard against Indian attacks, and by 1873 the town was a county seat, a U.S. port of entry, and an army depot.

During World War II, the Yuma Proving Ground was used to train bomber pilots, and General Patton readied some of his desert war forces for battle at secret areas in the city. Many who served here during the war returned to Yuma to retire, and the city's population swells during the winter months with retirees from cold climates who park their homes on wheels at one of the many RV communities. One fact may explain this: according to National Weather Service statistics, Yuma is the sunniest city in the United States.

GETTING HERE AND AROUND

AZ 8 runs through Yuma, which is approximately halfway between Casa Grande and the California coast. Most of the interesting historical sites are at the north end of town. Stop in at the Yuma Visitor Center, on the grounds of Colorado River State Historic Park, and pick up a visitor guide. You can also rent bikes here to ride along the riverfront.

Yuma is accessible by air through American Airlines, which has several direct flights daily between Yuma and Phoenix.

Amtrak trains run three times a week from Tucson west to Yuma (get your ticket or make a reservation beforehand as there's no kiosk or ticket window).

AIR CONTACTS Yuma International Airport (YUM). ☎ 928/726–5882 ⊕ www.yumaairport.com.

TRAIN CONTACTS Yuma train station. ✉ 281 Gila St. ⊕ www.amtrak.com.

VISITOR INFORMATION

CONTACTS Yuma Visitor Center. ✉ 201 N 4th Ave. ☎ 928/783–0071 ⊕ www.visityuma.com.

◉ Sights

Colorado River State Historic Park

NATIONAL/STATE PARK | On the other side of the river from Fort Yuma, the Civil War–period quartermaster depot resupplied army posts to the north and east and served as a distribution point for steamboat freight headed overland to Arizona forts. The 1853 home of riverboat captain G. A. Johnson is the depot's earliest building and the centerpiece of this park. The residence also served as a weather bureau and home for customs agents, among other functions, and

the self-guided tour through the house provides a complete history. Also on display are antique surreys and more "modern" modes of transportation like a 1931 Model A Ford pickup. You can visit a re-creation of the Commanding Officer's Quarters, complete with period furnishings. The Yuma Visitor Center and a pie shop are also here. ✉ 201 N. 4th Ave., between 1st St. and I–8 ☎ 928/783–0071 ⊕ azstateparks.com ⊠ $6 ⊗ Closed Mon. June–Sept.

Yuma Territorial Prison State Historic Park

JAIL | FAMILY | The most notorious tourist sight in town is now an Arizona state historic park, but it was built for the most part by the convicts who were incarcerated here from 1876 until 1909, when the prison outgrew its location. The hilly site on the Colorado River, chosen for security purposes, precluded further expansion.

Visitors gazing today at the tiny cells that held six inmates each, often in 115°F heat, are likely to be appalled, but the prison—dubbed "the Country Club of the Colorado" by locals—was considered a model of enlightenment by turn-of-20th-century standards: in an era when beatings were common, the only punishments meted out here were solitary confinement and assignment to a dark cell. The complex housed a hospital as well as Yuma's only public library, where the 25¢ that visitors paid for a prison tour financed the acquisition of new books.

The 3,069 prisoners who served time at what was then the territory's only prison included men and women from 21 different countries. They came from all social classes and were sent up for everything from armed robbery and murder to polygamy. R. L. McDonald, incarcerated for forgery, had been the superintendent of the Phoenix public school system. Chosen as the prison bookkeeper, he absconded with $130 of the inmates' money when he was released.

The mess hall opened as a museum in 1940, and the entire prison complex was designated a state historic park in 1961. ✉ *220 N. Prison Hill Rd., off I–8, Exit 1* ☎ *928/783–4771* 🌐 *www.yumaprison.org* 🎟 *$8* 🕒 *Closed Tues. and Wed. June–Sept.*

🍴 Restaurants

The Garden Café

$ | CAFÉ | Before or after a visit to the Sanguinetti House Museum, this adjoining café is a good place to stop for breakfast or lunch. The charming dining spot features lush gardens and aviaries on the outdoor patio, historical photos on the walls, and a menu of homemade salads, soups, and sandwiches. **Known for:** tortilla soup; fresh-baked bread and pastries; brunch spot. [$] *Average main: $11* ✉ *250 S. Madison Ave.* ☎ *928/783–1491* 🌐 *www.gardencafeyuma.com* 🕒 *Closed Mon. Closed June–Sept. No dinner.*

La Fonda

$ | MEXICAN | A Yuma institution, La Fonda opened as a tortilla factory in 1940, then added a colorful restaurant onto the original building in 1982; locals have been enjoying the carne asada, pollo asado, and chiles rellenos here ever since. Only canola oil is used (not lard), and all the sauces and marinades are made fresh, as are the corn tortillas, which many say are the best in town. **Known for:** classic Mexican; chipotle corn tortillas; best place to buy fresh tortillas. [$] *Average main: $11* ✉ *1095 S. 3rd Ave.* ☎ *928/783–6902* 🌐 *www.lafondarestaurantyumaaz.com* 🕒 *Closed Sun.*

★ Lutes Casino

$ | SOUTHWESTERN | Packed with locals at lunchtime, this large, funky restaurant and bar claims to be the oldest pool hall and domino parlor in Arizona. It's a great place for a burger or tacos and a brew. **Known for:** the "Especial" cheeseburger–hot dog combo; friendly atmosphere; great bar. [$] *Average main: $10* ✉ *221 S. Main St.* ☎ *928/782–2192* 🌐 *www.lutescasino.com.*

River City Grill

$$$ | AMERICAN | This hip downtown restaurant is a favorite dining spot for locals and visitors, and though it gets a bit loud on weekend nights, the camaraderie of diners is well worth it. Owners Nan and Tony Bain dish out a medley of flavors drawing on Mediterranean, Pacific Rim, Indian, and Caribbean influences. **Known for:** best upscale dining in Yuma; large, eclectic menu; vegan and gluten-free selections. [$] *Average main: $24* ✉ *600 W. 3rd St.* ☎ *928/782–7988* 🌐 *www.rivercitygrill.com* 🕒 *No lunch Sun.*

🛏 Hotels

★ Coronado Motor Hotel

$ | HOTEL | Built in 1938, this Spanish tile–roofed motor hotel has been well cared for and was where Bob Hope used to stay during World War II, when he entertained the gunnery troops training in Yuma. **Pros:** convenient location near AZ 8 and a short walk from the historic downtown area; great retro property; full breakfast at neighboring restaurant. **Cons:** some highway and street noise; older property might not appeal to some; rooms are somewhat small. [$] *Rooms from: $99* ✉ *233 S. 4th Ave.* ☎ *928/783–4453, 877/234–5567* 🌐 *coronadomotorhotel.com* 🛏 *86 rooms* 🍴 *Free breakfast.*

Hilton Garden Inn Yuma-Pivot Point

$ | HOTEL | One of the newer hotels in town, the Hilton Garden Inn Yuma caters to families and business travelers equally, with well-equipped rooms, an on-site restaurant, a pleasant pool area, and convenience to historic sights and the highway. **Pros:** comfortable rooms; pool, hot tub, and gym; easy walk to riverfront park and historic area. **Cons:** generic property; higher rates on weekdays. [$] *Rooms from: $109* ✉ *310 N. Madison Ave.* ☎ *928/783–1500* 🌐 *www.hiltongardeninn.com* 🛏 *150 rooms* 🍴 *No meals.*

🛍 Shopping

Art studios, antiques shops, and specialty boutiques have taken advantage of historic downtown Yuma's face-lift. The town's largest shopping center, Yuma Palms, sits just to the east side of U.S. 8 (at the 16th Street exit). A nice selection of regional gifts can be found at the Yuma Visitor Center.

Brocket Farms

FOOD/CANDY | This is the place for freshly picked Medjool dates, the high-fiber, fat-free fruit grown in this region. Stock up on local honey, jams, and chocolate treats, too. ✉ 102 E. 3rd St. ☎ 928/257–1440 ⊕ www.brocketfarms.com.

Colorado River Pottery

CERAMICS/GLASSWARE | This shop in the heart of Yuma features locally handcrafted bowls, vases, and dishes. ✉ 67 W. 2nd St. ☎ 928/343–0413 ⊕ www.coloradoriverpottery.com.

Imperial National Wildlife Refuge

30 miles north of Yuma on U.S. 95.

Something of an anomaly, this 25,765-acre wildlife refuge, created when the Imperial Dam was built, is home both to marshy-river species and creatures that inhabit the adjacent Sonoran Desert—coyotes, bobcats, desert tortoises, and bighorn sheep. Mostly, though, it's a major bird habitat, with waterfowl and shorebirds year-round and masses of migrating flocks during spring and fall.

GETTING HERE AND AROUND

From Yuma, take U.S. 95 north and follow the signs to the refuge; it's about a 40-minute drive. Between January and March look for army paratroopers taking practice jumps as you pass the Yuma Proving Ground.

👁 Sights

Imperial National Wildlife Refuge

NATURE PRESERVE | FAMILY | A guided, volunteer-led tour is a good way to visit this wildlife refuge and birder's paradise. The peak seasons for bird-watching are spring and fall, when you can expect to see everything from pelicans and cormorants to Canada geese, snowy egrets, and some rarer species. Mid-October through May is the most pleasant time to visit, as it's cooler and the ever-present mosquitoes are least active.

Kids especially enjoy the 1¼-mile Painted Desert Trail, which winds through the different levels of the Sonoran Desert. From an observation tower at the visitor center, you can see the river as well as the fields where migrating birds like to feed. You can sign up for guided walks from November through March. ✉ 12812 Wildlife Way, Yuma ☎ 928/783–3371 ⊕ www.fws.gov/refuge/Imperial ⊠ Free ⊙ Visitor center closed weekdays Apr.–mid-Nov.

Chapter 10

NORTHWEST ARIZONA

WITH LAUGHLIN AND HOOVER DAM

Updated by
Teresa Bitler

◉ Sights	🕹 Restaurants	🛏 Hotels	🛍 Shopping	🍸 Nightlife
★★★☆☆	★★★☆☆	★★☆☆☆	★☆☆☆☆	★★☆☆☆

WELCOME TO NORTHWEST ARIZONA

TOP REASONS TO GO

★ **Make a splash:** Boating, fishing, and water adventure top the list of favorite activities on the cool Colorado River and the adjoining lakes of Havasu and Mohave.

★ **Drive the open road:** Take a road trip on legendary Route 66 and cruise the longest remaining stretch of the Mother Road from Seligman to Kingman.

★ **Experience a slice of England:** Pass under on a boat or take a guided tour over London Bridge in Lake Havasu City.

★ **Hike Hualapai:** Take a break from the desert and climb the cool climes of Hualapai Mountain Park—the highest point in western Arizona.

★ **Take a walk on the wild side:** For Vegas-style gambling and glitz, spend some quality play time in the twin riverside cities of Laughlin, Nevada, and Bullhead City, Arizona.

In the far northwestern corner of Arizona, the fast-growing communities of Lake Havasu and Laughlin/Bullhead City are good bases for outdoor recreation and gaming, respectively. Kingman, the Mohave County seat and a historic shipping center, is an ideal launchpad for exploring historic Route 66.

The Colorado River flows out of the Grand Canyon to the north and then sweeps directly south, serving as the western border of the state of Arizona and supplying the lifeblood to the otherwise desolate desert region. Created from dams on the mighty Colorado River, lakes Mohave and Havasu provide a common link in the tristate area by offering some of the best water recreation around.

1 Kingman. The Mohave County seat and historic shipping center is an ideal launchpad for exploring historic and quirky Route 66.

2 Lake Havasu City. A mecca for water fun, Arizona's beach city is home to the London Bridge.

3 Bullhead City, AZ, and Laughlin, NV. Casinos and water sports attract 2 million visitors per year to these Colorado River cities.

4 Hoover Dam. The monumental Colorado River dam is considered one of history's greatest engineering feats.

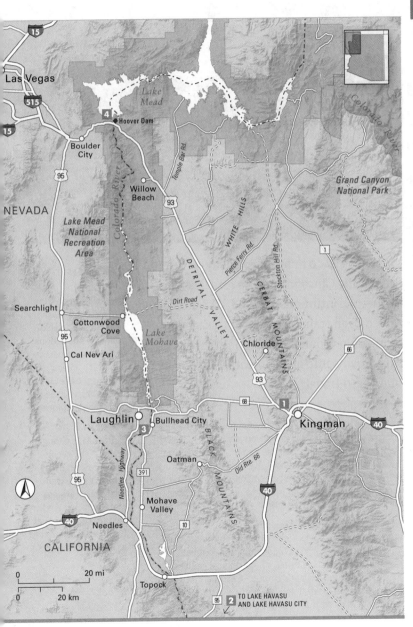

GET YOUR KICKS ON ROUTE 66

Historic Route 66 is the ultimate American road trip.

In 1938 the 2,400 miles of roadway connecting Chicago and Los Angeles was declared "continuously paved." U.S. Route 66 had been transformed from a ragged string of local lanes connecting isolated small towns into an "all-weather" highway that eased travel.

Just as the road crews changed what had been a string of rutty dirt roads into a paved roadbed, Route 66 changed the social landscape as communities adapted to the new road. The needs of travelers were met by new concepts, such as the gas station, the diner, and the motel. Nostalgic remnants from this retro road-tripping culture still exist along this stretch of the "Mother Road."

Most of old Route 66 has been replaced by the modern interstate system, but at Exit 139 from Interstate 40 you'll find yourself at the beginning of the longest remaining continuous stretch of the original Route 66. This 160-mile journey leads through Seligman, Peach Springs, Truxton, Valentine, Hackberry, Kingman, and Oatman, and on to the Colorado River near Topock.

BEST TIME TO GO
Although Route 66 is accessible year-round, spring and fall are the best times to explore roadside attractions or partake of nearby hikes. It's an easy side trip from Lake Havasu or Las Vegas; save a full day to explore.

FUN FACT
Route 66 is no longer an officially recognized U.S. highway—it hasn't appeared on maps or atlases since 1984, except for certain sections that have been designated as special historic routes.

BEST WAYS TO EXPLORE

SHOP FOR RETRO SOUVENIRS IN OATMAN

Cool Springs Station. This restored way station at the base of Sitgreaves Pass sells Route 66 T-shirts, hats, handmade jewelry, and souvenirs. It also houses a small museum dedicated to Route 66. ⊠ *8275 W. Oatman Rd., Kingman* ☎ *928/768–8366* ⊕ *www.route66cool-springsaz.com.*

Fast Fanny's Place. A Main Street fixture for more than 30 years, Fast Fanny's Place specializes in silver and turquoise jewelry, wind chimes, and Oatman souvenirs. ⊠ *141 Main St., Oatman* ☎ *928/768–7400* ⊕ *www. facebook.com/etueart.*

Oatman General Store. Oatman T-shirts, tongue-tingling hot sauces, Coca-Cola memorabilia, and other collectibles fill this general store, located across the street from the Oatman Hotel. ⊠ *180 Main St., Oatman* ☎ *928/768–9448* ⊕ *www.oatmangeneralstore.com.*

SIGN HERE
One of the joys of exploring Route 66 is admiring the vintage signage along the way.

Delgadillo's Snow Cap Drive-in. In Seligman, you can stop here for a "small soda" and to view the old Coca-Cola and Burma Shave signs. In fact, the whole town is rife with old signs and cars. ⊠ *301 W. Chino Ave., Seligman* ☎ *928/422–3291.*

Hackberry General Store. At this store, both a shop and museum dedicated to Mother Road memorabilia, you can pose for pictures with vintage cars, kitschy signs, ancient gas pumps, and highway memorabilia while sipping a bottle of sarsaparilla. ⊠ *11255 E. AZ 66, Hackberry* ☎ *928/769–2605* ⊕ *hackberrygeneralstore.com.*

The Oatman General Store is a slice of nostalgia.

QUICK BITES

Joe & Aggie's Cafe. A popular and quirky spot for hearty Mexican and American fare in downtown Holbrook since the 1940s, this restaurant is perfect for huevos rancheros, chiles rellenos, Navajo tacos, or a chicken-fried steak meal en route to nearby Petrified Forest National Park. **Known for:** Southwestern staples; historic diner status; Route 66 mural. ⊠ *120 W. Hopi Dr., Holbrook* ☎ *928/524–6540,* Average Main: $11.

Oatman Hotel. This allegedly haunted landmark (there are no overnight accommodations anymore) is on Oatman's historic main drag. Claims that Carole Lombard and Clark Gable honeymooned here have been definitively debunked, but this quirky establishment contains a fun little restaurant that's renowned for its juicy buffalo burgers and addictively filling "burro ears"—house-made potato chips served with tangy salsa. **Known for:** money-covered walls; burgers and chips; cowboy singers. ⊠ *181 Main St., Oatman* ☎ *928/768–4408,* Average Main: $11.

Bisected by a dramatic stretch of the Colorado River, home to the longest unbroken section of old Route 66, and anchored at opposite ends by the gaming town of Laughlin and the water-sports recreation hub of Lake Havasu City, Northwest Arizona and Southeast Nevada comprise a unique blend of deserts, mountains, and miles of shoreline. This sparsely populated region between Las Vegas and Phoenix appeals strongly to road-trippers, who appreciate the wide-open roads and scenic byways, and to boaters enthralled with the basaltic canyons and dammed lakes.

The defining feature of the region is the Colorado River, which affords visitors myriad opportunities to view local wildlife, Jet Ski, fish, and even rent houseboats. Since the late Pleistocene epoch when Paleo-Indians first set foot in the river that was once described as "too thick to drink and too thin to plow," the Colorado has been a blessing and a barrier. Prehistoric traders from the Pacific coast crossed the river at Willow Beach on their way to trade shells for pelts with the Hopi and other Pueblo tribes farther east. When gold was discovered in California in 1848, entrepreneurs built ferries up and down the river to accommodate the miners drawn to the area by what Cortez called "a disease of the heart for which the only cure is gold." Prosperity followed, particularly for Kingman.

Every spring the snowmelt of the Rocky Mountain watershed of the Colorado River rushed through high basaltic canyons like water through a garden hose and washed away crops and livestock. Harnessing such a powerful river required no ordinary dam. In 1935, notched into the steep and narrow confines of Black Canyon on the border separating Arizona and Nevada, 726-foot-high Hoover Dam took control of the Colorado River and turned its power into electricity and its floodwaters into the largest man-made reservoir in the United States: Lake Mead. In 2010 the similarly dramatic Hoover Dam Bypass (also known as the

Mike O'Callaghan–Pat Tillman Memorial Bridge) opened just south of the dam, vastly reducing the time it takes for automobiles to cross over the Colorado River.

MAJOR REGIONS

In **northwest Arizona,** take a drive down memory lane on the longest remaining stretch of Route 66—roll down the windows and watch the sweeping desert views pass you by. Along the way, check out the funky little ghost towns of Oatman and Chloride and make a splash in the cool blue waterways of Lakes Mohave and Havasu.

Take a quick jaunt into **southeast Nevada** for a look at monumental Hoover Dam and a hand or two of blackjack in a riverside casino. The fast-growing community of Laughlin is a good base for laid-back gambling and elite entertainment—all of the glitz and glamour of Las Vegas without the high prices and large crowds.

Northwest Arizona Planner

When to Go

Unlike many destinations, the communities in northwest Arizona don't have distinct high and low seasons. The arid climate and clear winter skies attract "snowbirds," retirees flocking south to escape the harsh northern climes. On the flip side, the hot, sunny summer months attract sports enthusiasts looking to cavort in the cool, blue waterways—despite searing temperatures that occasionally top 110°F.

Lake Havasu City plays host to hordes of college revelers during spring break in March, and Kingman fills up fast during the annual Route 66 Fun Run drive in May. Things simmer down a bit during the rest of spring as well as the fall months. Overall, expect fairly busy

weekends during the summer months and sold-out rooms during sporting events and fishing tournaments.

Hualapai Mountain Park is the one part of northwest Arizona that is high-altitude enough to get occasionally heavy snow in winter.

FESTIVALS AND EVENTS

Andy Devine Days

FESTIVALS | The September festival honors the film and television actor with a parade, art show, and an impressive rodeo and incorporates a Route 66 element with car shows and live music. ☎ ⊕ *www.andydevinedaysfestival.com* ⌕ *Free.*

London Bridge Days

FESTIVALS | Lake Havasu City heats up in October with a week of British-themed festivities celebrating the bridge and culminating in a parade on Saturday. ☎ *928/453–8686* ⊕ *www.golakehavasu. com.*

Route 66 Fun Run

FESTIVALS | This three-day event in early May is a 140-mile drive along the longest remaining section of the "Mother Road." More than 800 classic and custom automobiles participate. ☎ *928/753–5001 Historic Rt. 66 Association of Arizona* ⊕ *66funrun.com.*

Planning Your Time

Kingman is an ideal base for exploring Lake Mead National Recreation Area, the ghost towns of Oatman and Chloride, and the forested Hualapai Mountain Park. You'll need at least a day to enjoy water sports on Lake Mead, whereas an hour or two is enough to explore the funky little ghost towns. Visitors to Lake Havasu should spend a night or two to get a real sense of this recreation hub, although you can get a quick taste by making a day trip from Bullhead City.

Water activities dominate the scene here, but in a shorter visit you can check out London Bridge, go on a birding expedition at Havasu National Wildlife Refuge, or foray into the quaint if touristy shops in English Village. Fans of gambling can just hop across the Colorado River to Laughlin and spend hours or days reveling in the glitz and glitter. There are also casinos near Lake Havasu City, one on the Arizona side in Parker, an hour south, and the other easily reached across the lake in California.

■ TIP→ Remember that Arizona, in the mountain time zone, doesn't observe daylight saving time, but the neighboring states of Nevada and California, both in the Pacific time zone, do. When scheduling interstate travel, double-check all times to avoid confusion and missed connections.

Getting Here and Around

AIR
Kingman (IGM) no longer offers commercial air service. Laughlin-Bullhead City (IFP) has limited, chartered air service. Most visitors arriving by plane reach this part of the state after first flying into Las Vegas (two hours from Laughlin) or Phoenix (four hours from Kingman or Lake Havasu City) and renting a car.

CAR
Most visitors drive to this corner of the state—after all, Kingman is on the longest remaining stretch of Route 66. At first glance the countryside can seem a bit stark and remote, but there are many surprises in this part of the world, including the strange-looking Joshua tree, the defining plant of the Mojave Desert. Historic Route 66 crosses east–west and curves north of Interstate 40, which provides the fastest path across the region. U.S. 93 is the main route for north–south travel. All these roads are in excellent condition. On Interstate 40 high winds occasionally raise enough blowing dust to restrict visibility. In winter ice may be present on Interstate 40 east of Kingman and on sections of Route 66. Most of the county roads are improved dirt roads, but washboard sections bounce you around a bit, so take your time and drive no faster than prudence dictates. Be aware that many maps and GPS devices show what appear to be viable dirt roads that may actually be unmaintained or even abandoned—stick with established routes.

■ TIP→ Fuel up while you're in this part of Arizona—all grades of gasoline can be as much as $0.50 to $0.75 per gallon less in Kingman and Bullhead City than across the border in Nevada and California.

TRAIN
Kingman is the only city in this region served by Amtrak; the *Southwest Chief* stops in Kingman on its daily run between Los Angeles and Chicago (via Albuquerque).

Hotels

Midprice chain accommodations abound in Kingman and Lake Havasu and to a lesser extent Bullhead City—though the casino resorts across the river in Laughlin are among the best values in the region. Lake Havasu City has a few popular resorts, as does Laughlin, with its several glittery but reasonably priced gaming properties. Staying in a houseboat on Lake Havasu or Lake Mead puts a decidedly different twist on water recreation. These floating rooms with a view can be maneuvered into countless coves and inlets, allowing for peaceful solitude rarely found on the busy beaches and popular waterways.

Restaurants

Dining in this remote corner of the state is quite casual, though also affordable. You're more likely to find a 1950s-inspired diner, a taquería, or a family-owned café than a sophisticated, high-end eatery. For the most part you'll find home-cooked

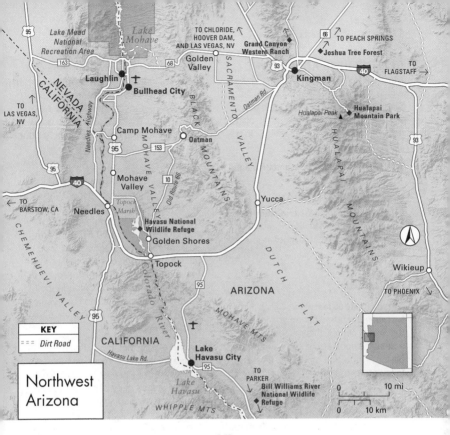

Northwest Arizona

KEY
=== Dirt Road

American and Southwestern favorites. The few higher-end dining options are in Lake Havasu and across the Colorado River in Laughlin's casinos, where steak houses proliferate.

Hotel and restaurant reviews have been shortened. For full information, visit Fodors.com.

What it Costs			
$	**$$**	**$$$**	**$$$$**
RESTAURANTS			
Under $12	$12–$20	$21–$30	Over $30
HOTELS			
Under $140	$140–$175	$176–$250	Over $250

Kingman

200 miles northwest of Phoenix, 149 miles west of Flagstaff via I–40.

The highway past Kingman may seem desolate, and the city itself doesn't have a ton of attractions, but the mountains that surround the area offer outdoor activities in abundance, especially along the Colorado River. Water sports play a big part in the area's recreation because about 1,000 miles of freshwater shoreline lie within the county along the Colorado River and around lakes Havasu, Mohave, and Mead—all of which are within a one-hour drive of this major stopping point for fishing and boating aficionados. And for those interested in the region's mineral wealth, the nearby "ghost" towns of Chloride and Oatman offer a glimpse of the Old West.

GETTING HERE AND AROUND

Most visitors to the region arrive by car, which is by far the best way to explore Kingman and area sites. Additionally, Amtrak's *Southwest Chief* stops daily in Kingman. The ride-share service Uber is also available.

CONTACTS Kingman Transportation Service. ☎ *928/753–1222.*

VISITOR INFORMATION

CONTACTS Kingman Visitor Center. ☒ *The Powerhouse, 120 W. Andy Devine Ave.* ☎ *928/753–6106* ⊕ *www.gokingman. com.*

 Sights

Arizona Route 66 Museum

MUSEUM | FAMILY | Sharing space with the visitor center, this museum provides a nostalgic look at the evolution of the famous route that started as a footpath followed by prehistoric Native Americans and evolved into a length of pavement that reached from Chicago, Illinois, to Santa Monica, California. The Route 66 Electric Vehicle Museum, a semipermanent display inside the museum, features electric vehicles on loan from the Historic Electric Vehicle Foundation. **Memory Lane,** also inside the Powerhouse building where the museum is housed, is a store crammed with kitschy souvenirs. ☒ *The Powerhouse, 120 W. Andy Devine Ave.* ☎ *928/753–9889* ⊕ *www.gokingman. com* ☒ *$4, includes admission to the Bonelli House and the Mohave Museum of History and Arts.*

Bonelli House

HOUSE | History buffs should check out the 1915 Bonelli House, an excellent example of Anglo-territorial architecture, featuring a facade of light-gray quarried stone and whitewashed-wood accents, a very popular style in the early 1900s. It is one of more than 60 buildings in the Kingman business district listed on the National Register of Historic Places and contains period pieces including a large wall clock that was once the only clock in Kingman. Because of the narrow hallways, only 10 visitors are allowed to tour the property at a time. ☒ *430 E. Spring St.* ☎ *928/753–1413* ⊕ *www. mohavemuseum.org/bonelli-house.html* ☒ *$4* ⊗ *Closed Sat.–Mon.*

Chloride

TOWN | The ghost town of Chloride, Arizona's oldest silver-mining camp, takes its name from a type of silver ore mined here. During its heyday, from 1900 to 1920, some 60 mines operated in the area: silver, gold, lead, zinc, molybdenum, and even turquoise were mined in the rugged terrain. Around 375 folks live in and around Chloride today; there's a restaurant, saloon, convenience store, RV park, and a smattering of old buildings.

Western artist Roy Purcell painted the large murals on the rocks on the eastern edge of town—10 feet high and almost 30 feet across, they depict a goddess figure, intertwined snakes, and Eastern and Native American symbols. To reach the murals, follow signs from the eastern end of Highway 125 along the unpaved road—it's a slow, twisting drive best attempted with four-wheel-drive vehicles. Outdoors enthusiasts can take advantage of the miles of hiking trails and explore the mineral-rich hills with excellent rock-hounding opportunities.

Mock gunfights in the streets mark high noon on the first and second Saturdays of the month. In October, the entire town turns out for Old Miner's Day—the biggest event of the year, featuring a parade, bazaar, bake sale, and family-friendly contests (St. Patrick's Day is also a big to-do here).

The marked turnoff on Highway 125 for Chloride is about 12 miles north of Kingman on U.S. 93. ⚠ **Give wide berth to abandoned mine entrances and shafts, which are often unstable and can cave in without warning.** Experts believe there are more than 200,000 abandoned mines in Arizona, many in the rich mineral regions such as the one surrounding Chloride. ⊠ *Chloride* ⊕ *www.visitchlorideaz.com.*

Desert Diamond Distillery

WINERY/DISTILLERY | Located at the Kingman Airport Industrial Complex, this distillery in an unassuming red building pours samples of its award-winning barrel reserve–aged rums and popular agave rum (along with two other rums, two whiskeys, and a vodka). Tours of the distillery explain the process of converting blackstrap molasses into fine spirits. ⊠ *4875 Olympic Dr.* ☎ *928/757–7611* ⊕ *www.desertdiamonddistillery.com* ⊠ *$7 for tour; $10 for tasting* ⊘ *Closed Tues. and Wed.*

Grand Canyon Western Ranch

FARM/RANCH | Sprawling at the base of Spirit Mountain, this historic 106,000-acre working cattle ranch about a 75-minute drive from Kingman takes guests on an adventure to the Old West. Corriente cattle still roam the hills and their cowboy caretakers guide horseback tours and horse-drawn wagon rides through the rugged countryside. Tap Duncan (a member of the Hole-in-the-Wall Gang) lived here, and Andy Devine supposedly spent some time working here. The ranch now offers rustic cabins, home-cooked meals, horseback riding, wagon rides, and a helicopter tour of Grand Canyon West. Located just 14 miles southwest of Grand Canyon West, the ranch is a popular stopping-off point for day-trippers seeking spectacular canyon views in this remote region. Several activities packages are available, with or without meal plans. ⊠ *3750 E. Diamond Bar Ranch Rd., Meadview* ☎ *928/788–0283, 800/798–0569* ⊕ *grandcanyonwesternranch.com* ⚠ *Reservations essential.*

★ Hualapai Mountain Park

NATIONAL/STATE PARK | You haven't truly hiked in northwest Arizona until you've hiked in Hualapai Mountain Park. A 15-mile drive from town up Hualapai Mountain Road leads to the park's more than 2,300 wooded acres, with 10 miles of developed and undeveloped hiking trails, picnic areas, ATV trails, rustic cabins, teepees, and RV (full hookups) and tent areas. Along the park's trail system, you'll find a striking variety of plant life such as prickly pear cactus and Arizona walnut. Abundant species of birds and mammals such as the piñon jay and the Abert squirrel live here, and pristine stands of unmarred aspen mark the higher elevations. Any of the trails can be hiked in about three hours. Keep in mind the terrain in the park ranges from 5,000 to 8,500 feet above sea level, and snow—sometimes heavy—is common in winter. ⊠ *6250 Hualapai Mountain Rd.* ☎ *928/681–5700, 877/757–0915 for cabin reservations* ⊕ *www.mcparks.com* ⊠ *$10 a day per vehicle.*

Kingman Railroad Museum

MUSEUM | Developed by Kingman's active legion of railroad aficionados, the Whistler Stop Railroad Club, this museum is set inside the town's vintage 1907 Santa Fe Railroad depot and contains vintage model-train layouts from the 1940s through the 1960s, plus additional memorabilia chronicling the region's rail history. ⊠ *402 E. Andy Devine Ave.* ☎ *928/753–7995* ⊕ *thekingmanrailroadmuseum.org* ⊠ *$2* ⊘ *Closed Mon. and Tues.*

Mohave Museum of History and Arts

MUSEUM | This museum includes an Andy Devine room with memorabilia from Devine's Hollywood years and, incongruously, a portrait collection of every president and First Lady. There's also an exhibit of carved Kingman turquoise, displays on Native American art and artifacts, and a diorama depicting the mid-19th-century expedition of Lt. Edward Beale, who led his camel-cavalry unit to the area in search of a wagon road along the 35th parallel. You can follow the White Cliffs Trail from downtown to see the deep ruts cut into the desert floor by the wagons that came to Kingman after Beale's time. ⊠ *400 W. Beale St.* ☎ *928/753–3195* ⊕ *www.mohavemuseum.org* ⊠ *$4,*

Did You Know?

Kingman, one of the main towns along Route 66, is awash in colorful murals and kitsch.

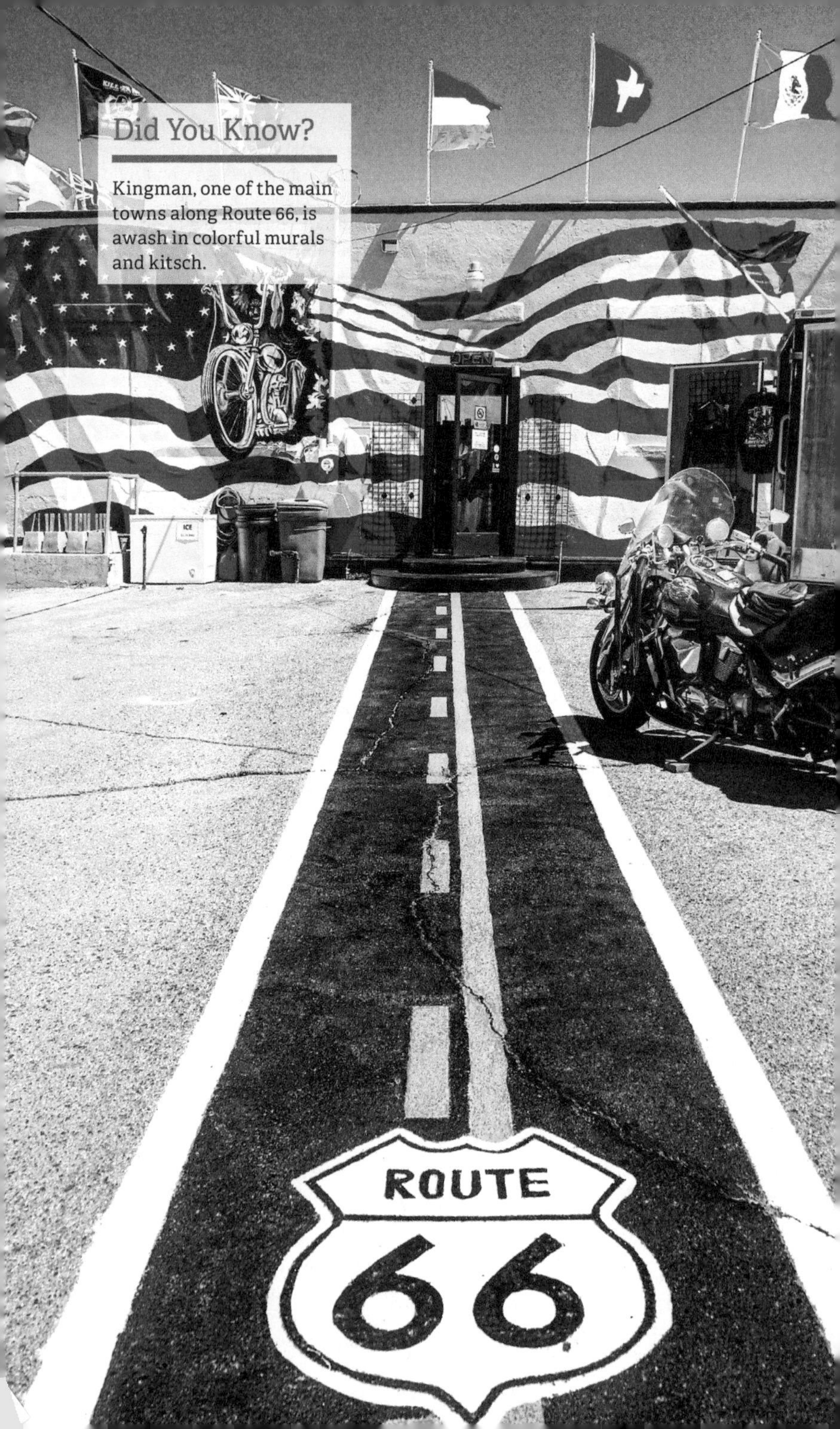

Joshua Trees

Traveling north from Kingman, keep an eye out for the strange-looking namesakes of the **Joshua Tree Forest** (*Yucca brevifolia*). This native of the dry Mojave Desert isn't a tree, but actually a member of the lily family. Standing as tall as 40 feet, the alien-looking plant can be recognized by its gangly limbs ending in dense clumps of dark-green, bayonet-shaped leaves.

Why are they called Joshua trees, anyway? Mormon emigrants traveling through the area in the mid-19th century named the towering plants after the biblical figure Joshua.

From February through March, Joshua trees bloom in clusters of creamy white blossoms. The trees don't branch until after they bloom, and, because they rely on perfect conditions to flower, they don't bloom every year—you're most likely to see blossoms following a rainy December or January.

includes admission to Arizona Route 66 Museum and the Bonelli House ⦿ Closed Sat.–Mon.

Oatman

GHOST TOWN | A worthwhile if hokey stop between Kingman and Bullhead City, the ghost town of Oatman lies along old Route 66. It's a straight shot across the Mojave Desert valley for a while, but then the road narrows and winds precipitously for about 15 miles through the Black Mountains. Oatman's main street is right out of the Old West; scenes from a number of films, including *How the West Was Won,* were shot here. It still has a remote, old-time feel: many of the natives carry sidearms, and they're not acting. You can wander into a saloon or visit the shabbily endearing **Oatman Hotel,** which now contains a restaurant but no longer rents overnight accommodations. Several times a day, resident actors entertain visitors with mock gunfights on the main drag.

More than 20 curio shops and eclectic boutiques line the length of Main Street. The burros that often come in from nearby hills and meander down the street, however, are the town's real draw. A couple of stores sell carrots to folks who want to feed these "wild" beasts, which at last count numbered about a dozen and which leave plenty of evidence of their visits in the form of "road apples"—so watch your step. For information about the town and its attractions, contact the **Oatman Chamber of Commerce** (☎ 927/768–6222 , ⊕ www. oatmangoldroad.org). ✉ Oatman.

🍴 Restaurants

Floyd & Co. Real Pit BBQ

$$ | **BARBECUE** | Drop by this unassuming storefront eatery in Kingman's historic downtown for tender, perfectly seasoned and smoked barbecue. Pulled pork sandwiches, Cajun-style andouille sausage platters, and racks of hickory-smoked pork ribs are favorites with sides of mac 'n' cheese, baked beans, and chunky potato salad. **Known for:** Memphis-style barbecue and wood-fired pizzas; homemade peach cobbler topped with vanilla ice cream; Arizona craft beers on tap. $ *Average main: $12* ✉ *420 E. Beale St.* ☎ *928/757–8227* ⊕ *www.floydandcompany.com* ⦿ *Closed Sun. and Mon.*

Mr. D'z Route 66 Diner

$ | **AMERICAN** | **FAMILY** | This popular spot—even Oprah and Gayle King stopped here—serves up road food with a '50s flair for breakfast, lunch, and dinner. The jukebox spins favorites, and tributes to Elvis and Marilyn Monroe adorn the walls in this old-fashioned diner decked out in bright turquoise and hot pink. **Known for:** house-made root beer; great '50s diner atmosphere and grub; across the street from the Kingman Visitor Center. $ *Average main: $10* ⊠ *105 E. Andy Devine Ave.* ☎ *928/718–0066.*

Rickety Cricket Brewing

$$ | **PIZZA** | This two-story brewery taps up to 25 beers crafted on-site, from the easily drinkable Birdcage Blonde to the much more potent Fruity Bruty, a raspberry imperial stout. The pizzas, which have medaled in international pizza competitions, are just as much a draw as the brews. **Known for:** ice rail on bar to keep your beer cold; plenty of seating, including two patios; arcade games and fun photo ops. $ *Average main: $15* ⊠ *312 E. Beale St.* ☎ *928/263–8444* ⊕ *www. ricketycricketbrewing.com* ⊗ *Closed Sun. and Mon.*

🛏 Hotels

Best Western Plus–King's Inn & Suites

$ | **HOTEL** | Conveniently located at the intersection of Interstate 40 and U.S. 93, this hotel has clean, spacious rooms and is a good base for visiting Hualapai Mountain Park, Laughlin, and the ghost towns of Chloride and Oatman. **Pros:** several restaurants are within walking distance; nicely kept, comfortable rooms; hot breakfast included. **Cons:** traffic noise from the highway; unimpressive exterior; popular with groups. $ *Rooms from: $100* ⊠ *2930 E. Andy Devine Ave.* ☎ *928/753–6101, 866/237–6365* ⊕ *bestwesternkingman.com* ↝ *101 rooms* ❖ *Free breakfast.*

Home2 Suites by Hilton Kingman

$ | **HOTEL** | **FAMILY** | This extended-stay hotel just off the interstate features a sleek, contemporary design, suites with kitchenettes, and a firepit on the patio. **Pros:** newest hotel in Kingman; fast Internet; separate parking lot for large vehicles. **Cons:** nonrefundable pet fee of $15 per pet, per night; some freeway noise; sliding shower doors don't close completely. $ *Rooms from: $120* ⊠ *1121 Sunrise Ave.* ☎ *928/529–5500, 855/618–4702 for reservations* ⊕ *www.hilton.com* ↝ *91 rooms* ❖ *Free breakfast.*

🌙 Nightlife

★ Diana's Cellar Door Wine Bar

WINE BARS—NIGHTLIFE | With more than 20 wines by the glass (priced at a very reasonable markup) plus a noteworthy selection of imported and craft beers as well as craft cocktails, this wine bar provides a sophisticated but low-key after-dark option in historic downtown Kingman. There's live music many evenings, and you can accompany your wine-sipping with food delivered from nearby local restaurants. ⊠ *414 E. Beale St.* ☎ *928/753–3885* ⊕ *www.dianascellardoor.com* ⊗ *Closed Sun.–Tues.*

Lake Havasu City

60 miles southwest of Kingman on I–40 to AZ 95.

If there's an Arizona Riviera, this is it. Lake Havasu has more than 400 miles of lake shoreline—it's actually a dammed section of the Colorado River—and the area gets less than four inches of rain annually, which means it's almost always sunny. Spring, winter, and fall are the best times to visit unless you plan to spend your day in or on the lake; in summer, temperatures often exceed 100°F. You can rent everything from water skis to Jet Skis, small fishing boats to large houseboats. The lake area has about a dozen RV parks and campgrounds, more than 120 boat-in campsites, and hundreds of hotel and motel rooms. There are golf and tennis facilities, as well as fishing guides who'll help you find, and catch, the big ones. This city of about 55,000 has grown rapidly over the past couple of decades, and downtown has become steadily more upscale—at least compared with the rest of northwest Arizona.

Learn about the purchase and reconstruction of London Bridge at the exhibit showcased at the Lake Havasu City Visitor Center, which is also a great place to pick up other information on area attractions.

GETTING HERE AND AROUND

You can explore downtown and the lakefront easily on foot, but most visitors arrive by car—the city lies about 25 miles south of Interstate 40 via AZ 95, and about 100 miles north of Interstate 10 via AZ 95. Vegas Airporter offers service from Lake Havasu to several Laughlin casinos and then on to McCarran Airport in Las Vegas.

CONTACTS Elite VIP Shuttle. ☎ 928/846–0069 ⊕ elitevipshuttle.com. **Vegas Airporter.** ☎ 928/854–5253, 888/948–3427 ⊕ vegasairporter.com.

VISITOR INFORMATION
CONTACTS Lake Havasu City Visitor Information Center. ✉ 422 English Village ☎ 928/855–5655 ⊕ golakehavasu.com.

◉ Sights

Bill Williams River National Wildlife Refuge
NATURE PRESERVE | This 6,055-acre desert oasis contains the largest surviving cottonwood-willow woodland in the region. The refuge is a favorite byway of neotropical migratory birds such as the flashy vermilion flycatcher and the brilliant summer tanager. ✉ 60911 AZ 95, between mile markers 160 and 161, Parker ⊹ 23 miles south of Lake Havasu City ☎ 928/667–4144 ⊕ www.fws.gov/refuge/Bill_Williams_River ⊠ Free.

Andy Devine ◉

Kingman's most famous citizen is Andy Devine (1905–77). The raspy-voiced Western character actor appeared in more than 400 films, most notably as the comic cowboy sidekick "Cookie" to Roy Rogers in 10 films. He also played "the Cheerful Soldier" in *The Red Badge of Courage* and was in several John Wayne flicks, including *The Man Who Shot Liberty Valance*, *Stagecoach*, and *Island in the Sky*. On the last weekend of September each year, Kingman celebrates its favorite son with the Andy Devine Days (⊕ www.andydevinedaysfestival.com), a festival that includes a rodeo, parade, and community fair.

★ **Havasu National Wildlife Refuge**
NATURE PRESERVE | Situated between Needles and Lake Havasu City, this spectacular 37,515-acre refuge is home to wintering Canada geese and other waterfowl, such as the snowy egret and the great blue heron. More than 315 species have been observed resting and nesting here. ✉ Off Oatman–Topock Hwy., Topock ⊹ Take Exit 1 off I–40 at California/Arizona border, then follow signs to refuge entrance ☎ 760/326–3853 ⊕ www.fws.gov/refuge/Havasu ⊠ Free.

Lake Havasu Museum of History
MUSEUM | This museum takes an in-depth look at the history of the region with exhibits on the Chemehuevi Indian Tribe, London Bridge, Parker Dam, the mining industry, and historic steamboat operation. ✉ 320 London Bridge Rd. ☎ 928/854–4938 ⊕ havasumuseum.com ⊠ $7.50 ☉ Closed Sun. and Mon.

★ London Bridge

BRIDGE/TUNNEL | Remember the old nursery rhyme "London Bridge Is Falling Down"? Well, it was. In 1968, after about 150 years of constant use, the 294-foot-long landmark was sinking into the Thames. When Lake Havasu City founder Robert McCullough heard about this predicament, he set about buying London Bridge, having it disassembled, shipped more than 5,000 miles to northwest Arizona, and rebuilt, stone by stone. The bridge was reconstructed on mounds of sand and took three years to complete. When it was finished, a mile-long channel was dredged under the bridge and water was diverted from Lake Havasu through the Bridgewater Channel. Today the entire city is centered on this unusual attraction. Walking tours are offered Tuesday, Thursday, and Saturday at 11 am from January through March (and group tours are also offered from October through April); the cost is $10 per person, and reservations are required. These guided strolls leave from the Lake Havasu City Visitor Center at the eastern base of the bridge, where you'll find a colorful re-creation of an **English Village** that houses a few curio shops and restaurants and offers good views of the channel of cool blue water flowing under London Bridge. On the western side, you'll find a handful of more urbane restaurants as well as the hip **Heat Hotel**. ✉ *1550 London Bridge Rd.* ☎ *928/855–5655 for tours.*

🍴 Restaurants

Barley Brothers Restaurant & Brewery

$$ | **AMERICAN** | In the little Island Mall on the west side of London Bridge, Barley Brothers is most acclaimed for its microbrewed ales on tap, especially Bighorn IPA and the Kickstart Oatmeal Stout. The casual cooking is hearty and filling with dishes ranging from standard salads and burgers to specials such as Jamaican barbecue salmon and savory peppercorn-topped sirloin. **Known for:** postcard-perfect view of London Bridge; six award-winning brews; wood-fired pizza and calzones. [$] *Average main: $17* ✉ *1425 McCulloch Blvd.* ☎ *928/505–7837* 🌐 *barleybrothers.com.*

★ Cha-Bones

$$$ | **AMERICAN** | Contemporary artwork on the walls, mod hanging lamps, and water sculptures create a contemporary vibe at this hip, elegant restaurant a short drive north of London Bridge. Superbly prepared steaks and seafood are the key draw, from 24-ounce porterhouse cuts to cioppino in a saffron-tomato broth, but also consider the barbecue ribs and linguine with chicken and poblano chiles. **Known for:** the best steaks in town; daily happy hour specials 3–6; extensive tapas menu. [$] *Average main: $22* ✉ *112 London Bridge Rd.* ☎ *928/854–5554* 🌐 *chabones.com.*

Chico's Tacos

$ | **MEXICAN** | This always-hopping taquería in the nondescript Basha's Shopping Center serves reliably good Mexican food. It's not fancy, but the clean and comfortable short-order joint turns out tasty tacos, burritos, tostadas, enchiladas, and taquitos served with chicken, grilled fish, carne asada, and other meat and veggie options. **Known for:** full service bar serving margaritas and more; hearty Mexican breakfasts; designated line for pick-up orders. [$] *Average main: $8* ✉ *1641 N. McCulloch Blvd.* ☎ *928/680–7010* 🌐 *www.chicostacoslakehavasu.com.*

College Street Brewhouse

$$ | **MODERN AMERICAN** | Although it's in a somewhat industrial area a short drive north of downtown, this lively, high-ceilinged restaurant and microbrewery with an enormous patio enjoys nice views of the lake. The craft beers, especially the crisp but balanced IPA and refreshing unfiltered American wheat, are reason alone to stop by, but the kitchen also turns out consistent comfort food including hefty sandwiches,

More than 400 miles of sandy beaches line Lake Havasu, where boaters can pass under London Bridge.

pizzas, and Cajun-influenced dishes. **Known for:** Big Blue Van blueberry-flavored wheat beer; lake views; inconsistent (and sometimes indifferent) service. $ *Average main: $16* ✉ *1940 College Dr.* ☎ *928/854–2739* ⊕ *www.collegestreet-brewhouseandpub.com.*

Juicy's "The Place With Great Food"

$$ | **AMERICAN** | Pairing great service with reasonable prices, this downtown locals' favorite fills up fast, especially for breakfast, thanks to its eggs Benedict dishes, biscuits and eggs, and loaded pancakes. The varied menu of lunch and dinner standards includes burgers with barbecue sauce, cheddar, and smoked bacon; meat loaf; pot roast stroganoff; and homemade soups and desserts. **Known for:** outstanding hearty breakfasts; varied menu of burgers, noodle dishes, and American standards; friendly service. $ *Average main: $16* ✉ *42 S. Smoketree Ave.* ☎ *928/855–8429* ⊕ *www.juicys-greatfood.com.*

La Vita Dolce

$$ | **ITALIAN** | This informal, bustling, family-run restaurant with indoor and outdoor seating serves reliably tasty, straightforward Italian fare, from classic pastas and grills—spaghetti and meatballs, portobello-mushroom ravioli, veal piccata—to a small but creative selection of thin-crust pizzas. The Maui Waui pizza with capicola ham, sweet pineapple, and marinara sauce is a local favorite. **Known for:** hands-down best Italian food in the area; several gluten-free options; daily happy hour from 3 to 6. $ *Average main: $15* ✉ *231 Swanson Ave.* ☎ *928/680–5885* ⊕ *www. facebook.com/lavitadolceitalianbistro.*

Shugrue's

$$$ | **AMERICAN** | This attractive space set on a bluff overlooking London Bridge has one of the best wine lists in town, plus consistently well-prepared steaks, seafood, and other traditional American and international dishes. Highlights include flatbread with Havarti cheese, portobello mushrooms, and olive-to-mato tapenade for a starter, and baked

Dijon-garlic-crusted halibut with sea scallops and tomato concasse as a main course. **Known for:** classic steak house dishes such as tournedos Oscar and French onion soup; fine dining with view of London Bridge; wine list with more than 100 selections. $ *Average main: $28* ✉ *1425 McCulloch Blvd.* ☎ *928/453–1400* ⊕ *shugrueslakehavasu.com.*

🛏 Hotels

If you're looking for an alternative to a hotel, consider a houseboat. What houseboats lack in speed and maneuverability they make up for in comfort and shade. **Lake Havasu Houseboats** has some of the most luxurious boats on the lake and the crew makes certain that boaters get the best instruction and tips for their travel into cool blue waters. Boats sleep 10 or more and have sundecks, waterslides, kitchens, and plenty of other amenities. Expect to pay $1,100 to $2,600 per night during the summer high season—the longer you rent, the less costly it is per day. ✉ *1000 McCulloch Blvd., Lake Havasu City* ☎ *800/843–9218* ⊕ *www.lakehavasuhouseboating.com.*

Heat Hotel
$$$ | **HOTEL** | The rooms at this sleek, angular boutique hotel on the west side of London Bridge capture the see-and-be-seen playfulness of Vegas, making it a hit with well-heeled, stylish visitors. **Pros:** stylish and posh decor; steps from London Bridge and many restaurants; swanky bar and cabana area; special packages for pet owners. **Cons:** might be a bit too trendy for some; bar and pool area can be a scene on weekends and during spring break; pounding music from bar can be heard in some rooms on the weekend; no on-site restaurant. $ *Rooms from: $200* ✉ *1420 McCulloch Blvd.* ☎ *928/854–2833, 888/898–4328* ⊕ *www.heathotel.com* ➹ *25 rooms* ❍| *No meals.*

★ Lake Havasu State Park Cabins
$ | **RENTAL** | **FAMILY** | Managed by Arizona State Parks, these 13 bare-bones but immaculate cabins in Lake Havasu State Park can accommodate up to six in two to three air-conditioned rooms and feature a picnic table, firepit on the beach, and enough parking space for several cars and a camper trailer. **Pros:** steps from the lake; photo-worthy sunset views; ideal for families who enjoy water sports and fishing. **Cons:** shared campground bathrooms and showers; BYO linens, pillows, and towels; pets are not permitted. $ *Rooms from: $99* ✉ *699 London Bridge Rd.* ☎ *928/855–2784* ⊕ *azstateparks.com/lake-havasu* ➹ *13 cabins* ❍| *No meals.*

London Bridge Resort
$ | **RESORT** | If you want to be close to the bridge, this hotel is a dependable choice with plenty to see and do on site. **Pros:** great views of London Bridge; suites come with sleeper sofas for extra guests; nightlife and business center. **Cons:** limited availability during the busy summer months; sales pressure from the resort's time-share options; popular with rowdy partiers, especially on weekends. $ *Rooms from: $135* ✉ *1477 Queens Bay* ☎ *844/335–3581, 928/855–0888* ⊕ *www.londonbridgeresort.com* ➹ *122 rooms* ❍| *No meals.*

The Nautical Beachfront Resort
$$ | **RESORT** | **FAMILY** | This expansive waterfront resort on a scenic stretch of Thompson Bay is a favorite choice of families and sports enthusiasts: boat rentals, a water park, golf (with reasonable rates), and a stunning infinity-edge pool with a bar and grill keep guests of all ages happily entertained. **Pros:** lots of on-site recreation amenities; set on a beautiful and relatively quiet section of lakefront; spacious rooms. **Cons:** $25 daily resort fee; 20-minute walk to restaurants and shops at London Bridge; ongoing renovations. $ *Rooms from: $169* ✉ *1000 McCulloch Blvd. N* ☎ *928/855–2141, 800/892–2141* ⊕ *www.nauticalbeachfrontresort.com* ➹ *139 suites* ❍| *No meals.*

🍸 Nightlife

Clubbing and barhopping are increasingly popular pastimes among visitors to Lake Havasu. Most of the top venues in town are located in hotels and restaurants, including Heat Hotel and Cha-Bones.

BlueWater Resort & Casino

CASINOS | A big nightlife draw around Lake Havasu is BlueWater Casino, 40 miles south in the town of Parker. The gaming area comprises more than 500 slot machines, plus blackjack, poker, and bingo, and it adjoins a full-service resort with a concert hall, bars, a movie theater, restaurants, a 164-slip marina, and a 200-room hotel. ✉ 11300 Resort Dr., Parker 🕿 928/669–7777, 888/243–3360 ⊕ www.bluewaterfun.com.

★ Desert Bar

BARS/PUBS | Along a remote mining road in the Buckskin Mountains roughly midway between Lake Havasu City and Parker, the quirky Desert Bar, aka the Nellie E. Saloon, is one of the region's most fabled curiosities. It's only open on weekends and occasional holidays (noon–6), Labor Day through Memorial Day. This cash-only, solar-powered entertainment compound is a work in progress, comprising indoor and outdoor bars, a stage with live music throughout the day, a horseshoe pit, a covered footbridge, and a nondenominational church that's the occasional site of weddings. ✉ Cienega Springs Rd., off AZ 95, Parker ⊕ 5 miles south of Lake Havasu City (follow signs) ⊕ www.thedesertbar.com.

Havasu Landing Resort and Casino

CASINOS | Just across the Colorado River from Lake Havasu, this small but lively casino and bar, which has live music most weekends, has become extremely popular thanks to the ferry service that zooms passengers over from London Bridge between 6:45 am and midnight (until 2 am on Friday and Saturday). The ferry costs $2 round-trip, and the scenic ride takes 17 minutes. You can also tie up your own boat at Havasua Landing's marina. The casino has 245 slots, plus blackjack and three-card poker tables, and there's live music Friday and Saturday nights. ✉ 13145 Havasu Lake Rd., Havasu Lake 🕿 760/858–4592 ⊕ www.havasulandingresortcasino.com.

🏃 Activities

There's no white water on the Colorado River below Hoover Dam. Instead, the river and its lakes offer many opportunities to explore the gorges and marshes that line the shores. If you prefer to do it yourself, look into the canoe and kayak rentals available on Lakes Mead, Mohave, and Havasu. Raft adventures will take you through the Topock Gorge near Lake Havasu, or you can boat upriver from Willow Beach 12 miles to the base of Hoover Dam. Along the way, chances are good you'll see bighorn sheep moving along the steep basaltic cliffs, and depending on the season, you can view hundreds of different types of migrating birds.

BOAT TOURS

BlueWater Jet Boat Tours

BOATING | From October through May, BlueWater Jet Boat Tours takes guests on a 2½-hour narrated trip up the Colorado River to Topock Gorge in the climate-controlled Starship 2010. A 1½-hour sunset cruise tours the lake's lighthouses. ✉ 70 London Bridge Rd. 🕿 928/855–7171 ⊕ www.coloradoriverjetboattours.com 🖃 From $50 🕙 Closed June–Aug.

Rubba Duck Safari

BOAT TOURS | FAMILY | "Mother Duck" leads a parade of seven rigid inflatable boats (RIB), piloted by guests, on a 2½-hour tour of Lake Havasu, including Pilot Rock, Balancing Rock, and Copper Canyon. The journey begins with 20 minutes of boating instruction and includes a mid-tour swim break. ✉ 402 English Village 🕿 928/208–0293.

The Colorado River separates the neighboring towns of Bullhead City, Arizona and Laughlin, Nevada.

CANOEING
Jerkwater Canoe Co.

BOATING | Jerkwater offers three different one-day canoe trips, including exploratory excursions in Topock Gorge and Black Canyon. Multiday paddling trips along several scenic stretches of the Colorado River are also available. ✉ 13003 Powell Lake Rd., Topock ☎ 928/768–7753, 800/421–7803 ⊕ www.jerkwatercanoe.com ⛵ From $46.

KAYAKING
Desert River Outfitters

BOATING | **FAMILY** | Kayakers can choose from several trip options, including Davis Dam to Rotary Park, half-day paddling trips on Lake Mohave, and all-day trips from Topock Gorge to the upper reaches of Lake Havasu. Full-day trips are for intermediate kayakers and are available only from mid-October to mid-April; the others are suitable for beginners and can be undertaken year-round. Some excursions are offered in the evening, by moonlight. ✉ 2472 Miracle Mile, Bullhead City ☎ 928/763–3033 ⊕ www.desertriver-outfitters.com ⛵ From $40.

Western Arizona Canoe & Kayak Outfitter (WACKO)

KAYAKING | This outfitter gets the outdoor adventure going with paddling trips in Topock Gorge, Lake Havasu, and the Bill Williams Wildlife Refuge. Despite the name, WACKO is a kayak-only operation. ✉ Lake Havasu City ☎ 928/855–6414, 888/881–5038 ⊕ www.azwacko.com ⛵ From $35.

GOLF
Lake Havasu Golf Club

GOLF | You can play on two beautifully laid-out 18-hole courses at this golf club with stunning views of Lake Havasu and the surrounding mountains. The East Course runs a bit shorter than the West Course, but both are similarly challenging, with tight fairways and demanding, relatively small greens on the former and ample bunkers and water hazards on the latter. ✉ 2400 Clubhouse Dr. ☎ 928/855–2719 ⊕ www.lakehavasu-golfclub.com ⛳ $65 ⛳ East Course: 18 holes, 6140 yards, par 72; West Course: 18 holes, 6466 yards, par 71.

WATER SPORTS

When construction of Parker Dam was completed in 1938, the reservoir it created to supply water to Southern California and Arizona became Lake Havasu. The lake is a 45-mile-long playground for water sports of all kinds. Whether it's waterskiing, Jet Skiing, stand-up paddling, powerboating, houseboating, swimming, fishing, or you name it, if water is required, it's happening on Lake Havasu.

With a boat, you have more options: you can find a quiet, secluded cove or beach to swim or fish. If you have a need for speed, you can plane up and down the lake with or without a skier in tow.

Cattail Cove State Park

WATER SPORTS | On the eastern shore of the lake 15 miles south of Lake Havasu City is 2,000-acre Cattail Cove State Park, a popular spot for fishing and boating (you can rent boats at the marina). There are 61 first-come first-served campsites ($30; four largest are $35) with access to electricity and water, and public restrooms with showers. ✉ *AZ 95* ✛ *15 miles south of Lake Havasu* ☎ *928/855–1223* ⊕ *azstateparks.com/ cattail-cove* 🖃 *$10 per vehicle weekdays, $15 weekends.*

Lake Havasu State Park

WATER SPORTS | Near London Bridge, Lake Havasu State Park has an interpretive nature garden and a level 1¾-mile trail that's perfect for watching the sunset. With three boat ramps, extensive docking, electrical hookups, and about 55 reservable campsites ($35–$40 daily, including day-use fee), it's an extremely popular spot in summer. ✉ *699 London Bridge Rd.* ☎ *928/855–2784* ⊕ *azstateparks.com/lake-havasu* 🖃 *$15 per vehicle weekdays, $20 weekends.*

EQUIPMENT AND RENTALS
Arizona WaterSports

WATER SPORTS | You can rent Jet Skis, jet boats, ski boats, and pontoon boats here, as well as a variety of other water toys, from wakeboards to inner tubes, and off-road vehicles. The company also has branches down at Parker Dam and at Blue Water Resort & Casino in Parker and delivers to most area campgrounds. ✉ *655 Kiowa Ave.* ☎ *928/453–5558, 800/393–5558* ⊕ *www.arizonawatersports.com.*

Bullhead City, Arizona, and Laughlin, Nevada

35 miles west of Kingman via U.S. 93 to AZ 68.

Laughlin, Nevada, is separated from Arizona by the Colorado River. Its founder, Don Laughlin, bought an eight-room motel here in 1964 and basically built the town from scratch. By the early 1980s Laughlin's Riverside Hotel-Casino was drawing gamblers and river goers from northwestern Arizona, southeastern California, and even southern Nevada, and his success attracted other casino operators. Today Laughlin is the state's third major resort area, attracting more than 3 million visitors annually. The city fills up, especially in winter, with retired travelers who spend at least part of the winter in Arizona as well as a younger resort-loving crowd. The big picture windows overlooking the Colorado River lend a bright, airy, and open feeling unique to Laughlin casinos. Take a stroll along the river walk, then make the return trip by water taxi ($5 one way, $20 all day). Boating, Jet Skiing, fishing, and plain old wading are other options for enjoying the water.

GETTING HERE AND AROUND

To get to Laughlin from Kingman by car, follow U.S. 93 north for 3 miles, and then head west on AZ 68 for about 30 miles.

Mills Tours and Tri State Shuttle offer regular service from McCarran International Airport to Laughlin/Bullhead City. Reservations for all shuttle services are required.

Lucky Cab & Limo Company of Nevada services Laughlin and Bullhead City. For another approach to getting from casino to casino in Laughlin, hop aboard a water taxi with River Passage. Fares can be purchased at the casino dock ticket booths.

Harrah's and Do Laughlin's Riverside Resort Hotel and Casino charter flights in and out of Laughlin/Bullhead International Airport for their players' club members and sell extra seats to the public.

AIRPORT CONTACTS Laughlin/Bullhead International Airport. ✉ *2550 Laughlin View Dr., Bullhead City* ☎ *928/754–2134* ⊕ *www.flyifp.com.*

TIMING

The state of Nevada is in the Pacific time zone, while Arizona is in the mountain time zone. Arizona doesn't observe daylight saving time, however. As a result, in summer Nevada and Arizona observe the same hours.

VISITOR INFORMATION

CONTACTS Laughlin Chamber of Commerce. ✉ *1585 S. Casino Dr., Laughlin* ☎ *702/298–2214, 800/227–5245* ⊕ *laughlinchamber.com.* **Laughlin Visitor Information Center.** ✉ *1555 S. Casino Dr., Laughlin* ☎ *800/452–8445, 702/892–0711* ⊕ *www.visitlaughlin.com.*

◉ Sights

Christmas Tree Pass Road

SCENIC DRIVE | FAMILY | Christmas Tree Pass Road is a dirt road that provides a gorgeous drive through the Lake Mead National Recreation Area to an extensive petroglyph site in Grapevine Canyon. This side route runs 16 miles through a desert landscape sacred to several historical and modern native tribes. The pass cuts through the rough-cut Newberry Range near legendary Spirit Mountain, with several turnouts (but no designated hiking trails) before the Grapevine Canyon trail. It's the kind of drive you imagined

when you bought your SUV, one that also should make sedan drivers extremely wary. Sedans can take a shorter, easier route to the Grapevine Canyon trail by instead approaching from the Laughlin side (U.S. 163), which reduces the dirt-and-gravel drive to two of its easier miles. The Grapevine trail has a parking lot with latrines (no running water) and a ¼-mile walk to the springs, which served as the central gathering point for Yuman- and Numic-speaking tribes, whose messages are etched on the canyon boulders. It's a more pleasant walk in the winter, when water is often channeling through the canyon. The trail around the springs also offers a chance to see desert wildflowers and blooming cacti in spring and early summer. The drive reconnects with U.S. 163 15 miles northwest of Laughlin. ✉ *U.S. 95, Searchlight* ✛ *14 miles south of Searchlight.*

Colorado River Museum

MUSEUM | FAMILY | Now located in Bullhead City Community Park, the Colorado River Museum displays the rich past of the tristate region where Nevada, Arizona, and California converge. Earnest volunteers guide you through the haphazard array of artifacts from the Mojave tribe and the gold rush era in nearby Oatman. There are also exhibits on the building of Davis Dam, 18th-century explorer Father Francisco Garcés, and the experimental use of camels in the area by a pre–Civil War U.S. Army. ✉ *1239 AZ 95, Bullhead City* ☎ *928/754–3399* ▱ *$2* ☉ *Closed June–Aug. and Sat.–Mon.*

Laughlin Labyrinths

TRAIL | FAMILY | Looking for a place to stroll with a view? These eight labyrinths ranging in length from 25 to 55 feet blanket a hill overlooking the casinos and the Colorado River. Watch for a small sign and parking area halfway between Bruce Woodbury and South Casino drives. ✉ *Thomas Edison Dr., between Bruce Woodbury and South Casino Dr., Laughlin.*

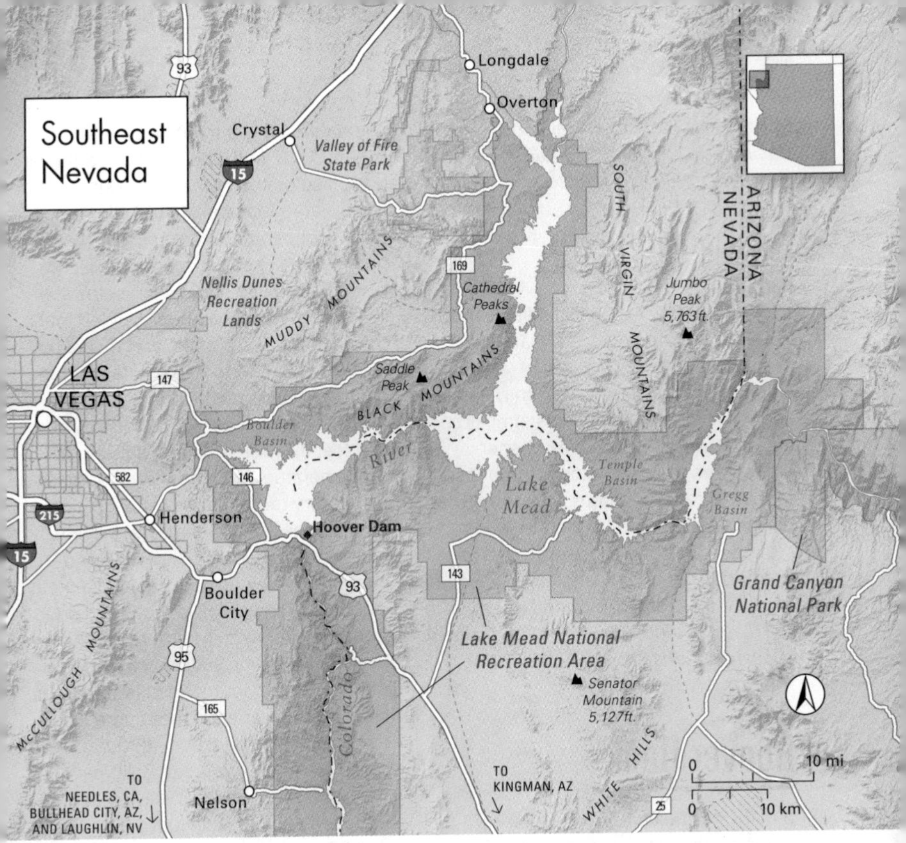
Southeast Nevada
93
Longdale
Overton
Crystal
Valley of Fire State Park
15
SOUTH VIRGIN MOUNTAINS
ARIZONA
NEVADA
169
Cathedral Peaks
Jumbo Peak 5,763 ft.
Nellis Dunes Recreation Lands
MUDDY MOUNTAINS
Saddle Peak
BLACK MOUNTAINS
LAS VEGAS
147
Boulder Basin
River
Lake Mead
Temple Basin
Gregg Basin
582
146
215
Henderson
Hoover Dam
15
143
Boulder City
93
Grand Canyon National Park
Lake Mead National Recreation Area
McCULLOUGH MOUNTAINS
95
165
Senator Mountain 5,127 ft.
Colorado
WHITE HILLS
0
10 mi
0
10 km
25
TO NEEDLES, CA, BULLHEAD CITY, AZ, AND LAUGHLIN, NV
Nelson
TO KINGMAN, AZ

Riverwalk Exploration Trail

TRAIL | FAMILY | An extension of the Laughlin Riverwalk, this 2-mile hike begins on the west side of Casino Drive, crosses U.S. 95 by a pedestrian bridge, and follows the Colorado River to Pyramid Canyon, where you'll find spectacular views of Davis Dam. ✉ *Laughlin.*

Searchlight Historic Museum

MUSEUM | FAMILY | Searchlight was once the biggest boomtown in southern Nevada, and some of its rich mining and railroad history is now compressed into a one-room museum inside the local community center. Visitors will find an assayer's office, outdoor mining display, and exhibits devoted to notables with ties to the area, including silent-screen star Clara Bow and early aviation heroes such as record-breaking test pilot John Macready. ✉ *200 Michael Wendell Way, Searchlight* ⊕ *On way to Laughlin from Las Vegas on U.S. 95, turn off at Cottonwood Cove Rd., drive almost a mile to end of town and turn left on Michael Wendell Way* ☎ *702/297–1642* 🌐 *searchlightmuseum.org* 🎟 *Free* 🕒 *Closed Sun.*

🍴 Restaurants

Bumbleberry Flats

$$ | AMERICAN | FAMILY | The New Pioneer Hotel's signature restaurant starts the day off right with hearty breakfasts that locals claim are the best in town; late risers don't need to fret—breakfast is served all day. As the day progresses, the kitchen also serves up huge portions of comfort-food classics such as burgers, fried chicken, and meat loaf. **Known for:** breakfasts big enough for two; beer taps at the table; friendly, attentive service. [$] *Average main: $14*

✉ *The New Pioneer Hotel, 2200 S. Casino Dr., Laughlin* ☎ *800/634–3469* 🌐 *www.laughlinpioneer.com.*

Hotels

Harrah's

$ | **RESORT** | **FAMILY** | The classiest joint in Laughlin comes with a private sand beach and two casinos, one of which is smoke free. **Pros:** separate family and adults-only towers and pools; smoking and smoke-free casinos; air-charter flights from all over the country to resort for player card members. **Cons:** pools can fill up fast; lines can be long for guest services, promotions; resort fee ($19) charged for free Wi-Fi and gym. [$] *Rooms from: $65* ✉ *2900 S. Casino Dr., Laughlin* ☎ *702/298–4600, 855/673–1206* 🌐 *www.caesars.com/harrahs-laughlin* 🛏 *1,561 rooms* 🍴 *No meals.*

Hoover Dam

8 miles northeast of Boulder City, 67 miles northwest of Kingman via U.S. 93.

GETTING HERE AND AROUND

Hoover Dam is about a 75-minute drive from Kingman via U.S. 93; it's about 15 minutes from Boulder City.

Sights

★ **Hoover Dam**

DAM | **FAMILY** | Originally referred to as Boulder Dam, this colossal structure, widely considered one of the greatest engineering achievements in history, was later officially named Hoover Dam in recognition of President Herbert Hoover's role in the project. Look for artist Oskar Hansen's plaza sculptures, which include the 30-foot-tall *Winged Figures of the Republic* (the statues and terrazzo floor patterns were copied at the new Smith Center for the Performing Arts in Downtown Las Vegas). The tour itself is a tradition that dates back to 1937, and you can still see the old box office on top of the dam. But now the ticketed tours originate in the modern visitor center (or online), with two options. The cheaper, more popular one is the **Powerplant Tour**, which starts every 15 minutes. It's a half-hour, guided tour that includes a short film and then a 537-foot elevator ride to two points of interest: the chance to stand on top of one of the 30-foot pipes where you can hear and feel the water rushing through to the generators, and the more impressive eight-story room housing still-functional power generators. Self-paced exhibits follow the guided portion, with good interactive museum exhibits and a great indoor/outdoor patio view of the dam from the river side. The more extensive **Hoover Dam Tour** includes everything on the Powerplant Tour but limits the group size to 20 and spends more time inside the dam, including a peek through the air vents. Tours run from 9 to 5 all year, with the last Powerplant tour leaving at 3:45 pm daily, and the last Hoover Dam Tour at 3:30. Visitors for both tours submit to security screening comparable to an airport. January and February are the slowest months, and mornings generally are less busy. The top of the dam is open to pedestrians and vehicles, but you have to remain in your vehicle after sundown. Visitors can still drive over the dam for sightseeing, but cannot continue into Arizona; you have to turn around and come back after the road dead-ends at a scenic lookout (with a snack bar and store) on the Arizona side. ■ **TIP→ The dam's High Scaler Café offers fare such as cold drinks, ice cream, and hamburgers.** ✉ *U.S. 93, east of Boulder City, Boulder City* ☎ *702/494–2517, 866/730–9097, 888/248–1259 security, road, and Hoover Dam crossing information* 🌐 *www.usbr.gov/lc/hooverdam* 🎟 *Powerplant Tour $15, Hoover Dam Tour $30, visitor center $10; garage parking $10 (free parking on Arizona-side surface lots).*

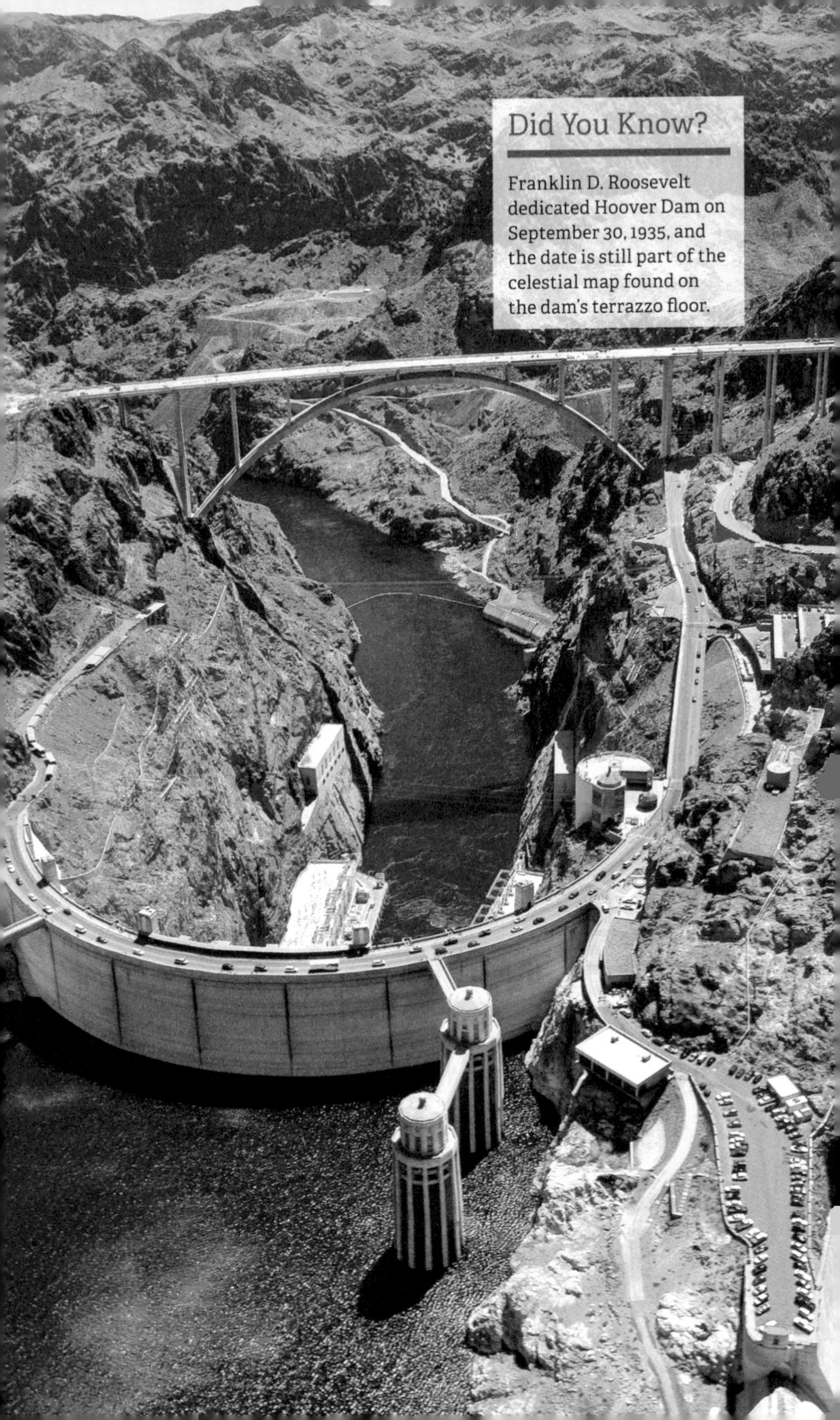

Did You Know?

Franklin D. Roosevelt dedicated Hoover Dam on September 30, 1935, and the date is still part of the celestial map found on the dam's terrazzo floor.

⚡ Activities

RAFTING

Black Canyon, just below Hoover Dam, is the place for river running near Las Vegas. You can launch a raft here on the Colorado River year-round. On the Arizona side, the 11-mile run to Willow Beach, with its vertical canyon walls, bighorn sheep on the slopes, and feeder streams and waterfalls coming off the bluffs, is reminiscent of rafting the Grand Canyon. The water flows at roughly 5 miles per hour, but some rapids, eddies, and whirlpools can cause difficulties, as can headwinds, especially for inexperienced rafters.

If you want to go paddling in Black Canyon on your own, you need to make mandatory arrangements with one of the registered outfitters. They provide permits ($12) and the National Park Service entrance fee ($10), as well as launch and retrieval services (the road in and out is in a security zone for the dam). You can get a list of outfitters at ☎ *702/294–1121*, or by going to the paddle-craft and rafting-tours section on the Bureau of Land Management's website (⊕ *www.usbr. gov/lc/hooverdam*).

Black Canyon/Willow Beach River Adventures

WHITE-WATER RAFTING | FAMILY | If you're interested in seeing the canyon and Hoover Dam on large motor-assisted rafts, Black Canyon/Willow Beach River Adventures has group excursions launching from the base of the dam for both 3-hour and 90-minute tours. The half-day excursion includes lunch; the shorter "postcard" tour lasts about 90 minutes but includes only 30 minutes on the raft. Round-trip Las Vegas transportation is available. All tours depart from Lake Mead RV Village. ⊠ *Lake Mead RV Village, 286 Lakeshore Rd., Boulder City* ☎ *800/455–3490* 🖃 *From $69*.

Index

Photo Credits

Notes

Notes

Notes

Notes

Notes

Notes

Notes

Fodor's ARIZONA & THE GRAND CANYON

Publisher: Stephen Horowitz, *General Manager*

Editorial: Douglas Stallings, *Editorial Director*; Jill Fergus, Jacinta O'Halloran, Amanda Sadlowski, *Senior Editors*; Kayla Becker, Alexis Kelly, *Editors*

Design: Tina Malaney, *Director of Design and Production*; Jessica Gonzalez, *Graphic Designer*; Mariana Tabares, *Design & Production Intern*

Production: Jennifer DePrima, *Editorial Production Manager*; Elyse Rozelle, *Senior Production Editor*; Monica White, *Production Editor*

Maps: Rebecca Baer, *Senior Map Editor*; Mark Stroud (Moon Street Cartography), David Lindroth, *Cartographers*

Photography: Viviane Teles, *Senior Photo Editor*; Namrata Aggarwal, Ashok Kumar, Carl Yu, *Photo Editors*; Rebecca Rimmer, *Photo Intern*

Business & Operations: Chuck Hoover, *Chief Marketing Officer*; Robert Ames, *Group General Manager*; Devin Duckworth, *Director of Print Publishing*; Victor Bernal, *Business Analyst*

Public Relations and Marketing: Joe Ewaskiw, *Senior Director Communications & Public Relations*

Fodors.com: Jeremy Tarr, *Editorial Director*; Rachael Levitt, *Managing Editor*

Technology: Jon Atkinson, *Director of Technology*; Rudresh Teotia, *Lead Developer*; Jacob Ashpis, *Content Operations Manager*

Writers: Teresa Bitler, Mara Levin, Elise Riley

Editor: Kayla Becker

Production Editor: Elyse Rozelle

13th Edition

ISBN 978-1-64097-353-4

ISSN 1559–6230

All details in this book are based on information supplied to us at press time. Always confirm information when it matters, especially if you're making a detour to visit a specific place. Fodor's expressly disclaims any liability, loss, or risk, personal or otherwise, that is incurred as a consequence of the use of any of the contents of this book.

SPECIAL SALES
This book is available at special discounts for bulk purchases for sales promotions or premiums. For more information, e-mail SpecialMarkets@fodors.com.

PRINTED IN CANADA

10 9 8 7 6 5 4 3 2 1

About Our Writers

Teresa Bitler, who updated the Northeast Arizona and the Northwest Arizona and Southeast Nevada chapters, moved to Arizona before her first birthday and has spent most of her life exploring the state. She regularly writes about Arizona destinations for AAA Highroads, contributes content to the Arizona Office of Tourism's online destination guide, and has authored two Southwest guidebooks. Her work has appeared in *National Geographic Traveler, American Way, Sunset,* and dozens of other periodicals.

Tucson, Grand Canyon, North-Central, Southern Arizona, and Travel Smart updater **Mara Levin** divides her time between travel writing, traveling, and social work. A native of California, Mara now lives in Tucson, where the grass may not be greener, but the mountains, tranquillity, and slower pace of desert life have their own appeal.

A Phoenix-based freelance writer and editor, **Elise Riley** left her native Arizona to report for newspapers across the country. She quickly learned that no place had Mexican food like the Valley, and eventually found the way back to her favorite salsas and enchiladas. Today she appreciates the striking desert sunsets more than she did in her childhood, and eagerly awaits the next out-of-state visitor she can take on a tour of her favorite local restaurants. Elise updated the Experience; Phoenix, Scottsdale, and Tempe; and Eastern Arizona chapters.